MASTERPLOTS II

NONFICTION
SERIES

MASTERPLOTS II

NONFICTION SERIES

4

Sha-Z

Indexes

Edited by

FRANK N. MAGILL

SALEM PRESS

Pasadena, California   Englewood Cliffs, New Jersey

∞ The paper used in these volumes conforms to the
American National Standard for Permanence of Paper
for Printed Library Materials, Z39.48-1984.

Library of Congress Cataloging-in-Publication Data
Masterplots II: Nonfiction series/edited by Frank N.
Magill
    p. cm.
    Bibliography: p.
    Includes indexes
    1. Literature—Stories, plots. etc. 2. Literature—
History and criticism. I. Magill, Frank Northen, 1907-
    . II. Title: Masterplots 2. III. Title: Masterplots
two.
PN44.M345   1989   89-5877
080'.2'02—dc19   CIP
ISBN 0-89356-478-8 (set)
ISBN 0-89356-482-6 (volume 4)

PRINTED IN THE UNITED STATES OF AMERICA

LIST OF TITLES IN VOLUME 4

LIST OF TITLES OF VOLUME 4

MASTERPLOTS II

NONFICTION
SERIES

SHAH OF SHAHS

Author: Ryszard Kapuściński (1932-   )
Type of work: Travel writing
Time of work: 1925-1979
Locale: Iran
First published: Szachinszach, 1982 (English translation, 1985)

Principal personages:
MOHAMMAD REZA PAHLAVI, the Shah of Iran from 1941-1979
THE AYATOLLAH KHOMEINI, the spiritual leader of the Iranian
Revolution

Form and Content

Born in 1932 and a graduate of the University of Warsaw in 1952, Ryszard Kapuściński has since pursued a highly successful career in journalism in his native Poland. He was on the staff of *Sztandar mlodych* (banner of youth) from 1951 to 1958; of *Polityka* (politics) from 1959 to 1961; and of *Kultura* (culture), of which he was deputy editor in chief from 1974 to 1981. He has also worked as a free-lance writer: from 1972 to 1974, and again since 1981. Of particular significance for his development as a journalist, however, and as the catalyst for his reputation as a writer outside Poland, was his service with the Polish Press Agency in Africa, Asia, and Latin America between 1962 and 1972, which sowed the seeds of an abiding interest in the Third World and its problems, on which this highly perceptive Polish observer, citizen of a country without traditions of overseas imperialism and a centuries-old victim of Great Power rivalries, has uniquely incisive insights. In his study of the corruption and decrepitude of the government of Haile Selassie of Ethiopia, *The Emperor: Downfall of an Autocrat*, published in 1983 in a translation by William R. Brand and Katarzyna Mroczkowska-Brand (originally published in Polish as *Cesarz* in 1978), Kapuściński artfully constructed, through a sequence of commentaries by palace officials and employees, an insider's picture of the rottenness at the core of the Ethiopian empire. Very different in style was his *Another Day of Life*, published in English in 1987 by the same team of translators from his *Jeszcze dzień życia*, published in Poland in 1976, which was a diary of a visit to Angola during 1975 at the time of Portugal's transfer of power and at the time of South African and Cuban military intervention.

Shah of Shahs, published in English in 1985 from the Polish *Szachinszach* of 1982, was the outcome of a visit to Tehran at the time of the establishment of the Islamic Republic, which early in 1979 replaced the despotic rule of Mohammad Reza Shah, who had mounted the throne in 1941. In writing an account of that event, one that would make sense in terms of what he had witnessed and one that would make comprehensible to his readers one of the most dramatic and seemingly least predictable upheavals of the twentieth century, he designed a highly flexible structure which would allow him to balance his personal observations with what he had learned from interviewers and what he knew of the complex historical background to the revolution. In particular, he had to convey to faraway Polish readers the intricate and highly ambiguous nature of traditional Iranian social and political relationships.

This he achieved with extraordinary success by separating his text into three sections of unequal length. The first, "Cards, Faces, Fields of Flowers," sets the scene in the Tehran hotel where he was staying. The second, which he called "Daguerreotypes," is a series of brilliant portraits relating to the shah's life and antecedents, and to the style of life which characterized his rule. This section, in turn, is followed by one titled "The Dead Flame," which enabled the author to move to front of stage and ruminate on the causes and consequences of what he reckoned to have been "the twenty-seventh revolution I have seen in the Third World."

Analysis

Ryszard Kapuściński was writing about a regime—the venal, cruel, and ostentatiously banal monarchy of the shah, and of its nemesis in the form of a revolution headed by profoundly conservative Muslim clerics, which must have seemed indescribably remote and exotic to his Central European readers. How, therefore, was he to convey to such readers the personality and inner workings of Iran's *ancien régime* and its headlong course toward self-destruction? His answer, since he could not provide a monographic analysis within the requirements of effective journalism, lay in his creation and careful placing of a series of vignettes of recent Iranian history, his "Daguerreotypes." These were prefaced by an opening twelve-page section in which he conveyed the atmosphere in Tehran following the monarch's departure and the triumphal return of Ayatollah Khomeini as seen from his hotel bedroom, with the employees playing cards and whiling away their time, with the television programs dominated by Khomeini's charismatic presence on the screen, and with his personal imperative to organize and make sense of the quantity of notes, photographs, and tapes which littered his living quarters.

The "daguerreotypes" become, in fact, a skillful history lesson. There are twelve "photographs," a "cassette," and seven "notes." Their alignment appears casual, but in reality they are precisely and deliberately arranged. The "photographs" set the scene and serve as recurring motifs, like faded pictures in a scrapbook: the shah's father (then a mere trooper) guarding the assassin of a former shah; the shah's father as an officer in the Persian Cossack Brigade; the shah's father standing forbiddingly beside his seven-year-old son. Then there is the 1943 meeting of Winston Churchill, Franklin D. Roosevelt, and Joseph Stalin in Tehran, followed by Mohammad Mosaddeq in his moment of triumph as the newly chosen prime minister in 1951. Next, the shah is seen in exile (Rome, 1953). Then comes a street scene, with a SAVAK informer (SAVAK was the shah's dreaded secret police organization), followed by a child victim of SAVAK brutality. The succeeding

vignettes are of the shah in 1973, at the time of the explosion of oil prices, announcing Iran's commitment to "the Great Civilization"; his posturing as a Napoleonic
warlord; a jet loaded with his courtiers flying off on a day-trip to Germany; and a
revolutionary caricature of "the Great Civilization" as "the Great Injustice." Taken
as a whole, these "photographs" encapsulate a certain view of the Pahlavi period
(1925-1979), the period when Iran was ruled by Mohammad Reza Shah and his
father.

Among these "photographs," the single "cassette" stands by itself, an anonymous Iranian commenting upon the career of Mohammad Mosaddeq, reminiscent
of the structure of Kapuściński's earlier study of Haile Selassie of Ethiopia. On this,
and on the "photographs," the various "notes" provide either glosses or serve to
carry the narrative along. Thus, one discusses the shah's egomania and isolation
from reality; another pinpoints the crucial role of oil; yet another looks at the so-
called monarchical tradition in Iran. One touches on the origins of religious opposition and the rise to public prominence of Ayatollah Khomeini. There is a perceptive
account of the way in which SAVAK pervaded every aspect of Iranian life, and of its
methods of repression, and there is a thumbnail sketch of Shi'ism as an opposi-
tional creed. Finally, and forming the culminating phase of this section, there is an
extended account of an Iranian intellectual (presumably a composite figure derived
from several different case studies) who returns from exile abroad during the last
months of the Pahlavi regime in time to experience surveillance and harassment
from SAVAK operatives, but at the same time to witness the beginning of the
collapse of the system of monolithic repression. This section, in particular, demonstrates very effectively Kapuściński's ability "to get under the skin" of Iranian
society in a way few foreign journalists were able to do.

In the final section of the book, "The Dead Flame," the author himself emerges
from behind these "photographs," these explications of recent Iranian history, these
impressions of the *ancien régime* provided by the assimilation of reading and
interviews, to interpret the fall of the monarchy in terms of direct experience: what
Kapuściński himself saw and felt. The cumulative effect of this section, following as
it does upon the skillfully constructed series of "Daguerreotypes," is a brilliant
indictment of the cruelty, the pettiness, the extravagance, and the pointlessness of
Pahlavi's Iran. In describing the abuse of authority under the shah, Kapuściński
shows how his rule, reinforced as it was by very large, well-armed, and well-paid
security forces, ultimately became unendurable. At the same time, he fears for
Iran's future, anticipating new tyrannies which will in time produce their own
retributions. For Kapuściński, as a reviewer in the Summer, 1985, issue of *The
Virginia Quarterly Review* duly noted, "Iranians, like many other peoples in the
world, are helpless against generic tyranny."

Kapuściński recognizes that the so-called causes of revolution—poverty, oppression, the abuse of power—are virtually ubiquitous in the Third World, yet true
revolutions (as opposed to revolts, *coups d'état*, and palace takeovers) are rare
indeed. Why was Iran different? In his view,

The indispensable catalyst is the word. The explanatory idea. More than petards or stilettoes, therefore, words—uncontrolled words, circulating freely, underground, rebelliously, not gotten up in dress uniforms, uncertified—frighten tyrants. But sometimes it is the official, uniformed, certified words that bring about the revolution.

Thus he pinpoints the opening of the Iranian revolution to January 8, 1978, when the shah ordered the publication of a scurrilous article on Khumaini in the government-controlled press, which triggered the series of protests and government killings that produced the great rhythms of Shi'ite mourning that eventually merged into the image of an entire nation demonstrating against its government. In such a crisis, the systematic state-sponsored terror of the past becomes self-defeating, only exciting the nation to fresh acts of heroism.

Kapuściński asserts that it is erroneous to assume that all nations wronged by history (and the Pole in him adds, "they are in the majority") necessarily live in constant contemplation of revolution. They do not. "Every revolution is a drama, and humanity instinctively avoids dramatic situations." Iran, however, was different. There, the nature of the despot and of the despotism made for drama. "In every revolution," he observes, "a movement grapples with a structure." The structure was what he calls "the theatre of the Shah," with the ruler as the self-absorbed director mounting the play of "The Great Civilization," with himself perpetually on front stage, backed by a huge cast of largely inanimate extras—courtiers, generals, policemen, lackeys. The movement, which he did not even deign to notice until it was too late, was the traditional faith of his people, quickened to flash point by his regime's excesses, and taking its bearings from mosque and mullah.

A student of dictatorships and state-sponsored violence in the Third World, Kapuściński provides his readers with a coherent account of the inner workings of revolution in Iran in a form which few other scholars, experts, or observers have attempted. In that sense, *Shah of Shahs* is likely to outlive much of the ephemeral literature evoked by the events of 1978-1979. Yet behind the penetrating analysis, the brilliant impressionistic brushstrokes which convey so much to the stay-at-home reader, there is a profound pessimism, a product not merely of his stay in Iran but also of his years of firsthand acquaintance with the Third World. As he watched the new order replace the old, Kapuściński mused that "one thing was invariable, indestructible, and—I dread saying it—eternal: the helplessness." Drawing to the end of his stay in Tehran, he visits a carpet-seller whom he knows in his shop in Firdausi Avenue. As his eyes run over the sumptuously decorated surfaces, the merchant tells him:

> You must remember . . . that what has made it possible for the Persians to remain themselves over two and a half millennia . . . is our spiritual, not our material, strength—our poetry, and not our technology; our religion, and not our factories. What have we given to the world? We have given poetry, the miniature, and carpets. As you can see, these are all useless things from the productive viewpoint. But it is through such things that we have expressed our true selves.

Critical Context

In the genre of travel literature, there are those writers who give to the reader what Lawrence Durrell has called "the spirit of place"; among such are the classics, the works of Alexander Kinglake, Charles Doughty, Freya Stark. Others seek to use their wanderings as a vehicle for social and political commentary, and in most cases, such works, even when they achieve an immediate success, enjoy only an ephemeral reputation. To this generalization, Kapuściński is likely to prove an exception. One clue to his uniqueness is to be found in a statement printed in an issue of *Contemporary Authors:*

> . . . I think that because the social and political structures of unstable third world countries are not quite so sophisticated as those of the developed world, one can more easily observe man and his behaviour in those countries. It is easier to observe the essence of modern conflicts, their generation. The field of observation is sharper, more focused.

In *Shah of Shahs*, he has provided a brilliant and evocative portrait of Iran in revolution such as is unlikely to fade much with the passage of time. The Iranian Revolution inspired an enormous literature, yet leaving aside the academic monographs and the fascinating (although often self-serving) memoirs by participants, the sheer complexity and subtlety of the context eluded the visiting journalist, whose quest for instant information within an unfamiliar historical setting frequently kept him oscillating between the bizarre and the commonplace. Somehow, Kapuściński avoided both these hazards and wrote in *Shah of Shahs* a minor classic of travel and of informed observation which may well take its place alongside the classic works on Iran by European travelers.

Sources for Further Study

Ajami, Fouad. Review in *The New Republic*. CXCII (April 8, 1985), p. 36.

Fox, Edward. Review in *Nation*. CCXL (June 22, 1985), p. 772.

Kaufman, Michael T. "Autocrats He Has Known," in *The New York Times*. CXXXVI (Feburary 15, 1987), p. 12.

Kennedy, Moorhead. Review in *The New York Times Book Review*. XC (April 7, 1985), p. 7.

Leonard, Louise. Review in *Library Journal*. CX (March 15, 1985), p. 52.

Lyons, Gene. Review in *Newsweek*. CV (March 4, 1985), p. 66.

Massing, Michael T. "Snap Books: Big Writers and Little Countries," in *The New Republic*. CXCVI (May 4, 1987), p. 21.

Gavin R. G. Hambly

SILENCES

Author: Tillie Olsen (1913-   )
Type of work: Literary history
First published: 1978

Form and Content

Silences is divided into two major parts of equal length: "Silences" and "Acerbs, Asides, Amulets. Exhumations, Sources, Deepenings, Roundings, Expansions." Through essays, quotations, and comments, Tillie Olsen presents the history of both well-known and obscure literary figures, stressing how cultural injustices and inadequacies have deterred these and other individuals, especially women, from fulfilling their literary potential.

Part 1 consists of three essays. The first, "Silences in Literature," was originally delivered from notes at a colloquium at the Radcliffe Institute in 1962, then edited from a taped transcription, and published in *Harper's Magazine* in October, 1962. In it, Olsen discusses the various types of unnatural creative silences, the conditions for full functioning, and the results of inadequate time and energy.

The second essay in part 1, "One Out of Twelve: Writers Who Are Women in Our Century," was first addressed to university literature teachers at a Modern Language Association Forum in 1971 and appeared in *College English* in October, 1972. Here, Olsen declares that in the twentieth century, for every four or five books written by a man, a woman writes one. Only one woman out of every twelve writers, however, receives recognition equivalent to that of her male peers. Why are so many more women than men silenced? Blaming history, attitudes, education, motherhood, the literary-critical establishment, and internalized literary gynophobia, she requests that teachers read, teach, criticize, and write about women writers, encouraging first-generation female writers so that gender equality will eventually result.

The final essay in part 1, "Rebecca Harding Davis: Her Life and Times," appeared first in 1972 as an afterword for the Feminist Press reprint of Davis' *Life in the Iron Mills: Or, The Korl Woman* (1861). Davis' instant fame and acceptance by such figures as Nathaniel Hawthorne, Louisa May Alcott, and Ralph Waldo Emerson diminished significantly after she was married and had devoted her life to her family. Although she continued to write prolifically and profitably, she never gained her former literary stature, lacking the time and energy to do so. A forerunner of social realism unable to maintain her artistic greatness because of social and cultural attitudes and constraints regarding women, Davis remains important not only for *Life in the Iron Mills* but also for her contributions to American social history.

Part 2 of *Silences* also consists of three major sections, each a development of its counterpart in part 1. "Silences in Literature: II" relies primarily on brief quotes from well-known writers, upon which Olsen comments. She illustrates several factors, including poverty, religion, and lack of support from established writers, which have dispirited and silenced great writers, stressing that lesser writers are even more easily silenced. Unnatural silences result from censorship, politics, marginality, and substance abuse. Then she sets forth the conditions necessary for the full functioning of creativity, as shown through journals, letters, notebooks, and accounts of such major writers as Herman Melville, Joseph Conrad, and Virginia Woolf. Conditions include "constant toil," "unconfined solitude," and freedom from other labor; especially crucial is abundant time to feed one's creative force, wait for it to develop, and be available to work whenever the creation ripens for expression.

Using entries from Woolf's diary covering her creation of *The Waves* (1931), Olsen provides a detailed account of the unforced process of creativity. Quoting Conrad, Sherwood Anderson, and Hart Crane, Olsen illustrates the despair of writers who realize that they have not done their best work; she cites Katherine Ann Porter's remark that talent does not always emerge: People "can be destroyed; they can be bent, distorted and completely crippled." Finally, Olsen reveals that in 1976 only one hundred American writers earned enough to support themselves by their writing, and she quotes William Blake's statement that contrary to popular belief, affluence is more conducive to artistic productivity than is poverty.

She then sings the blues regarding the social climate for modern writers, warning practicing writers to skip this depressing section. She speaks of such factors as the indifferent reading public, commercialism, and competition, asking what is wrong with a world which does not want people to do their best. Nevertheless, she stresses the importance of establishing a cooperative spirit among writers and quotes Porter's advice to writers to pay no attention to editors' and publishers' debasing influences: "You are practicing an art and they are running a business and just keep this in mind."

Olsen next concentrates on female writers in "The Writer-Woman: One Out of Twelve: II." She notes that few women have created a large body of work, then comments on the historical discovery that the women portrayed in literature by male authors are far different from actual women. Tracing the gains in women's literature, she reveals that two-thirds of the world's illiterate are female and that only 6 percent of the authors taught in twentieth century literature classes in 223 undergraduate course offerings from 1970 to 1976 were female. She then explores the causes of such inequity and discusses the causes of women writers' breakdowns and suicides. Concluding with a brief section considering the general question of stunted creativity in adults, Olsen talks about first-generation writers and notes special challenges for this emerging breed. She ends this section with a quote from Woolf: "English literature will survive if commoners and outsiders like ourselves make that country our own country." To illustrate her points further, Olsen concludes *Silences* with a condensation of Davis' *Life in the Iron Mills*, the story of a potential sculptor, Hugh Wolfe, destroyed by being born into the wrong social class.

Analysis

Although Olsen's work is rather subversive, the literary establishment lauded it when it appeared in 1978, and she increasingly has become a literary heroine. Olsen explicitly sets out the boundaries of her work's content: She is "concerned with the relationship of circumstances—including class, color, sex; the times, climate into which one is born—to the creation of literature." Dealing only with "unnatural" social and economic silences, she does not attempt to account for "natural," personal silences. Her book is a sociological analysis of literary creativity.

She organizes her material clearly, part 2 echoing part 1. Through the repetition of key phrases and passages, she keeps the reader in a circle of discovery, emphasizing, expanding, explaining, then reemphasizing her central points. The reoccurrence of such lines as "when the seed strikes stone; the soil will not sustain; the spring is false" provides images which, when validated by the experience of both famous and obscure writers, become increasingly charged with association and meaning. Also, the reoccurrence of quotes from Woolf's works prepares those readers for whom this writer may seem socially privileged to accept her as a member of the "outsiders" with whom Woolf classes herself.

Olsen's methodology is definitely more literary than scholarly. She emphasizes that her work "is not an orthodoxly written work of academic scholarship." Her numerous footnotes therefore sometimes lack complete citations or have an informal quality to which traditional English teachers would probably object. She offers "abashed apologies" to Hortense Calisher for using excerpts somewhat unfairly from her "superb essay" and admits her reluctance to quote John Gardner's comments on using his wife as an unacknowledged collaborator because the "true 'leech' writers," which she would rather have quoted, are not as honest as Gardner. Such honesty flies in the face of the "objectivity" of formal footnoting methods.

One critic accuses Olsen of "a deliberate misreading" of some of the excerpts she uses, such as these lines by Sylvia Plath: "Perfection is terrible./ It cannot have children/ It tamps the womb." Making an intuitive rather than a logical leap, Olsen comments that until recently most famous women writers have been childless. Using quotes as a springboard for thought is not a common method used in formal scholarship, but a creative writer such as Olsen would more likely rely on an intuitive instead of an analytical approach.

Such leaps underscore the patchwork effect of *Silences*, Olsen's "refusal to integrate or discipline her raw materials." This type of objection again illustrates that Olsen's work is not scholarly, that she has, as she explains, gathered her materials piecemeal over a period of fifty years with no intention of writing on the subject of stifled creativity. The laxity of her methodology would probably appeal more to the silenced artists and first-generation writers to whom she dedicates her book than to established, professional scholars and writers.

That *Silences* does not fit an established genre illustrates the unscholarly nature of this work. Because it is a blend of literary history, sociology, literary criticism, and the psychology of creativity, it defies conventional classification. This is, indeed, part of the subversive nature of this work: It blurs boundaries, explores new territory.

Overall, Olsen's departures from traditional scholarship argue eloquently that this book was written by an author with "no academic training in notation," one too busy to attend to the niceties of documentation and too honest to pretend that she alone knows the objective truth about the subjects under discussion.

Her style and tone also emphasize Olsen's commitment to making the world of letters accessible to the uninitiated. Never pedantic, she writes clearly, directly, and lyrically. For example, she begins by asking,

> What *are* creation's needs for full functioning? Without intention of or pretension to literary scholarship, I have had special need to learn all I could of this over the years, myself so nearly remaining mute and having to let writing die over and over again in me.

Olsen poses her questions so lucidly that any reader can grasp her meaning. She displays no need to absent herself from the text, to appear as an infallible authority, or to apologize for her motivations and her failures.

Such informality pervades the work, allowing Olsen to express her emotions honestly. When she talks of her first reading of Davis' *Life in the Iron Mills* in a "water-stained, coverless, bound" edition of *The Atlantic Monthly* which she bought for ten cents, she admits that she discovered the work by accident in an Omaha junkshop and was too ignorant of library methods to discover the book's author. Tracing the slow chain of events which eventually led to her discovery that Davis was the author, she writes of her own surprise and eagerness during her search and again admits her fallibility: "It did not occur to me to try the index of periodicals." Olsen preserves and communicates the enthusiasm with which scholars pursue their research.

Fragments and elliptical statments abound in *Silences*, again adding to the work's informality and accessibility. Especially near the end of *Silences*, Olsen's prose takes on the breathless, hurried quality which so many writers experience when nearing completion of the long task of composition.

Olsen speaks as a woman with a message who does not have time to waste on superfluities or empty gestures. Through her refusal to refine her work, her honesty of style and tone, she again illustrates her major points: Working-class people and women have as much to contribute to literature as do the more leisured classes; however, they have less time and energy in which to do so.

Olsen states as one of her principal purposes that she intends "to rededicate and encourage" silenced people and first-generation writers from minority groups. Through her informality and casual use of scholarly protocol, she speaks that language of those whom she encourages and provides a role model for her readers who also may be able to speak their own minority language with as much clarity and courage as she possesses.

Critical Context

Published one year before Adrienne Rich's classic feminist work *On Lies, Secrets, and Silence: Selected Prose, 1966-1978* (1979), in which Rich refers to Olsen several times, *Silences* has also been acknowledged as a feminist classic. Rich participated with Olsen in 1971 on a panel sponsored by the Commission on the Status of Women on the topic of "The Woman Writer in the Twentieth Century," at which time she presented her seminal essay, "When We Dead Awaken: Writing as Re-Vision." Describing the Modern Language Association as an old-boys' network, a "marketplace and funeral parlor for the professional study of Western literature in North America," Rich speaks of the "cynicism and desperation" of junior scholars, whipped by the publish-or-perish dictum, "rehearsing their numb canons in sessions dedicated to the literature of white males." Such an attitude is clearly reflected in Olsen's unscholarly methodology, style, and tone in *Silences*. Rich and Olsen have been two major forces behind subsequent changes in the content of sessions at the Modern Language Association, which ranged in the 1987 South Central regional conference from literature by contemporary Australian women to that of practicing Southwestern poets.

Writing not only as a feminist but also as a humanist, Olsen deals in essay form in *Silences* with the same concerns she brings to life in her two other published works: *Tell Me a Riddle* (1961), and *Yonnondio: From the Thirties* (1974). In her short stories she lets the reader hear voices usually silenced, such as that of a mother standing at her ironing board thinking of the ways in which she has failed her eldest daughter and of a sailor who never had close ties with his family. In her novel, *Yonnondio*, she presents the devastating effects of poverty upon one family during the Great Depression. *Silences* makes explicit some of the universal concerns which Olsen expresses in her fiction.

Finally, *Silences* is an educational treatise. Urging American society to refuse to waste the potential of some of its most talented members because of their class, race, or gender, Olsen stands with courage against the strength of traditional educational practices. *Silences* is a work of rare honesty.

Sources for Further Study

Adams, P. L. Review in *The Atlantic Monthly*. CCXLII (September, 1978), p. 96.

Atwood, Margaret. "*Silences,*" in *The New York Times Book Review*. LXXXIII (July 30, 1978), p. 1.

Miller, Nolan. "*Silences* by Tillie Olsen," in *The Antioch Review*. XXXVI (Fall, 1978), p. 513.

Oates, Joyce Carol. "*Silences* by Tillie Olsen," in *The New Republic*. CLXXIX (July 29, 1978), pp. 32-34.

Shelley Thrasher

SILENT SPRING

Author: Rachel Carson (1907-1964)
Type of work: Science
First published: 1962

Form and Content

Experiments conducted during World War II gave rise to the chemical pesticide industries. As a result of the widespread use of these pesticides, widespread destruction has been wreaked upon the earth, the atmosphere, the water, and all the inhabitants thereof, including man. Rachel Louise Carson's *Silent Spring* is the story of that destruction.

Carson, a trained biologist and a member of the U.S. Bureau of Fisheries (now the Fish and Wildlife Service) from 1936 to 1952, was well equipped to write the story that she knew had to be told. She had been concerned about the use of pesticides since the 1940's, at which time she tried to interest the editors of a magazine in an article on the effects of DDT. She was aware of the intense dissatisfaction and controversy over the Department of Agriculture's program to eradicate the fire ant in the South. She had followed with interest court cases in which citizens struggled to protect their environment—for example, the Long Island case in which the plaintiffs sued to prevent the spraying of their lands with DDT to control the gypsy moth. In the decade prior to the publication of *Silent Spring*, Carson had realized that an undercurrent of distrust regarding federal and state pest-eradication programs was gaining momentum. Finally, Carson received a letter from a close friend, Olga Huckins, who was outraged that spray airplanes had destroyed a private bird sanctuary on her property in Duxbury, Massachusetts. At that point, Carson became aware that what she had originally conceptualized as an article was rapidly becoming a book.

The following four years (1958 to 1962) were devoted to a massive research task: Carson perused thousands of scientific papers and articles and corresponded with scientists and medical doctors in both the United States and Europe. By 1962, the material had been amassed and awaited only the writing and rewriting that would produce a finished manuscript. That was no easy task, for the subject matter consisted of a welter of scientific details which would have to be made accessible to the layman.

Finally, the complete book was published by Houghton Mifflin Company on September 27, 1962. Attractive in format, including drawings by Lois and Louis Darling, it contained 297 pages of text, with an additional fifty-five pages that listed Carson's principal sources.

Silent Spring is a scientific work written for the general reader. Its seventeen chapters fully detail the effects, both immediate and long-range, of pest-eradication programs conducted in post-World War II America. Chapters 1 and 2 set forth the rationale for the book, concluding with these words of Jean Rostand: "The obligation to endure gives us the right to know." Chapter 3 provides background on the discovery, manufacture, and widespread use of chemical pesticides. Synthetic chemicals with insecticidal properties are products of World War II, an outgrowth of the development of the agents of chemical warfare. Prior to World War II, pesticides had been developed from inorganic chemicals, principally arsenic. With the impetus given to synthetic chemicals in the 1940's, however, two large groups of synthetic insecticides became widely used. One group, known as the chlorinated hydrocarbons, includes the familiar DDT; the other consists of the organic phosphorus insecticides.

Chapters 4, 5, and 6 examine the way in which these chemicals have contaminated particular areas: "Surface Waters and Underground Seas," "Realms of the Soil," and "Earth's Green Mantle." Man seems to have forgotten, Carson laments, that the earth's vegetation is a part of the whole of life and that there is a delicate and intricate balance among all living organisms. Furthermore, in the pollution of his environment, man has subjected himself to the risk of the contamination of public water supplies with poisonous and cancer-producing substances.

Chapters 7, 8, and 9 extend the analysis of the pesticides' lethal effects on the life surrounding the "target" pest. Entire populations of certain species of birds and fish have been annihilated in sprayed areas. Chapter 10, "Indiscriminately from the Skies," examines the massive devastation which ensues when aerial spraying is conducted over extensive areas. Two campaigns whose effects are analyzed in detail are sprayings of DDT to eradicate the gypsy moth in the Northeast and the fire ant in the South. Chapter 11, "Beyond the Dreams of the Borgias," presents evidence for the pervasiveness of poisonous substances in the human environment, including chemical residues on food.

In chapters 12, 13, and 14, Carson directs her investigation to the effects of chemical poisons on the tissues and organs of the human body. She projects the possibility of genetic changes in cellular organization and describes, further, the way in which normal cells turn into cancer cells. In chapter 14, she establishes a direct link between chemical pesticides and cancer in man.

Chapters 15 and 16 review the way in which "nature fights back." Pest insects continue to thrive, abundantly, because chemical spraying has often created unfavorable imbalances in the populations of the insect world. Planners of modern insect-control programs have not considered that nature itself, in its precarious balancing of living organisms, has already established an effective control of insects. This control is lost, however, when the destruction of natural enemies greatly enhances a species' ability to reproduce. Moreover, the ability of the insect population to develop resistance and immunity to the sprays is astounding and has created grave concern not only in agriculture and in forestry but also—and especially—in the field of public health.

The final chapter, "The Other Road," presents a choice which involves either continued destruction or the setting of a new direction based on preservation. This preservation requires alternate methods of pest control. Man should employ biological rather than chemical solutions, solutions which will not destroy the balance of nature. Carson affirms, "The choice, after all, is ours to make."

Analysis

Since *Silent Spring* had been serialized in *The New Yorker* beginning June 16, 1962, the heated controversy concerning the book's content had already begun before its publication as a book. Conservationists and wildlife societies, such as the National Audubon Society, were extremely enthusiastic. The National Agricultural Chemicals Association, on the other hand, had already initiated an extensive public relations campaign to discredit the book. Spokesmen for the opposition claimed that the book was "one-sided" and often "unscientific." The general public, however, did not have to rely on the book's advocates or critics. As the author intended, the public could now become the jury, for the whole case had been clearly and painstakingly laid bare in the seventeen chapters of this book.

As the audience, the American public, became engrossed in this work, many quickly recognized that it was not the recounting of man's violations against life that gives *Silent Spring* its permanence but rather its ethical dimension. Carson asks a series of questions which will always be integral to the human experience: "The question is whether any civilization can wage relentless war on life without destroying itself, and without losing the right to be called civilized." While admonishing man throughout for his imprudent and injudicious behavior, his "shotgun approach to nature," she never lets him forget his essential humanity and his humble place in the scheme of life. She urges man to preserve the harmonious balance in nature, she invites his humility, and she begs for his "reverence" before the great and precious miracle that is life.

While celebrating life, Carson knew that she must educate and caution her readers. Grave mistakes had been made, perhaps unwittingly, yet such mistakes constituted heinous crimes against nature and against humankind. Repeatedly, Carson underscores the inadequacy of the research that was to test the chemical pesticides before they were marketed. Although laboratory tests were conducted to determine the effects of the lethal substances on their designated targets, little or no regard was given to the effect the pesticide would have on the surrounding ecology. Nature endures and survives through the interdependence of many life forms. In many instances, not only were the "pests" eliminated but other creatures were destroyed as well. Ironically, very often in the aftermath of a toxic deluge there emerged a species of insect resistant to the chemical, requiring even more lethal dosages. In launching this warfare, this chemical "rain of poison," then, people had succumbed to a strategy which often not only did not eradicate the initial problem but also wrought heedless and senseless devastation.

Birds and fish have been particularly susceptible to death by chemical pesticides, but man is not exempt. Of grave concern to Carson are the long-range effects on the ecology and on humans, effects that result from a chain reaction of disasters, all precipitated by the initial lethal event. Body tissues in other life forms and in man have the proven capability to store toxic substances. Thus, a chemical, laboratory-tested for a "harmless" dosage, may not prove quite so innocuous once it accumulates or when it interacts with other substances which render it even more lethal.

The unknown long-range consequences should hold people back from their precipitous campaigns against insects and weeds, campaigns which not only are severely disturbing the balance of nature but also, in some instances, are producing changes in cells' genetic structure or creating cancer-producing substances, or carcinogens. *Silent Spring* validates pesticides' link to cancer, either directly or indirectly. Carcinogens have the capability to disturb the natural respiratory function of the cell, the oxidation process. In the ensuing desperate effort of the cell to survive, often through a process called fermentation, the cellular control and balance go completely out of control. Other chemicals impair the normal functioning of the liver. This damage to the liver reduces the body's supply of the B vitamins, leading to the escalation of the body's production of estrogens. The latency period for many types of cancer in humans is quite lengthy (blood disorders are a notable exception); therefore, it is not always easy to trace the cause-effect relationship. When the medical case histories are researched, however, quite often victims can be shown to have been exposed to cancer-producing chemicals. Moreover, with the pervasiveness of these substances in the environment, humans are frequently subjected to more than a single exposure.

Silent Spring is an alarming book, but its primary aim was neither to frighten nor to shock, but to caution. Bleak as the message is, it is not without hope. Carson reminds the reader that man has won other great battles, notable among these being the victory over infectious disease in the nineteenth century. She never adopts a tone of defeat. Rather, she emphasizes that people must recognize that solutions which are not compatible with the ecology are not viable solutions. While not wishing to diminish the funds and the effort expended in the research to find a cure for the most dreaded twentieth century scourge of man, cancer, she advocates an equal commitment to research directed at prevention.

The prose style of *Silent Spring* is rational and straightforward, but a deep emotional involvement permeates every page of this factual, scientific text. Occasionally an arresting figurative comparison explodes to underscore the emotional intensity of this work. For example, "This system, however—deliberately poisoning our food, then policing the result—is too reminiscent of Lewis Carroll's White Knight who thought of 'a plan to dye one's whiskers green, and always use so large a fan that they could not be seen.' " In our consumption of poisonous substances, says Carson, "we are in little better position than the guests of the Borgias."

Never was a voice more sincere, more committed, and never was a tone more urgent. Carson realized, perhaps, that time for her was running out (she died, from cancer, just nineteen months after the publication of the book), as she predicted it may be for the life of man, who is sustained by the good earth. Yet her legacy to mankind, in the form of this impassioned warning, if heeded, may abet man's survival.

Critical Context

Paul Brooks, former editor in chief at Houghton Mifflin and biographer of Rachel Carson, believes that *Silent Spring* "may have changed the course of history." Whatever may be its future claims to greatness, the work stands today as one of the most influential books of the twentieth century: It was pivotal in launching the environmental revolution and in making "ecology" a household word.

Silent Spring was Carson's fourth book. Some critics were quick to note that *Silent Spring* lacked the beauty and grace of *The Sea Around Us* (1951). One feels quite certain, however, that if Carson could choose one of her works as her legacy that work would be *Silent Spring*. That choice would be based not on the book's polemical character but on its transcendent message: Man must reexamine his relationship to nature and reaffirm the interdependence of all living organisms. It is the same theme which was clearly articulated by Carson when she was named the recipient of the Schweitzer Medal of the Animal Welfare Institute on January 7, 1963, four months after the publication of *Silent Spring*. An excerpt from her acceptance speech, reprinted in Paul Brooks's *The House of Life* (1972), expresses her deepest belief:

> Dr. Schweitzer has told us that we are not being truly civilized if we concern ourselves only with the relation of man to man. What is important is the relation of man to all life. This has never been so tragically overlooked as in our present age, when through our technology we are waging war against the natural world. It is a valid question whether any civilization can do this and retain the right to be called civilized. By acquiescing in needless destruction and suffering, our stature as human beings is diminished.

The sustaining beauty and power of *Silent Spring* derives from Carson's moral conviction and tone. *Silent Spring* is not merely a "who's who of pesticides," written in clear prose for the general public. It is not, as a few may have initially feared, a bludgeon to smash the chemical pesticide industries. The book does address itself to the destruction wrought by dangerous chemical pesticides, fungicides, and herbicides, but the implicit message throughout is simply a love of all nature. Carson, a very shy, unassuming, private person, had the great courage in the last years of her life to step forward as nature's advocate to plead for the survival of the earth.

Sources for Further Study

Brooks, Paul. *The House of Life: Rachel Carson at Work*, 1972.

Cox, Donald William. *Pioneers of Ecology*, 1971.

Graham, Frank. *Since "Silent Spring,"* 1970.

Marco, Gino J., Robert M. Hollingworth, and William Durham, eds. *"Silent Spring" Revisited*, 1987.

Sterling, Philip. *Sea and Earth: The Life of Rachel Carson*, 1970.

Kae Irene Parks

THE SINGER OF TALES

Author: Albert B. Lord (1912-   )
Type of work: Literary criticism
First published: 1960

Form and Content

The Singer of Tales has its origin in work begun by Albert B. Lord's teacher Milman Parry. It was Parry's theory that the language of the Homeric poems is to a large extent a language of traditional formulas, created over a long period of time by poets who composed their songs without the aid of writing. Homer, according to Parry, was an oral poet who composed as he performed, using ready-made and largely inherited phrases varying in length from one or two words to several lines. In the approximately twenty-eight thousand verses that make up the eighth century B.C. *Iliad* and *Odyssey*, about one-fifth of the verses are repeated word-for-word from one place to another; there are also some twenty-five thousand repeated phrases. It is the repetition of verse or phrases that makes it a formula and marks it as a product of oral poetry.

Between the years 1933 and 1935, Parry made two trips to Yugoslavia to confirm the conclusions he had formed about the Homeric texts by observing a living tradition of epic poetry as practiced by illiterate (for the most part) Serbo-Croatian singers of tales. At the time of his accidental death in 1935, Parry had collected 12,500 texts—some on phonograph records and some taken down during dictation—which form the Milman Parry Collection in the Harvard University library. Parry had been able to publish some of his work, but it was supplemented and carried on by one of his students, Albert Lord, who had accompanied him as an assistant on his second trip. Lord not only was with Parry when he made his collection but also made three later trips to Yugoslavia (in 1935, 1950, and 1951), during which he was able to record the same poets singing the same songs they had sung sixteen years earlier.

At the time of his death, Parry had written the first few pages of a book to be titled *The Singer of Tales*, which was to deal in a comprehensive way with the material he had collected in Yugoslavia. Beginning afresh, Lord carried on Parry's projected work as a doctoral dissertation at Harvard in 1949; he later revised it for publication under the same title in 1960.

Lord's book (309 pages) is divided into two parts. The first part gives an admirable account of exactly how Yugoslavian oral poetry is produced. In five chapters he considers the training and performances of singers, exactly what a formula is and how it works, the themes about which the singers compose their songs, the status of a finished song, and the relationship between tradition and writing.

The second part of the book attempts to apply the knowledge gained from Yugoslavian material to Homer as an oral poet and to the two poems attributed to him, the *Odyssey* and the *Iliad* (in that order, though the *Iliad* is generally considered to have been composed first). The last chapter is devoted to short essays on *Beowulf* (sixth century A.D.), *Chanson de Roland* (c. 1100; *The Song of Roland*), and the Digenis Akritas epic. A series of six appendices offers a comparison of two different poets singing the same song, different versions of the same song performed by the same poet on four different occasions, summaries of a number of "return" and "reurn-rescue" songs, an example of father-son transmission, and the text and translation of the "Song of Milman Parry," produced by an oral poet at Neesnje in 1933.

Analysis

The introductory chapter provides the necessary definition of terms to be used in the subsequent discussion (for example, the precise meaning of the word "oral") and a historical survey of Homeric scholarship and the status of "the Homeric Question." Next, Lord sketches the typical stages of the apprenticeship of a *guslar*, an oral poet who sings his trochaic pentameters to the accompaniment of a *gusle*, a one-stringed instrument that has the ambit of five notes. He describes, in addition, the conditions under which a poet usually performs: When a poet has reached his full development, he can shorten or lengthen his song effortlessly to suit the very fluid requirements of his audience and the occasion.

In his remarks on the formula, Lord adopts Parry's definition: "a group of words which is regularly employed under the same metrical conditions to express a given essential idea." He then describes and illustrates the use of the formula by examining the songs of Salih Ugljanin, Avdo Medjedović, and others. Lord's discussion of theme follows naturally on his analysis of formula. Here Lord shows how incidents or events are regularly used in the telling of a traditional tale, events such as an assembly of heroes, a wedding party, and the writing of a letter or a decree. He shows how such themes may be expanded (ornamented) and combined with one another to form a complex of themes.

Next Lord stresses the multiformity of the oral song. The oral poet rarely sings the same song twice in the same way. Modes of variation may include elaboration, changing the sequence of events, and even changing the ending of a story. Lord warns his readers to avoid applying to oral poems standards and preconceptions derived from an understanding of written literature. The meaning of "oral" in this context refers not to the recitation of a poem during a performance but rather to the composition of a poem during a performance. There is no "original" poem in the sense that the term is applicable to different versions of a written poem. Each oral poem sung by the poet on a given occasion is itself an "original."

In the concluding chapter of this part of the book, Lord deals with writing and oral tradition. He believes that the introduction of writing into an illiterate society may for a long time have no effect on oral traditional poetry because oral songs are the product of an old and perfected compositional technique, whereas written poems in a newly literate society tend to show the fumblings of an art in its infancy. Once literacy becomes a real factor in the creation of poems, however, the traditional way of composing oral song—the use of formula and themes as Lord has described it—tends to die out quickly, as it seems to have done in Yugoslavia. Once an oral composition is written down, it begins to be viewed as the single, correct text and becomes fixed in that form, which is then memorized for performance. When poets memorize their texts, they become merely performers, not creators of poems in the traditional oral way.

Throughout his first part, Lord addresses the Homeric Question in passing, referring to it as he observes the practices and products of the Yugoslavian singers. He observes, for example, that Yugoslavian singers rarely use more than one formula for one idea at a given metrical position in a line and that this is a characteristic of individual singers but not of the collected songs of a number of singers. This thriftiness in the use of formulas can be found in Homer's use of them. Lord concludes that the Homeric poems are the product of a single individual. Not only does Lord believe that the *Iliad* and the *Odyssey* manifest unity of authorship individually, he also thinks that both poems are by the same great poet, Homer. In this regard, Lord is clearly hostile to the analytical view of Homer. On the other hand, Lord is critical of the views of many Unitarians, who he believes have been too ready to praise Homer for subtle beauties which can be of no concern to the oral poet, as in the use of ornamental epithet, for example. In their general conclusions, the Unitarians are correct, Lord thinks, but often for the wrong reasons.

In the second part of the book, Lord applies his findings to Homer and the Homeric poems. Although he does not aim to give a complete account of Homer as an oral poet, he does show how the Yugoslavian material can shed light on Homer's practices. Lord had observed, for example, that the Yugoslavian poets have trouble in dictating their poems. Because they are accustomed to composing rapidly, they seem to become flustered and confused when asked to slow down for dictation. Once accustomed to this novelty, however, the poets tend, in dictating their poems, to produce longer and better organized poems than they would otherwise. The dictated version of Avdo Medjedović's *The Wedding of Smailagić Meho*, in twelve thousand verses—about the length of the *Odyssey*—serves Lord as proof of this contention. On the basis of Medjedović's performance, Lord thinks that the length, ornamentation, and organization displayed in Homer's poems show that Homer must have dictated his poems at his leisure in his old age (in Lord's experience there are no very good oral poets who are also young). If Lord's conclusions are correct, there may be a good chance that the transcribed texts of the Homeric poems go back to Homer himself, assuming that Homer's followers were content merely to memorize and reproduce his dictated text.

Throughout the thematic discussion of the *Odyssey* and the *Iliad*, Lord acknowledges an obvious handicap: The modern reader must read isolated texts in a tradition. The other poems of Homer's epic tradition have been lost, and this means a considerable loss of perspective. Here, as Lord notes, Hesiod and fragments of the epic cycle may be of some help in supplying hints of formulaic use and variant thematic treatments. Even Greek tragedy may be of help in reconstructing the epic tradition in which Homer worked, insofar as the tragedians draw on epic themes. Lord also makes use of the late versions of the story of the Trojan War by Dictys of Crete and Dares of Phrygia, even though their versions are the product of a self-conscious literary tradition.

Because of his experience with the way the Yugoslavian poets often conflate variant themes, Lord is able to argue that there was a version of the *Odyssey* in which Telemachus left Ithaca, met Odysseus, perhaps rescued him, but at any rate returned to Ithaca with him and another version in which Telemachus met his father in Ithaca at Eumaeus' hut—but only after his return. In the *Odyssey*, the second version prevails, but Lord thinks that there are vestigial signs of the first version in the poem, and this leads Homer into a certain occasional awkwardness and actual inconsistencies. Again, Homer seems to know and use three different versions of Penelope's recognition of the ragged beggar as her husband, Odysseus: one in which she recognizes him from the trial of the bow, another in which she recognizes him after he takes a bath, and a third in which she recognizes him from his knowledge of their bed's construction. Penelope clearly recognizes Odysseus from his knowledge of their bed's construction, but Homer keeps in his account the trial of the bow and the bath, and this causes a certain strain on the narrative. All this, according to Lord, is in keeping with the manner of the Yugoslavian oral poets when they are elaborating their stories in dictation.

Lord's treatment of the *Iliad* is in the same vein. In fact, he says that the essential pattern of the *Iliad* is the same as that in the *Odyssey* in that both poems tell the story of an absence that brings trouble to the loved ones of the absentee and of his return to set things right. In addition, Lord sees as common to both stories certain more fundamental and archetypal patterns. Achilles and Odysseus (and Beowulf for that matter) are mythic figures of death and resurrection. Beneath the story of the Trojan War and all stories of bride-stealing and rescue, according to Lord, lies the rape of Persephone as a fertility myth. Lord frequently alludes to these more basic mythic patterns of action in his discussion of the two poems.

The final chapter in this part of the book provides hints for the wide application of the book's thesis. A brief analysis of *Beowulf* and other Anglo-Saxon epics shows that they are oral in character. *The Song of Roland* and the Digenis Akritas epic, though they survive in literary texts, are also based on an oral tradition.

Critical Context

The Singer of Tales shows how oral composition is possible during an actual performance. The poet relies on traditional formulas and themes; he does not memorize his composition but is able to draw on a large stock of ready-made phrases and themes to compose a new poem every time he performs. Perhaps the best illustration of the oral poet's technique is the example cited in *The Singer of Tales*. Avdo Medjedović, certainly the most accomplished singer in Parry's and Lord's experience, was present when another poet, not so accomplished as Medjedović, performed a poem which Medjedović had never heard before. After the song was over, he was asked if he could now sing the same song. He immediately proceeded to do so but to a length nearly three times as long as that of the song he had just heard—6,313 lines as compared with 2,294. Medjedović was relying on his mastery of traditional formulas and on his ability to elaborate using traditional themes.

Since its publication, Lord's *The Singer of Tales* has held its position as the fountainhead of research in oral literature of all sorts, not only in epic poetry, for it was the first to show the way, and it continues to do so in this vast field of study. Lord's method is analogical. He applies his observations of a living oral tradition in Yugoslavia to earlier literature, primarily to the Homeric poems in *The Singer of Tales*, and thereby illuminates the form and structure of those earlier literatures. Since Lord's book, scholars may no longer impose on oral literature an often irrelevant model drawn from written literature, with its emphasis on a fixed text and on an "original" and "correct" version. Moreover, scholars now understand more clearly the important relationship between tradition and originality in oral composition. Although the oral poet relies on traditional formulas and themes (that is, on the work of his predecessors), he displays his individual creativity in the actual singing of his song.

Thus, from *Beowulf* to Xhosa and Zulu oral poetry in South Africa, the research of many scholars progresses following the pattern established by *The Singer of Tales*. Lord's own special interests are in Slavic literature, and his research since the publication of his monumental work continues in that area primarily, though he comes back to Homer from time to time. As for *The Singer of Tales*, it is generally still regarded as the single most important work in the field.

Sources for Further Study
Finnegan, Ruth. *Oral Poetry: Its Nature, Significance, and Social Context*, 1977.
Foley, John Miles. Introduction to *Oral Traditional Literature: A Festschrift for Albert Bates Lord*, 1981.
Kirk, G. S. *The Songs of Homer*, 1962.
Parry, Adam, ed. *The Making of Homeric Verse: The Collected Papers of Milman Parry*, 1971.
Young, Douglas. "Never a Blotted Line? Formula and Premeditation in Homer and Hesiod," in *Essays on Classical Literature Selected from "Arion,"* 1972. Edited by Niall Rudd.

H. J. Shey

SKETCHBOOK, 1946-1949
and
SKETCHBOOK, 1966-1971

Author: Max Frisch (1911-   )
Type of work: Cultural criticism
First published: Tagebuch, 1946-1949, 1950 (English translation, 1977);
   Tagebuch, 1966-1971, 1972 (English translation, 1971)

Form and Content

Although the English word "sketchbook" in many ways describes the seemingly random and tentative jottings in these volumes, Max Frisch employed the German term *Tagebuch*, or diary, to hint at its spontaneous and private nature, with the further implication that he would discuss issues of the day, that is, contemporary political topics, social problems, and world events. In a preface to the first volume, Frisch insists that his authority to write such a book derives not from his person but from his qualification as a contemporary. Though a citizen of a neutral country spared the destruction of World War II, Frisch does not consider himself an isolationist, or even a Swiss nationalist, but a thoughtful, politically engaged citizen of Europe. Significantly, Frisch has published sketchbooks which encompass the two most challenging periods in the second half of the twentieth century. His first volume covers the period directly following World War II, when Europeans had a unique opportunity to confront the mistakes and crimes of their immediate past and, more important, to reconstruct Europe along new designs. The second volume covers the six years of political and social upheaval surrounding the conflict in Vietnam, the Israeli-Egyptian war, the invasion of Czechoslovakia by Warsaw Pact troops, the imposition of a military dictatorship in Greece, as well as the attendant student revolts in Europe and the United States.

These so-called diaries are seldom presented in strict chronological order. In *Sketchbook, 1946-1949*, dated entries of his many travels are frequently interrupted for long stretches by essays, reports on the construction of an architectural project, discussions with acquaintances, or literary sketches. Nevertheless, the careful reader will discover that the various entries are grouped with subtlety to form distinct themes or situations. In the preface mentioned above, Frisch requests that his book, despite its fragmentary appearance, be read from beginning to end, thereby explicitly reinforcing its thematic nature. This composition is especially apparent in the second volume, where various and distinct typefaces illuminate categories of entries—some purportedly factual, as if taken directly from newspapers or wire services; some obviously literary fiction; and still others which seem distinctly personal. In their groupings, these entries contrast with or complement one another to present a multifaceted picture of a specific event, issue, or person.

Each volume is formally divided according to the years under consideration. *Sketchbook, 1946-1949* contains a table of contents which lists each individual entry, ranging from frequent café visits in peaceful Zurich to Frisch's European journeys to such war-ravaged cultural centers as Genoa, Milan, Florence, Prague, Vienna, Paris, Warsaw, Munich, Nuremberg, Frankfurt, Berlin, Hamburg, and Stuttgart. Important elements of the remainder of *Sketchbook, 1946-1949* include his meetings with the dramatist Bertolt Brecht as well as Frisch's work as architect and dramatist. The style is predominantly essayistic.

Sketchbook, 1946-1949 was originally published in 1950, three years after the initial appearance of his *Tagebuch mit Marion* (1947; diary with Marion) which was incorporated in the first part as the entries up to fall, 1947. The sections concerning Marion emphasize the importance of puppetry for Frisch; he sees this as the only form of modern theater which allows distance between the play and its audience, since in the puppet play there is no direct relation to real life; the play occurs beyond the bounds of reality. This encourages the viewer's imagination and gives added emphasis to speech.

In the second sketchbook, representing the years from 1966 to 1971, his chosen topics range from those of world politics, such as the use or abuse of power, exploitation, political indoctrination or concealment, to the more mundane and personal, such as aging, marriage, or the enjoyment of life within a tedious daily routine. Especially noteworthy are such rhetorical devices as the "questionnaires" and "interrogations"—closely structured formats which attempt to involve the reader in specific topics, including love, death, humor, happiness, hope, marriage, friendship, home, money, possessions. Yet another thoughtful fiction is that of the "Voluntary Death Association" and its attempt to lower the earth's population and median age by the voluntary suicide of its members over the age of sixty. Again, his numerous travels are interspersed with fictive fragments, while his style becomes increasingly notational, that is, composed of lists or of stories with individual sentences highlighted for effect.

Analysis

For many writers such as Max Frisch, the diary as literary form replaces the novel in an age when an omniscient narrator is suspect, if not ridiculous. Many critics consider Frisch's *Blätter aus dem Brotsack* (1940; papers from my mess kit), his third work, to be a conventional diary, that is, an autobiographical account of his military service at the outset of World War II. With the revision and expansion of his *Tagebuch mit Marion* as the beginning of *Sketchbook, 1946-1949*, however, scholars have noted the development of a unique idea of the contemporary diary, a model Frisch has followed in subsequent works: In the traditional diary form, the reader receives the impression that he or she is reading something spontaneous and private, thus credible and true. Frisch plays on these traditional expectations, though he creates a structured work of art at once as fictional as the most imaginative novel. Thus, Frisch may give his reader the impression that these sketchbooks are, in fact, personal diaries. In reality, they are tightly structured works of literature, works of fiction, which have from the outset been composed with publication in mind.

As a professional architect during the 1940's, Frisch simply had no time to write expansive works. The brief sketches, ideas, and literary fragments which character-ize the first sketchbook are a symptom of this shortage of time, though the strict composition of the final version belies this casual tone. In a 1961 interview, Frisch drew the distinction between his private diaries and those written for publication, emphasizing three volumes to be considered under the latter category: *Blätter aus dem Brotsack* and the two sketchbooks. Moreover, he considered two of his novels, *Stiller* (1954; *I'm Not Stiller*, 1958) and *Homo Faber* (1957; *Homo Faber: A Report*, 1959), diaries. With this in mind, the scholar Horst Steinmetz has gone so far as to assert that indeed all Frisch's works—be they drama or prose—are simply compo-nents of a greater, comprehensive diary.

In that same interview, Frisch pointed out that his first sketchbook was more than simply a logbook of historical events; it was intended to portray reality through fiction as well as through facts. Frisch further explained that his first sketchbook was to be a "confrontation" between three different realms: that of "fact," meaning the political and social events of the day; of "fiction," that is, of imaginary literary fragments (later often expanded to become independent works of prose or drama); and of "personal life," those incidents, anecdotes, travel descriptions, observations, and experiences such as his meetings with Brecht or the development of his archi-tectural projects. These two volumes are therefore much more than casual sketch-books or private diaries with literary inserts.

One of Frisch's repeated exhortations is the biblical commandment: "Thou shalt not make unto thee any graven image." In varying forms Frisch consistently repeats his conviction that one should cultivate no preconceived, and thus limiting, opin-ions. If an opinion of someone else has been formed, that person is then trapped in the preconception; regardless of what that person does, only those things that reinforce the observer's prejudice will be seen. No development will be possible, for either party. This commandment reflects Frisch's own postwar experiences and discoveries. For example, there are no "good" and no "evil" nations: There are only good or evil individuals. Despite the complexity of the task, each person must somehow be able to differentiate between the two by their actual deeds, not by preconceived notions.

According to Frisch, this philosophical approach can best be expressed in certain types of fiction. In writing novels and dramas Frisch has had to posit a beginning and an end, thus creating a finished work with developed or "fixed" characters in time and space to which the reader can react only after the fact. In the diary—as sketch or fragment—possibilities are only intimated:

> It is conceivable at least that a late generation, such as we presumably are, has particular need of the sketch, in order not to be strangled to death by inherited conceptions which preclude new births. . . . The sketch has direction, but no ending; the sketch as reflection of a view of life that is no longer conclusive, or is not yet conclusive; it implies mistrust of a formal wholeness which pre-empts the spiritual

content and can only be a vehicle for borrowed ideas; mistrust of ready-made formulas which prevent our time from ever achieving a perfection of its own.

Individuals or ideas should be seen as capable of development in several possible ways, and the reader should participate in this process. In this way, Frisch creates his own alienation effect to distance the reader's emotions from these important questions: Only through the conscious juxtaposition of "fact," "fiction," and "personal life" can Frisch arrive at a work that is at once distanced from his own subjective, thus limited, personality and yet is of general interest for a broad readership.

Critical Context

Though regarded as only a promising dramatist by the early 1950's, Max Frisch became a respected commentator on European affairs with the publication of *Sketchbook, 1946-1949*. His measured remarks—especially as an objective observer, a consequence of his Swiss citizenship—were welcomed by many in the German-speaking countries during postwar reconstruction. Yet not until the appearance of his first novel, *I'm Not Stiller*, in 1954 did Frisch gain worldwide recognition and popularity; during that decade, he and the dramatist Friedrich Dürrenmatt were to become the two most influential Swiss writers of the twentieth century.

For a writer who has since become renowned for his novels and dramas, it may seem a bit odd when critics insist that Max Frisch's entire work revolves around the diary form or that many of his works, introduced embryonically in the diaries, are even more effective there than in their later reincarnations as novel or drama. The seemingly autobiographical elements in his most popular fiction and drama—in *I'm Not Stiller, Mein Name sei Gantenbein* (1964; *A Wilderness of Mirrors*, 1965), *Homo Faber, Der Mensch erscheint im Holozän* (1979; *Man in the Holocene*, 1980), *Dienstbüchlein* (1974; service record), *Montauk* (1975; English translation, 1976), *Graf Öderland* (1951; *Count Oederland*, 1962), *Biedermann und die Brandstifter* (1958; *The Firebugs*, 1961), *Andorra* (1961; English translation, 1963), and *Biografie* (1967; *Biography*, 1969)—are introduced in embryonic form in the sketchbooks. In fact, they are more effective there, since they are still sketches and thus have many possible conclusions to which the reader can thoughtfully contribute. Though Frisch will not be best remembered for his sketchbooks, they form a seminal part of his artistic reflection and his literary development, and his oeuvre is unthinkable without them.

Sources for Further Study

Butler, Michael. *Frisch: Andorra*, 1985.
Peterson, Carol. *Max Frisch*, 1987. Translated by Charlotte La Rue.
Publishers Weekly. "Max Frisch Wins Twenty-Five-Thousand-Dollar Neustadt Prize." CCXIX (April 11, 1986), p. 23.
Steinmetz, Horst. "Frisch as a Diarist," in *Perspectives on Max Frisch*, 1982. Edited

by Gerhard F. Probst and Jay F. Bodine.
World Literature Today. LX (Autumn, 1986). Special Frisch issue.

Todd C. Hanlin

SLOUCHING TOWARDS BETHLEHEM

Author: Joan Didion (1934-   )
Type of work: Cultural criticism
First published: 1968

Form and Content

Slouching Towards Bethlehem is a collection of twenty essays on various subjects written by Joan Didion between 1961 and 1968. In the book's preface, Didion discusses the origin of the title, a phrase taken from William Butler Yeats's apocalyptic poem, "The Second Coming." She relates that in writing the title piece, about the gathering of hippies in the Haight-Ashbury district of San Francisco in 1967, she suddenly realized that the world as she knew it no longer existed. When one reviews the essays included here, it is obvious that the forces of chaos and change form the thematic adhesive that binds most of the collection.

The work is divided into three sections, the first of which, "Life Styles in the Golden Land," contains eight pieces that deal with personalities or incidents that seem quintessentially Western, if not Californian. Thus, one finds the story of Lucille Miller, who is convicted of murdering her dentist husband in San Bernardino; a profile of an exhausted John Wayne as he completes another film after cancer surgery; a wary look at Joan Baez's Center for the Study of Nonviolence in Big Sur; a meditation on Howard Hughes and his asocial behavior; and a satiric view of the Center for the Study of Democratic Institutions, among others.

In the second section, "Personals," Didion shifts the focus from society to herself. Here similar thematic concerns prevail; however, they are developed in decidedly subjective ways. She discusses abstractions such as self-respect and morality, ponders the implications of keeping a notebook, criticizes the film industry, and examines the complex network of tensions and affections that arise on any trip home to her parents' house.

The last section, "Seven Places of the Mind," strays even further from the social scene; on the surface, it would appear to have little to do with "personal" statements. Yet the locations Didion considers—Alcatraz, Sacramento, Guaymas, Mexico, Hawaii, Los Angeles, New York, and Newport, Rhode Island—all reveal her unique perspective. Here the intimate connection between setting and psyche is explored, as she argues for influence of place on human behavior.

As a result of these and other pieces, Didion has frequently been mentioned as a New Journalist, a writer who, along with Norman Mailer, Truman Capote, Tom Wolfe, and Gay Talese, pushes against the conventions of traditional reporting to offer idiosyncratic, personal viewpoints. Although some of the essays were commissioned, most were initiated by the author herself and first appeared in *The Saturday Evening Post* (a magazine she defends in her preface), *The American Scholar*, *Vogue*, *The New York Times Magazine*, and *Holiday*.

As a social critic, Didion can indeed be polemical—but never in the service of a particular "cause" or ideology. Thus, for example, the treatment of Joan Baez shifts from one of initial respect for her political poise and determination to a view of a rather shallow woman whose confused ideas center on an insipid desire to remain an adolescent. Didion never adopts the expected stance—such as criticizing Baez for her politics or celebrating her as a champion of the disaffected; instead, Didion searches for the individual behind the public persona and laments what she finds.

In her important uncollected essay, "Why I Write," Didion defines her purposes as a writer when she asserts, ". . . writing is the act of saying *I*, of imposing oneself upon other people, of saying *listen to me, see it my way, change your mind.* It's an aggressive, even a hostile act, . . . an invasion, an imposition of the writer's sensibility on the reader's most private space." First and foremost, then, writing becomes a way for Didion to define and assert herself; as she reveals later in the essay, it also leads to discoveries of what she does and does not know. This thrill of discovery animates the pieces in *Slouching Towards Bethlehem* and results in some highly charged, invigorating prose.

Analysis

As disparate as the pieces are, certain themes emerge; not the least of them involves Didion's theory of "atomization, the proof that things fall apart." Inspired by Yeats's poem, Didion appears convinced that the United States, in the last half of the twentieth century, is undergoing a cataclysm, a major unraveling of the individual and social fabric, in which chaos has come to define the ordinary course of events.

The first essay, "Some Dreamers of the Golden Dream," recounts Lucille Miller's sexual infidelity and presumed murder of her husband. As Didion depicts it, Miller's story becomes a modern morality play, complete with greed, lust, and homicide. As the title suggests, the principal players stumble about in states of delusion, dreaming the wrong dreams, misinterpreting the implications of the American Dream, and eventually allowing "the dream [to teach] the dreamers how to live."

In "Marrying Absurd," Didion aims her sights at Las Vegas and the "quickie" marriage industry which thrives there. Here she argues that Las Vegas, in all of its impermanence and unreality, operates as a fitting metaphor for a prototypical American industry. While her tone is wryly cynical throughout, she also strikes a note of despair when pondering the implications of transforming one of the most profound human experiences into a tawdry commercial venture.

"On Keeping a Notebook" details the often-inscrutable minutiae Didion includes in her notebook. As she reveals, these objects (napkins from a bar, for example) and observations mean nothing to anyone but herself and often appear to have no clear purpose or importance. In rather Proustian ways, however, they recover the past, bringing Didion back to where she once was and how she once felt. In one of her most eloquent passages, she writes:

Perhaps it is difficult to see the value in having one's self back in that kind of mood, but I do see it; I think we are well advised to keep on nodding terms with the [people] we used to be, whether we find them attractive company or not. Otherwise they turn up unannounced and surprise us, come hammering on the mind's door at 4 A.M. of a bad night and demand to know who deserted them, who betrayed them, who is going to make amends.

Atomization is not merely a theme but a structural device she frequently invokes. Its most dramatic appearance comes in "Los Angeles Notebook"; the essay opens with a description of the effects of the Santa Ana winds on the inhabitants of Southern California. Many readers assume that Didion is arguing for a causal relationship between the Santa Anas and aberrant behavior. Her point, however, is that they reveal "something deep in the grain," something already lying dormant: "The unpredictability of the Santa Ana affect the entire quality of life in Los Angeles, accentuate its impermanence, its unreliability. The wind shows how close to the edge we are."

The remainder of the essay is then divided numerically into four separate vignettes—one dealing with a radio talk-show, another with the author's encounter with a woman in a supermarket, a third with a nasty Beverly Hills party, and the fourth with a conversation in a piano bar. On first reading, these completely independent anecdotes make no apparent point, but on closer examination they reveal a divided, hostile society where predatory impulses have replaced all sense of shared purpose and community.

Another important Didion concern involves the antithesis of illusion and reality, and one of the most dramatic examples of this disjunction occurs in "John Wayne: A Love Song." Didion took this assignment reluctantly, for she had always admired Wayne and the larger-than-life image he portrayed in all of his films. While Wayne still conveys that presence on the screen and even in some personal conversations, he is an older, definitely ill man. Recovering from surgery and suffering from a severe cold, Wayne must retreat each day to an inhalator. As much as she wants to retain the silver-screen image of Wayne, Didion is also forced to consider the actor's weakness and vulnerability.

"7000 Romaine, Los Angeles 38" centers on Howard Hughes, the eccentric millionaire who once dominated the news media with stories about his peripatetic wanderings throughout the country. Like everyone else, Didion is fascinated by Hughes's escapades; unlike other journalists, however, she is more concerned with the implications of his eccentricities and the public's insatiable interest in him. In her view, Hughes is the quintessence of the American Dream, someone with "absolute personal freedom, mobility, privacy." Hughes is an American hero but one whose heroism Americans cannot admit to themselves because it is "socially suicidal." As she reveals,

It is impossible to think of Howard Hughes without seeing the apparently bottomless gulf between what we say we want and what we do want, between what we officially

admire and secretly desire, between, in the largest sense, the people we marry and the
people we love. . . . He is the last private man, the dream we no longer admit.

Given her preoccupations with chaos, atomization, and the illusory, many readers
have assumed Didion is nothing more than a pessimistic naysayer, but there is
ample evidence to the contrary. In fact, Didion's best pieces reveal a genuine moral
seriousness, a hard-nosed determination to strip the veneer away and reveal uncomfortable, but necessary, truths. In "On Self-Respect," the author sets herself an ambitious task: to define in clear terms an abstraction. Here she argues against common notions of self-respect, which usually emanate from the opinion of others. In
her view, what others think is beside the point; self-respect is something intrinsic, a
habit of mind which can be developed. While exhibiting signs of character and
moral nerve, self-respect ultimately involves "the willingness to accept responsibility for one's own life." Self-respect "free[s] us from the expectations of others, . . .
give[s] us back to ourselves."

"On Morality," another of her attempts to wrestle with an abstraction and make
some concrete sense of it, stands as a direct response to what Didion regards as
widespread, but nevertheless vapid, assumptions. She assaults the ethic of conscience as being "intrinsically insidious." She insists that "we have no way of
knowing—beyond loyalty to the social code—what is 'right' and what is 'wrong,'
what is 'good' and what 'evil.' "

Instead, she advocates "wagon-train morality," a primitive code which replaces
the ideal (and, in her opinion, the unknowable) good with survival. In a time when
the word "moral" is used to justify any action and to mask personal desire with
some idealized quality, Didion pleads with her audience to return to fundamental
issues, particularly loyalty to those one loves. To do otherwise is to consign oneself
to a form of hysteria which she sees as rampant.

In making her points in "On Morality," Didion reveals one of her most important
rhetorical techniques: concreteness. In "Why I Write," she insists that she does not
think abstractly: "My attention veered inexorably back to the specific, to the tangible, to what was generally considered, by everyone I knew then and for that matter
have known since, the peripheral." Such is the case in "On Morality," as the writer
composes her piece in a motel room in Death Valley.

The discussion is frequently interrupted by seemingly mundane and irrelevant
anecdotes, but each of these becomes part of the writer's distinct way of illustrating
how and where morality enters everyday lives. Integral to her argument is the contention that moral issues can be understood only in clear, definite particulars and
not in the windy speculations of theorists.

Many of the pieces in "Seven Places of the Mind" particularly exhibit Didion's
insistence on concreteness. In "Rock of Ages," for example, the focus rests continually on specific abandoned objects on Alcatraz. The sheer enumeration of
details in such a short piece leads one to question exactly where all of this is
headed—until the last paragraph, when Didion remarks, "But the fact of it was

that I liked it out there, a ruin devoid of human vanities, clean of human illusions." In its hard particularity, Alcatraz stands as a dramatic contrast to the confusion of the times.

Something similar occurs in "Guaymas, Sonora," as the author describes traveling with her husband on a Mexican vacation. In itself, the destination pales in comparison to the journey, and the passage through the desert reveals the essay's thesis. In the oppressive heat of the desert, one becomes "disoriented, shriven," forced to get outside oneself and emerge "like Alcestis, reborn."

In keeping with her theme of atomization and with her personal inclination to view matters concretely, Didion often structures her pieces around a cluster of fragments. In "Slouching Towards Bethlehem," she narrates a series of loosely related anecdotes in which certain figures meander about. To portray adequately "the social hemorrhaging" she witnesses, Didion assembles successive blocks of experience and dialogue which reveal the chaos about her. Ultimately, however, the point is weakened through diffusion, whereas a similar technique in "Los Angeles Notebook" is far more telling because of its intense concentration.

Still another favorite Didion technique is the use of multiple references and allusions to historical and especially literary sources. "On Morality" is peppered with numerous references, both obvious and arcane, to Alfred Rosenberg, the Mountain Meadows massacre, Klaus Fuchs, Daniel Bell, the Jayhawkers, the Donner-Reed Party, and the like. "7000 Romaine, Los Angeles 38" mentions Shoeless Joe Jackson, Warren G. Harding, and Charles Lindbergh, among others.

Clearly, though, the references and allusions Didion invokes most often are literary. For example, in "7000 Romaine, Los Angeles 38," she mentions both Raymond Chandler and later his novel *The Big Sleep* (1939); in "Los Angeles Notebook" the opening paragraph is an imaginative rewriting of the first paragraph of Chandler's "Red Wind." Another favorite literary reference is F. Scott Fitzgerald, who appears by name in "7000 Romaine, Los Angeles 38," and whose character, Jordan Baker from *The Great Gatsby* (1925), is invoked as an illustrative example in "On Self-Respect." The impression all these and other rhetorical techniques (such as parallelism, incongruity, and antithesis) make is one of daring experimentation and genuine erudition. Didion is well-informed and has read widely, and she makes effortless and often-artful use of her considerable knowledge.

Critical Context

Didion's concern with aesthetics and moral truth extends throughout her writings. Her career has been marked by an almost-even oscillation between fiction and nonfiction. Each of her four novels and three works of nonfiction stringently examines both the broad social panorama and its impact on individual lives. Individuality, continually assailed by forces outside it, forms the core of many of her writings.

Since the publication of her first novel, *Run River*, in 1963, Didion has developed into one of the most distinctive and important voices in American letters. Her essays and reviews appear in major newspapers and periodicals, and one measure by which the esteem with which her work is held can be gauged is how frequently her works are anthologized and taught in college classes.

In many of her works, especially *Slouching Towards Bethlehem* and her novel *Play It As It Lays* (1970), Didion reveals an awareness of and sympathy with existential thought. She knows the existentialist's feelings of rootless anxiety and dread, and like the existentialist she has faced the void of existence and returned determined to make something of life. Furthermore, she realizes that the world is not an ordered place; events often occur randomly and chaotically but, also like the serious existentialist, Didion believes that the meaning of life lies in individual decisions. Her determination to view existence through the lens of commitment and responsibility demonstrates her belief that existence need not be meaningless.

With each publication, Didion's stature has risen. One of her critics has described her as an "antiromantic realist"; as such Didion often holds a glass up to her times and scrutinizes what she finds there. Her vision is not always a popular or comfortable one, but it remains unflinching in its search for truth.

Sources for Further Study
Friedman, Ellen G., ed. *Joan Didion: Essays and Conversations*, 1984.
Harrison, Barbara Grizzutti. "Joan Didion: The Courage of Her Afflictions," in *The Nation*. CCXXIX (September 29, 1979), pp. 277-286.
Henderson, Katherine Usher. *Joan Didion*, 1981.
Johnson, Michael. "New Journalists Writing on the General Scene and the Race and War Scene," in *The New Journalism*, 1971.
Kakutani, Michiko. "Joan Didion: Staking Out California," in *The New York Times Magazine*. VI (June 10, 1979), pp. 34-36.
Kuehl, Linda. "Joan Didion, the Art of Fiction LXXI," in *The Paris Review*. XX (Spring, 1978), pp. 142-163.
Stimpson, Catharine. "The Case of Miss Joan Didion," in *Ms*. I (January, 1973), pp. 36-41.
Winchell, Mark Royden. *Joan Didion*, 1980.

David W. Madden

SMALL IS BEAUTIFUL
Economics As If People Mattered

Author: E. F. Schumacher (1911-1977)
Type of work: Essays
First published: 1973

Form and Content

E. F. Schumacher's essays in *Small Is Beautiful* comment on the state of economics and the functioning of the economy; he is critical of both. In his opinion, economists are too tied to the notion that profits should be a determining factor in economic affairs; thus, they are blinded to many of the economy's negative features. The features on which Schumacher focuses his attention are related to the form of modern technology, which employs the techniques of mass production. As a result, modern business firms have grown increasingly large and human beings have become dwarfed by their own creations. Nevertheless, Schumacher offers more than a critique. His book is a plea for a return to organizations and technologies more reflective of human needs and values. As he states,

I have no doubt that it is possible to give a new direction to technological development, a direction that shall lead it back to the real needs of man, and that also means: *to the actual size of man.* Man is small, and, therefore, small is beautiful.

In form, the book brings together nineteen essays, most of which were derived from articles and lectures presented by Schumacher between 1967 and 1972. From 1951 to 1971 Schumacher had worked as an economist for the British Coal Board, and his concerns with the environment, large-scale technology, energy, resources, and large organizations reflect that experience. Nevertheless, the essays are not highly technical, although some knowledge of economics is needed if the reader is to appreciate Schumacher's criticisms of that discipline. Schumacher, who at one time converted to Buddhism, writes in a gently reproving manner. His work follows in the steps of that of other critics of industrialism, such as Leo Tolstoy, William Morris, and the counterculture of the 1960's and 1970's. His search for intermediate technologies and organizational structures suitable for meeting human needs is influenced by principles set forth by Mohandas K. Gandhi.

The book is divided into four parts, each containing four or five essays. The nineteen essays are all of approximately equal length (ten to twenty pages), with footnotes included at the end of the book. Part 1, "The Modern World," is concerned with modern efforts to use science to enhance economic production and the problems this causes. Part 2, "Resources," details the ways by which modern economies misuse their resources, especially those that are not renewable. In part 3, "The Third World," Schumacher argues against taking the latest industrial techniques of richer countries as methods of fostering economic development in the poorer countries; instead, Third World nations should find intermediate-scale technologies to help them. In part 4, "Organization and Ownership," Schumacher considers the patterns of ownership, including nationalization, and structures of organization that would be more compatible with human needs.

Because many of the essays were written earlier, there is some repetition of material. To help tie them together, Schumacher refers to previous points. In addition, he finishes the book with an epilogue in which he restates his basic themes.

Analysis

The subtitle of this book, *Economics As If People Mattered*, is more indicative of its content than is the title, for Schumacher is deeply concerned with the human condition. Modern science, with all the gains that it has brought the world, is often thought to be humanity's greatest accomplishment. Modern capitalist economies, because of their application of science to the technology of industrial production and their emphasis on motivating economic activity through individual self-interest, are held by specialists to have brought about the greatest material comfort and individual freedom ever. In Schumacher's view, however, the proponents of these claims have never really looked at what is happening to the people in those societies that have made the most progress. If they did look closely, they would find a different result:

> In the excitement over the unfolding of his scientific and technical powers, modern man has built a system of production that ravishes nature and a type of society that mutilates man. If only there were more and more wealth, everything else, it is thought, would fall into place. . . . The development of production and the acquisition of wealth have thus become the highest goals of the modern world in relation to which all other goals, no matter how much lip-service may still be paid to them, have come to take second place.

Schumacher is concerned with showing that these goals are unhealthy for both human beings and the world as a whole.

He begins by debunking the notion that modern advanced societies have solved the problem of production through technological development. Because they have removed human beings from direct contact with nature, industrial methods of mass production also have negative side effects. When nature is thought of as something outside human activity, humans become careless about how they treat it. As a result, resources tend to be considered, to use economic terms, as an income (a flow of services) rather than as capital (a stock of goods). Resources such as petroleum and other forms of energy and minerals are used as quickly as possible in the creation of wealth instead of being thought of as something that should be conserved. This carelessness also applies to the environment, which is being polluted by the rapid use of material resources, and to the treatment of human beings, who are reduced to little more than appendages to the machinery they service in factories.

While science has abetted these deplorable conditions, Schumacher places most of the fault on economics. He finds that most current economic thinking is based on greed as manifested in the efforts of business to maximize profits. Economists who believe in the ability of markets to lead to sound social decisions place profits at the center of their philosophy because businesses can make profits only by serving the needs of the public. Because of the centrality of profits in economics, Schumacher finds it to be not a science but a religion, although a very influential one.

The canons of economics do not serve society well according to Schumacher. Individual consumers become bargain hunters who have no concern for what was needed to produce those bargains in terms of using resources, despoiling the environment, or harming workers. Schumacher finds shortsighted the idea that the profits of individual businesses can serve society as a guide to what is needed and what is not. Under that system, neither business nor the consumer has a larger responsibility beyond this to themselves.

According to economists, all those self-interested individual choices are supposed to benefit society ultimately—a result Schumacher considers highly problematic. Instead, there exists a system in which the world's richest society, the United States, even with all of its resources, uses an inordinate share of the world's resources. While other economists may recommend that all societies, especially the poorer ones, emulate the United States by increasing their standards of living, Schumacher holds that this would be impossible, given the world's resource base and the amount of pollution the environment can tolerate. In place of profit-oriented economics, Schumacher proposes an economics of permanence, one that takes a long-term view.

A part of that economics of permanence is to be found in "Buddhist Economics." Most economists consider human labor a burden, so humans must be paid to work. Buddhists, according to Schumacher, see life as a process of building character, with work being the main force for building it. Buddhists criticize economics for putting goods and consumption before creativity in work. For them, work undertaken with dignity is good, not a burden. Work should help humans develop and fully utilize all of their physical and intellectual facilities, it should help them overcome their egos by working with other humans in a common task, and it should produce the goods needed for existence. Machinery that can help humans in this sort of work is seen as good, but machinery that makes man a slave to it is not. The important point is to have production methods that are appropriate to human values.

In his search for a human scale in economics, Schumacher is concerned with the problem of balance. He finds all life to be a struggle to reconcile extreme visions of human behavior. In modern societies, for example, large-scale production is efficient and large organizations are suitable for controlling both it and the humans who work with it; yet people want to work in small-scale organizations, with as much freedom as possible. Schumacher's espousal of intermediate technology aims at attaining this balance.

A part of the failure of present industrial societies to find balance has to do with education. Schumacher believes that there is too much emphasis on science, thus producing only people trained in how to do things. What is needed is an education in values, which will teach what to do as well as how to do it. This training would stress the humanities, for that is where values are to be learned. In striving for the good, each person needs a clear sense of values.

For the remainder of the book, Schumacher consistently applies his concept of balance to show how the modern world has gone wrong and what might set it right, to help it achieve balance. He shows, for example, how agricultural land is being ruined by too heavy an application of science to food production, with little emphasis on conservation for the future. He describes how modern technology cannot help poorer countries become richer, because that technology aims at reducing the needs for labor when labor is the most abundant resource in those places. Again, Schumacher opts for an intermediate technology that will both increase productivity and provide many jobs. For example, older methods, such as those that existed in the United States in 1900, would be more beneficial than modern automated technology.

Schumacher also endeavors to show how balance could be achieved between the need for control and the need for freedom within large-scale organizations and between private and public ownership of organizations. While he sees some potential for socialism and nationalization of industry, Schumacher is not doctrinaire. He believes individual ownership is beneficial as long as the units are small; once an organization becomes large enough to exert an influence over a wide region, however, it should be subjected to some form of public ownership or control. Nevertheless, if that public control is not guided by a broad social vision, then it would be best to leave the organization in private hands. Yet for Schumacher, maintaining production is merely the means. The ends to which it will be put are a matter of human values which cannot be derived from science or economics, but which can only come from religious values, the wisdom of the ages.

Economists would not accept as legitimate Schumacher's critiques of their discipline. Although they do believe that an economy which produces more goods and services is better for its members, they also maintain that the decisions of what to produce, how much of it to produce, and how to produce it are best left to the individual, because that is the only way all the diverse human values that exist in society can enter into economic affairs. Thus, economists would argue that Schumacher, when he writes of religious values, is really imposing his own values on society. When values conflict, as they must, the marketplace is one arena, but not the only one, in which they can be mediated. Schumacher nowhere explains how one set of religious values can be chosen by society, an omission economists would find troublesome even if they were to agree with him.

Critical Context

The advanced economies of the West have had nearly a century of experience with industrialization and economic growth. During that time, the standard of living in those countries has risen dramatically. Along with this improved economic well-being has come a host of problems—social, political, and environmental. For most of this period, economists have extolled the successes and ignored the problems. Even when they have recognized the problems, they have maintained that science and technology would be able to solve them. In holding to this view they have argued that they, too, were dispassionately applying a science.

According to Schumacher, these economists are espousing a religion: Their theory that greed and profits will secure the best social decisions has no scientific basis. Although he mounts a strong attack on these presumptions, Schumacher is really seeking to attain balance in economic thinking. Economic decisions do need some measure of their worth, and profits serve this function well. Nevertheless, economic decisions that are not made within the context of a larger system of values become meaningless. Schumacher wants to incorporate into economics a system of values that combines Christian and Buddhist teachings. As a result, he can be criticized for seeing his own economics as a religion. Yet his infusion of religious values into economics is conscious, whereas traditional economists rarely appreciate the element of religiosity in their own thinking.

Schumacher also puts too much stress on the social influence of economics. Economists and economics tend to be influential only to the extent that they reflect dominant social values. Those who write about the virtues of the present economic system are heard because their views are in accord with powerful social forces, in this case the business community. Discordant voices are thus seldom needed. This applies to Schumacher as well. *Small Is Beautiful* was published at an opportune time, immediately after a decade of concern about the environment and just before a decade of energy crisis. Thus, Schumacher spoke almost as a prophet to a generation concerned with ecological problems and the difficulties that would exist as efforts were made to use nuclear energy as a replacement for fossil fuels. *Small Is Beautiful* is and will remain an influential book as long as there is concern over energy and the environment.

Traditional economists are interested in these problems, but their solutions rarely go beyond measuring the costs of environmental safety versus the lost benefits if a high standard of living is sacrificed. They continue to hope that profits can be used to solve the environmental and energy problems. Despite its inability to influence economists, Schumacher's message that a standard of living is no substitute for a life worth living is an enduring one.

Sources for Further Study
Barnes, Peter. Review in *The New Republic*. CLXX (June 15, 1974) p. 29.
Brynes, Asher. Review in *The Nation*. CCXVIII (June 8, 1974), p. 725.
Economist. Review. CCXLVII (June 23, 1973), p. 113.
Henderson, Hazel. "The Legacy of E. F. Schumacher," in *Environment*. XX (May, 1978), pp. 30-37.

Love, Sam. "We Must Make Things Smaller and Simpler: An Interview With E. F. Schumacher," in *Futurist*. VIII (December, 1974), pp. 281-284.

Donald R. Stabile

THE SNOW LEOPARD

Author: Peter Matthiessen (1927-   )
Type of work: Travel writing
Time of work: 1973
Locale: Himalayan Nepal
First published: 1978

> *Principal personages:*
> PETER MATTHIESSEN, the author
> GEORGE SCHALLER "GS," a zoologist
> TUKTEN, a Sherpa guide

Form and Content

When zoologist George Schaller ("GS") invited Peter Matthiessen to join the 1973 expedition to northwest Nepal (adjacent to Tibet), the two had already known each other for four years, having met on the Serengeti Plain of East Africa. Nor was this to be Matthiessen's first journey to Himalayan country, for he had toured there some twelve years before. Their plan this time was to observe the rut of the *bharal* (Himalayan blue sheep) and perhaps see the rarely observed Snow Leopard. Yet if the invitation came easily and was as easily accepted, the journey itself was to be an arduous and dangerous 250-mile trek through the rugged, breathlessly steep, and scarcely traveled ranges of the frozen Himalayas known as Inner Dolpo. This was not to be a typically modern expedition, with air drops, expensive support teams, abundant medical supplies, sophisticated equipment, and comfortable tents. This was to be an ordeal, a death-defying adventure, and a pilgrimage.

The Snow Leopard is arranged in four major parts (each having one or more epigraphs of spiritual writing) which are simply titled "Westward," "Northward," "At Crystal Mountain," and "Homeward." The periodic journal entries are individually headed by the date, as in a diary. The most treacherous hiking in "Northward," for example, begins on October 10 and ends with the hikers near exhaustion on October 31, on their final approach to Crystal Mountain; there, the cliff ledges they traverse are inches narrow, the steep slopes so extremely dangerous that drops are measured in hundreds of yards, and the snow so deep and ice-coated that it is passable only by planting one's stave and kicking a foothold into the snow wall.

Nature is not the only obstacle. There are also the incessant challenges of locating trustworthy porters, of having to dispense with already limited gear and pack animals as the snow deepens, of staying dry when crossing and recrossing the precarious glacier streams, and of breaking and reestablishing camp. Through it all, a handful of Sherpas (Tibetan-speaking Buddhist tribesmen), especially the one called Tukten, who gradually emerges as the spiritual mentor Matthiessen has been seeking, prove to be faithful guides over the steep cliffs of the mountains, and of the soul.

The book's first two pages provide maps locating Inner Dolpo and outlining the entire route covered in several hard months of travel; these the reader constantly checks to follow the trekkers' arduous progress. Throughout are meticulous notations of geography, direction, and particularly altitude: This lake is seen at 12,500 feet; northward, Dhaulagiri's lower flanks are 26,810 feet high; a prayer flag in one cairn near the Namdo Pass is crossed at 17,000 feet. There are entries that capture the awful beauty of these life-defying snow peaks: a sense of the extreme "top of the world" remoteness is gleaned from descriptions of deep azure sky, frozen white cliffs, and sunless, bone-chilling northern slopes.

The sense of peace, stillness, and the awesomeness of the great void experienced by the author, his friend "GS," and even more so, Tukten, forms the deepest impression on the reader. A simple remark, "Do you realize we haven't heard even a distant motor since September?" drives home to the armchair reader their isolation, their independence, their courage, and their total immersion in the wilderness. The reader will recognize that the journey is as much, or even more, an inward journey than a travel expedition. Still, the detailed checkpoints of inner progress are sparsely located, the sense of purpose is but faintly sketched, and the undefined spiritual objective is as difficult to gauge as the time-distance between snow-cone peaks.

Analysis

When asked why he has undertaken such a hard and treacherous journey, Matthiessen is clearly abashed. His curvilinear rationale goes like this: He has set out to observe sheep goats in Nepal because near Shey Gompa, "Crystal Monastery," the *bharal* are plentiful as they enjoy there the protection of the Buddhist Lama. Also, because the Lama of Shey is the most revered of all that region's religious leaders, and because Tibetan Buddhism is a final citadel of humanity's longed-for wisdom, and since, anyway, simply to glimpse the Snow Leopard would make the trip worthwhile, he has come to traverse the way step-by-step on foot. As this rugged "way" is clearly an image of the religious path, so the glimpsing of the Snow Leopard (rarely seen by anyone, especially Westerners) gradually emerges as an analogue of *kensho*, the first comprehended breakthrough to enlightenment.

It was Karma (or his personal destiny) that brought this invitation from "GS" to visit the holy place of Tibetan Buddhism shortly after Matthiessen had been introduced to Zen Buddhism by his wife, Deborah Love; her death by cancer soon thereafter interrupted their Zen practice together but spurred his quest to a greater intensity. The book's first epigraph, to "Westward," by Lama Govinda, clearly establishes the connection between the travel and religious dimensions of the author's pilgrimage:

> Just as a white summer cloud, in harmony with heaven and earth freely floats in the blue sky from horizon to horizon following the breath of the atmosphere—in the same way the pilgrim abandons himself to the breath of the greater life that...leads him beyond the farthest horizons to an aim which is already present in him, though yet hidden from his sight.

It gradually becomes clear that Matthiessen means to walk his readers, and himself, through the origins of Hinduism in India, through the Buddha's life and refinement of Hinduism from its more speculative philosophy to the more concrete experience of personal enlightenment, and then through all the major stages of Buddhism's later development in Tibet as well as China and Japan, where it became Zen.

Along the way, the author offers the genesis and history of Nepal itself, legends and traditions of various Tibetan tribes, insightful comparisons and parallels (if not historical influences) between the myths cherished by Asian and American indigenous villagers, and a host of fascinating details about the plant, animal, mythic, and geographical life of these Himalayan ranges. Steadily the focus narrows in on Matthiessen's central theme: The jewel in the heart of the lotus (the OM MANI PADME HUM) that he thirsts for, weeps over, dreams about, and fantasizes upon is his own parturition of self-knowledge in its deepest sense.

Still it seems that the goal of the quest forever eludes him. He never gets inside the Crystal Monastery (though "GS" does and describes its interior); he encounters, without recognizing (at least the first time), the Shey Lama; he never solves his koan, or Zen problem, assigned to him by his Zen teacher (partly because he expects its resolution to come in a calamitous upheaval; and he never catches a glimpse of the yeti (known generally as the legendary Bigfoot), let alone the nearly invisible Snow Leopard. Ultimately true enlightenment is less easily accessible (because much closer) than a remote monastery, and it requires more than a vigorous expedition of several months.

Yet Matthiessen is indeed the beneficiary of great teaching, which becomes clear when the Shey Lama (with twisted legs) reveals that his own happiness at being marooned in his isolation at Tsakang is even greater because of his very physical limitations: "Of course I am happy here! It's wonderful! *Especially* when I have no choice!" With that insight gained, Matthiessen ends his November 14 journal entry with rhetorical questions posed in typically enigmatic Zen fashion: "Have you seen the Snow Leopard? No! Isn't that wonderful?" Hence, only three days later, the last entry of "At Crystal Mountain" (which immediately precedes the final part, "The Way Home") shows that Matthiessen realizes his koan practice in a wholly different yet still wholly invincible way:

> Homecoming is the purpose of my practice . . . of my koan: 'All the peaks are covered with snow—why is this one bare?' To resolve the illogical question would mean to burst apart, let fall all preconceptions and supports. But I am not ready to let go, and so shall not resolve my koan, or see the snow leopard. . . . If the snow leopard should leap from the rock above and manifest itself before me—S-A-A-O!— then in that moment of pure fright, *out of my wits,* I might truly perceive it, and be free.

So much for his teacher's advice to expect nothing.

That enlightenment and delusion are one is further seen by the second epigraph to "The Way Home": Dogen Zenji's expression is "Do not be amazed by the true dragon." Now the carp, which must hurl itself to the very top of whatever waterfall lies between it and its spawning place, is a favorite symbol in Zen training because its self-transcending effort is emblematic of the Zen aspirant's wholehearted dedication and effort. The carp is said to become a dragon when it reaches above the falls to its home waters. In this way, the Lama Govinda's epigraph to part 2 is mirrored in Dogen Zenji's epigraph here: the goal, though hidden, is present within, and the practitioner ought not be amazed by his own dragon. While there are times when Matthiessen's descents from the great heights leave him exhausted, irritable, and thin-skinned (he is distressed, for example, by the bright tents and foreign faces of other mountaineers espied at Murwa, four thousand feet below Shey), and while, in his fatigue, he compounds his own distress by chastising himself for such foolishness (" . . . have I learned *nothing?*"), still the parturition of his homecoming is started, and he himself offers a splendid metaphor of this emergence:

> A change is taking place, some painful growth, as in a snake during the shedding of its skin—dull, irritable, without appetite, dragging about the stale shreds of a former life, near-blinded by the old dead scale on the new eye. It is difficult to adjust because I do not know who is adjusting; I am no longer that old person and not yet the new.

Critical Context

The Snow Leopard may have left Peter Matthiessen wandering between two worlds (one dead, the other struggling to be born), but when eight years later he brought out his second spiritual quest book, written in the same journal format (*The Nine-Headed Dragon River: Zen Journals 1969-1982*, 1986), its subtitle's frank disclosure indicated that his ever-sharpening focus had finally narrowed to the most seminal aspects of his inner pilgrimage. Indeed, since his first encounter with Zen was the Rinzai sect's Spartan and driving asceticism (the teachers to whom his wife had introduced him had pushed the intellect to the brink, and then beyond into the pure mind itself, by means of the koan and sudden-illumination method), and since the maturation of his Zen practice came with his emersion in Japan into the Soto sect's more patient and subtler method of sitting quietly to bring about a mellow but deep self-awareness, Matthiessen believed that some transition was needed in the complete record of his Zen journals. Therefore, in between part 1, "America: Rinzai Journals" and part 3, "Japan: Soto Journals," *The Nine-Headed Dragon River* reproduces at its center forty-five pages of *The Snow Leopard* and titles it "Nepal: Himalayan Journals." From this alone, one can readily see how organically holistic are his writing and his spiritual pilgrimage; one can also see the pivotal and climactic place *The Snow Leopard* occupies in that journey.

The Snow Leopard is critically important and summative in other senses as well. In addition to more than a dozen full-length nonfiction works, Matthiessen has written half a dozen novels: His initial *Race Rock* (1954) was heralded as a good first novel; his second and third (*Partisans*, 1956, and *Raditzer*, 1961) received mixed reviews; his fourth, *At Play in the Fields of the Lord* (1965), was nominated for the

National Book Award and considerably enhanced his reputation as a writer; his highly experimental *Far Tortuga* (1975) evoked both high praise and condemnation but was awarded the "Editor's Choice" citation by *The New York Times Book Review*. Matthiessen's steady and high acclaim as a wilderness writer has eclipsed his fame as a novelist, but without this novel-writing experience, he could hardly have brought to *The Snow Leopard* its dramatic suspense, its intricately woven texture of symbol and plot, and certainly not its evocation of such fine character development as that of Tukten.

Nevertheless, it is as "one of the most important wilderness writers of the twentieth century," to quote Anne Jannette Johnson, that Matthiessen has established himself, and *The Snow Leopard* is regarded as the masterpiece of the genre. There are others: Matthiesen's first study, *Wildlife in America* (1959), was chosen for the permanent library at the White House; his sixth, *Sal Si Puedes: Cesar Chavez and the New American Revolution* (1970), won the Christopher Book Award, 1971; his tenth, *The Tree Where Man Was Born / The African Experience* (1972), garnered a second National Book Award nomination. It was *The Snow Leopard*, however, that brought home the 1979 National Book Award for contemporary thought, and the paperback edition won the 1980 American Book Award. Two years later, *Sand Rivers* won both the John Burroughs Medal and The African Wildlife Leadership Foundation Award. Finally, crowning his work as naturalist, anthropologist, and geographical explorer, the Academy of Natural Sciences in 1985 awarded Matthiessen their gold medal for distinction in natural history.

Sources for Further Study
Begley, Sharon. "'Crazy Horse' Rises Again: A Win for Author's Rights," in *Newsweek*. CXI (February 1, 1988), p. 47.
Hoagland, Edward. Review in *The New York Times Book Review*. LXXXIII (August 13, 1978), p. 1.
Johnson, Anne Jannette. "Peter Matthiessen," in *Contemporary Authors*. N.s. XXI (1987), pp. 278-283.
Matthiessen, Peter. Interview by Wendy Smith in *Publishers Weekly*. CCXXIX (May 9, 1988), p. 240.
_____. *Nine-Headed Dragon River: Zen Journals 1969-1982*, 1986.
Prescott, P. S. Review in *Newsweek*. XCII (September 11, 1978), p. 89.
Sheppard, R. Z. Review in *Time*. CXII (August 7, 1978), p. 78.
Zwieg, Paul. Review in *Saturday Review*. V (August, 1978), p. 44.

                                                                    Paul R. La Chance

THE SOCIETY OF MIND

Author: Marvin Minsky (1927-   )
Type of work: Science
First published: 1986

Form and Content

Defining how the mind works and how intelligence is built out of smaller components, *The Society of Mind* posits the idea that the mind is a society made up of small processes called "agents," which work together to produce action, thought, commonsense reasoning, emotion, and memory. Marvin Minsky uses examples of computer programs and artificial intelligence to demonstrate how intelligence or mind can be created out of small, repetitive steps.

The form of the book reflects this idea of mental societies; it is made up of 270 page-length essays which present a single idea or theory or demonstration that is connected in different ways to those of the other essays. The form does not impose any hierarchical order on the material, as there are numerous cross-references incorporated in the text, the glossary, and the index. The form also reflects the way the mind itself cross-connects its agents. The book makes extensive use of diagrams and drawings to demonstrate its concepts. Literary quotations are also incorporated in the text to provide examples of cultural cross-references. While the book does not use a considerable amount of technical psychological terminology, Minsky has created many new terms to describe mental processes. Definitions are given in the text and in a glossary. There is also an appendix which discusses the relationship of the mind to the brain.

To introduce the idea of agents, Minsky describes a computer program, "Builder," which he and Seymour Papert developed in the late 1960's. It combined a mechanical hand, a television eye, and a computer into a robot which could build a tower out of children's blocks. The program had to use agents to "see" the block "grasp" it, "place" it, and "release" it. In addition, "Builder" had to be programmed or taught such concepts as not using a block already in the tower and how to begin and end the tower. Each of these agents, individually, is simple and not an activity which would normally be considered intelligence. "Builder" itself merely activates each separate agent. To understand the system as a whole, one must know how each part works, how it interacts with those to which it is connected, and how they combine to accomplish a given function. Intelligence or mind operates the same way. An additional complexity is the fact that the mind can perform a virtually unlimited number of procedures. Therefore, there needs to be an agent which decides which procedure will take precedence. A variety of agents such as non-compromise, hierarchies, and heterarchies can serve this function. Pain and pleasure are also agents which help the mind determine which procedure to give priority. From these simple agents, the mind builds the self, a sense of individuality, consciousness, and meaning.

Intelligence is defined as the ability to solve "hard problems" fairly rapidly and individually. Minsky excludes from intelligence instinctive behavior. The ability to solve hard problems often relies on the use of memory. A theory of memory must be able to answer questions about knowledge such as how it is represented, stored, retrieved, and used. The theory proposed is that "we keep each thing we learn close to the agents that learn it in the first place." The mind can activate an agent called a "knowledge-line" to do all these things. Knowledge-lines can attach to other knowledge-lines, which in turn create societies. These societies are organized into various "level-bands"; thus, any given mental process operates at any given moment only within a specified range of the structure of the agent. The idea of a level-band explains how it is possible for one process to concentrate on details while other processes are concerned with large-scale plans. From the concepts of agents, knowledge-lines, and level-bands, learning, reasoning, emotions, and language can develop.

There are at least four different ways of learning or "making useful changes in the workings of our minds": "Uniframing" combines several specific instances into a generalization; "accumulating" collects examples which violate the generalization; "reformulating" modifies the uniframe or accumulation; and "trans-framing" bridges structures, functions, and actions. These learning strategies, and problem solving, depend on the short-term memory in order to be able to modify strategies, remember what has just been done, and do something differently. There are many kinds of memory, some attached to time frames and others totally detached from time. These different kinds of memory allow for the interruption of mental processes and also allow them to be broken up into smaller units.

Reasoning is often divided into two different types: logical and common sense. Logical reasoning is often perceived as more difficult than commonsense reasoning, but actually the reverse is true. Logic follows rigid rules for creating chains of reasons. In fact, it is easier to program a computer to express logical reasoning than the commonsense variety. Commonsense reasoning makes chains through causes, similarities, and dependencies.

Although Western, scientific culture tends to emphasize that thought and emotion are very different, emotions are varieties or types of thoughts built up out of different brain agencies. Emotions may be necessary for certain kinds of learning to take place, especially for constructing coherent value systems or participating in a culture. The emotion of attachment may be requisite for developing a knowledge of language.

To explain how cultural concepts and language are processed, Minsky introduces the idea of "frames," or a sort of skeletal outline with slots to be filled. Each slot can be connected to other structures and is connected to a "default assumption," or a basic idea which can be modified or changed as more specific information is gained. For example, for most people the frame for "bird" is a feathered, winged, creature that flies. When it is known that the particular bird under discussion is a penguin, that slot in that frame is modified but the basic default assumptions about birds do not change. Frames such as grammatical structures help in the understanding of sentences. Frames such as cultural contexts and knowledge help in the understanding of language and stories. Most human communication is possible because frames of reference and meaning are constructed.

The power of intelligence comes from its diversity, because it can be made up of many different parts. Humans have many effective, although imperfect, means of achieving and expressing intelligence. The society of mind provides duplication and alternative perspectives which give intelligence versatility and durability.

Analysis

Describing the relationship between the brain or another physical entity and the mind has become an important part of many diverse disciplines. Understanding how the brain gives rise to thought and intelligence is one of the most profound questions in contemporary science and one to which Marvin Minsky has devoted his career at the Artificial Intelligence Laboratory at the Massachusetts Institute of Technology (MIT). *The Society of Mind* is a compilation of his theories and ideas about intelligence and the possibility of its creation in machines.

One of the major points Minsky makes about intelligence is that commonsense reasoning is more difficult to describe and explain than is logical rule-bound reasoning. Thus, it has been easier to program computers to play chess than to build a children's tower. When Minsky makes this assertion, however, he neglects to specify that computer chess-playing programs do not recognize the pieces through a visual mechanism nor do they physically grasp and move the pieces, which are part of the requirements for his computer program "Builder."

The Society of Mind is primarily concerned with explaining how humans learn to think and solve problems. The theory of intelligence formulated here is indebted to the concepts of learning investigated by Jean Piaget. Small children, as they gain knowledge, motor skills, and the ability to understand sensory data and relate them to a meaningful reality, are the model for learning and intelligence. Minsky has collaborated with Seymour Papert, a student of Piaget, to recognize and formulate some understanding of the principles which underlie human learning strategies. One example discussed in detail throughout several essays is the way children learn to recognize amounts. For example, a five-year-old child will watch as water is poured from one container into a taller, thinner container and will say that the taller container now has more water in it. By the time a child is seven, he or she will typically realize that it is the same amount of water. Minsky places this specific and universal process into a large and complex "society-of-more." The concept of "more" applies to many diverse elements, all of which need some organizing principles in order to relate to one another and to the larger society. This requires hierarchical systems which relate the lower level agencies to the higher level concepts. Minsky's diagrams demonstrate Papert's principle: "Some of the most crucial steps in mental growth are based not simply on acquiring new skills, but on acquiring new administrative ways to use what one already knows."

Minsky presents the way children learn meaning as primarily through an experience of trial and error. His examples are drawn from a physical experience that the child has which relates to an understanding of a concept or a definition. Various aspects of learning can have an impact on understanding—including recognizing repetition and realizing that humans tend to see things as wholes, adding missing elements. Nevertheless, people learn not only from physical experience but also from language and other abstractions. Minsky tends to define language as an agency of its own which is connected with other agencies. He does acknowledge that language creates one's image of reality, although he qualifies that statement: "Yet words themselves can't be the substance of our thoughts. They have no meanings by themselves; they're only special sorts of marks or sounds." Language is one of the most powerful controlling agencies; it seems to regulate what consciousness does. This makes language one of the higher level, or managing, agencies in the society of the mind.

According to Minsky's definition, a word "makes various agents change what various other agents do." Words are tied by knowledge-lines to other agents, which are activated or changed by the use of the word. In fact, the meanings of words only become totally clear in relationship to other words; that is how the inherent ambiguity of language is handled. Language is also intimately associated with the way connections between agencies are made. Out of language arise expression and creativity. Minsky's argument is that creativity and intelligence must originate from the language agency, which is in turn related to other smaller agencies. He expands the concept of meaning to describe how the ambiguity of all isolated knowledge is resolved through larger contextualizations. Stories and other verbal narratives have cohesion because they are related to a context that makes sense. Just as humans tend to see partial designs as complete forms, they tend to complete stories and narratives as well.

In order for a story to be truly understood, there must be recognizable connections between the various phrases, and these connections can also activate specific knowledge about contexts in the mind. In addition to these recognition agents which lurk in the mind, Minsky draws on Freudian psychology to describe suppressor agents and censor agents which prevent one from acting on certain thoughts or even from recognizing certain thoughts and ideas. He uses these agents to develop a definition of humor and to discuss how humor relates to learning. His discussion of jokes also is influenced by Freudian psychology and defines jokes primarily as stories which fool the censors. Minsky goes on to hypothesize that humor plays an essential role in learning because it allows one to escape the censors, which may be limiting new ideas and stifling creativity. Humor allows connections and analogies, which may be misleading or which may lead to new insight, to be explored. Clearly, in Minsky's scheme humor and even laughter are built out of smaller agencies and serve a necessary function in the learning process.

The Society of Mind demonstrates how intelligence, problem solving, learning, and models of reality can all be built from lower level agencies. Minsky asserts that "minds are simply what brains do," and he claims that brains are primarily machines. Yet he makes it clear that he means an extremely complex machine and even acknowledges that it is correct to deny that the brain is similar to a simplistic machine. Nevertheless, this mechanistic emphasis is also responsible for some of the omissions of the book as a complete presentation of intelligence and the learning process. He ignores all studies of animal intelligence and even seems to want to define intelligence in such a way that animals cannot possess it. For example, when discussing the problem solving inherent in an activity such as the dam building of beavers Minsky states that this knowledge is genetically based rather than truly learned. According to his theory, the ability of a beaver to build a dam is not a sign of intelligence or learning ability.

One other major limitation of the theory of mind as presented by Minsky is that it does not acknowledge some of the significant aspects of human memory. For example, some recollections are much more vivid than others; some are much easier to recall; some are sublimated entirely. In addition, humans are not always aware of the distinction between memories of actual events and fictional memories. Minsky simply does not discuss these aspects.

Critical Context

Marvin Minsky is one of the founders of the science of artificial intelligence, one of the first people to combine psychology, mathematics, and computer science to reach an understanding of such mental processes as memory, thought, and recognition. In 1958, he and John McCarthy created the Artificial Intelligence Laboratory at MIT. According to physicist Jeremy Bernstein, it is "one of the most creative and distinguished scientific enterprises of its kind in the world." Many of the most significant researchers of artificial intelligence have been Minsky's students. Among his most important contributions to the field have been the focus on commonsense reasoning, as opposed to purely logical systems, and his research on the problems of visual recognition. *The Society of Mind* represents a synthesis of Minsky's previous work on mental process.

Sources for Further Study

Bernstein, Jeremy. "Mind and Machine: Profile of Marvin Minsky," in *Science Observed: Essays Out of My Mind*, 1982.

Johnson-Laird, P. N. "Minsky's Mentality," in *Nature*. CCCXXVIII (July 30, 1987), pp. 387-388.

McCorduck, Pamela. *Machines Who Think*, 1979.

Meer, Jeff. "Mind Models: How Far Have We Come?" in *Psychology Today* XXI (May, 1987), pp. 102-103.

Winston, Patrick H., and Richard H. Brown, eds. *Artificial Intelligence: An MIT Perspective*, 1979 (3 volumes).

Diane Dowdey

SOME AMERICANS
A Personal Record

Author: Charles Tomlinson (1927-   )
Type of work: Memoir/essays
Time of work: 1945-1979
Locale: The United States and Italy
First published: 1981

> *Principal personages:*
> CHARLES TOMLINSON, a British poet and painter
> WILLIAM CARLOS WILLIAMS,
> MARIANNE MOORE,
> LOUIS ZUKOFSKY,
> GEORGE OPPEN, and
> EZRA POUND, American poets
> GEORGIA O'KEEFFE, an American painter

Form and Content

In a one-paragraph introduction to this brief volume, British poet Charles Tomlinson attributes its origin to the American literary critic Hugh Kenner, "who suggested the making of this book" out of essays that Tomlinson wrote between 1976 and 1979. Most of the essays the poet had already published in *Contemporary Literature*, *Paideuma*, and *The Hudson Review*. Gathered loosely around the theme of American influence on his work, the essays make a "Quantum Book" in the series of that name—the physicists' term for a unit of emitted energy—published by the University of California Press at Berkeley, as a "short study distinctive for the author's ability to offer a richness of detail and insight within about one hundred pages of print."

Some Americans consists of four essays of varying length, each one recounting how Tomlinson came to meet one or more American luminaries—poets or painters—and giving his retrospective impressions in acute detail. When a first meeting is preceded by an exchange of letters, these are described and frequently quoted. When acquaintances thus initiated flower into friendship, the progress of the friendship is memorably recounted. The book is peppered with references to contemporary writers and their books: Twelve columns of names in the index attest the sheer number of Americans with whom the young Tomlinson made contact in the course of his pilgrimage through the United States and through his dedicated and devoted reading.

The first and longest chapter (43 of the book's 134 pages), written in 1976 and 1977, chronicles Tomlinson's discovery of American poetry—despite its near invisibility in the England of his youth—and his first attempts to write poetry in an English idiom that was not distinctly British. He discusses the poets whose work he was reading, alludes frequently and happily to the positive reception publicly and privately accorded his own poetry, and describes his successful efforts to establish personal contact with the American poets William Carlos Williams, Yvor Winters, Robert Lowell, Marianne Moore, and others.

Chapter 2, eighteen pages long, focuses closely on the objectivist poets Louis Zukofsky and George Oppen, with mention of Tomlinson's indebtedness to American poet Robert Creeley for guidance and consultation about their work. The essay, written in 1978 and published that year in *Paideuma*, describes the summer of 1963, during which Tomlinson and his wife lived in Brooklyn, near both Zukofsky and Oppen. It recounts the conversations the three poets had and the breaking of the friendship between the two American poets. The narrative also serves to explain why Tomlinson's projected edition of an anthology to be called "Seven Significant Poets" never appeared: Zukofsky refused to be included, allegedly because of his resentment of Oppen, who was also one of the seven.

Chapter 3, at sixteen pages the shortest in the book and written in the same year as chapter 2, describes Tomlinson's one meeting with the American painter Georgia O'Keeffe. In it, he discusses her influence on his own painting, for Tomlinson is both poet and painter. The encounter with O'Keeffe is the least comfortable one described, because his intrusion into O'Keeffe's personal life was clearly resented. Tomlinson shows some courage in revealing this resentment, because it points up an undercurrent running through the book as a whole, his deliberate—sometimes almost relentless—pursuit of the people whom he reveres. (He visits more than a few of these artists in the midst of serious illnesses.) Tomlinson admits that he gained entrance to O'Keeffe's house under dubious pretenses and that she reprimanded him for this, but he also makes it clear that he might well be excused because he is her diligent admirer. In fact, Tomlinson even reviewed slides of O'Keeffe's work the night before he and his wife lunched with her. He mentions that O'Keeffe was so impressed by an acute observation about one of her paintings that she relented enough in her displeasure to bid him a gracious farewell.

Unlike the previous three, the final chapter, written in 1978 and 1979, finds Tomlinson and his wife not in the United States but in Italy, although still primarily in the company of Americans. Here he remembers his meetings with the aging American poet Ezra Pound and Pound's daughter Mary and her family. Tomlinson also recalls other Italian adventures, including his being fired by the editor and critic Percy Lubbock, an insult which he counters with a very unflattering portrayal of the man, in life and death (Lubbock's embalming is the closing scene of the book). Apart from its anecdotal significance, the main feature of this chapter is the detailed and informative description of the ways in which direct experience of the sights and landscapes of Italy improved Tomlinson's readings of the poems of Ezra Pound.

Analysis

It is fitting that *Some Americans* should end with the work of Ezra Pound, as it begins with Tomlinson's precocious interest in Pound, his purchase of a book of Pound's poetry while still in grammar school, and his amazement that American poetry was disregarded in his university assignments. As he says at the outset, "A boy from the provinces, going up to read English at Cambridge in 1945, as I did, will have learned little of American poetry from his university teachers. None of them seemed to mention it." That opening establishes several of Tomlinson's themes: his youth and his outsider status (the "boy from the provinces" at Cambridge), his enthusiasm for American verse and his hunger for guidance in his reading of it, and his self-possession, even pride, because he knows more than his peers and supposed superiors (the Cambridge professors' failure to "mention" contemporary American poetry rather strongly implies their ignorance of the matter).

These themes, suggested at the outset of this slim volume, are woven throughout the whole, where they serve the interests of the larger theme: Tomlinson's great regard for, and conscious debt to, American poetry. The book fits comfortably into the category of study that elucidates what William Wordsworth famously called the growth of a poet's mind, and it is valuable precisely because it provides insight into the ways in which Tomlinson adapted what he saw as the best features of American writing (and painting) to his own artistic purposes. In so doing, it also explains why he has seemed to his fellow poets in Great Britain to be rather outside their tradition: It is highly unusual for British poets to adjust their voice to American tonalities, but that is precisely what Tomlinson has done.

From his first shocked delight at the freedom and vigor of Ezra Pound's lines, what impressed Tomlinson the most was the verbal clarity, simplicity, and immediacy with which American poetry conveyed reality, what he calls "a regard for [the] minute particulars of language." He recalls his delight in the opening chapter, which also describes the depth and breadth of his exposure to such writers as Hart Crane, Wallace Stevens, Marianne Moore, Yvor Winters, and William Carlos Williams. From each he learned another refined technique; Tomlinson was drawn to resonant simplicity of statement, to arresting precision of language. He is careful to point out in detail exactly where American influence can be found in a particular poem of his own, where the evidence of his reading and his personal contacts with American writers can be seen at work in his own lines, both as originally conceived and as finally revised.

Once past the initial discussion of his indebtedness to the work of American poets, Tomlinson tells a series of pointed personal anecdotes about his contacts with living American legends. He seems never to have been content merely to read and to appreciate the work of those he admired; he seems always to have hungered for something more, some sort of reciprocal affirmation. As he recounts it here, he achieved this either by writing poems dedicated to a particular poet—a natural sort of compliment that would eventually catch the poet's eye—or by direct correspondence, often over an extended period and usually leading to a personal visit as well.

Tomlinson put to good use a year he spent teaching at the University of New

Mexico, taking the opportunity to conduct a sort of pilgrimage to the Americans he most admired: writers Ezra Pound, Louis Zukofsky, George Oppen, Marianne Moore, and painter Georgia O'Keeffe. All of them welcomed him, some more than others. The degree to which they welcomed him or did not is carefully made clear. Tomlinson's recollection of events is acute; he seems always to be aware of exactly how much time he spent with each person, the precise circumstances of their encounter, and virtually all of their conversation. All of this detailed information is provided at length, with significant quotation from letters and painstakingly reconstructed conversations. He does not hesitate to give the genesis of whole poems, including other writers' share in shaping and revising them, and this description is in itself an edifying study of the creative process at work.

Tomlinson is a master of nuance as well as of recall, and an attentive reader can glean from this memoir not only a string of interrelated anecdotes about some of the most luminous names in twentieth century art and letters but also a psychological portrait of the artist. He is sensitive, for example, to every word and gesture of praise or criticism, and he does not shrink from recounting both. Moreover, when he recalls instances of imperfection in his idols, he gives as good as he gets, subtly undercutting these famous poets with tremendous skill, not out of malice but rather from a desire to maintain proportion, giving their portraits a more human dimension. He is convincingly grieved by the split between Zukofsky and Oppen, for example, not only because it ruined his plans for an anthology of objectivist poetry but also because he sensed a fundamental misunderstanding at the root of the quarrel and tried unsuccessfully to mediate the breach. The second essay of the collection seems to be all that he was able to salvage from the effort.

Although the chapters are uneven in their orientation and purposes, each has its strengths. The first, "Beginnings," successfully portrays the author as a bright and aggressive student, writer, and entrepreneur of his own poetry. The scope is broad, pulling together all the significant influences on Tomlinson's developing style as a writer. The second chapter chronicles Tomlinson's experience of the Zukofsky-Oppen split from a concerned outsider's view. It is filled with fondly remembered detail of the happy time in Tomlinson's life when his family lived in New York City and he could visit with the celebrated objectivist writers, but it also conveys vividly his sense of frustration and of wasted time. The third chapter, infused with a quiet tension, briefly recounts the Tomlinsons' uneasy dinner with Georgia O'Keeffe. The most satisfying of all, however, is clearly the last chapter, with its nostalgic glimpses of the elderly Ezra Pound counterpointed by the vividly rendered direct experience of the various places in Italy mentioned in poems that Tomlinson had long been reading. This part of the book succeeds in making the reader share his sense of wonder and delight in finding in the objective reality a perfect analogue to the words of poems that he has already internalized.

The overall impression that Tomlinson creates in the volume is not so much one of a student among tutors—by the end of the book he is remembering himself as a well-established poet—but rather of a fine and capable artist among his peers, someone not in the least outclassed by those he reveres. Moreover, the continual exposure to poetry-in-the-making that this memoir offers is valuable itself. Tomlinson is not only a good writer, but also a good reader of the works of others. In this volume, he offers his readers precisely the sort of guidance in reading that he wished someone had given him during his undergraduate years.

Critical Context

Despite the obvious debt of modern English poetry to the Missouri-born T. S. Eliot, very few contemporary British poets have made much of American poetry. Donald Davie, Thom Gunn, and Charles Tomlinson are exceptions, however, and in *Some Americans*, Tomlinson makes clear the extent of his interest in modern American poets and his indebtedness to them. The memorable clarity of the essays in this book has much in common with the rigorous attention to detail and painterly description that characterize Tomlinson's poetry.

While Davie and Gunn lived and worked in the United States for extended periods, Tomlinson's stay, described in these essays, was far briefer. He returned to England to live and work, after the time described in the book. There, as before, his poetry continued to be met with some misunderstanding or lack of sympathy among his compatriots. *Some Americans* can be seen, at least in part, not only as a historical record of his American influences but also as a patient explanation and a potent defense of his work.

The language of the prose bears the hallmark of the poetry in its artful simplicity of diction, its lucid exactness of representation, and its honest personal statement. The record of events is rendered so clearly that there is little room for further excavation by critics and scholars: Apart from reviews when it first appeared, this work has been left to stand on its own as the straightforward autobiographical account that it is. *Some Americans* is an important historical and literary document, because Charles Tomlinson is a significant and unusual poet and because, beyond elucidating the sources and stimuli for some of his best early poems, he provides insight into the lives and work of important modernist figures.

Sources for Further Study

Beaver, Harold. "Crossing Rebel Lines," in *Parnassus: Poetry in Review.* X (Spring/Summer, 1982), pp. 117-124.

Hall, Donald. "Poet's Progress," in *The New York Times Book Review.* LXXXVI (March 1, 1981), pp. 12, 16-17.

Hennessy, Michael. "Discovering America," in *Contemporary Literature.* XXIII (Spring, 1982), pp. 254-258.

Pettingell, Phoebe. "Outer and Inner Landscapes," in *The New Leader.* LXIV (June 1, 1981), pp. 14-15.

Wilmer, Clive. "Masters in Modernism," in *The Times Literary Supplement.* February 5, 1982, p. 141.

Mary FitzGerald

A SORT OF LIFE

Author: Graham Greene (1904-   )
Type of work: Autobiography
Time of work: 1904-1932
Locale: Berkhamsted, Oxford, and London, England
First published: 1971

Principal personage:
GRAHAM GREENE, a novelist and playwright

Form and Content

The circumstances surrounding Graham Greene's publication of his first book-length autobiography, *A Sort of Life*, illustrate the duality that characterizes the author and his work. Greene once told a meeting of the Leicester University Literary Society that he had begun writing the book as therapy. Suffering from such deep depression that he feared a complete mental breakdown, Greene asked his psychoanalyst to administer electric shock treatments; instead, his analyst told Greene to write down a description of his earliest memories. Undoubtedly, Greene uses *A Sort of Life* to explore the psychological foundations of his life, but critics have noted that his autobiography appeared in the same year as a collected edition of his writings to which he wrote new introductions. These concurrent publications may have demonstrated Greene's desire to move beyond popularity and financial success to assume a position in the English tradition of conscious artistry alongside Henry James, Joseph Conrad, James Joyce, and Ford Madox Ford. It is possible that such contradictory motives were equally true, illustrating Greene's fastidious distinction between his public self, which he associates with his role as author, and his private self.

A Sort of Life is an example of Freudian self-analysis; it is a work which is founded on Greene's belief in the importance of formative influences: "The whole future must have lain all the time along those Berkhamsted streets." Nevertheless, in *A Sort of Life* Greene does not attempt to prove this causality through a sequential exposition of his childhood experience; instead, he distorts the unities of time, place, and action in order to concentrate on an abstract vision of his own developing character. The book is, therefore, at once intimate in Greene's effort to face the horror of self and evasive in his refusal to account for the factual details of his private life or to discuss the people who affected his early years. Greene tells little of his parents, brothers, sisters, school companions, or the many literary figures he came to know. Even his wife, Vivien, is barely mentioned, although she was the primary cause of his conversion to Catholicism and shared the agonizing years in which he struggled to establish himself as a novelist.

A Sort of Life is an impressionistic text in which Greene strings together arbitrarily related images that hint at the essence of the multiple Greenes hidden in his early years. The dreamlike memories he recounts, and frequently discounts by questioning their accuracy, serve as an escape from the depressing reality of his contemporary life, yet his book is not escapist, for it is through his intuitive use of dreams that Greene seeks to confront the grim realities of his own character. As Greene points out, he has always used autobiographical material in his fiction, and he approaches the writing of his autobiography in much the same way as he would approach the writing of a novel. Believing that any attempt to present a factually complete account would be lifeless and inaccurate, Greene accepts the necessary role of the imagination. He argues that a writer must have "a greater ability to forget than other men—he has to forget or become sterile. What he forgets is the compost of the imagination." He says that his motives for writing an autobiography are similar to his motives for writing novels: "a desire to reduce a chaos of experience to some sort of order, and a hungry curiosity."

The book's title underscores the limitations that Greene believes are inherent in autobiography, primarily the limitations of the author's memory, which "begins later [than a biographer's] and . . . ends prematurely." Although *A Sort of Life* was published in 1971, Greene chose to narrate his life only as far as what he calls the "years of failure which followed the acceptance of my first novel." Because "failure too is a kind of death," this temporal limitation provides Greene with a novelistic sense of closure. His decision to conclude on a note of uncertainty fits Greene's vision of himself as a victim, an author who maintains that "for a writer, . . . success is only a delayed failure." In actuality, *A Sort of Life* concludes with the publication of *Stamboul Train* (1932)—published in the United States as *Orient Express*—the novel which established Greene as a popular and successful author. Nevertheless, Greene's decision to end the autobiography at this point may be psychologically appropriate, for by 1932 Greene's character was set; indeed, despite superficial differences of setting and event, his subsequent work displays a remarkable consistency.

In *A Sort of Life*, Greene recounts events of his childhood in Berkhamsted, highlighting incidents that collectively portray a childhood of alienation and desperate rebellion, a dark portrait of Greene's inner state that contrasts with the objective perception of the secure and privileged life of an English headmaster's son. Greene's impressionistic narrative builds toward his adolescent breakdown, suicide attempts, and his parents' surprising decision to send him into psychoanalysis with Kenneth Richmond. Greene describes his treatment with Richmond, which initiated his lifelong interest in psychoanalysis and dreams, as "the happiest six months of my life." Greene goes on to recount his college years at Balliol College, in Oxford, his early years as a journalist, his conversion to Catholicism, his marriage, the disappointment that followed the initial success of his first novel, *The Man Within* (1929), and the failure of his two subsequent novels, *The Name of Action* (1930) and *Rumour at Nightfall* (1931); he concludes with the renewed promise of his fourth novel, *Stamboul Train*. Although the book contains useful commentary on the events of Greene's early life and the relation of these events to his later writings, politics, and travel, the autobiography is circumspect. Greene focuses on revelatory images of loneliness, violence, boredom, alienation, and despair. The book is particularly effective in its evocation of the unhappiness of Greene's school days—"weeks of monotony, humiliation and mental pain"—portraying him as torn between a desperate fear of rejection and an equally desperate need for isolation.

Analysis

In *A Sort of Life* Greene suggests that an appropriate epigraph for all of his novels would be some lines from Robert Browning's "Bishop Blougram's Apology":

> Our interest's on the dangerous edge of things.
> The honest thief, the tender murderer,
> The superstitious atheist, demi-rep
> That loves and saves her soul in new French books—
> We watch while these in equilibrium keep
> The giddy line midway.

The quotation underscores Greene's love of paradox, his rebellious sympathy for the nonconformist, his persistent disbelief in the capacity of words to capture in some final form the truth of existence, and his implicit belief that any honest search for meaning is a dangerous balancing act. Yet Greene is neither an absurdist who celebrates chaos nor a relativist who rejects the significance of moral meaning. Although recognizing that any search for meaning is unfinished, Greene sees such quests as essential to full human existence. Because the central concern of his writing is salvation, theological, societal, and personal, the question of truth is dangerous—a matter of life or death.

Just as Greene compares his writing to a high-wire act in which he carefully balances between moral opposites, he emphasizes separation as well. In *A Sort of Life*, barriers and borders are important symbols of alienation and the obstacles to knowledge. After his exile to the dormitory, where he suffered miserably from the public life he had to endure, the green baize door that stood between the school quarters and his family's rooms came to represent his irreparable separation from the security and innocence of his early childhood. More graphic is Greene's description of the flower border that separated the school grounds from an adjacent, ancient cemetery. He notes that the boundary was ill defined; each spring, when the school's gardener would replant the border, he would uncover bits of bone. Greene's dark memoir of his childhood is marked by many similar warnings to be mindful of death.

The settings of Greene's novels are so consistently sordid that critics have coined the term "Greeneland" to refer to his literary environment. In *A Sort of Life*, the Berkhamsted of Greene's childhood becomes another part of Greeneland, a habitat devoid of beauty and scarred by incidents of banal violence and cruelty. The crude sounds and smells of the dormitory, the stifling bourgeois conformism, the lack of privacy, and images of irrational and unpredictable violence and death become the focus of the narrative. Greene claims as his first memory an incident in which his nurse placed his sister's dead pug in his baby carriage in order to carry it home, an image he later used in *The Ministry of Fear* (1943). He recalls stopping with his nurse to watch a desperate man cut his throat at an almshouse window, the horror of his days as a World War II air-raid warden, and the anguish of receiving telegrams that first informed him of his father's death and then informed him of his father's illness.

Throughout *A Sort of Life*, Greene portrays himself as a victim, crushed by loneliness and boredom. As a schoolboy, his position as son of the headmaster alienated him from his mates and forced him into difficult questions of loyalty: "I was surrounded by the forces of the resistance, and yet I couldn't join them without betraying my father." His reaction is to rebel or seek escape. The ancestor he most admires is his father's father, who ran away from the bourgeois comforts of English family life to seek his fortune on the island of Saint Kitts. Greene clearly identifies with his grandfather's "irrational desire to escape from himself," and as a young man his rebelliousness often took self-destructive forms. In *A Sort of Life* he recounts running away from the school and using aspirin and other chemicals in unsuccessful suicide attempts. Most dramatic is his description of experimenting with Russian roulette, a desperate game he would play in solitude at the University of Oxford when the tedium of his existence became too great. His "discovery that it was possible to enjoy again the visible world by risking its total loss" was repeated in later years, when Greene sought to escape depression through travel, sexual exploits, alcohol, drugs, psychoanalysis, and writing.

Greene's rebelliousness and belief in the elusive nature of truth are demonstrated in the fragmentary style of *A Sort of Life*. The process of reconstructing his life is compared to "a long broken night. As I write, it is as though I am waking from sleep continually to grasp at an image, which I hope may drag in its wake a whole intact dream, but the fragments remain fragments, the complete story always escapes." Rather than presenting a chronological account of Greene's early years, *A Sort of Life* actually subverts the idea of a sequential narrative. Greene moves freely through time, associating incidents from his early years and events that occur outside the time frame of this autobiography. He employs a range of voices, building his book in an elliptic, enigmatic manner that is at once revealing and evasive. In the book's final pages, Greene describes an evening spent in Thailand with a literary acquaintance from his college days. The once-promising friend had long since given up writing in favor of opium, but a scene which the reader expects to highlight Greene's contrasting success focuses instead on the two men's similarity. The two "analyzed our differing failures without guilt or regret."

Greene also recounts his youthful offer to serve as a spy for Germany, and the image of the spy, particularly the double agent, illuminates Greene's approach to autobiography. Like a double agent in one of his novels, Greene refuses to present his readers with a single authoritative account of his life. He wears a series of literary disguises and shrouds his purpose in ambiguity. He tells his reader that his information is acquired indirectly through faulty and fragmentary memories and emphasizes its unreliability. Greene's approach displays his distrust of authority and easy answers. Like a double agent who manipulates both sides to his own advantage, Greene asserts his literary independence. His autobiography assumes the importance of self-analysis while admitting the impossibility of finally defining that self. The triumph of *A Sort of Life* is the book's successful portrait of Greene, not perhaps the historical Greene known by others but the youthful Greene imagined in maturity by the author himself. Greene openly identifies himself as an unreliable narrator, and he refuses to be limited by the specifics of fact because his purpose is to discover the more lasting nature of his being.

Critical Context

Graham Greene's literary reputation has been limited by his own unfortunate subdivision of his fiction into "novels" and "entertainments." He based this distinction on several factors: the entertainments were written with great speed during manic periods, and the novels were written more slowly during depressive periods; the entertainments focus on crime, and the novels treat larger subjects; the entertainments are seen as lay works, and the novels are viewed as Catholic. Many of these distinctions are accurate, but the unfortunate result of this too easy classification has been to encourage critical neglect of Greene's entertainments. The concurrent publication of *A Sort of Life* and a collected edition of his works, in which, for the first time, all of his works were labeled novels, marked an invitation for critics to reexamine the body of his work. It cannot, however, be said that his invitation has resulted in a great resurgence of critical interest in Greene's work.

A Sort of Life is complemented by other autobiographical writings, including essays such as "The Lost Childhood" and "The Revolver in the Corner Cupboard"; travel books such as *In Search of a Character: Two African Journals* (1961); and Greene's second book-length autobiography, *Ways of Escape* (1980), which roughly continues his life from the point in the 1930's at which *A Sort of Life* ends. In addition, Greene collaborated with Marie-Françoise Allain to produce *L'Autre et son double: Entretiens avec Marie-Françoise Allain* (1981; *The Other Man: Conversations with Graham Greene*, 1983). The relative wealth of autobiographical material and the fact that Greene's fiction has revealed so much of his character may have discouraged the production of a full-length biography.

Sources for Further Study

DeVitis, A. A. *Graham Greene*, 1986 (revised edition).

Kelly, Richard. *Graham Greene*, 1984.

Lamba, B. P. *Graham Greene: His Mind and Art*, 1987.

Spurling, John. *Graham Greene*, 1983.

Stannard, Martin. "In Search of Himself: The Autobiographical Writings of Graham Greene," in *Prose Studies*. VIII (September, 1985), pp. 139-155.

Wolfe, Peter, ed. *Essays in Graham Greene: An Annual Review*, 1987.

Carl Brucker

SOUND-SHADOWS OF THE NEW WORLD

Author: Ved Mehta (1934-   )
Type of work: Autobiography
Time of work: 1949-1952
Locale: Little Rock, Arkansas
First published: 1985

> *Principal personage:*
> VED MEHTA, a blind teenager

Form and Content

Ved Mehta was born in India of upper-class parents—his father being a fairly prosperous government official in the health department. Ved became totally blind as a result of illness at the age of three. At first he lived at home with his parents, four sisters, and two brothers. Later, his father sent him to school in Bombay before sending him to the Arkansas School for the Blind. This book is an account of his experience at this high school from August, 1949, until his graduation in May, 1952, and departure for college in California. Throughout his sojourn in the United States, Mehta wrote letters home on a typewriter and kept a journal. Thirty-five years later, these letters and his journal became the basis for a series of articles which first appeared in *The New Yorker.* They were then published in book form in 1985.

The book forms part of an ongoing autobiography. *Vedi* (1982) and *The Ledge Between the Streams* (1984) cover his childhood; two earlier volumes, *Daddyji* (1972) and *Mamaji* (1979), center on his father and mother. *Face to Face* (1957) was the forerunner of Mehta's autobiographies, covering his life through his college days and introducing many of the themes developed in the later works that focus on particular periods in his life.

Sound-Shadows of the New World follows Mehta through his experiences in high school and offers a glimpse into his thoughts, his hopes, his victories, and his defeats. The book contains 430 pages and is divided into eleven chapters. The first chapter deals with the difficulty of getting Mehta accepted into school, his final acceptance by the Arkansas School for the Blind, his journey to the United States, and his first days in New York and Little Rock. The last chapter deals with his final months in school, his problems in getting accepted into the university, and his graduation. Between these two chapters the book offers a narrative of Mehta's daily life interspersed with letters and entries from his journal.

Analysis

Sound-Shadows of the New World paints a picture of the world of the blind as perceived by one of its members. It speaks of the fear that the blind have as well as of the skills they are able to master and the life they are able to live in what they call the sighted world. As one follows Mehta through his adolescence one also learns about Indian values and Indian ideas. Mehta's family was from a high caste—the second highest caste in India—and as such had firm ideas of how life should be lived.

In particular, Mehta's values were shaped by his father, who had been educated in England and often reminisced about his days at the university. Thus, the already determined Ved Mehta became even more eager to go abroad for study. The first problem for Mehta was to gain admission into a school in the United States; the second was to finance his education, as the family had limited means, having lost most of their wealth when they emigrated from Pakistan when India became independent from Great Britain. Money was always a problem and was often on Mehta's mind. A scheme to raise money by selling ivory statues and carvings and other semiprecious materials in Little Rock came to nothing.

Throughout his first year, Mehta also had another worry; he had entered the country with a visitor's visa, as the Arkansas School for the Blind was not on the immigration authority's list of approved schools for foreign students. Only after intense efforts on the part of school officials did Mehta receive approval for him to stay and complete his education.

In chapter 1, Mehta raises the question of the cultural differences between India and America. The topic was an emotional one: girls and marriage. Just before seeing him off in New Delhi, his father asked him if he would ever marry a Western woman. Mehta replied rather haughtily in the negative, as a good Hindu should; his father noted that it might not be a bad idea, that India is a harsh land and marriage there is like a business transaction. Indian parents carefully measure their children's liabilities and assets; because of Mehta's blindness they would never be able to find a wife for him in their caste. Hindus would look down on him. A Christian woman might make him a much better wife than a Hindu woman, in any case, as Christians are taught love and compassion whereas Hindus learn only fate and duty.

Further, in a Western marriage, Mehta's father noted, "there is the possibility of intellectual companionship of equals—something that doesn't exist in an Indian marriage at all. Once you've seen that kind of marriage, you may want a companion equal to yourself, even if that means staying in the West."

This conversation—indeed, the entire subject of romance—was an embarrassing one for Mehta. It "wound a tightly coiled spring inside me." His ambivalence on the subject is well illustrated in an episode concerning a visit he received from his eldest cousin, who had been studying engineering at Oregon State University and was now on his way home to India. Mehta eagerly raised the question of dating, and their conversation illuminated the differences between America and India. Mehta, isolated in Little Rock and hanging on to what he remembered of India, was stymied by the Indian conception of purity. Fascinated by the idea of dating, he was also repelled by it; in India, if young people associated with members of the opposite sex before marriage they acquired a bad reputation and lost their purity. In India, purity, or the threat of its loss, determines a person's status and governs all actions and relationships between people. The Arkansas School for the Blind, which was coeducational, held dances on Saturday evenings, and all students were required to attend. Mehta had been much too shy to take an active role. He was shocked to discover that his cousin held the belief (common to Indians) that what one did abroad did not count. Since dating was part of the American teenage scene, his cousin believed that he too should date. Moreover, his cousin admitted that he himself had been dating since he first arrived in the United States.

This discussion did nothing to reassure Mehta. His confusion on the subject emerges periodically throughout the book. Feeling that he represented his country in Little Rock, he saw himself himself as responsible for projecting a proper image.

It was, in fact, as a spokesman for India that Mehta became quite renowned in the community. The local newspaper had carried stories about this boy who had traveled all the way from India to study at the local school for the blind. It was a time when India was in the news. India's independence in 1947 and the assassination of Mahatma Gandhi in 1948 had made people aware of that country. Mehta was occasionally asked by various organizations to give talks about his homeland, which, with help from his father, he did. In some ways, as he himself recognized, Mehta was mature for his age, and in other ways he was quite the opposite. This public speaking showed his more adult side.

Also during this period Mehta's interest in journalism was growing. One evening, feeling ill, he went directly upstairs after supper. Someone had left the radio on and Mehta heard a voice on the radio reading the news. He stood transfixed, listening to this man bringing him the world. He had never heard the voice before. The newsman filled a vacuum in his life, a gap whose existence he had not known until that moment. He became an inspiration to Mehta, just as he had become an inspiration to many others. The man was Edward R. Murrow. Mehta asked for, and was given, a room of his own (a tiny broom closet) in which he could put his typewriter, his radio, and his tape recorder. He also purchased a timer so that he could record programs from the radio even when he was in class. Murrow's broadcasts became Mehta's inspiration.

Determined on a career as a writer, he was ever conscious of finances. By taking correspondence courses during summer vacation, which he spent alone at the school, he was able to skip a year of instruction, thus relieving his father of some of the financial burden. Mehta also took a summer job in an ice-cream factory after he had learned to get around outside the school alone. He was also elected the school senate's president in his senior year.

Asked at graduation to name the most precious thing he was taking from the school, Mehta replied, mobility. For Mehta, mobility meant freedom and independence—which this sensitive, proud, talented person had always craved.

Critical Context

As noted above, *Sound-Shadows of the New World* is the fifth installment in a serial autobiography; excerpts from a sixth installment, following Mehta to Pomona

College in California, appeared in *The New Yorker* in 1987 and 1988. Two qualities distinguish Mehta's ongoing autobiography from most products of the genre: the copious detail of his account, and his perspective as a blind person.

By the time *Sound-Shadows of the New World* appeared, the scope of Mehta's project had become evident, and some reviewers found fault with the pace of his narrative. It had taken him five books simply to get himself through high school; why did he not simply tell his life story once and for all and have done with it? Such objections miss the intent of Mehta's work, which is more than a chronicle of events. While his style is unpretentious, his ambitions are high: He seeks to re-create the growth of a mind, the shaping of consciousness from childhood through youth and into adulthood. His is a philosophical autobiography grounded in the particulars—the trivia, even—of everyday life.

Add to that the unique contribution of the work as a document of a blind person's experience, and one can begin to appreciate Mehta's achievement. Of the auto-biography's installments, *Sound-Shadows of the New World* is one of the richest, as it recounts Mehta's immersion in an entirely new culture. Its virtues, though, are representative of the entire series.

Sources for Further Study
Gerrity, Mary T. Review in *School Library Journal*. XXXIII (September, 1986), p. 155.
Goffman, Amy D. Review in *Library Journal*. CXI (February 1, 1986), p. 77.
Kureishi, Hanif. Review in *The Times Literary Supplement*. May 30, 1986, p. 589.
Mehta, Ved. *Daddyji*, 1972.
_____. *Face to Face*, 1957.
_____. *Mamaji*, 1979.
_____. *Vedi*, 1982.
Sternhell, Carol. Review in *The New York Times Book Review*. XCI (March 9, 1986), p. 14.

Roger D. Long

THE SOVEREIGNTY OF GOOD

Author: Iris Murdoch (1919-   )
Type of work: Philosophy
First published: 1970

Form and Content

As a philosopher interested primarily in ethics and aesthetics, Iris Murdoch has contributed significantly to debates over the direction of modern philosophy. For many years a Fellow at St. Anne's College in Oxford, where she taught philosophy, Murdoch has offered a distinct vision of how the contours of contemporary philosophical thought ought to take shape. She has presented her critical philosophical reflection in a few technical papers and in more extended formats, as her well-received philosophical books *Sartre: Romantic Rationalist* (1953) and *The Fire and the Sun: Why Plato Banished the Artists* (1977) attest. Despite her stature as one of Great Britain's leading moral philosophers, however, it is for her fiction, to which she devotes most of her writing time, that Iris Murdoch is best known.

Iris Murdoch is recognized as one of the world's leading literary artists. She has penned four plays, including *A Severed Head* (1964), with J. B. Priestley, and several volumes of poetry, but it is as a prolific writer of fiction that she has received widespread attention and popular, as well as critical, acclaim. Murdoch has produced a novel every eighteen months after 1954, when her first novel, *Under the Net*, appeared. With subsequent novels, including such works as *The Bell* (1958), *The Red and the Green* (1965), *Bruno's Dream* (1969), *A Fairly Honourable Defeat* (1970), *The Philosopher's Pupil* (1983), and *The Book and the Brotherhood* (1987), her reputation as a serious, first-rate novelist was established. Critics have hailed her fiction for its intricate plotting, subtle symbolism, and philosophical complexity, and her nineteenth novel, *The Sea, The Sea*, published in 1978, earned for Murdoch the Booker Prize of that year. In recognition of her literary accomplishments, Great Britain's "First Lady of Fiction," as Murdoch has sometimes been called, was awarded a D.B.E. (Dame Commander of the Most Excellent Order of the British Empire) in 1987.

Although her philosophical work is certainly distinct from her fiction, Murdoch's sensitivity to the artist's role has shaped her vision of the philosopher and informed her view of the relation of ethics to aesthetics. *The Sovereignty of Good* demonstrates how the aesthetic dimension contributes to Murdoch's understanding of moral philosophy. Moral philosophy, she argues, demands the philosopher's commitment to a point of view, which is to say that the scientific spirit of detachment so prevalent in modern intellectual endeavors ought to be avoided: Murdoch denies "that moral philosophy should aim at being neutral." In saying that, Murdoch is advocating a way of doing philosophy that seeks kinship with the essayist and novelist, with the imaginative and committed artist who attends to details, even the details of the nonpublic inner life. Because "the good artist, in relation to his art, is brave, truthful, patient, humble," the good moral philosopher will in like manner bring virtue, not merely talent, to his or her work. The philosopher, that is, will be as concerned with virtue, love, and goodness as any artist who, by attending to such things, finally "alters consciousness in the direction of unselfishness, objectivity and realism." In this slender volume (104 pages), Murdoch exemplifies a way of thinking about values that reveals the aesthetic calling of the ethicist; for "art," she says, "is an excellent analogy of morals; . . . it is in this respect a case of morals."

The Sovereignty of Good assumes the form of the philosophical essay. The book comprises three essays ("The Idea of Perfection," "On 'God' and 'Good,' " and "The Sovereignty of Good Over Other Concepts"), all of which had previously appeared in print. The essays are unified by a common theme, namely, the supreme value of goodness, the preeminence or "sovereignty" of good. It is from goodness, Murdoch argues, that all other values derive their significance and worth. Further-more, the human mind is attuned by nature to the form of goodness, which is to say that goodness, which affects every moral and aesthetic experience, is finally a need of the moral personality. Some literary critics have found that *The Sovereignty of Good* elucidates issues raised by Murdoch in her fiction, and clearly this text clarifies themes central to her theory of literature. Yet because *The Sovereignty of Good* assumes the form of a discursive philosophical reflection, it should be read as a work in moral philosophy. The book not only responds critically to issues of concern in contemporary philosophical debates, but also, as a constructive philo-sophical effort, offers its own perspective on the nature of value and on the issue of how the moral person is constituted. The essays are meant to address the contempo-rary philosophical community with a new vision of what is at stake in moral philosophy. In this study, which is both a critique of modern scientific rationalism and a proposal for an alternative moral psychology, Murdoch defends the impor-tance of the idea of perfection and the role that goodness plays, or ought to play, in shaping moral thought and in advancing the moral lives of ordinary people.

Analysis

The Sovereignty of Good opens by critically examining certain assumptions that Murdoch believes modern philosophers have failed to assess adequately. The target of Murdoch's attention is the work of philosopher Stuart Hampshire, author of *Thought and Action* (1959), whose ideas she regards as "fairly central and typical," yet of greater benefit than most since they "state and elaborate what in many modern moral philosophers is simply taken for granted."

Murdoch finds Hampshire arguing first, that the self can be identified with the will; second, that thought and belief are separable from will and action; and third, that the human being should be understood through the metaphor of movement. Murdoch challenges all these positions, which are, she argues, based upon an implausible picture of human nature, one that is inattentive to the historical com-plexity of actual persons' lives. Furthermore, because these ideas confuse the moral world with the world of science, the moral life is reduced to almost exclusive concern with the will and with outward observable acts. For Murdoch, this view overlooks the positive role that thought and belief play for the developing moral personality.

In response to Hampshire, Murdoch proceeds to reconceive several notions important to ethics. Her task, like that of the artist, is to clarify what is real and what is illusion in the moral life. *The Sovereignty of Good* does not offer "new" ideas, if by that is meant Murdoch has a new theory of personality to advance. Actually, what Murdoch does is to reclaim a way of conceiving ethics long out of favor with professional philosophers. She argues for reestablishing at the heart of moral thinking the practical ethics of virtue which were so central to the ancient Greek philosophers, particularly Plato and Aristotle. Finding the modern conceptions of the self inadequate, Murdoch offers a revision in contemporary thinking about such topics as the meaning of the will, freedom, and goodness itself.

Murdoch's position rests on a particular analysis of the human will, which is a fundamental concept in Western ethics. Rather than accepting the familiar picture of the will as that endowment of personality wherein resides the power to make decisions in the vacuum of freedom, Murdoch defines the will as "obedience to reality." She challenges the idea of the free will, that is, the will unencumbered by the weight of character and history and unimpeded by the lure of excellence, and ties this picture of the will to the rational scientific thinking of the Enlightenment. The Enlightenment view that the self is ideally will and the will is the ultimate creator of values can be found, according to Murdoch, not only in the great rationalist philosopher of the eighteenth century, Immanuel Kant, but in more modern thinkers similarly committed to a rational or scientific view of, for example, persons (Sigmund Freud), history (Karl Marx), consciousness (Jean-Paul Sartre), or even language (analytic philosophers such as A. J. Ayer). By emphasizing the will as the essence of self, these perspectives (Freudianism, Marxism, existentialism, behaviorism, and logical analysis) assert the primacy of self while sponsoring the ever-increasing degradation of goodness. Murdoch believes that "in the moral life the enemy is the fat relentless ego," which is to say she singles out for criticism philosophical views that empower and authenticate the willful self. Such perspectives, she argues, distort reality, foster illusion, and obscure the role that goodness plays as the supreme value in human existence. Murdoch's view is that moral philosophy, like good art, ought to remind persons of the self's tendency to fall victim to its own act of blind deception. It ought also to encourage persons to counter such tendencies by helping persons "attend" to reality, an idea Murdoch takes from Simone Weil.

For Murdoch, attending to reality means contemplating goodness. Contemplating goodness leads the self away from itself, away from self-assertion, away from "the consolation of fantasy, romanticism and self-consciousness" to a vision of goodness, which she identifies as "a distant transcendent perfection, a source of uncontaminated energy, a source of *new* and quite undreamt-of virtue." This is the ideal of a perfect transcendent reality; this identifies the form of The Good. Murdoch's case is that the self achieves its true end and affirms its true nature to the extent that it attends to the form of goodness that announces itself in the human yearning for perfection. The will, for Murdoch, appears not as that which defines the essence of the self but as that which occasions "the disciplined overcoming of self." Murdoch's position is that an adequate theory of human nature must take into account the human propensity to selfishness and self-deception, for which the necessary tonic is "seeing the order of the world in the light of the Good" and achieving through humility "selfless respect for reality."

Murdoch identifies other implications of the Enlightenment idea that the will identifies the essence of the person as moral being. For example, if the will constitutes the essence of the self, the "inner life" is relegated to being merely an introduction to the outward action. In other words, persons' thoughts and beliefs are not morally relevant. Murdoch offers a counter-example to this assumption, showing in a brief story how a person (M) changes her attitude toward her daughter-in-law (D), not by a change in outward behavior but by the kind of moral reflection and reconsideration that directs M toward becoming more just and compassionate in her evaluation of D. From this example, Murdoch is able to argue that the inner life is directly relevant to moral life and that as such, thought and belief cannot be separated from action and will in any instance of moral evaluation.

A distinctive contribution of *The Sovereignty of Good* is the eloquent plea it makes for restoring the "vision" metaphor to ethics. Stuart Hampshire offered the idea that the metaphor of "movement" best captures the reality of the moral life, since the person can be considered "an object moving among other objects in a continual flow of intention into action." Murdoch objects, arguing that this is not true to the reality of human persons: People are not like that and should not be like that. Her alternative view is that the moral person is not an isolated will moving from intention to outward act. She argues for a picture in which the self presents itself as a complex of emotion, belief, thought, and volition seeking unity. Rather than enjoying a context of perfect freedom, persons are bound by the particularities of historical circumstance and condition, and from this position they seek the integration or unity which the idea of perfection—the lure of goodness, the yearning for excellence—provides. Murdoch's case is that the moral life is constituted not by movement but by vision.

The vision that unifies the moral life and makes the moral life in both its inner and outer dimensions possible is the vision of perfection, the vision of the Good. Murdoch offers an exposition of goodness in order to show that goodness exerts an influence on persons as they struggle to progress and improve, as they go about the work of " 'reassessing' and 'redefining' which is a main characteristic of live personality. . . ." Murdoch draws on the aesthetic experience to support a case that goodness "is a kind of intellectual ability to perceive what is true, which is automatically at the same time a suppression of self," thereby reclaiming goodness as a moral rather than a logical concept. Goodness, which Murdoch construes as the disinterested awareness of the world outside the self, reveals the truth about the moral personality as it is grounded in the reality of historical persons. Contrary to Kant, Murdoch holds that the moral life is misconstrued if considered as the product of thinking clearly, making rational choices, and acting. The moral life, rather, is vision; that is, it is a way of seeing the world, attending to it, looking at it, beholding it. With these alternative metaphors, Murdoch offers an aesthetic ethic that returns to pre-Enlightenment thinking, to the philosophy of Plato in particular, to find, as Plato found, that the ideal form of The Good is indispensable to moral thought and to the cultivation of moral excellence (virtue). Attending to The Good, directing one's "just and loving gaze . . . upon an individual reality," is the self's most ennobling and realistic activity, the activity that can overcome the self's natural tendency to spurn objectivity and unselfishness. The self that attends to the transcendent Good achieves realistic understanding not only of goodness and all the values for which goodness is the wellspring. The self that attends to The Good finally comes to see the self's own insignificance and accept death: Made humble by this insight, the self comes to understand that what should concern the self is all that is not the self.

Murdoch's picture of the moral personality makes clear its own assumption about human nature, namely, that despite the natural selfishness of human persons in an aimless and purposeless world, "we are spiritual creatures, attracted by excellence and made for the Good." This idea, associated with Plato and with Platonic thinkers such as Saint Augustine, places Murdoch in a premodern ethical tradition, one in which the moral life is inseparably tied to a vision of excellence itself, The Good. This vision, according to Murdoch, yields an understanding of the moral personality and even reality itself, reality untainted by the human tendency to be blinded by self. In developing an ethics of virtue around a vision of goodness, *The Sovereignty of Good* claims finally to be offering an ethic of reality.

Critical Context

The Sovereignty of Good offers not only an alternative to the picture of self that finds its source in Enlightenment rationalism; it separates the moral world from the scientific world and seeks to liberate philosophy as a study of human nature from the domination of science. Because of this move, *The Sovereignty of Good* has been considered a groundbreaking book in modern moral philosophy. As she reconsidered the nature of the moral personality, offering an analysis of goodness, a mysterious and indefinable concept so important to the work of the philosopher and the artist, Murdoch initiated a rethinking of the moral life itself, placing the ideas of character, of virtue, and, as Murdoch would argue in other works, even the idea of the story as the center of attention in philosophical deliberations about the nature of the moral life. Although Murdoch's Platonism has its detractors—philosophical Idealism is not without problems and always finds competent critics—the call for a return to an axiological ethics of virtue has met with a receptive audience. Murdoch stands with such philosophers as Stephen Toulmin, who has written often on the need for thinking about ethics as practical wisdom or *phronēsis*, as Aristotle termed it; and Alasdair MacIntyre, whose significant book, *After Virtue* (1981), brought a resurgence of interest in an ethic of vices and virtues. In the realm of religious ethics, the Christian ethicist, Stanley Hauerwas, has explicitly acknowledged a debt to Murdoch as he, too, has called for a turn from Kantian and utilitarian ethics to an ethics of virtue in which "story" is valued as a primary ethical category (narrative ethics).

Some critics have found the tone of *The Sovereignty of Good* to be severe, puritanical, even pessimistic; others have found ambiguities in the work itself. For example, although Murdoch has disclaimed belief in the Christian God and suggests that the concept of God is outdated, she seems inconsistent in suggesting that the practice of attending to God does serve to help persons in the modern era come into true selfhood. One could also ask whether Murdoch's invocation of the Platonic realm of ideas necessarily neglects the physical and bodily realm so important to certain ethical perspectives. The issue, then, is whether her moral theory preserves a form of the very moral isolation she has herself attacked so vigorously in *The Sovereignty of Good*.

Sources for Further Study
Backus, Guy. *Iris Murdoch: The Novelist as Philosopher, the Philosopher as Novelist—"The Unicorn" as a Philosophical Novel*, 1986.
Conradi, Peter J. *Iris Murdoch: The Saint and the Artist*, 1986.
Cummings, P. W. Review in *Library Journal*. XCVI (April 15, 1971), p. 1372.
Downey, Berchmans. Review in *Best Sellers*. XXXI (April 1, 1971), p. 8.
Hauerwas, Stanley. "The Significance of Vision," in *Vision and Virtue: Essays in Christian Ethical Reflection*, 1974.
McClendon, James W. "Three Strands of Christian Ethics," in *The Journal of Religious Ethics*. VI (Spring, 1978), pp. 54-80.
Todd, Richard. "The Shakespearean Ideal," in *Iris Murdoch: The Shakespearean Interest*, 1979.

Lloyd H. Steffen

SPACE, TIME, AND ARCHITECTURE
The Growth of a New Tradition

Author: Sigfried Giedion (1888-1968)
Type of work: Cultural criticism
First published: 1941

Form and Content

In the late 1930's, Sigfried Giedion, a Swiss art historian, traveled from Europe to the United States to teach at Harvard University, where he was invited to give the Charles Eliot Norton lectures for the academic year 1938-1939. These lectures, with the seminars he gave during the same period, formed the basis for the text of the first edition of *Space, Time, and Architecture* (1941). Both the lectures and the text of the book were originally prepared in German, Giedion's native language and the one in which he had earlier published two books of architectural history.

Giedion states in the foreword to the first edition of *Space, Time, and Architecture* that it "was written in stimulating association with young Americans," and the book has the ambience of the university lecture hall, where the flow of ideas is often more important than the formality or completeness of their presentation. Although Giedion takes up clearly defined positions on many issues of art, architecture, and cultural analysis, his approach to his material is more illustrative than dogmatic; the book's many editions and reprintings are evidence both of the documentary value of the author's well-illustrated text and of the continuing interest of Giedion's insights into modern architecture.

Analysis

Unlike Sigfried Giedion's earlier books, *Space, Time, and Architecture* is directed to a general audience as well as to students of architectural history, and it retains the flavor of the series of popular illustrated lectures from which it arose. It is a highly diverse book both in style and in content, and can be seen as several books in one. On a very human level, it is a professor's tour of his favorite topics and an overview of his professional experiences, which Giedion is concerned to reveal as having both emotional and intellectual aspects. On the academic level, *Space, Time, and Architecture* is a survey of what the author calls "the modern movement in architecture" as exemplified by the works of Walter Gropius (1883-1969), Ludwig Mies van der Rohe (1886-1969), and Charles-Édouard Jeanneret (1887-1965), known universally as Le Corbusier. Finally, on the level of personal belief, the book is more than indirectly an invocation of Giedion's idea of a just society and of the culture that might support such a society.

Space, Time, and Architecture is divided into nine major parts, which are given topical titles though their contents are, to an extent, recognizably a chronology of architectural history since the Renaissance. The book, however, does have some pronounced structural peculiarities. In places, the passage from one section to another seems to reflect the change of pace of the skilled lecturer, but in others the break between one topic and the next is mechanical, occasionally even tangential. Giedion's margin notes are a convenience, but they are an uncertain guide to the text. Similarly, the illustrations are in a continually changing relationship to the text, sometimes giving essential data to support an analysis and at other times providing imaginative diversions or unexpected analogies.

These observations about the visual and textual presentation of *Space, Time, and Architecture* might easily be taken to suggest that the book is imperfectly organized, but in fact the book's structure is an ingenious and almost certainly intentional homologue to its content. Giedion's central argument in the book is that architecture has evolved, by an inevitable (though not foreseeable) sequence of developments, to a particular constellation of properties which can be referred to as "space-time." In Part 1 he refers to a book, *Space and Time* (1908), by the mathematician Hermann Minkowski, in which the author states that "space by itself, and time by itself, are doomed to fade away into mere shadows, and only a kind of union of the two will preserve an independent reality." This new conception of space and time, which was an aspect of the revision of Newtonian physics carried out by Albert Einstein and others during the same era, in Giedion's view was allied with the work of the artists known as the cubists. This group, represented by such artists as Pablo Picasso and Georges Braque, sought a new kind of representation in painting and sculpture in which objects were shown simultaneously from many points of view, interpenetrating one another in a complex, fluidly structured continuum. Giedion's thesis is that the work of Le Corbusier, Gropius, and others is the natural expression of the same concept in architecture, slightly delayed historically by virtue of the inertia of the "academic," or official, architectural attitudes of the nineteenth century. In this "modernist" spirit, *Space, Time, and Architecture*—to the extent allowed by the largely rational conventions of scholarly publication—has a many-faceted personality which encourages the reader to share the author's own "space-time" perception and historical experience, rather than merely to receive a report of his conclusions.

In order to justify the inevitability of the forms of modern architecture as they were developed by Le Corbusier, Gropius, and others, Giedion pursues historical examples of architecture and urban planning beginning with the Renaissance and extending through the Baroque period into the nineteenth century. In his discussion titled "Our Architectural Inheritance," he reveals his indebtedness to two early figures in the study of the Renaissance and Baroque periods, the art historian Heinrich Wölfflin (1864-1945), with whom Giedion studied in Munich, and the nineteenth century Swiss historian Jakob Burckhardt (1818-1897), who in turn had been Wölfflin's teacher at the University of Basel. The legacy of these scholars was, in Giedion's words, an approach to cultural history which sought "to grasp the spirit of an epoch" and to develop observations about art and history with the broadest possible significance. Giedion, like Wölfflin, is aware of the need for incisive analyses upon which to base generalizations, but in *Space, Time, and*

Architecture he is rarely as systematic as his predecessors, preferring to let enthusiasm for his subject provide the momentum for his arguments. Throughout the book there is an oscillation between descriptive documentation of architectural monuments and earnest interpretations of their significance; though Giedion is an expert guide to a remarkable variety of structures and is never lacking for interesting observations about them, the lack of a consistent method of relating observations to hypotheses makes *Space, Time, and Architecture* more stimulating than conclusive.

Giedion's review of the changing space conceptions of painting and architecture parallels Wölfflin's argument in *Kunstgeschichtliche Grundbegriffe* (1915; *Principles of Art History*, 1929?) that the signal contribution of Renaissance art to Western culture was the development of linear perspective, which was later transformed into the flexible and dynamic sense of space characteristic of Baroque art. The quintessential Baroque architectural monument, in Giedion's view, is the undulating wall of San Carlo alle Quattro Fontane, in Rome, by Francesco Borromini (1599-1667). Noting that Burckhardt had "angrily observed that the façade . . . looked like something that had been dried in an oven," Giedion takes a radically different view of it, praising the "progression and regression of the wall through the hollowing-out of niches and the building up of contradistinguished parts" which results in "a real molding of space, a swelling and receding that causes the light to leap over the front of the church." Formal innovations such as Borromini's treatment of this wall and its associated interior spaces belong, in Giedion's analysis, to a special category of historical processes which he calls "constituent facts." These are the "genuinely new trends" which produce a "new tradition"; it is the duty of the historian to distinguish these "constituent facts" from "transitory facts," the "short-lived novelties" out of which period styles in art are fashioned.

Giedion's overview of the central concerns of art and architecture since the Renaissance begins with the concept of linear perspective and its implication of the primacy of the independent, static, and isolated vision of the individual; it then moves to the paired concepts of the undulating wall and "flexible ground plan," which embodied the complex dynamism of developed urban society. The next step in this process of cultural evolution, according to the author, is the Industrial Revolution, which introduced a crisis in the collective spirit of European civilization. In the Baroque period, he states, new scientific discoveries had "immediately found their counterparts in the realm of feeling and were translated into artistic terms," but in the nineteenth century the paths of science and the arts diverged, and "the connection between methods of thinking and methods of feeling was broken." This isolation of two mutually dependent modes of human experience, Giedion believes, is a phenomenon peculiar to the nineteenth century, and the solution to the problem, in his view, is in large part the obligation of architecture, the branch of the fine arts most closely allied to mathematics and physics, and the one most capable of bridging the gap between machine-age production and the emotional requirement of art.

Nineteenth century architecture was largely a failure both in its design and in its social function, according to Giedion, because it failed to embrace the Industrial Revolution either in technique or in spirit. Innovative building technologies were extensively researched and were imaginatively employed in isolated projects, but they were seldom assimilated into major, officially prestigious building programs until the last decades of the century. Of principal interest to the author are the development of cast-iron columns and steel frames and the subsequent use of "ferroconcrete," or the steel-reinforced concrete framework. These innovations permitted great flexibility in the scale and design of structures ranging from warehouses to residences and bridges.

Giedion describes how the aesthetic potentialities of modern materials gained increasing professional and popular notice in the 1880's and 1890's. The Eiffel Tower, completed in 1889, is the author's favorite example of an important structure both loved and scorned from its conception. By the turn of the century, a growing body of adventurous buildings in Europe and America had begun to define a distinct modern direction in architecture. In Giedion's analysis, the aesthetic renewal which cubism contributed to European architecture was at last manifested in the years just after World War I, when the social situation in Germany, in particular, created opportunities for fresh thinking about the role of the artist in society. The example of Gropius, the architect-director of the Bauhaus, a new design school begun in Weimar, Germany, in 1926, is the author's primary point of reference in ideological and aesthetic matters, and he follows Gropius' teaching and practice of architecture through the 1930's and beyond, when he became one of the most influential architects in America.

In the central section, titled "Space-Time in Art, Architecture, and Construction," which makes up nearly a quarter of the earlier editions of *Space, Time, and Architecture*, two other architects are prominently featured: the French-Swiss painter-architect Le Corbusier and the Finnish architect Alvar Aalto. Of the two, it is clear that Le Corbusier is the more compelling figure for Giedion, though his appraisal of Aalto is more warmhearted. Le Corbusier was an entrant in a 1927 competition for the design of the League of Nations building in Geneva, which resulted in a somewhat scandalous victory for reactionary taste when many modern plans were passed over for a conventional design in an academic mode. Giedion himself was an onlooker in this episode, and his activity as an activist in architectural circles dates from it.

There may be substance to the criticism that *Space, Time, and Architecture* presents a somewhat mechanistic and teleological view of the origins of modern architecture. In discussing Le Corbusier's work, for example, Giedion says little about the man himself—a problem the author seems to have tried to address in the fifth edition of the book, where he adds some details about Jeanneret's youth taken from the architect's own writings. Giedion gives ample evidence, however, of the influence of personal factors in other architects' production. His treatment of Aalto's work, for example, characterizes it as arising from an interest in human beings as well as from an attachment to the landscape of his native Finland. Giedion sees

Aalto as an intuitive architect who brings "the organic and the irrational" to conciousness from "primitive" sources, but he also praises Aalto's ability to unite industrial standardization—as in his successful work with wooden furniture—with strong individual expression.

The illustrations in *Space, Time, and Architecture* are a significant part of the book's value. In addition to reproductions of plans and diagrams, there are hundreds of photographs, generally of very high informational content. More important, many of the photographs are excellent interpretations of the buildings they picture; collectively they suggest how photographic communication strongly influences both intellectual and emotional responses to architecture. Giedion's use of photographs of Aalto's architecture appeals to intuition, as does the work itself. The author pairs a picture of Aalto's 1939 World's Fair Pavilion with an aerial photograph of Finnish lakes and forests; in ground plan, the undulating shape of the pavilion's wall closely resembles the lake shore. Many of the photographs in the book are Giedion's own, and are of professional caliber.

Having extensively reviewed the architecture pertinent to his "space-time" thesis, Giedion turns to the topic of city planning. Earlier sections of *Space, Time, and Architecture* provide a series of observations about large-scale planning in connection with major building projects in the Renaissance and Baroque periods; the last three parts of the book are mostly devoted to explaining the increasing social and aesthetic significance of urban design. The most interesting part of Giedion's discussion of the history of urban planning is undoubtedly his account of the career of Baron Eugène Hausmann, who was responsible for carrying out the transformation of Paris in the third quarter of the nineteenth century. What follows the discussion of Hausmann, however, should be read more cautiously, particularly the passages concerning automobile parkways. The author is aware of the abstract beauty of early examples, such as the 1939 Merritt Parkway in Connecticut, but from the perspective of the early 1940's he could not have forecast the destructive impact of cars upon American cities and landscapes.

Critical Context

In its final pages, Giedion returns to many of the passionate themes with which he began *Space, Time, and Architecture*—the mission of the artist to "open up new spheres of the unconscious," the need for a "unity of culture," and the humanization of the environment. To the degree that he has established a firm basis for his aesthetic judgments about particular buildings and environments, Giedion successfully renews these generalizations, but only in their broad sense. The descriptive and historical elements of his text, taken together with the book's illustrations, seem well integrated on a deeply intuitive level, but they are more a safety net for his weightier concepts than a demonstration of them. Many of Giedion's conceptions of the individual in society are very reminiscent of those of the Swiss psychologist Carl Gustav Jung, particularly with regard to the consequences of the "split" between thinking and feeling. Such ideas require the scope of investigation that Jung gave them and that Giedion, as an architectural historian, could not, but Giedion's adaptation of them is both sincere and constructive.

Giedion shows little evidence of having wished to distill or refine the arguments in *Space, Time, and Architecture*, and he clearly wishes his affectionate advocacy for his subject to be the standard by which the book is judged. The success of his advocacy is shown by the fact that the book can continue to serve as a kind of partisan introduction to architecture since the Renaissance. It is highly selective in the examples used to support its points of view, but this fact is readily apparent, and the book is unlikely to stand in the way of further investigations; in any case, it has been a touchstone for most later architectural historians, including those whose views diverge markedly from the author's. A large part of *Space, Time, and Architecture* consists of documentation of buildings that belong in any history of modern architecture, such as the Eiffel Tower, the Crystal Palace (erected in London for the Great Exhibition of 1851), and the Villa Savoie of Le Corbusier, constructed between 1928 and 1930.

The epigrammatic and oracular elements in the author's presentation and the occasional disjunctive or repetitive passage seem insignificant in relation to the whole of *Space, Time, and Architecture*; Giedion's urgency and enthusiasm outdistance his rhetorical quirks and make the book more readable than the vast majority of studies in art and art history.

Sources for Further Study
Banham, Reyner. *Theory and Design in the First Machine Age*, 1960.
Blake, Peter. *The Master Builders*, 1960.
Conant, Kenneth John. Review in *Journal of Aesthetics and Art Criticism*. I (1941), pp. 126-129.
Haskell, Douglas. Review in *The Nation*. CLII (August 16, 1941), p. 145.
Jencks, Charles. *Modern Movements in Architecture*, 1973.
Pevsner, Nikolaus. Review in *Burlington Magazine*. LXXXII (January, 1943), pp. 25-26.
Watkin, David. *Morality and Architecture: The Development of a Theme in Architectural History and Theory from the Gothic Revival to the Modern Movement*, 1977.
Wolfe, Tom. *From Bauhaus to Our House*, 1981.

C. S. McConnell

SPEAK, MEMORY
An Autobiography Revisited

Author: Vladimir Nabokov (1899-1977)
Type of work: Autobiography
Time of work: August, 1903, to May, 1940
Locale: Russia and Europe
First published: 1951, in Great Britain (U.S. edition, *Conclusive Evidence: A
   Memoir*, 1951); revised as *Drugie Berega*, 1954; revised again as *Speak, Memory:
   An Autobiography Revisited*, 1966

Principal personage:
VLADIMIR VLADIMIROVICH NABOKOV, a Russian-born émigré
   American novelist, poet, essayist, and translator

Form and Content

Vladimir Nabokov was one of the many aristocrats and intellectuals who emigrated from Russia as the Bolsheviks rose to power during the revolution of 1917. Nabokov's family moved, first, some fifty miles north from their estate to St. Petersburg, then to the vicinity of Yalta in the southern Crimea, and finally in 1919, by way of Greece, to London. Nabokov's parents, along with his two sisters (Olga and Elena) and youngest brother (Kirill), left London to take up residence in Berlin, where on March 28, 1922, his father was shot to death by right-wing Russians. Nabokov and his younger brother Sergei, who was to die of starvation in a Nazi concentration camp in 1945, matriculated at the University of Cambridge. Nabokov, upon graduating from Cambridge, went to live in Berlin in 1923 and there, two years later, was married to Véra Evseevna Slonim, who would bear his only child, Dmitri, in 1934. After Adolf Hitler had established his dictatorship and had begun his persecution of German Jews, Nabokov and his wife, who was Jewish, moved to Paris. This was in 1937. A year earlier "Mademoiselle O," written in French and the first part of what would become *Speak, Memory*, had been published in Paris.

Nabokov, his wife, and their son embarked at Saint-Nazaire, France, for the United States on May 28, 1940. This is the event with which *Speak, Memory* ends, although the final form of the work, published in 1966, includes references to many events occurring between 1940 and 1966. In the United States Nabokov saw his first publication of an English-language novel, *The Real Life of Sebastian Knight* (1941), taught Russian grammar and literature at Wellesley College from 1941 to 1948, concurrently holding a research fellowship with the Museum of Comparative Zoology at Harvard University, during which time he became an American citizen (in 1945) and taught Russian and European literature at Cornell University from 1948 to 1959. After the great critical and commercial success of his novel *Lolita* (1955), Nabokov maintained financial independence through his writing. Retaining his much-prized American citizenship, he moved with his wife to Montreux, Switzerland, in 1960; he died there in 1977.

After his arrival in the United States, Nabokov's "Mademoiselle O" was translated into English by Hilda Ward, revised by himself, and then published in *The
Atlantic Monthly* (January, 1943). Ultimately it became chapter 5 of *Speak, Memory*. Edmund Wilson, a literary ally who would later challenge Nabokov's compe-
tence as a translator, brought him into association with *The New Yorker*, in which,
from 1948 through 1950, eleven autobiographical reminiscences, each to become a
chapter in *Speak, Memory*, were published. These were "Portrait of My Uncle"
(January 3, 1948; chapter 3), "My English Education" (March 27, 1948; chapter 4),
"Butterflies" (June 12, 1948; chapter 6), "Colette" (July 31, 1948; chapter 7), "My
Russian Education" (September 18, 1948; chapter 9), "Curtain-Raiser" (January 1,
1949; chapter 10), "Portrait of My Mother" (April 9, 1949; chapter 2), "Tamara"
(December 10, 1949; chapter 12), "Lantern Slides" (February 11, 1950; chapter 8),
"Perfect Past" (April 15, 1950; chapter 1), and "Gardens and Parks" (June 17, 1950;
chapter 15). Chapter 11 appeared initially as "First Poem" in *Partisan Review*
(September, 1949), which later included "Exile" (January/February, 1951; chapter 14). Chapter 13 first appeared in *Harper's Magazine* (January, 1951) as "Lodgings in Trinity Lane." Accordingly, the order of the original composition and publication of the individual fifteen chapters in *Speak, Memory* is 5, 3, 4, 6, 7, 9, 10, 2,
11, 12, 8, 1, 15, 13, 14.

The autobiographical pieces were substantially revised, given a generally chronological arrangement, and published in 1951 under the title *Conclusive Evidence* ("of
my having existed," Nabokov later explained) in the United States and as *Speak,
Memory* in England. Nabokov revised the autobiography in 1954 when he translated
it into Russian as *Drugie Berega* (other shores). Revisions and amplifications of
both the English and Russian versions resulted in *Speak, Memory: An Autobiography Revisited*, the final form of the work, the sequel to which, although planned,
was never completed.

The final form of the work is in the nature of an apostrophe to his wife, Véra, to
whom the book is dedicated but who is mentioned in it not once by name. In the
1951 edition of the work, only the last chapter includes repeated addresses to "you."
In the 1966 version, this second-person address to his wife in increased in the last
chapter and is inserted into chapters 6, 10, 13, and 14.

The biography of his father in chapter 9 was considerably enlarged for its final
version. Andrew Field calls this segment "wooden and constrained" and notes that
the new material had been rejected by *The New Yorker* in 1966. Others, who are not
conditioned to the sophisticated tone of *The New Yorker*, may accept the portrait of
his father as actually the least pretentious and the most profoundly restrained and
moving passage of the entire book. The portrait of his mother is filled with implicit
endearment and gratitude but is unmarked by such depth of admiration and love as
that which he expresses with quiet reserve in the chapter on his father.

In addition to the portraits of his parents, his uncle Dmitri, and his French
governess (Mademoiselle O)—the last presented humorously and almost larger
than life—the other major focuses in the autobiography are on Nabokov's two

young loves ("Colette" and "Tamara"), his enthusiasm for collecting butterflies (and his erudition in lepidopterology), the character sketches of his successive tutors in Russia (a Greek, a Ukrainian, a Lett, a Pole, "a Lutheran of Jewish extraction," a Swiss, and "a young man from a Volgan province"), and his Cambridge education. The autobiography is not so much chronological or capitular as it is serial, a series of vignettes bound, not by transitions, but by thematic and imagistic variations.

Analysis

The clue to Nabokov's autobiographical method is contained in the first chapter. General Aleksey Nikolaevich Kuropatkin, a friend of the family, amuses the five-year-old Nabokov with match sticks arranged to represent the sea in calm and then in stormy weather. Fifteen years later the general, now aged and impoverished, asks Nabokov's father for a light. Nabokov calls this twofold incidence of the use of matches "the match theme" and observes that the "following of such thematic designs through one's life should be, I think, the true purpose of autobiography."

Of the many themes woven into the design of this autobiography two have particularly sinuous threads, the light-and-darkness theme and the death theme; furthermore, the two themes are frequently intertwined so as to become one. In the first sentence of chapter 1 human existence is defined in metaphor as "a brief crack of light between two eternities of darkness" and the two eternities are "identical twins." The movement from the darkness before birth to the darkness after death is variegated by shadows, which are constant intimations of the two eternities, across the crack of light. The image of the variegation is the chiaroscuro, as in "a mesh of sunshine on the parquet under the canework of a Viennese chair," "the shadow . . . undulated in the warm candlelight," "the morning twilight of the nursery," "the changeable twinkle of remote village lights," "the room would be cleft into light and shade," "sun-flecked trails," and many similar phrases in which the image may be as patent as these examples or subtle, as in "an albino physician." Chiaroscuro flourishes in Nabokov's fiction and serves along with other constants of his style to preclude any partition between his fiction and his autobiography, both of which, he claims, are products of the imagination; memory is for him a subsumption of the imagination. The best study of Nabokov's chiaroscuro, indeed the best study of Nabokov's art, is *Nabokov's Dark Cinema* (1974), by Alfred Appel, Jr., in which Nabokov's theme of light and darkness is studied in conjuction with and as culturally coextensive with the film technique that came to be called *film noir*.

In the crack of light between his two eternities Nabokov's birthday coincides with those of William Shakespeare, Vladimir Sikorski, Shirley Temple, and Hazel Brown; Sikorski is his nephew, and "Hazel Brown" is the color of the author's eyes. Sharing a natal day amounts to sharing the two eternities and, in corollary, the crack of light, thereby negating differences in time. "I confess I do not believe in time," Nabokov writes; "I like to fold my magic carpet, after use, in such a way as to superimpose one part of the pattern upon another." He holds to the same superimposition in the matter of a concidence of decease: His uncle Dmitri and his father died in, respectively, 1904 and 1922 on the same day, March 28, and the identicalness of the day eliminates the distance of the years, just as a sameness of circumstances nullifies temporality in the case of Nabokov's brother Sergei and a family friend, I. I. Fondaminski, both of whom died in Nazi death camps. Such examples of coincidence as design are detailed by Carol Shloss, who concludes:

> Though it may seem that the autobiographer is exploiting random coincidence for the purposes of composition, artificially grouping events in the same plane of vision, Nabokov would argue that this technique is not only the prerogative of art—which constructs artifices—but also the procedure of nature. . . .

For example, as Shloss points out, camouflage "challenges us to exercise the discernment that enabled . . . the young Nabokov to see butterflies disguised against their backgrounds." Like a fold of space-time in Nabokov's *Ada, or Ardor: A Family Chronicle* (1969), coincidence eliminates the temporal space between events as camouflage eliminates the spatial separation of entity and background. That each elimination is a semblance, challenging discernment in the same way that an artwork does, amounts to the equation of semblance and reality.

"Hazel Brown," the personification of the autobiographer's eye color, is camouflage that challenges the reader to discern, from the writer's perspective, the background that is both concealed by and equated with the foreground. Similarly, against the background of émigré writers, such as Vladimir Hodasevich, Ivan Bunin, and I. I. Fondaminski, Nabokov places Vladimir Sirin, without informing the reader that V. Sirin was his own pen name from 1925 to 1940, just as the earliest readers of "Mademoiselle O," published as a short story and subsequently included in Nabokov's *Nine Stories* (1947) and *Nabokov's Dozen* (1958), were given no indication whatsoever that the story was actually autobiography.

The half-page segment on V. Sirin begins, "[T]he author that interested me most was naturally Sirin. He belonged to my generation. Among the young writers produced in exile he was the loneliest and most arrogant one." Field ties the pseudonym to the "siren" of Slavic mythology and applauds the choice as a good one "for a writer such as he became because the creature is connected with the idea of metamorphosis." Nabokov objected to this tie-in, perhaps because "Sirin" carries an echo of *siriy* (orphaned), an intonation appropriate to what the writer was, paternally at least, at the time he adopted the name. Another possibility is that "sirin" is an anagram of "iris": He relates that on the night of his father's assassination he was reading to his mother a poem in which the city of Florence is likened to "an iris" and his mother agreed that the city did look like a *dymniy iris* (smoky iris), just before receiving a telephone call announcing his father's death. The anagrammatization would be consistent with Nabokov's concealing the name of the cartoonist Otto Soglow in the phrase "so glowing," as he informs the reader in his 1966 foreword.

The arrogance to which Nabokov confesses in the Sirin passage is ingrained in the final version of his autobiography. He classifies "peasant girls" as objectively as he speaks of the classification of butterflies. He laments the lost greatness and glamour of the Nord-Express "when its elegant brown became a nouveau-riche blue." He labels certain Russian writers, among them Ivan Goncharov, "stupefying bores (comparable to American 'regional writers')." He dismisses Stendhal, Honoré de Balzac, and Émile Zola as "destestable mediocrities." Maxim Gorky is "a regional mediocrity." He refers to Sigmund Freud as "Sigismond Lejoyeux, a local aeronaut" and "the Viennese Quack." Much of this arrogance is tolerable within the context of strong opinions. There is, however, one instance of arrogant spite that fails as humor and does not befit an aristocrat, even the liberal one that he claimed he, like his father, was. Learning that a subspecies of butterfly which he thought to be his discovery had already been classified by a lepidopterist named Kretschmar, he took petty revenge: "I got even with the first discoverer of *my* moth by giving his own name to a blind man in a novel." The novel was *Kamera Obskura* (1932, in which the character is Bruno Krechmar; *Camera Obscura*, 1936, in which the name becomes Albinus Kretschmar; revised as *Laughter in the Dark*, 1938, in which the name is finally changed to Albert Albinus).

The Kretschmar incident, creditably admitted if ingloriously concluded, does illustrate the depth of his subjective devotion to lepidopterology. His passion for the collection and study of butterflies enlivens many pages of his narrative and is the topic of chapter 6. His passion for chess is only slightly less keen than that for butterflies, and he delights in chess problems which camouflage a sophisticated solution by a less satisfying simple one. His third great passion, for the beauties and intricacies of language, is explicit in his comments on Russian and English and pervades his autobiography, as it does his novels, in the forms of euphuism, chiasmus, punning, alliteration, anagrammatization, archaism, coinage, and many other configurations of orthography, rhetoric, and syntax. The lengths to which he will go to compose, for example, an alliterative chiasmus is evident in a clause such as "Dostoevskian drisk could not compete with neo-Thomist thought." The construction hangs upon the rarely used word "drisk," which compels many, perhaps most, readers, even after they have learned from an unabridged dictionary that it means "a drizzling mist," to give ample thought to it. He contrives numerous melodic, if sometimes ostentatious, phrases such as "marvelous melting fata morgana effects" and "proposed imitations of supposed intonations." The linguistic cleverness and playfulness that color his fiction do the same for his autobiography and contribute both to the modernism which eliminates barriers between literary genres and to a polished lyricism that can be moving as well as mocking.

Speak, Memory in its final form is a series of verbal gesticulations intended to recapitulate "the supreme achievement of memory, which is the masterly use it makes of innate harmonies when gathering to its fold the suspended and wandering tonalities of the past." Nabokov's achievement is his emulation of memory's achievement.

Critical Context

Nabokov's Russian-language novels, written between 1925 and 1940 and eventually translated into English with the sometime collaboration of his son, fall short of the greatness of his major English-language novels—*Lolita*, *Pnin* (1957), *Pale Fire* (1962), and *Ada*. *Speak, Memory* antedates these masterworks; *Speak, Memory*, the 1966 version of which adds references to *Lolita* and *Pnin*, antedates Nabokov's masterpiece, *Ada*. Autobiographies ordinarily follow the literary successes of their subjects. Nabokov, like Robert Graves (who wrote his autobiography at age thirty-five and published *I, Claudius* four years later in 1934), confounds custom but confirms his own sense of his worth.

The autobiography, although most closely akin to Nabokov's fiction, has much in common with his essays, criticism, and interviews. In *Strong Opinions* (1973), he mentions "the melodramatic muddle and phony mysticism of Dostoevski," which phrase could serve as a gloss on "Dostoevskian drisk." The phrase appears in a long defense of his 1964 translation of Alexander Pushkin's *Evgeny Onegin* (1825-1833; *Eugene Onegin*) against Edmund Wilson's charges of, among other faults, mistranslations and an "addiction to rare and unfamiliar words" (for example, rummer, dit, gloam, scrab, mollitude, stuss). Nabokov defends his work ably, although with some unpleasant arrogance and with occasional lack of convincingness.

If Nabokov's works were to be listed in two columns, the first comprising fiction, poetry, drama, and translations, and the second comprising essays, criticism, interviews, and lectures, *Speak, Memory*, in its final revision, would be the link belonging to and connecting both columns. The posthumous publication of his *Lectures on Literature* (1980), *Lectures on Russian Literature* (1981)—in which he rails at length at Fyodor Dostoevski and Gorky—and *Lectures on Don Quixote* (1983) offer readers the opportunity to appreciate Nabokov's literary criticism and to see it as an extension of the attitudes expressed in *Speak, Memory*. These attitudes are summed up on his anti-Dostoevski lecture with the statement that "art is a divine game"—divine because the artist is creator, and a game because "it is all make-believe"; for Nabokov there is no access to true creation other than that afforded by the camouflage of make-believe and there is no divine gamester more productive of this access than he himself.

Sources for Further Study

Appel, Alfred, Jr. *Nabokov's Dark Cinema*, 1974.

Field, Andrew. *VN: The Life and Art of Vladimir Nabokov*, 1986.

Lee, L. L. *Vladimir Nabokov*, 1976.

Quennell, Peter, ed. *Vladimir Nabokov: A Tribute*, 1979.

Shloss, Carol. "Speak, Memory: The Aristocracy of Art," in *Nabokov's Fifth Arc: Nabokov and Others on His Life's Work*, 1982. Edited by J. E. Rivers and Charles Nicol.

Stegner, Page. *Escape into Aesthetics: The Art of Vladimir Nabokov*, 1966.

Stuart, Dabney. *"Speak, Memory*: Autobiography as Fiction," in *Nabokov: The Dimensions of Parody*, 1978.

Roy Arthur Swanson

SPRIGHTLY RUNNING
Part of an Autobiography

Author: John Wain (1925-   )
Type of work: Autobiography
Time of work: 1925-1960
Locale: England
First published: 1962

> *Principal personage:*
> JOHN WAIN, the novelist

Form and Content

Though best known for his first novel *Hurry On Down* (1953; published in the United States as *Born in Captivity*, 1954), the press reaction to which placed him prominently but uncomfortably among the "angry young men" of the 1950's, John Wain was among the most prolific and versatile writers of the decade—during which he had also produced two volumes of poetry (1951 and 1956), a collection of short stories (1960), a book of criticism entitled *Preliminary Essays* (1957), numerous other reviews, and three additional novels: *Living in the Present* (1955), *The Contenders* (1958), and *A Travelling Woman* (1959). *Sprightly Running*, which was completed in September, 1960, as he "reached the exact half-way point in three-score years and ten," is his personal assessment of the major influences on his development as a writer, poet, and teacher.

"My 1930s," the first of the book's nine chapters, comprises more than one-fourth of its total length. Wain's depiction of his childhood painstakingly details the isolation of a sensitive and somewhat frail boy who, as a member of the middle class (the son of a dentist), finds himself resented as an outsider and bullied by lower-class "roughs" in the schoolyard and the community at large. Though such persecution is certainly not unique (and he omits its details, noting that its forms remain much the same in any decade), Wain's early experience as a victim of bullying and intolerance gave him an acute sympathy for victims of persecution elsewhere—particularly, during the late 1930's and early 1940's, those in Nazi Germany.

The second chapter, "Love and the War," begins with the diagnosis of a detached retina in his left eye that confined the sixteen-year-old Wain to bed for three months and left him partially blind, causing him to be rejected for military service at age eighteen. During this time, he also developed an intense and prolonged but unrequited adolescent infatuation with the daughter of an insurance salesman—a "wretched hopeless passion" that continued until his enrollment at Oxford several years later. Influenced by his parents' support of the pacifist cause in the 1930's, young Wain again saw himself in a minority that was "oppressed, despised, [and] in possession of the truth but powerless to impose its will," characterizing his attitude as the Pharisaism of "any youth growing up in the attitude of high-minded martyr-dom, such as prevails among pacifists in a liberal country during a war . . . a holier-than-thou attitude."

Although he had reacted intensely against formal education in his younger years and had received only haphazard grounding in educational fundamentals, he en-tered St. John's College, Oxford, in 1943; his experience there is described in the book's lengthy third chapter. Under the direction of his tutor C. S. Lewis, who taught him the importance of meticulous analysis and rigorously precise writing, he began to shape his identity as a writer, while his friend Charles Williams instilled in him a reverential love of great poetry. During this time he befriended the brilliant but eccentric E. M. W. Meyerstein as well as Kingsley Amis and Philip Larkin, who were soon to begin their own distinguished literary careers; he also developed an abiding fascination with the life and works of Samuel Johnson, an interest which culminated in Wain's noteworthy biography of him published in 1975.

About his first marriage (1947) and divorce (1956) Wain discloses very little, giving it only a four-page chapter and declining even to reveal his wife's name in order to avoid "an unwarranted intrusion on someone else's privacy." The mar-riage's ending came "slowly, messily, in a welter of tears and agony," leaving him at the end of

> nearly a decade of suffering . . . with the knowledge that parting from someone
> you care for is the worst kind of pain, the slowest to heal and the most deeply felt . . .
> the nearest thing to hell that life can offer; and that the most terrible of all words is
> Good-bye.

"A Literary Chapter," the book's fifth, is devoted primarily to Wain's career as a writer (beginning at age nine with parodies of detective novels) and, from 1947 to 1955, as a lecturer in English Literature at the University of Reading. Though he resigned to become a full-time free-lance writer, Wain's own university associations were to continue throughout his career, culminating in his position as professor of poetry at Oxford from 1973 to 1978. His assessment of contemporary poetry within *Sprightly Running* is forthright and acerbic, decrying "the collapse of the consumer wall of the literary triangle" that has allowed the ascendancy of (unnamed) ersatz poets and fame-building publicity-mongers "whose methods make Barnum look like an archbishop."

Following a brief chapter on "The Wains in History," describing his now-unknown working-class ancestors as "among the people who carried the heavy weight of England on their backs," a chapter titled "Thoughts in an Aeroplane" is devoted to his travels in the United States and the Soviet Union. For reasons discussed at length in an article published in truncated form in the *Observer* but included in full in the chapter called "Criminal Record," Wain found that, despite the physical beauty of its countryside and the friendliness of its people, "the total effect of being in the Soviet Union was to depress me almost suicidally." In "Going

Home," the final chapter, Wain assesses the meaning of his own Englishness and reasserts his view of the fundamentally tragic nature of human life.

The book's title and its epigraph are taken from act 4, scene 1 of John Dryden's tragedy *Aurengzebe* (1675)

> . . . None would live past years again,
> Yet all hope pleasure in what remain;
> And, from the dregs of life, think to receive
> What the first sprightly running could not give.

Analysis

Written at a relatively early point in his career, *Sprightly Running* records the growth of John Wain's artistic sensibility and traces the intellectual origins of the worldview of this erudite and versatile mid-twentieth century man of letters. With a stoical acceptance of life's hardships and a determination to focus on the effects of such events on his personality rather than their precise details, he typically offers few specifics about some of his particularly painful experiences. Thus, in a single sentence or paragraph he often dismisses—as already too familiar—those sources of sentimental and/or sensational anecdotal material with which more typical autobiographies abound (the persecutions endured as a schoolboy, the agonies of unrequited adolescent love, the problems and deprivations of day-to-day wartime existence, the miseries of an unhappy marriage). Instead, in an engaging and insightful narrative that is at times unsparingly self-critical as well, he reveals the deeply personal origins of thematic preoccupations that recur throughout his fiction and criticism.

Among the foremost of these are his self-confessed pessimism and his concern with the exploitation of power in interpersonal relationships of all kinds. The first chapter, for example, not only adeptly recaptures the intensity of childhood experiences but also places them within the context of a mature adult's understanding of power and a particularly English class consciousness. Even at the age of five, as he lived in fear of the bullying practiced by children living in The Sutton (a nearby housing project), he had

> learned the following lessons: (i) that the world was dangerous; (ii) that it was not possible to evade these dangers by being inoffensive, since I was surrounded on all sides by those who hated me, not for anything I had done, but for being different from themselves; (iii) that, although the natural reaction to all this was fear, I could not admit to feeling fear or I should be disgraced.

During his teenage years, his sense of life being essentially tragic was reinforced by the hardships of war as well as his unrequited love, so that by the time of his arrival at Oxford he had constructed a worldview that "excluded the very idea of happiness except for the gross, the naïve, or the unreflecting"—an attitude that he characterizes (from his more mature perspective) as a "dangerous web." The miseries of his first marriage, though undisclosed, also clearly confirmed the view to which he had long adhered.

From infancy onward, Wain felt an intense love of nature and the English countryside, though this too, he grew to realize, was constantly menaced and soon to be lost, a victim of the continual encroachment of industrial expansion and urban growth. Yet, like William Wordsworth, he retains an almost pantheistic reverence for the natural world as a restorative refuge from the man-made environment.

Notwithstanding Wain's pessimism and his ultimately tragic view of life, *Sprightly Running* is by no means a misanthropic book; his repeated self-characterization as an outsider makes possible not only a tone of wry detachment but also a dry humor that, however satirical it may be, is consistently based on a humane and compassionate understanding. Thus, for example, even though his portrait of members of academia's "half dead" middle-aged professoriate has much the same animus as his friend Kingsley Amis's novel *Lucky Jim* (1954), Wain also details (from personal experience) the causes of such burnout: "the horrible drudgery of a don's life—the stacks of essays to be waded through, the committee meetings with boring colleagues, the fresh wave of empty young heads, every October, that have to be filled somehow." Although he would hold a number of faculty positions later in his career (at the University of Bristol in 1967, at the Centre Universitaire Experimentale in Vincennes, France, in 1969, and at Oxford in the mid-1970's), at the time of writing *Sprightly Running* he felt pleased to have "got out" of the classroom, foreseeing a return to teaching only if he were to come under "the lash of poverty."

Given his distinctly antiauthoritarian predilections and his sympathies for the individual rather than the group (especially when the former is being persecuted or bullied by the latter), Wain's averse reaction to his one-month visit to the Soviet Union is not entirely surprising, though he acknowledges that it fundamentally changed his understanding of the world. Accustomed to the English atmosphere of political and social toleration, he found both the absence of individual liberties and the presence of univocal official propaganda to be oppressive.

Though his novel *Hurry On Down* had been translated into Russian and had reportedly sold out in an edition of 250,000 copies (from which his share of the revenues had to remain inside the Soviet Union), he found that his work was of interest there because it was viewed as a manifestation of the anti-Western rebellion of one of the renowned (and, the Soviets had obviously concluded, potentially revolutionary) "angry young men." His art, in short, had been suborned to a political purpose that he did not endorse, enlisted in support of a radical cause in which he did not believe, and used as confirmation of the government-sponsored propaganda whose unchallenged and vitriolically anti-Western worldview he deplored. Yet, Wain insisted, more offensive than the use of his (and others') writings for such purposes were the "Newspeak" and "Doublethink"—terms coined by George Orwell in *Nineteen Eighty-Four* (1949)—with which the Soviets feigned a sincere interest in Western literature and art.

Earlier in 1959, shortly before his visit to the Soviet Union, Wain had ended an eight-month sojourn in the United States, first at New Hampshire's Macdowell Colony, a retreat for artists and writers, and subsequently in New York's Brooklyn Heights. Although *Sprightly Running* contains very few details of his travels throughout America, the overall impression was a strongly favorable one, though not uncritically so; though exhilarated by the size and diversity of America as well as the helpfulness of its people, he was disconcerted by the relative impermanence of its culture, the devaluation of tradition, and the relentless barrage of advertising.

After having repeatedly portrayed himself as an isolated outsider—a wry, sensitive, and introspective if pessimistic and beleaguered observer—in his final pages Wain surprisingly contends:

> I have long recognized myself as a participator . . . the sort of person who rushes headlong at life, collides with it, and gets hurt. But the hurt of staying away, the dull ache of seeing life go past without you, is worse than the shock of participation.

The book's final line ("Spirits of my unknown ancestors, speak through me: green hills of Staffordshire, stand firm in my mind!") echoes the famous closing line of James Joyce's *A Portrait of the Artist as a Young Man* (1916): "Old father, old artificer, stand me now and ever in good stead!"

Critical Context

Now recognized as a journalistic catchphrase rather than the name of a full-fledged literary movement, the term "angry young men" was commonly applied to a number of writers of the mid-1950's, including Kingsley Amis, John Braine, Alan Sillitoe, John Osborne, and John Wain. Their individuality and diversity have often been overlooked as certain similarities in their writings have been emphasized— particularly their portrayal of working-class protagonists who ardently voiced their social discontent, as well as their forthright inclusion of formerly "unmentionable" subject matter, "vulgar" language, and raucous comedy. From the outset, however, Wain was particularly uncomfortable with the label, and *Sprightly Running* is in part an explicit declaration of literary independence:

> Speaking for myself, I reject the label, and will always continue to reject it, because (i) it is the creation of journalists who know nothing, and care less than nothing, for the art to which my life is dedicated, (ii) it is a hindrance to anyone who holds serious opinions and is able to be genuinely serious about them, and (iii) because I refuse to be institutionalized, whatever may be the immediate advantages in terms of hard cash.

Wain's autobiography is also a valuable guide to an understanding of the pessimism that becomes increasingly prominent in his later fiction, which lacks the comic verve of his earlier work. Appropriately, his favorite author is Samuel Johnson, whose observation that "human life is every where a state in which much is to be endured, and little to be enjoyed" epitomizes a point of view much like Wain's own.

Although he acknowledges in *Sprightly Running* that many have found his criticism to be stronger than his creative work (as many subsequent critics have agreed), he has continually refused to confine himself to one type of writing, though he admits a surprising preference for short fiction and poetry to the novel, for which he remains better known.

His middle-class family background and antileftist opinions also fundamentally differentiate him from many "angry young men," whose origins were more directly in the working class and whose political sympathies were more left-of-center. Like the occasional Cold War tenor of his anti-Soviet rhetoric (however justifiable it may have been), Wain's disclaimer of revolutionary intent is a recognizable product of the late 1950's and early 1960's—a reminder of the comparative mildness of the then-startling "anger" that would, less than a decade later, be supplanted by far more radical and convulsive expressions of revolutionary rage, both in literature and in life.

Sources for Further Study

Creber, J. W. Patrick. "Some Lessons from a Short Story," in *English Journal*. LXXVI (February, 1987), p. 82.

Gray, James. Review in *Time*. LXXXI (May 24, 1963), p. 102.

Pryce-Jones, Alan. Review in *Newsweek*. LXI (May 13, 1963), p. 108.

Ryan, F. L. Review in *Best Sellers*. XXIII (May 15, 1963), p. 69.

Salwak, Dale. *John Braine and John Wain: A Reference Guide*, 1979.

_____. *John Wain*, 1981.

William Hutchings

STARTING OUT IN THE THIRTIES

Author: Alfred Kazin (1915-   )
Type of work: Autobiography
Time of work: 1934-1945
Locale: New York City
First published: 1965

> *Principal personages:*
> ALFRED KAZIN, a writer, critic, and teacher
> JOHN CHAMBERLAIN, a reviewer for *The New York Times*
> MALCOLM COWLEY, the literary critic and editor of *The New Republic*
> MARY MCCARTHY, the critic and novelist
> SOPHIE, Kazin's spinster cousin

Form and Content

This second in a series of autobiographical works by Alfred Kazin covers his life from the summer of 1934 to the end of World War II in 1945. It includes a series of portraits of people whom he met each year and traces his career as reviewer, critic, and teacher during this time.

Each of the six chapters and the epilogue are titled with the dates of years during the 1930's and 1940's. The opening scene of the first chapter, "1934," captures the exuberance and vitality of the young Kazin. As he brashly enters the office of John Chamberlain, reviewer for *The New York Times*, the nineteen-year-old Kazin is full of intellectual ideas and hopes to convince Chamberlain to help him obtain a literary job. In a summer of the Dust Bowl and the rising Nazism of Adolf Hitler, the young socialistic Kazin is full of optimism in the power of the world. He looks "to literature for strong social argument, intellectual power, human liberation." In the series of portraits he gives of the literary intellectuals he meets and in the discussions of social issues he recounts, Kazin provides a kind of intellectual history of the 1930's. The strong political optimism he shares with others in this period of harsh social upheaval finally dissipates at the end of the book, with the revelations of Hitler's concentration camps.

Each of the chapters and the epilogue focus on major influences in Kazin's life and on major intellectuals of the New York literary scene. He praises Malcolm Cowley, editor of *The New Republic*, for his ability to bridge the worlds of 1920's and 1930's writers. The former were generally disgruntled upper-class writers, but those of the 1930's came from the working class, the lower class, and the immigrant class. James T. Farrell, author of the *Studs Lonigan* trilogy, is praised for his ability to portray accurately the emptiness and futility of the working class yet include the hope that the "facts will make you free. . . ." Kazin likes William Saroyan because of the exuberance he invests in his writing. Both writers are admired by Kazin because they reject literary traditions in favor of newness and freedom. The chapters also present favorable pictures of Marxist critic V. F. Calverton, who immediately saw the falsity of Joseph Stalin in 1936, and of Ralph Bates, a British novelist-adventurer, who speaks movingly in 1937 at a party to garner support for the Communists in the Spanish Revolution. Other critics, such as Max Eastman, Sidney Hook, Bert Wolfe, and Mary McCarthy, who were associated with the *Modern Monthly* and *Partisan Review*, are discussed.

The negative effects of the intense ideological debates of the 1930's are shown in the character of Francis Corcoran, a Catholic interested in Jews and a pedant drawn to Communism. Corcoran believes that all printed matter is the truth, and he is completely deceived by the accounts of the Moscow trials of 1936. By 1939 he rejects Communism, turns to new forms of authority, and becomes an informer during the rise of McCarthyism.

This work traces Kazin's life from his first summer of reviewing for Malcolm Cowley at *The New Republic*, through his sense of isolation as a Jew of parents not intellectually oriented, and to his attempts to become a literary critic. Kazin discusses his associations with various young women whom he considers marrying, and these culminate in his marriage to his first wife in 1938. Her Russian heritage, her beauty, her attachment to science as a bacteriologist, and her fervor for women's rights attract him. Kazin discusses fully his intense hope that the Soviet workers' state will become the climax toward which history has been moving. Eventually he will reject the Communists because of the Moscow trials of 1936 and the Soviet Union's signing of the nonaggression pact with Hitler. Kazin also describes his teaching and living with his wife in Provincetown in 1940 as he prepares a book of literary criticism on American writers of the 1880's and 1890's. William Dean Howells and Henry James appeal to him because they include much social criticism in their writings. By 1945, Kazin finally accepts the belief that American society and its radicals have changed since 1940. The world can never return to the idea of a better life in the future because of society's loss of optimism and because of the events of World War II.

The epilogue, titled "1945," a time five years after the final chapter of 1940 and America's entry into the war, gives Kazin's reactions to the events of World War II. He sees the rearmament of the United States as a protection against the mass unemployment and social hysteria of the 1930's. For him it was "a sacrifice to progress" which the more accomplished society of the 1940's demanded, but the intellectual optimism of the 1930's could not be maintained with it.

Analysis

In his work, Alfred Kazin traces the influence on his life of two important themes during the 1930's. Through his description of individuals, he shows how strongly social change and specifically Socialism shaped him and those around him. It loomed for Kazin as a utopian goal, a kind of American Dream that seemed to provide hope among intellectuals in the midst of Depression-era America. He also traces artfully how the hopes of Socialism raised by the Russian Revolution of 1917 begin to fall quickly as power struggles developed in the Soviet Union. As the Stalinists gained more power and as the Moscow trials of 1936 turned darker, Kazin's own hopes for America soured. In his portraits of Mary McCarthy and other writers for the *Partisan Review*, he shows how their social criticism lost its optimism. For Mary McCarthy, criticism seems only a way of showing her superiority over an opponent; she makes Kazin realize that "it would be possible to be a radical without any idealism whatsoever."

A second theme that permeates this work is isolation. Two female members of his family reveal how this isolation is associated in Kazin's mind with his Jewishness in America. His mother constantly worries so much about others that he sees her as "a slave to other people." Never is she able to enjoy any happiness of the moment. Kazin's own thoughts echo this outlook on life when he describes his viewing a newsreel of liberated prisoners from the Nazi concentration camp at Belsen in 1945. Amid the joy of the liberation Kazin feels embarrassed and describes the sight of these Jews who look like "sticks" as "unbearable."

In contrast to his mother, his cousin Sophie is alive, active, open to the world, and full of emotion. Fellow dressmakers from the surrounding factories gather in the young Kazin's home in the evening to drink tea and listen to Sophie entertain them on her mandolin. The vibrancy that exudes from Sophie at these times is in Kazin's mind the central emotion he associates with his memories of her. This is also the emotion Kazin has for the intellectuals he finds so stimulating in their discussions of Socialism and social change during the 1930's.

Because Sophie is unmarried, Kazin's mother sees her as incomplete, unfulfilled, and enduring a plight that only marriage can cure. In "1937," Kazin reveals Sophie's fate. After being rejected by many potential suitors and in middle age, Sophie accepts an offer to pose as the wife of a man who will try to begin a new life in the Midwest. In a few months the man deserts her, and she goes insane from the emotional shock. For the next twenty years until her death, she lives in the state insane asylum.

In Sophie's bedroom, which became Kazin's after her departure, hang two pictures to which he often refers. These symbolize the two major themes of the book. The first picture is Sir George Frederic Watts' *Hope*: ". . . a blindfolded young lady with bare feet sat on a globe earnestly listening for the vibration of the single string on her harp. . . ." The second picture is Pierre-Auguste Cot's *The Storm*. In it two lovers run together from an approaching storm with a gauze veil held over their heads. The hope in the first picture comes through strongly in Kazin's belief that American life can be improved by Socialism and that he can help foster this improvement through his writing. Seeing a performance of Clifford Odets' *Awake and Sing* in 1936 confirms his belief that this can happen, because in the play everything comes together: "Art and truth and hope could yet come together—if a real writer was their meeting place." In his life with his wife in Provincetown and in his own writing, he seems to have achieved this dream of hope. In Sophie's plight and his mother's constant guilt over it, however, Kazin is drawn much more strongly to the concept of loneliness. His mother's belief that "you were lonely as a Jew and lonely in a strange land, lonely, always lonely even in the midst of people" teaches him "the picture of a woman or man as an abject soul wandering about the world looking for the other" and seeking protection from the coming storm.

In the 1930's Socialism and literature offered hope to Kazin, but World War II was the storm which finally arrived and changed his world. In "1940," he says of the radicals such as Philip Rahv and Mary McCarthy that they are certainly intelligent, but they lack a desire to suffer for mankind. They are "sour outsiders" who "shift back and forth amid the ideologies like a fevered patient trying to find a cool place in bed." Most important, they lack "the faith in a wholly new society" which those radicals of the 1930's had.

Critical Context

Most readers of Alfred Kazin's works know him as a major critic of American literature. *On Native Grounds: An Interpretation of Modern American Prose Literature* (1942), his first work, was highly praised for its description of the rise of social realism in American literature. In it Kazin stresses that literature must always be studied from within the contexts of the culture in which it is written, in marked contrast to the New Critics of that time, who disregarded historical and social criticism in favor of a close analysis of the text and its form.

Kazin's autobiographical works have received much less critical attention. *A Walker in the City* (1951) describes his boyhood in the Brownsville section of Brooklyn during the early years of the Depression. *New York Jew* (1978) covers Kazin's life from 1942 to 1978, paying particular attention to the socially turbulent 1960's. As with *Starting Out in the Thirties*, in each of these works Kazin does not present a day-by-day account of his life but prefers to use the same principles that he uses in his literary criticism. In order to reveal Kazin the man, he focuses on key people and key ideas, presenting himself within the social context of his day. He captures even better the optimism that raged for improving the plight of all mankind through individual sacrifice—as well as the loss of that optimism, and a shift away from personal sacrifice and toward personal power, that grew out of World War II.

Sources for Further Study

Capouya, Emile. "The America with Some Regret," in *Saturday Review*. XLVIII (September 18, 1965), p. 101.

Kauffmann, Stanley. "Young in the Thirties," in *The New Republic*. CLIII (September 18, 1965), pp. 17-20.

Kramer, Hilton. "The Age of the Intellectuals," in *The New Leader*. XLVIII (September 27, 1965), pp. 23-24.

Kronenberger, Louis. "Thirties: Frayed Collars and Large Visions," in *The Atlantic Monthly*. CCXVII (January, 1966), pp. 79-81.

Marx, Leo. "A Literary Radical," in *Commentary*. XL (December, 1965), pp. 118, 120-123.

Alan T. Belsches

STOP-TIME

Author: Frank Conroy (1936-   )
Type of work: Autobiography
First published: 1967

Principal personage:
FRANK CONROY, the author

Form and Content

Stop-Time is a fictionalized account of the early life of its author. It ends as he emerges into young adulthood, after his acceptance at Haverford College. Between a prologue and epilogue which together form a distinct suspended narrative, Conroy offers twenty chapters that primarily focus on early adolescence. Each chapter is named for one of its images or scenes. While one event or image gives unity to each chapter, chapters may also include events or impressions that are thematically, rather than dramatically, related. The chapter "Nights Away from Home," for example, revolves around the adolescent Frank's attempt to run away from New York to his childhood world of Florida, but that narrative is interspersed with other recollections of nocturnal alienation and disorientation, some of them quite fragmentary and devoid of narrative context.

Conroy begins and ends the account of his childhood and adolescence within a frame, presumably located in the present. The writer, now married and living in England, appears to have secured a calm and productive life. Yet he is addicted to wild, dangerous drives in the country. Once or twice weekly he compulsively races without headlights through the streets of South London, driving his Jaguar alone through the English countryside at speeds of more than one hundred miles per hour: "anything at all," he says, "to keep the speed, to maintain the speed and streak through the dark world." At the end of his story, the speaker again describes the nighttime drives and ends with a near-death collision. Paralyzed yet peaceful in anticipation of an imminent crash and a seemingly welcome death, the narrator nevertheless escapes, laughing.

The frame not only confirms that Conroy has indeed escaped his childhood and become a living writer, but it suggests the drama and intensity of the story placed within it. Conroy's experiences growing up within a drifting, mentally unstable family continually veer between providing a sense of self and a sense of annihilation. The story is ostensibly structured around the chronology of his parents' wanderings but its internal organization is based on the maturing consciousness of the child. In Faulknerian fashion, the analysis of the child's thoughts and actions is not given through the dispassionate retrospection of an adult narrator but seems to emerge from the past under recall. It appears as the spilling-over of the child's unconscious: something felt and thought by the child regardless of his inability to have articulated it in quite the language the author gives him. With the intimacy, urgency, and detail of psychological self-analysis, this roughly chronological narrative of American youth combines vivid realism with the imagery of dreams. Its episodic structure alternates between many small plots, told with the compression and resonance of short fiction, and nearly actionless depictions of trancelike states of consciousness to which Conroy is attracted as a child as well as an adult. Conroy effectively communicates the disorientation of the child through his depiction of the extreme close-up, hallucinatory experiences, and complete subjectivism. He makes no attempt to present characters objectively, or even to give them much dialogue of their own. All is told through the consciousness of the emergent author, who even in childhood has a critical eye for detail and strong impressions, especially of the grotesque.

Events in the story carry narrative weight in proportion to their significance to the child. Thus a yo-yo contest occupies an entire chapter and provides one of the book's central metaphors. Of equal importance is young Frank's terrifying habit of playing on a tenement rooftop while fantasizing about jumping to the street below. From within the child's world, Conroy makes minimal reference to any life outside the family or school. He offers no claims to have participated in national events, to have known famous people, or even to have developed as a product of his age.

Analysis

As a portrait of an artist, *Stop-Time* bears comparison with others within that subgenre. It is not, however, simply a quest for artistic form; Conroy's autobiography relates the search for acceptable forms of human relationship. As *The New Republic* noted of his later short fiction, the book concerns "how to live in the world as an adult male" and the difficulty of establishing endurable relations with father figures, youthful comrades, and women. It recounts the growth of sexual self-consciousness with candor and humor, recapturing the bafflement, timidity, and desperate aggression of an adolescent boy. Although Conroy emphasizes the idyllic friendship between him and another elementary school boy in Florida, the book succeeds most in its depiction of the terrible isolation of adolescence. As part of a dysfunctional family on the fringes of American life, Frank is most often voyeuristic in all relationships, not only those explicitly sexual.

The story also provides insight into the world of bohemian life and utopian experimentation during the years following World War II. After leaving the anarchy of a "progressive school," young Frank is pulled from place to place by his Danish mother and her lover (later her husband), a displaced New Orleans Frenchman. For much of his childhood, the family moves back and forth between the wreck of a Socialist utopia in the sandy wastes of an abandoned South Florida housing tract and the streets of New York City, where his stepfather is engaged in a number of fruitless get-rich-quick schemes. Whether socialistic or financially opportunistic, all schemes are equally suspect, and Frank perceives them as the indulgence of the lazy and weak-minded. Any dogma, even his stepfather's preoccupation with "pure food," is a symptom of formlessness and lies dangerously close to the ultimate formlessness of insanity.

Conroy is clearly less interested in describing a certain period in American life than in revealing the manifold indications of the sheer madness which looms everywhere. The threat of psychic breakdown informs the entire book, from his father's insanity to that of his sister, the twisted cruelty of their boarder, the instability of his stepfather, the derangement of a wealthy woman with whom he has an affair, the mental fragility of a beautiful girl in a Danish language school, and the harrowing scenes inside the institution for the retarded at which his parents were night wardens. Attempting to escape the loneliness of his parents' cabin by staying the night with them in the mental institution, Frank is overwhelmed by the urgency of the inmates' cries. He feels himself standing "balanced on the pinpoint of my own sanity, a small, cracked tile in the floor." Throughout the story, as in the events of the frame, the narrator shifts uneasily at the edge.

The autobiography totters between sanity and madness, control and chaos, self-consciousness and self-annihilation. Its fragmentary bits are held together by a highly selective and technically astute arrangement of repeated motifs. Conroy explores the exceedingly narrow division between a sense of one's self and the loss of self, and posits the capacity for design and control as the lifesaving mediating force between the two extremes. In one of the book's central chapters, "White Days, Red Nights," Conroy describes the winter he endured for the most part alone in a makeshift cabin while his parents worked at the Connecticut state home for the retarded. The nightmare hallucinations of his nights, he explains, at least "came from inside my own head. I was *making* it all, and although it was terrifying, it was not, as were the days, cosmically threatening." The days, however, "were emptiness, a vast spacious emptiness in which the fact of being alive became almost meaningless. . . . I wasn't conscious of what was happening, I lived it. I became invisible. I lost myself."

Other silences are as intoxicating as they are frightening. He remembers awakening without memory in a white, sunlit room, and this moment he calls "the exact, spatial center of my life, the one still point." Of equal attraction is the "waking sleep" of total absorption in music. Silence takes even more forms: Some allow the most vivid sense of both the immensity of the surrounding universe and the particularity of one's own reality. Of his unsupervised days in the open spaces of the sandy Florida pine woods, he recalls how he and his companion sat alone in the complete silence around them: "We shouted in joy and fear, sending our voices ahead to animate the bleakness, supremely conscious of ourselves as pinpoints of life in a world of dead things. . . ." Alone under the stars, the two boys find themselves "nervous, filled with passion" at the infinitude of sky. Later, listening to the shrieks and moans of the mental patients at the Connecticut institution, Conroy says:

> It was if all the saints, martyrs, and mystics of human history were gathered into a single building, each one crying out at the moment of revelation, each one truly *there* at his extreme of joy or pain, crying out with the purity of total selflessness.

In such sequences Frank feels the terror of the impersonal and the overwhelming need to express the self. Afraid of the abyss of the universe, on the one hand, and the disorder of the purely personal, on the other, he begins a quest for the structured form, the static and self-sustaining configuration which will give meaning to a haphazard world of experience.

As part of the quest, Frank begins to read, since in reading the chaos of experience becomes ordered and capable of examination. He develops mastery of a difficult yo-yo stunt pointedly called "The Universe," and of his prowess says that he was "finally free, in one small area at least, of the paralyzing sloppiness of life in general." Eventually he sees art's capacity for organizing experience in his friend's sketch of a door lock, a drawing which within its own stasis captures motion and change. In a final scene, the procedure of college board examinations allows Frank to perform with great skill during the segmented, organized parcel of time represented by the stopwatch of the examiner. Similarly, the design and finality of his own book provides the essential structure for his past life. As *Stop-Time* ends with the narrator walking away from his demolished car, laughing, Conroy suggests that while self-annihilation remains a powerful, magnetic attraction for its author, the book—whose composition necessarily follows the crash chronologically—can harness that dark force into the tense strength of its own creative design.

While the events and persons depicted in *Stop-Time* appear to have existed, most names are changed and chronology altered. Childhood and adolescence are brought alive without any self-conscious apparatus of recall; except for the frame and one reference to the present (given in montage, without transition), Conroy makes no mention of any present outside the time of the narrative. Like what Irish author George Moore termed his own autobiography, "a novel about real people," *Stop-Time* reads with the immediacy of such autobiographical fiction as D. H. Lawrence's *Sons and Lovers* (1913) or Sylvia Plath's *The Bell Jar* (1963). Yet Conroy did not publish the book as a novel. A nonfictional text claims to represent in some sense the world outside itself; for Conroy the affirmation of an integrated self may depend upon the design his own autobiography imposes upon his lived experience.

Critical Context

Before publication of *Stop-Time*, Frank Conroy was entirely unknown as a writer. Since, he has produced occasional journalism and *Midair* (1985), a spare assemblage of short fiction with evident autobiographical elements. He remains primarily recognized for his first book. Despite the superb story, "Gossip," whose excellence has been recognized by Terrence Rafferty in *The Nation*, *Midair* covers much the same ground as the autobiography, from scenes of a boy tormented by an insane father to suicidal "car games" of reckless speed. While repeating its incidents and its frenetic mood, the stories lack the rich context of the autobiography.

Stop-Time itself extends the reaches of twentieth century autobiography, especially in the difficult subgenre of the autobiography of childhood. It has been postulated that since childhood is constructed of trivialities, true autobiographies of childhood were unknown until the techniques of the Symbolists allowed revelation of the most profound meaning in apparently insignificant events. Conroy has packed his book with such trivialities, and because of his skill in portraying juvenile consciousness, they become the highly potent details of a study in human perception. As Tony Tanner notes, Conroy is able to capture "this receptivity of the child's psyche, to communicate to us that feeling of the process whereby the individual consciousness gradually takes on definition as it allows its vacancy to be 'topped up' with the images of things, whatever they may be, which are always there."

Conroy also develops the autobiography as what Paul John Eakin calls "the art of self-invention" and overtly acknowledges that function. Conroy's emphasis on visual perception rather than language acquisition in the self-inventive process may result in his neglect by the dominant school of deconstructionist critics, who focus upon language as the primary mode of consciousness. *Stop-Time*'s achievement, however, is to be one of the first books consciously to model itself on what has now become a theoretical truism: that autobiography will be less the representation of a given reality than the existential act of self-creation.

Sources for Further Study

Dienstag, Eleanor. Review in *The New York Times Book Review*. LXXII (November 12, 1967), p. 22.

Eakin, Paul John. *Fictions in Autobiography: Studies in the Art of Self-Invention*, 1985.

Jenks, Tom. "How Writers Live Today," in *Esquire*. CIV (August, 1985).

Jonker, Howard. Review in *Newsweek*. LXX (November 6, 1967), p. 96.

Tanner, Tony. *City of Words: American Fiction, 1950-1970*, 1971.

Elizabeth Grubgeld

THE STORY OF A LIFE

Author: Konstantin Paustovsky (1892-1968)
Type of work: Autobiography
Time of work: 1892 to the 1920's
Locale: Moscow, Kiev, St. Petersburg, and Odessa
First published: Povest o zhizni, 1946-1964 (English translation, 1964-1974):
   Dalyokie gody, 1946 (*Childhood and Schooldays*, 1964); *Bespokoynaya yunost*,
   1955 (*Slow Approach of Thunder*, 1965); *Nachalo nevedomogo veka*, 1957 (*In
   That Dawn*, 1967); *Vremya bolshikh ozhidany*, 1959 (*Years of Hope*, 1968);
   Brosok na yug, 1960 (*Southern Adventure*, 1969); *Kniga skitany*, 1964 (*The
   Restless Years*, 1974)

> *Principal personage:*
> KONSTANTIN PAUSTOVSKY, a short-story writer, novelist, and
> journalist

Form and Content

   Konstantin Paustovsky, a Russian writer who is not ranked with such luminaries
as Boris Pasternak, Mikhail Sholokhov, and Aleksandr Solzhenitsyn but who nevertheless commands much respect, was born and intellectually formed before the
Revolution. In his long career, he wrote short stories, plays, and essays, but his best
writing is contained in the six-part autobiography *The Story of a Life*. Although he
showed considerable talent as a fiction writer, he was much more successful when
drawing directly from his plentiful experiences. No doubt his storytelling acumen
served him well in writing his autobiography, because the accounts of his personal
experiences often read like fiction. His flowing narration and his ability to experience deeply and thoroughly everyday occurrences gives his autobiography an aura of
authenticity and immediacy.

   The Story of a Life is divided into six parts, coinciding roughly with important
periods in Paustovsky's life. The first part deals with his boyhood up to his graduation from high school. The second covers the interval leading to World War I and
the first three years of it. The third part takes the author through the Revolution.
The last three parts, *Years of Hope*, *Southern Adventure*, and *The Restless Years*,
follow his life up to World War II. The chapters, of uneven length, usually present a
well-rounded episode or story.

   Paustovsky begins his autobiography by depicting one of the turning points in his
life—the death of his father. Although the two were not overly close, this death
marked the end of the boy's happy childhood and the beginning of a life on his
own. The first and the longest part of the autobiography features frequent flashbacks
to his happy boyhood. Paustovsky describes visits to relatives in rural Russia and his
attempts to adjust to their life. The recipient of their immeasurable love, especially
that of his grandparents, he nevertheless felt somewhat apart from them. He enjoyed

being alone; he also discovered early that he wanted to be a writer, but his relatives did not give him much moral support. His high school days are depicted vividly and with great warmth for his teachers and schoolmates.

Reared in an intellectual, middle-class Ukrainian family, Paustovsky led a life of relative security until his family began to fall apart shortly before the war; the disintegration worsened during the war, when two of his brothers fell in one day. Although he was not close to his brothers, their demise signified to him the depth of the familial tragedy brought on by the war and the Revolution. He himself was spared the worst because he was exempted from military service because of his severe nearsightedness. His ambivalence concerning the Revolution reflects the dilemma many Russians faced at that time. Paustovsky's difficulties were multiplied by his growing desire to be a writer in such difficult times and by several unsuccessful love affairs. In the end, Paustovsky emerges as a promising young writer who had reached an understanding of the direction his country had taken and who steeled himself for the difficult tasks of an uncertain future. Thus, what begins as a personal account develops into a chronicle of an entire nation, reflected in the coming of age of a sensitive boy.

Analysis

The Story of a Life offers an insight into the early life of a Russian intellectual at the beginning of the twentieth century. Paustovsky realized early that his propensity for dreaming and inventing a world of his own predisposed him toward writing. This vocation, in turn, made him of necessity a loner. At times, he realized that he was afraid of behaving differently from others. He often asked whether a man had the right to live the way he wanted, by which he implied his desire, indeed, his need, to do so.

Another important part of his maturation was the inspiration he received from nature. He describes with tenderness and sensitivity his relationship with nature— not only his vague love for its beauty, but also as something indispensable for developing one's full strength; indeed, he believed that a life in nature should be the constant vocation of every human being. Whether he developed into a romantic writer because of his peculiar relationship to nature or whether he was drawn to nature because of his romantic disposition is difficult to say, but he remained close to nature all of his life.

Paustovsky was inspired by the simple yet profound wisdom of his grandmother: "The world is wonderful and good, and a man should live in it and work in it just as in a big garden." He strove to live up to that philosophy, looking for what was good in everything around him and often finding it. The conviction that one should affirm life remained with him throughout his life, placing him in the best of the humanist tradition. At the same time, Paustovsky was aware that good and bad exist together and that good often shines brighter through layers of lies, poverty, and suffering. His optimistic attitude was often put to the test, especially during years of war and revolution. It also made him look for every flicker of humanity in even the worst people. The core of his belief was that there is something in every heart which must respond to even the weakest challenge of what is good. Nowhere is this better illustrated than in the episode in which he carried carnations onto a trolley during the war; all the passengers wanted a flower, awakened briefly to a memory of happiness buried by the litter of daily life, after years of deprivation.

Much of the book deals with the war and the Revolution. The majority of the people were not for the war and were utterly confused by the Revolution. Most swam with the tide, wishing only to survive. The reaction of the young Paustovsky was typical of such an attitude. From his earliest childhood he had heard from his father words about freedom, about a revolution that would bring to an end the misfortunes of the people. The young Paustovsky was attracted primarily to the romantic side of revolutionary activities, seeing the Revolution as something "desperately brave, inflexible, and selfless." This was a rather naïve stance, and he admitted as much: "Belief in universal happiness shone in us like the sun rising over our disordered lives. It was sure to come. It seemed to us, naïve as we were, that its guarantee was our desire to construct it and to see it." This belief that the Revolution would suddenly change people for the better and reconcile bitter enemies was, again, typical of the Russian intelligentsia, starved for honesty and fairness in government but helpless at organizing the state and realizing their dreams.

Strangely, Paustovsky blames the liberal intelligentsia for this failure, yet he was unwilling to accept the Bolshevik revolution completely. As a consequence, he experienced the first two or three years of the Revolution not as a participant but as "a deeply interested spectator." In this ambivalence lies an explanation for the failure of the Russian liberal intelligentsia and for the success of the Bolsheviks. If Paustovsky, personifying the humanist intellectual, was unclear about the future course of Russia, how could one expect it from the uneducated masses? Still, clinging to an expectation for the wonderful days ahead and freedom for all people, he joined the Revolution.

Yet not before he drew a frightening picture of the destruction of Russia, its culture, arts, and almost everything else. The happenings sometimes seem unreal, sometimes magnificent, but unnecessarily cruel nevertheless. Man forgot about nature and even love was regarded as a sentimental sickness. In the words of the poet Maximilian Voloshin, "What use are poets and artists in such tough times as these?" Even the barbarisms of the Middle Ages paled in comparison to the cruelty, the violence, and the ignorance that had erupted. "Where had all this been hiding, ripening, gathering strength, and waiting for its hour to strike?" Paustovsky wonders. History itself was sliding swiftly backward and everything was confused. Still, when faced with a decision regarding whether to emigrate, he decided, as a matter of conscience, not to leave his country: "A deep devotion to freedom, justice, and humanity, together with an honesty toward oneself, have always seemed to me the essential qualities of a man in our revolutionary times."

Written in a straightforward, realistic fashion, *The Story of a Life* has many literary, social, historical, and political resonances. Paustovsky presents his life story during a crucial period of Russian history in plain yet beautiful language. He excels in the creation of mood, penetrating beneath human relationships and motivations, couching his story in pastel colors and gossamer, despite the pain and destruction.

Paustovsky stands as one of the last practitioners in the great tradition of Russian realism. He touches upon a society undergoing cataclysmic transformations, not all of which were for the better, and offers a view of historical events that is much more objective than the official one, mainly because he did not belong to those who made history. Indeed, Paustovsky was more or less apolitical during the period of the Revolution and its immediate aftermath. It took him a long time to understand the events occurring around him, let alone to participate fully. Thus, his presentation of his early life is more faithful to reality.

The last three parts of Paustovsky's autobiography, *Years of Hope*, *Southern Adventure*, and *The Restless Years*, are somewhat weaker than the first three, perhaps because they no longer deal with the excitement of youth and because they depict life in the Soviet Union, with its lack of artistic freedom. In its totality, Paustovsky's autobiography covers most of his youth and adult life as well as the intellectual history of a turbulent era in Russia during the first half of the twentieth century.

Critical Context

The Story of a Life, which Paustovsky wrote near the end of his career, displays the maturity and wisdom acquired through a long and active life. For that reason, among others, it is considered his most important work. Clearly, however, *The Story of a Life* is closely related to Paustovsky's other works, in that it contains the same basic qualities—directness, poetic tone, dramatic quality, a strong understanding of human nature, and a belief in ethical principles—which are found in many of his short stories, plays, and essays.

As a memoirist, Paustovsky was working in one of the richest genres in Russian literature. Since Russian writers are generally considered the conscience of their people, often speaking out when others are silent, their autobiographical writings have added weight. This has been especially true during the Soviet period, when writers, censored more than at any other time, have still managed to speak their minds. Thus, Paustovsky joins such memoirists as Boris Pasternak, Korney Chukovsky, Nadezhda Mandelstam, Lev Kopelev, Evgeniya Ginsburg, and many others. The significance of Paustovsky's contribution derives primarily from his artful depiction of his personal experiences and from his role as a highly respected writer whose integrity as a defender of the artist's dignity is beyond reproach.

Sources for Further Study

Alexandrova, Vera. *A History of Soviet Literature*, 1963.
Bliven, Naomi. Review in *The New Yorker*. XL (January 2, 1965), p. 70.
Salisbury, H. E. Review in *The New York Times Book Review*. LXIX (May 3, 1964),
    p. 1.

Sendich, Munir. "The Translator's Kitchen," in *Babel*. XVII, no. 3 (1971), pp. 10-21.

Slonim, Mark. *Soviet Russian Literature: Writers and Problems, 1917-1977,* 1977 (second edition).

Viereck, Peter. Review in *Saturday Review*. XLVII (May 16, 1964), p. 38.

Vasa D. Mihailovich

STORYTELLER

Author: Leslie Marmon Silko (1948-   )
Type of work: Literary history
First published: 1981

Form and Content

In 1969, Leslie Marmon Silko's first story, "The Man to Send Rain Clouds," appeared in *New Mexico Quarterly*, and it was used as the title story of an anthology of Indian poetry edited by Kenneth Rosen in 1974. Silko is half Laguna Indian, and this piece signaled the beginning of her efforts (through her poetry and stories) to put Old Laguna on the map as a source of age-old materials. "This place I am from is everything I am as a writer and human being," she says. Laguna represents a life, a history, a liturgical culture that in her mind America should not ignore— even though it has been Christianized and many of the old ways forgotten or changed.

The Lagunas are Pueblo Indians for whom space and cyclic time are much more important than linear time and the progressive conquering of place. Such perspectives are evident in Silko's first book of poetry, *Laguna Woman* (1974). Here she expresses in meditative as well as humorous ways her reverence for the land and all things living on it. For her the earth is the mother of all, a "sister spirit" that permeates all life—plant, animal, and human. "There was a time," she says, "long long ago, when animals and humans talked to each other. . . ." This collection also includes reflections on the ways men have abused women, just as they have often mistreated the land.

In connection with America's bicentennial in 1976, Silko published her first novel, *Ceremony* (1977), which draws on a great body of Laguna myth on "the relationship of man's health and behavior to the fertility of his land." Though about a man, Tayo, returning from World War II to his native New Mexico, the novel really depicts a person who has lost his center of being because he is separated psychologically and spiritually from the land of his ancestors. It includes several women, among whom is Ts'eh, the universal feminine principle of creation, through whom Tayo is brought back to his own center of being, to a sense of wholeness. Consciously and unconsciously through ceremony he is healed or reborn to a new connection to the earth. He relives the old stories and is thereby able to close the gap between the isolate human being and the landscape beneath and around him.

In *Storyteller*, Silko gathered all the themes of her work to date. (In fact, *Storyteller* incorporates excerpts from both *Laguna Woman* and *Ceremony*.) *Storyteller* includes photographs, letters, and historical vignettes, but it is not a documentary. It includes stories, but it is not a work of fiction. It includes poems, but it is not poetry. Rather, it is a distinctive combination of these diverse forms, juxtaposed and interwoven to reveal the many-faceted nature of storytelling and its vital role in the life of her people.

Basic to the structure of *Storyteller* are eight short stories, beginning with one titled "Storyteller" and ending with a final (ironic and humorous) trickster story, "Coyote Holds a Full House in His Hands." These longer pieces show the indigenous place of stories in Pueblo life, including the abduction of women, the interdependence of death and life, the importance of the crops and hunting to survival, and the function of humor as a major ingredient in the Laguna culture. As a backdrop to her book Silko places twenty-six photographs, which tell her story in another way, depicting the people (the storytellers) who influenced her young life, the terrain— mountains, desert, horizon—of Old Laguna, the huge cornstalks, deer from the hunt, and the Pueblo buildings symbolic of her people's unique way of life.

Connecting and enlarging upon the main stories are poetic inserts—some highly evocative, some prosaic—that expand the main themes and cast them in a larger perspective. Some are mythic in scope, embodying balladlike legends passed on orally for centuries. They include self-conscious expositions of what storytelling is about, reflective pieces on the importance of human relationships and identity with the land, clan stories usually related to rooting out witchery, descriptions of the crops and hunting as basic to Pueblo life, and humorous episodes that expose a culture never afraid to laugh at itself. Near the end of the book is a photograph of Silko herself, set amid the rocky desert soil that she has made so real, indeed mythologized for her readers in *Storyteller*.

Analysis

For Leslie Silko, the story is basic to existence, for the Lagunas have always had a tremendous concern for language. She says that

> storytelling for Indians is like a natural resource. Some places have oil, some have a lot of water or timber or gold, but around here, it's the ear that has developed.

The story is not only about life, it is life, giving to as well as drawing meaning from it. In *Storyteller*, Silko uses different forms to tell her story, which is also her people's story, so thematically she begins with the intimate childhood relationships, such as those with Aunt Susie and Grandma A'mooh, from whom she heard her first tales. Throughout the book she uses photographs to reaffirm the poetry in the early sections, for both show the loving context in which the mythic episodes were first told to her and which she would later pass on to others as a writer. Stories depicting the girl jumping into the lake, whereupon her "clothes turned into butterflies," as well as the girl's choice of death in "Cottonwood," show the closeness of death and life, sadness and joy, love and hate as part of the ironic texture of the old stories.

These stories come from and belong to the community. In contrast to the white world, where individual success is so important (as in the myth of Horatio Alger), the Laguna Indian finds identity through the group. In "Geronimo," a group of Laguna soldiers act as guides for the whites in search of this great warrior, but the

Indians treat the hunt as just that—a hunt, realizing that the white soldiers are going the wrong way. Ironically, observes Per Seyersted, it is the Lagunas who feel superior, not inferior, to their white companions, as the group, not the individual, prevails.

Fundamentally, these stories are spiritual, but not in the traditional Christian sense. Historically the Lagunas were conquered and Christianized by the Spaniards, but they have maintained their identity through stories. In "The Man to Send Rain Clouds" the Indians invite the priest to sprinkle holy water on the body of a dead member of the community, but not for the reason the priest thinks. The water for the Indians is a way of ritually calling for rain, of maintaining the cycle of death and life, not simply ensuring the eternal condition of an individual soul. The coming of rain and growth of the crops are central themes in *Storyteller*, especially in the middle, poetic section, where in a typical clan story Sun Man outsmarts the Gambler—the trickster who has tied up the storm clouds in his bag—to free the rain and thereby the people.

The Lagunas' equivalent of the Christian idea of original sin is "witchery." It is that force which causes suffering and torment, sterility and death, and against which characters such as Spiderwoman continually battle. This power isolates and paralyzes Tayo in *Ceremony*, and Silko includes the poetic statement on witchery from that novel in *Storyteller*. It is related to "Tony's Story," which also exemplifies the Lagunas' keen awareness of the invisible evil forces that interfere with fertility and community happiness. Here Leon has returned from the war and is continually harassed by "the cops," whereupon Tony, poignantly aware of an evil spirit-world, kills the policeman and burns his body in the car, concluding, ". . . everything is O.K. now, Leon. It's killed. They sometimes take on strange forms."

Silko says that her stories are really about "relationships"—love relationships, as in "Yellow Woman," where a woman follows the "ka'tsina spirit" to the mountains, though she has a husband and children at home, or "Lullaby," in which a mother is deceived into signing away her children, a type of death which is matched only by her singing a lullaby to her deceiver dying in the snow at the end. Silko's favorite story, though, is "Storyteller" itself, which she wrote in Alaska, showing that the "interior landscapes of her characters" are related to but transcend particular types of terrain—in this case, the Alaskan tundra. Here a woman is limited by both the environment and the men who use her, though in the end "she does the guy in."

During their long history, the Lagunas have had to endure hostile Apaches, Spanish colonization, and extreme weather, to say nothing of boredom, in order to survive. To this end, their rituals and ceremonies, of which stories are a part, speak of relationships and survival amid all kinds of problems (witchery). "With these stories of ours we can escape almost anything," says the old storyteller. Perhaps this is true primarily because of the people's humor. For the Lagunas, to laugh is to live. In stories such as "Uncle Tony's Goat," the children fashion bows and arrows to shoot at an old, smelly goat that finally runs back to the mountains, whereupon Tony concludes in front of the children: "That damn goat got annoyed too easy anyway." The goat was not the only one who got annoyed.

In "Coyote Holds a Full House in His Hand," Silko concludes with a ribald tale reminiscent of Geoffrey Chaucer, in which the protagonist excites various types of women by rubbing their thighs—and without charging a cent. He reasons, "This is something I want to do especially for you," and everyone seems happy. Coyote is a tricky personage—half creator, half fool—characterized by his irreverence toward everything from sex to religion, but important for Indians because, says Paula Gunn Allen, "it is this spirit of the trickster-creator that keeps Indians alive and vital in the face of horror."

In *Storyteller*, Silko relies on an accretive structuring to build toward comprehensive significance in her work as a whole. It includes many forms, related to one another by association rather than by linear development, that build in meaning through repetition of themes as well as forms to create an overall effect—a wholeness or total appreciation of the Laguna perspective on the world.

Critical Context

Popular Indian literature is male-centered and rooted in conflict and crisis: Geronimo or Crazy Horse fighting the white settlers, for example. Leslie Silko and others have pioneered a type of literature that is rooted in what Allen calls "the centrality of the feminine power of universal being." Her concern is a tribal perspective centered in ritual and ceremony and designed to bring people together in harmony with Mother Earth.

In this context, the earth is not inanimate and separate from human beings, not an object to be subdued as in the Judeo-Christian tradition. For the Laguna Indians, the earth is sacred, not only because it has been consecrated by men but, more important, because it is alive, filled with power. The purpose of ceremony is— through song and dance and stories—to connect people to the earth, to generate peace and harmony among human beings, in short to create community. In the process, the private self is brought into a larger relationship to others and the entire mystical universe.

Storyteller is unique because it combines many kinds of literature to achieve this end. Silko's tribal perspective surfaces in various literary forms, some old and some new, which work together in ceremonial ways (repetition of words and phrases, juxtaposition of images and themes) to create a wholeness that reflects the unity of the universe itself and the interlacing of life on all levels.

Sources for Further Study

Allen, Paula Gunn. *The Sacred Hoop: Recovering the Feminine in American Indian Traditions*, 1986.

Chapman, Abraham. Introduction to *Literature of the American Indians: Views and Interpretations*, 1975. Edited by Abraham Chapman.

Fisher, Dexter, ed. "Stories and Their Tellers: A Conversation with Leslie Marmon Silko," in *The Third Woman: Minority Women Writers of the United States*, 1980.

Rosen, Kenneth. "Notes by the Contributors," in *The Man to Send Rain Clouds*, 1974. Edited by Kenneth Rosen.

Seyersted, Per. *Leslie Marmon Silko*, 1980.

Velie, Alan R. "Leslie Silko's *Ceremony*," in *Four American Indian Literary Masters*, 1982.

Thomas Matchie

THE STORYTELLER
Reflections on the Works of Nikolai Leskov

Author: Walter Benjamin (1892-1940)
Type of work: Literary criticism
First published: "Der Erzähler," 1936 (English translation, 1968)

Form and Content

Walter Benjamin is something of an anomaly in an era of literary criticism when every significant critic is the author of some major work and seems to "belong" to some unified theoretical school or another. Benjamin, a German-Jewish intellectual who committed suicide during the Nazi persecution, is primarily known as the author only of a number of essay-length studies which have been edited since his death. Moreover, although he did some writing in the late 1930's in connection with the so-called Frankfurt School, established in Germany for the study of Marxism, it is not easy to pigeonhole him or his views as belonging to a rigid theoretical framework. His best-known literary essays are "Das Kunstwerk im Zeitalter seiner Reproduzierbarkeit" (1936; "The Work of Art in the Age of Mechanical Reproduction," 1936), "Franz Kafka" (1934; English translation, 1968), and the 1936 essay on Nikolai Leskov as storyteller, which were unknown by most English readers until they appeared in *Illuminations* (1968), a collection of Benjamin's essays translated by Hannah Arendt.

Although the subtitle of the storytelling essay, one of Walter Benjamin's most famous pieces, indicates that its focus is on the fiction of the Russian writer Nikolai Leskov, what Benjamin actually develops in the essay is a definition of the nature of storytelling—an art which he laments is coming to an end for various sociological reasons. The essay lists what Benjamin considers to be the primary characteristics of the storyteller and examines each one in turn, in both theoretical and historical terms and as evidenced by the fiction of Leskov. As is typical of the style of Benjamin, the essay is deceptive in its simplicity, actually packing much more into its concise and sometimes epigrammatic style than a casual reading might reveal.

Made up of nineteen separate sections, the essay devotes only five sections to discussions of Leskov's works; even these are mostly generalizations about how Leskov was comfortable in distant places (and thus is aligned with the more general notion of stories coming from one's travels), about Leskov's being grounded in the classics (and thus aware of the timelessness of stories), about Leskov's awareness of the craftsmanship necessary for telling stories, and finally about the sources of Leskov's work in the myths and fairy tales of the peasantry.

It is the general nature of storytelling itself that really interests Benjamin; the discussion of Leskov seems merely to have offered him an excuse to engage in this theoretical exploration of the most ancient narrative art. Thus, Benjamin examines the sources of storytelling, analyzes its basic characteristics, points out its differences from other, similar narrative forms, suggests what in human experience gives it its most basic authority, and laments nostalgically its inevitable passing away in the modern world.

Analysis

The first criterion of storytelling Benjamin describes is its oral nature; moreover, he says, of those who write down stories the best ones are those who most closely stick to a simulation of this oral source. Benjamin says that there are two basic types of oral storytellers—those who come from afar and tell of their adventures (embodied in the figure of the traveling seaman) and those who stay at home and tell of events there (as represented by the stationary farmer). The second characteristic of the storyteller is an orientation toward practical interests; all stories contain something useful, Benjamin argues, whether that useful information is obvious and on the surface or is embedded within the narrative in some way. Thus, stories do not derive from idle gossip or even from the need to recount interesting experiences, but rather they spring from a basic human need to recount real-life examples of coping with the mystery of human reality.

However, storytelling is dying out, says Benjamin; people no longer seem to have the ability to exchange experiences. He offers several historical and sociological reasons for storytelling's demise. The most basic reason for the death of storytelling is the fact that the communicability of experience itself is dying out; thus storytelling, which always offers counsel, has no more place in the modern world. Indeed, wisdom itself, which Benjamin defines as counsel woven into the fabric of life and thus which has its origins in storytelling, is dying out. This process, which Benjamin links to the increasingly secular forces of history, has gradually removed narrative from the realm of living speech.

The rise of the novel is one of the primary symptoms of the decline of storytelling, Benjamin suggests. The novel is quite different from the story in that it neither comes from the oral tradition nor goes into it. Whereas the birthplace of the story is the teller's experience, the novel begins with the solitary self. Whereas the story springs from orality, the novel is bound to the form of a book. Whereas the storyteller takes his story from experience, either his own or what he has heard from others, the novelist is no longer able to express himself by giving examples of his most important concerns.

Furthermore, Benjamin says, another form of communication has come to predominate in the modern world, which threatens storytelling even more seriously than the novel; that is, "information," by which Benjamin means primarily the information of the news media. The difference between the forms of storytelling and forms of news information, argues Benjamin, is that whereas storytelling always had a validity that required no external verification, information must be accessible to immediate verification. Storytelling differs from information in that storytelling does not aim to convey the pure essence of the experience in some distilled way, but rather imbues the story with the life of the storyteller. Aspects of the storyteller cling to the story; that is why many storytellers begin with the circumstances by which they have gained access to the story that they are about to tell.

This distinction between storytelling and information points to one of the primary differences between the "truth" of story and the truth of other forms of explanation characteristic of discursive writing. Whereas, in such forms of discourse as history, sociology, and psychology, the aim of the work is to abstract from concrete experience so that a distilled discursive meaning remains, in story, the truth is somehow communicated by a recounting of the concrete experience itself in such a way that the truth is revealed by the details of the story, not by abstract explanation. The story has a compactness that defies psychological analysis; in fact the less psychological shading the story has, the more the listener will remember it and tell it to someone else later, says Benjamin.

Whereas story is borrowed from the miraculous and does not demand plausibility or conformity to the laws of external reality, information must be plausible and conform to such laws. When stories come through information, they are already loaded down with explanation, says Benjamin; it is half the art of storytelling to be free from information. Because the reader of story is free to interpret things the way he understands them, story has an amplitude lacking in information.

Another basic difference between story and information is that whereas the value of information does not survive the moment of its newness, a story is so concentrated that it retains its truth power for a long time. Moreover, story stays in the memory and compels the listener to tell it to someone. In fact, insists Benjamin, it might be said that storytelling is the art of repeating stories, for when the rhythm of the story seizes the reader, he listens in such a way that the ability to retell it comes by itself.

Benjamin does not, however, spend the entire essay focusing on such external characteristics of story as how it is transmitted. He is also concerned with what gives storytelling its validity, since he insists that, unlike information, it does not require external verification. Instead, the story finds its validity in the awareness of death, says Benjamin. One's wisdom and real life, the very stuff of stories, become transmissible at the moment of death, and thus death is the sanction for whatever the storyteller tells, for death is storytelling's ultimate authority. Since increasingly modern man has become distanced from the actual experience of death, Benjamin argues, one can see another reason that the art of storytelling is coming to an end. Whereas dying once was a public process for the individual, in modern times death has been pushed out of the perception of the living. In deriving its ultimate validity from death, Benjamin argues, story faces ultimate reality, not immediate reality; that is, story deals with man's most basic existential situation in the world.

In describing the craftsmanship required of story, Benjamin cites Paul Valéry, who notes that nature creates perfection through a long chain of causes; man once imitated nature, says Valéry, by elaborating things to perfection, but he does so no longer. Modern man is concerned only with what can be abbreviated and abstracted; he is no longer concerned with telling stories by the layering of various retellings so that multiple experiences of storytellers can imbue the story with concrete human meaning.

Benjamin also sets up a distinction between the chronicler and historian to clarify his definition of storytelling. Whereas the historian must explain the happenings he describes, the chronicler is content with displaying the events as models of the course of the world. Whereas the chronicler bases his tales on a divine plan of salvation and thus is relieved of the burden of explanation, the historian is bound to the abstraction process that explanation demands. The storyteller preserves the nature of the chronicle, Benjamin says, although in a secularized form.

The most basic relationship between the storyteller and the listener, Benjamin argues, is the listener's need to retain the story so that he can reproduce it. There is a crucial difference between the way memory is manifested in the novel and the way it is manifested in the story, Benjamin says. Memory is that which creates the chain that passes story from one generation to the next, much as a web is created in which one story attaches to the next. What distinguishes memory in story from memory in the novel is the perpetuating "remembrance" of the novelist as contrasted with the short-lived "reminiscences" of the storyteller. Whereas the remembrance of the novel is bound to one hero and one journey, the reminiscences of the storyteller encompass many diffuse occurrences.

As a result, story focuses on the relatively concrete "moral of the story," while the novel focuses on the more abstract "meaning of life." The first true storyteller, says Benjamin, is the teller of fairy tales, for the fairy tale provides good counsel. According to Benjamin, whereas realistic narrative forms such as the novel focus on the relatively limited areas of human experience that indeed can be encompassed by information, characters in fairy tales or stories encounter those most basic mysteries of human experience which cannot be explained by rational means, but which can be embodied only in myth. The wisest thing the fairy tale teaches is to meet the forces of the mythical world with cunning and high spirits. What the fairy tale, and therefore the story, does is to teach how to deal with all that which we cannot understand.

The storyteller is of the same company as that of teachers and sages, says Benjamin, for the storyteller has counsel for many based on a lifetime of experience. The gift of the storyteller is the gift of relating his life, for he is able to fashion the raw material of experience, both his own and the experience of others, in a solid and useful way. It is therefore unfortunate, says Benjamin, that storytelling—that is, the ability to exchange experiences—is slowly dying.

Critical Context

One of the earliest mentions of Benjamin's essay on the storyteller by an English-language critic of note is Susan Sontag's citation of the piece as an example of the kind of formal analysis for which she called in "Against Interpretation" (1966). The essay has been the source of some annoyance to the two groups of critics who have tried to claim Benjamin as their own in the 1970's and 1980's: the Marxist critics who align themselves with the Frankfurt School of Max Horkheimer and Theodor Adorno, and the structuralists and deconstructionists who try to see Benjamin as a forerunner of Michel Foucault or Jacques Derrida. For the Marxists, the storytelling essay represents a lamentable lapse into nostalgia and thus is uncharacteristic of Benjamin's "tougher" philosophical essays; for the structuralists and poststructuralists, the work depends too much on a sort of inherent mythic consciousness that does not align itself comfortably either with the "scientific" linguistic-based studies of the narratologists and the textualists or with the skeptical self-questioning of the followers of Derrida.

Moreover, although the essay is praised by Sontag as a model of the formal study of both a genre and an author, one of the best-known formalists, René Wellek, finds it doubtful in its assumptions about the relation between fairy tale and myth and just plain wrong in its reading of Leskov's stories. Wellek confesses finally that he sometimes does not understand the working of Benjamin's mind, particularly in this essay, which has been considered by some to be his masterpiece.

Because Benjamin has so often been identified with Marxist criticism, many critics and readers who are either hostile or indifferent to Marxism have not studied this essay very carefully. Its value lies not in its assertion of Marxist values, either socially or aesthetically, nor does it lie in its analysis of Leskov, for that is but a minor and, as Wellek has pointed out, a questionable part of the piece. Rather, the essay's real value lies in the suggestions it offers about the basic nature of narrative, particularly the primal nature of story as opposed to the more recent realistic narrative characteristic of the novel form. No one who wishes to understand the basic nature of story can afford to ignore Walter Benjamin's profound study of the storyteller.

Sources for Further Study
Eagleton, Terry. *Walter Benjamin: Or, Towards a Revolutionary Criticism*, 1981.
Jennings, Michael W. *Dialectal Images: Walter Benjamin's Theory of Literary Criticism*, 1987.
Roberts, Julian. *Walter Benjamin*, 1982.
Sontag, Susan. "Under the Sign of Saturn," in *Under the Sign of Saturn*, 1980.
Wellek, René. "Walter Benjamin's Literary Criticism in His Marxist Phase," in *The Personality of the Critic*, 1973. Edited by Joseph P. Strelka.

Charles E. May

THE STRUCTURE OF SCIENTIFIC REVOLUTIONS

Author: Thomas S. Kuhn (1922-   )
Type of work: History/science
First published: 1962

Form and Content

In *The Structure of Scientific Revolutions*, Thomas S. Kuhn has provided in essay form his views on the nature of the scientific endeavor. It is a subject that Kuhn believes is little understood by the general public, by students of science, and even by scientists themselves. In particular, he challenges the beliefs that the development of science has been linear and cumulative and that science is characterized by complete objectivity. These beliefs, he says, are propagated by contemporary textbooks and by many popular writings of scientists. In the preface, he describes the intellectual route by which he came to his views.

The circumstances surrounding and leading to Kuhn's writing of *The Structure of Scientific Revolutions* involved personal and institutional elements. In the late 1940's, Kuhn was a graduate student in theoretical physics at Harvard University. He has stated that during his years of studying physics he developed a strong interest in the philosophical aspects of science. As an advanced graduate student, he became a teaching assistant in a group of new science courses for nonscience majors that Harvard was developing at that time.

In the years immediately following World War II, the faculty of Harvard University came to the conclusion that the postwar generation of Harvard students needed to be more broadly educated than their predecessors had been with regard to their cultural heritage. A new set of "general education" courses were devised, which included science. It was thought that a historical approach would be appropriate for developing in all students an appreciation of what had been accomplished by Western (as contrasted to Eastern, or Oriental) scientists and how their accomplishments had been achieved.

In preparing himself for his new teaching duties, Kuhn made a particular study of the shift from Ptolemaic, geocentric astronomy to Copernican, heliocentric astronomy—a shift that is often called the Copernican Revolution. Kuhn brought some new insights to this transition, eventually writing *The Copernican Revolution: Planetary Astronomy in the Development of Western Thought*, which was published in 1957 with a foreword by James B. Conant, a former president of Harvard University and the architect of its general education program. This early work of Kuhn can be a valuable adjunct to the reading of *The Structure of Scientific Revolutions* for readers with some interest in and knowledge about astronomy.

After completing his doctoral work in physics in 1949, Kuhn turned his attention, full-time, to studying the history of science and its philosophical implications. He remained at Harvard, associated with the history of science department and the general education program, until 1956, when he accepted a position at the

University of California at Berkeley.

Kuhn's historical studies in the physical sciences focused on those periods during which radical changes took place in the scientific modes of investigation and explanation, that is, "revolutions," as he called them. In *The Structure of Scientific Revolutions*, first published in 1962 by the University of Chicago Press, he set forth details of the perspectives he had developed on this subject. The 175-page book is divided into thirteen chapters.

Soon after its publication, *The Structure of Scientific Revolutions* was widely reviewed, read, and discussed. It was reprinted several times. In 1972, a new edition was issued that was not a revision of the original text but did include a thirty-seven-page postscript prepared by Kuhn in 1969. In this postscript, he answered some of his critics and clarified some of his earlier statements.

By that time Kuhn was recognized internationally as a philosopher of science. (Both editions were also issued as volume 2, number 2 of the *International Encyclopedia of Unified Science*, a publication organized by an outstanding international group of philosophers of science.) By 1969, he was a professor at Princeton University, where he remained until he accepted a position as professor of philosophy and history of science at the Massachusetts Institute of Technology in 1979.

Analysis

Although the title of Kuhn's essay specifies revolutions, his presentation has a broader scope, namely, the nature of scientific enterprise. His perspectives developed from consideration of the sequence of steps, from ancient Greece to the present, that resulted in twentieth century physical science. His philosophy of science stems, primarily, from historical study. He has, however, also considered psychology and sociology and applied them to the scientific endeavor as a whole. His approach is an interdisciplinary one.

In each of the thirteen short chapters, a single idea is set forth, usually drawing heavily on examples from the history of physics, chemistry, or astronomy, as would be expected given the author's background. Yet the examples are secondary in importance to the notions that they are being invoked to explicate. Although familiarity with the physical science being cited is very helpful to the reader, lack of such knowledge is by no means a complete barrier to comprehension of Kuhn's points.

Two features which distinguish Kuhn's writing on the philosophy of science are his belief that revolution (not evolution) marks the development of science and his introduction of a set of terms to characterize scientific activity. Some of these terms were given new or expanded meanings by Kuhn and became identified with a "Kuhnian" approach. They have been seized upon by some readers and applied in fields widely divergent from the physical sciences.

Kuhn's thinking about the development of science may be briefly summarized. At most given times, scientists pursuing a "mature" science practice "normal science" and teach it to their students, initiating them and training them to carry on in the then-established tradition for their particular discipline. For sciences which have reached a state of "maturity," a "paradigm" has been established by consensus among the practitioners. For Kuhn, the term "paradigm" refers to a situation in which all the currently known information in a field is accessible, suitable lines of investigation to extend that knowledge are recognized, and a collection of laws, theory, applications, and instrumentation constituting a "model" are accepted. In Kuhn's view, before a science has reached mature status it is most often studied or investigated in relative isolation by scientists from a number of competing schools of thought and, in retrospect, would be viewed as being in a preparadigm state of development. During its preparadigm period, it cannot be regarded as being truly scientific because no consensus prevails.

To be an accepted member of a scientific profession at any given time, an individual is expected to accept and conform to the current paradigm, selecting appropriate problems to study. Kuhn regards such activity not as paradigm testing but as "puzzle solving" within the currently accepted paradigm.

Inevitably, such investigations reveal "anomalies," that is, instances that cannot be fitted into the current paradigm. (Accidental discoveries are another source of anomalies.) The presence of anomalies threatens a crisis in the paradigm. Initially, in the face of anomalies, efforts are made to modify the current paradigm to accommodate the new information. When that cannot be done or when that has come to involve cumbersome and far-fetched elements, the time is right for the introduction of a new paradigm.

A scientific revolution occurs when a new paradigm gains wide acceptance. Yet a revolution cannot occur unless a new paradigm has been made ready. It may take decades for a new paradigm to become established within the majority of a scientific community, and some older scientists may go to their graves never having accepted the new paradigm for one reason or another.

Acceptance by a scientific community of a new paradigm, that is, a scientific revolution, involves many changes that are not immediately clear. For example, a new conceptual vocabulary is required, new theories must be developed, new problems posed for solution, old lines of inquiry abandoned as irrelevant, metaphysical ideas (often unarticulated assumptions) examined for tenability.

Kuhn considers successive paradigms to be necessarily different and irreconcilable, their respective adherents seeming to operate in different worlds which prevent any meaningful communication among them. Scientists, in Kuhn's view, talk only to colleagues sharing the same paradigm and are usually insulated from other disciplines and from the public at large.

Kuhn recognizes the political connotations associated with the word "revolution" and does not shy away from its use, even noting some similarities between political and scientific revolutions—a point which brought him some criticism from scientists, many of whom prefer the word "breakthrough" to characterize marked changes in the course of the development of a scientific discipline.

Kuhn challenges the idea of what is typically regarded as scientific progress. In particular, he does not believe that each successive paradigm shift brings scientists closer to the "truth." At most, science can be said to have progressed from previous stages but not toward an ultimate goal.

Critical Context

With the publication of *The Structure of Scientific Revolutions*, Thomas Kuhn came to be recognized as a provocative contemporary philosopher of science. He joined the company of previously established figures as Karl Popper, Imre Lakatos, and Paul Feyerabend. While it is not appropriate here to compare and contrast the writings of these various philosophers of science, two comments are relevant.

In 1965, a symposium focusing on Kuhn's work was held in London under the auspices of the Division of Logic, Methodology, and Philosophy of Science of the International Union of the History and Philosophy of Science. Kuhn, Popper, Lakatos, and Feyerabend were all contributors to the resulting volume *Criticism and the Growth of Knowledge*, which was published by Cambridge University Press in 1970. Two essays by Kuhn are included, "Logic of Discovery or Psychology of Research" and "Reflections on My Critics." In these essays, Kuhn discusses the differences between himself and the other three; he also tries to correct some misinterpretations of his work.

Despite these attempts by Kuhn to clarify his writings, David Stove, an Australian philosopher of science, published a sharply critical commentary, *Popper and After: Four Modern Irrationalists*, with Kuhn one of the four. In particular, Stove charges these theorists with expounding the view that scientific knowledge is never true or false and that even the best scientific opinion at any given time is an unjustified conjecture, deeply influenced by its contemporary context.

Other philosophers of science who have found themselves at odds with Kuhn's views are Israel Scheffler and Dudley Shapere. Scheffler is disturbed by the subjectivity that Kuhn attributes to scientific investigation, and Shapere is critical of the notion of paradigms set forth by Kuhn. Margaret Masterson, another contributor to *Criticism and the Growth of Knowledge*, also criticizes Kuhn's use of the word "paradigm." Kuhn took note of and responded to some of those critics in the postscript to the second edition of *The Structure of Scientific Revolutions*. To some extent, it appears that misunderstanding of Kuhn's words has contributed to the disquietude which some readers have experienced. Nevertheless, the notion of paradigms and all that the word connotes for Kuhn, the importance Kuhn places on consensus within a scientific community, and Kuhn's strict use of the term "revolution" have resulted in considerable debate about his views, especially within the communities of scientists and historians, or philosophers, of science.

On the other hand, writing in 1980, Gary Gutting stated that *The Structure of Scientific Revolutions* "has had a wider academic influence than any other single book of the last twenty years." Gutting was particularly struck by the number of different disciplines that have found a Kuhnian approach useful. As the editor of *Paradigms and Revolutions: Appraisals and Applications of Thomas Kuhn's Philosophy of Science*, Gutting assembled a collection of fourteen essays responding to

Kuhn's views from the areas of philosophy, the social sciences, the humanities, and the history of science. Also, he has provided a bibliography of about 250 items (including sources in English, French, and German) whose publication was stimulated by their authors' consideration of Kuhn's writings. In addition to studies by scholars in the fields listed above, there are entries specifically related to theology and religion, to art and literature, and to education. Social scientist Barry Barnes is also very appreciative of the value of Kuhn's ideas for his discipline. Writing in 1982, when his book *T. S. Kuhn and Social Science* was published, Barnes stated that research into the sociology of knowledge had already benefited from Kuhn's work and would continue to do so in the future.

The extension of Kuhn's ideas to fields beyond the physical sciences had already begun before the second edition of *The Structure of Scientific Revolutions* was published. In his postscript, Kuhn seems somewhat surprised by the enthusiastic responses to his ideas coming from widely different disciplines, and he makes some cautionary comments.

Kuhn continued to expand upon his original writings and published a number of articles in line with the main themes set forth in *The Structure of Scientific Revolution*. Fourteen of those articles were republished in 1977 by the University of Chicago Press under the title *The Essential Tension: Selected Studies in Scientific Tradition and Change*. In one of the essays in this volume, he discusses the essential tension that he believes exists between tradition and innovation in scientific research. Regardless of the degree of agreement (or disagreement) with Kuhn's ideas that each reader experiences, it is impossible not to recognize how provocative they have been, and continue to be, stimulating scholars from diverse disciplines to examine and reexamine their methods and beliefs.

Sources for Further Study

Barnes, Barry. *T. S. Kuhn and Social Science*, 1982.

Gutting, Gary, ed. *Paradigms and Revolutions: Appraisals and Applications of Thomas Kuhn's Philosophy of Science*, 1980.

Lakatos, Imre, and Alan Musgrave, eds. *Criticism and the Growth of Knowledge*, 1970.

Scheffler, Israel. *Science and Subjectivity*, 1967.

Shapere, Dudley. "The Structure of Scientific Revolutions," in *Philosophical Review*. LXXIII (1964), pp. 383-394.

Stove, David. *Popper and After: Four Modern Irrationalists*, 1982.

Katherine R. Sopka

SUN AND STEEL

Author: Yukio Mishima (Kimitake Hiraoka, 1925-1970)
Type of work: Essays
First published: Taiyō to tetsu, 1968 (English translation, 1970)

Principal personage:
YUKIO MISHIMA, a brilliant Japanese author and playwright

Form and Content

On November 25, 1970, Yukio Mishima, a brilliant author of more than forty novels, short-story collections, plays, and essays, committed suicide after leading a group of his private army, the Tatenokai (shield society), into the office of a general in the Japanese Self-Defense forces in Tokyo and holding the officer hostage while he tried to rally the troops to cast off their role as a merely defensive force and honor the emperor by returning to the ancient Japanese traditions of the warrior. Mishima knew that the attempt to rouse the army was doomed and had already planned his death as a penance for having led a failed coup. He killed himself by seppuku, ritual disembowelment. (Hara-kiri, the term for this method of death which is more commonly used in the West, literally means "belly cut.") In the final act of seppuku, Mishima was beheaded by his best friend in the Tatenokai, who was then killed in the same fashion. Not only the literary world but also the global community was stunned by what seemed an insane act that ended a prolific artistic career.

Although the manner of Mishima's death was shocking, his suicide at the age of forty-five would not have surprised a careful reader of his works. Only two years before his death, Mishima had published *Sun and Steel,* in which he outlined his views on death as the ultimate tragic experience and the perfect fulfillment of the life of the warrior and the artist.

Sun and Steel consists of three parts: a long essay in which Mishima relates the story of his life from the standpoint of his intellectual, spiritual, and physical development; a shorter essay, "Epilogue—F104," in which he describes a ride in a jet fighter; and a short poem, "Icarus." In the long essay, Mishima describes how the growth of his mind and spirit was essentially backward; most people enter a world which they experience primarily in a physical way and then progress to the world of perception, thought, ideas, and words. Mishima, a bookish child who was overly protected by a domineering grandmother, began life by regarding words as primary and realizing only in late adolescence the importance of the body in the training of the total person. In his adulthood, he began a program of bodybuilding to which the title of the work refers—the sun on one's skin when exercising in the open air and the steel of the weights and swordplay used in developing muscles.

As his body becomes more finely tuned, Mishima discovers that too much emphasis on words have caused him to cloud reality with ideas. He rediscovers a language of the body and learns that to be truly alive is to experience the pain and suffering which is the mark of tragedy. Moreover, Mishima believes that the ultimate experience of pain and suffering is death. Thus, Mishima's physical and spiritual education leads him to the conclusion that a sound mind must be housed in a sound body, uniting the roles of intellectual and warrior, and that an early death in the full flower of both physical and mental vigor is desirable.

Analysis

Although Mishima's attempt to strengthen his body provoked the writing of *Sun and Steel*, the book is not a description of a bodybuilder's regimen. Rather, it consists of a series of philosophical speculations, many of which are farfetched and disturbing. Mishima's wild assertions have provoked many critics to voice their dismay. *Sun and Steel* expresses the romantic ideal of death as both the ultimate experience of life and its tragic fulfillment, a motif found in the works of such Romantic artists and thinkers as John Keats, Richard Wagner, Walt Whitman, and Friedrich Nietzsche. Indeed, Mishima was familiar with the works of these writers; unlike many contemporary Japanese artists, he had read widely in Western literature.

Mishima had set himself the difficult task of explaining the discoveries of the body in words. He notes that words are like "white ants" which eat away at reality, hiding and destroying it rather than revealing it. (Elsewhere he compares words to corrosive acid that eats at a plate on which an etching is made.) Since he must use words to explain an experience that transcends words, the book is frequently mystifying. It is easier to grasp what Mishima is trying to convey by examining the implications of certain key images that offer a glimpse of Mishima's transcendent experience.

The first of these is Mishima's description of a group of young men carrying a heavy portable shrine through the streets of a city during a religious ceremony. Their bodies are strained, yet each young man, although exhausted, wears an expression of happiness. Mishima notes that as they carry the shrine, they are looking at the sky, which he sees as an emblem of tragedy available to be seen and comprehended by any ordinary person. (The assumption that a clear blue sky is emblematic of tragedy is only one of many questionable assertions that the reader must accept in order to follow the progress of Mishima's emotions and spirit.) The person with an unfit body would not be able to perform the task of the shrine carriers and thereby would be denied access to the ultimate tragedy revealed by physical action. Mishima believed that his preoccupation with the written word had clouded that basic sense of tragedy. Thus, Mishima set about improving his body. Mishima would later carry such a shrine; photographs of him taken at the end of the run reveal the beatific face he had earlier described in the essay.

The next event to which Mishima refers is a striking awareness of the sun which he experienced in the summer of 1945 during the training he underwent in preparation for his induction into the army during what he calls "the summer of the defeat." The sun gleamed on the wings of the airplanes, destined for destruction, as it had on the blood and bodies of those killed by the war. The sun, another feature of that searing, tragic sky, becomes for Mishima an emblem of death which leads all creation on to its ultimate destruction.

Mishima notes that he then took refuge in his books and studies, hiding from the sun and its message of death, but he does not tell the reader that when he reported for his draft physical, he had a slight cold which the army doctor diagnosed as the beginning of tuberculosis and because of which the doctor disqualified Mishima for duty. Mishima did nothing to dissuade the doctor from his erroneous opinion, thus dodging military service and what would have been almost certain death. Thus, another possible interpretation of Mishima's fascination with violence, emperor worship, and sacrifice for one's country is that he was doing penance in this fashion for his failure to answer his country's call at its hour of greatest peril.

In a central image which defines the meaning of his essay, Mishima asks the reader to consider the existence of an apple. The skin of the apple is all that is visible, but deep inside is the core (like the human spirit). In order for the core to experience true existence, it must be visible, that is, exposed to the sun in its capacity both to create and to destroy. Thus, the apple must be sliced open so that the core can both see and be seen. That moment, its death, is the height of the apple's existence. To one familiar with the circumstances of Mishima's death, the metaphor is chilling.

Mishima writes that, having sought to achieve a concise, unadorned style to match his lean and finely tuned body, he found that style in the brief messages scribbled by kamikaze pilots who were about to fly into the tragic blue sky to die for their emperor. They had already honed their physical bodies to perfection in order to become pilots. With their last brief words they distilled the essence of tragedy. Mishima describes the ultimate style which he is seeking as like the hardwood entrance hall of a samurai mansion on a winter's day, an image which contains several key elements. The samurai mansion evokes solidity, formidability, and the sense of the heroic Japanese tradition; the winter's day, with snow shrouding every-thing, is emblematic of simplicity and death. The hardwood interior matches the result of bodybuilding in which Mishima was engaged. The wood has been cut open to reveal its musculature and it has been polished, indicating the peak of perfection. Perhaps most significant in this account is what is not there—the samurai is not there, only the entrance of his house is mentioned, as if to suggest that the spare style for which Mishima aims is only the beginning of a quest which will ultimately end in physical action.

With the recognition that tragic spirit must be fused with that of a group, the last piece of the puzzle of Mishima's death slides into place. To die merely for oneself would be only an egotistic romantic end; submersion in religion, as with the shrine bearers, is too limited and does not contain the possibility of death. To die for the emperor, however, is to die for Japanese culture—since the emperor is the foun-tainhead of that culture—as well as to fulfill one's own tragic fate.

The second essay in *Sun and Steel*, "Epilogue—F104," describes Mishima's ride in a fighter plane and adds nothing to the philosophical conclusions reached in the longer essay, but makes overt the eroticism suggested in that piece. The take-off is described in sexual terms; Mishima sees himself as "spermatozoon-like" when, strapped into the cockpit of the plane, he surmises that he will soon know what a sperm cell feels at the moment of ejaculation; the clouds through which he and the pilot pass are "semen-white." In another startling image, which combines resonances of wisdom, narcissism, and death by suicide, Mishima thinks of the band of clouds circling the earth as resembling a snake trying to swallow its own tail. Mishima and the pilot enter that blue sky at which he had seen the shrine bearers staring; near to death, he becomes a part of tragedy. As he encounters the gravitational force, his face is contorted by both pain and joy like that of a person experiencing an orgasm.

The short poem "Icarus," which ends *Sun and Steel*, is, significantly, named for one who tried to reach the clear blue of the sky on wings fashioned through art and who failed and died. The sixty-one-line poem consists of sixteen sentences, fourteen of which are questions. After a long explanation of his life, Mishima wonders why he must act out the strange fate which he has contrived for himself—or is it that it has been granted to him? He is not sure. That the writer thinks of himself as a failure is clear from his identification with Icarus. Having, at the beginning of the book, declared that words are inadequate and works of art effete, Mishima, ironically, concludes with a poem. His effort to explain himself through words has been a failure; clearly, the only way to find the answer to those questions was through violent action.

Critical Context

Mishima's revolt and suicide mimicked one of the most famous events of Japanese history, the Ni Ni Roku incident of February 26, 1936, in which army officers tried to force the emperor into a militaristic position by occupying parts of Tokyo. Their revolt was crushed, but Mishima wrote a laudatory short story, "Yūkoku" ("Patriotism"), about an officer who, although not actually part of the revolt, favored its objectives. He knows that he will be asked to lead an attack against his comrades and chooses seppuku as an honorable way out of his dilemma. His wife, a bride of only a few months, stabs herself. The couple make love before their suicides, so the story is an intense blend of eroticism and violence. Mishima also played the role of the officer in a film of the story that is so graphic that some members of the audience fainted.

The theme of tragic fulfillment through violent death which is the central idea of *Sun and Steel* appears frequently in Mishima's fiction, often coupled with an act of revolt like the attempted coup which triggered his suicide. Another of Mishima's works based, like "Patriotism," on an actual incident is the novel *Kinkakuji* (1956; *The Temple of the Golden Pavilion*, 1959), in which a Zen Buddhist student burns down a sacred temple. In *Homba* (1969; *Runaway Horses*, 1973), the protagonist commits seppuku. Yukio Mishima wrote works which scintillate with many ideas and emotions leading to a multiplicity of interpretations. It is therefore too much to say that *Sun and Steel* provides the answers to the meaning of his life's work, but it certainly does supply the key to the meaning of his death.

Sources for Further Study

Keene, Donald. "Yukio Mishima," in *Dawn to the West: Japanese Literature of the Modern Era*, 1984.

Lebra, Joyce C. "Mishima's Last Act," in *Literature East and West*. XV, no. 2 (1971), pp. 279-298.

Nathan, John. *Mishima: A Biography*, 1974.

Scott-Stokes, Henry. *The Life and Death of Yukio Mishima*, 1974.

Spurling, John. "Death in Hero's Costume: The Meaning of Mishima," in *Encounter*. XLIV (May, 1975), pp. 56-64.

Ueda, Makoto. "Yukio Mishima," in *Modern Japanese Writers and the Nature of Literature*, 1976.

Yamanouchi, Hisaaki. "Mishima Yukio and His Suicide," in *Modern Asian Studies*. VI (January, 1972), pp. 1-16.

_____. "A Phantasy World: Mishima Yukio," in *The Search for Authenticity in Modern Japanese Literature*, 1978.

James Baird

SURPRISED BY JOY
The Shape of My Early Life

Author: C. S. Lewis (1898-1963)
Type of work: Autobiography
Time of work: 1898-1929
Locale: Great Britain
First published: 1955

> *Principal personages:*
> CLIVE STAPLES LEWIS, a writer
> ALBERT JAMES LEWIS, his father
> FLORA AUGUSTA LEWIS (NÉE HAMILTON), his mother
> WARREN LEWIS, his brother
> WILLIAM KIRKPATRICK, his tutor
> OWEN BARFIELD, his friend

Form and Content

A longtime friend and literary executor of the Lewis estate, Owen Barfield, has suggested that there were, in fact, three C. S. Lewises. That is to say, there were three different vocations that Lewis fulfilled—and fulfilled successfully—in his lifetime. There was, first, Lewis the distinguished Oxford don and literary critic; second, Lewis the highly acclaimed author of science fiction and children's literature; and third, Lewis the popular writer and broadcaster of Christian apologetics. The amazing thing, Barfield notes, is that those who were familiar with Lewis in any single role may not have known that he performed in the other two. In a varied and comprehensive writing career, Lewis carved out a sterling reputation as a scholar, novelist, and theologian for three very different audiences. In *Surprised by Joy*, written seven years before his death, Lewis helps to shed light on all three of his personas.

Surprised by Joy represents one of the few works within the Lewis canon that speaks directly and unabashedly about his personal life. Given the almost stifling attention that Lewis' private life has received since his death in 1963, *Surprised by Joy* stands apart as an astonishingly candid yet self-effacing volume by one widely regarded as the premier Christian apologist of the twentieth century. Lewis proceeds in *Surprised by Joy* as one reluctant to reveal specific details of his life but who relents, as he suggests in the preface, in order both to answer "requests that I would tell how I passed from Atheism to Christianity" and "to correct one or two false notions that seem to have got about." Lewis' reluctance does not simply involve the conventional modesty of the autobiographer who wishes to downplay the importance of his life but stems as well from his conviction that no writer's work is especially illuminated by psychologial inquiry into his or her life. As a renowned literary critic and literary historian, he had witnessed too many works passed off as "literary criticism" that were instead imagined reconstructions of the author's composing process or thought life—poor substitutes for thoughtful attention to an author's text itself.

Lewis referred to this twentieth century critical preoccupation as "the personal heresy": the tendency to identify authors with their creations, assuming that each work is somehow and essentially a rehearsal of a writer's own life. Lewis believed that this critical heresy robbed works of their power and meaning by reducing all literary criticism to biographical skullduggery. He thus rejected out of hand the notion that an artist was obligated to lay bare his private life—either for the sake of celebrity or for its putative insights into his literary works. To accomplish the task he set for himself, then, Lewis was forced to overcome his "distaste for all that is public, all that belongs to the collective." The record of his life, to the extent that it contributed to his defense of Christianity, would be temporarily opened to the world at large—but only under his conditions. It would not be submitted for approval to those pundits or self-styled critics of his career who were merely seeking evidence to undermine his arguments for Christian faith. Nothing is recalled that is directly related to this purpose. Nevertheless, Lewis was clearly uncomfortable with the genre of autobiography and warns the reader in his preface:

> The story is, I fear, suffocatingly subjective; the kind of thing I have never written before and shall probably never write again. I have tried so to write the first chapter that those who can't bear such a story will see at once what they are in for and close the book with the least waste of time.

The subtitle of the book, *The Shape of My Early Life*, succinctly captures the scope of Lewis' autobiography; it deals almost exclusively with his adolescent search for "joy" and those events leading up to and just subsequent to his conversion at age thirty-one. It constitutes what Lewis himself would refer to as "spiritual autobiography," but not in the genre of "confessions" such as those of Saint Augustine or Jean-Jacques Rousseau. Lewis views himself in *Surprised by Joy* as no more or less a sinner than anyone else, but it is chiefly his intellectual journey that needs charting; his is not a grand repentance from fleshly indulgence but a recovery of a childlike wonder at the world and its mysteries. To further this specific goal, the volume contains only those people and events, ideas and contexts that help Lewis explain his conversion—first to himself, and secondarily to his readers. Never one to be accused of hyperbole, Lewis' grand climax to his journey of faith is announced in matter-of-fact, demure terms: "Every step I had taken, from the Absolute to 'Spirit' and from 'Spirit' to 'God,' had been a step toward the more concrete, the more imminent. . . . To accept the Incarnation was a further step in the same direction."

Analysis

Surprised by Joy is essentially an account of those factors that brought Lewis to a mature, adult Christian faith. The reader learns as much about what Lewis read as a child, an adolescent, and an undergraduate as he or she does about Lewis' friendships, military experiences, or love life—the staples of much midcentury biography. Lewis begins his work with an overview of the Lewis family and his early schooling. The Lewis household emerges as a particularly bookish home; the reality he found on the pages of his parents' extensive library seemed as tangible and meaningful to him as anything that transpired outside their doors. Lewis depicts himself and his brother, Warren, as comrades in arms, absolute confidants who shared their deepest longings and secrets without sibling rivalry—all in the happiness of the secure shelter of their parents' Belfast home. The tranquillity of the Lewis home was shattered beyond repair, however, by the death of his mother; the rest of his saga becomes the melancholy search for the security and settledness he had taken for granted during the peace and grace of childhood.

It is this theme, the longing for a restoration of the joy he experienced as a boy, that permeates the entire volume. By "joy," Lewis meant not mere pleasure but the sublime experience of the transcendent, the fleeting glimpse of the eternal that is occasionally mediated by earthly loves and beauties. Lewis believes that a full experience of joy will be possible only in heavenly glory at the consummation of the age, a joy to be found in the Creator who invented both world and word, person and personality. It is He alone who redeems His fallen creation and provides them with joy. From his earliest intimations of this joy, Lewis depicts himself in *Surprised by Joy* as precociously oriented toward the metaphysical and ultimate questions.

Lewis turned first to the written word as an outlet for this ongoing search, creating at age eight the land of Boxen, a world populated by dressed, talking animals, the precursor of what would someday be refashioned as the land of Narnia—Lewis' magical land of children's adventures that retell the story of the Creation, Fall, and Redemption of humankind. Later, Lewis embraced what he referred to as "northernness," the Norse mythology that represented for him the embodiment of otherness and an escape from the mundane realities of boarding school. Before his eventual return to orthodox Christianity, however, Lewis would experiment with adolescent atheism, various Eastern beliefs, and the Absolute of Aristotelian ethics on his way to the trinitarian God proclaimed by Christianity.

In describing this progression, Lewis paints fascinating pictures of early twentieth century Great Britain and its intellectual climate—especially the school system and the trials and tribulations of a nonathletic young boy whose aesthetic sensibilities were out of place among the concerns of his peers. The book's remaining chapters chronicle the steady ascension of Lewis' mind and heart—both his reason and his imagination—toward the reacceptance of the faith he had once shared with his brother and parents and had denounced as a young poet and philosopher. Most important here are two individuals and two authors whom Lewis cites as critical influences animating these gradual changes.

The first of these persons is the "Great Knock," William Kirkpatrick, Lewis' last real tutor before he entered the University of Oxford. "Kirk," as Lewis called him, taught Lewis the value of dialectic, that argumentative give-and-take that seeks truth through the relentless probing of an opponent's position, a fierce and, in Kirk's hands, exaggerated version of Socratic dialogue. As an atheist, Kirk lent no direct support to Lewis' metaphysial yearnings but taught him that while reason alone could never bring the inquirer to central truth, it was the foundation for all credible, defensible belief. Lewis' considerable debating skills can thus be seen as emanating from his beloved tutor. No less important to Lewis was his encounter and subsequent friendship with Owen Barfield, whom he met at Oxford in 1916. Barfield, a keen dialectician himself and a lawyer by profession, helped sharpen Lewis' understanding of both reason and faith. In their "Great War," a vibrant correspondence between the two covering many years, Lewis and Barfield debated the meaning of the supernatural and the identity of God. Barfield's chief contribution to Lewis' journey of faith, however, was his demolishing of Lewis' "chronological snobbery," the "uncritical acceptance of the intellectual climate common to our own age and the assumption that whatever has gone out of date is on that count discredited." Freed from the notion that the past was invariably wrong and that the present always the barometer of truth, Lewis was able to confront the possibility that the Christian message could have validity even in the twentieth century.

By his account, two authors also emerge as particularly influential in and crucial to his agonizing grope toward faith. The first of these was George Macdonald, the nineteenth century Scottish Presbyterian minister and novelist, whose works in his own time were more popular than those of Charles Dickens. Reading two of Macdonald's fantasy works, Lewis reflected later, had "baptized" his imagination, preparing him for a world beyond the material one of which he had grown so tired. The other author was G. K. Chesterton, a popular and prolific London journalist and a talented Christian apologist in his own right. Chesterton's work *The Everlasting Man*, a portrait of Christ and of His impact on culture, presented Lewis with a more global, comprehensive picture of Christianity and its place in human history. Lewis could thus say: "in reading Chesterton, as in reading Macdonald, I did not know what I was letting myself in for. A young man who wishes to remain a sound Atheist cannot be too careful of his reading. . . . God is, if I may say it, very unscrupulous."

From Lewis' perspective, the "joy" he had so long sought had been discovered in the least likely place within the least likely circumstances. Few Oxford professors of literature become ardent, vocal, internationally known promoters of religious faith. Lewis' personal account of this highly unusual occurrence thus makes *Surprised by Joy* compelling reading for believer and nonbeliever alike.

Critical Context

Lewis' life and work have been the focus of countless books since his death in 1963. Ironically, he may eventually suffer the same fate as other authors he himself championed and "rehabilitated" during his scholarly career. Surrounded by volume after volume of analysis, paraphrase, and critique, Lewis' own canon may be dwarfed by secondary sources, a development he opposed all of his life in reading others. One does not need the critics to enjoy Chaucer, he once said, but Chaucer to enjoy the critics. As it stands, both his fiction and his theological writings have been endlessly anthologized and hypercritically explored, creating a trail of footnotes and asides long enough to camouflage the essential viewpoints and facts about his life—thus discouraging even the most diligent student of Lewis. It must be said, however, that Lewis' own works remain the most reliable sources and insightful interpreters of his thought and personality. *Surprised by Joy*, while, as noted, emerging as one of the most personal of Lewis' books, retains the characteristic stylistic and thematic modes found elsewhere in his oeuvre.

It is in *Surprised by Joy*, for example, that one learns the extent to which Lewis is indebted to a romantic view of both life and culture, that is, a mind-set in which reason and imagination are held in tension at all times and neither is allowed to dominate or cancel out the other. Haunted in his search for joy, Lewis turned first in his youth to the strange and preternatural—the darker myths of the North. His youthful trek into the vagaries of philosophy landed him within various camps of pantheism and theism, and, finally, led him to the Christian theism wherein reason and imagination are married in the Eternal Logos, the "Myth Become Fact," which he discovered in Jesus of Nazareth. Despite his judgment that his text seems "suffocatingly subjective," the deliberate, methodical way in which Lewis narrates his life parallels the meticulous arguments with which he constructed his scholarly treatises and theological briefs. Here, as elsewhere, Lewis steadfastly refuses to include any details of his life to titillate the amateur psychologist or self-styled debunker.

Therefore, even when he is revealing innermost thoughts and private incidents, Lewis still maintains a distance from both the reader and his subject matter—as if he were creating a persona, a fictional Lewis (as he indeed did in the first volume of his space trilogy, *Out of the Silent Planet*, 1938), whose life and personality he must discern through the same careful historical research and fundamental objectivity that underlies such scholarly works as *The Allegory of Love: A Study in Medieval Tradition* (1936) and *A Preface to "Paradise Lost"* (1942). Even though Lewis' circle of friends include a veritable Who's Who of popular fiction, among them J. R. R. Tolkien, Charles Williams, and Dorothy L. Sayers, only those who had a direct influence on his coming to faith receive specific citation or focus. In a word, *Surprised by Joy* represents the kind of scholarship about his own life that Lewis practiced in his own literary criticism and theological works and remains an admirable model of autobiographical restraint and insight.

Sources for Further Study

Carnell, Corbin Scott. *Bright Shadow of Reality: C. S. Lewis and the Feeling Intellect*, 1974.

Edwards, Bruce L. *A Rhetoric of Reading: C. S. Lewis's Defense of Western Literacy*, 1986.

_____, ed. *The Taste of the Pineapple: C. S. Lewis as Reader, Critic, and Imaginative Writer*, 1988.

Green, Roger Lancelyn, and Walter Hooper. *C. S. Lewis: A Biography*, 1974.

Hannay, Margaret Patterson. *C. S. Lewis*, 1981.

Holmer, Paul. *C. S. Lewis: The Shape of His Faith and Thought*, 1976.

Howard, Thomas. *The Achievement of C. S. Lewis*, 1980.

Lindskoog, Kathryn. *C. S. Lewis: Mere Christian*, 1981.

Bruce L. Edwards

THE TEACHINGS OF DON JUAN
A Yaqui Way of Knowledge

Author: Carlos Castaneda (1931-   )
Type of work: Autobiography/cultural anthropology
Time of work: 1961-1965
Locale: The southwestern United States and northern Mexico
First published: 1968

> *Principal personages:*
> DON JUAN MATUS, a Yaqui Indian *brujo*
> CARLOS CASTANEDA, his apprentice

Form and Content

The Teachings of Don Juan: A Yaqui Way of Knowledge reads like a novel, but it was Carlos Castaneda's master's thesis. While gathering information about medicinal plants used by southwestern Indians, Castaneda was introduced to the enigmatic and supremely confident don Juan Matus. This Yaqui *brujo* (a medicine man, sorcerer, or witch) was to be his mentor in the arduous process of becoming what the Indian called "a man of knowledge."

Mescalito, the spirit of the peyote plant, has indicated to the *brujo* that Castaneda is the person to whom he should act as "benefactor" and pass on his age-old knowledge. As a youth, don Juan was selected similarly. There is no indication where his knowledge originates or how old it may be. As teacher, guide, and interpreter, don Juan introduces his student to an extraordinary world by teaching him the principles necessary for entering and utilizing "nonordinary" reality. Castaneda's unusual experiences during his apprenticeship both terrify him and make him violently ill, but they disclose marvelous possibilities.

Near the end of the fourth year of his apprenticeship, Castaneda experienced a particularly traumatic lesson. Late one evening, suddenly fearing for his life, he became convinced that the don Juan he seemingly observed was in fact a diabolical impostor bent on destroying him. With this experience, Castaneda's implicit sense of everyday reality was severely undermined; he began to have what might be described as a nervous breakdown and abruptly broke off his relationship with the sorcerer. *The Teachings of Don Juan* recounts events which took place during the first four years of the author's apprenticeship.

The book is divided into three parts: "Introduction," "The Teachings," and "A Structural Analysis." "The Teachings" (the largest section, comprising 131 pages of the book's 196) consists of dated field notes which describe the "ordinary" and "nonordinary" experiences Castaneda has with don Juan. In addition to descriptions of the procedures or rituals used to induce nonordinary experiences, these notes include question-and-answer sessions between teacher and student both before and after perception-altering experiences. In these conversations, Castaneda tries to clarify his encounters with nonordinary reality as well as reveal the content of don

Juan's beliefs. Because "The Teachings" includes the subjective version of what he experiences, this section is emotionally charged and reveals the author's confusion, amazement, and, at times, abject fear.

"A Structural Analysis" was written after Castaneda's experiences as an apprentice. An abrupt change of style is evident as this section reflects the objective and detached language of an anthropologist. In it the author attempts to establish criteria for analyzing the lessons, perceptual attitudes, and psychological states reported in "The Teachings" and to "disclose the internal cohesion and cogency of don Juan's teachings." A discussion of suggestibility is a prominent part of this section. Appendices briefly discuss the process of validating nonordinary reality and include a detailed outline of "A Structural Analysis."

Analysis

Like Aldous Huxley's psychedelic literature, Carlos Castaneda's *The Teachings of Don Juan* attempts to examine rationally what escapes the limits of logic. Unlike other works of the genre, however, which generally describe and discuss drug-altered experiences, this book identifies a structure to which halluncinatory experiences conform and teaches a coherent way of experiencing the world that is utterly foreign to Western consciousness. For this reason, the work intrigued an entire generation interested in both hallucinogens and altered states of consciousness and is considered a classic addition to the literature which chronicles the psychology of drug-altered perception.

Used separately and on different occasions, the hallucinogenic substances *mescalito*, *yerba del diablo*, and *humito*—peyote, Jimson weed, and mushrooms—play a significant role in Castaneda's introduction to the system don Juan attempts to elucidate. The bulk of his teachings, in fact, involve the preparation and use of these hallucinogenic plants. Each plant possesses different perceptual properties. In explaining the use of the "allies," as don Juan calls the entities present in these plants, the *brujo* warns Castaneda that they are powerful but dangerous teachers which can accept or reject the recipient. The capacity of these plants to produce a peculiar state of perception is an essential element in the learning process, guiding the initiate to a level of conceptualization that allows him to comprehend nonordinary phenomena. Castaneda learns further that the realm of nonordinary reality is not illusory but real, with its own inherent properties and, moreover, that it can be utilized in such a way as to draw points of reference which have value in ordinary reality. That this nonordinary reality has a form, structure, and logic of its own and that one can actually move around in it is undoubtedly one of the author's most startling and controversial revelations.

The interrelation of mind and matter, the processes of perception and knowing—these are some of the themes of don Juan's lessons. Again and again he forces his student to question the validity of his assumptions; nothing can be taken for granted. Don Juan's epistemology is as exacting and subtle as that of any contemporary theory, requiring the precise performance of sophisticated and complex techniques. Because these procedures collapse the façade of illusions on which most people depend, learning them demands the courage and discipline of a warrior. "A man goes to knowledge," don Juan tells his student, "as he goes to war, wide-awake, with fear, with respect, and with absolute assurance. Going to knowledge or going to war in any other manner is a mistake, and whoever makes it will live to regret his steps."

"Going to knowledge" also brings with it an ongoing reevaluation of the normal, everyday world and one's role in it. What constitutes worthwhile goals and what constitutes the highest knowledge must be reformulated to synthesize with the insights acquired in the learning process. Castaneda discovers, for example, that for the man of knowledge there are no regrets in the struggle for understanding, even though he is acutely aware that if he does achieve his goal, it will be only for a fleeting moment, and death will claim the final victory. Thus, for the man of knowledge—as for all enlightened individuals—it is the journey itself which must provide the meaning and the rewards.

The epistemology and ethics of the system don Juan teaches is founded on metaphysical presuppositions which differ radically from Western conceptions of reality. In fact, the prevailing notion of reality in the West is merely a facet of the more fundamental and holistic world to which don Juan is privy. The Cartesian duality of mind and matter, a supposition of Western metaphysics, is ignored. Mind and matter are categories which have a diminished role in the Indian's ontological paradigm, where physical and cognitive being are considerably more diverse than traditionally conceived by Westerners.

The companion world Castaneda is shown is not transcendental in the sense that it lies beyond the sensorium; rather, it is apprehended by utilizing and understanding sensoral data in a different way, guided by the insights provided with psychedelics. Mastering the *brujo*'s more sophisticated level of perception allows the apprentice to see the world's complexity more completely. Even something as innocuous as the light of day has deeper significance. The evening twilight, for example, is seen as an avenue to a separate reality, "the crack between the worlds."

Given the nature of don Juan's world, the man who has mastered the principles of the *brujo*'s system can see the future, leave his physical body, be in two places simultaneously, and he is capable of transforming himself into a bird, dog, coyote, or any other creature. Such acts conflict with the description of reality most Westerners understand, and Castaneda himself is skeptical that such possibilities exist. His own experiences, however, seem to corroborate the claims of his benefactor. After having smoked the hallucinogenic mixture *humito*, for example, he recounts his apparent transformation into a crow and his subsequent sensation of soaring above the mountains with other birds. Returning to ordinary reality, he finds himself naked in the open desert.

After such strange experiences, Castaneda is at times ecstatic, but more often exhausted and confused. The uncertainty about what he has actually experienced is apparent at every step of his apprenticeship, particularly when he begins to shift in and out of ordinary and nonordinary states without hallucinogenic mixtures. He describes these phenomena as they occurred—subjectively. Only afterward, during dialogues with his teacher (which are interpretative debriefings as well), does Castaneda attempt to understand what he has experienced. Rather than applying the methodology of modern scientific investigation, however, he and his teacher conduct these discussions using terms of the Indian's world. Although Castaneda's questions of his teacher are at times fumbling and redundant, they are a concerted effort to comprehend don Juan's order of conceptualization.

Castaneda's unique approach to his subject, as well as his considerable talents as a writer, results in a vivid and compelling exploration of an experiential paradigm previously undocumented. By describing the events of his apprenticeship with the same terror, ecstasy, wonder, and bewilderment he experienced as they occurred, he has made don Juan's amazing world tangible. The book is a story of discovery and revelation delineating a mysterious and fully elaborated worldview, a view which differs radically from Western cosmology but provides as much, if not more, cosmological satisfaction. As a story of discovery, it incorporates a familiar archetypical theme, Hesse-like in its presentation, of a young man's initiation into another way through the kind but emphatic tutelage of a wise old man.

Critical Context

The Teachings of Don Juan provided the foundation for Castaneda's further conversations and experiences with don Juan, related in the widely popular works that followed: *A Separate Reality: Further Conversations with Don Juan* (1971), *Journey to Ixtlan* (1972), *Tales of Power* (1974), *The Second Ring of Power* (1978), *The Eagle's Gift* (1981), and *The Fire from Within* (1984). The most frequent criticism leveled against these works, particularly upon the appearance of the first, questions their basis in fact: How much of the study is true?

The Teachings of Don Juan has the momentum and suspense of fiction and a narrative power unmatched by other anthropological studies. Castaneda himself calls his book an anthropological field study, but the testimony of leading scholars is mixed. Detractors claim that the book is a fraud, the work of a novelist rather than a scientist, although one with a unique knowledge of the desert and Indian lore. For example, how could an observer, under the conditions experienced by Castaneda, write down everything don Juan says verbatim?

Other criticisms revolve around three themes. First, there is no proof that don Juan really did what he said he did—or that he even exists; there is no bibliography, no corroboration at all, beyond the book itself. Castaneda is the only one who has seen him, so the accuracy of the events described depends solely on his reliability as a witness. Because there is virtually no information about don Juan's past (nothing is learned about his family), it is impossible to decide whether his "way of knowledge" has genuine ethnic roots or he is a harmless crank who fabricated his stories as mood and occasion suggested. (That Castaneda never considers don Juan's motivation is seen as another weakness of the study.)

Next, Weston LaBarre, the most distinguished researcher of peyoteism, is particularly critical of Castaneda's report, noting that it does nothing to advance the knowledge of ritualized hallucinogenic experiences and, moreover, that the entire study is at best pseudoscience, similar to that popularized by Thor Heyerdahl and Desmond Morris.

Finally there is the controversy concerning the source and originality of don Juan's teachings. Scholars have called attention to the striking similarity between the ideas of the *brujo* and those of Taoism, American Indian folklore, and European existential philosophy. It is no wonder, then, that experts can recognize in Castaneda's book much that is of anthropological validity.

Those who find the book enlightening are not only convinced of its cultural and historical accuracy but also believe it represents superior ethnographic scholarship. Because Castaneda attempts to go within rather than merely observe don Juan's world, the book's place among contemporary anthropological studies is unique, and the author has been seen as a major figure in the evolution of the discipline. Defenders of the work point out that don Juan's ancestry is unimportant because he is, after all, a loner, an outcast sorcerer who neither speaks for nor represents Yaqui culture or religion.

To the charges of plagiarism, the work's supporters find that the similarities between don Juan's ideas and those of others in no way undermine the credibility of the study; in fact, such similarities point to the universality and profound truth of don Juan's way of knowledge. Castaneda himself has responded to the charges by pointing out that Westerners are generally unwilling to look at another culture on its own terms, particularly when it conflicts with the vision of reality they have been reared to perceive and accept.

The question of its authenticity remains unanswered, but whether castigated or celebrated, *The Teachings of Don Juan* was widely read by a generation of young people in the 1970's and continues to fascinate readers. By providing a glimpse into another way of experiencing the world, it suggests that reality is not absolute but a culturally determined package of illusions. With this glimpse comes flexiblity, curiosity, and an open mind.

Sources for Further Study
Ash, Lee. Review in *Library Journal*. XCIV (March 1, 1969), p. 1014.
de Mille, Richard, ed. *The Don Juan Papers: Further Castaneda Controversies*, 1980.
Noel, Daniel C., ed. *Seeing Castaneda: Reactions to the "Don Juan" Writings of Carlos Castaneda*, 1976.
Roszak, Theodore. Review in *Nation*. CCVIII (February 10, 1969), p. 184.
Young, Dudley. "The Magic of Peyote," in *The New York Times Book Review*. LXXIII (September 29, 1968), p. 30.

Alan Pratt

THE TECHNOLOGICAL SOCIETY

Author: Jacques Ellul (1912-   )
Type of work: Cultural criticism/sociology
First published: La Technique: Ou, L'Enjeu du siècle, 1954 (English translation, 1964; revised, 1967)

Form and Content

Jacques Ellul, a professor of history and sociology of institutions at the University of Bordeaux and the author of forty books, wrote *The Technological Society* between 1952 and 1954. Little known until it was published in its English translation in the United States in 1964, the book reflects the twin paths of the author's life. First, he had a productive scholarly career, with specialities in history, sociology, and law. For a time, he tried to marry his academic interests to political activities. During World War II he was active in the French resistance to Nazi rule. After the war he began a promising political career as deputy mayor of Bordeaux, but he abandoned that to devote his time more fully to teaching and writing. Second, Ellul was an active lay ecclesiastic. Converted to Christianity when he was twenty-two, he became a leader of the Protestant Reformed Church of France. A third of his books have theological themes, as he focuses on the two ideologies that inform his intellectual worldview, Christianity and Marxism. He seeks no synthesis between these two, but instead tries to place them face to face, in order to determine what is real socially and spiritually.

The Technological Society is the first part of Ellul's sociopolitical trilogy about contemporary Western society. It was followed by *Propagandes* (1962; *Propaganda: The Formation of Men's Attitudes*, 1965) and *L'Illusion politique* (1964; *The Political Illusion*, 1967). In all three of these books, but particularly in *The Technological Society*, Ellul offered a powerful, if gloomy, analysis of the influence of "technique" in modern society. Ellul's work, largely an elaboration of his original philosophical and sociological insights, interprets the modern age in terms of a single phenomenon, technique. Technique, according to Ellul, is more than machine technology; it is "*the totality of methods arrived at and having absolute efficiency . . . in every field of human activity.*" The machine is merely symptomatic of technique. Everything touched by technique, however, assumes a machinelike quality. Thus, technique is exemplified in the General Motors assembly line but also in such varied aspects of human behavior as psychological counseling, dietetics, and media manipulation in American presidential politics.

The Technological Society investigates the phenomenon in three areas: economics, politics (the technique of organization), and human affairs (manipulation of humans through brainwashing, propaganda, advertising, and the like). Basically, Ellul contends that the predominant characteristic of the contemporary human condition is the technique developed by modern industrial society. Unlike premodern technology, technique has pervaded all aspects of life, becoming an autonomous force, independent of the humans who have collectively created it. Technique builds on itself, ceaselessly requiring more technique. Before its force, people are powerless; they cannot choose to ignore technique, let alone reverse it. Their only choice is to go ahead. As a consequence of this technological imperative, the traditional moral content of all societies is overwhelmed.

Not surprisingly, some critics often characterize Ellul's works as extreme and accept them only with caution. He is not simply a prophet of the apocalypse, for his thought is complex, subtle, and insightful. His profound pessimism, however, has led some critics to see him as a technological determinist, who underestimates the capacity of the human mind to comprehend and surmount the problems of technique.

Others, however, have defended Ellul as a trenchant critic of modern intellectualism, which has unbalanced the relationship between humanity and nature by its overemphasis upon reductionist science. It was precisely this kind of controversy Ellul hoped to provoke with his book, since his purpose in writing was to preserve values founded upon liberty and hope, which are deeper, more traditional, and more basic than rationalism.

Analysis

Ellul's main purpose is to explain the role technique has assumed in the contemporary world and to call attention to the need to bring it under control. He begins with an explanation of technique's origins and characteristics.

According to Ellul, technique arose in the eighteenth century as a consequence of five interrelated causes. First, it resulted from the fruition of a long history of technological experience. Every invention after about 1750 had necessary antecedents which had increased the momentum of technological discovery to the point where both quantitative and qualitative breakthroughs could occur. Second, population expansion fostered needs which could not be satisfied except by technical development. Population growth created not only the necessary market for technique but also the requisite human material. Third, the economic environment combined two seemingly contradictory traits: It was stable and yet in flux. Stability permitted research on well-defined problems, and flux permitted technical inventions to be quickly adopted. Fourth, the social milieu was sufficiently flexible to permit technological innovation. Two traditional restraints, social taboos and inflexible social structures, broke down. The traditional values that had caused earlier technological innovations to be carefully scrutinized before adoption lost their hold, and the breakup of traditional social groups led to migration to cities, where individuals were isolated and subjected to the power of technique. Finally, a clear technological intention, sponsored by special interests, particuarly the bourgeoisie, appeared. Ellul believes that the 1750's "adherence of the whole of society to a conspicuous technical objective" had occurred. All five of these factors occurred simultaneously, resulting in the emergence of technique.

Ellul lists eight characteristics of technique. Two of these, he says, are obvious.

First is its rationality. It brings mechanics to bear on all that is spontaneous and irrational and reduces them to the "scheme of logic." Second, technique creates artificiality. It destroys, absorbs, or subordinates the natural world and will not permit its restoration. Third, technique is self-directing. It is guided by the single criterion of efficiency. Technique seeks the "one best way"; if a better technological means exists, it will be used. Human choice has therefore little to do with technique. Fourth, technique is self-augmenting, in that it proceeds without decisive intervention by individual humans. Its growth is automatic and irreversible, developing according to laws of geometric progression. In its development, technique poses primarily technical problems that consequently can be solved only by technology. The result is a situation of self-reinforcing cycles. Technique thus assumes its own momentum and direction. Fifth, technique implies monism. That is, the technological phenomenon forms a whole and is unitary. The good uses of technique cannot be dissociated from the bad, nor the useful from the destructive. According to Ellul, phenomena as diverse as the organization of an office and the construction of an aircraft have certain identical features. Once the technical orientation has been adopted, it brings into existence all aspects of technique. It is impossible to accept some and reject others. Sixth, techniques become linked together; all require one another. So, for example, economic techniques require political techniques, which in turn require propaganda. Seventh, technique is universal; all peoples follow the same technological road. They are distinguished only by their relative places on the technological trajectory. Technological invasion crushes the independence of traditional civilizations. Finally, technique is autonomous and the prime mover of every other aspect of society. It is a closed system. It determines the conditions of social, political, and economic change. It is not guided by imperatives developed independently of it.

The result of technique's enormous influence is the inexorable loss of human freedom, according to Ellul. The ultimate technical accomplishment comes when people are manipulated into believing that they want to do what the state demands of them. The success of political propaganda in all societies, whether liberal-democratic or Marxist, reflects the fact that technique's domination has little to do with different political ideologies. Neither Marxist nor capitalist societies question the doctrine of progress through technique.

Perhaps the key concept in *The Technological Society* is that technique is autonomous, that it moves ahead with an inner direction and a force of its own making. Ellul contends that this autonomy has several causes. First, as new technologies emerge, they create problems which require more technology for their solution. A classic example is the automobile, which as it is perfected requires successive technological improvements in roads, social controls, and laws. Second, when certain technologies are created, they require others for their effective utilization. Mass production, for example, requires the assembly of parts and materials from a variety of locations, which demands improvements in communication and transportation techniques. Third, when a technological apparatus is assembled, it builds its own momentum because of the commitment of personnel and matériel. The combination of vast human and natural resources virtually assures that technique will continue to develop without direction by individual humans. In the end, national policies are shaped to a large extent by technological-industrial complexes.

The individual thus loses freedom of choice. Trained with a narrow focus on instrumentalities with little or no attention to cost-benefit analysis of the end results, the technicians are unable to see that technique is in fact controlling them. The result, to Ellul, is clear: "True technique will know how to maintain the illusion of liberty, choice, and individuality; but these . . . will be mathematically integrated into the mathematical reality merely as appearances! . . . The individual will no longer be able, materially or spiritually, to disengage himself from society." The individual cannot escape technique's domination.

Critics of Ellul's vision of technique have argued that he is unnecessarily negative and pessimistic and that he idolizes a nontechnical past that never really existed. They contend that while it is difficult to gainsay Ellul's realism about technique, since modern weapons and environmental problems are dangerous and pressing, he does not sufficiently recognize that technique has enhanced the lives of most ordinary people. In their view, technique has freed humanity from the conditions of hardship, starvation, and superstition that dominated history. To argue that technique has done nothing for humanity is patently absurd. Not every aspect of industrialization is necessarily enslaving and idol-producing. Ellul's critics also argue that he implicity assumes that things were better in the past. This idealization of a romanticized, pretechnical past leads to a serious misinterpretation of history.

Despite these criticisms, however, most evaluations of Ellul's work are favorable. Even those who do not share his fundamental premises agree that he has identified the central thrust of modern history and that his analysis must be taken seriously. Ellul himself stated the purpose of his books clearly: He wants to provoke a reaction of personal reflection and thus force readers to choose to do something. This aim explains the character of his writing: It is forceful, dialectical, and full of assertions sometimes unsupported by thorough factual analysis. He attempts not so much to explain as to argue, to convince others of what he believes to be true. He wants to force the reader to grasp the ironic contradictions of a society dominated by technique, and follow them through to their ultimate resolutions.

In describing things as they are and are likely to become, he appears to assume inevitability. In fact, his writings, taken as a whole, indicate that he believes that man has the ability to change technique and alter the ultimate course of social evolution. *The Technological Society* seeks to warn people of what is likely to happen so that they will take charge of their history rather than be carried away by events. He hopes that subsequent events will prove him wrong, but he fears that he is correct.

Critical Context

Ellul's work falls within the genre of studies that criticize the nature of modern technological society. Aldous Huxley, who introduced Ellul to the United States in conversations at the Center for the Study of Democratic Institutions in Santa Barbara in 1959-1960, said that Ellul's work made the case he had tried to make in his *Brave New World* (1932). Ellul's path-breaking analysis of the impact of technique on all aspects of society spawned a host of related studies in the two decades following the publication of his book in the United States. Fritjof Capra's *The Turning Point: Science, Society, and the Rising Culture* (1982) offers a penetrating critique of Cartesian-Newtonian thought, focusing particularly on what he calls the mechanistic view of life. Mihajlo Mesarović and Eduard Pestel's *Mankind at the Turning Point: The Second Report to the Club of Rome* (1974) argues, as does Ellul, that unbridled economic and technological invention are straining the carrying capacity of the world.

Ellul emphasized the threat posed to the natural environment by technique. His warnings in this area have been echoed by countless other authors, including David Ehrenfeld, whose *The Arrogance of Humanism* (1978) criticizes technique's confidence that progress is inevitable and that man can surmount any and all natural barriers to technological development. His criticism of technique is based upon his Christian faith. In this respect, E. F. Schumacher, a leading figure in the environmental movement of the 1970's, closely resembles him. Schumacher's *A Guide for the Perplexed* (1977) claims that the mad rush for technological development has reduced humanity to the level of productive machinery, and that modern industrial civilization has lost the meaning of human existence. In his words, contemporary science and education no longer provide social and moral maps that would enable humans to find the answer to life's most pressing questions.

Ellul's book is thus centrally situated among works that criticize the nature of technological civilization and call mankind back to values that are broader and more enduring than technique. The two main themes of his writings are the nature and influence of technique and the role of Christianity in civilization and individual existence. His work may be characterized as prophetic, in that he seeks to disturb the status quo, question what is taken as normal, shed new light on old issues, and offer new perspectives. Bringing criticism from outside the normal order of dis course, Ellul challenges the common assumptions of modern technological society.

Like that of all prophets, Ellul's perspective has its limitations. He does not give a complete, reasoned exploration of all of his arguments. Critics have noted blind spots, overstatements, and contradictions. As "prophecy," however, Ellul's work has been heard as a profound critique of technological society.

Sources for Further Study
Christians, Clifford G., and Jay M. Van Hook. *Jacques Ellul: Interpretive Essays*, 1981.
Ellul, Jacques. *In Season, Out of Season*, 1981.
Hanks, Joyce M. *Jacques Ellul: A Comprehensive Bibliography*, 1984.
Holloway, James Y., ed. *Introducing Jacques Ellul*, 1970.

Lovekin, David. "Giambattista Vico and Jacques Ellul: The Intelligible Universal and the Technical Phenomenon," in *Man and World*. XV, no. 4 (1982), pp. 407-416.

Menninger, David C. "Jacques Ellul: A Tempered Profile," in *Review of Politics*. XXXVII (April, 1975), pp. 235-246.

Nisbet, Robert A. "The Grand Illusion: An Appreciation of Jacques Ellul," in *Commentary*. L (August, 1970), pp. 40-44.

Ransom, H. H. Review in *Saturday Review*. XLVII (September 26, 1964), p. 48.

Theobald, Robert. Review in *The Nation*. CXCIX (October 19, 1964), p. 249.

Williams, Raymond. Review in *The New York Times Book Review*. LXIX (October 18, 1964), p. 32.

Loren W. Crabtree

TESTAMENT OF YOUTH, TESTAMENT OF FRIENDSHIP, and TESTAMENT OF EXPERIENCE

Author: Vera Brittain (1893-1970)
Type of work: Autobiography
Time of work: 1893-1950
Locale: England, France, Malta, Scandinavia, Germany, the United States, and India
First published: Testament of Youth, 1933; *Testament of Friendship,* 1940; *Testament of Experience,* 1957

> *Principal personages:*
> VERA (MARY) BRITTAIN, the author, a pacifist and a feminist
> EDWARD BRITTAIN, her brother, a war casualty
> ROLAND LEIGHTON, her fiancé, a war casualty
> GEORGE CATLIN, her husband
> WINIFRED HOLTBY, her closest friend
> JOHN CATLIN, her son
> SHIRLEY CATLIN, her daughter

Form and Content

The three autobiographical books written by Vera Brittain owe their popularity to the fact that they represent more than personal history. They are interpretations of a time when a secure old world was dying and a cruel, horrifying new era was being born. As a young woman who lost those she loved in World War I, who dedicated herself to the causes of pacifism and feminism after the war, and who then survived World War II, once again to plunge into the fight for peace and for the rights of women, Brittain represents the victories and defeats, the hopes and fears of her generation.

Testament of Youth covers the period from Brittain's birth in 1893 to her marriage in 1925. It is a book of 662 pages, with acknowledgments and a foreword by Brittain. Later editions include a preface by the author's daughter, Shirley Catlin Williams, which stresses the importance of the work as the only representation of World War I written by a woman and also as a book describing the death of an era. The twelve chapters are separated into three unequal parts, each of which ends with a milepost in Brittain's life—her fiancé's death, the end of the war, and finally, her marriage.

The thematic development of *Testament of Youth* is indicated by the epigraphs which introduce each part of the book and each chapter. The initial epigraph, a segment of a fairy tale, is repeated at the end of the later book, *Testament of Experience,* which takes Brittain's life from 1925, the year of her marriage, to 1950. In *Testament of Youth,* however, it is the epigraphs preceding the chapters that are particularly moving, because all of them are quotations from poems either by Brittain herself or by her brilliant and doomed fiancé, Roland Leighton.

Although it is somewhat shorter (480 pages), the third of Brittain's autobiographical works, *Testament of Experience*, repeats the format and the subject matter of her first book. Again, her personal life is dominated by the love of a man, her husband, George Catlin (referred to as "G."); again, her public life is dedicated to the struggles for women's rights and for peace; again, Brittain and those she loves, her husband and her two children, are endangered by war, just as her fiancé, her brother, and her close friends had been in *Testament of Youth*.

The structure is almost identical to that of Brittain's first autobiographical volume. After a foreword, there are twelve chapters, grouped into three unequal parts, each of which ends with an important event. The first part takes the author from her marriage to the beginning of World War II; the second, to the end of the war; and the third, on travels throughout the world, ending in London with Brittain once again in the arms of her husband.

Testament of Experience repeats the pattern of epigraphs preceding each part and each chapter. These epigraphs, however, vary greatly in form. There are lines from letters by G. or by Brittain, segments of poems or prose by the author, and—when the writing and publication of *Testament of Youth* is described—even a book-jacket blurb by Brittain's friend Winifred Holtby.

The second autobiographical work, *Testament of Friendship*, is different both in subject matter and in form from the other two volumes. While each of them concentrated on Brittain's attempt to survive a war and to be reunited with those she loved, in this book the threat comes from disease, which did indeed bring death to Brittain's closest friend, Holtby, when she was only thirty-seven.

Testament of Friendship covers a sixteen-year period, beginning with the initially hostile meeting between Brittain and Holtby at postwar Oxford and ending with Holtby's death in 1935. It covers some of the same time period as *Testament of Youth*, which ends in 1925, and *Testament of Experience*, which begins in 1925, and therefore it deals with some of the same events. In this volume, however, Brittain's perspective is different: She considers such events in her life as her relationship with G., her marriage, and her motherhood not in themselves, but as they affect and are affected by her friendship with Holtby. Furthermore, she shows the parallels between Holtby and herself, both of whom were torn between art and activism and both of whom, as women, were also torn between their desire to devote themselves to the men they loved and their need to realize their own potential.

Because the analysis of this relationship is so detailed, it is not surprising that *Testament of Friendship* is 442 pages in length, about the same as *Testament of Experience*, which deals with twenty-five years instead of sixteen. The book is divided into twenty-three chapters, with a prologue and an epilogue.

Like the other books, *Testament of Friendship* is elegiac in tone. Yet *Testament of Youth* and *Testament of Experience* derive their elegiac tone less from the descriptions of personal loss (though both do contain such passages) than from the evocation of the end of an era. In *Testament of Friendship*, the elegiac tone arises from the fact that the book is a tribute to a friend and an expression of personal grief at her loss, not in a cataclysm, but through disease.

Analysis

The epigraph to part 1 of *Testament of Youth* is also the final quotation in *Testament of Experience*. Briefly, it is a fairy tale about a girl who was permitted to choose between happiness at the beginning of her life and happiness at the end of it. Reasoning that it would be wiser to have something pleasant in the future than in the past, the girl chooses happiness in old age.

When Brittain completed *Testament of Youth* in 1933, she was happily married and the mother of two children. She could not be certain that her later years would be happy; she did know, however, that she had lost her golden years, along with her idealism and innocence, to the forces which produced World War I. *Testament of Youth* is Brittain's own story; it is also the story of the women and the men of her generation.

Brittain was a child of the Victorian period, born into a lesser branch of a prosperous manufacturing family, reared in a pleasant English country house, educated by a governess, at day school, and finally at boarding school. In 1912 and 1913, she lived the life of a debutante. Only when she determined to go to the University of Oxford did she begin to suspect that there might be disadvantages to her stable society. While it was assumed that her brother, Edward, would go to Oxford, her family could not imagine why Vera would wish to get a college education. Even after she had convinced her father to send her, Brittain had to overcome the fact that her preparation was inadequate; meanwhile, her mother had to contend with the scandalized community. Clearly, a stable society could be stagnant. In this first confrontation with society, Brittain set a pattern for her life. Thereafter she would question what others took for granted, she would act to change whatever social institutions she found to be flawed, and she would honestly record the internal conflicts and the external struggles in which she was involved, not merely as personal matters but also as reflections of the larger problems of her generation.

By deciding to go to Oxford, Brittain was asserting her intellectual equality with the male sex. Yet, before she could become involved in the struggle for women's rights, which later became so important in her life, her country had become involved in another struggle, which the idealistic young people of Brittain's England considered a crusade for freedom. By the end of World War I, Brittain was to believe that those young people had been tricked and betrayed, and as a result, she was to espouse her second cause, that of pacifism.

While Brittain was at Oxford during the first months of the war, she had become friendly with Roland Leighton, a brilliant and talented young man who appreciated and applauded her need for intellectual development. Although she knew that her society demanded that a woman lose her identity in marriage, she was certain that Leighton would never desire such a sacrifice. By the time Leighton left to fight what was expected to be a short war, he and Brittain were engaged. Believing that she, too, must help in the war effort, Brittain went into nurses' training in June, 1915. At Christmastime, Leighton was to return on leave. The day after Christmas, she rushed to answer the telephone, certain that he was calling to say that he arrived. Instead, she received a message informing her that he was dead.

During the next four years, Brittain discovered another weakness in that society which had seemed so comfortable. As she nursed maimed and dying men, as she received word of the deaths of Edward and all of her young male friends, she thought of the safe civilian leaders who were so quick to declare war and then to prolong the butchery as long as possible. Brittain had discovered that the German soldiers were not monsters; they had been lied to as thoroughly as had the young men of the Allied forces. Clearly, the war had been a horrible fraud; the society that justified it with patriotic slogans had been deceitful and hypocritical.

When peace came and Brittain returned to Oxford, she took her experience and her message with her. Yet she was once again disillusioned. The society that she had hoped to undeceive did not wish to hear her message. What she did not realize was that her bitterness was driving people away. It was an outspoken fellow student, Holtby, who made that unpleasant truth quite clear to her, and who later became her closest friend. Gradually, Brittain moved back into society; she worked for peace by lecturing on behalf of the League of Nations, she wrote a novel, and she fell in love again. At the end of *Testament of Youth*, with her wedding to Catlin just a few days away, Brittain once again could hope for happiness.

Brittain had delayed writing about her wartime experiences because, as she commented, the memories were simply too painful to recall. When she did write *Testament of Youth*, she had distanced herself enough to understand her own experience. In those traumatic wartime years, she had seen a new vision of her world, as a battleground between idealism and greed, peace and war, love and death. She had also come to the realization that women must often decide between preservation of the self and loss of the self in conventional marriage.

The fact that Brittain, unlike her friend Holtby, did not have to make that choice is one source of the optimism of *Testament of Experience*. Catlin, whom she calls G., shared her vision of the world, her passion for change, and her assumption that women's goals were as important as those of men. During the twenty-five years of marriage which are chronicled in the book, Brittain and Catlin were frequently separated, while one or the other traveled or lectured. Brittain makes it clear that the periods when they were apart were difficult; however, every reunion renewed their relationship. At the end of *Testament of Youth*, Brittain had met Catlin on a train; at the end of *Testament of Experience*, she meets him in a customs shed, rushing to him as enthusiastically as she had twenty-five years before. Her expectations for their future are indicated by her reprinting the fairy story with which *Testament of Youth* had begun. Clearly, she expects to have a happy old age with her husband.

The political events of which Brittain and Catlin were a part during that quarter century gave them less reason for optimism. Even while they worked for peace and freedom, they saw the rise of Fascism and the spread of war. When he went to Spain during the Civil War, Catlin realized that he was watching a dress rehearsal for the attack on Europe. At last the air war came to England, and at that point, once again, Brittain had to worry about those she loved. Fearful for their young children, Shirley and John, she and her husband sent them to the United States. The price she paid was the loss of three formative years in their lives. Still, she was more fortunate in World War II than she had been in World War I; those closest to her, her husband and children, all survived. When she traveled after the war, Brittain saw the devastation of Europe; she visited India and Pakistan; she met leaders from all over the world and heard their hopes and fears. Certainly she realized that atomic weapons posed a greater threat to the world than anything that had existed earlier. Nevertheless, the absence of personal tragedy makes *Testament of Experience* a much happier book from *Testament of Youth*.

Where *Testament of Youth* and *Testament of Experience* alternate between personal and public events, *Testament of Friendship* moves in parallel lines, alternating between the two women whose relationship is the subject of the book. After an initially hostile encounter at Somerville College, Oxford, Brittain and Holtby became close friends. Both women had war experience; the fact that she, too, had seen the war at first hand enabled Holtby to convince Brittain that she must move out of the bitter self-righteousness that was isolating her from her classmates. Both women were feminists, aware of the dangers of marriage. Both women were writers, struggling to make reputations for themselves. Both had a strong sense of social responsibility.

Their personalities, however, were quite different. Brittain was serious and emotional; she profited from the contact with high-spirited, outgoing Holtby, who regularly aided strangers and ended up their intimate friends. On the other hand, Holtby, whose writing was less polished than Brittain's, needed her friend's critical help. It is a testimony to the depth of their feeling for each other that it could transcend Holtby's success when Brittain was still unpublished and later occasions when the situation was reversed.

Because both women saw the need for social reform and yet were driven to write, they could talk about the conflict that is a major theme of *Testament of Friendship*: the opposition between the demands of the artistic self and those of the social self. The result may have been a dilution of effort, yet neither Holtby nor Brittain could exclude either drive from her life.

In another area, Brittain and Holtby took different paths. Persuaded that Catlin would enhance her career, not destroy it, Brittain left Holtby, with whom she had lived for three years, in order to marry, and then went to the United States with her husband. Initially, it seemed that Brittain's marriage would end the friendship, but after she returned, she and Holtby once again became close, and the latter also became fond of Catlin. For Holtby, marriage did not seem to be indicated, perhaps because she had chosen not to risk it, perhaps because the man she loved, who was charming and irresponsible, insisted on disappearing for months and years whenever he took a fancy. Only when she was dying did he seem to recognize her need; summoned, he came, and she died believing that they were to be married at last.

Although both Holtby and Brittain were public figures, this book is primarily an account of a private relationship. Antifeminists who insist that women cannot maintain close friendships should be convinced by this tribute that they are wrong. Neither college disagreements nor personality differences, neither one's early success nor the other's marriage, neither frequent separation nor final death could break the bond that is honored in *Testament of Friendship*.

Critical Context

For a long time, Vera Brittain was noted chiefly as the author of *Testament of Youth*, generally agreed to be the best, if not the only, account by a woman of the spiritual and psychological effects of World War I. Critics pointed out Brittain's own insistence that her life was typical; by studying it, they could understand both her generation's initial idealism, even gullibility, and its postwar disillusionment.

Testament of Friendship was generally regarded as interesting, but inferior to *Testament of Youth*; *Testament of Experience* brought mixed reviews. Many critics believed that it lacked the single focus of *Testament of Youth*; they resented Brittain's assumption that readers would find the details of her marriage and her travels as interesting as the significant observations on world affairs which she interspersed. Others, however, found *Testament of Experience* important because it did reveal a life that was whole. It might be argued that Brittain's later autobiographical book was intended to show a merging of idealism with reality, a reconciliation of the artistic and social selves, and, above all, a proof that marriage and motherhood need not negate a woman's being but can instead deepen her understanding of life. Even though *Testament of Youth* will probably always be ranked as Brittain's finest work, her story is incomplete without those two books in which she illustrates the triumph of hope over despair.

Sources for Further Study

Chambers, Peggy. "Vera Brittain," in *Women and the World Today*, 1954.

Delany, Paul. "Playing Fields, Flanders Fields," in *London Review of Books*. January 21-February 3, 1982, pp. 22-23.

Gray, James. "Hypatia at the Helm," in *On Second Thought*, 1946.

Haig, Rhondda Margaret. *Leisured Women*, 1928.

―――――――――. *This Was My World*, 1933.

Mellown, Muriel. "Vera Brittain: Feminist in a New Age," in *Feminist Theorists: Three Centuries of Key Women Thinkers*, 1983. Edited by Dale Spender.

Ringel, Fred J. "The 'Lost Generation,'" in *The Nation*. CXXXVII (October 18, 1933), pp. 454-455.

Rosemary M. Canfield Reisman

TESTIMONY
The Memoirs of Dmitri Shostakovich

Author: Dmitri Shostakovich (1906-1975)
Edited by Solomon Volkov
Type of work: Memoir
Time of work: 1906-1975
Locale: The Soviet Union
First published: 1979

Principal personages:
DMITRI SHOSTAKOVICH, a preeminent Soviet composer
JOSEPH STALIN, the General Secretary of the Soviet Communist
  Party and leader of the Soviet Union, 1928-1953
ALEKSANDR GLAZUNOV, a noted Russian composer, director of the
  Petrograd (Leningrad) Conservatory, 1905-1928

Form and Content

Testimony is the story of Dmitri Shostakovich's life from his childhood to just before his death in 1975. The autobiography was written in 1974 and 1975, with the assistance of the music critic Solomon Volkov, Shostakovich's friend, who transcribed his conversations with the composer, edited them, and wrote the introduction. Shostakovich undertook the project on the condition that Volkov would not publish the book until after his death.

Shostakovich asserts (not entirely convincingly) that his own life is not interesting, but he suggests that there is value in revealing the truth about those whom he has known. In the course of relating a series of vignettes about these diverse people and his relations with them, he provides a vivid history of Soviet culture, particularly its music and theater. The people whom Shostakovich discusses are chiefly Soviet figures, but some foreigners are included as well.

In the English translation Shostakovich's memoirs comprise 291 pages, with an additional forty-two pages of introductory material. The book also contains thirty-nine photographs, a listing of Shostakovich's major compositions, titles, and awards, an index, and detailed notes about most of the persons Shostakovich mentions. Although originally written in Russian, the work was first published in English, translated by Antonina W. Bouis. In his preface, Volkov recounts the origin of the book. Shostakovich, whom Volkov first met in 1960, asked Volkov to work with him on his memoirs beginning in 1971 after the latter had published a prominent work on Leningrad composers. Volkov suggests that Shostakovich chose him because of his youth and his devotion to music. He believes that Shostakovich decided to record his memoirs in order to justify himself, as he had been criticized for many years for not speaking out against the Soviet authorities. In an introduction following the preface, Volkov gives an overview of Shostakovich's life and work.

The text of the memoir is divided into eight untitled and unnumbered chapters, sustained sections appropriately combined by Volkov with Shostakovich's approval. The first deals with Shostakovich's reasons for recording his memoirs and his early training. In the second chapter, he talks about his life at the Petrograd Conservatory and his relationship to his teacher Aleksandr Glazunov. The third chapter concerns the late 1920's, when Shostakovich was at the Moscow Art Theatre; he reminisces about his relationship with Vsevolod Meyerhold and Marshal Mikhail Tukhachevsky. The fourth chapter is chiefly about the period during which Shostakovich was in disgrace (1936-1941) because of his opera *Ledi Makbet Mtsenskogo* (1934; Lady Macbeth of the Mtsensk District). The next includes some reflections on the harshness of the 1930's and on Glazunov. The last three chapters contain more of his reminiscences about Soviet and foreign intellectuals and their attitudes toward Stalin's Soviet Union in the 1930's and 1940's. These recollections, however, do not proceed in strict chronological order; throughout, Shostakovich refers to incidents from his past out of sequence. He only briefly touches on experiences he had after World War II. Furthermore, Shostakovich does not discuss his music very much except as it affected the society and politics of the time. This is a work portraying Russian society, not a technical monograph on musicology.

Analysis

Dmitri Shostakovich stands among the giants of modern music. He is also part of the paradox of Soviet culture. Both conservatives and liberals have accused Soviet authorities of stifling that culture, but it has survived and flourished in the twentieth century. Shostakovich is a prime example. In a long and productive career he wrote fifteen symphonies, six concerti, operas, film scores, preludes, sonatas, and scores of other works.

Shostakovich was born in 1906 into a family of Polish descent in St. Petersburg. His mother began to teach him piano at the age of seven (rather late for someone destined for such greatness). While still a child, he studied with Ignati Gliasser, but he left when he began to surpass his instructor. In 1917, Shostakovich entered the Petrograd Conservatory to study piano and composition with Aleksandr Glazunov.

Glazunov is one of the main heroes of *Testimony*. As the heir to composers such as Pyotr Ilich Tchaikovsky, Modest Mussorgsky and Nikolai Rimsky-Korsakov, Glazunov linked the golden age of nineteenth century Russian music with that of the twentieth. Shostakovich counts him among the best of Russia's composers, although at the time he was celebrated more at home than abroad. Shostakovich finds this odd, as he believes that Russian musicians attain much of their popularity at home from their reputations abroad, reflecting the paradoxical love/hate relationship Russians have with things foreign—an inferiority complex of sorts which the author finds irritating.

At the conservatory Shostakovich was a particular favorite of Glazunov. In 1919, during the Soviet Civil War, the government imposed a prohibition against alcoholic beverages—a ban enforced by draconian penalties. Shostakovich's father, a biologist who worked for the Bureau of Standards, had special permission to receive grain alcohol, which he supplied to the alcoholic Glazunov. Shostakovich's fellow students believed that his grades were based on this bootlegging rather than on merit, but the author claims that this was not true and gives examples when Glazunov judged his work rather harshly.

In his youth Shostakovich mocked Glazunov as a relic of the old era, but after reaching maturity and having lived through the tyranny of Joseph Stalin and the hypocrisy of Nikita Khrushchev he came to appreciate the lessons Glazunov taught on living—lessons which were even more important than his music. Ironically Shostakovich sums up Glazunov's life by recalling "an ancient prayer"—the serenity prayer of Alcoholics Anonymous: "Lord, grant me the strength to change what can be changed, Lord, grant me the strength to bear what can't be changed. And Lord, grant me the wisdom to know the difference." Shostakovich says he does not know whether he loves the prayer or hates it.

Shostakovich composed his first major work, *First Symphony* (1926), in 1924-1925. It was an immediate success, and his reputation in the Soviet Union was established. This was a period of artistic ferment and bitter conflict as rival groups sought to set the course of the arts in the new Soviet state. In this heady atmosphere Shostakovich joined the Moscow Art Theatre and worked with Vsevolod Meyerhold and Vladimir Mayakovski. The experimentation of the 1920's soon came to end, however, as Stalin consolidated his power over every aspect of Soviet life.

Shostakovich recalls this era with bitter sarcasm mixed with subtle wit and black humor. Tragedy soon becomes farce, he maintains; another person's fear seems ludicrous when retold. Shostakovich himself became the object of Stalin's wrath with his opera *Ledi Makbet Mtsenskoga*, part of a cycle of operas he planned depicting Russian women. This opera was based on a tragedy of pre-Revolutionary Russia by Nikolay Leskov ("Ledi Makbet Mtsenskogo uezda," 1865; English translation, 1922), but it was also an Aesopian fable lamenting contemporary conditions. Stalin was not fooled. After its debut, Shostakovich—on tour in Northern Russia having just returned from Turkey as an honored Soviet cultural figure—read an article titled "Muddle Instead of Music," attacking his opera. Some thought and still think that this vituperative piece was written by the hack David Zaslavsky, but Shostakovich is convinced that it was written by Stalin himself. Immediately, Shostakovich became an outcast, but he survived and indeed once more rose to the highest honors, even during the time of Stalin.

World War II was a period of liberation for Shostakovich. In the 1930's during the purges the intellectuals had to be silent, but when the war came they could openly grieve for their losses—not only for those killed in the war but for the victims of the purges as well. The world, Shostakovich maintains, does not understand his seventh and eighth symphonies, which constitute his interpretation of Anna Akhmatova's poem *Rekviem* (1963; *Requiem*, 1964)—a requiem for friends swept up in the terror.

During the war Shostakovich's international reputation grew. At one point he was the subject of a cover story in *Time* magazine (July 20, 1942). His standing in the Soviet Union also was restored. Later, however, Shostakovich aroused Khruschev's displeasure by introducing Jewish themes in his works. He had a keen interest in Jewish folk music and a great love for the pathos of Jewish folksongs. He also had a deep hatred of anti-Semitism, Russian as well as German. Although he was not Jewish, he had many Jewish friends and students.

The leaders of the Soviet Union move in and out of Shostakovich's autobiography, especially Stalin, the bogeyman of the Soviet intellectuals. (Indeed, Stalin rather than Shostakovich may be the central character of the work.) Shostakovich did not know any of these political leaders personally except the great general Marshal Tukhachevsky, whom Stalin had executed in 1937. Shostakovich in his bitterly ironic style castigates Stalin as the friend and spiritual brother of Adolf Hitler, but shows more personal contempt against those who claimed to be tricked by him. ("[W]ho was tricked? An illiterate old milkmaid?")

Stalin was exceptionally suspicious and, probably as a result of his early seminary training, had a great fear of priests. Shostakovich tells the story of how the eccentric pianist Maria Yudina, Shostakovich's classmate, once wrote an insulting letter to Stalin but survived because of its religious message. Shostakovich also dwells on the love of the Soviet intelligentsia for William Shakespeare's plays, particularly his favorites *Hamlet, Prince of Denmark*, *Macbeth*, and *King Lear*. Stalin, however, disliked Shakespeare—because of the violence against leadership in *Macbeth* and *Hamlet*, Shostakovich suggests.

Shostakovich does not have kind words for the West either. He visited the United States and Great Britain several times and was neither happy nor particularly impressed. Indeed, Shostakovich is frequently harsh in his judgments, and his barbs wound some of the greats of this century—Soviets and foreigners alike: Arturo Toscanini as well as Sergey Prokofiev; George Bernard Shaw as well as Aleksandr Solzhenitsyn. He is particularly intolerant of hypocrites and snobs. On the other hand he is a staunch defender of his friends and his mentors, many of whom suffered greatly during the purges of the 1930's.

Critical Context

When *Testimony* was published in the West after Shostakovich's death, his relatives denounced it as a fraud. This reaction was probably motivated by fear of reprisals, although Shostakovich does not attack Socialism, the Soviet system itself, or the Russian motherland. He was a great defender of Russia even though he himself was of Polish descent and his great-grandfather and grandfather had participated in the Polish uprisings against the czars in 1830 and 1863. With *Testimony*, Shostakovich stands not only as a musical giant of the twentieth century but also as an important witness of Soviet society, adding his voice to those of Nadezhda Mandelstam, Solzhenitsyn, and others who have recorded the horrors and absurdities of Stalinism. In particular, *Testimony* provides a picture of Stalin which can aid in evaluating one of the most controversial leaders of the modern age.

Shostakovich's autobiography is a book of contradictions. Here is a party man denouncing the Party. He relates a tale of hardship, sorrow, and fear. He describes the slanders and denunciations he underwent. Yet he was honored throughout his life, winning the Stalin Prize—awarded by the general secretary himself—thirteen times from 1941 to 1951. Nevertheless, honesty is the basis and survival is the theme of this autobiography. In one part Shostakovich tells of his enjoyment of the American musical comedy *Fiddler on the Roof*, which he saw in New York. He understood the message of the show to be a yearning for the homeland. Shostakovich himself, however, was also a fiddler on the roof, trying to hold his balance while scratching out a passable tune.

Sources for Further Study
Devlin, James. *Shostakovich*, 1983.
Norris, Christopher, ed. *Shostakovich: The Man and His Music*, 1982.
Roseberry. *Shostakovich: His Life and Times*, 1981.
Sollertinsky, Dmitri, and Ludmilla Sollertinsky. *Pages from the Life of Dmitri Shostakovich*, 1980.

Frederick B. Chary

THE THEATER AND ITS DOUBLE

Author: Antonin Artaud (1896-1948)
Type of work: Theater criticism
First published: Le Théâtre et son double, 1938 (English translation, 1958)

Form and Content

After he had completed his play *Les Cenci* (1935; *The Cenci*, 1969), Antonin Artaud conceived of the idea of collecting his writings on theater into a book that would outline his vision for a new kind of theater. Despite his failure to realize his vision in his production of *The Cenci*, Artaud continued to prepare new articles for his book and to crystallize his thinking on theater as he journeyed to Mexico to investigate the ritual performances of the Indians. In mid-voyage, Artaud settled on *The Theater and Its Double* as the title for his seminal work on theater, and he proofed the final copy upon his return to France. Artaud was an erratic genius plagued by a lifelong mental illness, to which he finally succumbed. By the time *The Theater and Its Double* was printed in 1938, Artaud had been institutionalized and remained so until 1946.

The Theater and Its Double is a collection of visionary essays, heated lectures, formal manifestos, defensive letters, and insightful reviews. All the works were written between 1931 and 1936. Some of them had already appeared in periodicals and pamphlets or had been delivered as lectures, while others were written specifically for publication in book form. Artaud himself arranged the order of the works, ignoring the chronological sequence in which they were written.

Although the book is by no means the work of a systematic thinker, it does have a loosely defined shape, moving from generalities to specifics. First, it discusses the metaphysical foundations for Artaud's plans to reform theater; then it shows how those plans would be put into action. In his preface, "The Theater and Culture," Artaud notes the demise of Western culture and its inability to confront the crucial needs of the modern individual. Because culture is impotent and ineffectual, Artaud calls for a new art form centered on a dynamic theater. Next, Artaud gives form to his revolutionary ideas by focusing on three metaphors: the plague, the metaphysics of action, and alchemy. In each of the first three essays in the book ("The Theater and the Plague," "Metaphysics and the *Mise en Scène*," and "The Alchemical Theater"), Artaud describes a violent upheaval, a process of transformation, and a rite of purification. In these essays, Artaud speaks with a voice of prophetic urgency, mixing graphic descriptions with deeply mystical pronouncements. He compares his theater to the plague. Both are violent and cataclysmic events which overturn the social order and purge the population. By reproducing the chaotic effects of the plague, theater can purify an audience through a "redeeming epidemic," much like a vaccine. Second, Artaud compares the theater to "metaphysics in action." Through the presentation of a series of signs and symbols, the theater becomes a transcendent experience which elevates the audience into a world of spiritual ecstasy. Finally, Artaud compares theater to alchemy. Both use essential ingredients and symbolic formulas to create a physical form and to distill it into a spiritual essence. By using these metaphors to explain his views on theater, Artaud sets the tone for the rest of his book: Theater is a powerful force that can work a magical transformation upon an audience. The next two essays in the book advance this theme as they contrast Western theater, which is detached and divorced from the crucial myths of humanity, with Oriental theater, which is vital, physical, and transcendental. Having established the purpose of his new theater and its roots in Oriental drama, Artaud, in his next essay, "No More Masterpieces," urges modern theater to abandon its traditional repertoire of time-worn and irrelevant works and to create a new theater that speaks directly to the needs of the times. Interweaving all his previous themes, Artaud finally pulls together his ideas into a plan of action. In two manifestos, interrupted by a series of letters clarifying his position, Artaud clearly outlines the form of his new Theatre of Cruelty, detailing its structure and purpose. Artaud concludes with an article on acting, followed by two reviews that illustrate his ideas. Thus, *The Theater and Its Double* moves clearly from the abstract to the concrete, from theory to practice.

All the works in the book hammer home Artaud's major theme. The modern age is one of anxiety and uncertainty. Art and culture have grown stagnant and detached. Modern theater, in particular, has lost touch with its audience. Artaud's remedy is a new, revitalized theater based on violent images and on ritualized performance techniques that have the ability to move an audience intensely. For this transformation to take place, theater must be reformed in all of its aspects.

Analysis

Artaud saw the modern age as a time of great uncertainty in which all the old values had disintegrated. With the sense of a prophet who has an urgent mission to accomplish, Artaud vehemently attacked the culture of his day. For Artaud, art had become fossilized, detached, and elitist. It had become much more concerned with form and aesthetics than with the underlying mystery of being. The theater had become a slave to the written text, a subgenre of literature, and a showcase for tired old masterpieces written in a language that was dead and that failed to speak to the needs of the present generation. This outmoded theater probed into psychological problems and scrutinized the petty conflicts of particular individuals. It was concerned with analyzing and dissecting the human psyche in order to reduce the unknown to the known. Characters constantly used words to explain and jabber away about their feelings. By engaging in endless debates, the old dramas reduced theater to an intellectual exercise devoid of mystery. Furthermore, Artaud saw the audiences of his day as a group of voyeurs watching theater like Peeping Toms. He attacked this theater as a "digestive theatre," where audiences merely absorbed performances but were not deeply affected by them. He wanted to replace this theater with a Theatre of Cruelty.

For Artaud, cruelty did not mean bloodshed, torture, or mere sensationalism. He believed that humanity's fate is locked into a rigid determinism and is controlled by dark, sinister forces. This determinism creates a sense of cruelty that humanity must face. Thus, Artaud wanted to create a theater that would act like a magic rite of purification and would impinge on all the senses of the audience members, assaulting their nervous sytems in order to reach deep down into their unconscious minds and bring to the surface of their consciousness a new sense of self-awareness. Such shock therapy would evoke in the audience members a transcendent experience and would elicit from them a powerful upsurge of feelings.

For theater to have this effect, it had to be completely revolutionized. Thus, Artaud carefully delineated his plans for a new, revitalized theater. First, since verbal language was dead, sterile, and ineffectual, theater must end its attachment to the written text and create a visual, nonverbal language of sights, sounds, and gestures. Artaud was perceptive enough to realize that theater had the potential to go beyond staged dialogue. He wanted the theater to use its ability to create startling pictorial and kinetic images. Words would be transposed and used in unusual contexts. They would be reworked into incantations, chanted for their sound effects, or spoken with unusual inflections. Screams, shrieks, and singsong melodies would replace much of the traditional dialogue. The traditional author, divorced from the production, would be replaced by a director/creator. This director, acting like a divinely inspired shaman, would create his own theatrical work within the rehearsal process and would completely control all aspects of production. Artaud was ahead of his time in seeing the potential for the director to become the dominant creative artist in the nonrealistic theater. He also saw that directors did not have to be completely faithful to the text. The standard series of classical plays would be abandoned or would be adapted and stripped of their texts "using only accouterments of period, situations, characters, and action." Performances would be created out of themes, events, or other sources, not from a written text.

Artaud realized that theater could go beyond the bourgeois concerns of love and money. He wanted his Theater of Cruelty to explore cosmic themes, focusing on wars, revolutions, and cataclysmic events. Theater would return to myths and sacred texts, to a world of ritual and exorcism. Artaud suggested that theater use such grandiose events as the fall of Jerusalem or the conquest of Mexico. The theater would not, however, simply mirror history. Characters would no longer be psychological types concerned with individual problems; instead, they would be raised to the stature of gods, heroes, and monsters, engaged in cosmic warfare. Performance would not center on conflicts between individuals but on conflicts between spiritual forces.

Such a theater would be based on a series of violent and sensual images. Gestures would become a part of a codified language of signs and symbols. Artaud realized that the true spiritual idea could be reached only through symbols. Even facial gestures needed to be codified into a series of meaningful symbolic types. For Artaud, "an image, an allegory, a figure that masks what it would reveal [has] more significance for the spirit than the lucidities of speech and analytics."

Artaud also wanted to use all the elements of the theater to create a bombardment of vivid images. Musical instruments able to produce dissonant tones would accompany performances, creating piercing sounds. Costumes would be neither modern nor historical but would resemble ritual garb. Lighting would strain the range of the color spectrum and would be shot across the audience in waves and bands in order to create sensations of heat and cold. Artaud's theater would not need a set. The characters would be walking hieroglyphs. Objects would be distorted in size and shape. Enormous manikins and puppets would populate the acting area, and actors would be masked.

Artaud realized that his new style of performance would call for a new acting space, and thus, he helped revolutionize the concept of theater architecture. Theater would abandon the traditional auditorium and take place in found spaces, such as barns or hangars. In order to establish direct contact between the spectator and the spectacle, the audience would be located in the center of a vacant area and would be seated in swivel chairs as they watched a performance surround them. The action would envelop the audience, taking place not only in all four corners of the theater space but on overhead galleries and catwalks. Scenes would pop up unannounced anywhere in the theater space, and actions would fluctuate from one area to another. Sometimes several actions would take place simultaneously. Lights would be focused on the audience as well as the performers. Such a performance area would allow for the maximum use of space.

Artaud's book is a revolutionary document, indeed, for Artaud turned the realistic theater topsy-turvy. He foresaw a theater that would operate in a spatiotemporal dimension instead of a verbal one. He proposed a plan for making the audience an essential part of the spectacle, and he realized that theater could have a profound effect if it returned to its primitive origins. He clearly sums up his position in one of his oracular pronouncements, proclaiming that "a play disturbs the senses' repose, frees the repressed unconscious, incites a virtual revolt . . . and imposes on the assembled collectivity an attitude that is both difficult and heroic."

Critical Context

Artaud lived in a time in which realism was under attack from a number of literary movements. One such movement was surrealism, which stressed dream visions and advocated striking juxtapositions of disparate images. Artaud was active in the surrealist movement but soon broke away from it for political reasons. Most of his critical writings focus on the experimentation with language and on the anarchical nature of poetry. *The Theater and Its Double* is the culmination of his thinking. In it, he sees theater as the ultimate art form, one that can totally escape language and logic. Unfortunately, Artaud was not able to realize his dreams; his own ventures in theater were dismal failures. His ideas were to come to fruition in the artistic revolution of the 1960's. His book reads almost like a blueprint for the changes in the avant-garde theater that were to occur more than two decades later. Traditional theater spaces were abandoned, and theater moved into the streets, into churches, into abandoned warehouses, into rock quarries. Partially influenced by Artaud, American director Richard Schechner produced plays in a garage, put the audience in the center of the action, and created multilevel theater spaces. Julian Beck, another American influenced by Artaud, created ritual theater encouraging direct contact with audience members. British director Peter Brook helped organize a company called The Theatre of Cruelty. Its productions experimented with chants, ritual dance, symbolic props, and other techniques proposed by Artaud. During this period, enormous puppets replaced actors, classical plays were rewritten, performance pieces were created without using playwrights, and psychedelic light shows became the craze. Realistic productions gave way to a theater of fantastic and phantasmagoric images. Artaud was alive and well and his book became a best-seller among the leading theater practitioners of the avant-garde.

Dramatic criticism was also influenced by Artaud. Major theater journals abandoned literary criticism and began to focus on the science of performance studies as theater branched out into the fields of anthropology and structuralism. Everything from voodoo rituals to modern carnivals became the subject matter for this discipline. Artaud's vision of a mystical theater thus radically changed the concept of theatrical performance. Whether one agrees with its theories, *The Theater and Its Double* has become required reading for any serious student of the theater. Artaud stands with Bertolt Brecht as one of the leading voices in modern theater.

Sources for Further Study
Bermel, Albert. *Artaud's Theatre of Cruelty*, 1977.
Costich, Julia F. *Antonin Artaud*, 1978.
Esslin, Martin. *Antonin Artaud*, 1976.
Greene, Naomi. *Antonin Artaud: Poet Without Words*, 1970.
Hayman, Ronald. *Artaud and After*, 1977.
Knapp, Bettina. *Antonin Artaud: Man of Vision*, 1969.
Sellin, Eric. *The Dramatic Concepts of Antonin Artaud*, 1968.

Paul Rosefeldt

THESE THE COMPANIONS
Recollections

Author: Donald Davie (1922-)
Type of work: Autobiography
Time of work: 1922-1979
Locale: Great Britain, Ireland, the Soviet Union, the United States, and Italy
First published: 1982

Principal personages:
DONALD DAVIE, an English poet, teacher, and literary critic
F. R. LEAVIS, an English literary critic
YVOR WINTERS, an American literary critic
PHILIP LARKIN, an English poet
C. S. LEWIS, an English writer, literary critic, and Christian
　　apologist
AUSTIN CLARKE, an Irish poet
WACŁAW LEDNICKI, a Polish scholar

Form and Content

Donald Davie is a well-traveled and well-respected poet, literary critic, and academic. His life has centered on words, the makers of words, and those places where works of the imagination are valued. In this autobiography he remembers some of those words, those makers, and those places. Davie realizes that many people do not share his love of words and the imagination, and that others will not think his life particularly enlightening on these things. Yet his sense of responsibility to record a perhaps disappearing notion of literary culture triumphed over the paralyzing "Who cares?"—and the result is an engaging series of scenes from a literary life.

These the Companions: Recollections is an autobiography which is only indirectly concerned with its author. Much like Ernest Hemingway in *A Moveable Feast* (1964), Davie reveals himself primarily by writing about those around him. He takes his title from a phrase in Ezra Pound's *The Pisan Cantos* (1948), a work written at a similar time in Pound's life in a similar spirit of gazing back over a life and assessing its accomplishments and failures. Like Pound, Davie finds much of the value of his life to have derived from the people and places he came to know, and from an attitude toward culture to which he has tried to contribute.

Along with his title, Davie seems to derive part of the book's methodology from Pound. Pound's infamous "ideogrammic method" for writing poetry called for placing side by side "luminous details," those apparently insignificant details from life that are in fact carefully chosen to illuminate surrounding circumstances, the significance of which is left to the reader to ascertain or construct. Davie uses a similar strategy in *These the Companions*. Rather than offer an exhaustive recounting of his life, he focuses on a handful of times and locales, capturing in relatively few strokes the tone and temper of the time, the people, and himself. The relationship between one episode and the next—say between his war years in the Soviet Union and his postwar years at Cambridge—is left largely unstated, but the cumulative effect is to create an increasingly rounded picture of a man of letters and of a fading idea of culture.

Another insight into the style of *These the Companions* is found in the chapter titled "Americans," in which he notes the American love of "feeling their way" along in their approach to life. Something of that sort describes the strategy and tone of these recollections as well. Davie repeatedly makes a proclamation or sketches a memory or offers an evaluation only to qualify or cancel it with a phrase to suggest that he has not got it right, or that he is putting on airs, or that he is wearied of his own attempts at self-justification. This self-deprecation is in part a conscious strategy with specific intended effects, one of which is to lend a relaxed, intimate, and appealingly nondogmatic quality to the work.

Yet Davie the autobiographer is also still Davie the poet. His ability to evoke place, and the aesthetic implications of place, is crucial to the success of these recollections. For example, he muses on poetry in his beloved Cambridge:

> But now as when Leavis began, the poems that come out of Cambridge are just what they always were: at best sensitive, intelligent, well-mannered, but never conclusively and passionately *clinched*. I am prepared to believe, now, that this is inevitable. It is a matter of light, and the climate. As the fog swirls into Trinity Street in the early afternoon, or hangs there until nearly midday, as the warm lights high in the walls wink on and glow through the haze, I recognize the irremediably Gothic Cambridge that I best know and love. And how can the art that comes of such weather be anything but crepuscular, approximate, a composition of fugitive or hulking shadows?

As with most effective autobiography, Davie's gift with words and his guiding sensibility make compelling what would otherwise be the mundane details of a seemingly unexceptional life.

Another part of the attraction of this book is the names and reputations to which Davie's remembrances give flesh: F. R. Leavis, Yvor Winters, Hugh Kenner, C. S. Lewis, and numerous less known figures. To some he offers homage; with others he settles scores, unable to resist the writer's ultimate last weapon—having the last word. (Davie is usually more generous to others, however, than he is to himself.) In the process, he lightly seasons his recollections with the kind of insider literary anecdotes that delight the bibliophile. He recounts Kenner's story of Pound's response to a critical comment about T. S. Eliot: "Never under-estimate the Possum [Eliot]; he has a lot of low vitality—like a crocodile."

Analysis

These the Companions displays an ambivalent attitude toward the past it is trying to recapture. Davie declares in the preface, with the protective self-deprecation that he uses throughout, that he is "presumptuous not for myself but on behalf of . . . the imagination." His problem, however, is "to recollect in the imagination a past that all the same shall not be imaginary." Davie repeatedly questions the accuracy or validity of his own memory. It is tempting to remember the slag heaps of his northern England home as ugly and blighting, but he doubts they ever appeared to him that way in his boyhood. Elsewhere he warns himself against rigging evidence in retrospect to support a present bias. On another occasion, he concedes that memory simply can lie.

Davie's response to the problem, like that of many modern writers, is, in part, to embrace it. Memory cannot be separated from imagination. Eliot affirmed that not only does the past shape the present, but the present shapes our understanding of the past as well. So Davie concedes the power of the imagination to create a past which one can never fully verify. It is perhaps no accident that he begins the book by recounting not his boyhood directly, but a dream he had as an adult of a return to his boyhood home. In dream the imagination rules absolutely; in memory perhaps only somewhat less so.

A richly imaginative exercise of memory is one of the qualities Davie prizes most highly—and sees most in decline in contemporary society. He laments the almost complete lack of "the faculty of pious memory" in his philistine southwest England in-laws, and he wonders at what point England will have so little left of its cultural heritage that there will be no point in trying to rekindle it.

Davie laments the decline of this kind of imagination, which he also describes as a kind of "cherishing," not only in England but indeed in modern culture as a whole. He contrasts it with more radical, apocalyptic views of the imagination which see it as inventing or remaking reality, a romantic outlook that goes against Davie's neoclassical grain.

Davie's view of the imagination is only one indication of his sense of being out of step with his age. He feels himself to be a citizen of a passing world, one where the written word was sovereign, where aesthetic and moral values intertwined, where great works of literature defined the cultural landscape. His mother had memorized most, if not all, of the most popular anthology of English literature of her time, and Davie sees this love of words in his home as having shaped him: "If I am so literary myself that I sometimes despair of breaking through a cocoon of words to a reality outside them, that is above all my mother's doing. And I am grateful, mostly." Characteristically, his memories of the Soviet Union during the war are woven through with the books with which he filled his young mind. While many distinguish between books and the so-called real world, Davie asserts that "reality is measured and underwritten . . . by the records of the imagination."

Davie labels himself an anachronistic survivor of a literary civilization whose very idea is now widely ridiculed. Ironically, among its greatest enemies are current writers and critics. Davie is an unrepentant cultural conservative in an avant-garde, pluralistic age. The latter part of *These the Companions* particularly takes up arms against the contemporary deification of literary criticism and theory coupled with a slackening of poetic standards, the vulgarization of sex in literature, the loss of moral vision, and, particularly in England, the general antipathy (in the name of egalitarianism) to excellence.

Davie finds refuge from such foolishness in, among others, the great Russian writers of the past and present. He contrasts their ability to affirm life despite suffering (or because of it) with the sterile nay-saying of so many of his contemporaries. Davie's own moral earnestness, his tendency toward didacticism in his poetry, draws him to the Russian expectation that writers should be teachers—even prophets—as well as witnesses. Alexander Pushkin, he saw, "was a conscience as well as a consciousness," a combination that squares well with Davie's boyhood Baptist understanding of "witness."

A common thread in this autobiography is a sense of a lost center in modern life, one manifestation of which is lowered artistic standards and a dulled historical and ethical sense. Davie is aware that linking aesthetic, ethical, and social values together has been out of favor since the latter part of the nineteenth century. He is unapologetic about doing so, but at the same time aware that his own temperament and choices have their limitations as well.

Critical Context

In *These the Companions*, as in both his poetry and his scholarly work, Davie consciously goes against the tide of contemporary culture. The contemporary literary scene is dominated by theories of language and texts according to which genuine meaning is nearly impossible because of the ambiguous, self-destructing nature of words. Ethical and moral considerations, whether arising from the text or brought to it, have long been seen as irrelevant. In many circles, close attention to the craft and tradition of poetry has been secondary to notions of self-expression or to sincerity of feeling or politics.

Davie registers his complaint against these trends, and records his own different path, without expending much effort to refute them. There is a sort of diffidence in Davie's autobiography that perhaps grows out of his sense of his own shortcomings and from the awareness that he has fought the good fight in other contexts.

Those other contexts include both his poetry and his academic writing. Davie is known in both these areas as a defender of classical qualities: restraint, control, urbanity, wit, formal elegance, and public morality. In the 1950's he was associated with a loose affiliation of writers known as "the Movement," who reacted against what they saw as the romantic excesses of the Anglo-American modernists and later poets such as Dylan Thomas, Robert Lowell, and Sylvia Plath, whose poetry was marked by verbal and emotional self-indulgence.

These the Companions is consistent with Davie's lifelong work. It is sometimes poignant yet emotionally restrained. It speaks out for classical values in a romantic age, yet with a certain sense of defeat that is also found in Davie's later poetry. It reflects Davie's desire for something more stable than that provided by twentieth century culture, yet also demonstrates once again his great interest in poets such as

Pound (about whom he has written two books) whose basic approach to poetry is at odds with his own.

Sources for Further Study

Bedient, Calvin. "Donald Davie," in *Eight Contemporary Poets*, 1974.

Dekker, George, ed. *Donald Davie and the Responsibilities of Literature*, 1984.

Powell, Neil. *Carpenters of Light: Some Contemporary English Poets*, 1980.

Rawson, Claude. Review in *The New York Times Book Review*. LXXXVII (November 21, 1982), p. 9.

Simpson, Louis. "Review" in *The Times Literary Supplement*. October 8, 1982, p. 1097.

Daniel Taylor

THE THIRTIES, THE FORTIES, and THE FIFTIES

Author: Edmund Wilson (1895-1972)
Edited by Leon Edel
Type of work: Autobiography
Time of work: 1930-1960
Locale: The United States, Europe, the Soviet Union, Haiti, and Israel
First published: The Thirties: From Notebooks and Diaries of the Period, 1980; *The Forties: From Notebooks and Diaries of the Period*, 1983; *The Fifties: From Notebooks and Diaries of the Period*, 1986

> *Principal personages:*
> EDMUND WILSON, a literary critic and writer of poetry, fiction, and plays
> MARY BLAIR, an actress, his first wife
> MARGARET CANBY, his second wife
> MARY McCARTHY, a novelist, his third wife
> ELENA MUMM THORNTON, his fourth wife
> F. SCOTT FITZGERALD, a novelist, his friend
> JOHN PEALE BISHOP, a poet, his friend
> EDNA ST. VINCENT MILLAY, a poet, his lover
> CHRISTIAN GAUSS, a professor at Princeton University, his mentor

Form and Content

These three books consist chiefly of Edmund Wilson's notes to himself about his life during the decades between 1930 and 1960. Less formal than his critical works or his studies in culture, they are not the day-by-day records of a diary, even though he sometimes recorded specific events: a party, a visit to New York, an argument with one of his wives, the death of a friend.

For the most part, however, Wilson's journals chronicle the events of a period of time, for example a two-month stay at his house in Wellfleet, on Cape Cod, or a summer spent in the family home he inherited in Talcottville, New York. Extensive entries in *The Thirties* detail his trips to various economically depressed areas of the United States and reflect his political commitment during that troubled decade; these observations formed the basis for his book *The American Jitters: A Year of the Slump* (1932; revised in 1958 as *The American Earthquake: A Documentary of the Twenties and Thirties*). A series of long entries in *The Forties* provides his impressions of Europe just after World War II, when he was sent abroad by *The New Yorker* to do a series of articles. These impressions were eventually formalized in his book *Europe Without Baedeker: Sketches Among the Ruins of Italy, Greece, and England* (1947). These are extended notes for novels which were never written, but also detailed entries in *The Thirties* about a working-class woman with whom Wilson had an affair that is the basis for an important segment of *Memoirs of Hecate County* (1946).

These journals are not random jottings. Like everything else Wilson wrote, they are for the most part formal and highly literate in style. Also like everything else he wrote, they were intended for publication; Wilson selected Leon Edel for the task of editing the journals long before his death. Edel, known chiefly for his five-volume biography of Henry James, was one of the few academic scholars Wilson respected, and he wanted his journals edited by a scholar. Edel performed his task conscientiously, providing explanatory notes for the many people mentioned in the journals (there is, however, a major omission in the absence of any index entry for Elena Mumm Thornton Wilson, Edmund Wilson's fourth wife, in *The Fifties*).

While they are carefully written, the journals are less formal in content and approach than any of Wilson's other writings. They are detailed, frank, and casual, for example, about his marriages and other sexual involvements, including his affair with and marriage to Elena Mumm Thornton, descendant of a once-wealthy German family. He records their sojourn in Reno, where he was getting a divorce from the writer Mary McCarthy and Thornton was obtaining one from her first husband; he is interested equally in Thornton's sexuality and the scenes and scenery of the West. Their wedding, late in 1946, is mentioned only casually. There is a strong contrast between the cool, measured cadences of Wilson's deliberate prose style and the explicit nature of some of his descriptions. This contrast grows more pronounced as he grows older, reaching a high point in *The Fifties*, when he speculates somewhat ponderously on whether his attraction to a lesbian friend shows a homosexual side to his own nature.

In the earlier volume, many of the entries are brief, dealing with scenes he observed, cities he visited, people he met, or gossip he heard. As time went on, he seems to have become more conscious of the likelihood that the journals would someday be published, and *The Fifties* is therefore less informal than *The Thirties*, more speculative and more coherent.

Analysis

The different emphases of the three sets of journals reflect the changing interests in Wilson's career. During the early thirties, as one of the editors of *The New Republic*, he was deeply engaged in left-wing politics and in reporting the ongoing labor struggles of the decade. He writes movingly of the long and bloody strike in Harlan County, Kentucky, and of Detroit in the early 1930's. Later in the decade he made a visit to the Soviet Union. He had completed much of the writing for his study of the evolution of French Socialism into Soviet Communism, *To the Finland Station: A Study in the Writing and Acting of History* (1940), but he considered that direct observation of the Soviet system at work was necessary to his book. He went as a detached observer; he liked many of the people he met but was aware of the flaws that were beginning to show in the system. During this decade he never turned his back on literature, always his consuming interest, but there are more references to writers with a political commitment and to political activists than to noninvolved writers. He is, for example, more interested in Upton Sinclair than in William

Faulkner; the index to *The Thirties* contains no references to Faulkner, who published five major novels during the decade.

In many ways, *The Thirties* is the most lively and exciting of these three volumes. Wilson had served his apprenticeship in the literary world during the 1920's; by 1930, he had written much of his groundbreaking critical book on literary modernism, *Axel's Castle: A Study in the Imaginative Literature of 1870-1930* (1931), and his reputation was firmly established. Divorced from his first wife, the actress Mary Blair, he embarked on a hectic and passionate (and brief) marriage to Margaret Canby. The Great Depression was under way, and with it the unemployment and social unrest that would last through the decade.

Wilson became more a reporter of politics than a literary critic. For him, as for many intellectuals, the emerging industrial labor unions and the politics of the Left seemed to hold the keys to needed changes, and they attracted his deep interest. He maintained his independence, however, never committing himself to a particular party or faction. His sympathy for the downtrodden was always to some degree tempered by his analytical nature. When others were becoming Communists or fellow travelers, Wilson made the origins and history of communism the subject of one of his finest historical studies, *To the Finland Station*.

Few journal entries or notes remain from the first half of the following decade, and *The Forties* is therefore the shortest and least informative of these volumes. His bibliography shows that he was highly active; between 1940 and 1943, he published *To the Finland Station*; worked at editing F. Scott Fitzgerald's *The Crack-Up: With Other Uncollected Pieces, Note-Books, and Unpublished Letters* (1945); and published critical studies titled *The Boys in the Back Room: Notes on California Novelists* (1941) and *The Wound and the Bow: Seven Studies in Literature* (1941), a collection of poems titled *Note-Books of Night* (1942), and a pioneering anthology of American literature, *The Shock of Recognition: The Development of Literature in the United States Recorded by the Men Who Made It* (1943). Nevertheless, by 1940, Wilson was middle-aged; Fitzgerald, who died in 1940, had been one of his best friends since they were at Princeton University together. In 1944, an even closer friend, the poet John Peale Bishop, also died. Canby had died in an accident in 1932, and he had been married to the novelist McCarthy, but by 1945 that marriage had deteriorated and he was deeply involved with Thornton, whom he would wed in the following year.

There were also financial problems. After living in New York City for twenty years, in 1941 he bought a house at Wellfleet on Cape Cod, which would continue to be one of his homes for the rest of his life, but he worried that he could hardly afford the purchase. His books were widely admired but were not widely sold, and he had no steady source of income until 1943, when he agreed to write regularly for *The New Yorker*, a commitment which paid him an annual salary and expense money to provide book reviews and extended articles on social subjects. His journal for this decade comes to life when he embarks on his postwar European voyage for *The New Yorker*.

The end of World War II marked a kind of watershed in Wilson's life and a time of renewal. His European trip confirmed his lifelong distrust of the British, but it also gave him an opportunity to be an early witness to the devastation wrought by the war. He traveled to Italy, to Greece, and to Crete, and learned at first hand about the atrocities committed by the German conquerors of Greece. *The New Yorker* gave his literary criticism a wide audience. At the age of fifty, he experienced with Thornton one of the most passionate episodes of his life; their marriage produced a daughter, Helen, in 1948. His second work of fiction, *Memoirs of Hecate County*, published in 1946, created a scandal because in one chapter, "The Princess with the Golden Hair," he included a number of sexual descriptions that were unusually explicit for the time. It also made him a considerable amount of money.

Later in the 1940's, he made other long trips. He traveled to the pueblo of Zuni in New Mexico to observe the traditional *shalako* ceremony, an experience which was to provide much material for *Red, Black, Blond, and Olive: Studies in Four Civilizations: Zuni, Haiti, Soviet Russia, Israel* (1956). His account of his stay in Zuni in 1947 is interesting in its descriptions of the pueblo itself, the Indian ceremonials, the masks, and the rituals. Additionally, it is acutely observant in Wilson's analysis of his hosts, anthropologists who were studying the Indians and who seemed to Wilson to be too far distanced from the people they studied. Two years later, he would make a trip to Haiti, where he was interested in another primitive society, but a very different one, on the verge of major changes.

The Fifties is the most poignant and magisterial of these three volumes. Early in the decade, Wilson was deeply depressed by another series of deaths among those closest to him. His great love from the 1920's, the poet Edna St. Vincent Millay, died in 1950; he had visited her last in 1948, and had been saddened to find her old. Her death was a stark reminder of his own advancing age and his mortality. His formal memoir of Millay is the concluding section of *The Shores of Light: A Literary Chronicle of the Twenties and Thirties* (1952); what he recorded in his journal was more open and intimate, less concerned to remind a later generation of what she had meant to him and to the 1920's. Early in 1951, Wilson's mother died, and later that year the great Princeton professor and dean Christian Gauss, Wilson's early mentor and lifelong inspiration, collapsed and died at Pennsylvania Station in New York.

As the decade progressed, however, Wilson's life became more and more satisfying. At his mother's death he had inherited her family's home at Talcottville, in upstate New York, and Wilson restored it and lived there for parts of the summers of the rest of his life. His wife disliked the old house and preferred to stay on Cape Cod; after several arguments, faithfully recorded in the journals, it was agreed that he would spend time at Talcottville by himself. The house and its furnishings gave him a strong sense of belonging to an old and valuable tradition, and its isolation provided him with time and solitude for undisturbed bouts of writing, away from the busy social round of Wellfleet.

By this time, Wilson was unquestionably the United States' best-known and most respected critic and its only genuine man of letters. The widely admired early study of modernism *Axel's Castle* had been followed by two wider-ranging studies, *Triple Thinkers: Ten Essays on Literature* (1938) and *The Wound and the Bow*, which had established even more clearly his preeminence among American literary critics. In addition to his criticism he had written novels, plays (such as *The Little Blue Light*, 1950, and *The Room and This Gin and These Sandwiches*, 1937), and poems (*Night Thoughts*, 1961). He was content in his marriage, although his sexual adventurings had not really ended, and he had achieved cordial relations with the children of his earlier marriages. The sales of his books and his occasional pieces in *The New Yorker* gave him financial security, despite careless bookkeeping which led to problems with the Internal Revenue Service; those problems dogged him throughout the decade and eventually gave him the subject for another book, *The Cold War and the Income Tax: A Protest* (1963).

He continued to be prolific. Early in the 1950's, he edited for publication his essays from the 1920's, 1930's, and 1940's, which appeared in two popular volumes, *Classics and Commercials: A Literary Chronicle of the Forties* (1950) and *The Shores of Light*. He became fascinated by the discoveries in the Middle Eastern Qumran caves of ancient scrolls dealing with the Essenes, traveled to Israel, and eventually wrote the controversial study *The Scrolls from the Dead Sea* (1955). He had learned several languages at preparatory school and at Princeton; he had learned Russian in the 1930's in connection with his trip to the Soviet Union. Now, in 1952, he returned to Princeton to learn Hebrew, the better to read the scrolls and discuss them with experts.

He made further trips to Europe, finding himself profoundly uncomfortable with his wife's German relatives but otherwise coming to a deeper appreciation of European culture. His interest in American Indians turned from the Zunis to the Iroquois of the Northeast, who were engaged in a struggle for their ancestral lands with state and federal governments. He made friends among the Iroquois, was introduced to some of their customs, and eventually wrote a book about their traditions and their difficulties, *Apologies to the Iroquois* (1960).

Perhaps most important, Wilson in the last years of the decade began planning and writing the essays on American history, culture, and literature which would become what many regard as his finest work, *Patriotic Gore: Studies in the Literature of the American Civil War* (1962). While he had been fascinated by exotic cultures, political movements, and social developments, he had never abandoned his love of literature. Now, at the height of his powers, he began a new study of a crucial period in the literature and history of his own country. More than any other book, this study of the American Civil War displayed his fascination with the interactions between public events, social and economic changes, and literary expression.

Critical Context

The journal form is one that relatively few writers have chosen, and the most famous of those who have (such as André Gide and the Goncourt brothers) have been French. Writers who choose to record their most intimate actions and thoughts ordinarily use diaries for the purpose, using journals, if at all, to note impressions and ideas they might use in more formal writings. Wilson's journals combine the two functions to an unusual degree.

In his own career, Wilson's journals fill a special role. He was a prolific, almost a compulsive, writer; thirty-one books of his writings have been published, testimony to the fact that he wrote about everything that interested him, and he found few things in the world that did not. Most of his other works, however, are relatively formal both in style and in content. They are also impersonal, in the sense that Wilson believed that the job of the literary and social critic was to act as an objective observer, commenting on what he saw in a detached fashion for the information and edification of his audience.

In the journals, Wilson was under no such constraints. He felt free to record gossip, to give vent to his dislikes, and to record his special passions. What is perhaps most impressive about these volumes is their confirmation of what the more formal studies imply: the amazing range of Wilson's interests and of his knowledge. The indexes of all three volumes are highly impressive in the diversity of references to the people Wilson knew, the books he read, the ideas he considered. There was nothing casual about his interests; if something attracted his attention, he studied it, read about it, and if possible examined it at first hand. Almost no one in the United States, for example, has ever been interested in or informed about the literature of Haiti, but when Wilson went to that island he was as deeply involved with its literature, and the connections between that literature and the island nation's Franco-African culture, as he had been with the Soviets he met in 1935 or the writers he knew on Cape Cod.

These volumes are important for several reasons. They will not add much to Wilson's already assured reputation as a critic, but with *Upstate: Records and Recollections of Northern New York* (1971) and *The Twenties: From Notebooks and Diaries of the Period* (1975) they provide a fascinating look at Wilson's private life and experience which will be of great use to biographers and historians in the future, and which provide for all readers insights into elements of his character not evident in the more formal writings. They provide rich evidence of the inquisitiveness as well as the occasional crankiness of Wilson's mind. Like other writers' journals and some biographies (for example, Richard Ellman's *James Joyce*, 1959, 1982), they show how the raw materials of experience are transformed by the writer's imagination into the stuff of literature. Finally, they provide a wide range of insights into the literary world—not only in the United States but in Great Britain and France as well—during much of the twentieth century.

Sources for Further Study

Costa, Richard Hauer. "Edmund Wilson: *The Forties*," in *Modern Fiction Studies*. XXI (Winter, 1985), pp. 751-753.

DePietro, Thomas. "Edmund Wilson, American," in *The Sewanee Review*. XCIV (Winter, 1986), pp. 160-166.

Epstein, Joseph. Review of *The Fifties* in *The New York Times Book Review.* XCI (August 31, 1986), p. 3.

Holloway, John. "Varieties of Dialogue: Wilson, Trilling, Leavis," in *Encounter.* LVI (February/March, 1981), pp. 67-77.

Kazin, Alfred. Review of *The Forties* in *The Atlantic Monthly.* CCLI (April, 1983), p. 126.

Levin, Harry. Review of *The Thirties* in *Saturday Review.* VII (August, 1980), p. 58.

Pritchett, V. S. Review of *The Fifties* in *The New Yorker.* LXII (January 5, 1987), pp. 83-85.

Vidal, Gore. *The Second American Revolution and Other Essays*, 1982.

John M. Muste

THOUGHT AND LANGUAGE

Author: Lev Vygotsky (1896-1934)
Type of work: Psychology/linguistics
First published: Myshlenie i rech, 1934 (partial English translation, 1962; complete
  translation, 1986)

Form and Content

Designed for the general reader, Lev Vygotsky's *Thought and Language* is a proposed resolution of the materialist-idealist split in Soviet psychology of the 1920's, a critical review of previous theories about the connection of language and thought, and an account of his and his colleagues' experimental results that supported a new formulation of the interrelationship of thought and speech. The study takes the form of an assessment of major theories, both Western and Soviet, in psychology and linguistics, with references to literary theory. Vygotsky finds such an interdisciplinary approach helpful for clarifying the different roots of thought and speech and for forming an "interfunctional interpretation of higher mental functions." Vygotsky's version of this relation grows out of and diverges from the developmental theories of Jean Piaget, with whom Vygotsky maintains a sort of running dialogue throughout the book. The underlying hypothesis of Vygotsky's work is that the developmental approach must be applied to thought and speech.

The book is organized in seven chapters, the first of which states the problem and Vygotsky's approach. Here he shows that previous studies of consciousness have focused on separate functions, though in principle psychologists accept the unity of consciousness and the interrelation of all psychological functions. He argues that they must shift to a study of developmental changes in the interfunctional structure of consciousness. He establishes word meaning as the minimal unit of verbal thought and makes semantic analysis his method in pursuing the nature of verbal thought—the development, function, and structure of this unit. Any word is already a generalization of reality and therefore an act of thought.

The second chapter critiques Piaget's developmental theory of thought and language in children, accepting much of Piaget's approach but challenging his explanation of egocentric speech. Piaget sees the child's talking aloud to himself as a midpoint between his asocial exclusive focus on self (autism) and his developing capability for directed thought—that is, his socialization. Vygotsky argues instead that speech is social from the beginning and that egocentric speech is an instrument of thought which seeks and plans solutions to problems, an intermediate stage leading not to socialization but to the inner speech of the adult.

In chapter 3, Vygotsky objects to William Stern's theory of language development on the grounds that the understanding of symbol comes much later than Stern thinks, but he likes Stern's realization of the great moment when the child learns the "grandiose signality" of speech. Vygotsky sees this phenomenon as the internalization of psychological tools. Human beings communicate through semiotic mediation.

In chapter 4, Vygotsky pursues the way in which this perception of speech as symbol comes into being, phylogenetically and ontogenetically. By distinguishing between communication among animals and that among human beings, he concludes that thought and speech have different genetic roots and that their curves of development come together in human beings at about age two, when words flood into the child's speech. Thought then becomes verbal and speech rational. At school the child begins the long process of internalizing speech, with the final achievement of "speech-for-oneself." With a rich cultural environment, that inner speech gradually becomes capable of greater abstraction and multileveled thought. In this chapter Vygotsky also shows how inner speech develops in stages: external speech, egocentric speech, and inner speech.

The following two chapters present Vygotsky's research group's experimental investigations on the development of word meanings in childhood and on the child's acquisition of "scientific" and "spontaneous" concepts. He uses the terms "complexes," "pseudo-complexes," and "potential concepts" as stages in the development of thinking. Concept formation, too, is shown to occur in stages, the highest stage being the application of an abstraction to new concrete situations that must be viewed in abstract terms. Mature thought, he says, must alternate between moving from the particular to the general and moving from the general to the particular.

This analysis has pedagogical application, and Vygotsky explores the way in which the different kinds of concepts can be supported by adult cooperation in the home and the school. He introduces the term "zone of proximal development" in explaining the point at which a child can most benefit from instruction.

The last chapter summarizes the outcomes of the study:

> (1) providing experimental evidence that meanings of words undergo evolution during childhood, and defining the basic steps in that evolution; (2) uncovering the singular way in which the child's "scientific" concepts develop, compared with his spontaneous concepts, and formulating the laws governing their development; (3) demonstrating the specific psychological nature and linguistic function of written speech in its relation to thinking and clarifying, by way of experiments, the nature of inner speech and its relation to thought.

His group found that thought and word are not connected by a primary bond; instead, their connection originates, changes, and grows in the evolution of thinking and speech. Study of the union of these elements in the unit, word meaning, made clear that not merely the content of the word changes but also the way in which reality is generalized and reflected in the word.

Vygotsky looks forward to further studies when he notes at the end of his work that "a true and full understanding of another's thought is possible only when we understand its affective-volitional basis." In reality, the development of verbal thought moves "from the motive that engenders a thought to the shaping of the thought, first in inner speech, then in meanings of words, and finally in words." He sees thought and speech as the key to human consciousness, and a word as a microcosm of human consciousness.

Analysis

Vygotsky's first interest was creativity, and his studies in psychology began as an attempt to explain the reason for the "inexpressible" in art. His first book, in 1925, was on the psychology of art (based on his doctoral thesis), and he had friends among the Russian Formalists, filmmakers, poets, and painters.

Alex Kozulin, translator and interpreter of Vygotsky's legacy, sees the psychologist's focus as the "problem of the structural transformation of the lower functions into the higher ones." This is a developmental problem, and Vygotsky, in an analogy to Karl Marx's notion of mechanical tools for the human transformation of nature, sees psychological tools as the way human beings master themselves by means of interaction with the environment. Marxist and Hegelian ideas of the material basis of reality and the mastery of human phenomena through the study of their origins and history underlie Vygotsky's work. Thus, he took a developmental approach to the study of the individual's acquisition of psychological tools, the stages of his or her transformation of natural psychological functions into higher ones, and the formative role of language in human thought. Vygotsky intended, too, to study the historical development of psychological tools and higher mental functions in human life, but did not live to accomplish this aim. Drawing from Émile Durkheim and Pierre Janet, Vygotsky sees "the very mechanism underlying mental functions [as] a copy from social interaction; all higher mental functions are internalized social relationships."

His evidence that thought and speech have different roots but flow together to interact at early stages of development ultimately suggests the interaction of higher mental functions—that is, functional systems. The ability to move between planes of these systems allows the highest understanding of reality an individual human being can achieve.

Thus it is that Vygotsky's theory of the nature of inner speech is an essential element of his view. Inner speech for Vygotsky is the internalization of the social world in the form of personal consciousness. Accepted symbolic systems are here remodeled into individual human thought. *Thought and Language* analyzes the process by which children develop the ability to use the symbols their society has generated. Mastery of generalizations at one level allows mastery of increasingly abstract generalizations. What the person eventually achieves is the interrelating of concepts in a system. Productive thought is based on the ability to move rapidly from one plane of generality to another.

Vygotsky's description of the most advanced stage of inner speech constitutes a guess at the nature of creative thinking and his explanation of why some experience is inexpressible. He makes a distinction between the *sense* of a word (the interiorization of the total context in which the word is encountered) and the *meaning* (its socially agreed upon definition). This distinction makes clear the intensely personal inner world of each human being. Sense is more important than meaning, the sentence more than the word, the context more than the sentence in inner speech. Unlike Piaget, Vygotsky believes that autistic dreaming persists into adulthood, as a response to frustrations and disappointments in the real world. The autism of the artist, however, can generate new symbols, new language which itself can enter the stream of intellectual life, changing reality. The history of language is a history of human conceptions of reality.

Vygotsky's theory of a child's developing ability to abstract has important implications for teaching practice. Understanding the way mental functions develop allows educators to find the best methods to foster that growth. Vygotsky's distinction between "scientific" and "spontaneous" concepts reveals the specialized function of school instruction: to introduce concepts for which the child's real experience has already prepared him or her to understand. Constant interaction between concepts encountered in education and rich natural experience in the world (itself permeated with concepts) enables the child to reach higher levels of thought. The young child thinks in complexes, giving "family" names to experience. Just prior to true conceptual thinking is the stage Vygotsky identifies as "pseudoconceptual," in which the child appears to be abstracting, but is in fact achieving the result on the basis of concrete, visible likenesses rather than principle. Because adult thinking occurs concurrently on several planes, including the pseudoconceptual plane, children's pseudoconceptual thinking makes possible an interchange between them and adults.

Vygotsky's analysis of the differences between written and spoken language also has relevance for teaching. Writing is a tool whose importance in the developing ability to use symbols is not at first apparent to the child. Writing is speech at its most formal: It uses more words, addresses an absent audience, and makes the greatest syntactical differentiation.

Vygotsky's developmental theory also has implications for testing. He finds that the measurement of mental age, or of concepts already mastered, or indeed the use of standardized tests in general is not so accurate as the measurement of the results a child can achieve in solving a problem with some slight help. The discrepancy between a child's actual age and the level he can achieve in solving problems with assistance is the zone of proximal development, a truer measure of intellectual progress.

An important part of the Vygotsky group's work is the devising of a new experimental methodology to study speech and thought. He insists that indirect as well as direct evidence is appropriate to the analysis of thought, and he applies the insights of the then-new linguistics to the study of children's and adults' speech. His account of the experimental investigation is integral to the formulation of his theory.

One other result of the work represented in this volume is Vygotsky's interest in the mentally and physically handicapped. He learned much about ordinary mental activity from his work with schizophrenics, and his ideas about schizophrenia have even in the late twentieth century been useful to Western psychologists.

Vygotsky's achievements, then, are the development of a new methodology of linking the world and the mind through study of word meaning as a basic unit; the understanding that word meanings evolve and that the level of abstraction a person achieves varies with behavioral and psychological circumstances; and the idea that the relation of word and thought is a process, and that thought is an inner movement through a series of planes. He showed that in mastering speech, the child moves from the part to the whole, but in meaning, the child moves from the whole to the part; that the increasingly complex movement from meaning to sound must be developed; and that the achievement of inner speech is part of the transition from the child's social activity to more individualized activity. Vygotsky's work did in fact make possible an experimental psychology of higher mental activity.

Language and Thought shows Vygotsky to have been a highly literate investigator. To illustrate the way in which the meaning of words can vary according to context, for example, he quotes Konstantin Stanislavsky's clarification of the subtext of lines from a play. He uses epigraphs from contemporary poets and shows how thought between sympathetic pairs can proceed almost without words by citing a famous passage from a novel by Leo Tolstoy. Furthermore, it is evident that Vygotsky brings to his study a sophisticated philosophical background. He is familiar with the work of major Western and Soviet psychologists, he knows the works of German and French sociologists and biologists, and he uses linguistics and literary theorists as resources. All this learning is worn lightly; he introduces quotes and allusions unobtrusively in the construction of his own argument. Since the book is not addressed solely to psychologists, explicit documentation does not overwhelm the reader, and the book is clear and accessible. Though full of new and fruitful ideas many as yet unexplored, it is never dense, but always stimulating.

Critical Context

Vygotsky's work on thought and language was exciting to a generation of Soviet psychologists and inspired many of the leading figures in the field through the half century after his own premature death. Most members of the group who worked with him on the experiments reported in *Thought and Language* went on to do major research in psychology, education, and anthropology. Filmmakers such as Sergei Eisenstein and poets such as Osip Mandelstam used some of his ideas in aspects of their own work. His challenge to then-existing psychological practices did in fact change the course of Soviet psychology.

Nevertheless, that influence was both misapplied and interrupted as a result of Joseph Stalin's political interference in linguistics and psychology. A subsequent book by Vygotsky (written with Alexander Luria), a comparative study of mental development in a section of the Soviet Union that represented several stages of human culture, was rejected for publication, as were other, shorter pieces. His Marxist orientation was called into question, and his citation of Western authorities bespoke what the Stalinist government considered an unhealthy bourgeois influence. As a result, his students, in developing his theories in a context which demanded strict Marxist applications, in fact distorted his work. Their theories of activity replaced his emphasis on semiotic mediation with a stress on behavior as well.

Only after the thaws following Stalin's death did fuller publication and more critical examination reveal the richness of Vygotsky's theoretical work. Themes in his papers and in the work under discussion which had remained undeveloped received new attention, both in the Soviet Union and abroad, where psychological emphases of the earlier period had given way to interests closer to Vygotsky's own. Advances in the field of semiotics supported Vygotsky's notion that words not only represent reality but actually mold it. Application of his theory of the role of the adult in children's learning gave a distinctive shape to Soviet psychology and education. Vygotsky's emphasis on the way culture changes over time, providing the available forms of knowledge, distinguishes his approach from Piaget's. His concept of the importance of systems in mental activity makes his work fully contemporary.

Sources for Further Study

Cole, Michael, and Sylvia Scribner. Introduction to *Mind in Society: The Development of Psychological Processes*, by Lev Vygotsky, 1978.

Emerson, Caryl. "The Outer World and Inner Speech: Bakhtin, Vygotsky, and the Internalization of Language," in *Critical Inquiry*. X (December, 1983), pp. 245-264.

Kozulin, Alex. "Psychological and Philosophical Anthropology: The Problems of Their Interaction," in *Philosophical Forum*. XV (1984), pp. 443-458.

_____. *Psychology in Utopia: Toward a Social History of Soviet Psychology*, 1984.

_____. "Vygotsky in Context," in *Thought and Language*, by Lev Vygotsky, 1986.

Lucid, Daniel P., ed. *Soviet Semiotics: An Anthology*, 1977.

Luria, Alexander. *The Making of Mind: A Personal Account of Soviet Psychology*, 1979.

Wertsch, James V. "The Semiotic Mediation of Mental Life: L. S. Vygotsky and M. M. Bakhtin," in *Semiotic Mediation: Sociocultural and Psychological Perspectives*, 1984. Edited by Elizabeth Mertz and Richard J. Parmentier.

_____, ed. and trans. *The Concept of Activity in Soviet Psychology*, 1981.

Martha Manheim

THE THREAD THAT RUNS SO TRUE

Author: Jesse Stuart (1907-1984)
Type of work: Autobiography
Time of work: The 1920's and 1930's
Locale: Rural Kentucky
First published: 1949

Principal personage:
JESSE STUART, a teacher and writer

Form and Content

Jesse Stuart was only sixteen when he began his teaching career at the one-room Lonesome Valley School in rural Kentucky. He had not planned on a teaching career and, in fact, had not completed his own high school education at the time. Nevertheless, having gone by mistake into a room where the county school board was testing teacher candidates, he decided to try the exam. He passed it and received a second-class certificate, which permitted him to teach the lower grades. He chose to go to Lonesome Valley School because his older sister had taught there and had been beaten up by the school bullies; Stuart enjoyed a challenge. In *The Thread That Runs So True*, he tells of the challenges he faced as a classroom teacher and school administrator in the Kentucky rural school system of the Depression years.

At Lonesome Valley School, Stuart learned how to engage his students' interest and win their respect. He learned how to improvise in a classroom when books and supplies were not available. He learned how to help his students apply their lessons to their everyday tasks and take pride in their accomplishments. Finally, he experienced the frustration of coping with politically elected school trustees, sometimes themselves illiterate, who ruled the teachers and curriculum in accordance with their private wishes.

After his initiation at Lonesome Valley, Stuart went on to obtain his own high school diploma. He then worked his way through Lincoln Memorial University in three years and received a baccalaureate degree in 1929. He took a straight academic program, not a teacher-training course, because he did not intend to go into teaching as a career. He thought to combine farming in his Kentucky homeland with a career of writing about the richness of life there. He left Lincoln Memorial in debt, however, and had to seek more immediate sources of income. Stuart worked for a year in the local steel mill but subsequently was persuaded to become the only teacher in a fourteen-student, rural high school for one hundred dollars per month. Though he had to scramble to keep ahead of them in their courses, his students excelled, winning prizes in competitions with larger and better financed high schools in the city system. Stuart became committed to fighting rural illiteracy and the impoverished, politicized school system that perpetuated it.

At the age of twenty-three, Stuart became a high school principal and began coping with underpaid teachers, opinionated parents, and a stubborn, miserly school board. With persistence and characteristic innovation, he dealt with these problems and helped make the school notable for its prizewinning students. At the same time, he took graduate courses in education and, as a result, was constantly in debt. When the school board rejected his request for an annual salary of fifteen hundred dollars, he decided to leave the teaching profession. He attended Vanderbilt University to complete a master's degree, but when all his clothes and his thesis were destroyed in a dormitory fire, he hitchhiked home without completing his program.

The following year, Stuart, at age twenty-four, accepted an appointment as superintendent of the rural school district in which he had grown up and taught. He found the system staggering under debts and competing with a city system for students and the state subsidy that went with them. He had to cope with an antiquated trustee system in which 246 elected rural trustees, many of them illiterate, tried to rule the local schools like petty dictators.

Confronting these problems head-on, he created such a controversy that his school district became involved in thirty-two lawsuits, winning "thirty-one and one-half." His life was even threatened, and many of his friends avoided him in public. He found consolation in writing poetry and fiction about the rich life of the Kentucky hill people, and he published the first of his twenty-eight books, *The Harvest of Youth*, in 1930. With the 1934 publication of his second work, a collection of poems titled *Man with a Bull-Tongue Plow*, his writing began to sell; he became a sought-after public speaker, traveling to many states beyond his native Kentucky. On the basis of his published stories and poems, he won a Guggenheim Fellowship and spent fourteen months in Europe. On his return home, he was married to his local sweetheart and returned to the struggle to improve Kentucky's education system.

In *The Thread That Runs So True*, a first-person narrative, Stuart enriches the story of his own education and development with a deep appreciation for his students and their accomplishments. They come alive as he conveys the richness of their speech and personalities. The book's title and chapter headings are taken from a folk song which the children would sing at Lonesome Valley School. With a poet's eye, Stuart captures the beauty and the aching hardships of the Kentucky hills. With candor, he analyzes the causes and impact of the neglect of rural schools that ranked the state next to last among the national school systems.

The book is divided into six sections of unequal length, each one subdivided into internal numbered chapters. Each of the six main sections deals with a different theme or stage of Stuart's learning about education. The subsections resemble individual short stories or essays. The autobiography follows a chronological pattern, but Stuart never subordinates narrative to time. Moreover, he does not allow himself to come between the reader and the community he describes; he functions as a guide, but the experiences he chooses to highlight help the reader to understand the unique culture and special problems of the Kentucky hill people. Ever sensitive to them, Stuart has disguised the names of the places and persons he depicts, thereby giving the work more artistic and analytical freedom.

Analysis

Jesse Hilton Stuart wrote some thirty books about Kentucky during his lifetime. He crafted his love for his home state into poetry, novels, and the numerous short stories for which he is especially famous. He wrote two autobiographical works in addition to *The Thread That Runs So True*, *Beyond Dark Hills* (1938) and *The Year of My Rebirth* (1956). The first of these, *Beyond Dark Hills*, was truly an exploration of self. During Stuart's year of graduate study at Vanderbilt University, his English instructor had assigned a "brief autobiography" with an eighteen-page limit. In eleven days, Stuart wrote 322 pages, "from margin to margin," because "I couldn't tell Dr. Edwin Mims what I wanted to tell him in eighteen pages." The manuscript was eventually published as his fourth book.

The Thread That Runs So True appeared after many of Stuart's stories and novels had been published. Like his fiction, it incorporates a profound love for nature, an appreciation for the soft rhythm and colorful metaphor of the Kentucky hill people's speech, and a pride in human accomplishment. The audience for this work, however, was very different. In a post-World War II world, Stuart was making an eloquent and pointed protest to those who controlled the fate of public education in Kentucky and across the nation. The son of an illiterate father and a mother with only a second-grade education, Stuart wrote in his 1958 preface to *The Thread That Runs So True*, "I know as surely as I live and breathe the positive proof of what education can do for a man." This work, then, is at once a plea for education and a testimony to its power. In it, Stuart acknowledges the important encouragement he received from his parents, teachers, and students: "I felt I could repay them by inspiring other youth. This means more to me than all the money in the world."

Stuart's natural ability as a writer is especially apparent in this book, with its skillful combination of narrative and analytical prose. It is a work that functions effectively at three levels. At its most basic, it is masterful storytelling. The characters described are interesting and recognizable; their conversation is colorful and holds attention. At this level, *The Thread That Runs So True* is a collection of integrated short stories, perfect for schoolchildren and readers of all ages. It allows readers to compare the problems of the Kentucky schoolchildren with their own and to be inspired by what these children were able to accomplish, despite the most primitive and impoverished circumstances. As Stuart intended, these stories are testimony to the love of learning. Just as important, they are fun and dramatic. As single selections or as a whole, *The Thread That Runs So True* is a marvelous work for oral interpretation.

At the second level, this book is an important autobiography. Stuart was described by one literary critic as a prolific and natural-born writer comparable to Thomas Wolfe. As an author, Stuart was remarkable not only for the amount of quality work he produced but also for his reach across the full range of creative writing, from poetry and the short story to the novel, the autobiography, and the essay. His works are intriguing for their simplicity and for his dynamic expressions of individuality. He engages his readers, and they wish to know more about him as a person.

The Thread That Runs So True portrays Stuart as a young man in the process of making important life choices. The reader sees him accepting the challenge to better himself through education, yet ultimately turning away from the rewards of upward mobility to invest himself and his talent in the Kentucky hill culture that had nurtured him. His dismay at the low salaries and prestige given to teachers and the entire school system documents that this is a story of conscious choice, not of blind self-sacrifice.

This autobiography profiles the development of Stuart's values and ethics. The tone is optimistic and positive, almost heroic in its assertion of individual worth and the promise of achievement through hard work. Although Stuart acknowledges that he was not typical of rural Kentuckians—there were fewer than ten local college graduates in his county—he works to demonstrate that his energy, native intelligence, and capacity for hard work were typical. He insists that these traits of his students were the real ingredients of his success as a teacher. He is an eloquent spokesman for Appalachia, and he demands that it be given its due.

At yet a third level, Stuart has selected stories and autobiographical elements to shape an indictment of the Kentucky school system, perhaps the most skillful aspect of the work. It is at this level that the book's structure and purpose become most apparent. Each section, its title echoing the voices of the children's song, uses colorful narrative and reconstruction of conversation to depict some problem of the Kentucky rural schools: the primitive buildings that housed the earnest, hardworking, barefoot elementary students; the community indifference and lack of respect; the insult of the trustee system, which gave local politicians more authority over school affairs than the professional educators; the pitiful budgets. Yet, the thread of student success runs throughout the stories, despite the system's handicaps.

At its most effective, this picture of the state education system is framed in the conversations and discussions of the participants. The descriptions of the arguments among the Greenwood County School Board members provide candid and humorous insight into the workings of small-town politics. At other points, where Stuart wished to convey specific facts or information which would not normally be part of local conversation, he steps in as an observer and critic. For the most part, however, he portrays himself as participant in the events that take place. He blends the polemic into the fabric of the narrative.

Because this book is an autobiography, a time line substitutes for plot. The ending is, accordingly, rather ambiguous and probably the least satisfying part of the work. Stuart returned from his year of study in Europe to find vast changes in the Greenwood County school personnel and no place for him to work. His own outlook had changed as well, as a result of his observing the rise of Fascism in Europe. There is a mood of apprehension in the final section, giving it a different tone from that of its predecessors. It is as though Stuart has had his say about the needs of education and is searching for a new subject. His description of teaching remedial English at a large Ohio school is cursory and lacks the warmth of the earlier chapters. He returned to Kentucky to wed Naomi Deane, to farm the family homestead, and to work on his uncompleted novel. The tale simply stops there.

Critical Context

Because of Jesse Stuart's stature as a unique and beloved author, *The Thread That Runs So True* has an assured place in American literature. What makes this work especially noteworthy is Stuart's use of it to make his case for public school education. Seldom have professional educators had at their side an author of such repute and, even more important, such wide and verifiable experience in the schools. Stuart has used his material strategically, couching it in writing so enjoyable that students, teachers, parents, administrators, and politicians can see the importance of their role in public education without being alienated by dull or preachy writing. In his selection of events and personalities, Stuart manipulates both his materials and his readers to make his case.

Stuart presented this work at a time when the nation was prepared to deal with the problem of illiteracy. Published in 1949, when the nation was recovering from decades of economic depression and war, *The Thread That Runs So True* reached a national audience eager to address the issues of education. Accordingly, the book was brought into the classroom by multitudes of teachers and was placed on recommended-reading lists. Students were inspired, teachers encouraged, and general readers informed by this gentle and enjoyable exposé. For contemporary readers, *The Thread That Runs So True* remains a masterful example of the writer's craft. It captures for all time the essence of the Appalachian heritage and remains an eloquent statement of the value of public education.

Sources for Further Study

Blair, Everetta Love. *Jesse Stuart: His Life and Works*, 1967.

Clarke, Mary Washington. *Jesse Stuart's Kentucky*, 1968.

Gilpin, John R., Jr. *The Man . . . Jesse Stuart: Poet, Novelist, Short-Story Writer, Educator*, 1977.

Herndon, Jerry A. *Land of the Honey-Colored Wind: Jesse Stuart's Kentucky, a Resource Book*, 1981.

Richardson, Edward H. *Jesse: The Biography of an American Writer, Jesse Hilton Stuart*, 1984.

Eleanor L. Turk

365 DAYS

Author: Ronald Glasser (1940-   )
Type of work: Essays/history/psychology
Time of work: 1968-1970
Locale: The United States, Vietnam, and Japan
First published: 1971

> *Principal personage:*
> RONALD GLASSER, a medical doctor working for the United States
> Army during the Vietnam War

Form and Content

As Ronald Glasser notes in his foreword to *365 Days*, he arrived at Camp Zama, in Japan, in September of 1968. Educated at The Johns Hopkins University, where he was a Phi Beta Kappa graduate in 1961, and at The Johns Hopkins Medical School, where he completed his M.D. degree in 1965, he undertook three years of specialized training in pediatrics at the University of Minnesota Medical School. With that background, he had expected to be treating the dependent children of those soldiers stationed in Japan. What he encountered, however, was the horror of war, for Camp Zama, with its seven-hundred-bed hospital, served as a United States Army evacuation center for soldiers needing more extensive care than was available in Vietnam. As he remarks, Zama is the only general hospital in Japan; Glasser is proud of having served in this large, modern, and efficient facility, where "literally thousands of boys were saved" during his two-year assignment in the army.

Glasser is also clearly proud of the soldiers he comes to know at Zama. Although these young soldiers are no more than "boys," they are brave and stoic and honest. They are also confused; as the soldier's poem which serves as the epigraph for the first story says, "Even those who make it home/ Carry back a scar." From knowing these soldiers, Glasser feels the obligation "to give something to these kids that was all theirs without doctrine or polemics, something they could use to explain what they might not be able to explain themselves." Because Glasser believes that "there is no novel in Nam, there is not enough for a plot," what he offers instead are "sketches, not finished stories." Yet here, as elsewhere, he understates his point, for the seventeen sketches contained in *365 Days* are built on a carefully interconnected series of motifs. Reminiscent in pattern of James Joyce's *Dubliners* (1914), the book also reminds one of the work of Stephen Crane, to whose memory the book is dedicated.

Of the seventeen essays, eight of them focus on the soldiers' lives in Vietnam, and one examines the training of a young officer before he departs the United States. Ranging in length from two to fifteen pages, the essays depict moments of crisis for the soldiers. In "Mayfield," for example, the central character is a forty-three-year-old first sergeant involved in the war in the delta of southern South Vietnam. The reader sees the war through Mayfield's eyes:

Strange war. Going for something they didn't believe in or for that matter didn't care about, just to make it 365 days and be done with it. They'd go, though; even freaked out, they'd go. They'd do whatever he told them. . . . They'd do it, and if led right, they'd do it well.

That quality of dedication, to survival and to their unit, is seen at the end of the sketch, when Mayfield himself is wounded but orchestrates his troops, F-4 tactical air support, and medical evacuation helicopters into an effective fighting team. Similarly, in "Track Unit," the reader observes Deneen, a young lieutenant assigned unexpectedly to tanks, take command in the heat of his first firefight. Although later wounded, Deneen recognizes his skill and is anxious to return to his position as a commander. The sketch ends with Glasser's admission that it is his duty to assign him a medical profile to make this possible.

The remaining eight sketches either directly or indirectly focus on the medical corps that cares for the wounded soldier. Like the soldiers' stories, these range in length also. At one extreme is a three-page sketch of an unnamed soldier who expires after being mutilated during the explosion of a Chinese Communist mine. A thirty-two-page piece titled "Gentlemen, It Works" centers on a transcription of a briefing which explains the psychological effects of combat stress. Several other sketches describe more directly the medical corps personnel: "Joan," for example, relates the story of a nurse working at a surgical hospital in Vietnam; "Choppers" tells of the rigors of medical evacuation helicopter duty; "Medics," similarly, consists of short, poignant vignettes of the medical troops assigned to frontline combat units.

The first and final sketches form a matched pair. Set in Camp Zama, these pieces depict graphically the interactions of the evacuation hospital's medical staff with the wounded soldiers. In the first, Dr. Peterson serves as the central figure, treating Robert Kurt, a member of the 101st Airborne Division in Vietnam. Despite a life-threatening leg wound, Kurt recovers; as he does, however, his confidence in his ability to rejoin the elite division declines. Close to the end of his tour, Peterson convinces the soldier to return home rather than rejoin his unit. In the final piece, Dr. Edwards fights valiantly, but in vain, to save the life of a badly burned soldier, David Jensen. The soldier's final dying words—"I don't want to go home alone"— remind Edwards of his own trip home with the casket of his dead brother and remind the reader of the irony of the book's title, *365 Days*: The war cannot simply be erased at the end of a finite tour of duty.

Both the foreword and the glossary are significant parts of *365 Days*. In the foreword Glasser comments, "If you survive 365 days . . . you simply go home," but the stories demonstrate that the war lives on indefinitely, both for the soldiers and for the medical corps—and particularly for the author. Indeed, in presenting a combined "Glossary of Military and Medical Terms" at the end of the narrative, Glasser is suggesting a close relationship between those who served in the medical corps and those who served as combat soldiers.

Analysis

It is appropriate that *365 Days* should begin and end with a sense of the interconnectedness of the medical and combat services, for their members are the true heroes and heroines of these sketches. Just as Glasser recognized that "there is not . . . a community in America that would not have been proud" to claim Zama's hospital for its own, so he himself is able to feel proud of the soldiers he comes to know and respect. In writing of moments in the soldiers' and medics' lives, Glasser emphasizes a pattern of naïveté, dedication, frustration, and personal sacrifice. This archetypal pattern of the loss of innocence links these diverse sketches together.

Ultimately, the author focuses on the naïve goodness of the soldiers and medics. In "The Shaping-Up of Macabe," for example, Glasser relates how Macabe evolves from an idealistic college Reserve Officers' Training Corps (ROTC) cadet into a pragmatic and efficient artillery officer. Glasser writes, "Hemingway had his Spain; Macabe would have his Vietnam." Macabe volunteers for one specialized training course after another, from artillery training to "jump" school to ranger training, and learns that this war is not romantic. He comes to focus, even while in training, "always on the immediate." According to Glasser, Macabe and the other soldiers in his unit "were learning how to live with someone trying to kill them." Thus Macabe's violent retributive actions become understandable in the context of his situation, for their "unit had been hit three nights in a row."

This American pragmatism, born of naïveté, is effective—"most of the time it works," notes Glasser. In "Gentlemen, It Works," Glasser interweaves the stories of two soldiers, Dienst and Washington, with a brief history of military psychiatric practices. Beginning with the errors of the past (the evacuation procedures used during World War I and the individual, intensive psychotherapy emphasized by Freudians during World War II), a psychiatric medical adviser suggests a newer, pragmatic approach, stressing that "health rather than disease" is the most efficient way of treating combat exhaustion. In depicting the successful return of both Dienst and Washington to their units, Glasser advocates the ultimate compassion of this approach, for "a year's problem does not become a lifelong disability."

Because of the essential goodness of both the soldiers and the medics, Glasser's focus on their psychic and physical wounds assumes an understated but tragic tone. When he mentions, at the end of "Come On! Let's Go!" that "4,114 Americans were killed, 19,285 were wounded, and 604 were lost," the cold statistics take on meaning because of the human story that introduces those numbers. The cumulative effect of the woundings and deaths described is a strong sense of loss.

More pervasive, however, is the theme of selfless sacrifice that runs through the seventeen sketches. Troops live where it is "115 degrees in the sun," where soldiers are required to spend the night in two-man perimeter defense positions armed only with bayonets and knives, where endless five-hour marches are punctuated with a deadly sniper round or pressure-detonated mine. For the medics—the "young [who] are suddenly left alone to take care of the young"—the situation is worse. Becoming deeply attached to their units, they sacrifice by "cutting down on their own water and food so they can carry more medical supplies." Even the doctors at Camp Zama, one step removed from direct combat, make their sacrifices, both in the long and grueling hours that they work and in their contact with the wounded and dying soldiers. As Glasser has noted in another context, "Doctors should be taught right through school to deal with grief, suffering, heartache and anguish." For the medics and doctors, as much as for the soldiers, personal sacrifice brings a muted tone of nobility to their stories.

Still, Glasser's view is not without cynicism. Embedded in these tales of sacrifice by essentially good and honest people is a sense of disgust at bureaucratic bungling, waste, and dishonesty. Macabe, for example, despite all of his extensive training as a ranger, is assigned duties as a forward observer, and Deneen, trained as an airborne officer, is assigned to a mechanized battalion. Glasser is also critical of the medical corps—for example, when certain of its personnel unthinkingly follow army regulations to the detriment of their patients. The majority of his criticism, however, is aimed at civilian contractors working in Vietnam. In "$90,000,000 a Day," Glasser describes how Herman London bribes a sergeant in headquarters to transport a case of liquor to a civilian construction site in the jungle.

Clearly, the prevailing tone of *365 Days* is that of an elegy. Amid the stories told from differing points of view there emerges an acceptance of pain and suffering and a stoic faith in one's unit and its individual members. The penultimate story, "Brock," brings many of these themes together. A member of a covert special forces unit working behind enemy lines, Brock visits wounded members of his team at the Camp Zama Evacuation Hospital. Disdainful of the army hospital's protocol, Brock places personal loyalty above regulations and continues to visit his men. Reticent about his accomplishments and sacrifices, he later quietly recounts the story of his specialized unit's professional pragmatism. In essence, Brock is the archetypal hero of these sketches. Yet the story ends in a fashion typical of the other stories. En route home at the end of his tour, Brock is told, "There's no one out there any more." Although that is literally the truth, it underscores a more substantial truth: that Brock, because of the depth of his experiences in the war, will always carry, within himself, vestiges of those experiences.

Critical Context

In commenting on "Brock," one early critic of Vietnam War literature observed that this piece demonstrates

> the unique serviceability of the shorter fictional modes in coming to terms with the sense of episodic randomness and strange fragmentation that so often seemed to characterize one's vision of the actual experience of the war.

Yet "Brock," which is not—strictly speaking—"fictional," does more than this in the context of the book as a whole, for it is here that the central themes coalesce most clearly. What appears in this story is reinforced, or repeated with variation, in other sketches in the narrative. Rather than being seventeen discrete sketches,

365 Days displays, in its concern for social, medical, and military issues, a thematic unity that emphasizes the encompassing nature of the Vietnam War experience. In this it bears a remarkable likeness to Walt Whitman's meditations on the Civil War, *Specimen Days and Collect* (1882-1883), and Ernest Hemingway's tales of World War I, *In Our Time* (1924).

Despite the artistry of this nonfiction narrative, however, it has not escaped social criticism. Ostensibly for its liberal use of obscenities, the narrative was banned in 1981 from a high school library in Baileyville, Maine. Reaching a federal district court in Bangor in December, 1981, the controversy received some press coverage and eventual notoriety. Indeed, the library had housed only fourteen books on Vietnam, two of them nonfiction; one of these, Philip Caputo's *A Rumor of War* (1977), used more obscenities than did *365 Days*. Several veterans testified in court that the obscene language in *365 Days* added verisimilitude, that the book told the truth about Vietnam, and that "to censor the language in that book would be to deprive them of their own history." Although Glasser himself appeared at the trial, it was not until the spring of 1982 that the book was allowed back on the library shelves.

In his next three books, Glasser turned more directly toward the medical profession: In *Ward 402* (1973), he focuses on an eleven-year-old-girl who dies of leukemia after receiving controversial medical treatment; in *The Body Is the Hero* (1976), he relates the history of the science of immunology, beginning with Louis Pasteur; and in *The Greatest Battle* (1976), he advances his own theories about the genesis and prognosis of certain types of cancers and the problems inherent in the accepted forms of research. These works, however, seem to have left him unfulfilled. In 1985, rejecting his own statement, "If there is more to be said [about Vietnam] it will have to be said by others," he returned to this subject in his first fictional narrative, *Another War, Another Peace*. In this book Glasser wrote explicitly about what is merely implied in *365 Days*—that, for the survivors of the war, its effects linger. The central figure, a young man stationed first in Vietnam and then reassigned to Camp Zama, exhibits the typical psychological manifestations of survivor guilt.

Sources for Further Study

FitzGerald, Frances. "A Reporter at Large: A Disagreement in Baileyville," in *The New Yorker*. LX (January 16, 1984), pp. 47-90.

Lask, Thomas. "Vietnam: Children's Crusade," in *The New York Times Book Review*. LXXVI (September 11, 1971), p. 25.

Polner, Murray. Review in *Saturday Review*. LIV (September 11, 1971), pp. 46-47.

Prescott, Peter S. "The 'Dignity' of Battle," in *Newsweek*. LXXVIII (September 13, 1971), p. 99.

Simpson, Louis. "Nothing to Show But Their Wounds," in *The Listener*. LXXXVII (June 1, 1972), pp. 735-736.

Charles J. Gaspar

TIME AND WESTERN MAN

Author: Wyndham Lewis (1882-1957)
Type of work: Cultural criticism/philosophy/literary criticism
First published: 1927

Form and Content

The form and content of *Time and Western Man* are, appropriately, given the author, not easy to explain. They are best understood by examining the complex artistic and intellectual personality of Wyndham Lewis, who by the mid-1920's was equally famous as a novelist, as a painter, and as a critic. In *Time and Western Man*, he has taken his interest in philosophy and wedded it to his disdain for certain nineteenth century and early twentieth century philosophers whom he believes have undermined the culture of post-World War I Europe. Their seemingly innocent confirmation of one another's positions, in Lewis' opinion, not only ruined philosophy but also seeped into the social sensibility. As a thinker, as a social critic, and as an artist of unusually wide gifts, Lewis is on the attack against the shoddy thinking, as he sees it, developed in Europe under the influence of Henri Bergson, Alfred North Whitehead, Oswald Spengler, and several lesser followers. The rot, he claims, did not stop with philosophers and historians; it also infested the artistic world, and Lewis is willing to take on the task of straightening up literature and the plastic arts at the same time.

There is, however, another aspect of Lewis' talent that must be understood. He is often (some would say always) a satirist, and as such is not satisfied with simply putting his arguments forward reasonably. A streak of Swiftian excess is often the best part of his work. Lewis is not usually the best source of the facts, but he is always lively and eccentric and occasionally bellicose. Whatever else it is, *Time and Western Man* is lividly, wittily aggressive and often smartingly comical in the best tradition of roughhouse satire.

Lewis divides the book, if only loosely, into two sections. In the first, "The Revolutionary Simpleton," he addresses, in the main, the way in which his philosophical enemies have encouraged sloppy thinking and behavior in society and particularly in the arts; he examines with some care specific artists whom he sees as the most serious examples of the problem. The second section, "An Analysis of the Philosophy of Time," is somewhat more complicated and more dependent on special knowledge. In it, Lewis explores the philosophical influences of the fad he calls "the time-cult."

Analysis

The basic theme of this work is Lewis' concern over the way in which Bergson and his followers have, in Lewis' opinion, undermined the twentieth century view of reality. Certainly the reader would benefit from having some substantial knowledge of the philosophical work of Bergson, Spengler, Whitehead, and Bertrand Russell.

The book would, then, seem to be of interest exclusively to professional thinkers. Lewis, with his enormous confidence, was not dismayed by professional scrutiny; nevertheless, he meant *Time and Western Man* to be a popular commentary on certain philosophers' work, and it can be read as such, if one remembers that he is a satirist and polemicist and therefore not to be completely trusted in his interpretation of complicated ideas.

The main idea to be grasped, if the book is to be read by the layman, is that Lewis is much exercised by Bergson's theory—which is accepted, with variations, by the other philosophers mentioned—that time and change are the ultimate realities, that things are only "real" in relation to their place within the constantly changing stream of becoming, and that intuition, rather than intellect, is mankind's most important tool for making sense of life. Defining reality as "temporal," or as constantly changing, Lewis believes, undermines everyday facts and normal trust in the human mind's ability to order reality. Common sense, according to Lewis' reading of Bergson and his followers, is discredited, and the immediate objects of human experience lose their authenticity.

Clearly, that is an oversimplification of Lewis' complicated argument, which is itself an oversimplification of the work of philosophers who question positivism. Very roughly, positivism embraces the idea that knowledge is based on sense experience. Lewis' enemies might be called "relativists" or "postrelativists," since they distrust objects as touchstones for truth and believe that immediate experiences are "true" only within the constantly changing stream of time.

The book may seem to be of limited interest, applicable only in the world of hairsplitting theorists and unworldly thinkers; Lewis, however, is not an academic but an activist, fighting for the life of society and the arts in the real world. It is in the first half of the book that the lay reader will feel most at home, since it is here that Lewis attempts to expose the relativists' pernicious influence, particularly in the world of art.

In book 1, appropriately titled "The Revolutionary Simpleton," Lewis claims that the relativists' emphasis on reality as a kind of sensational flux has debased the arts, which, in the hands of too many artists, have become romantically softheaded and infantile. If reality is sensation, the recording of sensations, however silly or unimpressive, is worthwhile. Artistic structures are repudiated as "artificial," and the subject of art can be anything, since all action is leveled. Lewis finds this kind of thinking manifested at its worst in the work of Gertrude Stein; he argues that for all of her claims of doing serious work, she is not to be taken any more seriously than one would take the work of the minor, popular literary "entertainer" Anita Loos. The belief that art is a product of high skill and imagination applied to interesting ideas, says Lewis, is abandoned by some artists for the celebration of the moment, for the recording of the most trivial sensation. Artists act like children, recording childish responses to banal phenomena which have been given authenticity by the philosophers whom Lewis despises.

Certainly there is something to be said for Lewis' argument, and Gertrude Stein, in particular, with her simplistic style and unstructured tales, has always been viewed with some skepticism. She may, in fact, seem small game for Lewis' sometimes lethal satirical attack. Yet he does not stop there. He is quite willing and able to take on other arts and other artists—some of considerable moment. Lewis' attack on what he sees as the intrusion of flaccid, relativistic ideas in the work of the Russian ballet impresario Sergey Diaghilev is mischievously healthy; he pricks the bubbles of artistic pretension, regardless of whether the reader agrees with him. Indeed, he often demonstrates in his attacks on the promotional hot air of the modern arts that skill which is the mark of a great satirist: the ability to make the reader enjoy arguments with which he strongly disagrees and which he would reject out of hand had they been presented with less brio.

In general, Lewis believes that the philosophy of "sensation," as opposed to the philosophy of "fact," has been taken up by too many modern practitioners of the arts as an excuse not only for sloppy work but also for simply bad art. He points to artistic presentations on the stage, in the plastic arts, in music, and in literature whose patent formlessness is passed off as "true" because it is just like the form-lessness of sensation. The works are inchoately simple and sincere and are therefore regarded as equal to, if not better than, the old works of skilled, polished calculation.

Yet there is more to the chapters on the artists than a blanket denunciation. Lewis is something of a crank on many occasions, but his charges are not entirely without foundation, particularly with respect to fringe characters such as Stein. He does pro-vide the kind of arguments which make it possible to think about new kinds of art with some defense against the excesses of faddishness and unthinking enthusiasm.

More than that, however, Lewis is often an extremely perceptive critic when he is dealing with artists whose works he does not wholly endorse but nevertheless recognizes as artistically important. He sees, for example, that James Joyce's *Ulysses* (1922) is an imposing contribution to the development of the novel, and he connects Joyce to the English tradition of humor as manifested in the work of the eighteenth century writer Laurence Sterne. What Lewis does not like about *Ulysses* is its seemingly indiscriminate piling up of brute detail. He claims that Joyce, Stein, and Ezra Pound are all under the influence of Bergson, all "time" writers, self-indulgent and disorganized; however, he also can distinguish the lesser talents from the greater. His comments on Pound, for example, are particularly interesting, as are his careful distinctions between Joyce and Marcel Proust, but he is unrepentant in accusing all of them of a flabbiness which he traces directly to the "duration-flux" of Bergson and his followers.

Whether the reader agrees with Lewis about the works' value and influence, there is much perceptive commentary on the arts of the post-World War I period in the first half of the book. The real danger faces the reader without much critical background. The major philosophical idea of this section is easy to understand and easy to take with some skepticism, but Lewis' arguments are uneven and sometimes eccentrically wrongheaded. The reader not only must be on the lookout but also should know the text of the original materials well, partly because Lewis is unashamedly attempting to persuade and partly because he is such a fine artist, so ebullient, so wittily seductive.

Book 2 is less successful, in part because it is more committed to point-by-point argument and to building, with considerable repetition, the case against the philosophers and their followers. There are, however, chapters which go beyond obsessive argument to consider the influence of Lewis' adversaries on particular aspects of the real world. This section really does demand some substantial preparation; one needs to have read some Bergson and perhaps some works of George Berkeley, whom Lewis admires but whom he sees as having precipitated the whole group into their sensationalism with his theory that there is no existence of matter without perception of the same.

Critical Context

Ultimately, *Time and Western Man* must be seen not as philosophy—or indeed, as an influential criticism of philosophy—but as a literary text. Even if one disagrees with Lewis' belief that the Bergsonians' influence was a bad thing, there is clear evidence that the influence existed and that many of the major artists of the twentieth century were determined to put it into action in their works. What Lewis provides is an articulate, sometimes extravagantly zealous attack on the excesses, the limitations, and the failures of those works. He is not always right, and one may well suspect that he is only occasionally right; nevertheless, he knows the danger that artists, particularly lesser artists, face when they record the minutiae of sensation. From Lewis' extreme position, the well-read student can move back into a more balanced, less prejudiced position, taking along some of the rigorous skepticism of a man who was not easily swayed by fashion and was not afraid of sometimes looking the fool.

The book must also be seen as part of the Lewis canon. He was always a propagandist, a satirist, a troublemaker, and a splendidly irreverent upsetter of literary applecarts. In this work, he turns philosophical polemics into something which looks suspiciously like fun, and he can be read just for the pleasure of watching him blasting his way across the landscape of modern thinking, throwing everything into disarray for the moment, and making it necessary to think again— or, indeed, for the first time—about ideas which have been taken for granted.

Sources for Further Study

Grigson, Geoffrey. *A Master of Our Time: A Study of Wyndham Lewis*, 1951.
Jameson, Fredric. *Fables of Aggression: Wyndham Lewis, the Modernist as Fascist*, 1979.
Kenner, Hugh, *Wyndham Lewis*, 1954.
Pritchard, William H. *Wyndham Lewis*, 1968.
Tomlin, E. W. F. *Wyndham Lewis*, 1955.
Wagner, Geoffrey. *Wyndham Lewis: A Portrait of the Artist as the Enemy*, 1957.

Charles Pullen

A TIME TO DANCE, NO TIME TO WEEP
An Autobiography

Author: Rumer Godden (1907-   )
Type of work: Autobiography
Time of work: 1907-1946
Locale: England and India
First published: 1987

> *Principal personages:*
> RUMER GODDEN, a writer
> ARTHUR LEIGH GODDEN, her father
> KATHERINE HINGLEY GODDEN, her mother
> JON,
> ROSE, and
> NANCY, her sisters
> LAURENCE FOSTER, her first husband

Form and Content

Rumer Godden, the second of four daughters of Arthur Leigh Godden and Katherine Hingley Godden, was born December 10, 1907, in Eastbourne, Sussex. Taken to India in infancy (her father worked for the oldest Indian inland navigation company), she began a childhood that was divided between India and England and that was to have great influence on her career as a writer. A prolific author of children's books, poetry, novels, and works of nonfiction, Godden has seen six of her stories become films. *A Time to Dance, No Time to Weep*, the first volume of her autobiography, covers the years 1907 to 1946.

It is clear that Godden's memories of childhood in India with her sisters are happy ones. Her contacts with servants and villagers of the smaller towns of India introduced her to the variety of religions, ethnic backgrounds, and class systems that made up the social fabric of the great subcontinent. This exposure developed in her a tolerance for diversity and a compassion for those who suffer economic or social exploitation. Unlike many of her compatriots, who never understood, or wished to understand, the rich cultural traditions of the various peoples of India, the young Godden immersed herself in them. Her own experiences as she moved from the warm, exotic beauties of India to the cold, rather puritanical household of her paternal grandmother in London, or a school run by an order of Anglican nuns, taught her the problems of being different. She has retained strong sympathies for Eurasians, who seemed suspended between two worlds, welcome in neither.

There is a balance in her memories of India, golden as they are. Not only did English children suffer separation from their families, but in residence in India they also endured many dangers, illnesses, and accidents. Bitten by rabid dogs, the

Godden girls had to endure the painful procedures of the Pasteur treatment to protect them against hydrophobia. Moreover, English husbands and fathers such as Arthur Godden spent months away from their families pursuing their work, and often their vacations were spent on hunting or exploratory expeditions. Of great benefit to the young Goddens was that they traveled widely over India, seeing its great cities and its outlying provinces. Godden's autobiography is characterized by themes that appear in her novels: the isolation and pain of being different, the contrasting and sometimes insurmountable differences between the outlooks of East and West, and the vagaries of relationships threatened by alienation, separation, and indifference.

Trained as a dancer from childhood, Godden dedicated the years from 1920 to 1925 to study of ballet in London. Returning to India, she opened a dancing school for children in Calcutta in 1928. In 1934, she was married to a young stockbroker, Laurence Foster. Following the birth of their son David, who lived only a few days, Godden continued teaching and began writing, something that had interested her from the age of five, when she had begun writing poems. Two daughters were born to Foster and Godden, Jane in 1935 and Paula in 1938. Both daughters were born in England. The publication of Godden's first book, in 1936, brought her some success, and in 1939 she achieved international attention with the publication of *Black Narcissus*.

In 1939, she returned again to India, fearing danger to her daughters as World War II began. Her husband joined the army, leaving her in serious financial straits because of his free-spending habits. The deteriorating marriage continued formally, but there was little left of the relationship. Godden's account of her struggle during the war years in Kashmir, in beautiful but primitive surroundings, is one of the most gripping parts of her memoir. Although this period ended in illness, fear, and eventually flight, she knew great happiness and satisfaction there.

Godden's last tour of the province of Bengal was undertaken for the Women's Voluntary Services to chronicle the part played by women of that province during the war; her report was published as *Bengal Journey: A Story of the Part Played by Women in the Province, 1939-1945* in 1945. In that year Godden returned to England, and in 1946 she wrote one of her finest stories of India, *The River*.

Her autobiography is characterized by the author's gift of storytelling, by her ability to handle time and flashbacks gracefully, and by her descriptive powers, which critics have always found formidable.

Analysis

A Time to Dance, No Time to Weep has been well received by critics because it clarifies the genesis of Godden's work. Always reticent about her private life and that of her family, with her autobiography Godden has put many ideas found in her novels into perspective. She is generous toward her first husband, who seems to have been unequal to his responsibilities, and honest in her evaluation of her own actions from the perspective of eighty years. What has been suggested by critics as important to her writing has also been important in her life.

Godden's autobiography, therefore, expresses cogently the strongly held principles that have always been evident in her writing. Her own experience speaks to the fact that all individuals are part of a culture, and even the best intentioned cannot expect to penetrate another culture fully. One can try to learn, understand, and appreciate the alien point of view, but Englishmen cannot become Indian, and Indians cannot become European, although they may try.

In the book *Kingfishers Catch Fire* (1953), Sophie Ward wishes to live as the peasants do in Kashmir. Her failure to understand local customs endangers her family, and when her daughter is badly beaten, she realizes that she must leave. During her stay at Dove House in Kashmir, where she went because she had so little money, Godden hoped to live simply, like the peasants; yet she experienced the same failure that Sophie Ward did. Her mistake in ignoring local advice on the hiring of servants led to danger to her and her children and the necessity of leaving.

Godden is frequently preoccupied with religion; three of her novels deal with women under monastic rule. All of her books indicate the acceptance of a divine presence, and she seems to believe that one's religion, however imperfectly followed, is a binding force. This is not to suggest that her writing is a vehicle for any particular religious belief, nor is it overly didactic. She holds simply that people are bound by their religious beliefs, as they are by their cultural origins.

The importance of the family is another constant in her life. She believes that it is within the family that children learn the basic facts of living. Life, birth, death, suffering, joy, supportive love, and selflessness are learned as one grows from childhood to adulthood. The continuity of the family is important, and it is worth noting that two of Godden's novels, *China Court: The Hours of a Country House* (1961) and *A Fugue in Time* (1945), are concerned with houses that witness several generations of human drama. *A Time to Dance, No Time to Weep* illustrates Godden's love of houses in which she has lived.

As a result of these positions, Godden has often been described as "conventional." It is pointed out that her males are "lordly" and domineering. Yet a reading of her autobiography reveals a very strong female whose resources seem limitless and who is equal to many challenges.

Godden's ability to handle time has long been admired by critics. They contend that her placement of past, present, and future events is the most remarkable characteristic of her best work. She may interest her readers in details and then, through a series of flashbacks, reveal important aspects of the lives of her protagonists. Such techniques give deeper meaning to her characterizations, allowing her to make them credible and well-rounded. In several of her books, Godden has experimented with sequence. Not satisfied with earlier efforts, she persevered in fashioning tales in which time is blurred, so that past and present seem one. Time is also important in the autobiography, which follows not only Godden's life but also the lives of those dear to her. The loves and sorrows, marriages and accomplishments, children and travels of her three sisters are incorporated into her own story.

She describes her father's retirement and return to England with her mother. Her parents' support of her and her daughters continued through the war years despite the distance which separated them.

All these comments on time, family, continuity, and wholeness in the autobiography point up Godden's preoccupation with craftsmanship. *A Time to Dance, No Time to Weep* opens with a preface in which Jon and Rumer Godden stand on the quay in Plymouth, watching as their luggage is unloaded from the ship that has brought them from India for formal education in England. The sisters are chilled not only by the weather but also by the realization that they are facing the end of childhood. As the book ends twenty-six years later, Godden stands on the quay at Liverpool. With little money, but with a valuable Indian rug under one arm and the newly finished manuscript of *The River* under the other, she is ready to begin again.

Godden's ability to describe natural settings—panoramic views of snow-capped mountains and the rivers of India—is mentioned by every critic. Her descriptions of the homes in which she lived with joy, as well as those that held less happy memories, are equally impressive.

More subtle, and possibly more important to her work, are her depictions of people, physical and psychological. Godden depicts children with particular skill. She conveys their innocence and vulnerability, for she knows the depth of humiliation and hurt that coldness and betrayal can evoke. Her memories of the nuns at St. Monica's, who used public humiliation as a punishment and who felt it their duty to break the spirits of those who did not fit the norm, are depicted vividly. Yet she is able to rise above the injured child's point of view, commenting that it must have been as hard for the nuns to deal with the "little fishes" from India as it was for the young Goddens to respond to the nuns. Whether *Black Narcissus*, which tells of the failure of the goals of a group of Anglican nuns in India, is a response to that unhappy time is not clear, although Godden suggests that the story was undertaken partly as retribution. Her description of the Indians whom she came to know well, trusted servants and friends such as the Kashmiri Jobara, and members of the older generation whom she admired for their wisdom, are well served by her artistry in delineating character.

Yet it is her portrayal of adolescence that is most insightful. She remembers the difficulty of growing up, the painful lessons learned, the heartaches and self-consciousness, and the vulnerability to criticism or unkindness. A growing awareness made her understand that life is a mixture of good and bad, that relationships between men and women are fraught with disappointment, that everything is more complicated than one might wish.

Godden's style is deceptively simple. It reads well and it is poetic. Godden quickly captures the reader's attention with her highly developed flair for the dramatic. Careful analysis indicates that her language is also subtle, precise, and rigorously honed. It is easy to miss the underlying unity and the scrupulous attention to pattern in *A Time to Dance, No Time to Weep*. In describing her work habits, Godden mentions that she read aloud one manuscript to her sister Jon, although she hated to have anyone read to her. When Godden finished, Jon said quietly that it simply would not do, and the author returned to her writing to rework the material to meet the exacting standards she had always employed. Most critics consider that only her first book lacked this craftsmanship. Since Godden was not formally prepared for her writing career, she had to find her own way, but she was also free of restrictions.

The only comprehensive study of Godden's work was published in 1973. Some of the previous criticism had examined the stream-of-consciousness portions of her work and her experiments with symbols. One critic commented that she belonged in the great symbolist movement, and while he would not place her beside Herman Melville, William Butler Yeats, or James Joyce, he looked forward to reading her future work with enthusiasm. Some of Godden's symbols are immediately evident: the river as the symbol for the continuity and flow of life which sweeps all before it; the garden as Eden; childhood as the age of innocence; the serpent as evil; the death of a child as the Fall and the loss of innocence. Yet others are far more subtle and are recognizable only after reflection.

Godden is gifted at creating an atmosphere of observations woven into a complex but satisfactory whole. As she calmly and dispassionately reviews her childhood, adolescence, and life as a young wife, mother, and author, she finds her life to have been painful, but also joyous, filled with humor and love, and eminently worth living.

Critical Context

Rumer Godden is one of the last English writers to have been influenced by the British colonial experience in India. As in the case of many others before her, she loved and hated much of what she remembered from her life there. The physical beauty of the country and the graciousness of many aspects of its culture clash with the cheapness of human life amid the grim poverty of great numbers of the population. The strict divisions of class and religion and the fanatic hatreds bred between groups contrast with the decency, devotion, and wisdom of individuals. The contrast with English traditions and behavior is often described in striking paradox. Parallel construction is one of Godden's preferred techniques, and her life in two cultures affords ample opportunity for its employment.

The autobiography also recalls the uneasy history of the period it covers, an era of two world wars which dislocated lives and too frequently caused loss of loved ones. Godden seldom baldly states her personal or political points of view, but she does recall that with many others of her generation, she had signed a peace pledge, vowing never to fight for king or country. With the suicide of her Jewish doctor, who had learned of the suffering of his people in Germany, she realized that she must renounce that pledge.

Despite her care in avoiding political stances, Godden does imprint her own vision and personality on the work. One of its greatest achievements is the illumination of her literary work. Clearly, art follows life here. Time after time Godden's experiences are mirrored in her work; indeed, no part of her experience seems wasted.

Finally, *A Time to Dance, No Time to Weep* is the portrait of a remarkable woman who through the changes of her life has developed a discipline and serenity of spirit, a "willed composure" that some have found very "close to wisdom."

Sources for Further Study

Billington, Michael. "Three Passions in Calcutta," in *The New York Times Book Review*. XCIII (January 3, 1988), p. 3.

Godden, Rumer. "On Words," in *The Writer*. LXXV (September, 1962), pp. 17-19.

_____. *Two Under the Indian Sun*, 1966.

Prescott, Orville. "The Essence of Experience: Godden, Winslow, Widgenden," in *In My Opinion*, 1952.

Simpson, Hassell A. *Rumer Godden*, 1973.

Tindall, William Y. "Rumer Godden, Public Symbolist," in *College English*. XIII (March, 1953), pp. 297-303.

Anne R. Vizzier

TIMEBENDS
A Life

Author: Arthur Miller (1915-   )
Type of work: Autobiography
Time of work: 1915-1987
Locale: The United States, Italy, the Soviet Union, Yugoslavia, and China
First published: 1987

> *Principal personages:*
> ARTHUR MILLER, a playwright and the author of the
>   autobiography
> MARY SLATTERY, the Ohio Catholic to whom Miller was married
>   despite her family's opposition
> MARILYN MONROE, the flamboyant and troubled actress who
>   became Miller's second wife
> INGE MORATH, a professional photographer and Miller's third wife

Form and Content

While *All My Sons* was opening in Boston in 1947, Arthur Miller was already dreaming of another play that would

> cut through time like a knife through a layer cake or a road through a mountain revealing its geologic layers, and instead of one incident in one time-frame succeeding another, display past and present concurrently, with neither one ever coming to a stop.

Two years later, *Death of a Salesman*, the American play most firmly established in the world repertoire, achieved that structure of simultaneity and, as far as anyone can predict, artistic timelessness. "Attention must be paid," says Linda Loman about her husband Willy, and audiences have concurred—even in Beijing, where, despite a lack of traveling salesmen, a Chinese production of the Miller play was a success in 1983.

Attention must also be paid to *Timebends*. Its eight sections are arranged in loose chronological order, but within each the author proceeds according to the dictates of thought and theme rather than the calendar. Past, present, and future blend in a Sargasso Sea, and anyone who would jump in and out abruptly is vulnerable to temporal caisson disease: "timebends."

Miller rehearses the story of a working-class Jewish childhood in New York, an early job in an automobile parts warehouse, and student days at the University of Michigan. He recounts the failures of his first two marriages. The first, to Mary Slattery, an Ohio Catholic, was opposed by her parents and is presented as a casualty of Miller's burgeoning success. The second, to Marilyn Monroe, was much more passionate and publicized, and Miller sees it as a victim of the troubled actress' private demons. He writes with satisfaction of twenty-five years of marriage to photographer Inge Morath.

Miller reviews the successes and disappointments he experienced writing for the theater and for film, and he provides telling portraits of such notable contemporaries as Lee J. Cobb, Elia Kazan, Lee and Paula Strasberg, Clark Gable, Clifford Odets, and Laurence Olivier. Throughout his very active career, Miller has been intent on maintaining sympathy for the plight of ordinary people, and he describes at some length how, for example, immediately after the triumph of *All My Sons* freed him to sit in a study and write, he instead sought out a menial job in a beer box factory. His wanderings through the Brooklyn waterfront and his visit to a devastated Italy after World War II shaped the compassionate vision behind *A View from the Bridge* (1955).

Miller was an active participant in the 1949 Waldorf Conference organized by cultural and scientific leaders to encourage a *rapprochement* between the United States and the Soviet Union. His refusal to subscribe to Cold War pieties and his activities to promote peace and justice led to a defiant appearance before the House Committee on Un-American Activities. Seeking greater publicity for its campaign to purge American society of leftists, the committee went after actors, directors, and authors during the 1950's. Subpoenaed in 1956, Miller was found in contempt of Congress when, genuinely contemptuous of a state that pried into private beliefs, he refused to cooperate. The conviction was overturned on the ground that the committee's patriotism inquests had nothing to do with legislation. Though its ostensible subject was the witch trials in seventeenth century Salem, Massachusetts, Miller's 1953 play *The Crucible* implicitly portrayed the social repression and Red-baiting prevalent during the reign of Senator Joseph McCarthy.

As president of the International Association of Poets, Playwrights, Editors, Essayists, and Novelists (PEN), Miller succeeded in revivifying that moribund world federation of authors. From the 1960's through the 1980's, he served as a kind of literary statesman, traveling to distant countries to affirm the principles of free expression. Whether as author or as artistic diplomat, Miller consistently acted on his belief that art is dependent upon a moral world. The author of an impressive body of work that includes the plays *After the Fall* (1964), *Incident at Vichy* (1964), and *The Price* (1968), Miller presents himself as a respected public figure chary of publicity. *Timebends* is a meditation on fame and fortune through a backward glance over memorable moments of a productive life.

Analysis

It is a willful amnesia that Miller finds so distressing in American society. Writing is impossible without any historical awareness, though making connections to the past can also be hazardous. Miller gave the title *Danger: Memory!* (1987) to two one-act plays he wrote immediately before *Timebends*. His description, in the autobiography, of their sense of "imploding time," of "moments when a buried layer of experience suddenly surges upward to become the new surface of one's attention and flashes news from below," is as applicable to the perilous exhilaration of *Timebends* itself as it is to the plays.

"In the sense that we lack any real awareness of a continuity with the past," he laments, "we are, I think, a country without a theatre culture." Miller's plays have been important to whatever such culture there is in the United States, though *Death of a Salesman* is the only one of his theatrical works to have received largely favorable reviews at its premiere. More than poets and novelists, playwrights are dependent on the verdict of critics, particularly of whoever is writing for *The New York Times*, and on the vagaries of avaricious producers. Describing his successful adaptations throughout the rest of the world, Miller presents himself as a prophet with little honor in his own country, which once even stripped him of his passport. True, he has been a guest at Democratic and Republican White Houses, but the America he describes is one in which serious drama is increasingly neglected. During the previous four decades, he saw the United States "devolving into a mania for the distraction it called entertainment, day-and-night mimicry of art that menaced nothing, redeemed nothing, and meant nothing but forgetfulness."

Timebends is a guerrilla action against the insidious appeal of oblivion and an effort to remember when, for all of its difficulties, theater mattered. Miller's ambitions from the outset were to offer something more important than diversion in the face of war and oppression. "I could not imagine a theatre worth my time that did not want to change the world," he declares. In its earnestness, this autobiography is worthy of Miller's seventy-two years and the several hours a reader might spend on it.

"Celebrity is merely a different form of loneliness," writes a man who, during the moments of his greatest public triumphs, mistrusted success and fled from the public gaze. "He is strongest who is most alone," according to a line Miller quotes from Henrik Ibsen's *En folkefiende* (1882; *An Enemy of the People*, 1890), a play he adapted into English. Though reticence is one of his themes, it is a disingenuous pose for an autobiographer. Critical of a culture in which "most people would much rather laugh than cry, rather watch an actor being hit on the head by a pig bladder than by some painful truth," Miller presents himself with self-righteousness and self-pity as a solitary seeker of truth who defies the frivolousness of the American public. He is wary of the kind of acclaim that is capable of destroying its own object: "The story of American playwrights is awfully repetitious—celebratory embraces soon followed by rejection or contempt, and this without exception for any playwright who takes risks and does not comfortably repeat himself." The story that this playwright tells of himself is of an author who refused to bask in early success and whose attempts to challenge himself and his audiences sabotaged his popularity. *Timebends* is a statement of artistic credo and a justification for the shape of its author's career.

Miller's extraordinary second wife made him the object of massive publicity, and, among those with more taste for melodrama than for drama, he probably remained best known as the husband of Marilyn Monroe. The marriage seemed a pairing of theater and Hollywood, of brains and beauty, of Jew and Gentile, and it did not survive the filming of *The Misfits* (1961), a screenplay that Miller wrote expressly to fortify a woman who was "dancing at the edge of oblivion."

Among the thirty-two pages of photographs in *Timebends* are four shots of Monroe, captioned "the best of times." Yet Miller also describes his twenty-five years with photographer Inge Morath, his third wife, as "the best of my life." First wife Mary Slattery, the Midwestern Catholic whom the Brooklyn Jew claims to have outgrown, is only a spectral presence.

Timebends is not the definitive biography of Arthur Miller. Too many omissions, such as the absence of any mention of his 1980 television film about the Holocaust, *Playing for Time*, keep this from being a complete record of the man who "wanted to write a play that would stand on the stage like a boulder that had fallen from the sky, undeniable, a fact." *Timebends* stands as the testimony of a decent, thoughtful, occasionally sanctimonious man. It is the self-portrait of a playwright in a world where theaters are going dark. His epitaph for Marilyn Monroe might do double service for himself: "She was a poet on a street corner trying to recite to a crowd pulling at her clothes." Miller wears his duds with dignity.

Critical Context

Ultimately, *Timebends* is not the principal work on which Arthur Miller's reputation will rest; if he had not written the handful of plays that have entered the standard theatrical repertoire, this autobiography would not be read, but then neither could it have been written. It is the summation, from the perspective of early old age, of Miller's growth, through 1987, as a writer and a human being. Miller has published one novel, *Focus* (1945); one volume of short stories, *I Don't Need You Any More* (1967); and numerous essays. He will be remembered, however, as he remembers himself—as a playwright—and this book is a drama of ideas brought to another stage.

Timebends provides suggestive but elusive insights into the creative process and will be a valuable resource to anyone investigating the genesis of Miller's plays. He presents his salesman uncle, Manny Newman, as in part a model for Willy Loman, and, while acknowledging that *After the Fall* draws on the circumstances of his troubled marriage to Marilyn Monroe, he refuses to concede that it exploits that relationship. The book is also a remarkable participant's account of the social, political, and theatrical history of the United States during the decades that followed World War II.

Age has not softened Miller's desire for social justice or his contempt for the unexamined life he sees too many of his countrymen living. Like Miller's plays, *Timebends* is a jeremiad, made compelling by the authority with which Miller's achievement as playwright endows him. Convinced that "there could be no aesthetic form without a moral world, only notes without a staff," he offers these notes of a career spent trying to reconcile the aesthetic and the moral. *Timebends* is ambitious in its literary design and in its designs on the reader's imagination. "A failure to imagine will make us die," declares Miller in this imaginative account of a playwright's life.

Sources for Further Study
Bloom, Harold, ed. *Arthur Miller*, 1987.
Corrigan, Robert W., ed. *Arthur Miller: A Collection of Critical Essays*, 1969.
Hogan, Robert. *Arthur Miller*, 1964.
Huftel, Sheila. *Arthur Miller: The Burning Glass*, 1965.
Martin, Robert A., ed. *Arthur Miller: New Perspectives*, 1981.
Martine, James J., ed. *Critical Essays on Arthur Miller*, 1979.
Moss, Leonard. *Arthur Miller*, 1980 (revised edition).
Murray, Edward. *Arthur Miller, Dramatist*, 1967.
Nelson, Benjamin. *Arthur Miller: Portrait of a Playwright*, 1970.
The New Yorker. Review. LXIII (December 14, 1987), p. 150.
Newsweek. Review. CX (November 16, 1987), p. 110.
Publishers Weekly. Review. CCXXXII (October 16, 1987), p. 76.
Time. Review. CXXX (November 23, 1987), p. 88.
Welland, Dennis. *Miller: The Playwright*, 1967.

Steven G. Kellman

TO KEEP THE BALL ROLLING

Author: Anthony Powell (1905-   )
Type of work: Memoir
Time of work: 1905 to the late 1970's
Locale: Great Britain, the United States, Japan, Bulgaria, and other countries
First published: 1983: *Infants of the Spring*, 1976; *Messengers of Day*, 1978; *Faces in My Time*, 1980; *The Strangers All Are Gone*, 1982

> *Principal personages:*
> ANTHONY POWELL, a British novelist
> VIOLET PACKENHAM, his wife
> CYRIL CONNOLLY, an editor and essayist
> ERIC BLAIR (GEORGE ORWELL), a writer
> EVELYN WAUGH, a novelist
> MALCOLM MUGGERIDGE, an editor at *Punch*

Form and Content

In 1976, Anthony Powell, author of the highly acclaimed twelve-volume series of novels, *A Dance to the Music of Time* (1951-1975), published *Infants of the Spring*, the first of the four volumes which make up his memoirs. The second, *Messengers of Day*, appeared in 1978, followed by *Faces in My Time* in 1980 and *The Strangers All Are Gone* in 1982. Together they make up *To Keep the Ball Rolling*, which in turn was published in an abridged one-volume edition in 1983.

Powell took the title for *Infants of the Spring* from William Shakespeare's *Hamlet* ("The canker galls the infants of the spring"). Born in London in 1905, Powell was descended from an old Welsh family. Avowing an avid interest in genealogy, he explained that what attracted him to a study of his family was "the vast extent of human oddness." In both Powell's novels and his memoirs, it is most often human eccentricities which capture the writer's attention and the reader's interest. His father, one of those human oddities, was a professional soldier, and many of the experiences of Powell's childhood were later transformed into his portrayal of the childhood of Nicholas Jenkins, the narrator in *The Kindly Ones* (1962), the sixth volume of *A Dance to the Music of Time*.

His family's middle-class aspirations and expectations for an only son made a private education mandatory, and Powell entered Eton College, the exclusive public school, in 1919. Disliking cricket and most other sports, Powell instead joined the Eton Society of Arts, a student group presided over by the future aesthetes Brian Howard and Harold Acton, and including the future novelist Henry (Green) Yorke. Also at Eton during those years were Cyril Connolly, the essayist and editor, and Eric Blair (George Orwell).

In 1923, Powell entered the University of Oxford, where he became a student at Balliol College, with its "arrogant brilliance." Powell admired his college's tradition of tolerance, a quality often expressed in his writings and his own temperament. Yet he was not as challenged at Balliol as he had been at Eton; his time at Oxford was seemingly less memorable, although during those years his friendship with Connolly grew and he became acquainted with Evelyn Waugh. His descriptions of those who crossed his path at Eton and Balliol make up a considerable part of *Infants of the Spring*.

The second volume of Powell's memoirs, *Messengers of Day* (a title taken from *Julius Caesar*), begins in 1926. Not yet twenty-one years old, Powell went to London to learn the publishing business at the firm of Gerald Duckworth and Company. His first months in London were socially difficult and dreary, but that changed with the reappearance of Evelyn Waugh, at that time writing *Decline and Fall* (1928). Waugh's London connections opened many doors, and he became a continuing character in *Messengers of Day*. The discussion of Waugh and his life — anecdotal, with occasional and often coincidental meetings during the many years before Waugh's death in the 1960's—is typical of Powell's memoirs. Through Waugh and others, Powell joined the London social scene, with its continuous round of parties and debutante dances. A socially acceptable, Oxford-educated young man, even if he had little money, was always welcome. He also came to know many members of London's artistic and intellectual community, and Powell, ever the observer, made much use of those experiences in his later novels, particularly in *A Buyer's Market* (1952), the second volume in *A Dance to the Music of Time*.

In *Messengers of Day*, Powell discusses various literary figures who influenced him during the late 1920's: E. E. Cummings and to a lesser degree Ernest Hemingway, but not, he claims, James Joyce, although Powell smuggled the forbidden *Ulysses* (1922) from France in 1927. He also discovered Robert Burton's *The Anatomy of Melancholy* (1621), about which his fictional alter ego, Nicholas Jenkins, would later write. Many critics have also noticed a connection to Marcel Proust, whose works Powell first read while at Oxford. According to Powell, everyone he knew was writing a novel at that time, and he was no exception, with his first novel, *Afternoon Men*, appearing in 1931. Somewhat to his surprise, it was received by the critics as a bitter satire, although he saw it rather as an "urban pastoral."

Shortly after the publication of *Venusberg* in 1932, Powell reduced his hours at Duckworth's, hoping, after the publication of two novels, to branch out into journalism. A third novel, *From a View to a Death*, appeared in 1933. As the second volume of his memoirs ends, Powell's publishing career has waned, but his three novels, although unrewarding financially, have been satisfactorily reviewed by the critics.

Faces in My Time (a title taken from *King Lear*) covers the years from 1934 to the early 1950's. This was perhaps the most significant period of Powell's life—it brought marriage and war—and proved to be seminal in the development of his later multivolume novel. Powell's fourth novel, *Agents and Patients*, published in 1936, continued the trend of his earlier novels by being more representative of the

1920's than of the politicized 1930's. In 1934, Powell met his future wife, Violet Packenham, daughter of an Anglo-Irish aristocrat, the Earl of Longford.

In 1936, Powell attempted to become a film scriptwriter, and he humorously describes his brief career at one of the London-based American companies, Warner Bros. Powell later transferred his London experiences to Hollywood, where he was no more successful, and he finally returned to England. Back in London and unemployed, Powell began writing book reviews for the British press and working on his fifth novel, *What's Become of Waring*, published in 1939. Rereading that novel later, he noted its reflection of that eve-of-war era "by a sense of nervous tension that seems to underlie a superficially lighthearted tone of voice." Even before the outbreak of World War II, Powell concluded that, given the climate of the times, it was impossible for him to write another novel. Instead he began a study of John Aubrey, the seventeenth century antiquary and author of *Brief Lives* (1813).

When war came, Powell, although overage, was able to get a posting as a second lieutenant in his father's old unit. In 1941, he was transferred to the Intelligence Training Centre at Cambridge and then posted to London, where he served for most of the remainder of the war as liaison to several of the governments-in-exile from German-occupied countries. During the war years Powell met old friends and acquaintances, made new ones, and then later used those characters and incidents in the composition of his multivolume novel. The end of the war found Powell's wife pregnant with their second child, while Powell returned to reviewing, which he describes in a chapter titled "Upper Grub Street," and to his study of Aubrey, which was published after much delay in 1948.

The Strangers All Are Gone ("Come, let's away; the strangers all are gone," *Romeo and Juliet*), the final volume of Powell's memoirs, carries the story to the end of the 1970's. The technique continues to be ironic and anecdotal, but the chronological narrative becomes more diffuse. In what was perhaps a defense against his critics, Powell wrote,

> I have chosen to make a kind of album of odds and ends in themselves at times trivial enough. In the course of my own reading I have often found the trivial to be more acceptable, even more instructive in the long run, than some attempts at being profound.

The volume continues his short descriptions of the faces he has known in a way that echoes John Aubrey's *Brief Lives*. In the early 1950's Powell, through an inheritance, was able to purchase The Chantry, a nineteenth century country house in the west of England, and he recites tales about life at The Chantry in his usual fashion.

In 1953, Malcolm Muggeridge, Powell's longtime friend and then editor of *Punch*, asked Powell to become the literary editor of the magazine. He accepted, no easy task given Muggeridge's strong personality and outspoken political opinions. Powell left *Punch* around 1960 and became involved in the obscenity trial of D. H. Lawrence's *Lady Chatterley's Lover* (1928). Powell, who had doubts about the novel on literary grounds, was asked to be a witness for the defense but was never called to testify. He is more enthusiastic about the memoirs of Casanova, which he discusses along with *Lady Chatterley's Lover* and the anonymous *My Secret Life* in a chapter titled "Fit for Eros."

In the early 1960's, his first novel, *Afternoon Men*, was produced on the London stage. Fascinated with the process, even though the play ran for only a short time, Powell notes the differences between a novel and a play; in the latter the actor can and will give his or her own interpretation of the character, while in a novel the writer is more in control. The reviews were mixed, and Powell expressed the traditional complaint of the playwright: Drama critics have too much influence. Nevertheless, he went on to write two plays, though neither was ever produced.

As the various volumes of *A Dance to the Music of Time* regularly appeared, Powell's fame increased and he traveled abroad to various literary gatherings. He visited the Unites States in 1961 for the first time since his brief Hollywood sojourn, and in 1964 Powell was invited to Japan to help commemorate the four hundredth anniversary of Shakespeare's birth. Powell records many humorous anecdotes about his visit, especially concerning the differences between East and West, and he reveals himself to be a rather traditional Englishman who, at least in his memoir, judges others by his own standards. He also participated in a writers' conference in Venice, some of which he recorded in *Temporary Kings* (1973). He writes amusingly of still another conference, in Bulgaria, in the company of C. P. Snow. At the conclusion, Snow told Powell, "You were a great success. . . . There was an argument as to whether you looked like a professor or a soldier." Powell then fell silent, seeming to ponder the strangeness of the personality with which he had lived so long. He adds, "I had often wondered about it myself."

At the end of his memoirs, in a chapter titled "Grave Goods," Powell attempted a summary of his life and work. Perhaps it might better be said that Powell alludes to and then escapes from any precise summary. He asks, "But if the consolation for life is art, what may the artist expect from life?" He then turns to Giorgio Vasari, the Renaissance artist and historian who recounted the time when the Medicis of Florence ordered Michelangelo to build a snowman in the palace courtyard. Powell notes that the result was undoubtedly the finest snowman in history. Furthermore, he observes, "If you want something done get the best executant available to do it; that minor jobs are often worth taking on; that duration in time should not necessarily be the criterion in producing a work of art." The reader is left to wonder if Powell, then well into his eighth decade, is alluding to his own literary career—that of the detached and ironic observer of a particular segment of British society during the twentieth century.

Analysis

At the beginning of *Infants of the Spring* Powell quotes Joseph Conrad:

> To keep the ball rolling I asked Marlow if this Powell was remarkable in any way. "He was not exactly remarkable," Marlow answered with his usual nonchalance. "In a general way it's very difficult to become remarkable. People won't take sufficient notice of one, don't you know."

To Keep the Ball Rolling was the overall title Powell chose for his memoirs, and some reviewers have indeed complained that the four volumes are in many ways unremarkable. Some argued that Powell was unwilling or unable to portray the deepest human emotions, that his female characters were generally underdeveloped, that, like his fictional alter ego, Nicholas Jenkins, Powell was overly passive and reflective, and that he refused to grapple with serious issues such as good and evil. Yet reviewers of his memoirs have also praised his wit, his ironic detachment, and his elegant literary style.

To Keep the Ball Rolling is a sequence of memoirs, not an autobiography. The four volumes are less about Powell the individual than about what he observed in the world outside himself. The writer's ego and personality are of less importance than the lives and activities of others; his interest in family genealogy stemmed from a desire not to discover who he was but to explore and comment upon the rest of humanity, the close study of which Friedrich Nietzsche described as fundamentally comic. In this sense, Powell might be seen as a post-Freudian, in that he only incidentally analyzes the inner human being. Many critics have also noted similarities between Powell and Marcel Proust; both wrote long novels, both were concerned with the essence of time, and both discussed societies and social classes undergoing a process of disintegration. Powell's sensitivity, however, is more external than internal—unlike Proust's.

Other reviewers of his memoirs praise Powell for his ironic common sense. To these critics, his so-called passivity is actually a kind of comic acceptance of the uniqueness of individual human beings. As a conservative Englishman, he was not one to urge change on society, much less advocate a particular ideology or worldview. His mission, if any, was to deflate the pretensions of human beings: not only those of the many characters who populate his writings but also his own—and those of the reader.

Some complain that for all Powell's discussion of the many authors in his memoirs, he tells the reader little about writing. He wittily describes writers and their personalities but generally not their works, and he is no more forthcoming about himelf as a writer. His explanation for choosing to write a multivolume novel—so he would not be restricted by the usual eighty-thousand-word novel and so he would not need to invent new characters for each book—seems both specious and superficial. Harold Acton, Powell's contemporary at Eton, commented that Powell was the last of the polite novelists, whose forte was civilized conversation, and although Acton agreed with Powell's descriptions of other writers, most of whom Acton knew himself, he argues that perhaps Powell's happy marriage had aborted certain other sensitivities and perceptions.

Most critics comment upon Powell's apparently conscious decision to distance himself from the reader. His own deeper feelings remain generally hidden, at least in the pages of his memoir. The reader senses that there is a civilized or, better yet, a classical sensibility at work, one drawn to a certain traditional society and its civilized values: the English upper-middle classes. The age of the mass man is not

Powell's, and he maintains his discreet distance from much of the modern world through his elegant sentences, his cool style, and his ironic wit.

In his memoirs, Powell states that his writings have sold as well in the United States as in England, which is interesting given their firmly British grounding. It could be argued that Powell is merely writing about the twentieth century in general, for his novels, especially *A Dance to the Music of Time*, are a brilliant portrayal of a broad group of generally upper-middle-class characters in a society experiencing much trauma if not disintegration—wars, economic depression, the rise of working-class politics, the general loss of community. Yet his work also very much reflects his class and his country. American readers of Powell's works might simply be fond of things British, such as the British monarchy and thatched cottages, or it may be that the best of Powell's writing, although rooted in a particular time and place, also transcends them. At worst, his novels could be enjoyed as the literate person's soap opera, full of conversation and incident, in itself no mean accomplishment.

His memoirs, however, pose a different problem for the reader. His elliptical and anecdotal style often depends on the reader's having some considerable knowledge of the numerous figures he discusses. Here even many of his fellow countrymen would be at a disadvantage at the time the volumes were published. Among the authors he discusses from the 1930's and 1940's, Waugh and Orwell are still widely known, and many readers will have some knowledge of writers such as Kingsley Amis and V. S. Naipaul. Still, most of the persons he briefly describes are figures who have sunk into anonymity, even for most readers in England. Because of his wit and style Powell makes many of those anecdotes interesting and amusing, but without some greater knowledge of the characters portrayed the stories often remain only partially appreciated.

Powell must have known that only a few of his readers would be able to follow him through his many stories. Some have complained that Powell's memoirs are much inferior to his novels, that he merely repeats old tales. It is doubtful that Powell was merely lazy when he composed his memoirs. It is even less likely that Powell had exhausted his abilities as a result of his long labors on *A Dance to the Music of Time*. After the four volumes of *To Keep the Ball Rolling* had been published, he wrote other novels of wit and substance. It seems more likely that Powell's choice of subject matter and style—his acquaintances and his brief observations of them—was a decision intentionally made. Powell was not writing his memoirs for the average reader.

Critics have often commented on the relationship between John Aubrey and Powell, noting that the latter's memoirs are a series of "brief lives." In his study of the seventeenth century writer, Powell praised Aubrey for his sensitivity, his descriptive anecdotes, his penetrating observations of a wide variety of individuals, his feeling that the present is rooted in the past. According to Powell, Aubrey was there to "watch and record," and he urged the reading of Aubrey, "for there, loosely woven together, is a kind of tapestry of the good and evil; the ingenuity and the folly; the integrity and the hypocrisy; the eccentricity, the melancholy . . . of the English race." It could well be an epitaph for Powell's own writings.

Critical Context

Although not the last of Powell's literary works, his memoirs were published when Powell was in his seventies, after a long and productive literary career. *Afternoon Men*, his earliest novel, had appeared in 1931, almost half a century before the first volume of *To Keep the Ball Rolling*. In the many years between, Powell wrote sixteen other novels as well as two volumes about Aubrey, in addition to composing innumerable reviews and other articles for various newspapers and magazines. In one sense his memoir is similar to those of many other literary figures, coming as it did toward the end of a literary life. Less personally revealing than the remembrances of some other figures of the twentieth century, Powell's memoirs are more traditional in form and content and perhaps more British than American in point of view.

What makes his memoirs of particular interest to many readers, however, is what they might reveal about the relationship between Powell's life and his masterpiece, *A Dance to the Music of Time*. The multivolume novel, written over many years, is in the opinion of many literary critics one of the major fictional works of the second half of the twentieth century. It is so monumental an accomplishment that it cannot help but cast a long shadow over the four volumes of *To Keep the Ball Rolling*. One wonders to what degree the fictional Nicholas Jenkins is a copy of the real Anthony Powell, how closely the many characters of the novel are modeled on persons known to Powell, and who those persons are. Whatever else Powell tells about his experiences, literary and otherwise, readers of the novel want to know how near art is to life.

Some critics of *To Keep the Ball Rolling* have claimed that one is best advised to read *A Dance to the Music of Time*, that the memoirs are an unsatisfactory and faint echo of those novels. When discussing his experiences with Welsh soldiers in the early days of World War II, Powell admits that the pertinent novels of his multivolume work "throw more light on the experience than can be achieved in memoirs." Frequently in his memoirs he refers to his colleagues and acquaintances who were later transformed into characters in the various novels in the series. Often the transformation was such that individuals assumed that they had been the model for a particular character when in fact they had not. If art imitates life, sometimes life wishes to imitate art. Powell confesses that many of his fictional characters are based on people he knew but argues, somewhat persuasively, that once invented elements come into play, the fictional persons begin to take on lives of their own; the individuals in *A Dance to the Music of Time* are not those whom Powell knew in the real world. Art might borrow from life, but it then becomes art. Readers of Powell's memoirs and his many works of fiction will continue to ponder that connection between fiction and reality.

Sources for Further Study

Barber, Michael. "Anthony Powell," in *The Paris Review*. XX (Spring, 1978), pp. 46-79.

Bayley, John. "The Artist as Raconteur," in *The Listener*. XCIX (May 11, 1978), p. 615.

Bergonzi, Bernard. *Anthony Powell*, 1971.

Brennan, Neil. *Anthony Powell*, 1974.

Gaston, Paul L. " 'This Question of Discipline': An Interview with Anthony Powell," in *The Virginia Quarterly Review*. LXI (Autumn, 1985), pp. 638-654.

Gorra, Michael. "The Modesty of Anthony Powell," in *The Hudson Review*. XXXIV (Winter, 1981/1982), pp. 595-600.

Morris, Robert K. *The Novels of Anthony Powell*, 1968.

Pritchard, William H. "Anthony Powell's Gift," in *The Hudson Review*. XXXVII (Autumn, 1984), pp. 363-370.

Russell, John. *Anthony Powell: A Quintet, Sextet, and War*, 1970.

——————. "Definitive Days," in *Modern Age*. XXVI (Summer/Fall, 1982), pp. 418-421.

Tucker, James. *The Novels of Anthony Powell*, 1976.

Eugene S. Larson

THE TONGUE SET FREE,
THE TORCH IN MY EAR,
and
THE PLAY OF THE EYES

Author: Elias Canetti (1905-　　)
Type of work: Autobiography
Time of work: 1905-1937
Locale: Europe
First published: Die gerettete Zunge: Geschichte einer Jugend, 1977 (*The Tongue Set Free: Remembrance of a European Childhood*, 1979); *Die Fackel im Ohr: Lebensgeschichte 1921-1931*, 1980 (*The Torch in My Ear*, 1982); *Das Augenspiel: Lebensgeschichte 1931-1937*, 1985 (*The Play of the Eyes*, 1986)

> *Principal personages:*
> ELIAS CANETTI, a writer
> JACQUES CANETTI, his father
> MATHILDE ARDITTI, his mother
> VENETIA (VEZA) TOUBNER-CALDERON, his wife
> KARL KRAUS, a writer and lecturer
> ROBERT MUSIL and
> HERMANN BROCH, his friends and fellow writers
> HERMANN SCHERCHEN, a conductor
> ALBAN BERG, a composer

Form and Content

An autobiography often sheds light on the major works of a writer. It is preferable to diaries or notebooks, since those can contain fragmentary thoughts which may or may not be fully developed. Some writers produce well-researched memoirs, which may give the appearance of justifying thoughts and actions after the fact.

The three volumes of Elias Canetti's autobiography leave readers with the impression that they have just listened to an elderly gentleman tell the story of his early life. Canetti thinks back fifty or more years and recalls events that made a significant impression on him. Sometimes the impression was crucial for only that moment; at other times, it was so profound that it endured throughout his life. Although the first and second volumes are arranged in chronological order—the third volume is divided topically—Canetti's interest seems to be more in telling a good story than in revealing logically ordered information.

These three volumes cover the period of time from Canetti's birth in 1905 until the death of his mother in the summer of 1937. This formative period of his life encompassed the years when he wrote his important novel *Die Blendung* (1935; *Auto-da-Fé*, 1946) and two plays, *Hochzeit* (1932; *The Wedding*, 1984) and *Komödie der Eitelkeit* (1950; *Comedy of Vanity*, 1983). During this time Canetti also began work on his monumental lifelong study *Masse und Macht* (1960; *Crowds and Power*, 1962).

When Canetti won the Nobel Prize in Literature in 1981, there was considerable confusion on the question of which country could claim him as its writer. He was born in Russe (Rutschuk), Bulgaria. His family belonged to the group of Sephardic Jews who had been expelled from Spain in the fifteenth century and settled in Andrianople, Turkey. Since his paternal family had retained Turkish citizenship, Canetti was a Turkish citizen at the time of his birth. At home he spoke Ladino, an old form of Spanish that was spoken in the community of Sephardic Jews. In this environment he also learned Bulgarian and Hebrew, as well as several other languages.

When Canetti was six years old, the family moved to Manchester, England, where he learned English. When his father died in 1912, his mother decided that the family should move to Vienna, which meant that Canetti had to learn German. This stage of his life was an important one since he now had the opportunity to learn the language that his parents had used as their "secret language" at home. In the next decade, he learned three different types of German: From 1913 to 1916 he learned the German spoken in Vienna, from 1916 to 1921 that of Zurich, and from 1921 until 1924 the German of Frankfurt am Main. Upon completing secondary school in Frankfurt, he returned to Vienna, where he studied chemistry at the University of Vienna, completing his studies with a doctorate in 1929. For almost another decade he remained in Vienna, devoting himself completely to writing.

It must be mentioned that in late 1938 Canetti and his wife were among the last Jews to flee Vienna, which had been annexed to Adolf Hitler's Germany earlier that year. They settled in London in 1939, where Canetti would continue to reside. All of his writings are in German. Given his great admiration and affection for Vienna and the German language, the only country that might legitimately claim him as its Nobel laureate is Austria. Canetti, however, has never claimed a national or political identification. The Nobel Prize citation identified him correctly as the "exiled and cosmopolitan author" who has "one native land, and that is the German language."

From this multilingual and multiethnic background came Canetti's intense interest in the use and power of language. Even the titles of his autobiography allude to this great concern. The first volume, *The Tongue Set Free*, begins with Canetti's earliest remembrance. When he was two years old, his family spent the summer at Carlsbad, a spa in Czechoslovakia, where he was cared for by a young nanny. This girl enjoyed a liaison with a young man who lived in a room across the hall. In order to assure that the child not say anything, the man threatened every day to cut off his tongue with a jackknife. Although the young people were found out, the threat to the boy was so effective that Canetti "literally held his tongue for ten years."

The title of the next volume, *The Torch in My Ear*, makes direct reference to the journal *Die Fackel* (the torch), written and published by Karl Kraus, the most influential critic and polemicist in Vienna during the first third of this century. Kraus was an absolute master of the word. His writings and lectures attacked everything in society that he considered to be negative or corrupt. Yet, says Canetti, "Kraus was so fair that no one was accused unless he deserved it. Kraus never made a mistake; he couldn't make a mistake. Everything he produced was one hundred percent accurate." Although this may be a slight exaggeration, Canetti certainly did learn some of the power of the spoken and written word from Kraus.

The third volume of the autobiography, *The Play of the Eyes*, makes reference to yet another aspect of the word: the unspoken word. In his relationship with Alma Mahler, a most influential woman in the cultural life of Vienna, Canetti gleaned answers, replies, and attitudes from her appearance long before she spoke.

Throughout the autobiography, Canetti explains a concept which he developed in his early years: the "acoustic mask." He maintains that each individual has a unique manner and way of speaking, similar in uniqueness to fingerprints. This concept is articulated in his descriptions of the people he encounters, even if they speak a language he does not understand. When Canetti, for example, read his plays to Viennese audiences during the last years of his time there, he would assign a specific "acoustic mask" to each of the two dozen characters in the play in order to demonstrate the specific individuality he had assigned them.

The autobiography also reveals the preliminary investigations Canetti conducted for his major sociopsychological study *Crowds and Power*. Although the work was not completed until almost forty years after Canetti's early experiences with crowds, it is of considerable interest to learn how his initial involvement with large groups of people engaged in destructive activites compelled him to investigate this important phenomenon. Unfortunately, these three volumes of autobiography do not cover the very interesting period of Canetti's life from 1937 until 1960, when *Crowds and Power* appeared.

Analysis

It is not surprising that the autobiography of one of the major intellectual figures of the twentieth century pays homage to his literary heritage. In his three volumes, Canetti discusses a total of 111 authors and 118 works of literature, many of them at some length. For Canetti, the most influential writers from world literature are Aristophanes, Miguel de Cervantes, Dante, Fyodor Dostoevski, Homer, William Shakespeare, Jonathan Swift, and Leo Tolstoy. He is thoroughly familiar with the German classical writers of the eighteenth and nineteenth centuries such as Johann Wolfgang von Goethe, Friedrich Schiller, Georg Büchner, Heinrich von Kleist, Jakob Michael Reinhold Lenz, Gottfried Keller, Conrad Ferdinand Meyer, and Eduard Friedrich Mörike. Among his contemporaries, Canetti holds Karl Kraus, Hermann Broch, Robert Musil, Heinrich Mann, Thomas Mann, and Robert Walser in the highest regard. Many other writers are mentioned; all of them have influenced his thinking and writing. These belletrists are all members of Canetti's literary family.

A writer needs ancestors. He must know some of them by name. When he thinks he is going to choke on his own name, which he cannot get rid of, he harks back to ancestors, who bear happy, deathless names of their own. They may smile at his importunity, but they do not rebuff him. They too need others, in their case descendants.

Access to this world of literature was made possible by a few teachers; Canetti's mother, however, was the most influential force in assuring that he acquired this host of ancestors.

Following the death of Canetti's father in England when the boy was only seven years old, his mother decided to return to her favorite European city, Vienna. So that he could continue his schooling without interruption, the mother taught him German in three months. She also continued the daily reading and discussion periods which the father had started at an earlier time. Mother and son read Shakespeare in English and Schiller in German.

After each scene, she asked me how I understood it, and before saying anything herself, she always let me speak first. . . . The more intelligently I responded and the more I had to say, the more powerfully her old experience [for example, of going to the theater as a young woman] surfaced in her. . . . She spoke to me as to an adult.

Canetti admits that his understanding of these plays at that age was limited, yet the discussions served as a means of education that he would continue with his mother for many years. His mother was a stern teacher, demanding rigorous thinking and carefully articulated commentary. This very methodical and conscientious manner of reading and thinking is one which Canetti has continued throughout his life. This fact becomes especially evident when one reads his essays and the nonfiction study *Crowds and Power*.

Canetti experienced a most problematic relationship with his mother. As a young child he had been very devoted to his father, who had a joyous, loving, and extroverted personality. When the father died at age thirty of a stroke, the seven-year-old was devastated. Gradually, he came somehow to blame his mother for causing the death through intellectual infidelity. As his mother took on the task of rearing the three children alone, Elias, being the oldest, was given and assumed the role of the husband and father. He became his mother's intellectual partner when they read Shakespeare and Schiller. Occasionally he also was charged with the responsibility of caring for his younger brothers. As the years passed, the relationship between mother and son became more and more hostile—each making extraordinary demands on the other. An acute Oedipal complex apparently developed, ultimately resolved only through complete separation. The relationship between these two very powerful personalities remained antagonistic and unredeemed, even more than four decades after the mother's death.

In addition to revealing the impact his parents had on his development, Canetti writes about his encounters with grandfathers, uncles, and other members of the family. Both grandfathers seem to have been rather successful businessmen in

Bulgaria; the maternal grandfather even had several sons conducting business in Manchester, England. Canetti's father, who undoubtedly would have been a much happier man if he could have pursued his interests in playing the violin and in acting, was forced to enter the family business. Canetti's parents had met when both were students in Vienna, where they were enraptured by the magic of the theater performances at the Burgtheater (the royal theater). With the memory of his father as a jovial, creative, and playful person, and of his mother as a teacher of great dramatic literature, it is not surprising that the young Canetti was strongly attracted to a life of creativity and the mind. In his early years, however, he was not infrequently told by grandfathers, uncles, and others that he must abandon his fierce dedication to a life of learning and prepare himself for the task at hand: to be a successful businessman. The family reluctantly supported him while he studied chemistry at the University of Vienna, because they believed that his expertise in that field would enhance the business. Although Canetti completed his studies with a doctorate in chemistry, he never did—nor did he ever intend to—work as a chemist in business. Frequently, even at a young age, he expressed his abhorrence of business activities and his strong contempt for the acquisition of material wealth that he associated with the business world.

During his student years, from 1924 to 1929, Canetti became a member of the cultural and literary community in Vienna. Undoubtedly the most important experiences in this rich intellectual life were his meetings with Kraus and with Veza.

Kraus at that time was considered to be the greatest satirist since Jonathan Swift. As the founder and soon sole writer of the most influential magazine in Austria, *Die Fackel*, Kraus contributed brilliantly idiosyncratic social and literary criticism. His great drama *Die letzten Tage der Menschheit* (1918; the last days of mankind) is a visionary satiric tragedy of mankind, made up of a vast assemblage of scenes that intend to document the banality of an apocalypse during the years from 1914 to 1919. Although the play has never been performed (it is more than 800 pages long), Kraus often used selections from it for spellbinding public readings to large, devoted audiences in Vienna. Kraus was a master when it came to using the German language. Not only in the periodical and the plays but also in aphorisms and essayistic commentaries, Kraus demonstrated an unequaled linguistic creativity. Canetti attended almost every public reading and lecture that Kraus held during a decade. Kraus's readings of the different roles of characters in his play confirmed for Canetti the validity of his concept of the "acoustic mask" which every individual has. Furthermore, the nineteen-year-old Canetti must have experienced profound lessons in the use of language at the Kraus readings. Although he had demonstrated a sensitivity for the power of language at an early age, this proclivity surely became a lifelong obsession as a result of these encounters.

Veza was Venetia Toubner-Calderon, the woman Canetti wed in 1934. She was a highly intelligent and educated woman whom he met at the Kraus readings in 1924. Not unlike his mother before, Veza was Canetti's intellectual soulmate, but without the great personality conflicts. They discussed not only the Kraus readings and lectures but also all of their readings of classical and contemporary literature. Veza was the first sympathetic but intelligent critic of his novel *Auto-da-Fé* and his plays *The Wedding* and *Comedy of Vanity*.

From his student days until he left Vienna in 1938, Canetti remained at the center of Viennese literary and cultural life. In addition to discussing the artistic work of nearly all the people who are today considered significant from that period and place, Canetti describes his personal relationships with, for example, Robert Musil and the equally important writer Hermann Broch, who had published his novel *Die Schlafwandler* (1931-1932; *The Sleepwalkers*, 1932) just as Canetti was finishing his own major novel. Canetti was also a good friend of the conductor Hermann Scherchen, who specialized in modern music, as well as of the composer Alban Berg. In the field of the visual arts, Canetti reports on meetings with Oskar Kokoschka and the sculptor Fritz Wotruba, on whom he would later write a book.

In 1928, Canetti spent some time in Berlin, the other great cultural center of the German-speaking world. He had been invited to translate several works of the American writer Upton Sinclair. While there he met many artists, among them the playwright Bertolt Brecht, the painter George Grosz, and the Russian short-story writer and dramatist Isaac Babel. Canetti was happy, however, to return to Vienna, a city which was more appropriate to his quiet and thoughtful personality.

In addition to showing Canetti's development as a playwright and novelist, the autobiography traces the evolution of his interest in crowds and power, the topic of his great socioanthropological study examining the origin, constitution, and behavior of crowds from primeval to modern times. Canetti's first personal experience with a crowd came during a workers' demonstration in Frankfurt following the assassination by nationalist and anti-Semitic fanatics of Germany's secretary of state Walter Rathenau. What puzzled Canetti at the time was the manner in which he had become a part of the crowd even though he was merely an uninvolved bystander. His second and by far most influential experience with a crowd came in Vienna on July 15, 1927. On that date there was a spontaneous workers' demonstration protesting an unjust verdict in the trial of the assassins of some workers in Burgenland some months earlier. The demonstrators set fire to the Palace of Justice, and when the mayor ordered the police to shoot, some ninety deaths resulted. This demonstration had been spontaneous, and so had Canetti's participation in it. He became fully involved in the activities of the crowd and suggests in his autobiography that the remembrance of this experience gave him the most important insights for *Crowds and Power* some thirty years later.

Critical Context

Elias Canetti has never been a popular or an easy writer. Neither the popular press nor the academic community has been extensively involved in discussing and analyzing his work. Perhaps one can blame historical events: He was a promising young writer when he was forced into exile as a result of Hitler's expanded persecution of Jews following the annexation of Austria. Perhaps one can blame the Western non-German-speaking countries: Even when his works appeared in translation, not many scholars and critics were willing to assume the challenging task of reading and working on this difficult writer. Perhaps one can also blame Canetti himself: He has always been a very private person who does not promote his own work.

The three volumes of Canetti's autobiography can change the public's lack of understanding of one of the most important men in the literary and intellectual world of the twentieth century. These three books offer a good introduction to the novelist and playwright. They provide a fine insight into the life and thinking of the scholar who wrote an extraordinary analysis of crowds and power. They serve as a prelude to the volumes of aphorisms and essays which Canetti wrote during the four decades following the period described in the autobiography.

Yet this autobiography can also be read as a work of history. The subtitle of the translated first volume is *Remembrance of a European Childhood*. The next two volumes are remembrances of a young European artist and intellectual. They examine that very creative period in the arts that ended only with the establishment of a dictatorship and the subsequent outbreak of World War II. Canetti was a marvelous observer and a critical analyst of the times.

Finally, the autobiography can be read as a work of fiction. It is written not unlike a *Bildungsroman*, a psychological novel of education and development. It is not necessary to have previous knowledge of the individuals or the times that are mentioned in these three volumes. Canetti is a marvelous storyteller.

Sources for Further Study
Barnouw, Dagmar. "Elias Canetti: Poet and Intellectual," in *Major Figures of Contemporary Austrian Literature*, 1987. Edited by Donald Daviau.
Hulse, Michael, ed. and trans. *Essays in Honor of Elias Canetti*, 1987.
Modern Austrian Literature. XVI, nos. 3/4 (1983). Special Canetti issue.
Seidler, Ingo. "Who Is Elias Canetti?" in *Cross Currents: A Yearbook of Central European Culture*, 1982.
Sontag, Susan. "Mind as Passion," in *Under the Sign of Saturn*, 1980.
Turner, David. "Elias Canetti: The Intellectual as King Canute," in *Modern Austrian Writing: Literature and Society After 1945*, 1980. Edited by Alan D. Best and Hans Wolfshutz.

Thomas H. Falk

TOTEM AND TABOO
Resemblances Between the Psychic Lives of Savages and Neurotics

Author: Sigmund Freud (1856-1939)
Type of work: Psychology
First published: Totem und Tabu: Einige Übereinstimmungen im Seelenleben der Wildren und der Neurotiker, 1912-1913, serial; 1913, book (English translation, 1918)

Form and Content

Totem and Taboo is a formal intellectual essay which elaborates on ideas fundamental to Sigmund Freud's theories of the developmental structure of the personality and its relation to the nature of human society. Specifically, it examines the origins of modern social institutions (such as the family), religion, law, myth and totemism, the incest taboo, and exogamy. The essay is divided into four major sections which deal with various aspects of primitive society. In order to understand how Freud derived the themes contained in *Totem and Taboo*, a word concerning his overall theories of the psyche should be said first.

During the latter part of the nineteenth century, Freud, a Viennese neurologist, began to explore the phenomenon of the unconscious through techniques of hypnosis, free verbal association, and the analysis of his patients' dreams. The unconscious is the repository of strong elemental desires which influence much of the individual's behavior. The conscious, rational self is much like the tip of an iceberg; below the surface irrational urges dictate, he suggested, a large proportion of the choices a human being makes. In his *Die Traumdeutung* (1900; *The Interpretation of Dreams*, 1913), he theorized that certain elemental wishes and desires were unacceptable and were subsequently repressed or sublimated through the symbolism of the dream process.

Freud came to posit in his subsequent writings a genetic structure for the personality. The newborn infant is an organism dominated by the Id, a center of libidinal, or (broadly speaking) sexualized, energy that demands immediate gratification of its elemental desire for pleasure (the release of states of tension). This instinctive condition Freud called the pleasure principle (*Lustprinzip*). The constraints of human existence, as well as those of society, mean that such demands cannot always be met. A sense of identity, or self—the Ego—develops in the infant; the Ego is in part formed by such frustrations and the neurotic blocks that mark them.

These blocks (or cathexes) often accompany the socialization of the individual to what Freud called the reality principle (*Vernunftsprinzip*), the demands of physical and social existence that necessitate the sublimation or repression of libidinal desires. The reality principle is transmitted through the agents of socialization and civilization—that is, parents, teachers, religions, and governments. This transmission is accomplished primarily through commands, prohibitions, guilt, and punishment. A sense of conscience—the Superego—develops in the individual and serves to restrict prohibited behaviors.

The infant also undergoes a maturation process in which the locus of bodily pleasure changes in the organism. During infancy and early childhood, the anal and oral orifices are tension-charged areas because of the physical necessity to defecate and eat. As the child grows, pleasure centers shift to the genital region. There are, however, problematic areas during this stage of development, and here Freud introduced the Oedipus complex, an aspect of the neurotic male personality. The infant's psychology is for Freud the most intense in the life of the individual, and the relationship of the male child to the mother is crucial. According to Freud, the son comes to perceive himself as being in competition with the father for the mother's love. That produces anger and jealousy toward the father figure as well as fear and guilt because of the son's desire to eliminate him. The Oedipus complex develops in all male children but is overcome by most men when love and sexuality are transferred to adult females outside the family unit. If this issue remains unresolved within the male personality, then a neurotic fixation develops. Freud focused for the most part on the development of the male personality and gave less attention to the female psyche and the possible neurotic fixations on the father—the Electra complex—that may develop. He called his method of investigation "psychoanalysis" and claimed that therapy based on his ideas could cure the problems of the neurotic personality.

Analysis

In *Totem and Taboo*, Freud discusses how the developmental patterns of the psyche shape the course of human civilization. His discussion assumes that the behavior of primitive peoples will illustrate certain aspects of the unconscious, as well as the mechanisms of repression/sublimation, in a clearer manner than the behavior of more civilized peoples. He turns to the almost universally recognized cultural taboo against incest and examines how it structures primitive societies. The focus of his discussion is on the totem system that structures many primitive groups. The totem is a sacred animal which a certain tribe or clan has elected and which its members are forbidden to kill or eat except during certain special rituals. Members of the same totem clan are also prohibited from having sexual relations with one another. The totem is usually passed on to succeeding generations of the tribe through the female line.

The first section, titled "The Savage's Dread of Incest," utilizes the works of early ethnographers, such as Andrew Lang's *The Secret of the Totem* (1905) and J. G. Frazer's *Totemism and Exogamy* (1910), as source material. The totem prohibition—the violation of which involves death or social exclusion)—occurs invariably among primitive peoples and covers all manner of familial relations (son/ mother, brother/sister, son-in-law/mother-in-law). Psychoanalytic studies, Freud concludes, show that such taboos necessitate the repression of sexual drives and are the major source of neurotic behavior in the individual of modern society.

In the second section of the essay, "Taboo and the Ambivalence of the Emotions," Freud argues that ambivalence is central to the concept of the taboo. Because it represents powerful desires within the individual that must be repressed, the focus of the taboo is the object of strong attraction; because of the extreme negative consequences of transgression, people also have a strong aversion to the desires that generate the taboo. Thus, the taboo system in primitive cultures affords the individual a kind of ambivalence which reduces any potential neurotic conflict. Taboos in primitive societies are usually institutionalized (ritualized) within a particular cultural pattern through their association with concepts of a demon or a deity. This institutionalization is an example of a defense mechanism known as projection, in which feelings are transferred to external objects. In such primitive cultures in which projection is thus a prominent and codified feature of the society, prohibitions do not necessarily give rise to neuroses, since acceptable and nonacceptable action is openly defined for all members.

In modern European societies in which these prohibited behaviors are often not even publicly acknowledged (much less institutionalized in socially sanctioned cultural patterns), the tendency toward the development of neurotic compulsions is more pronounced because the resultant conflict is internalized. Religion does codify prohibitions against certain sexual behaviors, but religious taboos are often not clearly integrated into secular institutions in European societies. This lack of clearly structured taboos occasions the phenomena of conscience and guilt. Modern society thus produces, Freud concludes, many more neurotic individuals who are caught in an inner conflict of repressed emotions. Thus, according to Freud, civilization is achieved at the price of repression and subsequent neurotic disorder.

Freud also discusses the relationship between totem prohibitions and repression and the psychic phenomenon of *Verschiebung*, or transference and displacement. Objects or actions that are tangentially or contiguously related to the original prohibition become compulsively restricted or repressed. For Freud, the mechanisms of displacement represent the major modes of operation in the unconscious. The displaced objects cannot be touched or, sometimes, even mentioned without severe consequences. Again, such behavior occurs in primitive societies but is often institutionalized as ritual and serves therefore as a more consciously reflected aspect of the culture.

The third section of Freud's essay bears the title "Animism, Magic, and the Omnipotence of Thought." Animism is the primitive belief that the inanimate world is populated by spirits or demons. This belief, as well as the various types of primitive magic, is an example of the transference of unconscious elements of the psyche onto the external world. In these aspects of the primitive mind—myth, magic, and ritual—Freud sees the "omnipotence of the thought," or the power of the Id and the force of the unconscious in the human personality. The Id does not distinguish between real and unreal but operates only on the strength of its libidinal energy. With these ideas, Freud thus presents a theory of religion that suggests that the religious impulse is not an aspect of some transcendent part of human nature but rather a mere projection of a dimension of the neurotic self. Freud's intellectual position is that of a confirmed atheist. The concept of a loving "Father God" is an infantile remnant of the unconscious childhood wish to be protected. This "magical" thinking is, according to Freud, apparent in the compulsive behavior patterns of certain neurotics.

In the final section of *Totem and Taboo*, "The Infantile Recurrence of Totemism," Freud returns to a discussion of the riddle of totemism and its relationship to the incest taboo. He examines theories concerning the sociological and psychological origins of totemism. At this point, Freud begins what is probably the most famous part of the *Totem and Taboo* essay, that is, his ideas concerning the Oedipus complex and its relationship to the incest taboo. He again assumes that the psychological state of primitive man corresponds to that of the developing child. He therefore discusses several case studies of animal phobia in young male children as parallels to the totem experience. He finds that these case studies reveal Oedipal conflicts and asserts that the totem animal is a substitute for the father figure.

The conditions of the totem taboo represent primitive re-creations of the Oedipal situation, in which the male child covets his mother and lives in fearful respect of his father. The periodic ritual sacrifice and consumption of the totem animal that occur in most tribes—a symbolic transformation of parricide—represent a structured and institutionalized means of releasing the repressed anxiety and guilt that remains in the unconscious. The primitive man thereby both slays and becomes one (through eating during the totem feast) with the figure of power (that is, the god/father). This sacrifice thus also has strong religious meaning.

Freud discusses Charles Darwin's concept of the primal horde with its violent competition for power and position—the survival of the fittest—in relation to the Oedipal situation and the development of the totem taboo. One might think here of certain animal groups, such as wolves or certain apes, in which there is a rudimentary social ranking order. The dominant male of the group—the strongest and most aggressive—defeats in battle the younger males and thereby lays first claim to the females as well as to the group's food resources. As the dominant male ages and weakens, he is killed by one of the younger males. That parallels the Oedipal situation in humans—except in the latter case, the son's guilt over the slaying or displacement of the father becomes a major issue. Human groups, Freud asserts, developed the totemic system as a symbolic means of sublimating, or defusing, the guilt experienced by the son. That constituted the first step toward human social organizations such as government and religion. These institutions are based on the psychological displacement of libidinal desire and the guilt that accompanies prohibited urges. The sense of guilt and conscience continues as a safeguard against the eruption of these violent desires.

Since the psychological origins of religious belief are a favorite topic of Freud, he elaborates upon this theme in *Totem and Taboo*. He discusses the meaning of totem sacrifice and its relationship to the constellation of son and father. The original animal sacrifices of the totem were symbolic displacements of the Oedipal wish to remove the father and have been replicated in various forms of religious worship.

The totem feast sublimated this desire and its guilt in ritual sacrifices, thereby establishing a sense of a religious brotherhood and community. This original sense of the sacred sacrifice was preserved in ancient cultural forms such as Greek tragedy as well as in the rites of Christianity.

Critical Context

Without such a system of symbolic displacement of violent emotions, social order—and therefore civilization—would have been impossible. The notion that civilization is based on the sublimation of instinctive urges represents a central Freudian idea that was developed at length in *Das Unbehagen in der Kultur* (1930; *Civilization and Its Discontents*, 1930). In *Totem and Taboo*, Freud sets out to illustrate how certain ideas fundamental to his early views of the personality—particularly that of the Oedipus complex—can be found within the ritual patterns of less developed cultures; the book is an application of psychoanalytic theory to the field of anthropology. This book was written to provide more evidence that psychoanalytical theories can account for all varieties and historical stages of human behavior. These ideas concerning the psychological origins of primitive religion presented in *Totem and Taboo* are also expanded upon (in the context of the Judeo-Christian tradition) in Freud's later work *Der Mann Moses und die monotheistische Religion: Drei Abhandlungen* (1937-1939; *Moses and Monotheism*, 1939). He clearly had realized relatively early that his ideas concerning the individual psyche were applicable to broader areas of human activity.

In *Totem and Taboo*, Freud broadens the scope of his work from the structure of the individual personality to the history of cultural and societal development. This book has had important ramifications for subsequent theories of unconscious psychological mechanisms operating within certain social institutions—such as politics and warfare, justice and the legal system, religious belief and ritual organization. For example, the philosopher Herbert Marcuse's book *Eros and Civilization: A Philosophical Inquiry into Freud* (1955) is a good example of the application of Freudian ideas to political theories of social and economic development. Also, Fredric Jameson's *The Political Unconscious: Narrative as a Socially Symbolic Act* (1981) represents the use of Freudian concepts in the area of Marxist literary theory and interpretation.

Sources for Further Sources
Benjamin, Nelson, ed. *Freud and the Twentieth Century*, 1957.
Brown, J. A. C. "Psychoanalysis and Society," in *Freud and the Post-Freudians*, 1961.
Huxley, Francis. "Psychoanalysis and Anthropology," in *Freud and the Humanities*, 1985.
Levin, Gerald. "Neurosis and Culture," in *Sigmund Freud*, 1975.
Roheim, Geza. *Psychoanalysis and Anthropology*, 1950.

Thomas F. Barry

TRIBUTE TO FREUD

Author: H. D. (Hilda Doolittle, 1886-1961)
Type of work: Memoir
Time of work: 1933-1934
Locale: Vienna and London
First published: 1956; expanded, 1974

Principal personages:
SIGMUND FREUD, the founder of psychoanalysis
H. D., one of his patients, a well-known poet

Form and Content

In March of 1933, H. D. went to Vienna for the special purpose of beginning a series of psychoanalytic sessions with Sigmund Freud because, as she later noted, "there was something that was beating in my brain," and she believed that Freud would help her "take stock of her modest possessions" and guide her in discovering "how best to steer her course" through her troubles.

H. D.'s sessions lasted until the middle of June. She returned for a five-week series in the autumn of 1934, and she saw Freud briefly four years later, after he moved to London to escape from Nazi-occupied Vienna. From London in 1944, during the conflict that was part of the troubles she had feared and that had brought her to Freud, H. D. described her psychoanalysis with Freud, her "whole translation of the Professor and our work together"; this short work she called "Writing on the Wall," but it was published as *Tribute to Freud*.

H. D.'s memoir interweaves details from her sessions with idiosyncratic insights about psychoanalysis and personal feelings about Freud, whom she called the "Professor" or the "Master." The eighty-five separate entries of "Writing on the Wall" vary from one paragraph to several pages. They provide as much of a profile of Freud as they do of H. D., as she reveals details about her ancestry, childhood, and imagination.

"Writing on the Wall" and "Advent," the diary H. D. wrote while in Vienna during the first sessions, were published together in 1974 as an updated version of *Tribute to Freud*. Many editions since 1974 have included selected letters that Freud wrote to H. D. between 1932 and 1937. "Advent" comprises nineteen entries that H. D. made from March 2 to March 25, 1933. Freud sensed that she was writing these entries; by preparing for her daily sessions, she was inhibiting them, he thought, and so he insisted she stop writing the diary. H. D. made one final entry on June 12, after the sessions were over and she was preparing to leave Vienna.

Written a decade apart, "Advent" and "Writing on the Wall" are nevertheless similar in format, style, and content, so *Tribute to Freud* can be appreciated and legitimately discussed as one work. Neither section is organized by topic, place, or time. In literary terms, the style is known as stream of consciousness; in psychoanalytic terms, free association. In H. D.'s own words, "I wish to recall the impressions, or rather I wish the impressions to recall me. Let the impressions come in their own way, make their own sequence." Consequently, H. D.'s description of Freud's consulting room in ,Vienna in 1933 leads, without transition, to the steps outside her father's study in Bethlehem, Pennsylvania, in 1901 or to a small hotel room in Corfu, Greece, in 1920. A description of Freud blends into a reflection on Asclepius or Hermes or Thoth.

H. D.'s memoir is structured by her repeatedly returning to reconstruct and reexamine specific experiences, thoughts, and dreams. She is obsessed, for example, with memories of her childhood, particularly her dominating and distant Victorian father. As an astronomer, her father, like Freud, with whom H. D. often identifies, uncovered mysteries of the universe.

H. D. repeatedly relates her traumatic experiences during and immediately after World War I: the death of her first child at birth in 1915 and her subsequent failed marriage; her relationship with D. H. Lawrence and his later repudiation of it (Lawrence's troubling letter, stating, "I hope never to see you again," resounds throughout the memoir); her brother's death in World War I and her father's after he hears of his son's; and finally, her pregnancy in 1919, in which pneumonia and depression threaten her baby's life and her own. All contributed to her psychological near-collapse at the end of the decade.

H. D. describes recurring dreams and psychic visions, particularly her central psychic experience, which occurred in her hotel room on the island of Corfu in April, 1920, where her friend, the novelist Bryher (Winifred Ellerman), took her to recover after her breakdown. H. D.'s vision, which Freud assessed as a dangerous symptom, consisted of a number of images she saw cast on the wall: a series of reversed *S*'s or question marks, an outline of a goblet or cup, a tripod, and the head and shoulders of a nondescript figure. H. D. believed that interpreting this mysterious vision would free her of all her pent-up troubles:

> Upon the elaborate build-up of past memories, across the intricate network made by the hairlines that divided one irregular bit of the picture puzzle from another, there fell inevitably a shadow, a writing-on-the-wall, a curve like a reversed, unfinished *S* and a dot beneath it, a question mark, the shadow of a question—*is this it?*

Tribute to Freud, then, can be categorized as a memoir; yet it is not only that. It is part diary, part homage; it is also a case study in psychoanalysis and an affectionate, poetic portrait of Freud. As an autobiography, it includes H. D.'s real and imagined experiences, her view of both the real and the psychic worlds.

Analysis

"This is obviously not an historical account of . . . a new branch of psychological research and a new form of healing called psychoanalysis," H. D. reminds her readers. *Tribute to Freud* can be read as a case study of H. D.'s attempt to rid herself of her psychological burdens, but as she searches to satisfy this aim by seeking to interpret her visionary experience on Corfu, it also becomes evident that she looks to Freud for support and confirmation of her previously held belief in the healing power of the imagination and of art.

In her Freud-inspired and -directed search, H. D. recovers threads of her life to discover personal and universal patterns: "It was not that he conjured up the past and invoked the future. It was a present that was in the past or a past that was in the future." She found her own personal pattern to be bound with Freud's, professing further, "The years went forward, then backward. The shuttle of the years ran a thread that wove my pattern into the Professor's."

H. D. and Freud shared a love and fascination for the antique world—its art, culture, and mythology. They discussed the rare artifacts collected in Freud's study as great appreciators of art as well as interpreters of symbols and universal patterns of the collective unconscious.

Freud's theories about the unconscious, or H. D.'s interpretation of them, helped her clarify ideas which she had been developing in her poetry and fiction and which she attempted to codify in 1919 in a brief psychological tract she titled "Notes on Thought and Vision." In this work, which she alludes to in *Tribute to Freud*, she distinguishes different states of mind; her state of "over mind" comes close to Freud's notion of the unconscious. She also distinguishes between temporal events, which she defines as occurring in "clock time," and universal experiences, which occur in moments "out-of-time," a state similar to Freud's universal consciousness.

In the memoir, H. D.'s most direct homage to Freud emphasizes these ideas and Freud's personal integrity in expressing them:

> He had dared to say that the dream came from an unexplored depth in man's consciousness and that this unexplored depth ran like a great stream or ocean underground. . . . He had dared to say that it was the same ocean of universal consciousness, and even if not stated in so many words, he had dared to imply that this consciousness proclaimed all men one; all nations and races met in the universal world of the dream; and he had dared to say that the dream-symbol could be interpreted.

As H. D. explains it, Freud believed that by exploring this great ocean of dreams, humanity could better understand itself and save itself. Understanding her own dreams and visions, particularly her Corfu vision, was H. D.'s way to recovery.

To understand her vision, H. D. strove to discover how her individual pattern related to those universal patterns. Seemingly unrelated events or details, she claims, "make up a group, a constellation, they make a groove or a pattern into which or upon which other patterns fit, or are placed unfitted and are cut by circumstance to fit." Her childhood memory of her brother, without her father's permission, playing with his magnifying glass to set a paper afire with the sun's rays, fit the pattern of Zeus and Prometheus. Freud was cut from the pattern of great healers: Thoth, Hermes, and Asclepius. H. D. identified her own search with the Egyptian resurrection myth of Isis and Osiris. She gathered memories as Isis gathered the scattered limbs of her murdered and dismembered brother Osiris. For Isis and for H. D., these efforts effected a physical healing and a spiritual regeneration.

H. D. and Freud had different views, however, regarding rebirth, resurrection, and the immortality of the soul. Freud believed in an afterlife only in the sense of his life being carried on through his children and grandchildren. "It worried me," H. D. states several times, "to feel that he had no idea—it seemed impossible— really no idea that he would 'wake up' when he shed the frail locust-husk of his years, and find himself alive."

Although Freud helped H. D. steer herself to and through her Corfu vision, each interpreted its meaning differently. Freud interpreted it as H. D.'s desire for a union with her mother. H. D., again recognizing a mythological pattern, saw the indistinct figure in her vision as Nike, the winged goddess of victory. For H. D., Nike symbolized the triumph of the soul and, since she believed that the past was also found in the future, forecasted survival of her troubles and spiritual rebirth. In a parallel fashion, in clock time, Nike symbolized the triumph of good over evil—Adolf Hitler's defeat in World War II.

H. D. dramatizes this spiritual affirmation and, despite her independent analysis, acknowledges her indebtedness to Freud in the final entries of "Writing on the Wall." In this climax to the memoir, she interweaves allusions to many of the experiences related earlier with lines from Johann Wolfgang von Goethe's lyric poem "Mignon" (1794). Here H. D. seems to cut the poem's pattern to fit her own, asserting that "the whole poem in its symbolism follows the soul's progress." Throughout this fantasia, she uses the lines from "Mignon" to highlight and confirm her own salvation and healing, by poetry as well as by psychoanalysis. "We are dealing here," she informs the reader, "with the realm of fantasy and imagination, flung across the abyss, and these are a poet's lines." The final lines she cites, the concluding lines of "Mignon," serve as her final homage to Freud and suggest that through his guidance she has at last found her way: "There! There/ Goes our way! O Father, let us go!"

Critical Context

In *Tribute to Freud*, H. D. brings alive a figure that has dominated much of twentieth century thinking. The book is an indispensable record, too, as it captures Sigmund Freud, seventy-seven years old when H. D. meets him, at the end of his long, prestigious, and controversial life. He is still active, perceptive, crafty, affectionate. While clearly not an academic study of psychoanalysis, *Tribute to Freud* is a valuable overlay providing a range of illuminating details, from descriptions of Freud's famous study and horsehair sofa to personal anecdotes about Freud at work.

As a product of H. D.'s eclectic mind, interests, and experience, *Tribute to Freud* also highlights other central events and important figures of the century. H. D. records the oppressive feeling accompanying the rise of Nazi political power and Jewish persecution in Vienna of the early 1930's. Among other signs she witnesses, swastikas are chalked outside Freud's home. Freud is forced to exile himself in 1938 to England, where he died in 1939.

Tribute to Freud reveals valuable information about its author, who, by the time she met Freud, had herself shaped literary history. She lent her signature, "H. D., Imagiste," and exemplary poems to the Imagist movement of poetry, which flourished early in the second decade of the twentieth century. Those persons whom she reveals in her memoir as inseparable from her psyche are also inseparable from a study of twentieth century letters: Ezra Pound, to whom she was once engaged; Richard Aldington, to whom she was married and divorced; and D. H. Lawrence, with whom she had a psychological, literary, and perhaps sexual affair.

Tribute to Freud is another instance of H. D.'s keeping alive through her writing those inseparable from her imagination. *By Avon River* (1949) is a poetic tribute to William Shakespeare and a prose tribute to the Elizabethans. Two intensely personal works are *End to Torment* (1979), her memoir of Ezra Pound, and *Bid Me to Live* (1960), her novel that reconstructs her relationships with Richard Aldington and D. H. Lawrence.

H. D. wrote *Tribute to Freud* at a pivotal time in her life, a time when she was searching for support for her personal and artistic beliefs. The work is a testament to the creative power of the mind and memory, to imagination and art, and to the ability of all of these to survive personal and cultural tragedies. *Tribute to Freud's* themes, language, and imagery are at the center of *Trilogy* (1946), the long poem H. D. was writing through the war years, and in the poetry she would yet write, *Helen in Egypt* (1961) and *Hermetic Definition* (1972).

Sources for Further Study

Barron, Louis. Review in *Library Journal*. LXXXI (September 15, 1956), p. 1996.
Davidson, H. A. Review in *The New Republic*. CXXXV (September 10, 1956), p. 20.
Friedman, Susan Stanford. *Psyche Reborn: The Emergence of H. D.*, 1981.
Robinson, Janice S. *H. D.: The Life and Work of an American Poet*, 1982.

Steven P. Schultz

TRISTES TROPIQUES

Author: Claude Lévi-Strauss (1908-   )
Type of work: Memoir/travel writing
Time of work: 1927-1941, 1950
Locale: France, Atlantic ocean liners, Brazil, the Caribbean, Pakistan, and India
First published: Tristes tropiques, 1955 (English translation, 1964; also known as
  A World on the Wane, 1961)

Principal personage:
CLAUDE LÉVI-STRAUSS, a famous French anthropologist

Form and Content

Claude Lévi-Strauss began *Tristes Tropiques* as a novel, and among the remnants of his novelistic intentions are the book's title (literally, "sad tropics") and a long description of an ocean sunset, a tedious purple passage that illustrates why Lévi-Strauss is not a modern master of the novel. Generally, however, his original intentions seem to have exercised a beneficial influence. Throughout most of the book his style is highly literary and readable, not the abstract scholarly style one might expect from the great structuralist anthropologist, and this engaging style in part explains the work's history as a best-seller. Another part of the explanation is the work's equally engaging content, which shows the young Lévi-Strauss finding his vocation as an anthropologist and going on his first (and actually most important) forays into the field—travels among the Indians of Brazil's Mato Grosso and Amazonia during the 1930's. Both the style and the content make *Tristes Tropiques* the best introduction to Lévi-Strauss and his work.

If *Tristes Tropiques* became an autobiographical instead of a fictional work, it nevertheless retains revealing parallels to fictional form. The overall work is reminiscent of a *Bildungsroman,* or novel of development of the main character. *Tristes Tropiques* shows Lévi-Strauss not only finding his vocation but also developing the views that underlie his later achievement, particularly his views on primitive and modern cultures. This development has a retrospective quality, since Lévi-Strauss is narrating it fifteen to twenty years later—a common technique in the *Bildungsroman* in order to give the work perspective. His later perspective enables Lévi-Strauss to look upon his earlier struggles somewhat indulgently, perhaps romantically, and no doubt with more humor than he felt at the time: His earlier self resembles a Conradian hero setting off into the heart of darkness, only to discover that the more dangerous darkness resides in the culture from which he came. This journey of personal and cultural discovery takes, as Clifford Geertz noted, "the form of the standard legend of the Heroic Quest," earning for Lévi-Strauss the title "the anthropologist as hero" from Susan Sontag.

Lévi-Strauss' perspective also permits him to depart from chronological order, to use flash-forwards and flashbacks at will. These techniques enable him to compare and contrast his experiences in Brazil during the 1930's with his experiences in Pakistan and India in 1950. They also allow him to group his material roughly by subject matter, thus combining expository with narrative principles and leading to the book's strange circular movement.

Tristes Tropiques consists of nine parts, each containing from three to seven chapters. Part 1 treats Lévi-Strauss' transatlantic journeys: It begins in France in 1934, on the eve of his first departure for Brazil, but soon jumps ahead to a 1941 crossing. Most of part 1 is devoted to this 1941 trip aboard a crowded steamer with other Jews fleeing France's Nazi conquerors. Part 2 then circles back to France in 1934, telling how young Lévi-Strauss got the job to go to Brazil and teach sociology at the University of São Paulo; circles further back to relate his university studies in philosophy and law, then his decision to become an anthropologist; and concludes with the 1934 voyage and a six-page description of an ocean sunset. Part 3 continues with the 1934 voyage and eventually reaches São Paulo. Part 4 describes São Paulo and other parts of Brazil, then jumps ahead to 1950 and three chapters describing Pakistan and India. Part 5 circles back to 1930's Brazil and finally begins the narrative proper—that is, a series of anthropological expeditions to study Brazil's primitive Indian tribes. The expeditions follow in chronological order, with the names of the tribes studied—Caduveo, Bororo, Nambikwara, and Tupi-Kawahib—providing the titles for parts 5 through 8. Part 9 concludes with a summary of an unpublished play along French neoclassical lines ("The Apotheosis of Augustus") that Lévi-Strauss wrote in the jungle, a summing up of the book's themes, and a return to Pakistan and India for some final slams at Islam and Western civilization.

This potent mix is further stirred by incidental or digressive commentary on personal, geographical, sociological, linguistic, philosophical, and anthropological matters. Apparently the hidden reason Lévi-Strauss became an anthropologist is that it allowed him to comment on anything and everything. In any event, his postmodernist freedom of form and range of content in *Tristes Tropiques* make Lévi-Strauss the Milan Kundera of the anthropological set, with this vital difference: Whereas the contemporary Czech novelist was inspired by Denis Diderot (1713-1784), the great rationalist, Lévi-Strauss was inspired by Jean-Jacques Rousseau (1712-1778), the great Romantic. Toward the end of *Tristes Tropiques*, Lévi-Strauss freely acknowledges his debt to "Rousseau, our master and brother, to whom we have behaved with such ingratitude but to whom every page of this book could have been dedicated, had the homage been worthy of his great memory."

Analysis

Like Rousseau, Lévi-Strauss was born on the fringes of French society: Rousseau to Huguenot parents in Geneva, Switzerland, and Lévi-Strauss to Jewish parents in Brussels, Belgium. When Lévi-Strauss was still a child, his family moved to France, where his marginalized background apparently encouraged him to play the role of the outsider right up through his university studies at the Sorbonne (anti-Semitism was prevalent at the time but, significantly, is mentioned in *Tristes Tropiques* only in its virulent Nazi form). His role as outsider could have disposed Lévi-Strauss to take up anthropology and to move to Brazil, where, paradoxically, he was accepted as a representative of admired French culture.

Yet in the early chapters of *Tristes Tropiques*, Lévi-Strauss himself cites intellectual reasons for his choice of anthropology as a profession. His intellectual development involved two false starts, first in philosophy, then in law, both of which he studied at the Sorbonne and in which he passed his examinations with honors. Critics of structuralism will find his reason for rejecting philosophy ironic: He thought the study of philosophy at the time sterile because it involved "the application of an always identical method" to "every problem, whether serious or trifling." Essentially, philosophy at the time consisted of "mental gymnastics" and "verbal artifice" with dichotomies. His reason for rejecting law seems more consistent with his role as outsider: He discovered the extroverted people going into law to be obnoxious. Thus he left the ranks of the extroverts and joined the introverts, "prematurely aged adolescents, discreet, withdrawn, usually Left-wing," who hewed to the arts and sciences. Among the arts and sciences, the introverts found "ambiguous activities which can be classed either as a mission or a refuge," with anthropology being "the most extreme form of the second term of the contrast."

Lévi-Strauss, however, did not become an anthropologist simply by default; more positive reasons also motivated his choice of vocation. Anthropology was concerned with the larger patterns beneath surface details of phenomena, much like psychoanalysis, geology, and Marxism—three strong influences on the young man. Anthropology also appealed to his vast curiosity: "As a form of history, linking up at opposite ends with world history and [Lévi-Strauss'] own history," it offered "intellectual satisfaction" and "a virtually inexhaustible supply of material." His choice of anthropology as a vocation was clinched by his excited reading of American anthropologist Robert H. Lowie's *Primitive Society* (1920). More than anything else, perhaps, it was the romantic appeal of primitive cultures that drew the young Lévi-Strauss to anthropology.

In *Tristes Tropiques*, the romantic appeal of primitive cultures is balanced by the equally romantic critique of modern culture, forming a dichotomy much like those Lévi-Strauss had rejected in philosophy and linking him solidly to his mentor Rousseau, who taught the superiority of primitive society over "civilized" society. Describing modern civilization as a creeping "monoculture," Lévi-Strauss finds it typified by stultifying sameness, destructive exploitation of people and nature, overpopulation, and the garbage that litters the world's beaches. The modern world is settling into a scientific and technological dark age marked by "a progressive welding together of humanity and the physical universe, whose great deterministic laws, instead of remaining remote and awe inspiring, now use thought itself as an intermediary medium and are colonizing us. . . ." Lévi-Strauss sees the future of the modern world foreshadowed in the wretched poverty of overcrowded India and the closed thought system of Islam. The ultimate result will be entropy and the end of man: "The world began without man and will end without him."

The early chapters of *Tristes Tropiques* show Lévi-Strauss himself as a victim of some of the forces of entropy loose in the modern world. These forces are represented by World War II and the Nazi political regime from which he has to flee, but they are especially epitomized by the French military authorities on the Caribbean colonial island of Martinique, where Lévi-Strauss is forced to make a lengthy stopover on his way to the United States. Isolated from the French homeland and uncertain whether to side with the Free French or the Vichy government, the local military contingent has developed "a collective form of mental derangement": Further, "Their one assignment, which was to guard the gold of the Bank of France, had degenerated into a kind of nightmare, for which the excessive drinking of punch was only partly responsible. . . ." In particular, they are paranoid about a possible takeover by the Americans, whose "warships cruised continuously outside the harbour." Yet the Americans are hardly any less paranoid: In San Juan, Puerto Rico, another lengthy stopover on his odyssey, Lévi-Strauss is detained for investigation by the United States Federal Bureau of Investigation when authorities discover his index card citing a classic anthropological work in German, *Unter den Naturvölkern Zentral-Brasiliens* (1894).

It is no wonder that Lévi-Strauss prefers the company of primitive Indians living in the Mato Grosso and Amazonia. While emphasizing the need for anthropological objectivity, Lévi-Strauss clearly grows attached to his subjects as people. Individual Indians are given names and personalities at the same time Lévi-Strauss studies their tribal language, customs, artifacts, and kinship patterns. Perhaps living out his childhood fantasies, Lévi-Strauss enjoys sharing the Indians' homes, food, stories, and daily existence. There is no condescension toward them, only fascination that sometimes develops into admiration. Probably for these reasons, plus a few gifts that he brings along, Lévi-Strauss seems to have remarkable success in being accepted by the Indians (in contrast to a number of missionaries who disappear).

The details of Indian life that Lévi-Strauss records are indeed fascinating, though only a few of the more exotic or bizarre can be noted here. Among those would have to be the diet of the foraging Nambikwara during the seven-month dry season in the harsh *sertão* (semi-desert scrubland). A typical family repast might consist of "a few orange-coloured *buriti* fruits, two fat poisonous spiders, tiny lizards' eggs, one or two lizards, a bat, small *bacaiuva* or *uaguassu* palm nuts and a handful of grasshoppers." The Caingang, on the other hand, prize "the *koro*, pale-coloured grubs which . . . had the consistency and delicacy of butter, and the flavour of coconut milk," while the Tupi-Kawahib imbibe an excellent alcoholic drink called *chicha* into which virgins "spit copious quantities of saliva." For this purpose, the village Lévi-Strauss visits has to make do with three young girls; the shortage of virgins can be attributed to the sexual practices of the Tupi-Kawahib, among which are homosexuality, polygamy, and wife-sharing (including sharing with guests). The constricting penis sheaths worn by the otherwise naked men seem to do no good. In this regard, the performance of Chief Taperahi, who has four wives, is remarkable, but an even greater achievement of this truly creative person is his virtuoso solo performance (over two consecutive nights) of an eight-hour play, "The Farce of the Japim Bird."

Chief Taperahi puts so much of himself into his performance because possibly it is the last time "The Farce of the Japim Bird" will ever be heard on Earth. After him, no one seems left who is capable of remembering and acting all the parts. His solo performance symbolizes the plight of the Brazilian Indians, whose numbers were rapidly declining (mainly from disease and assimilation) even as Lévi-Strauss studied them. In turn, the plight of the Brazilian Indians is no different from that of primitive peoples throughout the world. Like plant and animal species, whole cultures have disappeared or are disappearing before the encroachment of modern civilization. The loss to the human race is incalculable, as the rich range of possibilities narrows to the same sterile "monoculture" everywhere. Perhaps some of those disappearing cultures carry with them important secrets, such as how to live in harmony with nature, that modern civilization lacks and on which its survival depends. So far, the real tragedy belongs to the disappearing cultures, through whom Lévi-Strauss is able to record and foreshadow what it is like to say good-bye.

Critical Context

Though Lévi-Strauss lacks the strident tone of a Jeremiah, there is no doubt that he speaks like an Old Testament prophet in *Tristes Tropiques*. From his world perspective, it is not simply the tropics that are "sad." If the human race does not change its ways, he warns, it will become a teeming world of beggars and finally end its days like the Nambikwara tribe—a few survivors wandering the *sertão*, eating insects and lizards, and clinging together at night in the ashes of the campfire. His warning recalls the prophetic messages of other modern geniuses, such as Sigmund Freud and Albert Einstein, to whom the world seems not to listen.

Yet Lévi-Strauss also speaks out of another, more optimistic tradition in *Tristes Tropiques*, a tradition that began with Plato's *Politeia* (388-368 B.C.; *Republic*). This tradition asks the question "What is the ideal society?" Like his mentor Rousseau, Lévi-Strauss seems to find the ideal society in simple social structures that exist in harmony with their environments and within a rich folk culture—to the tribe, the rural community, the village, the small town. His version of an ideal society resembles the simple rural village that Socrates and his friends first envision in book 2 of the *Republic*, or the old small towns of Europe, or Jeffersonian democracy as perhaps once embodied in Appalachian folk culture. For Lévi-Strauss, Brazil's expiring Indian tribes retain the structures of such a society even while they present images of the end.

Within Lévi-Strauss' own career, *Tristes Tropiques* is, as already indicated, a central work. Instrumental in initially drawing his wide audience, it provides an important foundation for understanding his life and thought. Although describing the beginnings of Lévi-Strauss' career, *Tristes Tropiques* followed a number of his other anthropological studies and immediately preceded the vastly influential *Anthropologie structurale* (1958; *Structural Anthropology*, 1963).

Sources for Further Study

Donato, Eugenio. "*Tristes Tropiques*: The Endless Journey," in *MLN*. LXXXI (May, 1966), pp. 270-287.

Geertz, Clifford. "The Cerebral Savage: On the Works of Claude Lévi-Strauss," in *Encounter*. XXVIII (April, 1967), pp. 25-32.

Hayes, E. Nelson, and Tanya Hayes, eds. *Claude Lévi-Strauss: The Anthropologist as Hero*, 1970.

Leach, Edmund. *Claude Lévi-Strauss*, 1970.

McNelly, Cleo. "Natives, Women, and Claude Lévi-Strauss: A Reading of *Tristes Tropiques* as Myth," in *The Massachusetts Review*. XVI (Winter, 1975), pp. 7-29.

Mehlman, Jeffrey. *A Structural Study of Autobiography: Proust, Leiris, Sartre, Lévi-Strauss*, 1971.

Pace, David. *Claude Lévi-Strauss: The Bearer of Ashes*, 1983.

Harold Branam

THE TRUE CONFESSIONS OF AN ALBINO TERRORIST

Author: Breyten Breytenbach (1939-   )
Type of work: Autobiography
First published: 1983

Form and Content

Breyten Breytenbach made his reputation in South Africa first as a member of the Sestiger movement of the 1960's, which sought to modernize both the language and the themes of Afrikaner poetry. Until this point, Afrikaans authors had loyally celebrated the historical, puritan virtues of Die Volk and left more controversial commentary to English-language writers.

Breytenbach spoke against the political and racial injustices in South Africa, enraging the traditionalist Afrikaners while exciting their radical young. His literary achievement and his linguistic verve were admired, even while his denunciations were condemned. The fact that he used Afrikaans for his writing limited his audience until his work was translated. Later he decided to write in English. *The True Confessions of an Albino Terrorist* was his first work to receive international acclaim.

The genesis of this book is political. Breytenbach became a member of the banned African National Congress and was driven into exile. He chose Paris, where he worked as a painter. He wedded a Vietnamese woman, an act deemed miscegenation under the Race Relations Act of his country, which forbade interracial marriage. In spite of academic invitations, his marriage prevented his legal return. In 1975, he chose to enter South Africa on a forged French passport, intending to set up a new white revolutionary organization to be called Okhela. It is clear that he had passionate political convictions, but he proved an inept revolutionary.

Breytenbach was immediately recognized and followed by the police throughout his stay. On his attempted departure he was detained, arrested, and charged with "terrorism"—a blanket accusation in South Africa. He was unskillfully defended by lawyers, themselves fearful of being tainted with the stigma of being terrorist sympathizers. Since he refused, out of loyalty, to name the friends who might have testified for him in the witness box, he was, not surprisingly, found guilty. The judge, calling him "dangerous," imposed a prison sentence of nine years, a term longer than even the prosecution had demanded.

The True Confessions of an Albino Terrorist is a record of Breytenbach's experiences, from his arrest at the airport to his release and return to Paris in 1982. Soon after Breytenbach's arrest, a security officer, believing that the prisoner was a Russian agent, demanded that he write the story of his life, hoping that evidence of his treasonous behavior would surface. Breytenbach's hesitant attempts were regularly torn up, since his refusal to pen a simple confession indicated to the police a lack of honesty in his self-assessment. He was repeatedly forced to rewrite his diary. Later, when Breytenbach came to write of the events in retrospect, he imposed a literary structure on what would otherwise have been simply reportage. This work thus reaches a depth of psychological understanding beyond a relation of events.

Ostensibly, the structure of the book is chronological. There are fifteen chapters. Chapter 1 begins with Breytenbach's arrest at the airport in Johannesburg. Subsequent chapters deal with his trial and his experiences in the different jails where he was imprisoned and where he suffered various degrees of hardship. The last chapter describes the happiness of his release, when, after urgent appeals by his international literary and diplomatic friends and advocates, the last two years of his sentence were waived, provided he accept permanent exile—a repudiation of South Africa that he ardently desired.

At the end of each chapter, Breytenbach interposes "inserts," in which reminiscence and introspection combine to survey the circumstances within his upbringing and education that brought about his radical commitment and subsequent capture. At the conclusion of this personal history, he adds an extended appendix in the form of brief essays which comment separately and somewhat randomly on general topics: interrogation tactics, the state of South African prisons, evidence of police torture, the nature of Afrikaans, and the future of Azania, as free South Africa will be called. He reprints the Okhela Manifesto, which he openly and injudiciously took with him to South Africa. This document, demanding militant resistance against the state, became the basis for the charges of terrorism made against him. There are also thirteen poems composed in prison. Their tone is more intellectual than accusatory. Breytenbach's writing remains consistently introspective and personal in tone even when his subject is urgently political, and the poems speak of his love for his wife and his ardent desire for freedom.

Analysis

The overall structure of this book is conceived as an extended series of conversations with "Mr. Investigator." The presence of this formidable, nebulous, almost abstract personality seems intended to symbolize a kind of mythic spirit of ultimate authority to which all thinkers must address their innermost thoughts and by so doing justify their convictions. He is clearly not one of the actual police interrogators. In fact, on one occasion during an extended monologue, Breytenbach apologizes for having accidentally called the investigator "Interrogator." The actual military interrogators are designated by name and title.

The Investigator is assumed to be seeking not only to control illegal activities but also to examine the thought processes that allow them to occur. Like the torturer in George Orwell's *Nineteen Eighty-four* (1949), he can confidently defend his own depraved version of moral truth. In contrast to the real tormentors, he is depicted as a man of rational if immoral understanding. Although ultimately he is committed to the side opposite to decency and truth, he is not an unimaginable monster; he functions within the same ambit as the author and is assumed to be capable of debating issues in the open and logical manner of normal intellectual discourse. The Investigator becomes a receptive sounding board for ideas, a kind of alter ego with whom Breytenbach argues and to whom he appeals in tones of modest reason rather than belligerent confrontation. Within this dialogue one sees how Breytenbach is attempting to resolve the tensions and contradictions within his own actions and examine the complex patterns of belief that he has used to justify them. Thus, the book is not only a passionate denunciation of the regime that has imprisoned Breytenbach but also a work of introspection, an examination of the principles at stake and the personality that finds confrontation at the moral level unavoidable.

Everywhere he saw the disintegration of human dignity. Among his fellow prisoners, decency melted into an inevitable violence that is directed not toward warders but toward one another. Stuffed socks made brutal coshes. Spoon handles were so regularly sharpened into daggers that the angry authorities eventually made convicts feed themselves with their hands. Violence turned inward; suicides were common. Homosexuality was rampant. The presence of those awaiting execution put a pall over the entire institution. Breytenbach records the dozen nationalities that were found within the South African prison system. Most European countries were represented, from France to Yugoslavia. Apartheid ruled inside as well as outside the prison walls. Japanese were classed as "white," Chinese as "coloured" under the spectrum of the system. Breytenbach's stress on the fate of these members of diverse nations indicates his sense of the universal nature of the affront that South African policy imposes, a cruelty that stretches far beyond the penalizing of its own citizens.

By some standards, his own treatment was scarcely inhumane. His penalties had few of the gross cruelties he observed being inflicted on the black prisoners in this radically segregated environment. Perhaps this relatively easy fate allowed a certain dispassion and ironic vision to flourish in his writing. His descriptions of the warders are of twisted personalities, petty, silly men reminding one of Hannah Arendt's recognition of "the banality of evil." These creatures are not dramatic enough to be villains, though their willing acceptance of their degrading duties does make them evil. Sometimes it is the sheer absurdity of the system that provokes his derision, more the stuff of Franz Kafka than of the gulag. Breytenbach, by extrapolation, demonstrates how apartheid imprisons even those who are privileged within the South African society.

Breytenbach's account is animated by a tension between his pride in his radical service and the humiliating consequences of his arrest. In a sense his capture could be considered a triumphant result of his activism: The police have regarded his intervention as sufficiently serious to require severe penalty. On the other hand, Breytenbach resents the consequences that follow from his dabbling in the coming revolution. He seems to need to have it both ways. He condemns, on grounds of moral justice, the sentence imposed upon him by a regime known to be despotic and its attendant courts, assumed to be biased. But to the extent that he demands a verdict of "innocent of the charges," and argues a legal defense in the courtroom, it is difficult to see how he can maintain his status as a terrorist, unquestionably guilty for intending, by his own admission, violently to bring down the regime that condemns him for the destructive intention of which he openly boasts. His situation is unlike that of many other contemporary prisoners who are incarcerated without accusation, trial, proof, and sometimes even reason, who spend their time in their cells trying to imagine for what reason they were brought to their present state.

Indeed, Breytenbach exhibits a sublime innocence that makes the idea of his being a genuine revolutionary absurd. The international appeals for his release were based on the improbability that such a person could be considered a dangerous and efficient terrorist. Breytenbach was not sure that he approved of this evasive line of self-defense, since it diminished his sense of radical commitment. His carefully composed manifesto for Okhela might be considered treasonous even in countries much less restrictive than South Africa. It is based on the fundamental proposition that no political change can possibly occur unless it is enforced through total and violent social uprising. Only deliberate acts of violence will shatter allegiance to the continuing political oppression and wrest power from the hands of those who enjoy the opportunities that segregation and discrimination provide. Breytenbach in essence is a man of letters who is condemned by his spiritual sympathies to become directly engaged in the political struggle. This obligation satisfies his intellectual convictions, but he would surely serve the cause better as its articulate spokesman than as an active soldier. Like many liberal thinkers, Breytenbach discovers that when revolutionary theories are put into practice, the results may be antagonistic to his gentler inner nature as a man of letters.

The mixed tone of the writing exactly reflects the psychological ambivalence of Breytenbach's position. It rarely has the documentary directness that one might expect from his situation. The eleven-line subtitle of part 1 seems a parody of the quaint wit of an eighteenth century novelist: "Being the veritable account in words and in breaks of how a foolish fellow got caught. . . ." Even as irony this is a curious tone in which to record his circumstance, for it mocks the seriousness of his fate. The book itself ranges across two levels of diction. There are sections in which with blunt accuracy and directness he describes his experiences and the suffering he observes. Occasionally he employs a deliberately tough rhetoric. Yet philosophical and speculative ideas always intrude, necessitating a more complex and eloquent form. This change of tone is especially noticeable in the "insert" sections that terminate the chapters; these sections are virtually prose poems.

The thirteen poems composed in prison exhibit the same instinctive concentration on the analysis of his own nature rather than that of the regime. He dreams and writes of the outside world, quite colloquially reminiscing about his wife, delighting in her letters. He is eloquent about the prospects of freedom, detailing the pleasures that the streets and restaurants of Paris will bring. The subject is hard but the feeling is eager and positive, so that in the last couplet he can write, "Burn, burn with me, love—to hell with decay/ to live is to live, and while alive to die anyway."

Critical Context

Unhappily, in the twentieth century a new genre of autobiographical writing—the prison diary—has come into being. On all continents, provocative and innovative writers have been incarcerated for their principles and have suffered the torments devised by oppressive regimes. Wole Soyinka's *The Man Died: Prison Notes of Wole Soyinka* (1972) is another example of books in this mode. Breytenbach's work fits this pattern as he describes his years of internment in South Africa. It brings together two complementary themes that are of wide international concern: the denunciation of dictatorial atrocities—by governments of both the Left and the Right—and, specifically, the condemnation of South African racism.

The South African situation has been described in innumerable studies, scholarly and anecdotal, statistical and literary. Breytenbach's book is a powerful exposé of the degraded system and addresses fundamental issues of the century. By deliberately calling himself an albino, he proclaims that he is white only on his outside skin; in his heart he identifies with black people, the oppressed and the dispossessed. In this way he links himself with the revolutionary proletariat. Overall, however, the book is a very personal and human record. Breytenbach does not strike any calculated political pose. His moral convictions are based on humanistic decency rather than political principles. Thus, he lacks the coherent intellectual creed that has helped to sustain Communist as well as Christian prisoners in similar circumstances. Breytenbach has only an inner conviction of the immorality of his country's government: "I believe, more than ever, that the system existing in South Africa is against the grain of everything that is beautiful and hopeful and dignified in human history. . . . It is totally corrupt and corrupting."

The harsh experience of Breytenbach's prison days made him more fully aware of his own nature, the spiritual essentials by which he chooses to conduct his life. He learns from his deprivation the intensity of his need for beauty, even in its humblest forms. His confinement allows intellectual purgation, permitting him to see more clearly the reasons for which he has chosen to reject his country and seek, at the cost of a cultural schism, an exile that provides at least a physical freedom. In this way his work links to the profound statements made by many Soviet "refuseniks," who have sought the resolution of their own intellectual impasses in a departure that is no less painful for being emotionally essential.

Sources for Further Study

Cope, Jack. *The Adversary Within: Dissident Writers in Afrikaans*, 1982.
Des Pres, Terrence. "Rimbaud's Nephew," in *Parnassus*. XI (Fall/Winter, 1983, Spring/Summer, 1984), pp. 83-102.
Moore, Gerald. "The Martian Descends: The Poetry of Breyten Breytenbach," in *Ariel: A Review of International English Literature*. XVI (April, 1985), pp. 3-12.
Roberts, Sheila. "South African Prison Literature," in *Ariel: A Review of International English Literature*. XVI (April, 1985), pp. 61-73.
van Der Merwe, P. P. "Breyten Breytenbach and the Poet Revolutionary," in *Theoria*. LVI (May, 1981), pp. 51-72.

John Povey

THE TRUTH AND LIFE OF MYTH
An Essay in Essential Autobiography

Author: Robert Duncan (1919-1988)
Type of work: Literary history
First published: 1968

Form and Content

Robert Duncan's subtitle for his study of myth, *An Essay in Essential Autobiography*, serves to describe the work's general form. About halfway into this small book, however, Duncan steps outside the flow of his thinking to comment on how the piece is being written and his uncertainty about its contents:

> The voice, I felt, was not yet in the words, or I couldn't hear it. Nowhere in what I was doing did I feel right about the thing having begun; everywhere it was about to begin; I did not have the "opening" words. For the essay must move, I knew, as the poem moves, from the releasing pattern of an inspiration, a breathing.

Such reflection distinguishes Duncan's essay from the formal essay, which is written with such care as to assure the reader that the author knows exactly where he is going. Duncan admits to composing a poet's essay, or one sustained by an elusive muse. The subtitle also announces the personal character of the work, and the essay includes lengthy narrative of autobiographical details, along with quotations from Duncan's previously published poems. This blending of forms—essay, personal narrative, poetry—marks the work as modern. Yet the admitted recourse to "inspiration" places the writer in an ancient context. The essay is traditional in its development of a theme, modern in its author's admitted anxiety about what is being said, and primordial in its acknowledgment and acceptance of help from outside: "They came, the words that keyed in the work of this paper, not in my own writing, but in an early poem of Denise Levertov's."

The Truth and Life of Myth was taken from a paper Duncan presented to a 1967 conference in Washington, D.C., on religion and myth in poetry. Its central concern is to illustrate Duncan's absolute reliance on myth for inspiration when writing poetry. The first of the essay's three sections includes Duncan's recollections of his childhood impressions while listening to stories and poems and analysis of how these readings formed his consciousness. The topic Duncan discussed in 1967 was in line with theological and philosophical issues of the time, and his essay serves as a defense of poetry against attitudes then current. Early in the essay Duncan quotes a statement made by Rudolph Bultmann: "Modern man is convinced that the mythical view of the world is obsolete." (Bultmann advocated "demythologizing" Scripture to keep the modern mind, which was scientific and unsentimental, from embarrassment when confronted by Scripture.) Duncan's discussion of the so-called modern mind and the "sentimental" poetic mind is at the core of the essay.

The audience addressed in the essay would include Duncan's fellow poets, who were typified during the 1970's as seeking inspiration through mysticism and Oriental religion. Yet the essay reflects the "spirit of the times," generally described as pragmatism. Pragmatism speaks to the poet with a voice "that has again and again, sneering or pitying or condescending, reproved the poet for his pathetic fallacies, his phantasmagoria, his personifications, ecstatic realizations, pretensions." Duncan's audience of doubters includes literary critics, who sneer along with Bultmann at the poet's ascription of deep meanings to common experience.

The essay's second section argues that the last two thousand years of world history have been a stage on which mythological stories have been acted out, reacted against, rejected, and reaffirmed. Duncan discusses the history of Christianity, with special attention paid to Saint Francis and Ignatius of Loyola, the founders of lasting movements whose original inspiration was reversed by followers who were not living the same "story" as their founder. This section also introduces what Duncan calls the "retraction of sympathies," by which he means the overestimation of reasonableness. Duncan shows how this "retraction" occurred, and how it is a criticism of mythological thinking that even he as a follower of myth can understand. Duncan shows how mythological thinking carried out in the real world by religious enthusiasts created a nightmare from which men defended themselves by becoming reasonable.

The essay's brief third section discusses the poet's condition, faced as he is with his "inspiration" and his need to participate in primordial reality while remaining wary of the delusions in which he might be trapped. The essay concludes with an affirmation of the poet's place amid such uncertainty, since that is the only place inspiration will reach him.

Analysis

Duncan's essay begins with a definition of the poet which appears to play into the hands of those who privilege the modern, demythologized mind, those who see the poet as deluded and irrational:

> When a man's life becomes totally so informed that every bird and leaf speaks to him and every happening has meaning, he is considered to be *psychotic*. The shaman and the inspired poet, who take the universe to be alive, are brothers germane of the mystic and the paranoiac.

Madness has been the traditional accusation leveled at poets, but Duncan intends psychosis as an analogy for, not a judgment of, the poetic mind which seeks meaning from the universe. Revelation, says Duncan, always comes into the world through myth, which is to say that a human consciousness mediates a message given to its apprehension. Though the demythologizer might like to run away from the myths of Scripture, he cannot run away from the apparatus of his consciousness which is attuned to meaning. By running away, like Jonah from the voice of God, the demythologizer must treat a part of himself as if it did not exist. The poet is willing if wary: "We at once seek a meaningful life and dread *psychosis*, 'the principle of life.' "

The demythologist's attitude is much discussed in this essay. According to Duncan, the demythologist assumes arrogantly to know the most—simply because he has a modern attitude. Duncan finds the ignorance of this attitude worse than the arrogance, for demythologists ignore the greatest insights of very modern thinkers, such as Ernst Cassirer and Claude Lévi-Strauss, for whom myth is man's way of knowing reality. Yet more than showing the errors of modern doubters, Duncan is concerned to establish the reality of the message which comes to the poet. His title emphasizes that myth is both truth and life. The truth that stirs the poet is not a reality of ideas or images, but a reality of presences. When the subject of one of Duncan's poems was Cupid and Psyche, he was not writing about the ancient Cupid and Psyche but inspired by their presence in his consciousness: "I cannot make it happen or want it to happen; it wells up in me as if I were a point of break-thru for an 'I' . . . that may like the angel speaking to Caedmon command 'Sing me some thing.' "

Duncan counters the modern objection that this experience is simply a fantasy cooked up by an overactive imagination by illustrating the poet's connection in a community existing since the beginning of human time. The myth of Cupid and Psyche has stirred many others before Duncan. He did not invent it. It is an old story, a bedtime story, and the humbleness, the familiarity, of the myth allows the poet to approach it, and, dependent on his gifts, release its deeper contents which Duncan finds no less than "perilous." The poet finds the truth and life within his consciousness, as something inherited in the process of being a man. The contact between the natural and supernatural, the transfer of communication between the poet's working self and his soul, is awe-ful. The rational demythologizer, who knows nothing of the experience, can easily reject the contents of such contact. A poet might turn away as well, but only because the contents are too much to bear.

For Duncan, what is reaching out to the poet from the supernatural part of himself is the presence of "Love":

> Our sexual pleasure is a protective appetite that distracts us or blinds the psyche to the primal Eros, as all the preoccupations of our poetic craft preserve a skin of consciousness in which we are not overtaken in fear of the Form that works there.

For Duncan, this Eros (the Cupid of the "Cupid and Psyche") is a transcendent reality, a living presence he senses while writing the poem. Again and again in Duncan's essay the poet is described as someone barely adequate to comprehend the mystery which he confronts. Describing the composition of the poem, Duncan says, "I was hard pressed to keep up with the formulations as they came." Poetry, the craft and techniques of writing, Duncan calls a defensive operation, a "skin of consciousness" which protects the poet from that "Form" he fears.

No poetic could be more religious than Duncan's. It is diametrically opposed to the trend of modern thought summed up in René Descartes' familiar proposition, "I think, therefore I am." Duncan brings the arrogance of the writer into question with his depiction of forces which overshadow human consciousness. Yet it is at the point where the poet openly admits his weakness and dependency that the modern critic finds him most aggressive and proud, as the poet is aspiring to a world of supernatural knowledge which the modern mind knows cannot be known. This struggle between the mystical poet's apprehension of reality and the modern critic's denial of this apprehension is at the core of Duncan's essay. Yet Duncan's purpose is not to argue with unbelievers but to depict the craft of poetry as a deeply serious endeavor, much different from the fancy saying of things everyone knows already, a view of poetry which developed in the eighteenth century.

Duncan's essay works as an invitation as well as a caution to poets, who in the twentieth century have less and less contact with an audience beyond their fellow poets. Poets, Duncan says, must take the risk of believing in the profundity of their contact with myth. Since the essence of poetry is vision, the cult of personality is diminished: "Wherever we open ourselves to myth it works to convert us and to enact itself anew in our lives. Every sympathy is the admission of a power over us, a line in which sympathetic magic is at play." Contrary to what the modern critic thinks about the visionary poet, that he pretends to know more than can be known, Duncan's ideal poet works primarily from a sense of not knowing, and, especially, a sense of waiting for the voice of the poem—"the voice comes from a will that strives to waken us from our own personal will or to put that will to sleep." Still, since the poet does not know the voice which inspires his poem, he must be wary of, or certainly uneasy in, its presence. Duncan's image of the poetic process is therefore a wrestling, like Jacob with the angel, and, ultimately, a crucifixion and passion, like that Jesus Christ experienced; the poet loses his identity so a new identity can be created: "The poet understands the truth of the anguish of Christ's passion as a truth of poetic form," and "in every true poet's voice . . . you will hear also a counterpart of the Son's sorrow and pain of utter undergoing."

The struggle the writer undergoes is felt by the reader following Duncan's thinking through the essay. A sentence will break off, a line of discussion will be interrupted. As well, Duncan frankly admits where he is affected by the modern distrust of myth. He questions his own tears, his own capacity to be affected by "fairy stories." The modern voice cautions him that his visions are only imaginary. Yet another voice, nothing less than a commanding voice coming from the poem, orders him to hold the vision steady, to receive it, and "to admit, beyond my sense of contemporary proprieties, that it was not 'sentimental' to come upon weeping as one came upon seeing."

While emphasizing the poet's dependence on the presence of myth, Duncan's poetics is not simply a passive apprehension: "The poet who thunders with the voice of God speaks from a reality that is not only inspired but has to be realized in terms in which the craft and wishes of the man are thoroughly complicit." The poet, for Duncan, is both empathizer and creator. Like William Shakespeare, he can become myriad human forms, but it is his power to give these forms presence in the words they speak that is his and his alone. In this sense, the myth needs the poet for its existence. The "truth" of all religion, philosophy, and science—as well as the material of literature—is, Duncan says, made up by the human mind through the imagination. The picture of the universe Charles Darwin imagined from his "data," while creating the modern sense of unbelief in myth, can inspire a poet like Duncan to see the reproduction of myth through history as an evolution of the myth's form. Ancient myth, a transcendent presence for Duncan, can assimilate all new knowledge the modern mind has about the universe. As Duncan shows, Darwin's scientific perceptions were a confirmation of the myth of metamorphosis and "shapeshifting" with which ancient poets found themselves occupied. That individual minds in science and poetry, two seemingly opposite activities, have analogous perceptions of what the world is confirms the existence of myth for Duncan.

Critical Context

Duncan's essay places him with other poets of his generation, writers such as Charles Olson, Gary Snyder, and Allen Ginsberg, who turned to earlier civilizations, mysticism, and Eastern religion in search of myths which they found lacking in the American consciousness. American civilization was criticized for any number of evils during the 1960's—aggression in Vietnam, destruction of the environment, dehumanization of workers, pragmatic affluence—and poets were involved in public protests as well as writing their visions of how life should be lived and what gods deserved reverence. Duncan's sense of the poet connected to the myth, dependent upon myth, allies him with this movement which was characterized by an emphasis on the primitive and romantic experience of which the modern, rational man was not aware.

This neoromantic movement also went against the poetics of earlier twentieth century poets. Duncan criticized T. S. Eliot, Wallace Stevens, and Ezra Pound for their excess of rationality, and for worrying too much about being reasonable so as to fit in with reasonable, educated opinion. Also, these poets for Duncan placed too much emphasis on the poem as a work of highly conscious art and not enough emphasis on the meaning given in the poem which a poet cannot assume full credit for stating. Duncan's experience of hearing a William Blake poem read aloud in the early 1950's released "the wonder of the world of the poem itself" and broke "the husk of my modernist pride and shame, my conviction that what mattered was the literary or artistic achievement."

Reading Duncan's poetry in the light of the poetics he declares in this essay confirms that Duncan practiced what he so passionately advocated. In his poems, mythological persons are characters, and ancient lore impinges on immediate sensation. Speaking to monarch butterflies in the title poem of *Roots and Branches* (1964), Duncan says; "There are/ echoes of what I am in what you perform/ this morning. How you perfect my spirit!" This book testifies that poetry is not a craft but a presence or a body of some kind, a container like a boat or a lake, in which the poet is held and from which he is asked to speak. The condition is partly a departure from reason, as the poet is open to seizures and being beside himself, overwhelmed by the radiance of vision. Above all, such poetry is religious, harking back to writers such as Henry Vaughn and George Herbert, who spoke prayers to God in the form of poems. A poem celebrating H. D.'s birthday concludes, "Father whose signature is in the chemical bond,/ how long you have searcht for me;/ I am your son."

Sources for Further Study

Altieri, Charles. *Enlarging the Temple: New Directions in American Poetry During the 1960's*, 1979.

Bertholf, Robert J., and Ian Reid, eds. *Robert Duncan: Scales of the Marvelous*, 1979.

Duncan, Robert. *Fictive Certainties: Five Essays in Essential Autobiography*, 1979.

Gunn, Thom. *The Occasions of Poetry: Essays in Criticism and Autobiography*, 1982.

Martin, Robert K. *The Homosexual Tradition in American Poetry*, 1979.

Thurley, Geoffrey. *The American Moment: American Poetry in the Mid-Century*, 1977.

Bruce Wiebe

TRUTH AND METHOD

Author: Hans-Georg Gadamer (1900-   )
Type of work: Philosophy
*First published: Wahrheit und Methode: Grundzüge einer philosophischen
Hermeneutik,* 1960 (English translation, 1975)

Form and Content

Truth and Method is a formal and difficult philosophical treatise. Its German
subtitle, translated as "foundations of a philosophical hermeneutics," indicates its
focus on the topic of hermeneutics, or the philosophical study of the science of
interpretation and analysis. The book is organized into three major sections: a
discussion of the issue of truth/validity in the context of aesthetics, an expansion of
this theme into the domain of the humanities and social sciences in general, and an
examination of hermeneutics in terms of language. A number of discussions of
related topics are appended.

Hermeneutics—the term derived from the Greek demigod Hermes, the mes-
senger of the gods and inventor of language and writing—involves the study and
analysis of the methodologies and theoretical approaches by which one arrives at
the truth content of a particular object of inquiry (an art object, a text, or a
historical epoch, for example). Hermeneutics has a long history in the fields of
biblical and religious studies (interpretive commentaries on biblical passages) and
legal studies (interpretive commentaries on the law). It becomes particularly significant in the modern age with respect to methodological questions in the social
sciences (historiography) and the fine arts (literature).

A brief overview of the history of hermeneutic studies will be helpful in understanding the tradition from which Hans-Georg Gadamer's work emerges. Individuals such as Johann Gottfried Herder, Friedrich Schleiermacher, and Wilhelm
Dilthey were leading eighteenth and nineteenth century critical thinkers who developed central concepts in the field of hermeneutics. Dilthey is particularly important because of his efforts in distinguishing the types of inquiries and methodologies
unique to the natural sciences (*Naturwissenschaften*) versus the humanities and
social sciences (*Geisteswissenschaften*) and because of his theoretical model of
the "hermeneutic circle." According to Dilthey, the natural sciences "explain"
(*erklären*) phenomena of nature (as facts or hypotheses) whereas the humanities
seek to "understand" (*verstehen*) the activity of the human spirit. Dilthey's notion
of the hermeneutic circle implied that understanding occurs through a structural-
historical process involving part and whole (or subject and object) and is based
on the phenomenon of subjective experience (*Erlebnis*) and the ability to feel
empathetically the experiences of others (*Einfühlung*). The mediation of subject
and object in the hermeneutic circle results in an objective understanding of
truth. Dilthey's ideas were important for the development of later hermeneutic
theories.

The work of the German philosopher Martin Heidegger was especially influential on the formulation of Gadamer's thought. According to Heidegger's ontological philosophy, understanding—and therefore hermeneutics—is not merely a cognitive faculty: It is the mode in which the human being exists. To be human means to seek understanding, to reveal or uncover the truth of Being. The communication of Being—the events of language, conversation, questioning, and answering—is the task of human existence. The work of art (especially literature) is a particularly significant mode of communication for Heidegger since the artist or writer seeks in essence to "speak" Being. All communication is grounded in human existence and is therefore temporal, intentional, and historical. These ideas played a major role in shaping Gadamer's discussions of hermeneutics.

Analysis

The first section of *Truth and Method* examines the question of truth in terms of aesthetic consciousness. In it, Gadamer attempts to illuminate the phenomenon of understanding. The concept of aesthetic perception is a phenomenon of post-Cartesian (modern) philosophy, and it implies a subjective, nonempirical domain of experience that represents in the aesthetic image a transformation and revelation of the truth of human existence. Although different from the "knowing" of empirical sciences, art is to be acknowledged as a form of timeless knowledge, a mode by which humanity comes to understand itself. The work of art presents a form of dynamic play (*Spiel*) that is not a static and objective subject-object relationship but rather a dynamic and subjective event of consciousness that transforms the onto-logical status of both the viewer and the artwork. The meaning, or truth, of a work of art is not in the object itself but is established in the one who views it. The subjective self-understanding of human existence achieved in aesthetic perception—the hermeneutics of art—is a model for the nature of hermeneutics in general.

In the second section of his work, Gadamer discusses the nature of understanding in the humanities and social sciences. All forms of human understanding (and human existence) are temporal, finite, and therefore historical. That there is ul-timately no objective or absolute vision of truth is fundamental to the existential view of the finitude and perspectivity of human existence and represents a major aspect of Heidegger's thought. This idea is very different from the Enlightenment view of the primacy and universal validity of reason that structures the concepts of truth in most disciplines of science and the humanities. It also differs from the theories of previous hermeneutic thinkers, such as Dilthey, for whom the act of interpretation produces an objective sense of the meaning of a given thing.

Gadamer's ideas suggest that every hermeneutic act is already structured by both conscious and unconscious preconceptions (*Vorurteile*) that determine the ways in which an object is seen. There is no completely objective view of an issue; a bias is always present in the viewer. A major form through which such preconceptions are transmitted is in language and the notion of "tradition," itself primarily a construct of language. Tradition, a historical phenomenon, is the previously established (and institutionalized) mode of approaching an object—be it a work of art, a biblical passage, or a literary text. It follows that any attempt to understand an object or issue—to derive its meaning—must take into account the historicity of its own understanding. Every act of interpretation is structured by such preconceptions, or the already established "horizon of expectations" *(Erwartungshorizont)* that is held by the one who interprets. This idea also implies that there is not necessarily any correct interpretation. Meaning is not an objective property of the object but is relative to the point of view of the interpreter.

For Gadamer, the hermeneutic act involves coming to terms with the reality of tradition as a major factor in the process of interpretation. Understanding means that one must mediate between the past (tradition) and the present (the situation of the one who interprets). For Gadamer, the acknowledging of the weight of tradition does not imply, as it did for earlier hermeneutic philosophers such as Schleiermacher, the attempt to reconstruct the historical context out of which a work of art, for example, originates—that is, a re-creation of the original. Such a re-creation is impossible, because the act of understanding is inextricably tied to the present. Even if it were possible to rethink the situation of a prior time, the significance that a work of art might assume is conceivably different in the past from what it would have been in the present.

Gadamer's hermeneutics presupposes an issue of application in the act of understanding that must involve an objective and authentic awareness of the operation of tradition within the context of the present. The interpreter must develop a consciousness of the historical reception of the object as it influences its reception in the present *(wirkungsgeschichtliches Bewusstsein)*. This consciousness is characterized by a relationship of openness to the "other" (the object of interpretation), a willingness to allow the Being of the other to affect the Being of the interpreter. This state of hermeneutic consciousness is again defined existentially, that is, in terms of the experiential, a receptiveness to experiencing as the other experiences.

Gadamer goes on in this section to elaborate on his notion of hermeneutic experience. He criticizes the theoretical stance of the sciences which holds that only verifiable data (rather than subjective experience) provide the source material for objective knowledge. Gadamer's definition of experience is dialectical, although not in the Hegelian sense of the dialectical objectification of consciousness. It is rather a dialogue. For Gadamer, experience is an encounter with the other in which the existential finitude of the individual is revealed, a sometimes painful confrontation in which the historicity of the self in the world is experienced. This process is dialectical because expectations are often thwarted by what is experienced and the individual is compelled to synthesize a new understanding.

This dialectical process of understanding is structured as question and answer, an open hermeneutic dialogue between subject and object. Authentic questioning is characterized by openness to experience and the encounter with negativity, in the sense that a true question presupposes no answer. Although it assumes no answer, the open question does specify the domain to be examined. Thus it is always essential that the right question be asked. The subject does this by immersing himself in the object. The text or work of art to be understood can be regarded as an answer to a question posed by its context. Both the interpreter and the object of interpretation must, therefore, also be seen within the historical (and linguistic) context of tradition.

In the third and final section of *Truth and Method*, Gadamer discusses the nature of language as a determinant of the hermeneutic experience. He stands against much of modern linguistic (structuralist) theory, which regards language as a formal system of signs, mere symbolic forms or concepts that perform the function of designation. In accord with Heidegger's earlier views, Gadamer stresses the suggestive, poetic power of words to evoke or reveal the mystery of the human experience of Being. Language is more than a system of formal relations. It is intimately tied to the existential nature of man's subjectivity and thought. Language opens, or discloses, the world as a phenomenological construct of human experience (consciousness); it is in and through the medium of linguisticality that man exists.

Thus, understanding is an act mediated by language. The work of art or text to be interpreted resides within the context of tradition, and this heritage is transmitted (as well as concealed) by language. The common ground for an authentic historical awareness is the linguistic nature of both interpreter and tradition; man "belongs," as Gadamer phrases it, to a "community" that is linguistically a "speaking." In the dialogue between subject and object that is the hermeneutic act, one must learn with an attitude of openness to "hear" what tradition and the text speak.

Gadamer, like Heidegger, tends to privilege poetry as a special mode of "speaking." Language is essentially speculative: That is, it never fully captures in words what it seeks to comprehend. In all statements, there is always a dimension of what is unsaid, ineffable. This speculative, or unspeakable, aspect of all language is, for Gadamer, the ground of Being in which all exist. Poetry, and all imaginative uses of language, is quintessentially speculative; it seeks to speak the unspeakable that is Being by creating new visions, new possibilities of existence.

At the conclusion of the volume, Gadamer makes a claim for the universality of his hermeneutic theory. He maintains that it is not limited to the humanities or aesthetic criticism but is a model for all modes of philosophical inquiry. The speculative nature of language characterizes the hermeneutic posture in general and is grounded in the experiential foundation of human existence. Thus, because he links his methodology to ontology, Gadamer can make his claim for the universal applicability of hermeneutics to all disciplines.

Critical Context

Gadamer's *Truth and Method* represents a major contribution to the field of hermeneutics in the humanities, and it expands the range of discussion far beyond that established by earlier thinkers such as Schleiermacher and Dilthey. Gadamer's treatise also presents an extended commentary on and elaboration of certain central ideas concerning the ontological nature of understanding in the thought of Martin Heidegger.

Upon the original publication of *Truth and Method* in 1960, a controversy developed between Gadamer and the German social philosopher Jürgen Habermas. The debate centered on the definition of and role ascribed to language and tradition in Gadamer's hermeneutics. Gadamer's notion of these concepts is ontological, metaphysical, and, as some might add, quasi-mystical. Habermas, whose thinking comes from a Marxist orientation, suggested that language cannot be divorced from its social and political contexts and that Gadamer's position of openness to tradition in the hermeneutic act does not adopt a sufficiently critical posture toward its subject. Language and tradition often serve as a means of social power and political hegemony that shapes and manipulates consciousness in at times rather subtle ways. They can function as a mode of legitimizing systems of social oppression and violence. Hermeneutics, Habermas maintained, must be transformed into an ideological criticism (*Ideologiekritik*) that examines the oppressive social and political implications of language and tradition.

Hermeneutics also shares with another major twentieth century philosophical movement, deconstruction, a debt to the ideas of both the phenomenologist Edmund Husserl and the ontological thinker Heidegger. Gadamer's hermeneutics carries on the Husserlian-Heideggerian tradition and focuses on the act of interpretation and the establishment of meaning. Deconstruction—as expressed in the theories of Jacques Derrida, especially—emphasizes the indeterminacy of meaning and suggests a multiplicity of ways in which texts can be read. Whereas Gadamer regards language as an ontological revelation, or disclosure, of Being, Derrida sees the notion of Being as simply another kind of reading, a linguistic "myth of presence." Derrida's position presents a revision of Husserl and Heidegger in terms of subsequent developments in structuralism, semiology, and post-Freudian theory.

Such controversies notwithstanding, Gadamer's *Truth and Method* has broadened and revitalized the field of hermeneutics. In the mid-twentieth century, critical theory has come to occupy a prominent position in many intellectual disciplines, and Gadamer's work represents a significant contribution to the overall philosophical reflection upon the nature of understanding.

Sources for Further Study

Bleicher, Josef. *Contemporary Hermeneutics: Hermeneutics as Method, Philosophy, and Critique*, 1980.

Dockhorn, Klaus. "Hans-Georg Gadamer's *Truth and Method*," in *Philosophy and Rhetoric*. XIII (Summer, 1980), pp. 160-180.

Hinman, Lawrence M. "Gadamer's Understanding of Hermeneutics," in *Philosophy and Phenomenological Research*. XL (June, 1980), pp. 512-535.

Hogan, John. "Gadamer and the Hermeneutical Experience," in *Philosophy Today*. XX (Spring, 1976), pp. 3-12.

Kisiel, Theodore. "The Happening of Tradition: The Hermeneutics of Gadamer and Heidegger," in *Man and World*. II (August, 1969), pp. 358-385.

Palmer, Richard E. *Hermeneutics: Interpretation Theory in Schleiermacher, Dilthey, Heidegger, and Gadamer*, 1969.

Thomas F. Barry

TWELVE YEARS
An American Boyhood in East Germany

Author: Joel Agee (1940-   )
Type of work: Memoir
Time of work: 1948-1960
Locale: East Germany
First published: 1981

Principal personages:
>JOEL AGEE (also known as JOEL UHSE), the author of this memoir, who recalls his coming-of-age during a turbulent period in history
>JAMES AGEE, his father, an American writer
>BODO UHSE, his stepfather, an East German novelist and editor
>ALMA MAILMAN AGEE UHSE, his mother, James Agee's former wife
>STEFAN UHSE, Joel Agee's stepbrother

Form and Content

Twelve Years is a lyrical evocation of Joel Agee's passage toward manhood; it is a moving autobiographical record of the failures, fumbles, and epiphanies of a boy who lands in the Soviet sector of East Germany in 1948, when he is eight years old. The boy is in the company of his mother, his stepbrother, and his stepfather, Bodo Uhse. Uhse, an "Old Communist," and those like him, who "had fled and fought the Nazis, . . . were expected to be the leaders of the New Germany, which would be built on the ruins of the old." For the next twelve years, until his family is finally wrenched apart by the failure of his parents' marriage, Agee is shaped by the disappointments and repercussions of his uncontrollable adolescent individuality in a restrictive sociopolitical climate.

Following the well-known traditions of the literary self-portrait, Agee reveals himself as a benighted, sexually frustrated "young misfit," a transplanted Huckleberry Finn who struggles to find his elusive identity and its particular artistic voice just as wretchedly as he struggles to lose his virginity. These are struggles that are neither won nor lost within the boundaries of the text, for when the twenty-year-old high school dropout turned shipyard laborer, Joel Uhse—as he is known in East Germany—leaves his home of twelve years for the United States in 1960, his identity as a man and an artist is not yet firmly established.

There are no chapters in the memoir. It is divided chronologically into three sections, three divisions of the titular twelve years. The first section, "1948-1955," explores the first seven years of Agee's life with his family in East Berlin, until he is sent away at the age of fifteen to a boarding school in Thuringia. The next section, "1955-1958," concentrates on the years between age fifteen and age eighteen, years of almost unavoidable failure and increasing sexual longing and frustration. This part relies on substantive passages from Agee's adolescent journals to textualize the process of remembering. The third section, "1959-1960" (by far the shortest), focuses on his final year in East Germany, spent as a shipyard laborer.

In the first section in particular, Agee investigates not only events and emotions but also the mysterious workings of his memory and its incomprehensible selective process. In the second section, these discursive passages are largely replaced by "documentary" entries from his diaries, including, in particular, a short and poignantly bitter play he has recorded both to illustrate and to distance himself from the horror and the guilt of his parents' rapidly deteriorating marriage. The third and final section is appropriately less literary; the simplified style and more coherent nature of the prose are in accord with the rhythm of his shipbuilder's hammer. The memoir ends abruptly; the past self that Agee has re-created moves as unceremoniously into the reader's past as the train on which he and his mother are installed— they are on the first leg of their journey back to the United States—jerks roughly toward his future. The circular nature of Agee's experiences is reflected in the structure of his writing.

Analysis

The narrative opens as Joel Agee Uhse sets out with his parents and his stepbrother on the Russian freighter *Dmitry Donskoy*. The family is embarking on a journey from Mexico to Leningrad, and then on to the small East German village of Gross-Glienicke. Aware of the conscious and necessarily literary act of remembering, Agee "casts out the net for memories." The reader is made pointedly aware of the writer's struggle to grasp the truth of his own experience.

Agee is often a frustrated witness to his known yet unremembered past. Unable to control the quixotic wellsprings of his memory, he is concerned with documenting not only his past but also the inevitable present-tense frustrations of the artist engaged in the act of writing autobiography. He is puzzled by his inability to focus his inner eye on his stepfather, and he investigates the ambiguity of his own recollection. At times, it seems that Agee is no more certain of the reality of his past experience than of the reality of his younger brother's many imaginary friends. He ponders the reasons for "the spectral impression" of Bodo Ushe's presence and the tenuousness of his early memories in general.

In these passages, Agee is investigating the whole genre of autobiography—not only his particular boyhood. He deliberately involves the reader in the immediacy of the textual act of re-creation, while his unrelenting search for the truth of the past gives rise to some of the most lyrical passages in the work: "Trying to remember the village from which I've been absent for so long, I find myself floating over it, like a ghost. But it's difficult to haunt a past that is itself becoming ghost-like, losing its features."

Limited by chronological boundaries, the composition of the text as a whole relies heavily on juxtaposition and association. Disparate "swatches" of memories, impressions, and events are arranged to reflect the pattern of the author's life, in a narrative quilt that lacks one clear overriding and coherent style. Moments of high comedy alternate with moments of crude realism and tragic vision. Agee's efforts at lyrical evocation are not always completely successful. For the most part, however, the almost pedantic attention to the stylistic details of each individual section of prose lends the work a kind of narrative unity. Leitmotifs throughout the work, such as his mother's predilection for New Orleans jazz and American dancing, also serve to bond Agee's separate memories into the general fabric of the text.

The failure of Agee's poetic aspirations is a consistent theme in the text. The natural son of one of the most famous and most troubled American writers, and the stepson of an acclaimed East German critic and writer of social realist novels, Agee is stifled between the extremes of his own expectations and the expectations of those around him. The stepson of one of the privileged "intelligentsia," one of the first literary families of the East German state, Agee never sparkles with that flash of genius—a genius he perceives and envies in his stepbrother. Agee's first literary act is to copy out a Rudyard Kipling poem and present it as his own, and from that moment on, he can find no public poetic voice which will earn for him the admiration he so craves. All of his efforts toward artistic fulfillment end in failure and in an intolerable sense of personal ignominy. These artistic difficulties are paralleled and reflected in his stepfather's inability to satisfy the state's literary expectations by producing those tomes for which he has already received payment.

Agee never seeks exculpation for his literary failings in sociopolitical musings. His inadequacies of talent are presented with all the terrible finality of an adolescent consciousness: They are intensely personal failures, symptomatic of the more general failure of his own private and public self. In fact, *Twelve Years* is written in the tradition of the novel of the antihero, the promising but doggedly failing young man whose existence belies his potential. After he has initial success in the eighth grade, Agee's academic career takes a decided turn for the worse. He cannot interest himself in the boringly adult responsibilities of schoolwork, the repetitious monotony of English, math, and chemistry. Yet, even as he sabotages all possibilities for his own success, he dreams of recognition and longs to be known as a witty sophisticate in his parents' intellectual world. Daydreaming and a dedicated truancy mark his unhappy struggles with the socialized remnants of the Prussian education system.

Agee feels as stigmatized by these failures as he does by the indelible stain of his virginity. His plans for a pleasurable initiation into the world of adult sexuality, his urgent need to establish his manhood (and thereby achieve a sense of personal validity), is the one sustaining goal of his adolescent consciousness. The recollected progression of his pornographic dreams and fantasies, masturbatory triumphs, and humiliating encounters with a selection of temptresses occupies a major part of the work. The autobiography depicts the universal agonies and concerns of adolescence, concerns which recognize no cultural or political borders, reflecting events which could have taken place in New Jersey, rather than in East Berlin and Thuringia.

Indeed, several critics have commented on the inappropriateness of Agee's emphasis on developmental concerns, given the geopolitical setting of his autobiography. Yet while the memoir can in no way be classified as a sociopolitical document, Agee's recorded experiences necessarily reflect the political conditions and upheavals of the time—translated and transposed into the quotidian realm; indeed, deft use of juxtaposition renders authorial comment unnecessary. His boyishly naïve recollections of postwar life in the privileged village of Gross-Glienicke resonate with the peculiar paradoxes typical of the East Germans' ambiguous relationship with the occupying Soviet forces. His instinctive reactions to the West, to all that was "over there"—accessible and yet untempting—foster greater insight into the complexities of the situation than any political record.

His reactions reflect a boyish loyalty to his home, and to the established philosophies of his home, rather than an indoctrinated political position. Joseph Stalin's death is important to him because school is canceled for a week, but still he judges the Western celebrations to be rather churlish. He and his friend Peter always defended the political status quo against the "reactionaries" among their peers, yet both must stand trial before a tribunal of Communist Party members for their decadent petite bourgeoise schoolboy antics. References to the blatantly elitist social system and the explosive political climate appear in the text as personal memories, recorded because of their emotional, rather than their political, significance. Agee's confusion and terror during the Hungarian uprisings are revealed in a desperate present-tense journal entry:

> Meanwhile, the West broadcasts dramatic and, I suspect, invented appeals from alleged rebel radio stations in Hungary. Who to believe in? One side lies, the other keeps silent. *Is our silence not deception as well?* . . . I'm afraid the West might see its chance here to deliver a decisive blow against the suddenly vulnerable Soviet Union. But that would mean a world war. God protect us!

His stepfather had even hidden a bottle of chloroform "with the idea of killing us and himself in case of a Fascist takeover: he was afraid we would be tortured."

The title's emphasis on the "American-ness" of this particular boyhood has been judged by some to be catchpenny and improbable, for the young Agee was only one year old when he departed the United States, and he soon felt very much at home among the privileged intelligentsia of the new East German regime. Yet while it is true that the major concerns of the work are with the general themes of adolescence and autobiography, it is also true that Agee's first halting German words, "Ich bin ein Amerikaner," proclaim him alien, as does his obvious relationship to his irrepressibly un-German mother. On another level, his refusal to conform to the mores of the school and social system brand him as "bourgeois" and "bohemian," terms which are in turn linked to decadent American behavior.

At the conclusion of the Party tribunal, convened because of his all too apparent incorrigibility, one of the teachers argues for immediate expulsion, on the grounds that "keeping this young man and his like in our schools . . . will continue to infect the student body with the virus of bourgeois individualism." Reprimands notwithstanding, Agee continues on his appointed path to failure, and the reader may speculate that perhaps these particular labels had an unperceived, positive resonance for the first son of James Agee, as he battled himself and his environs to establish his own true identity. At any rate, it is significant that at the time of preparing the manuscript he is again Joel Agee, and no longer the Joel Uhse of his memoir.

Critical Context

The concerns that Agee re-creates in his finely organized network of separate, self-contained memories are not those of political parties: They are the concerns of a typically narcissistic and nihilistic adolescence that has rejected both itself and the adult world to which it paradoxically aspires.

Agee's unattainable boyhood goal seems to be to forsake the childish realms of virginal ignominy without passing through the equally offensive gates of responsible maturity. The painfully slow resolution of this problematic dilemma occurs in the social and political climate of East Germany after the war, and to this extent, Agee chronicles not only his own development but also that of his adopted home. Still, *Twelve Years* never attempts to answer the question "What was East Germany like between the years of 1948 and 1960?" Instead, the memoir is a response to Agee's own internal quest for memory, an answer to a self-posed question: "What did it *feel* like to grow up in East Germany between the years of 1948 and 1960?" The location is not central, but never irrelevant, to the author's primary goal: the literary re-creation of his former boyhood self.

Twelve Years is not intended as a political or sociological document, but as an artistic re-creation and interpretation of a former self via the paths of memory. Literary accuracy, the correspondence between the written word and the event, between the expression and the experience, was Agee's principal goal, and the formal beauty of the prose is generally acknowledged by most readers, although some have found fault with an autobiography that is so clearly "self-absorbed . . . in a world raw from its recent history and pervaded with politics."

East German texts are often devoured by their cultural context; American texts often ignore theirs. Joel Agee's sensitively written autobiography provides the best of both worlds: a memoir that chronicles the development of a child and a country, devoid of bitterness or propaganda yet filled with a "reflective political intelligence" and an engaging sense of self-parody. Agee documents the cultural conflicts that informed his youth with a perplexingly aggressive, yet understated, humor, best exemplified, perhaps, in his description of members of the East German intelligentsia battling one another for hotels and utilities around an American Monopoly game board. The work strives to address universal questions of adolescence and identity while recording the writer's self-conscious quest for the script of his own memories. *Twelve Years* is a work which has earned consideration in many critical contexts: theoretical, literary, and sociopolitical. It is a welcome and finely crafted addition to the genre of the literary memoir.

Sources for Further Study

Adams, P. L. Review in *Atlantic Review*. CCXLVII (June, 1981), p. 101.

Coles, Robert. "Growing Up East German," in *The New York Review of Books*. XXXIII (July 16, 1981), p. 49.

Reed, J. D. "Young Misfit," in *Time*. CXVII (May 11, 1981), p. 90.

Richardson, Jack. "Growing Up German," in *The New York Times Book Review*. LXXXVII (April 26, 1981), p. 12.

Street, J. B. Review in *Library Journal*. CVI (May 1, 1981), p. 106.

Ingrid Walsoe-Engel

TWICE ROUND THE BLACK CHURCH
Early Memories of Ireland and England

Author: Austin Clarke (1896-1974)
Type of work: Autobiography
Time of work: The late 1890's to the mid-1920's
Locale: Dublin, Liverpool, Manchester, and London
First published: 1962

Principal personage:
AUSTIN CLARKE, an Irish poet

Form and Content

Together with *A Penny in the Clouds: More Memories of Ireland and England* (1968), *Twice Round the Black Church* constitutes a rare account of growing up, culturally and spiritually, in Dublin at the turn of the century, an account which to some extent parallels and amplifies the classic treatment of the same subject by James Joyce in *A Portrait of the Artist as a Young Man* (1916). Such parallels are interesting in their own right, and are made more so by the fact that Austin Clarke is one of the major Irish poets to emerge in the generation of writers who succeeded Joyce and W. B. Yeats.

The focus of *A Penny in the Clouds* tends to be on the public and cultural events of the author's boyhood and youth, as though to complement the private and personal orientation of the earlier work. Like the young Joyce, Austin Clarke was born to the newly emerging Irish Catholic middle class, and, though the term "Victorian" is used in a familiarly pejorative manner throughout *Twice Round the Black Church*, as a child Clarke clearly benefited from some of the term's positive, materialist connotations. Unlike that of Joyce, his family background remained stable and disciplined, and his physical needs and social aspirations (including an expensive education, received largely, like Joyce's, from the Jesuit Order) were attended to if not quite automatically at least with comparatively less strain.

As a result, in one sense *Twice Round the Black Church* is a loving inventory of Dublin in its material aspects at the turn of the century. The author vividly recalls the street scenes, small shops, and back lanes of his boyhood, recollections which are replete with the spontaneous ebb and flow of childish perception. Since many of the places commemorated in *Twice Round the Black Church* have gone the way of the wrecking ball or have otherwise sustained modern development, there is an antiquarian as well as an aesthetic pleasure to be derived from the book's faithful transcriptions of childhood's fugitive, evanescent observations. Moreover, since these observations are not confined to the author's home territory on the city's near north side but include all areas of presuburban Dublin, this work is valuable to students of the city in the final stages of its existence as "the second city of the Empire." In addition, the author's intermittent animadversions on the growth of

Dublin's suburbs provide an introduction to one of his most characteristic poetic roles, that of social satirist.

The main interest of Clarke's imaginative recapturing of the city scenes of his childhood, however, is not so much cultural as it is aesthetic. In the fluency of his recollective gestures, the reader is at once impressed by this author's superb sense of, and appreciation for, detail. This sense is best displayed in the accounts of the author's excursions on family outings from the city. In these there is a wonderful sensitivity to light and color and a boldly expressive testament to the author's belief in the delights of knowledge and in experience as a source of wonder and uniqueness. These accounts of the countryside around Dublin, and of the English countryside, also provide important insight into the author's poetic character.

Such depictions of city and country, however, while not functioning solely as background, are of secondary importance to the main subject of *Twice Round the Black Church*, which is the author's psychological and spiritual development. A recurring preoccupation in Clarke's mature verse addresses the role of the Catholic church as a source of spiritual nourishment and guidance in matters of social and personal behavior. The origins of these interests is detailed in this work of autobiography. Given this focus, it might well be concluded that *Twice Round the Black Church* is an idiosyncratic distillation of the concerns of Joyce's *A Portrait of the Artist as a Young Man* and William Wordsworth's *The Prelude: Or, The Growth of a Poet's Mind* (1850), since it portrays with great candor the impressionable intelligence of a sensitive, sickly child and the forces that contend in the making and marring of that intelligence.

An appreciation for the issues involved may be gained from a study of the work's title. Local childish superstition considered it foolhardy in the extreme to circle more than twice a notable local ecclesiastical landmark, the "Black Church" (Saint Mary's Chapel, an idiosyncratic construction, gothic in style and built in black stone, hence its colloquial Dublin name), located close to the Clarke family home, because on a third circuit the devil would pounce. From this point of departure, *Twice Round the Black Church* deliberates upon the childishness and potency of superstition.

As though in part to show that though superstition may be childish it is not confined to childhood (the author strongly implies that he lost his job as a lecturer in English at University College, Dublin, because he was married in a civil rather than a religious ceremony), this autobiography is not presented chronologically. The author ranges freely and without apparent method over, roughly, the first thirty years of his life. The intention seems to be to dispense with the cause-and-effect implications of a linear approach to his material. Since, in effect, *Twice Round the Black Church* is the autobiography of a spirit, enacted through the representation of certain recurrent—and perhaps archetypal—moods (though Clarke does not directly expound an archetypal approach), the author has understandably seen fit to depict those moods, together with their effects and consequences, in a manner which reproduces the involuntary, irresistible, and patternless character of their initial occurrence. In addition to its various other attributes, therefore, *Twice Round the Black Church* succeeds in making an interesting comment on the problem of form and autobiography.

Analysis

The claim that this poet's volume of autobiography has something in common with one of the definitive poetic autobiographies, *The Prelude*, is not merely a means of underlining the interest of the material contained in *Twice Round the Black Church*. The passage with which Clarke opens his autobiography suggests that the poet-in-making is drawing on the example of Wordsworth, with its emphasis on fear and wonder as primary stimulants of the imagination. (Clarke has an unexplained aversion for the term "imagination," but its implication is clear.) Perhaps Wordsworth is merely a comparatively modern example of how fear and awe may overwhelm a growing mind, fear and awe being the two experiences considered so powerful by Aristotle in the generation of meaningful experience. Quite possibly it is Aristotle whom Clarke invites the reader to call to mind, since mention of this philosopher may perhaps lead to thoughts of Joyce, an author noted for his Aristotelian attachments, as *A Portrait of the Artist as a Young Man* eloquently testifies.

The overtones of Joyce suggested by *Twice Round the Black Church* are also neither adventitious nor pedantic. From a strictly documentary point of view, Clarke's recollection of his encounter with Joyce in Paris is no doubt this memoir's most valuable contribution to literary history. On the other hand, however, the author's numerous crises of faith—precipitated by emotional hypersensitivity, an excess of moral scruple, and difficulties in contending with a burgeoning sexual nature—are strongly reminiscent of the material presented in Joyce's celebrated autobiographical work. In Clarke's case, however, there is no specific denouement: The young man, tormented by the intellectual and emotional demands of his own nature, does not end up transforming himself into an artist. Indeed, the links between Clarke's inner life and the development of his poetic vocation are tenuous in *Twice Round the Black Church*. Given Clarke's renowned anticlericalism, it may be surmised that he declined to give the Church any credit for the coming into being of his poetic personality.

Although, like Joyce, who invented the persona of Stephen Dedalus for himself, Clarke accepts the possibility of "a governing myth," such a facet of his development receives much less attention than his sensory enjoyment of color and texture, both in the actual world and in the world of words. Perhaps the relish provided by language is at times overstated in *Twice Round the Black Church*, as in the dazzling but surely strained analysis of the verbal texture of the banal sentence, "I've swum the Liverpool Docks." On the other hand, Clarke also recounts, "My first experience of the evocative power of verbal rhythm . . . brought back my earlier experiences of Nature." It is as if the mind's enthrallment with particularity provides the consciousness with a realization of the distinctiveness of the world, of the innate resistance of worldly phenomena to being subsumed into system. The preservation

of this particularity—obvious here as elsewhere in Clarke's work in a love of naming, a casual but piquant enjoyment in using technically precise and sometimes obscure terminology—is a basis for a sense of distinctiveness on the part of the
preserver.

The need to undertake acts of preservation is a response to wonder, and wonder,
in turn, may be the intimate counterpart of fear. At one point, speculating on his attraction to the "ancient pity and awe" of the traditional Irish sagas (which provided
him with the subject matter of his earliest published poems), Clarke attributes it to
fear. He remarks, "Such seconds of fear become as valuable to us as years." "Rich
in experiential material" is perhaps one of the meanings of "value" in this context.

Not surprisingly, however, Clarke's vision also had the effect of inducing derision of, if not downright hostility to, most social institutions and of expressing a
strongly satirical attitude to what he—and many other members of his generation
of Irish writers—considered the smug repressiveness of the newly established Irish
Free State, "our ill-fare state" as it is called here. At the same time, however, as the
deliberately unprogrammatic form of *Twice Round the Black Church* makes clear,
Clarke is not interested in creating systems which might replace any given set of
social circumstances. On the contrary, this volume of autobiography is a tribute to
the author's impenitent sense of his own distinctive, particular, and to some extent
forbidding individuality (in emotional tone and intellectual drive, Clarke is one of
the major assassins of the stage Irishman). It is also a tribute to the lifelong struggle
to retain a sense of his own particularity—a struggle which was evident in the
poetry, plays, novels, and criticism written by this exemplar of Irish independence,
Austin Clarke.

Critical Context

Because of Clarke's emphasis on personality and the paradoxically formative
repressions and permanent transitory moments which governed its formation, the
reader may get the impression from *Twice Round the Black Church* that the Dublin
of the poet's youth was a rather stagnant backwater of the British Empire. Students
of literary history will know, however, that Clarke's formative years coincided not
only with a devotional revolution in the Irish Catholic church (in part, the product
of a reaction against clerical modernism) but also with the coming into prominence
of the foundation of the Abbey Theatre, the attempts to rehabilitate the Irish
language, and the general efflorescence in Dublin of imaginative writing prior to
World War I. Apart from a few brief, though sincere, tributes to the excitement of
discovering the lost world of literature in the Irish language, *Twice Round the Black
Church* conveys little of the public temper of those times. As such, it may be
considered very much an expression of Clarke's career, lacking in opportunism and
facile character sketches to a virtually perverse degree.

Yet, it is clear from Clarke's early works that the Irish Literary Revival was a
significant means of self-realization. One implication of *Twice Round the Black
Church* is that the self-realization was inevitable, irrespective of prevailing cultural

conditions (his emigration to England and the demoralizing years spent as a book reviewer and minor poet there—touched on in this work—may be cited in evidence of such independence of mind). Part of Clarke's significance in the history of modern Irish poetry derives from the manner in which he outgrew the mode of his youthful pastiche epics and began the difficult task of making his own witnessing the source and justification of his poetic utterance.

In the context of Clarke's career as a poet, this autobiography occupies a particularly revealing position. Coming between the somewhat inexpressive bitterness of the 1950's satires and the attempt at greater spontaneity and freedom of his late verse, *Twice Round the Black Church* could be viewed as a necessary preamble to the final, freeing phase of one of the century's more notable poets.

Sources for Further Study
Halpern, Susan. *Austin Clarke: His Life and Works*, 1974.
Harmon, Maurice, ed. *Irish University Review*. IV (Spring, 1974). Special Clarke issue.
Schirmer, Gregory. *The Poetry of Austin Clarke*, 1983.
Tapping, G. Craig. *Austin Clarke: A Study of His Writings*, 1981.

George O'Brien

TWO WORLDS
An Edinburgh Jewish Childhood

Author: David Daiches (1912-   )
Type of work: Memoir/autobiography
Time of work: 1919-1944
Locale: Edinburgh and Fife, Scotland
First published: 1956

> *Principal personages:*
> DAVID DAICHES, a developing writer, later a biblical-literary
>   scholar, teacher, and diplomat
> SALIS DAICHES, his father, a rabbinical leader in Edinburgh
> FLORA DAICHES (née LEVIN), his mother
> LIONEL DAICHES, his elder brother
> SYLVIA and
> BERYL, his sisters
> ISRAEL DAICHES, his grandfather, a rabbi in Leeds

Form and Content

In the summer of 1937, having found his father's religious-secular synthesis personally untenable, David Daiches, son of Salis Daiches, a leading rabbi in Edinburgh, departed from a tradition that had produced an unbroken line of Daiches rabbis from the time of the Middle Ages. He resigned his fellowship at Balliol College, University of Oxford, where he had been writing his doctoral dissertation on English translations of the Hebrew Bible; he accepted an academic position at the University of Chicago so that back in Edinburgh his father "would not feel embarrassed," and he was married to his beloved Isobel Mackay.

By the late 1980's, Daiches had written and edited more than twenty-five books and taught as a tenured and visiting professor at more than fifteen major universities, including Cornell University and the University of Cambridge. His books include *The Novel and the Modern World* (1939), *Poetry and the Modern World: A Study of Poetry in England Between 1900 and 1939* (1940), *Virginia Woolf* (1942), *Robert Louis Stevenson* (1947), *A Study of Literature for Readers and Critics* (1948), *Robert Burns* (1950), *Milton* (1957), *The Present Age After 1920* (1958), *A Critical History of English Literature* (1960), *Willa Cather: A Critical Introduction* (1971), *Sir Walter Scott and His World* (1971), and *God and the Poets* (1984).

Two Worlds: An Edinburgh Jewish Childhood, one of three autobiographical works, is best described as a memoir, since it deals exclusively with a life segment so influenced by Daiches' father. Daiches first reveals himself as a lonely six-year-old and ends as a mature adult twenty-six years later, at the time of his father's death. In the second work, *A Third World* (1971), Daiches describes his life in the United States: at the University of Chicago, at Cornell, and at the British Embassy in Washington, D.C. The third work, *Was: A Pastime from Time Past* (1975), is more experimental in style than the two previous books and may be an attempt to reconcile differences for a mature synthesis.

Two Worlds is relatively short, 152 pages, and carefully focused. In eight chapters Daiches describes his life as a child about to enter Watson's Boys' College; his experiences at school and at home with his family—brother, sisters, mother, father, and paternal grandparents; his family vacations; his father's great legal battle and triumph against a rabbinical impostor; and the resolution Daiches achieved of conflicts generated by his life in two worlds.

Analysis

If *Two Worlds* is a "tribute" to his father, it is also a son's selective recapitulation of formative experiences. Despite Rabbi Daiches' ability to reach dissident groups within his own religious community and in the secular world of Edinburgh and beyond, his son was lonely as a child. He had few close friends in the small Jewish community and few at the secular Watson's Boys' College, where his orthodox observance of the Sabbath precluded participation in sports and debating. Food at the schoolboys' favorite eating place was not kosher, so here too David felt excluded. Even on vacation at the shore, the family seems to have been a fairly separate unit. Grandfather Daiches, rabbi of an Orthodox Jewish congregation, Beth Hamedrash Hagadol in Leeds, is described as a wonderfully loving person, but David saw him quite infrequently; the mature Daiches suspects that his father was trying to escape a ghetto mentality.

Assessing his own break with tradition, Daiches describes the "enormous change" once he entered the University of Edinburgh. He was popular and participated actively in university life—including leadership in the literary and debating societies, closed to him earlier at Watson's because of Sabbath scheduling.

One alternative to Orthodoxy, Liberal Judaism, was closed to him by his father's convincing argument:

> My father's chief objection to Liberal Judaism was thus that it made the individual conscience the arbiter of what was good and worth preserving and what was valueless and expendable in the law which had come down as the word of God. Once you take that view, divine authority is gone and chaos is come again.

Somehow, this argument left only agnosticism as an alternative. He says,

> I came to see the Hebrew Bible as a fascinating record of the spiritual development of a people rather than as a book of conduct inspired by God. . . . I read much Zionist literature as well as modern Hebrew poetry. . . . Unconsciously, I was preparing for a showdown with my father. Whatever happened, I was not to be accused of lack of knowledge of or affection for my ancestral heritage.

Daiches explains that he also began to question the separation between Jews and non-Jews, wondering whether it was "healthy, desirable," or even "possible."

Indeed, at university he found that many of his new non-Jewish friends were intelligent and thoughtful. It was somewhat threatening to discover that on some level he had more in common with them than with his relatives and Jewish friends.

Realizing that he had often experienced earlier life in "an abyss" between worlds, Daiches defined his ideology, married Isobel Mackay, and discovered the impossibility of a real "showdown" between the generations, because of the presence of love.

Critical Context

The reviewers who discussed *Two Worlds* in 1956, the year of its American publication, primarily considered the specific identity of the author. David Daiches was a distinguished scholar, writer, and university lecturer descended from a long line of Orthodox Jewish rabbis. George Adelman, reviewing the memoir for *Library Journal*, Saul Bellow, writing for *Saturday Review*, Milton Hindus, writing for *Chicago Sunday Tribune*, and several others saw the book as one written by a master of language and literature, humorous and appealing, a Jewish story of a memorable father by his son.

What seems to have been ignored is the implicit but universal struggle of the son. In that sense, the true story has much broader appeal and wider relevance. Twelve years after the first American publication of *Two Worlds*, William G. Perry, Jr., published *Forms of Intellectual and Ethical Development in the College Years* (1968), in which he discussed results of interviewing large groups of students at Harvard University during their undergraduate years. He concluded that normal development involves a questioning and reassessment of family and community values and a final definition of oneself related to an informed choice of vocation. In the same year, Erik H. Erikson first published *Identity, Youth, and Crisis* (1968) and confirmed many of Perry's conclusions about adolescent development.

Stories of such quests usually begin with the hero's leaving home to test his powers in the larger world. In *A Portrait of the Artist as a Young Man* (1916), James Joyce strikes a familiar note when his hero, Stephen Dedalus, identifies himself by placing his name at the top of a list of locations. The locations start with Stephen's presence in his schoolroom class in chemical "elements" and the list continues, suggesting widening concentric circles, so that, finally, "the world" is followed by the ultimate in one's address, "the universe." When Stephen leaves home, he leaves his mother, his father, his siblings, Catholicism, and Ireland, calling on an adoptive father, Daedalus, to help him. Perhaps he may return after a broader perspective helps him clearly sort out who he is. This biographical novel was first written as *Stephen Hero* in 1903.

Ralph Ellison's hero in *Invisible Man* (1947) is forced to search actively for a meaningful identity in order to be perceived as a man. The conflicts are infinitely complex and symbolic in this novel of growing up, but they certainly involve a testing of worlds and a quest for identity.

If *Two Worlds* is significant, it is so at least partly because the youthful agony of divided loyalties makes the story vital. The conflict between childhood dreams and parental hopes, between personal needs and real or imagined family expectations, is not new. The search for identity, if new in any respect, is merely newly recognized.

Sources for Further Study

Adelman, George. Review in *Library Journal*. LXXXI (February 1, 1956), p. 436.
Bellow, Saul. Review in *Saturday Review*. XXXIX (March 24, 1956), p. 19.
Hindus, Milton. Review in *Chicago Sunday Tribune*. April 8, 1956, p. 9.
The New Yorker. Review. XXXII (March 24, 1956), p. 151.
Russell, Francis. Review in *The Christian Science Monitor*. April 30, 1956, p. 3.

Judith B. Schnee

UNDERSTANDING MEDIA
The Extensions of Man

Author: Marshall McLuhan (1911-1980)
Type of work: Cultural criticism
First published: 1964

Form and Content

"The medium is the message" is one of those phrases that seem to summarize in a synthetic, almost formulaic way a major insight of the twentieth century. As such, it has acquired the true mark of popular notoriety: It sounds both familiar and profound, but its meaning is only vaguely understood and its source is often unknown. In fact, tracing this phrase to the book in which it is first discussed at length and to the argument which its originator builds around it is instrumental to a full understanding of its relevance.

Marshall McLuhan's *Understanding Media*, in which the cryptic phrase appears as a chapter title, was first published in 1964, but it did not attract wide attention until the following year, when extensive review articles appeared in *The New Yorker* and in other influential journals. From that moment on, the international debate over McLuhan's controversial theory gained momentum, and *Understanding Media* rapidly became one of the most discussed books of the 1960's.

That was probably a most unexpected turn of events for those who had followed the development of McLuhan's intellectual career. A Canadian by birth, he had studied engineering and then literature at the University of Manitoba. He had subsequently specialized in literary criticism at the University of Cambridge in England. McLuhan greatly admired James Joyce, Ezra Pound, and T. S. Eliot and traced some of these authors' stylistic innovations to the symbolism and linguistic dexterity of the Elizabethans. This early interest stimulated McLuhan's own delight in the inventive use of unusual grammatical constructions, in the creation of puns, and in a formulaic style that very probably contributed to the popular impact of *Understanding Media*. Yet McLuhan's early works seem to be squarely in the tradition of rather esoteric academic production, directed at a limited and specialized audience.

Some of the themes he was to develop fully in *Understanding Media* appear as early as 1951, in his book *The Mechanical Bride: Folklore of Industrial Man*. A subsequent work, *The Gutenberg Galaxy: The Making of Typographic Man* (1962), takes up similar themes in a clearer form and presents the gist of McLuhan's main theoretical contribution. The publication of *The Gutenberg Galaxy*, which received the Canadian equivalent of the Pulitzer Prize—the Governor General's Literary Award—caught the attention of Canadian intellectuals, but in general McLuhan was still considered a marginal phenomenon, a maverick academic with an unusual turn of mind. All that would change dramatically with the publication of *Understanding Media*.

This book expands on some of the ideas McLuhan had already introduced in previous works, but the theories are presented in a much more accessible, less specialized format. The style is both entertaining and slightly baffling. Ideas are organized in short, snappily written chapters, and concepts are repeated again and again, for emphasis and for clarification. The book is organized in two parts, each subdivided into a number of chapters. Part 1, containing seven chapters, lays down the theoretical foundations of McLuhan's argument; part 2, divided into thirty-three shorter chapters, illustrates the argument in a systematic way.

The argument, which the phrase "the medium is the message" aptly summarizes, centers on the idea that the reality shared by people living in a certain culture or age is determined by the kind of psychic framework created by their senses. The five senses, however, do not always contribute equally to the creation of this framework for the simple reason that in the process of evolution humanity develops specialized forms of communication—the "media" of the title—which, by being extensions of particular senses, automatically reinforce the function of one sense at the expense of all others.

With the introduction of Johann Gutenberg's printing press, for example, the visual function underwent a tremendous overdevelopment, and this shift created societies that were fundamentally different from those typical of preliterate times, when people's reality was based on the sense of hearing. This particular example, fully discussed in *The Gutenberg Galaxy*, is taken up again in *Understanding Media*, but here the focus expands from a description of the particular consequences of one technological innovation to the investigation of the very nature of media and their impact on the human psyche. The fundamental point McLuhan emphasizes is that all human technological innovations may significantly shape perception and cognition. Thus, they carry a communicative message that is rooted in their form rather than in their content. It is to this form and to the particular way it expands the functions of certain senses that human beings must pay attention in order to understand the process of social change affecting societies.

Furthermore, McLuhan suggests that this understanding is made urgent by the shift in perception being created by what he defines as "the new electric age." As this shift gains momentum, the older forms of "typographic perception," typical of Western civilization until the mid-twentieth century, lose their relevance and power. It is only through a full understanding of the mechanism by which media affect psychic constructs that one can prepare for this shift and for the new society it is creating.

Analysis

McLuhan's theory of communication, laid out in part 1 of *Understanding Media*, is centered on four major concepts. First, there is the idea that any invention or technology is an extension of human sensory organs and constitutes a new medium of interaction with the environment. Second, it is argued that media, as extensions of man, have characteristics that mold people's experience quite independently from their possible use or content. Third, McLuhan defines media as either "hot" or "cool" and points out that this major difference determines the characteristics of the psychic reality they help to create. Fourth, and finally, it is theorized that a shift in the media orientation of a society inevitably leads to major patterns of change, particularly striking when the shift is from a hot to a cool medium or vice versa.

While the theory encapsulated in the phrase "the medium is the message" is perhaps the most misunderstood of McLuhan's contributions, the distinction between hot and cool media is perhaps equally confusing to some. That may be because it derives from the communications engineer's concepts of information density and semantic redundancy, concepts unfamiliar to most readers of social critiques. The distinction McLuhan makes, however, is quite clear: "Hot media are low in participation and cool media are high in participation or completion by the audience." In other words, a medium that provides the recipient with much precise, standardized information—such as, for example, a photograph—is "hot." A medium that requires the user to do a considerable amount of "filling in" through inference and imagination, such as in the case of a cartoon, is definitely "cool."

The distinction between hot and cool media and the hypothesis that a shift in orientation from one to the other is likely to create major social upheavals are central points of *Understanding Media*. In the conclusion of *The Gutenberg Galaxy*, in which McLuhan fully discusses the impact on Western civilization of the phonetic alphabet and printing—typically hot media—a question is raised: What kind of perception and judgment would characterize "the new electric age." *Understanding Media* tries to provide an answer to that question by examining how the print-oriented, grammar-bound, linear-thinking individual constituting the prototype of Western man for the last five centuries is reacting to the bombardment of the senses brought about by electric and electronic media, the first of which was the telegraph and the most typical of which is television. Through a systematic analysis of the characteristics of the major media affecting the Western world, McLuhan points out how the electric/electronic media are strikingly different from those that preceded them. Thus, they herald the radical breakdown of all the social forms human beings take for granted but which are in fact correlates of the "Gutenberg way of perceiving."

In McLuhan's view, literacy, especially literacy based on the type of phonetic alphabet that made the printing press technologically feasible, had a variety of consequences. The artifical dissociation of sight, sound, and meaning into a linear sequence organized through the eyes led to a parallel dissociation of the individual from the web of social relations typical of preliterate, tribal societies. The use of standardized symbols to signify sounds and their arbitrary combination into units of meaning led to similarly arbitrary abstract concepts of time and space. The lineality of the printed page led to a particular type of belief in sequential causality and encouraged abstract representations of space.

The description of the characteristics of the "Gutenberg way of perceiving" is a rather gloomy one. The reason is that the overdevelopment of the visual sense brought about by phonetic literacy is seen by McLuhan as a truly reductive phenomenon. In preliterate times, the primary means of communication was speech. Thus, the hearing organ was the door to perception and experience. A reliance on the auditory in contrast to the visual implies important differences. The hearing organ is a cool medium, since it requires much "filling in" by the listener. The privileging of cool media leads to the contemporaneous stimulation of the other senses and inherently requires a much broader social involvement. The sensuous richness and human interdependence of preliterate societies is seen, by McLuhan, as truly lost by print-oriented Western man.

Nevertheless, the overall tone of *Understanding Media* is determinedly cheerful. The author seems to fashion himself as the prophet of a new golden age, an age in which people are slowly led back by electric/electronic technology to the multisensory richness of preliterate times. As the new media are making written language obsolete, Western man is gaining freedom from the individualistic cage in which he has lived for so long and is slowly assuming a place in the web of social interdependence characterizing the "global village."

Furthermore, the impact of the new media brings positive changes of another kind. "The electronic age," McLuhan states, "is literally one of illumination":

> Just as light is at once energy and information, so electric automation unites production, consumption, and learning in an inextricable process. . . . The very same process of automation that causes a withdrawal of the present work force from industry causes learning itself to become the principal kind of production and consumption.

The final message of *Understanding Media* is that the scope of the electronic means of communication is so vast that they can be seen as an extension not of one sense organ but of the entire nervous system. Thus, human beings are returning to the sensual completeness of tribal life but at a higher level—a level that allows for much imaginative participation in society, particularly through the role of students, teachers, and artists.

The optimism with which McLuhan depicts the golden age ushered in by changes in the media orientation of society has stimulated the criticism of more somber social observers. Harold Rosenberg represents well the feeling of a large group of McLuhan's detractors when he accuses him of being "a belated Whitman singing the body electric with Thomas Edison as accompanist." Certainly, the sweep of the prophetic vision McLuhan presents in *Understanding Media* and the style of its presentation may be disconcerting. It has also been pointed out, however, that the importance of *Understanding Media* has little to do with its scholarly worth or literary style. In this book McLuhan presents a theory, no matter how simplistic or overblown, that explains some of the sweeping changes affecting civilization. Speaking in 1967, George T. Elliott praised McLuhan by saying that his teaching "is radical, new, capable of moving people to social action. If he is wrong it matters." Hindsight allows the expansion of this statement with the suggestion that the ideas McLuhan presented in *Understanding Media* should be periodically reexamined. Regardless of whether they are right, they certainly deserve attention.

Critical Context

The concept that the expressive form of a work of art is its true "message," quite independent from its representational content, has been the mainstay of aesthetic theory since the beginning of the twentieth century. McLuhan's familiarity with this concept, derived from his background in literary criticism, may be seen as one of the stimuli behind some of the ideas proposed in *Understanding Media* and may also help to explain the intuitive appeal of the phrase "the medium is the message."

Furthermore, some of the other themes used by McLuhan in his theory of communication are also derived from works which had already received considerable attention by the time of his writing. In particular, one must remember that two American anthropologists, Edward Sapir in the 1920's and Benjamin Lee Whorf in the 1950's, had developed a theory of linguistic relativity which proposes that a culture's language determines that culture's overall worldview. Also, as early as the 1930's, a full-blown theory of technological determinism was developed by the influential Chicago school of sociology. Writing in 1940, Robert Ezra Park summarized this theory by saying, "Technological devices have naturally changed men's habits and in doing so, they have necessarily modified the structure and functions of society," an idea not unlike the one McLuhan was to present in his own work.

Yet the phenomenal popular success of *Understanding Media* and the greater critical attention attracted by McLuhan can only be understood in the context of the special intellectual and social atmosphere of the 1960's. By 1965, when the McLuhan phenomenon was in the limelight, the unusual characteristics of this decade had become apparent. People felt as if they were living through a nodal moment in history, and that caused both excitement and bewilderment. As a consequence, and as it often happens during periods of major social change, people looked for prophets, wise persons who provide explanations for changes and offer predictions for the future. McLuhan was easily identified as one of these prophets on the basis of his theories; the messianic fervor of his tone, the immediacy of his literary style, and the insouciance of his personality combined to make him a popular icon.

In a way, the success of *Understanding Media* proved to be the undoing of McLuhan's theories. By the beginning of the 1970's, his ideas had been either completely assimilated or totally rejected, and the works in which they had been presented were receiving less and less attention—but then, the progressive obsolescence of the printed word (and of the belief in linear theories of causality) is one of the predictions McLuhan himself had made.

Sources for Further Study

Finkelstein, Sydney Walter. *Sense and Nonsense of McLuhan*, 1968.
Miller, Jonathan. *Marshall McLuhan*, 1971.
Rosenthal, Raymond, ed. *McLuhan: Pro and Con*, 1967.
Stearn, Gerald, ed. *McLuhan: Hot and Cool*, 1967.

Theall, Donald. *The Medium Is the Rear View Mirror: Understanding McLuhan*, 1971.

E. L. Cerroni-Long

AN UNFINISHED WOMAN
A Memoir

Author: Lillian Hellman (1905-1984)
Type of work: Memoir
Time of work: 1905 through the 1960's
Locale: New Orleans, New York City, Hollywood, the Soviet Union, and Spain
First published: 1969

> *Principal personages:*
> LILLIAN HELLMAN, a famous playwright
> MAX HELLMAN, her father
> JULIA NEWHOUSE HELLMAN, her mother
> DOROTHY PARKER, her close friend
> HELEN JACKSON, her maid
> ARTHUR KOBER, her first husband
> DASHIELL HAMMETT, her lover and an important American
> novelist
> SOPHRONIA, a servant who had a great influence on Hellman

Form and Content

Lillian Hellman was sixty-four years old when *An Unfinished Woman* was published. She had had twelve plays produced and published, most of which had been highly successful. The plays had long runs on Broadway, and Hellman was viewed as one of the most important American dramatists. Her last play, however, had been a failure, and she was inclined to think that her playwriting career was over. She had also been a very successful screenwriter in the 1930's and 1940's, but that career had been suspended when she was blacklisted in the 1950's. In addition, her last screenplay, written in the early 1960's, had not been well received.

As she turned to teaching college classes, Hellman began to think of writing nonfiction. She was not attracted to the form of autobiography, having no wish—as she says in *An Unfinished Woman*—to be the "bookkeeper" of her life. She did not have the memory or the interest to chronicle her existence from its beginning—but the memoir form was appealing. She could concentrate on the dramatic incidents of her life and narrate her experiences in story form. Early in her career she had tried writing novels and short stories, without success. Memoir writing provided a fresh approach to the narrative prose she had always wanted to write.

Because of her public prominence as a playwright and her participation in politics, Hellman had written a significant amount of journalism. Her first thought was to collect and revise her articles. When she examined them, however, she realized that they were quite ephemeral pieces—perhaps good enough for their time but not important enough to justify reprinting. Instead, Hellman turned to memories of her personal life, to her childhood in New Orleans and New York, to diaries of her trips to Spain and the Soviet Union, and to people—such as Dorothy Parker (one of her closest friends), Helen Jackson (her maid), and Dashiell Hammett (her lover)—who had meant so much to her.

The title of Hellman's first memoir evokes the myth of herself as a person who never quite matured. She brilliantly conveys the image of an older woman reflecting on the gaps in her life, admitting her faults, and finding the origins of her formidable character. Her memories are often fragmentary—they literally break off because she has forgotten something or has failed to formulate her opinions about someone or something. She quotes liberally from her diaries—which are themselves unfinished bits of writing—to suggest the disjointed quality of her life. At the same time, her power as an artist comes through in the portraits that conclude the memoir.

Analysis

The first two chapters of *An Unfinished Woman* describe the first seventeen years of Hellman's life. They convey a wonderful sense of her years in New Orleans and New York. An only child who was spoiled by her parents and who experienced wildly divided feelings about her mother's rich relatives (the Newhouses) and her father's poor ones, Hellman swings from absolute identification with her handsome lady-killing father, Max Hellman, a charming salesman, to fascination with her mother's powerful, ruthless kin. Julia Newhouse Hellman is presented as a rather weak figure, taken care of by her husband's two sisters, Hannah and Jenny, who are deeply devoted to her husband.

Hellman is especially good at dramatizing the intensely private, egocentric world of an only child. She speaks lovingly of her retreat to her favorite tree, where she would spend many hours reading, sometimes skipping school, and living in the world of her imagination. It is from her cherished fig tree that Hellman throws herself when she learns of her father's infidelity. She catches a glimpse of him out on the town with his girlfriend, one of the boarders in the house run by Hannah and Jenny. In a murderous mood, Hellman impulsively inflicts punishment on herself rather than on her father and his lover. She breaks her nose in the fall from the fig tree and goes to her beloved black nurse, Sophronia, for comfort. Sophronia admonishes her never to talk about what she has seen, never to go around making "bad trouble" for others.

This early scene in *An Unfinished Woman* sets the tone for all Hellman's memoirs. The fig tree has been her source of comfort. She describes it as a kind of Eden of her own making, with the tree's limbs almost literally embracing her. When she falls from the tree, she is shattering her paradise and entering the world of sin and corruption. Her broken nose is her badge of courage; it leads to the lesson that she should never betray a confidence, never violate a friendship. She learns, at a very early age, what it means to have a conscience and to act in accord with it. The fig tree scene also expresses Hellman's great anger. Throughout her life she will lash out at others and at herself when she is displeased. Hammett will replace her father as her unfaithful hero. Like her father, Hammett will teach her much—about politics, about integrity, and about writing. She will remain loyal to his memory even as she rails against him for turning to other women.

Chapters 3 through 6 briskly cover Hellman's early career: a marriage to Arthur Kober (writer and publicity agent), various odd jobs working for New York and Hollywood producers and publishers, fitful attempts to write fiction, and travel to Europe. Hellman presents herself as an intelligent, rebellious woman who has not yet developed the talent to write. Not until she meets Dashiell Hammett in Hollywood in 1930 does she begin to submit to the discipline of a creative mind. She lives with Hammett, watches him write, listens to his stories about being a Pinkerton detective, and follows his advice on adapting a historical event to the stage. The resulting play, *The Children's Hour* (1934), is a huge success on Broadway and leads to a lucrative screenwriting contract with Samuel Goldwyn.

Hellman portrays her years in the 1930's as energetic, creative, and dissolute. Drinking for both her and Hammett was an enormous problem but also part of the glamour of the times. Striking vignettes of F. Scott Fitzgerald and Ernest Hemingway suggest the milieus in which she traveled as a major figure in the theater. While Hellman earned enormous amounts of money, she spent most of it and implies that her life lacked stability until she purchased a farm in Westchester County, New York, with the profits from her play *The Little Foxes* (1939).

The center of the memoir, chapters 8 through 14, contains Hellman's memories and diary entries from trips to Spain (1937), the Soviet Union (1937, 1944, and 1967), and Eastern Europe (1967). Although she does not provide much historical background, Hellman suggests that she was part of a generation of writers who were staunchly anti-Fascist and pro-Soviet. It seemed in the early 1930's that the Soviet Union was building a new, more democratic world. Hellman went to Spain because she hoped it would be the place where Adolf Hitler and Benito Mussolini would be halted in their drive to dominate Europe. She makes no great claims for herself as a political thinker, but she does excuse her naïveté by evoking the sense of solidarity everyone who visited Spain felt. Here writers, workers, people from all walks of life and from all parts of Europe and the United States had come to fight for the Spanish republic, which had been invaded by Francisco Franco's Fascist-backed forces.

Hellman was in Spain for only a few weeks. Her diary entries are an effective way of presenting how difficult it was for her to grasp the meaning of events, to make sense of the conflicting arguments she heard. Hellman knows she could not be much more than a tourist at a war and that, next to the suffering Spanish people, her own preoccupations are silly and out of place. Her diary entries reveal her efforts to understand her motivations and to rid herself of cant:

> Last night I packed a jewelry case—what a ridiculous thing to have brought to Spain. . . . I have twice put off my departure: each day I tell myself that I will stay until the war is over and be of some use, but at night, when I don't feel well, dizzy and weak, I want very much to leave.

In the Soviet Union, Hellman was lionized as a great figure of the theater. She admits that she was blind to much that was happening—for example, Stalin's purges of Communist Party members in the so-called show trials were taking place during her first trip there. Her excuse is that the diplomats in the American embassy were so biased against the Soviet Union, so mean-spirited in their observations about Russian life, that she could not believe them.

Hellman's 1967 trip to the Soviet Union is presented as her opportunity to reflect on the wartime years when she was a guest in the American embassy. She has a reunion with her translator, who took her to the front in 1944. She hears stories about Stalin's evil but still cannot quite fathom what has happened to Soviet society. The shabbiness of Moscow in the late 1960's bothers her, and it is clear that she misses the camaraderie she experienced during the war. In 1979, in the collected edition of her memoirs, Hellman added an italicized section on her attitude toward Stalinism and took the issue up at greater length in *Scoundrel Time* (1976).

An Unfinished Woman closes strongly, with three powerful portraits. Their strength derives from the fact that Hellman has only to deal with her personal attitudes toward these people she knew quite well. In contrast to the sections on Spain and the Soviet Union, the chapter on Dorothy Parker is full of wonderfully concrete metaphors that summarize Hellman's reading of human character. Parker "was, more than usual, a tangled fishnet of contradictions: she liked the rich because she liked the way they looked, their clothes, the things in their houses, and she disliked them with an open and baiting contempt." Parker was a socialist who could not abide "the sight of a working radical"; her sense of style, in other words, attracted her to the people she opposed on principle while it repelled her from the people she was supposed to support. Similarly, Helen Jackson, a black woman, reminds her of Sophronia, who had a very human, very contradictory nature, including a "real-pretend love for white people."

Hellman's paradoxical uses of words, her reliance on hyphenated expressions, is a stylistic trait suggestive of her belief that human character is something less than complete and often conflicted. Hammett is the epitome of the conflicted human character—the "sinner-saint" Hellman simultaneously adores and condemns. No man treated her affection with less loyalty (Hammett always had other women in his life), but no man was more devoted to her writing (he insisted that she write the very best she could and kept sending her back to write draft after draft of her plays until they were right).

It is clear from *An Unfinished Woman* that neither her life nor her career gave Lillian Hellman a sense of completeness. She ends her memoir lamenting the fact that she never made sense of her experiences. The last word of her memoir is "however," an ambiguous ending that implies that more could be said. Thus, *An Unfinished Woman*, true to itself, ends with an unfinished thought.

Critical Context

When *An Unfinished Woman* appeared in 1969, it was greeted by reviewers as a triumph of memoir writing. Hellman was hailed as a survivor of the political battles of the 1930's, a strong woman who made her fame and fortune in a man's world, a pillar of honesty, and a role model for a whole new generation of women. While she had been a public figure for many years, her memoir made her a national celebrity and won for her an audience of readers largely unfamiliar with her plays and not especially knowledgeable about her political background.

Several reviewers commented on Hellman's elliptical style. So much seemed to be left out of her stories. That is what made her fascinating and tantalizing. There was a craving for more of her memories, especially since she virtually ignored the writing and reception of her plays. She had yet to explain adequately her leftist politics. Hellman did not disappoint her audience, producing *Pentimento* in 1972, *Scoundrel Time* in 1976, and *Maybe* in 1980. As with *An Unfinished Woman*, these books were memoirs, not autobiographies; that is, in each book Hellman concentrated on important periods in her life—her testimony before the House Committee on Un-American Activities, more episodes from her childhood, the production of her plays, her years in Hollywood—but did not offer a detailed chronology or explanation of her personal and political development.

Pentimento, which employs the portrait format of the last three chapters of *An Unfinished Woman*, was considered to be an unqualified artistic success. *Scoundrel Time* was at first greeted with enthusiastic reviews and then became the subject of virulent attacks by critics who accused Hellman of lying about her Stalinism and fabricating parts of her past. By the time *Maybe* appeared, her memoirs were received much more skeptically, with reviewers commenting on the self-serving nature of her memories. Although the veracity of her memoirs has been under attack, and the style of her nonfiction writing has been criticized for imitating Ernest Hemingway and Dashiell Hammett, there seems little doubt that Hellman's powerful imaginative depiction of herself will secure for her an important niche in American literature.

Sources for Further Study

Dick, Bernard F. *Hellman in Hollywood*, 1982.
Falk, Doris V. *Lillian Hellman*, 1978.
Lederer, Katherine. *Lillian Hellman*, 1979.
Martin, William B. "Lillian Hellman's Table Talk," in *Conference on College Teachers of English Studies, 1981*. XLVI (September, 1981), pp. 29-35.
Rollyson, Carl. *Lillian Hellman: Her Legend and Her Legacy*, 1988.
Ross-Bryant, Lynn. "Imagination and the Re-valorization of the Feminine," in *Journal of the American Academy of Religion*. XLVIII, no. 2 (1981), pp. 105-117.
Spacks, Patricia Meyer. *The Female Imagination*, 1975.
Wright, William. *Lillian Hellman: The Image, the Woman*, 1986.

Carl Rollyson

UNFRAMED ORIGINALS

Author: W. S. Merwin (1927-   )
Type of work: Autobiography
Time of work: The 1930's and 1940's
Locale: New York City, New Jersey, and Pennsylvania
First published: 1982

Principal personages:
    W. S. MERWIN, a well-known American poet and translator
    HIS FATHER, a Presbyterian minister
    HIS MOTHER, a reticent woman of profound feeling
    HIS GRANDFATHER, a mysterious figure for Merwin

Form and Content

W. S. Merwin's *Unframed Originals* is made up of six sections written at intervals over a span of several years. As Merwin points out in a brief prefatory note, "Each was intended to stand by itself, but each was part of the whole enterprise." Each was "a product of a single impulse," the attempt to recapture the past. Born in 1927 in New York City, William Stanley Merwin spent his early years in Union City, New Jersey, and Scranton, Pennsylvania, where his father, a Presbyterian minister, held pastorates. As a young adult, Merwin lived in France, Portugal, and London, supporting himself as a tutor and translator. Merwin's autobiography concerns itself largely with the people and places surrounding his earliest years.

Merwin is known primarily as a lyric poet and translator of poets. His mature poetry includes *The Carrier of Ladders* (1970), for which he was awarded the Pulitzer Prize. His translations range from the ancient *The Poem of the Cid* (1959), to the more modern *Twenty Love Poems and a Song of Despair* (1969), by Pablo Neruda. His prose reflects a poet's distrust of generalizations and analysis. His past, as he recollects it, is not historical but poetic, evoked in a metaphorical but plain style, minutely and sensuously detailed. Neither the individual sections themselves nor the narratives within the individual sections are chronologically ordered. Their order, rather, is one of mood and memory, or, as Merwin puts it, "a presentation of things that originally happened in sequence but now occur in the same moment in my mind, and so have become simultaneous, like flakes of snow that have fallen from different heights into the sea." While *Unframed Originals* is clearly autobiographical and Merwin's memory serves to unite the different sections of the book into a coherent whole, unlike most autobiographies, the primary concern is not Merwin himself, but "reflections of other people," particularly his immediate family and relatives.

The opening section, "Tomatoes," serves to introduce several of the book's central thematic concerns. In it, Merwin, then nine years old, meets his grandfather for the first and last time. They discuss, briefly and inconsequentially, the art of growing tomatoes. Divorced from Merwin's grandmother long before his birth and banished from the family, his grandfather is absent throughout Merwin's life. Nevertheless, in his absence, this man exerts a mysterious influence because he can never be fully known.

In the sections which follow—"Mary," "The Skyline," "Laurie," "Hotel," and "La Pia"—the reader is led, as one reviewer put it, more deeply into Merwin's "intricate family webs." Each section centers on a figure peripheral to young Merwin's life but essential to an understanding of his parents' inner lives and, consequently, his own. "Hotel," for example, focuses on the character of Aunt Margie, actually his grandmother's first cousin. For his mother, she "represented family not only in the sense of blood tie and continuity, but in that of shared assumptions, attitudes, conduct, gesture." Aunt Margie stayed with the Merwins only briefly, finding the household atmosphere repressive. For his mother, however, she remained, even in her absence, "a private source of strength." Upon Margie's death, young Merwin, "for whatever unknown reason," was made the sole heir to an estate consisting of "one large black and black-green folding steamer trunk" and a small sum of money. Both were significant gifts. The trunk, "this grown-up object appearing out of my mother's absent family," came to represent "a past older than either of my parents"—a past that was "in fact mine." The money was put to use some years later to buy a small farmhouse in France. The price of the house was, coincidentally, "exactly the amount, in francs," that Margie had left him. His ties to Aunt Margie were tenuous, even accidental, but real—a link, as Merwin writes, to "a life and world before mine."

Analysis

In the opening paragraph of "Mary," Merwin writes, "Once I imagined, with no way of saying it, that my parents, and everyone of their age, kept somewhere among them the whole of the past." In many respects, *Unframed Originals* represents Merwin's quest to recover the "whole of the past." Yet from the outset it is a quest haunted by a sense of ultimate failure. Too much of his elders' living memory was left unrevealed and then lost forever after their deaths. James Finn Cotter calls Merwin "a master of color and line" and suggests that *Unframed Originals* "belongs in the gallery of great word-portraits." What is most important for Merwin, however, is not the portrait itself but what lies beyond the frame. In an interview with Ed Folsom and Cary Nelson, he states, "One of the main themes of *Unframed Originals* is what I was not able to know, what I couldn't ever find out, the people I couldn't meet." Indeed, *Unframed Originals* describes absence and loss.

Socially, the conditions of loss center on the changing nature of the American family. As Merwin puts it, "I was convinced that I knew less about my family, and my parents' families, than it was usual to know." Yet the reasons for his ignorance are hardly unusual; the modern American family is marked by wide geographic dispersal: "My father referred to his family as 'the family,' and he called us 'our family.' His family was related to our family, but lived far away. Or we lived far away." The family had been stretched thin by distance—a distance both caused and only partially alleviated by modern transportation. Images of trains and automobiles, for example, recur throughout *Unframed Originals* and take on a symbolic importance: "It seemed to [my father] then, probably, that many things, even most things that he considered his, were slipping from him. And that must have had something to do with his idea of going, in the new car, to visit the rest of Grandma's children. . . ." Yet visits were brief and transient. The continuing day-to-day contact which reveals the lives of others in depth had been irretrievably lost.

Geographic distance is mirrored by a personal distance. Throughout *Unframed Originals*, one detects an aversion to self-revelation. "Reticence," as Merwin puts it, "was one of the main things I was writing about. Indeed it was a very reticent family." Merwin can only speculate tangentially on the conflicting motives for silence. He reveals the resentments and shame his excessively pious grandmother felt for his grandfather, but the explanation for their divorce goes no deeper than the simple pronouncement, "He drank." While his own parents were never divorced, his mother, in a rare moment of candor, revealed that there was a time when she might have left his father for another man but decided against it. The motives for her temptation and her decision to remain were both lost within silence: "She would say nothing more on the subject." Of his relationship with his mother, Merwin writes that "she has been so secret, and I have grown up in the habit of being so reticent with her, that it cannot be easy now to find what we want to say to each other."

Perhaps even more insidious than personal reticence is personal indifference. Of his relationship with his father, Merwin writes,

> The past itself, the past of others, of places, of his family, most of his own past, seemed to hold no more than a wan, flickering interest for him, apart from a thin collection of dependable references treasured as proofs and names of feelings that he wanted to believe still existed and were his.

Whether caused by the changing conditions of social life, the personal reticence born of shame, or a simple indifference, the result is the same: The past slips away. As Mark Irwin points out, *Unframed Originals* is "haunting in the final realization that the past cannot be reconstructed, only glimpsed during privileged moments."

Those privileged moments, however, serve as the rationale for Merwin's recollections. There is an intimate revelation of detail in which one can glimpse "pieces of an order." As Merwin observes, "I felt if I could take any detail, any moment, anything I could clearly see, and pay enough attention to it, it would act like a kind of hologram. I'd be able to see the whole story in that single detail."

The order, however, is not so much personal as transcendent. W. H. Auden, on the publication of Merwin's first book, characterized him as a mythological poet. The observation is no less true of Merwin's prose. In the final section of *Unframed Originals*, "La Pia," he writes,

A line and its passage from the *Purgatorio* that have been running in my head all week on the mountain, like a tune, start up again: *e riposato della lunga via.* "And (you have/ thou hast) rested from the long way." *Via*, the journey, with its continuing echo or reminder of *vita*; the journey through death that is the way of life, and of the poem. Not in the text, that echo, but summoned by it.

Like Dante's Vergil, Merwin too makes a "journey through death." As he attempts to come to terms with his mother's death, she blends symbolically with the figure of La Pia, a minor character in Dante's *La divina commedia* (c. 1320; *The Divine Comedy*, 1802). Dante reveals very little of La Pia, essentially only her name and her plea to be remembered. Yet the figure of La Pia haunts Merwin. He reads over Dante's lines "in the hope of hearing through them what is here to be remembered, something more, La Pia." In much the same spirit, he recounts the remembered bits and pieces of his life, less for their own sake than for the echoes they summon. He would have the reader hear "something unplaceable but distantly familiar." He would strike "a note that led back through [his] grandparents' lives to the beginning, and before." He would have each reader hear mythic echoes of his own originals.

Critical Context

Part of the difficulty critics have had in categorizing Merwin's work lies in Merwin himself. When asked if he thought of himself "as belonging to a specific generation of poets who share similar experiences," he agreed that he felt a part of his generation but went on to say, "I don't feel part of any school or approach or movement or anything like that. I never have. In the late fifties, all of American poetry was supposed to be divided into two camps. That never made any sense to me at all." Neither of the two schools, the "projectivist" and the confessional, adequately describes Merwin's work. Although Merwin was politically active in the peace and antinuclear movements, unlike that of the projectivists his work reveals that activism only obliquely; although his work is intimate in tone and style, Merwin himself is too reticent for the obsessive self-revelation of the so-called confessional poets.

If Merwin is to be categorized at all, it is perhaps best to place him within a larger American tradition. As the critic Harold Bloom wrote, Merwin belongs within "the revival of the Native Strain or Emersonian vision." Like his contemporary, John Ashbery, also born in 1927, Merwin explores what the critic Richard Howard called "a quality of life which used to be called visionary, and which must be characterized by its negatives, by what it is not, for what it is cannot be spoken." While Ashbery and Merwin are strikingly different in style, they share a concern with revealing in the little that can be said all that cannot. Both explore absence and loss.

Merwin is uncompromising in this exploration. One critic, Helen Vendler, finds Merwin's work so "starved and mute" that she has "a relentless social-worker urge to ask him to eat something, anything, to cure his anemia." Others, however, find it "apocalyptic and agonized," an evocation of contemporary despair. Yet for all Merwin's obsession with absence and loss, he would not wholly abandon himself to a nihilistic despair: "We try to save what is passing, if only by describing it, telling it, knowing all the time that we can't do any of these things. The urge to tell it, and the knowledge of the impossibility. Isn't that one reason we write?"

If *Unframed Originals* is not itself lost in time, it will be remembered for the little it has said. It will be remembered for what it has preserved, in a language both evocative and spare, against loss. Merwin would reveal, as he writes near the end of *Unframed Originals*, "the stone, the humanly prized thing out of the earth, the crystal, the focus, the symbol, the gauge, the promise, the enduring impersonal source of radiance."

Sources for Further Study

Bloom, Harold. "The New Transcendentalism: The Visionary Strain in Merwin, Ashbery, and Ammons," in *Chicago Review*. XXIV, no. 3 (1972), pp. 25-43.

Cotter, James Finn. "Poets Then and Now," in *America*. CXLVIII (January 29, 1983), pp. 75-76.

Folsom, Ed, and Cary Nelson. "W. S. Merwin," in *American Poetry Observed: Poets on Their Work*, 1984. Edited by Joe David Bellamy.

Fuller, Edmund. "Autobiographies of a Satirist in Line and a Gifted Poet," in *The Wall Street Journal*. CCI (January 3, 1983), p. 22.

Hirsch, Edward. "The Art of Poetry XXXVIII: W. S. Merwin," in *The Paris Review*. XXIX (Spring, 1987), pp. 56-81.

Howard, Richard. *Alone with America: Essays in the Art of Poetry in the United States Since 1950*, 1980 (revised edition).

Irwin, Mark. Review in *World Literature Today*. II (Spring, 1983), p. 294.

Oates, Joyce Carol. "Family Portrait," in *The New York Times Book Review*. LXXXVII (August 1, 1982), pp. 7, 29.

Vendler, Helen. "W. S. Merwin," in *Part of Nature, Part of Us*, 1980.

Christopher L. Picard

THE UNQUIET GRAVE
A Word Cycle

Author: Cyril Connolly (1903-1974)
Type of work: Cultural criticism/autobiography
First published: 1944

Form and Content

In his introduction to the 1950 edition of *The Unquiet Grave*, Cyril Connolly wrote at length about his intention for the work, which, as he acknowledged, could look very much like a loose, somewhat precious series of melancholy comments upon life, supported by lavish quotations from an impressively wide range of literature and philosophy. It could also be read as simply a kind of vade mecum, an English gentleman's vaguely autobiographical record of emotional states precipitating snatches of elegant quotation.

It was, in the main, on this level that its early success rested, and it became something of a cult book among sophisticated intellectuals, particularly in Great Britain. Although the book was supposedly written by someone hiding behind the name "Palinurus," it was well-known that Cyril Connolly, one of the brightest members of the British literary world and the editor of its finest literary magazine, *Horizon* (in which the work was originally printed), was its author. It was no surprise that Connolly, admired for his astonishingly deep knowledge of world literature, would be able to put so much of his knowledge so gracefully into this modestly sized work.

The source of the book was a set of journals that Connolly wrote in London between autumn, 1942, and autumn, 1943, during World War II. During this time he was unhappily attempting to deal with the failure of his first marriage and with his sense of not attaining the success as a writer which his brilliant career as a student had suggested was inevitable. "Palinurus" was the fictional guise he rather half-heartedly hid behind in print, but the comments are clearly those of Connolly about his own life.

In his introduction, Connolly suggests that the book goes beyond aimless, if intriguing comment by a man in emotional turmoil. He suggests that it has a definite structure. In the first section, his views of life in general, of love, of religion, and of literature are placed in the context of his middle-aged crisis. In the second section, the crisis is discussed in terms of two kinds of philosophers, those who espouse pessimism and destructiveness and those who teach one to accept failure with courage and the determination to get on with life. In this section, the contemplation of innocent nature leads him out of his despair. Finally, he remembers the happy times in his past and is brought around to accept life with all of its pains and pleasures.

The reason Connolly chose this form of self-examination can best be understood if something is known of his failures as a husband and as a writer. He was, in fact, a very famous man, and his work as the editor of *Horizon* was widely acclaimed. That might well have satisfied anyone else, but Connolly from the time that he was a schoolboy had been singled out for even finer things. He won a scholarship to Eton College, the most prestigious boys' school in Great Britain, and while there he proved that his intellectual and literary gifts were of the highest order, at a time when Eton was educating some of the finest literary minds in the country. As a result of his work there, he won a scholarship to Balliol College, University of Oxford, and he was again recognized as one of the most promising students of his generation. Connolly, however, did badly in his examinations, and he came out of Oxford rather at loose ends. He taught for a time, and then he drifted into journalism. He wrote one novel, *The Rock Pool* (1936), which was well received but hardly a work of genius, and he watched as his contemporaries developed literary reputations of far more substance than his. He was supposed to have led them all but had found himself on the fringes of success. The failure of his marriage seemed to confirm his failure as a man, consonant with his failure as an artist. *The Unquiet Grave* might be seen, then, on its surface, as an exercise in self-pity, if expressed with a formidable show of learning.

Analysis

What saves *The Unquiet Grave*, in large part, from being simply a lachrymose exercise in elegiac regret is the way in which Connolly imposes one kind of literary form upon another. The basic form is that of the occasional essay, which has a centuries-long tradition in European letters. Indeed, the question of the value of life (which is part of Connolly's theme) can be seen in the dialogues of Plato— sometimes with a very serious tone, sometimes with a kind of sophisticated playfulness. That thinking about subjects of importance can, in itself, be entertaining as well as enlightening was an idea put into practice throughout the history of Western literature, by Michel Eyquem de Montaigne on the Continent and by Sir Thomas Browne, Jonathan Swift, Samuel Johnson, and Charles Lamb in Great Britain. Connolly is at one with that tradition, knowing that his personal problems can, if expressed intelligently and within the context of other writers' work, go beyond the particularity of the single situation and can, in the best sense of the word, "delight" the reader.

The essay, however, is not the only form used in *The Unquiet Grave*: Connolly imposes another structure on top of the civilized musings about life which are common to the essay tradition. What he develops is a prose version of what is commonly known in poetry as the "dramatic monologue," which reached its most successful expression in the work of the nineteenth century English poet Robert Browning. A character, possessing some qualities, some social position, some peculiar gift or task, is brought by those peculiarities to a moment of crisis; sometimes the character is quite deeply affected by the situation, sometimes he or she is insensitive to what is happening, but ultimately the pattern of the poem leads to a moment of enlightenment. The poem itself, in its pattern of working through the problem, provides the solution, and the character is able to move forward into conduct consistent with the understanding of what must be done to survive. In "Childe Roland to the Dark Tower Came," Roland is full of doubt, chagrin, and a sense of betrayal; in the end, having thought the problem through as he approaches his task, he is prepared to fight—whatever the odds, however badly he has been used. Melancholy stasis gives way to action. That is exactly what Connolly, through the character Palinurus, achieves in his prose version of the usually poetic form.

Palinurus, the pilot of Aeneas' ship in the epic poem (c. 29-19 B.C.) by Vergil, falls asleep at the helm. He falls overboard and manages to get ashore, but he is killed by savages. Since Palinurus is left unburied, his soul cannot be carried over the River Styx to eternal peace in the Underworld. Connolly identifies with him, in part, because there is, in some versions of the myth, a suggestion that Palinurus deserts Aeneas. Palinurus' fall from the boat is a failure to do his duty, just as Connolly failed to fulfill his early promise as a writer. Moreover, Palinurus' moping on the shores of the River Styx parallels Connolly's unhappiness about his personal life, surrounded by and mirrored in the chaos of wartime London.

Connolly's use of Palinurus is, in part, comparable to T. S. Eliot's use of Tiresias in *The Waste Land* (1922), which had some influence on *The Unquiet Grave*. In both works, figures from classical myth are used to represent modern man, caught in the dilemma of twentieth century angst. Yet, Palinurus has a much more specifically personal connection: He stands for Connolly, and the details of his life are drawn from Connolly's own life (including his tendency, given his enthusiasm for the food and drink of the good life, to overindulge himself). More seriously, it is Connolly's voice that is heard, and his impressive intelligence is displayed in the short, informal comments upon life, love, literature, philosophy, religion, and social change.

Just as his life is on the decline, literature—the novel especially—has peaked with the successes of Marcel Proust, James Joyce, and Virginia Woolf. There is no chance for the fame to which he had aspired, and life in general comes to nothing. The dominant figures of the first section are the great pessimists Blaise Pascal, Giacomo Leopardi, and Gérard de Nerval, the latter advocating suicide as a solution. Connolly remembers four friends, all of them suicides. While this section is despairing, the narrator has such an energetic and astonishingly informed personality that the work is never simply an exercise in self-pity.

The second section, though no less entertaining, tends to be tied more often to a kind of diary entry which relates the material more intimately to the personality and personal habits of the author. Connolly remembers his life in Paris and traces his difficulties back to that time, but, in the process of remembering, he moves slowly from bitterness and defeat to memories of the pleasures of that time. Ultimately, he remembers, with some considerable tenderness, the lemurs which he and his first wife kept for a few years. These memories of Paris at its best, and the affection which he had for those animals, slowly soothe him, and he turns away from the negativism of the first section to see life as both comedy and tragedy. Happiness must be man's goal, even in the face of the destruction of the war, which is still going on as the book ends.

The latter part of the book is much less agitated, often sweet-natured, without sacrificing the keen intelligence which Connolly establishes at the beginning. Palinurus in the very process of complaint, recrimination, revaluation, and remembering has learned how to make the best of a bad job, to bear the pain of being human, and relish the pleasure. He has reached the shore.

By turning his personal dilemma into a work of art, Connolly has exorcised his demons. He does not, however, stop there. In what may seem an artistic error, he adds an epilogue, in which he explores the Palinurus myth with the help of modern psychological theories, theories which he uses in an unsystematic way throughout the work. He sees this exercise as a relief from the emotional passages extolling the pursuit of happiness, and it has a pawky charm about it as an exercise in scholastic hairsplitting. It may, however, seem to some to undermine the feeling of quiet exultation which is so successful in bringing Palinurus to an understanding of how life can be lived serenely. Thus, while intellectually amusing, the epilogue may be an artistic error.

Critical Context

Connolly was to go on to have a respected career as a critic in the best London newspapers. He continued to edit *Horizon* until it closed in 1950. He became the literary editor of the *Observer*, and later the main book reviewer for the *Sunday Times*. Yet he never wrote the great book that he thought he was capable of producing. His critics suspected that he failed to write that great book simply because of his enthusiasm for the pleasures of life, exactly the kind of self-criticism he makes in *The Unquiet Grave*.

This may be Connolly's best work, although there is some support for his earlier work, *Enemies of Promise* (1938), about his school days at Eton. *The Unquiet Grave* is, perhaps, too self-interested, too indulgent of his ability to produce examples of his knowledge of European literature and, as a result, too diffuse to be taken quite as seriously as he wanted it to be taken. It is, however, a popular book, and it has been added to the list of Penguin Modern Classics, something of a sign of long-term interest, if not necessarily of "classic" status. The work successfully brings together the essay, the dramatic monologue, and the confessional journal; with considerable charm and occasional wit, Connolly expresses the state of mind which may be taken as a symbol for the intellectual confusion of the war years.

Sources for Further Study

Baker, Carlos. Review in *The New York Times Book Review*. L (October 7, 1945), p. 6.

Erdman, Irwin. Review in *Saturday Review*. XXVIII (November 17, 1945), p. 12.

Marshall, Margaret. Review in *The Nation*. CLXI (October 20, 1945), p. 405.

Pryce-Jones, David. *Cyril Connolly: Journal and Memoir*, 1983.
Time. Review. XLVI (November 5, 1945), p. 108.
Wilson, Edmund. Review in *The New Yorker*. XXI (October 27, 1945), p. 88.

Charles Pullen

USHANT
An Essay

Author: Conrad Aiken (1889-1973)
Type of work: Autobiography
Time of work: The early twentieth century
Locale: England, Europe, Georgia, Massachusetts, and aboard a ship crossing the Atlantic Ocean
First published: 1952

Principal personages:
    D., the narrator of Conrad Aiken's mythologized life story
    HIS PARENTS, who died in a murder-suicide
    EZRA POUND and
    T. S. ELIOT, poets who influenced Aiken

Form and Content

Conrad Aiken's *Ushant*, the poet's major prose work, falls into no clear literary category. It is at once an autobiography, a confession, and a participatory novel which involves the reader in the journey of remembrance, creation, and imagination on which Aiken sets forth. Following the precedents of such writers as Laurence Sterne and James Joyce in his use of free-association and stream-of-consciousness techniques, Aiken created a literary form to suit his needs, allowing the contents of his memory and the honesty of his self-analysis to give shape and meaning to his circular narrative. *Ushant*, which is divided into six sections, is a journey of return to the "beginning without beginning" of his life. The book is Aiken's synthesis of his life as a poet, and it is linked to the modernist view of man as the creative artist of his life.

In the book, which draws on the author's past experiences so that he may fully realize his creative ego, Aiken often portrays himself as a cultural artifact rather than as a person. The circular journey that returns him to his roots is paralleled by the journeys of many other "travelers." Along the way there are numerous contacts with the world of a whole generation of American and British artists who contributed to the vital movement of modernism in the first half of the twentieth century.

The central image of the narrative is that of the tiny ship at sea amid a dream seascape, approaching the mythical island of Ushant. In cabin 144 are twelve sleeping travelers returning from the United States to England two weeks after the close of World War II. Among them is the main character D. (for Demarest, the main character in Aiken's novel *Blue Voyage*, written in 1927). D. details the lives of several of his cabin mates and compares their need to return to England with his own. His empathy with their compulsion to revisit England underscores the fact that these passengers link him with the rest of humanity. D. is the "eye" and the "I" of the book. He is returning to Ariel's Isle (England) and to Saltinge, the country house of which he has many memories.

The form of the narrative is governed by D.'s mental associations, so that the tale resembles a series of double-exposure photographs. D.'s narrative scenes, each containing two or three superimposed images, begin with his dream of the sea and Ushant. From there they glide into his consciousness as he considers the others in the cabin, and then through free associations to which he gives symbolic significance. In this way, D. arranges his narrative material like a film montage, moving from dream to reality to the making of symbolic order, the very process of art. These three forms of consciousness—reality, dream, and symbol—change and blend just as they would in a writer's creative work. Given this approach, the reader reviews not only D.'s conscious and unconscious past but also his construction of a work of art from these materials.

In his dream, which initially seems vague and ambiguous, D. sees himself with three other persons translating a novella about his life which may be written in German, Spanish, or Provençal. As the dream progresses, he realizes that he is all four of the persons engaged in the translation of his life and that these translators provide various interpretations of his past actions and failures, both human and literary. Thus, D. is not only reviewing his life but also dreaming and translating a book, *Ushant*, whose actual creation is taking place before the reader's eyes. As D.'s plan unfolds before the reader, the book is being written; its central aim is D.'s acquisition of self-knowledge, his embarkation on a project which would be

> an integral part of the very vision—of the . . . indecipherable, or nameless land, a land of which one could make oneself the possessor by a mere strictness of aware-ness . . . [a land] architected, with its own intrinsic and natural spiral of form, as a whole drama of the human soul, from the beginningless beginning to the endless end. Too difficult altogether.

Despite this difficulty, D. tries because he believes that "this pursuit [is] possibly the most essential of dramas, . . . since that pursuit is the central undeviating concern of every living individual human being; and thus, in aggregate, on the grand evolutionary scale, of all mankind." It is not surprising that facing such a formidable task, Aiken puns with the book's title, writing it as "You shant."

Ushant, or Île d'Ouessant, is a real island off the coast of France whose lighthouse guides the traveler toward the coast of England. It was once the western limit for Europeans, and its fog-shrouded shores suggest the Celtic myth of the western land of the dead. D. regards it as a point at which East and West (England and America) are reconciled. It is also the place where D. the writer will find the most complete state of consciousness, the ultimate point at which he will attain self-knowledge. That point is never reached in the autobiography, because the "journey" lasts for a lifetime. Yet D. believes that despite the unresolved nature of his vision, "we rise, we rise, ourselves now like notes of music arranging themselves in divine harmony, a divine unison, which, as it had no beginning, can have no end. . . ."

Analysis

The "beginning without beginning" that affects D. throughout his life, and which is the source of his creative voyage toward both Ushant and the self-destructive elements in his life, lies in his discovery, at age eleven, of the bodies of his parents, whose bitter quarrel had resulted in a murder-suicide. He sees part of his quest as the attempt to reconcile these parents in himself and to deal with their deaths through his art. The chosen action for D. is to journey back and forth across the Atlantic, and the resolution of his odyssey will be the reconciliation of the opposites of his life through creativity.

The book's six sections follow in the most general way the chronology of events in D.'s life, shifting time and place continuously. After the initial introduction to the form and method of the book and the appearance of D.'s cabin mates and the four translators of his life, D. returns to the world of his childhood and the images of his parents: the lackluster mother and the elegant, handsome doctor father. D. describes his house in Savannah and its two doors, one leading to the stately lawn and graceful garden and the other to the back streets and raw adventures. This dualistic view pervades the entire book, especially when D. is comparing England and the United States, his mother and father, Savannah and Boston, or East and West, and it clearly adds to his fears as a child and the ambiguities of his self-image as a man and an artist. At this point, D. does not tell how his parents died but only of his sense of dislocation when he was moved from Savannah to New England to be cared for by cousins, aunts, and uncles.

Section 2 of *Ushant* moves to the world of New England; it describes D.'s first recognition that he is caught between two worlds, a pattern which is repeated throughout his life and which leads him ultimately, though with difficulty, to a reconciliation of the two. D. remembers himself as a source of embarrassment to the family because of his parents' deaths. He is passed from house to house until the family recognizes that it needs him as much as he needs them in order to deal with the guilt and sadness connected with past events. The portrayals of Aunt Sybil, the Beloved Uncle, and the powerful Aunt Maud are striking, particularly when D. contrasts their northern coolness and firmness with exciting, passionate Savannah, a place of beauty and "incredible and cruel fertility." Nevertheless, it is in Boston, Concord, and later Cambridge that D. develops his poetry, that "deepest and most secret habit of his nature."

These accounts of D.'s childhood are the most affecting sections of the book, because they are mainly centered on character portraits of the family past. The influences of environment and heredity become marvelously mixed when D. tells of ninety-five-year-old Aunt Jean, who, in her delirium, confuses D. with various family members who lived in the nineteenth century. In this scene, D. becomes a composite portrait of five generations; he feels a queer combination of anonymity and identity within the structure of his family, an ambiguity which he in turn passes on to the three D.'s who are his children. In his way, all D.'s relatives help compose the moving pattern of his life. Perhaps most significant, Aunt Sybil and the Beloved

Uncle allow D. to see the portfolio of his father's poems, thereby helping him to exorcise his guilt and shame and encouraging his desire to write by showing him that writing was a "family habit."

The third section of the narrative centers on D.'s excursion into the world of Bloomsbury after his break with Harvard University. It begins with a contrast between D.'s adventurous Cousin Del, whose passion for ships and the sea D. shares, and the Frightened Uncle, who always sat on the fence and never learned to live. Though D. is not given to some of the dangerous exploits of his cousin, he does heed the words of the uncle who tells D. not to make his mistake. Consequently, D. decides to leave Harvard after a year and spend time in London. It is here that he meets Tsetse (T. S. Eliot), of whom he had heard at Harvard, and other American literary lights, most of whom, in the tradition of Nathaniel Hawthorne and Henry James, have returned to the motherland of the English language. D., speaking now as the poet, sees this as symbolic and describes people and places in England metaphorically. For example, he refers to his three wives as Loreleis I, II, and III, to T. S. Eliot as Tsetse (perhaps because of his somnolent voice), to Ezra Pound as Rabbi Ben Ezra (a sharp reference to Pound's anti-Semitism), and to Malcolm Lowry, who is given to theatricality, as Hambo. More relevant to *Ushant*'s major themes is the symbolic juxtaposition of places and persons. D.'s parents, especially, are associated in his mind with England and America. He sees England as an ordered, social, traditional, and maternal influence and America as a chaotic, individualistic, iconoclastic, and paternal influence in his life.

D. also sees this duality in the attitudes toward England and America expressed by various American writers. At first, he connects himself to writers such as James and Hawthorne, for whom England and Europe held a greater fascination, at times, than America, even though both writers had their roots squarely in the American romantic and puritanic spirit. Yet as D. spends more time in England and on the Continent, he is drawn to comprehend and empathize with those writers, such as Walt Whitman, Edgar Allan Poe, and Emily Dickinson, who "stayed at home" and drew heavily on their own individual resources rather than a traditional sense of society. After his own struggle, D. accepts the American scene, "changing by realizing and accepting by changing," or fusing the two worlds in himself as he had done with the opposing worlds of Savannah and Boston.

His voyage back to the United States provides D. with the characters for his novel *Purple Passage* (Aiken's facetious title for his earlier autobiographical novel, *Blue Voyage*). Most significant of these characters is Cynthia, whom D. sees as the precipitator of his break with the United States, his fatherland. It is she who underscores the great differences between the two worlds: shaped, traditional Europe and raw, unfinished America, where the "sense of freedom is priceless." While his affair with Cynthia lasts, he makes his break with Harvard and gives himself to the continental scene. Always, however, he struggles with his attraction to the United States and the need to explore and face his origins.

Breaking off from his explorations of his past, D. returns to the present aboard the eastbound ship. He emerged from the cabin at the start of section 3; now, at the beginning of section 4, he makes his way to the ship's bar, where he hears the voices of some of his cabin mates. His physical movement parallels his spiritual growth, and as he leaves the cocoon of self to enter a larger world, his memories follow him. He recalls his meeting with Tsetse in Paris and the parting of their ways, Eliot returning to Harvard to study Sanskrit and D. visiting Naples, Rome, and the graves of John Keats and Percy Bysshe Shelley. D. remembers, too, that Europe was a way to deal with what he had thought of as the family madness, the insanity that caused him to break off his studies and come to Europe seeking experience. He sees his fate affected by Tsetse and by Irene, an English courtesan, who waits for him in Leicester Square in London. For D., these two influences— Eliot in art and Irene in sex—are intertwined, ambiguous yet determining voices in his life as an artist. He asks himself a question: Is the artist the healthy child of nature, her spokesman and her celebrant, or is he the unhealthy rebel pitted against the determining forces? D.'s answer is to celebrate those moments of expanded consciousness while maintaining an awareness of the underlying chaos of life.

Painful experiences with an Italian Berlitz teacher in Venice and later with a German waitress reveal D.'s timidity with women, a timidity based partly on his sense of inadequacy and partly on his fear of marriage. It is Irene Barnes, the Englishwoman he meets in London, who helps D. to "put on a new body and a new mind." His brief interlude with her opens D. to the love of others and frees him from his narcissism. Even though he spends only a brief time with Irene, a time described by Aiken in a comic Joycean manner, she evokes in him a genuine feeling of love. This sense is augmented by an incident in which D. overcomes his repulsion and feels compassion for a man with a hideously scarred face sitting opposite him in a railway car. Small episodes of disclosure like these are at the very center of *Ushant*. Unlike other autobiographers, Aiken concentrates not on the chronology of events but on the minor experiences that brought about major changes in the growth of his soul.

D.'s recollection of the years before and after World War I become his main preoccupation in part 5 of *Ushant*. It is then that he makes the important decision to leave England and return to his roots in the United States. For Eliot and Pound, remaining in Europe meant turning away from America and American themes; Aiken was unable to do that. D. leaves England, sure of his place there. He will not return until after World War II. D. finds his enforced exile good for him; looking back on his life in England, he sees himself as a man who was writing with his eyes shut.

The final section of the book brings all the various elements that have made up D.'s complex life into focus. He recognizes that he had to journey to England to understand his American roots and to undertake the psychologically circuitous journey back to himself. In that journey, he learned to love and to value all experience.

The completed book, which the reader sees emerging from Aiken's memory and imagination, reflects and refracts the author's self. The book is by its nature both subjective and objective, and it is not always easy to comprehend everything that Aiken is trying to say. Aiken himself recognized this in a letter he wrote just before the book appeared. "[I was] early convinced that I should have to plump for an all or nothing nebular and tensionless spiral," he says. "[*Ushant*] will thus select the particular reader I want. . . . [The] whole effect will be there for him if he wants it."

Critical Context

Ushant reflects the tone of the early twentieth century, a time of artistic discovery and creativity for American artists of the modernist group. Aiken was an important poet, one whose poetry was highly subjective and autobiographical and one who relied on musical elements, an oddly ironic humor, and a powerful love of life to shape his work. All these elements are present in *Ushant*, and with them is Aiken's strong attraction to the abstract and the divine essence at the center of everything. Aiken felt modern man's need for roots and the "rage for order," as did his contemporaries Eliot and Wallace Stevens, and it is in this book that he makes his spiritual journey, shared with everyone, leading toward that "indecipherable land."

Sources for Further Study

Denney, Reuel. *Conrad Aiken: Pamphlets on American Writers*. Vol. 38, 1964.

Hoffman, Frederick J. *Conrad Aiken*, 1962.

Martin, Jay. *Conrad Aiken: A Life of His Art*, 1962.

Rountree, Mary. "Conrad Aiken's Heroes: Portraits of the Artist as a Middle-Aged Failure," in *Studies in the Literary Imagination*. XIII (Fall, 1980), p. 82.

Spivey, Ted R. *The Writer as Shaman: The Pilgrimages of Conrad Aiken and Walker Percy*, 1986.

Marc L. Ratner

THE VANISHED WORLD, THE BLOSSOMING WORLD, and THE WORLD IN RIPENESS

Author: H. E. Bates (1905-1974)
Type of work: Autobiography
Time of work: The early 1900's to the early 1970's
Locale: Great Britain, the United States, France, India, Burma, and Tahiti
First published: The Vanished World: An Autobiography, 1969; *The Blossoming World: An Autobiography*, 1971; *The World in Ripeness: An Autobiography*, 1972

> *Principal personages:*
> H. E. BATES, a well-known author of novels and short stories
> MARJORIE COX, his wife
> EDWARD GARNETT, a reader for the publisher Jonathan Cape
> CONSTANCE GARNETT, his wife, a translator

Form and Content

In *The Vanished World*, English novelist and short-story writer H. E. Bates describes his early life, up to the point when his first novel, *The Two Sisters*, was accepted for publication by Jonathan Cape in 1926. Bates was born in 1905 in the small town of Rushden, Northamptonshire, in the English Midlands. In this first volume of his three-part autobiography, he describes two formative influences in his working-class upbringing.

The first formative influence was his close relationship with his grandfather, a shoemaker who became a small farmer when the days of the handcraftsman in the shoe industry came to an end. Bates owed his love of music to his grandfather, and also the paradisaical days of his early childhood, many of which were spent on the five acres of land that his grandfather worked hard to make productive. The second formative influence was that of his father, a stern Methodist who devoted himself to music but who frowned upon such pastimes as cardplaying, drinking, and dancing. Bates and his father would take long walks in the countryside, and the joy of these walks still remains with him as he writes, more than fifty years later. Bates's love of the English countryside, and the way of life in the Edwardian villages of the Midlands, is apparent throughout *The Vanished World*. Indeed, it is this world, which disappeared forever with the coming of World War I, which gives the book its title.

Bates was a fine student at a local working-class school and was quickly given work of far greater difficulty than that given to the other pupils. Yet this progress did not continue at Kettering Grammar School, where Bates went in 1916 after failing to win a scholarship to a prominent private school. He recalls that at the time he was an apathetic, rather rebellious student who was not interested in literature, who had no grasp of scientific or technical subjects, and whose only ambition was to be a painter. In 1919, however, a new teacher of English awakened him to the power of the English language, first through John Milton's *Areopagitica* (1644) and the authorized version of the Bible and then through a whole stream of English poets—from Geoffrey Chaucer to John Keats. That was the first intervention, according to Bates's interpretation of the events of his life, of that "Divinity which shapes our ends, rough-hew them how we will" (William Shakespeare's words). This benevolent, shaping power is seen in dramatic events which change the course of an individual's life, events which cannot be willed, foreseen, or resisted. It provides Bates with a loose organizing principle and injects a feeling of drama and destiny into his life's story.

Bates left school at the age of sixteen, declining to pursue a place at the University of Cambridge. That was a decision, he says, that he never regretted. For a brief period he worked as a junior reporter on *The Northampton Chronicle*, and he evokes the Dickensian atmosphere of the newspaper office with a novelist's skill. He was bored there, however, and to his relief was fired after a few months. After that he became a warehouse clerk, a job which required him to do very little, and he took advantage of the situation by reading voraciously. It was while he was a clerk that he began his first novel, at the age of seventeen, writing surreptitiously while at work. The resulting work was a rambling, immature effort, as he soon found out after submitting it for expert opinion. He immediately wrote another novel, also in the warehouse, which was to become his first published work, *The Two Sisters*. By the age of twenty, Bates had written short stories, poems, and plays, in addition to his novel, which was rejected by ten publishers, before Cape gave him his first success.

In *The Blossoming World*, the second volume of his autobiography, Bates describes his entry into the literary world and the growth of his skill and reputation as a writer up to the end of World War II. This volume opens with Bates in the first flush of early success. He had sold a one-act play to the British Broadcasting Corporation and short stories to *The Nation* (then edited by Leonard Woolf), *New Statesman*, *The Adelphi*, and *The Manchester Guardian*. He began to meet some of the notable literary figures of the day, including Edward and Constance Garnett, who became his mentors, benefactors, and close friends. Edward Garnett at the time was a reader for Jonathan Cape, and his wife was a translator of Ivan Turgenev and Leo Tolstoy. Bates provides memorable and affectionate portraits of both the Garnetts. He also describes an amusing incident involving T. E. Lawrence, his meetings with Graham Greene, and his friendships with Sir Rupert Hart-Davis and David Garnett.

Bates was married to Marjorie Helen Cox in 1931, and he and his new wife moved to a converted barn in the southeastern county of Kent. Bates decided that he wanted to be nothing else but a writer and would therefore never accept another job. Not surprisingly, he often found himself in financial hardship and would write reviews and articles for quick money while his next novel was in progress. Throughout the inevitable vicissitudes of the writer's life, he showed considerable resilience and determination, and a complete dedication to his chosen craft.

In 1938, his novel *Spella Ho* became his first commercial success both in Great Britain and in the United States, where it was serialized in *The Atlantic Monthly*. Bates traveled to the United States in order to supervise personally the cuts needed for serialization. He makes some acid comments on American insularity, appalled at having been asked to amend the Midlands dialect of his novel in order to make it more acceptable to American readers. He appears not to have been much impressed by the United States; the only thing he enjoyed was a trip to watch the Boston Red Sox play baseball.

Bates concludes *The Blossoming World* with an account of his experiences during World War II, up to 1941. He gives a fascinating account of life in Kent during the early stages of the war: how the sight of the German bombers darkened the sky like a gathering of giant starlings on their way to London; how remote and unreal the Battle of Britain appeared when viewed from the ground, and how the natural world seemed to take on a heightened beauty when human life and civilization had so suddenly become uncertain and precarious.

In 1941, Bates was commissioned by the Royal Air Force (RAF) in the unusual capacity of short-story writer—the first such commission in the history of the armed forces. The story of his success in this unusual endeavor—to bring the exploits of heroic RAF pilots home to the public in a more vivid way than statistics or newspaper reports ever could—is the subject of the first chapters of volume 3, *The World in Ripeness*. These wartime stories, written under the pseudonym Flying Officer X, were so successful that they were soon published in book form, with an initial printing of 100,000 copies.

Much of *The World in Ripeness* is a travelogue. Bates visited France just after it had been liberated from Nazi rule, and in February, 1945, he traveled to India and Burma, commissioned by the RAF to write stories for the American market about the war in the East. He was shocked by the squalor and chaos he discovered in Calcutta, and he found the heat oppressive. Traveling to the cool of the north, within sight of the Himalayas, he found himself charmed by the sweetness of Indian culture, if somewhat puzzled by its fatalism. From India he flew to Burma, where he encountered many of the refugees driven out of Rangoon by the invading Japanese. He was impressed by the quiet grace of the Burmese, and his experiences in Burma were recorded in his novel *The Purple Plain* (1947), which was later made into a film starring Gregory Peck.

The World in Ripeness is shorter than the other volumes, and Bates covers the twenty-five years of his life after the war in the final fifty pages. These pages describe an enjoyable trip to Tahiti and the genesis of his highly popular series of novels about the boisterous, unconventional Larkin family, beginning with *The Darling Buds of May* (1958).

Analysis

Throughout his autobiography, Bates reveals the qualities which distinguish his best writing—clarity, economy, directness, and honesty. His writing is imbued with rich descriptive power; some of the finest passages in *The Vanished World*, for example, are those in which life in the English countryside during the Edwardian era is recorded in exact, minute, appreciative detail. Such passages, with their accompanying feeling of a childhood paradise now lost, recall the autobiographical reminiscences of Bates's contemporary the English poet Kathleen Raine in her *Farewell Happy Fields* (1973).

True to his working-class background, Bates reveals himself as pugnacious and sometimes blunt, always ready with a strong opinion. He is quick to like or dislike both people and ideas. His scorn can sometimes be extreme, as when he took an instant dislike to a nameless member of *The Atlantic Monthly* editorial board ("talentless, phoney, pompous, the worst kind of literary snob") and when he attended a session of the Bengal Assembly in 1945 ("never . . . had I seen the mark of evil and corruption so indelibly bitten into so many human faces at one time"). He loses few opportunities to contrast the days of his own youth with the horrors of modern life: Drugs and violence have replaced the innocent fun of street games, the quality of workmanship is everywhere on the decline, and, as far as the "present generation of young writers" is concerned "many . . . appear never to have taken the trouble to learn anything of the use of language." Literary critics also arouse Bates's contempt, and he likens them to wasps, stinging everyone in sight for no reason other than spite. It is difficult to avoid the conclusion that Bates was disappointed by the adverse critical reaction to much of his postwar work, which for the most part acquired the label "popular fiction." The notion that popularity might be one of the deadly sins was not one that Bates could accept.

The most important aspect of Bates's autobiography is probably the light it sheds on his development as a writer, and on the creative process itself. His early reading was in Arthur Conan Doyle, Rudyard Kipling (whom he professed to dislike), and other writers now forgotten. This early literary education taught him the value of economy in the use of language, which he took as a guiding principle for his short-story writing.

Later he absorbed the work of Joseph Conrad (who was the major influence on *The Two Sisters*), Arnold Bennett, H. G. Wells, John Galsworthy, Edith Wharton, Willa Cather, and Stephen Crane. To Crane Bates owed his first conscious desire to write stories. After *The Two Sisters*, he developed an interest in Ivan Turgenev, Anton Chekhov, Guy de Maupassant, Maxim Gorky, Gustave Flaubert, and Knut Hamsun. Flaubert was the major influence on Bates's second novel, *Catherine Foster* (1929).

In the 1930's, Bates admired the work of W. H. Hudson, Edward Thomas, Ernest Hemingway, and Sherwood Anderson. Yet, on the other hand, he had harsh words for a number of other writers of high reputation. A particular animus toward D. H. Lawrence is noticeable on more than one occasion. *Women in Love* (1920), for example, is described as "absurd and grossly overpraised, . . . the worst novel ever written by a writer of international reputation"; *Lady Chatterley's Lover* (1928) is "that silliest of books." The attack on Lawrence is so virulent (Lawrence "hadn't enough imagination to invent Mickey Mouse") that one can only wonder at its cause. Thomas Hardy, whose novels resemble Bates's in more ways than Bates chooses to acknowledge, is "one of George Eliot's many miscarriages," and Bates remarks somewhat immodestly that as early as the 1920's he himself was getting more atmosphere into ten words than Hardy and his kind (who are never identified) could in a page. Such controversial opinions lose some of their credibility through Bates's error of chronology when discussing writers active in the 1930's—he includes both Lawrence, who died in 1930, and Hardy, who died in 1928.

Although Bates is sure of his own worth as a writer, he also reveals that the price of distinction is ruthless self-criticism. In spite of his prodigious output, which amounted to about one book per year for nearly fifty years, he destroyed many short stories and three entire novels simply because he thought they were not good enough. He managed to combine the virtues of the disciplined craftsman with those of the commercial writer, for whom speed is of the essence. He claims, for example, that he wrote twelve thousand words of *The Two Sisters* in one day while at his job in the warehouse. Sometimes he would be under such pressure that he would bash out a story between breakfast and lunch, an article between lunch and tea, and a review between tea and supper.

Bates never minimizes the exacting demands of his profession, and his comments on his own craft are frequently illuminating. He likens a short story to a horse race; it is the beginning and the end which count the most, and of the two, the beginning is probably the more important. The success of a novel or story often rests on the ability of the writer to sense at the very outset, like a composer, the right key for the work. Setting it in the right key will make the difference between a story which flows effortlessly and one which continually causes difficulty for the writer.

One of Bates's most important points is that a highly developed imagination is far more useful for a writer of fiction than acute powers of observation. The writer deals not in truth but in lies, but he so shapes the lies to make them appear more true than life itself. Bates returns to this idea again and again: He points out that *The Two Sisters*, unlike most first novels, did not have a single autobiographical element in it. None of the characters was based on living people—the novel was pure invention from start to finish. (This idea seems to be the root of his argument with D. H. Lawrence, whose novels, Bates claims, were always autobiographical. Lawrence never had to invent much because he always had a hero at hand: himself.)

The same principle, fidelity to imagination over observation, informs Bates's novel *Fair Stood the Wind for France* (1944), which takes place in the French provinces during wartime. At the time, Bates had never set foot in France, but he trusted his imaginative instincts to guide him. The novel turned out to be one of his most successful. Bates cites as the best example of his principle Stephen Crane's *The Red Badge of Courage: An Episode of the American Civil War* (1895), in which Crane captures the atmosphere of the American Civil War, although he had not even been born when the war took place.

In addition to Bates's comments on the creative process, he gives many insights into the origins of particular works. The basis for his most popular character—Uncle Silas, featured in *My Uncle Silas* (1939)—turns out to have been Bates's roguish granduncle, who made a deep impression on him in childhood. It was typical for Bates to store impressions for many years before they emerged in his work. When the right creative stimulus occurs, which cannot be predicted or planned, the story unfolds. His story "The Hessian Prisoner," from the collection *The Black Boxer* (1932), was based on an incident from Bates's childhood, when a German prisoner of World War I turned up in Bates's hometown of Rushden. The incident remained with Bates some twenty years before finding its place in the story. Similarly, what may well be Bates's finest novel, *Love for Lydia* (1952), was based on his experiences as a reporter for *The Northampton Chronicle* thirty years previously. These examples present the other side of Bates's creativity—he was not only a highly imaginative writer but also one whose work was as often as not firmly rooted in his own experience and his own environment.

Critical Context

With the exception of two collections of short stories, one of which was published posthumously, Bates's three-volume autobiography was his last work. These volumes add yet another genre to Bates's varied output, which includes not only novels and short stories but also essays, children's literature, plays, general nonfiction—principally a survey of the modern short story—and biography (of Edward Garnett).

Bates's autobiography gives the reader a fair idea of some of the topics and themes he treated with such distinction in his fiction, particularly the way of life in the small farms and cottages of rural England, which as he says in *The Vanished World* had at the time of his childhood changed little since William Shakespeare's day. Because volume 1 captures so effectively a "moment in time" (to use the title of one of Bates's novels) it is valuable as a social document.

Other Bates fictional themes which are apparent from his autobiography are the effects of war on both combatants and civilians (his indignation at the disgusting, pointless business of war is noticeable in all three volumes) and the effects of industrialization on the social fabric. His gift for evoking mood, atmosphere, delicate feeling, and the intensity of the strong emotions of joy, sorrow, love, and anger is everywhere apparent.

What the reader might not guess from the autobiography is that much of Bates's best work is tragic. He often depicted people who were lonely, isolated, frustrated, or otherwise handicapped. He was as acutely aware of what life takes away as what it bestows; indeed, very few of his characters could share Bates's own belief in the beneficent divinity that shapes the lives of men. Bates, by his own account a contented and fulfilled man, most resembles, as he points out, the carefree Pop Larkin of his Larkin family series: "a passionate Englishman, a profound love of Nature, of the sounds and sights of the countryside, of colour, flowers and things sensual; a hatred of pomp, pretension and humbug; a lover of children and family life; an occasional breaker of rules, a flouter of conventions." Such might be Bates's epitaph.

Sources for Further Study

Baldwin, Dean R. *H. E. Bates: A Literary Life*, 1987.
Choice. Review. X (June, 1973), p. 671.
The New Yorker. Review. XLVII (January 8, 1971), p. 86.
The Times Literary Supplement. Review. October 8, 1971, p. 1217.
Vannatta, Dennis. *H. E. Bates*, 1983.

Bryan Aubrey

VEDI

Author: Ved Mehta (1934-   )
Type of work: Autobiography
Time of work: 1939-1943
Locale: Lahore and Bombay, India
First published: 1981, serial; 1982, book

> *Principal personages:*
> VED MEHTA, the author and narrator
> MR. RAS MOHUN, a headmaster
> MRS. MOHUN, his wife

Form and Content

Though blinded at the age of three by meningitis, the Indian-born writer Ved Mehta has always been relentlessly self-reliant. After his first book, the auto-biographical *Face to Face* (1957), Mehta ignored the subject of his blindness. He joined *The New Yorker* as a staff writer in 1961 and focused his attention on postcolonial India, especially its political situation. He went so far in his refusal to make any concession to his blindness as to keep mention of it off the dust jackets of his books. Starting in 1972, however, he began a multivolume autobiographical project, which deals at great length with his handicap and his adaptation to the sighted world. The first two books, serialized before publication in *The New Yorker* like all subsequent volumes, were biographies of his parents, *Daddyji* (1972) and *Mamaji* (1979).

Vedi, its title taken from Mehta's childhood nickname, is the third volume and deals with his experiences from when he was almost five to the age of nine at the Dadar School for the Blind in Bombay. The narrative is roughly chronological, but most chapters are organized by themes (indicated by titles such as "Activities and Outings" and "Holidays"), and an epilogue relates the author's return to the school while writing the book. Mehta balances the boy's sketchy but vivid memories with the mature reflections of the adult Mehta. Interwoven throughout are his father's commentary about past events and a selection of the correspondence between his father and the headmaster, Mr. Ras Mohun, a use of letters characteristic of Mehta, who makes extensive use of interviews, letters, and diaries in all of his au-tobiographical writing.

Vedi was a normal boy, despite his blindness, but with the fatalistic Indian attitude toward blindness, his prospects for a normal life were bleak. Conditions in the country's few schools for the blind, most of which were started by American missionaries, were generally deplorable. The lucky few who were helped could not aspire to much more than learning a simple craft and often died young. The rest were expected to beg or, if they came from a high-caste family such as Vedi's, live as perpetual invalids without any prospect of marriage or career.

It was with the hope that an education would help Vedi avoid this fate that his father sent the very young boy more than a thousand miles away from his home in the Punjab to a school located in a polluted and poverty-stricken industrial area of Bombay. Unlike the other boys and girls, indigent orphans, Vedi, the pampered son of a Western-educated doctor with an important post in the Anglo-Indian medical administration, was not prepared for the school's harsh conditions.

This is not the story of a sensitive boy suffering the torments of boarding-school life. To the contrary, Vedi, a fiercely independent, even willful, young boy, adapted quickly to the Dadar School. Despite the caste differences, he was readily accepted by the boys once they recovered from the initial shock of his fat cheeks and soft clothes.

Exposed to disease and the countless physical injuries of an active childhood, Vedi spent more and more of his time in bed, but he thrived in other ways. Spoiled at home, Vedi learned at school to fend for himself. Mrs. Mohun would not put up with his "jungly boy" ways and taught him some manners. She also made Vedi sleep in the dormitory despite an understanding to the contrary with his parents, but Mehta expresses no rancor against her: "I soon learned that there was no point in refusing [since] there was no one to run to with my complaints and appeals. Besides, I wanted to be a good child. . . ." Vedi was a good-natured child, entering into all the activities of the school—its classes, games, and outings—and the heady mysteries of growing up with an enthusiasm that makes for lively retelling.

Though most of the book is about his school life, some of it deals with Vedi's two lengthy stays at home because of diseases contracted at the school, typhoid and ringworm among them. Despite his love for his family, it is clear that Vedi felt more comfortable among the blind children. Though he was allowed to have his way and run wild at home, he had to fight constantly for attention, since no one in his family seemed to encourage his attempts to be an equal part of it (with the important exception of his father, always frank and supportive, whose voice figures throughout the book as a soothing presence, always explaining and extolling). Instead, his sighted relatives seemed to use him for their own purposes, sentimental or superstitious. One aunt cried over him every time she saw him, and his mother had him shuffle her cards to bring her luck, but no one bothered to explain how the game was played until a boy at school did.

Consequently, when the threat of bombing raids brought the boy's stay at the Dadar School to a close, he did not consider it liberation but banishment. Though the grown-up Ved Mehta knows the Dadar School must have been a horrible place, it retains for him, and therefore the reader, a definite appeal in memory.

Analysis

In the first paragraph of *Vedi*, the boy's father voices the two most important themes of the book, self-reliance and memory: "'You are a man now,' he said. This sentence of my father's was to become the beginning of my clear, conscious memory."

It was Vedi's good fortune to have a father who wanted his son to become self-reliant and had the resources to help. Consistently rational in a society permeated with supersitition and hidebound traditions, the father took what steps he could to secure his son's future. On the other hand, Vedi's mother, though loving and supportive, embodied the fatalistic Eastern attitude he had to resist. Torn between the conflicting needs for independence and security, Vedi was finally oriented toward the West by his father. Necessary as this was, it makes *Vedi* a book about loss: of sight, of friends, of family. Vedi was always an outsider, the blind among the sighted and the rich boy among the poor. Rejecting pity, he had an impatient, almost imperious need for love, which he demanded of people but which never provided him with the security he sought. There is no self-pity in this book. As crucial to his achieving self-reliance as his father's support was Vedi's cheerful self-assurance, which reflects his mother's emotional, irrational nature as much as his father's enlightened ways. With a playful imagination that still shines in this writing, Mehta could pretend a cold shower was rain or that his fingers were his friends competing to see who could read Braille letters the fastest. When Mohun first saw him, he thought Vedi was a sighted boy because of his open expression, and this openness and curiosity, along with a sometimes mulish self-confidence, were the boy's main strengths.

> Sometimes the wish to touch a thing I had heard about, like Mr. Ras Mohun's ruler, would so agitate me that I couldn't stop thinking about it. The name of the thing would go on repeating itself in my head . . . like a permanently stuck record.

This agitation made Vedi stubborn in his refusal to acknowledge limitations. For example, he insisted once that he could see a photograph, and on his first visit to the ocean, he went racing "toward the roar and the rush," exhilarated by the sense of having nothing in front of him but the wide open ocean.

Beneath his self-confidence, however, is an undercurrent of anxiety running throughout the book. Parting from his family at the train station to return to the school, Vedi heard a blind beggar approach the family. "I remember thinking that I could end up like him, and feeling even more frightened." This fear was grounded in the sense of powerlessness that came with blindness. All the children felt something malevolent in the sighted world, with its objects that seemed to lunge out at them. "Whenever we hurt outselves on anything at all, we would kick it and beat it and cry out, 'The sighted bastards!'" Their crude equation of sight and power, so strong that the boys hardly believed there could be schools for the blind in America, was mainly associated with the dormitory proctor, the Sighted Master, who handed out beatings with a discarded shoe that he kept under his bed. In the one really shocking incident in the book, the Sighted Master uses a board one night to silence the whimpering of two boys, one blind and deaf, the other retarded, who then mysteriously vanish by the following morning.

Such extreme abuse was the exception, but the children's fears were not groundless. Returning years later to the school, Mehta found that while one of the boys went on to become a teacher of the blind, several others died young of tuberculosis, and the rest apparently returned to the poverty that had spawned them. He interviewed a woman who had been lucky enough to wed a sighted teacher, but after her husband's death, she was reduced to such destitution that she had to beg Mehta for money. Though sympathetic, he fled, "her begging tone having stirred up . . . an old fear."

After years of fleeing this fear of poverty and dependence, Mehta faces it squarely in his autobiographical project, undertaken to recapture the lost places of his youth and assuage the pain of separation and exclusion. He is not interested in dramatizing his past but in rediscovering and reclaiming it. Painful incidents, such as his helping another boy kill a cat to learn what death is like, are not included to shock but because they are part of what the adult has to accept to bring his past into the present.

Toward the end of the book, Mehta relates how one of his sisters stepped on a pin, necessitating an operation and some physical therapy. While he was helping her, Vedi remembered how he had been helped to learn to walk again after his meningitis. In this way, as Mehta explains in the introductory note to this book,

> memory expands by some kind of associative process, so that a remembered scene that at first seems hardly worth a line grows in the act of thinking and writing into a chapter, and this full-blown memory uncovers other memories, other scenes, which in their turn expand and multiply.

By pursuing this associative process, Mehta succeeds in re-creating the experience of the blind boy. Though he fills in gaps not only of a child's memory but also of his perspective, the "judgment and experience, which, as a boy, I could not have had," this is predominantly a memory book, a book about what the child felt and not what the adult knows it must have been like.

Throughout, the writing is clear and forceful, its main stylistic characteristic being the absence of visual detail. The writing abounds with description that relies on his memories of the other senses: the smell of orange fingernail polish, the taste of a flower, the sound of a bouncing ball, the feel of shapes in dough. Limited to four senses, the writing conveys some of the limits of Vedi's blindness while in no way restricting the power of his writing to create images. "They were all named Nurse," Mehta writes about a nurse he recalls from a stay in the hospital,

> but one who was named Nurse was different. I would hear her sandals jauntily stepping toward my bed. She was always quietly humming some tune or other, and there was a scent of jasmine in her hair and on her clothes, which, though faint, seemed to defy the germicidal air.

Mehta imbues even simple sounds with great emotional weight, as when he recalls the jangling of his mother's jewelry, betraying her furtive signing about him to the rest of the family.

Although the use of English expressions such as "tiffin" (snack break) and "draughts" (checkers) in a book written for an American audience may seem strange at first, they convey the atmosphere of his Anglo-Indian childhood. Similarly, the many lively metaphors make it possible for the reader to understand something of how a blind boy imagines the world. When Vedi was trying to understand what a mirror's reflection must be like, for example, he thought of an echo. When he first experienced the ocean, "The school compound and the racing track suddenly shrank in my mind, like a woollen sock Mamaji had knitted for me which became so small after Heea's ayah washed it that I could scarcely get my hand in it." In this way, careful always to root his images in the concrete experiences of the child, Mehta draws the reader into a shared rediscovery of his lost childhood.

Critical Context

While *Vedi* stands on its own merits, it is the first part of an ongoing autobiographical project and has to be seen within that framework. The thirteen-hundred-mile trip from his home in the Punjab to the school in Bombay was only the beginning of a lifelong odyssey. Still a child, Mehta went on to a school for the blind in Arkansas, before going on to a successful college career at Pomona, Oxford, and Harvard, preparatory to becoming a writer. Intending to chronicle his entire life, Mehta recognizes that the labor and time needed for each book means that he may never bring the story up to the time of its writing. Moreover, some critics, such as Carol Sternhell, acknowledge the heroism of the undertaking while questioning the need for such extensive self-absorption, suggesting that such self-indulgence will get tiring long before the project is done.

Also problematic is the book's depiction of India. It is not surprising that Clark Blaise can say about a book by a man who has written so much on his native country that, "Being blind in colonial India . . . is a kind of personal reflection of the handicap and dependence of the nation itself." This parallel is not, however, made explicit in the book, and Mehta has said that his autobiography is not intended to explain India to Westerners but to be read like a novel. Though *Vedi* deals extensively with life in India and differences between Eastern and Western attitudes, Mehta restricts his perspective to a very personal one. A self-styled archaeologist of his own life, Ved Mehta insists that he is content to let the sociologists explain India.

Sources for Further Study

Blaise, Clark. "Four Senses and Imagination," in *The New York Times Book Review.* LXXXV (October 17, 1982), p. 12.

Dong, Stella. "Ved Mehta," in *Publishers Weekly.* CCXXIX (January 3, 1985), pp. 57-58.

Dowd, Maureen. "A Writing Odyssey Through India Past and Present," in *The New York Times.* June 10, 1984, sec. 6, p. 50.

Malcolm, Janet. "School of the Blind," in *The New York Review of Books*. XXIX (October 7, 1982), pp. 3-5.
Sternhell, Carol. "A Donkey Among Horses," in *The New York Times Book Review*. XCI (March 9, 1986), p. 14.

Phil McDermott

A VERY PRIVATE EYE
An Autobiography in Diaries and Letters

Author: Barbara Pym (Mary Crampton, 1913-1980)
Type of work: Autobiography/diary/letters
Time of work: 1932-1980
Locale: Primarily England; Italy, Portugal, Germany, and Central Europe
First published: 1984

Principal personages:
BARBARA PYM, a novelist
HENRY (LORENZO) HARVEY, an older contemporary at the
    University of Oxford with whom she fell in love
ROBERT (JOCK) LIDDELL, a mutual friend at Oxford, later a
    novelist, critic, and travel writer
PHILIP LARKIN, a poet, instrumental in Pym's rediscovery
HILARY PYM, Barbara's younger sister

Form and Content

British novelist Barbara Pym began keeping a diary while a student at the University of Oxford in the 1930's. Using excerpts from these diaries, from her later, less formal notebooks, and from some of her letters, Pym's younger sister Hilary and her friend and literary executor Hazel Holt have put together a different kind of autobiography. Pym tells her own story in her own words, but the two editors have also written small amounts of introductory and explanatory material to fill in the gaps with facts, ideas, and feelings that were not recorded originally to serve such a direct and organized autobiographical function. Yet the author regularly shows that she expected her diaries and notebooks to be published.

Holt's three-page preface sets forth her personal and professional relationship with Pym, which included twenty-five years together as editors and writers for the International African Institute in London. Hilary Pym, in five pages, provides background details of the Pym family and briefly sketches the childhood of the sisters in Oswestry, Shropshire.

The body of the book is divided into three main parts. Part 1, "Oxford," covers the 1932-1939 period, when Pym was studying English literature. She remained in Oxford, at least part-time, after completing her degree. During that period she began work on her first novel, which was not actually completed until 1950, when it was published under the title *Some Tame Gazelle*. Part 2 covers the years of World War II; during that time, Pym joined and ultimately became an officer in the Women's Royal Naval Service. The four subdivisions reflect both chronological and thematic concerns: "Adapting to the War" covers the period from 1940 to 1942, when England was suffering air raids; Pym wrote in a letter to Henry Harvey and his wife, Elsie, in Stockholm, "Wars aren't what they used to be in Victorian times, when they were fought abroad decently by professional soldiers!" Demonstrating both the passing of time and the connections between Pym's private life, the war, and "ordinary" life, the editors cover 1943 and part of 1944 with two sections related to when she started new diaries. They are titled "Christmas I" (1942) and "Christmas II" (1943). Sometimes there are large gaps in time unaccounted for during these war years; for example, the ten-month period between diary entires of November 21, 1943, and September 17, 1944, includes but one letter, written to Harvey, on May 26, 1944. The last section of her war and prepublication years is titled "Naples" and reflects her life in Italy with the navy, working at her job as a censor. This part of her life came to an end with her discharge on January 11, 1946.

Although she went to work that same year for the International African Institute, the entries in the autobiography do not begin until early in 1948. The last of these three main parts of the book, "The Novelist," consists of three sections, the first devoted to the 1948 to 1963 period, when six novels were published in rapid order. The second covers the 1963 to 1977 period, when no publisher wanted to print what she wrote. It concludes with the period from 1977 until her death in 1980, when renewed publication brought greater fame than before. Four new novels were published, three during her lifetime and one posthumously. The 334 pages of the autobiography itself are followed by a bibliography and brief publication history of the novels and a comprehensive index and glossary, the glossary being the inclusion of nicknames and other aids to cross-referencing. The book contains twelve pages of photographs.

The principal recipients of her letters were Henry Harvey, her first love at Oxford and later a professor at the University of Helsingfors; Robert Liddell, a staff member at the Bodleian Library, Oxford, when Pym met him and later a novelist and critic living primarily in Athens; Philip Larkin, poet, writer on jazz, and librarian at the University of Hull; and Robert Smith, an Oxford graduate and professor of history at the University of Lagos in Nigeria.

Analysis

Barbara Pym's diaries, letters, and notebooks show that she had four major interests in life: writing novels, reading literature, being a faithful supporter of the Anglican church, and getting married. Her words do not necessarily establish the priority of these goals in the order listed. She achieved the first three; she was never married. Had she not been the author of ten published novels, however, her autobiography probably never would have been published. Thus, it is the relationship between how she viewed her life and what she says in her fiction that gives this book its primary reason for being. The book probably conveys special impressions to the readers of Pym's novels, but it still draws, in its own right, a fascinating portrait of a vibrant, sentimental, and loving woman whose life and thoughts can be enjoyed for their own sake.

Pym knew by the age of twenty-one that she wanted to be a writer, saying in a diary entry of September 1, 1934, that she had started writing a novel about herself and her sister living together as spinsters in their fifties. Her youthful prediction, in what eventually became *Some Tame Gazelle*, was in large part true. Her sister was married but then divorced, and the two of them lived together in their later years. Her expressions of the pleasures and pains of being a writer occupy a large portion of the book. She saw herself as fulfilled finally only by writing, yet writing was difficult and she was not, in the early years, being published. In a diary entry dated April 7, 1940, she tells of her reluctance to get down to writing while at the same time feeling that no day was a good one if a few pages of writing were not accomplished. She complained to herself about the small amount of writing she had done that year but also said that she did not have the motivation she had felt in the past: "I am no longer so certain of a glorious future as I used to be—though I still feel that I may ultimately succeed." She was still unpublished. She concludes this particular entry by saying that reading and domestic concerns may keep her "quite happy. But it isn't *really* enough, soon I shall be discontended with myself, out will come the novel and after I've written a few pages I shall feel on top of the world again."

If writing itself could put her on top of the world, rejection of her manuscripts by publishers put her into other states of mind. Writing to Harvey on August 20, 1936, Pym said that Jonathan Cape, a publishing house, had agreed to take another look at her novel, but that she was only mildly hopeful about its acceptance and expected to cry when she got it back. Yet there are no exclamations of joy (because she apparently did not record any) over the final 1949 acceptance of this first novel. The absence of her feelings at that time is an example of the gaps that this particular kind of autobiography leaves in the full depiction of a life.

The different numbers of entries that occur within similar time periods suggest that once publication came her way, Pym's writing of letters and of diary entries had to be forgone in favor of working on her novels. The entries for the period from 1949 to 1963 require only twenty-nine pages, but the equally long period from 1963 to 1977, when she could not get any new novels published, is covered in seventy-four pages. The entries for the 1963-1977 period regularly express her belief that most of her difficulty in achieving new publication was the result not of any diminution of her powers as a novelist but of changes in tastes and attitudes brought about in the tumultuous 1960's. She stated in a letter of January 26, 1970, that a publisher would not accept *The Sweet Dove Died* (published in 1978) "Only . . . because it seems a risk commercially." Speaking of another reader's praise of her manuscript, she says that from it she gained confidence that she could still write, even though the books that she was writing were not then publishable. Her explanation for the fourteen-year dry spell gains credence from what happened in 1977, in a world more ready to read Pym's satirical and witty novels about the social mores in English intellectual and middle-class circles.

On January 21, 1977, *The Times Literary Supplement* published a survey of literary figures naming the most underrated writers of the century. Pym was the only living author named twice, by Philip Larkin and Lord David Cecil.

Instant attention followed. As Pym herself says in a notebook entry of the following day, she had been contacted by a radio station official and her British publisher had said to a reporter that reprints of her earlier novels might be considered. Pym's comment was *"That'll* be the frosty Friday!" She turned out to be in error, however, because within two years, and following the 1977 publication of *Quartet in Autumn* in the United States, Cape had reissued all six of the earlier novels.

The resulting fame and the cancer that would take her life in less than three years did not affect Pym's ironic sense of humor and biting tongue. Writing to her friend Bob Smith on October 25, 1978, about her being made a Fellow of the Royal Society of Literature, she said, "I haven't yet been able to go up and sign the book (and have my hand held by the president at my inauguration) but I *have* paid my subscription and that surely must be the main point."

If being a writer was Pym's primary passion, being a woman who needed the love of a man certainly ran a strong second. Writing in her notebook in her forty-second year, she strongly implies her own failure to find a satisfying love: "Perhaps to be loved is the most cosy thing in life and yet many people, women I suppose I mean, know only the uncertainties of love, which is only sometimes cosy when one accepts one's situation (rarely perhaps)."

Although Pym may have in the course of her life written many letters to women, this book is composed almost exclusively of letters to men. The one female recipient is Elsie Harvey, the wife of Pym's first love, Henry; Pym wrote to her in an ironic, sometimes patronizing, tone. For example, she was only twenty-five when she wrote, "You would not expect an old woman to change her ways, would you?" She predicted that Elsie "would be shocked" if Pym were "suddenly to marry" but added that "there seems to be no chance of that." Five years earlier (in 1934), Pym had apparently been deeply in love with and, from her point of view, been badly treated by Henry. Writing about Henry's attention to another girl, Pym stated that she was so unhappy that she burst into tears and "cried more" than she had for a long time.

Henry was lost in the 1930's, but following two marriages he returned to her life in the 1970's. She records his coming to tea on February 17, 1976, at which time, because it was cold, she burned some pages of a 1943 diary. She says that the lover who "inspired" the diary is dead. Then she speculates in a way that neatly brings together her human and literary loves: "Could one write a book (a sort of novel) based on one's diaries over about 30 years? I certainly have enough material." Despite such lost diaries and the absence of any letters to members of her family, this is a book that has enough material about her personality and her thoughts to serve as an autobiography.

Critical Context

Upon its publication in 1984, *A Very Private Eye* received reviews in at least eleven major American periodicals, ranging from *The Wall Street Journal* to *The*

New Republic. A thesis running through most of these reviews is that this book accomplishes the primary biographical function of elucidating some relationships between fact and fiction. Readers of this book who have previously read Pym's novels can benefit from discovering the reasons behind her taking certain positions or expressing certain attitudes. There is the equal reward of getting her view of the real persons behind some of her fictional characters. Other readers of this book may well be led by Pym's strong, honest, open personality to want to discover her novelistic creations.

In addition to being placed within the context of the fiction, this book can be examined in its relationship with the more usual way of publishing an author's diaries and letters, that is, as separate volumes that do not purport to be autobiographies. Pym clearly meant to say what she says in all this material, and she clearly hoped that much of it would be published; the form it might take was not of her choosing, but she and her words are well served by this form of publication. Although this book does serve well as an autobiography, the reader should not take it as replacing a full biography, with interpretation of Pym by some writer other than Pym.

Sources for Further Study

Burkhart, Charles. *The Pleasure of Miss Pym*, 1987.

Goldstein, William. "A Novel, a Biography, a Play: A Peek Inside the Pym Estate," in *Publishers Weekly*. CCXXVIII (October 4, 1985), p. 43.

Long, Robert Emmet. *Barbara Pym*, 1986.

Nardin, Jane. *Barbara Pym*, 1985.

Rossen, Janice. *The World of Barbara Pym*, 1987.

Salwak, Dale, ed. *The Life and Work of Barbara Pym*, 1987.

J. F. Kobler

A VOICE FROM THE CHORUS

Author: Andrei Sinyavsky (as Abram Tertz, 1925-   )
Type of work: Letters/meditations
Time of work: 1966-1971 and 1973
Locale: The Soviet Union
First published: Golos iz Khora, 1973 (English translation, 1976)

Principal personages:
ANDREI SINYAVSKY, a Soviet literary scholar imprisoned in a labor
camp
MARIA SINYAVSKY, his wife

Form and Content

In September, 1965, a Soviet literary scholar named Andrei Sinyavsky, who was about to celebrate his fortieth birthday, was arrested and charged with subversion. Beginning in 1959, manuscripts of several works by Sinyavsky had been smuggled to the West, where they were published under the pseudonym Abram Tertz. These works included a literary manifesto, *Chto takoe sotsialisticheskii realizm* (1959; *On Socialist Realism,* 1960); a volume of short fiction, *Fantasticheskie povesti* (1961; *Fantastic Stories,* 1963); and two short novels, *Sud idyot* (1960; *The Trial Begins,* 1960) and *Lyubimov* (1964; *The Makepeace Experiment,* 1965). A small collection of aphorisms and reflections, *Mysli vrasplokh* (1966; *Unguarded Thoughts,* 1972), first appeared in the American periodical *The New Leader* a few months before Sinyavsky's arrest, under the title "Thought Unaware"; this work was particularly important for its revelation of Sinyavsky's devout Russian Orthodox faith.

There had been considerable speculation in the West concerning the identity of the mysterious Abram Tertz, and Sinyavsky's trial, in February, 1966, provoked international protest. (Yuli Daniel, another writer whose works had appeared pseudonymously in the West, was tried at the same time.) Receiving a seven-year sentence, Sinyavsky was sent to Dubrovlag, a complex of labor camps about three hundred miles east of Moscow, where there were sawmills and factories for producing furniture. It was during this time (he served more than six years of his sentence) that Sinyavsky wrote the bulk of *A Voice from the Chorus.*

The form of the book reflects the circumstances of its composition. In the labor camp Sinyavsky was allowed to write twice a month to his wife, Maria; everything he wrote had to be passed by the camp censor. Instead of allowing these circumstances to discourage him, Sinyavsky turned them to his own advantage. In addition to the meditations that became *A Voice from the Chorus,* Sinyavsky wrote a good part of a long critical study of Nikolai Gogol, *V teni Gogolia* (1975; in the shadow of Gogol), and a shorter study of Alexander Pushkin, *Progulki s Pushkinym* (1975; walks with Pushkin)—all this in the guise of letters to his wife. (As the critic Clarence Brown has remarked, the censor who inspected these letters "must have thought the Sinyavskys the most cerebral couple since the invention of marriage.")

A Voice from the Chorus (the title is that of a poem by Aleksandr Blok) is an unclassifiable book, one that does not fit in any clearly defined genre. It comprises two sharply contrasting kinds of material. On the one hand, there are Sinyavsky's meditations, reflections, pensées, aphorisms, ranging in length from a single line to several pages; the average page includes several entries. The subjects of these meditations are richly various, but there is among them a dominant theme: the nature of art. On the other hand, alternating with Sinyavsky's reflective voice, there is the "chorus": In these passages, which are italicized to distinguish them from Sinyavsky's own words, one hears the diverse voices of his fellow prisoners— slangy, pungent, ignorant, pious, mean, whimsical, fatuous, wise. Sometimes Sinyavsky comments on these voices or provides a context for them:

> In answer to a question about Christianity and the New Testament—with a hurt expression:
> *"Why weren't the apostles Ukrainians?"*

On other occasions he presents, without comment, a string of quotations from the chorus on a given topic, or simply a list of colorful expressions.

The book is divided into seven parts. The first six parts (comprising 316 of the book's 328 pages) correspond to the years of Sinyavsky's imprisonment, from 1966 to 1971. While most of the entries are not dated, there are a handful of dated entries scattered throughout the book, serving the reader as chronological markers. Similarly, while the text generally resembles a notebook or journal rather than a collection of letters, Sinyavsky has retained a few passages in which he directly addresses his wife, reminding the reader of the personal context of these meditations.

The seventh and final part of the book—by far the shortest—was written after Sinyavsky's release. (In 1973, he and his wife and son were permitted to emigrate to Paris, where Sinyavsky began teaching at the Sorbonne.) Here, he records some of his thoughts on returning to ordinary life: his sense of disorientation ("the feeling of a dead man appearing at life's feast") but also his awareness that the book he has made now has a sovereign existence of its own.

Analysis

It is fitting that *A Voice from the Chorus* should conclude with a vision of a book, "hundred-mouthed," fulfilling its destiny independent of its creator, for Sinyavsky believes that the writer serves as a "form" for a power greater than himself. "I have no program except art," Sinyavsky said in an interview in *The Times Literary Supplement* (May 23, 1975). "All my life I have wondered what art is and why it exists." Those questions are not definitively answered in *A Voice from the Chorus*; Sinyavsky suggests that it is of the essence of art to elude precise definition: "Art is always a more or less impromptu act of prayer. Try to catch hold of smoke." Nevertheless, he does not cease exploring the nature of art; that quest lends continuity to his wide-ranging reflections.

Above all, he emphasizes the absolute freedom of art. No demands for social utility, no partisan claims, may be allowed to constrain that freedom. Thus, despite the fact that it no longer serves the purpose of concealment, Sinyavsky continues to use the pseudonym Abram Tertz for most of his publications. Sinyavsky originally took this name from an underworld ballad; it suggests art's perennially subversive nature. By the same token, Sinyavsky rejects the demands of realism: "Art is not the representation, but the transfiguration of life." Indeed, Sinyavsky argues that "realism" is largely a fiction; so-called realistic painting, he notes, is a triumph of artifice, made possible by the viewer's unconscious acceptance of countless conventional devices.

What he says about art in general, Sinyavsky reaffirms for writing in particular: "From the start, from the very first paragraph," he declares,

> you must write in such a manner as to cut off every way of retreat and thereafter live only by the law of the train of words now set in motion. . . . not giving way to any hopes for some world other than this self-sufficient text. . . .

This emphasis on the freedom of the writer and the self-sufficient text would seem to align Sinyavsky with American postmodernists such as John Barth. Yet while it is true that Sinyavsky and the postmodernists have some common enemies, they are nevertheless separated by profound differences. The postmodernists typically stress the self-referential quality of literary texts, language feeding on language, texts feeding on other texts. For Sinyavsky, art is a vehicle for transcendence.

Sinyavsky frequently speaks of writing in religious, sometimes mystical, terms. The writer, he says, must learn to empty himself. In the realm of art, as in the spiritual realm, commonsense rules do not apply, and incapacity can become a virtue; a writer "knows nothing, remembers nothing, can do nothing," but it is this very "impotence" that allows him to forget himself and write. In such passages, Sinyavsky's aphoristic style recalls the deliberately provocative pronouncements of Viktor Shklovsky.

Since *A Voice from the Chorus* is not a treatise on aesthetics but is itself a work of art, the reader can readily see how Sinyavsky puts his principles into practice. Certainly, there is a "fairy-tale" quality to this book written in a labor camp. The twentieth century is unfortunately very rich in prison literature, but few works in this genre bear even a superficial likeness to *A Voice from the Chorus*. In one of his early entries, Sinyavsky writes, "Books resemble windows when the lights come on in the evening and begin to glow in the surrounding darkness." So amid the routine of forced labor and confinement, he writes about painting and architecture, folktales and jokes.

Because he views art as a transfiguration of reality and not merely as an escape from it, Sinyavsky includes along with his own voice the many voices of the chorus. His use of these voices is stylized (to take an obvious example, virtually all profanity is eliminated); the chorus grounds his book in everyday reality—his meditations can never become too highfalutin—yet at the same time that everyday reality is transfigured, heightened. It should be noted, too, that while Sinyavsky often quotes his fellow prisoners to humorous effect, his attitude toward them is not condescending. Indeed, there are passages in which Sinyavsky's voice is almost indistinguishable from those of the chorus: "I wonder what mice make of birds, and beetles—of butterflies? They are obviously able to see each other. But what do they think?" For the reader, coming across such a passage is like turning a corner on a busy street and discovering a plum tree in full blossom. Art, Sinyavsky says, is gratuitous, an extra; yet it is also "the very seal and token of existence, the means by which being is made manifest."

Critical Context

Readers in the West frequently encounter Russian literature in what might be called an artificial environment, in which literary works are detached from their cultural context. This leads to misunderstanding, since the reader is likely to overlook significant differences between Russian and Western perspectives.

Western critics often contrast Sinyavsky with his countryman Aleksandr Solzhenitsyn. Clearly the two men represent diametrically opposed approaches to literature. Solzhenitsyn the novelist has assembled a vast historical archive to authenticate his fictional re-creation of Russia in the years leading up to the Revolution. Sinyavsky is a creator of fantastic fictions, scornful of the pretensions of realism. Solzhenitsyn is the foremost representative of what has been called the authoritarian-nationalist wing of the Russian émigré community, while Sinyavsky is one of the leading figures of the liberal-democratic wing. Many critics, dismayed by Solzhenitsyn's apparent contempt for Western institutions, have pointed to the grounding of his political program in his Russian Orthodox faith, which they regard as dangerously archaic.

While there is unquestionably a real basis for the contrast between Solzhenitsyn and Sinyavsky, it is misleading on both sides, particularly with regard to Sinyavsky's alleged affinities with liberal humanism. In an essay titled "Dissent as a Personal Experience" (*Yearbook of Comparative and General Literature*, 1982), Sinyavsky defines his position. As a writer, he says, he is in opposition to not only the Soviet government but also his fellow émigrés: "I am an enemy—an enemy as such— metaphysically, in principle." He rejects Solzhenitsyn's mixture of religion and authoritarian politics, but also—in *A Voice from the Chorus* as in *Unguarded Thoughts*—he rejects such dearly held Western notions as "freedom of choice," "human dignity," and "the inviolability of the person," dismissing them as nothing more than cant. In *Unguarded Thoughts* he writes that truly Christian attitudes and actions are "abnormal," against human nature; in *A Voice from the Chorus*, he describes the process of writing as equally abnormal and paradoxical. In some ways, from the viewpoint of secular Western society, Sinyavsky may be more "extreme" than Solzhenitsyn.

Sources for Further Study

Brown, Clarence, ed. *The Portable Twentieth-Century Russian Reader*, 1985.

Brown, Deming. "The Art of Andrei Sinyavsky," in *Slavic Review*. XXIX (December, 1970), pp. 663-681.

Fanger, Donald. "A Change of Venue: Russian Journals of the Emigration," in *The Times Literary Supplement*. November 21, 1986, pp. 1321-1322.

_____. "Conflicting Imperatives in the Model of the Russian Writer: The Case of Tertz/Sinyavsky," in *Literature and History: Theoretical Problems and Russian Case Studies*, 1986. Edited by Gary S. Morson.

Hayward, Max. *Writers in Russia: 1917-1978*, 1983.

Labedz, Leopold, and Max Hayward, eds. *On Trial: The Case of Sinyavsky (Tertz) and Daniel (Arzhak), Documents*, 1967.

Lourie, Richard. *Letters to the Future: An Approach to Sinyavsky/Tertz*, 1975.

John Wilson

A WALKER IN THE CITY

Author: Alfred Kazin (1915-   )
Type of work: Autobiography
Time of work: 1920-1951
Locale: Brooklyn and Manhattan
First published: 1951

Principal personage:
ALFRED KAZIN, the author and narrator

Form and Content

Brooklyn-born literary critic Alfred Kazin established his credentials as a leading authority on American literature with his very first book, *On Native Grounds* (1942), published when he was twenty-seven years old. That first study sought to show that American prose writing came of age as something distinctively American only with the work of William Dean Howells and his contemporaries, during the second half of the nineteenth century. Kazin argued that the predecessors of Howells and his group had looked primarily to Europe for inspirational models and for recognition; the exponents of American realism and naturalism, he said, were the first to address the American public directly, with depictions of the daily life they saw around them, thereby creating a literature that was, in every sense, indigenous to their native soil.

Recognizing that there was something inherently contradictory, or at least puzzling, in this strong advocacy of what was most American about American literature by a child of recent immigrants to the United States, Kazin soon followed *On Native Grounds* with a personal essay designed to explain—perhaps to himself as much as to his readers—how it was possible for a young man who had grown up in the insular and impoverished world of the Jewish ghetto of Brownsville, in East Brooklyn, to develop so passionate a commitment and so firm a sense of belonging to American culture. The essay gradually expanded, taking the form of painful yet lyrical reminiscences of his entire Brownsville youth, from childhood to graduation from high school, at which time he symbolically left the ghetto and crossed the Brooklyn Bridge to enroll in Manhattan's College of the City of New York. The reminiscences were not intended to constitute a systematic and complete autobiography; rather, they were impressionistic and selective, focusing on the details that illuminated the process by which immigrant parents with little formal education produced a son who grew up with a passion for reading and a well-developed taste for literature, music, and painting. The reminiscences were organized into four chapters which traced Kazin's journey—in time and space, in body and spirit—from Brownsville to Manhattan, the heart of American cultural life. Because most of the stages of the journey had been accomplished on foot, during the many exploratory walks the young Kazin liked to take beyond the ghetto, he called his book *A Walker in the City*.

The memoir begins with an account of the sensations experienced, and the consequent memories recalled, whenever Kazin, as a young Manhattan-dwelling critic, returned by subway to Brownsville to visit his family. This chapter, titled "From the Subway to the Synagogue," uses the opening walk between the subway station and his old home as a springboard to the world of his childhood, which was limited to the few streets and landmarks of the five city blocks that made up his old neighborhood. Each of the landmarks passed on the walk triggers a host of memories, the richest by far being evoked by the school, the cinema, and, at the end of the walk, within sight of the tenement in which his family lived, the small wooden synagogue that was the social and spiritual center of his family's life. The second chapter focuses on the quality of Kazin's home life as a child. Titled "The Kitchen," it describes the central roles played by his mother, who held the family together, and by the kitchen, the main stage on which his childhood unfolded. All Kazin's contacts with the world beyond the neighborhood—effected by visits from family and friends, the New York newspaper his father brought home every evening, and the English books owned by an unmarried cousin who lived with the Kazins— are made in the kitchen. The third chapter, "The Block and Beyond," concentrates on Kazin's early teens, when his experiences and contacts widened considerably, taking him into other parts of Brownsville and beyond Brownsville into the more prosperous central sections of Brooklyn. By the final chapter, "Summer: The Way to Highland Park," Kazin is a high school student, the Depression has begun, and he has formed friendships with contemporaries who have intellectual and political interests like his own. He has ventured into "the real world," taking summer jobs in Flatbush and Borough Park and beginning to put distance between himself and Brownsville. He has a steady girl with whom he regularly walks to Highland Park, near the border of Queens, where from the hilltop reservoir it is possible to look across at the skyscrapers of Manhattan, the promised land, soon to be his home.

These four "chapters of the journey," as Kazin designates them, actually describe a circle, which returns Kazin from his adult home in Manhattan to his origins in a far corner of eastern Brooklyn and then follows him, step by step, on walks of ever-increasing length until he is back home in New York's literary world. During the journey, the reader not only experiences vicariously the author's emotions and struggles but also arrives at an understanding of how the outsider became an insider: how the intensely Jewish child of poor immigrant parents entered the American literary mainstream helped, not hindered, by his strong ethnic and religious heritage.

Analysis

The essential drama at the heart of this memoir is already present in embryo in its opening sentences: "Every time I go back to Brownsville it is as if I had never been away. From the moment I step off the train at Rockaway Avenue . . . an instant rage comes over me, mixed with dread and some unexpected tenderness." These emotions are symptoms of the love-hate relationship all first-generation

Americans seem to have with the world of their origins. On the one hand, the warmth of family life and the nurturing environment of a supportive culture give shape and meaning to existence, forging unbreakable bonds. On the other hand, the squalid poverty in which recent immigrants were usually forced to live and the endless struggles to survive and somehow advance one's fortunes engendered deep resentments and fears of authority, of the system, and of the ever-present threat of violence generated by the frustrations inherent in those social and economic conditions. Sensitive youngsters growing up in such communities necessarily feel the contradictory emotions of the desperate desire to escape and the tender need to belong. Such are the emotions that Alfred Kazin places at the heart of *A Walker in the City*, emotions he reawakens in himself every time he returns to the scenes of his childhood.

The range and variety of those emotions probably suggested to Kazin the impressionistic mode of presentation that he chose for the intricate drama of his growing up. Instead of trying to separate the emotions and depict and explain them one at a time, Kazin makes almost every paragraph into a strong mixture of contraries. He shows himself to be constantly angry with his parents, for example, over their complacent acceptance of their poverty at the same time as he is sympathetic toward their suffering and even grateful for the antimaterialistic values they gave him. Similarly, his recollections of his school days, his teachers, his synagogue and cinema visits, and his neighborhood associations all inspire an interplay of opposite feelings which he tries to communicate through a tumbling, pell-mell writing style. The observations and the accompanying emotions flow forth profusely, tripping over one another as they emerge and creating a mélange of irritation, apprehension, and warm nostalgia. This technique of constantly fusing contrasting reactions evoked by objects observed and tastes, smells, and sounds experienced gives the prose of *A Walker in the City* its distinctive rhythmic pattern and its lyrical tone.

The danger of an undisciplined outpouring of emotion has been effectively countered by the conscious use of several organizing principles and devices. The clearest sense of order is provided by Kazin's attention to the different stages of growing up. The first chapter is based predominantly on the earliest memories of childhood, when Alfred was perhaps five or six years old and his world was confined to the immediate vicinity of home. The second chapter depicts a boy of perhaps ten, more literate and articulate, curious about the concerns and conversations of the grown-ups who frequent the house and bring intimations of the great world beyond the neighborhood. By the third chapter, the narrator is usually recalling his teenage self, when he first began to see and know "the beyond" outside Brownsville and to sense the excitement it offered. Finally, in the last chapter, graduation from high school is the central event, suggesting arrival at the threshold of maturity and a readiness to leave Brownsville behind and plunge into the wider world.

To the seasons of youth, Kazin adds the seasons of the year to help give some sense of orderly progression to his book; each of the four chapters is given over, in the main, to the evocation of a single season, starting with fall in chapter one and concluding in chapter four with the narrator's favorite among the seasons, summer, when he feels liberated from the disciplined routines of the school year and exhilarated by the freedom to pursue his interests.

A final device is the use of recurring motifs and symbols, several of which are repeated at least once in every chapter. For example, the neighborhood practice of releasing pet pigeons from their rooftop cages in the evening is described in every chapter; it is a symbol of the need to escape Brownsville for a while, even though the pigeons are seen to follow the same circular sweep each time they are released and to return safely to their cages. Mention is also made in every chapter of the sweet sadness Kazin experiences when he hears the plaintive melody of *kol nidre*, the prayer sung at the start of the evening service on the Day of Atonement. That memory is intended as a symbol of the narrator's unbreakable bond with his cultural heritage. Other customs, places, persons, and cultural artifacts are brought repeatedly into the narrative, where they function as a refrain to make the reader comfortably familiar with the world the author is re-creating. Moreover, these devices help the reader to understand the tension Kazin experienced between the lure of the cultural world beyond Brownsville and the bond he felt with the family and community of his origins. With those organizing and unifying devices, Kazin is able to communicate fully the bewilderingly contradictory themes of *A Walker in the City*, an angry yet loving memoir, in the form of a prose poem, about the discovery of a literary vocation in a remote section of Brooklyn.

An important concluding point must be added to this analysis. Although *A Walker in the City* is autobiographical, it is not solipsistic, self-important, or even narrowly ethnic. Kazin avoids those faults by steering a middle course between the particular and the general. Whether speaking of himself, the Jewish cultural environment, or Brownsville, Kazin gives enough specifics to provide the ring of authenticity but never enough to become embarrassingly personal or local. The particulars he chooses to record always reflect something universal in human nature. *A Walker in the City* is indeed about a sensitive Jewish boy, a stammerer, growing up in a Brooklyn ghetto in the 1920's, but in a larger and more important sense, it is the story of every first-generation American born to recent immigrants and growing up in the impoverished environment to which most immigrant groups were confined for the United States' expansionist years. Kazin's book is a poetic account of the immigrant experience in America as seen through the eyes of their American-born children.

Critical Context

Alfred Kazin's conscious reason for writing *A Walker in the City* was certainly personal. The success of his first book, *On Native Grounds*, doubtless inspired in him the desire to explain himself more fully, to resolve the apparent paradox that he seemed to many to represent as a non-American critic of American literature. It is not likely, however, that that was Kazin's sole motivation. With the perspicacity of hindsight, it is possible to associate Kazin's autobiographical memoir with other events then occurring in the literary world, and particularly with the remarkable post-World War II flowering of American-Jewish writing. From 1945 to 1970 there poured out, mainly from New York, an incredible body of writing—including poetry, drama, fiction, and essays—by Jews and on overtly Jewish themes. Such writers as Delmore Schwartz, Arthur Miller, Saul Bellow, and Lionel Trilling, not to mention influential publications such as *Commentary* and *Partisan Review*, constituted a major new presence in American literature in those years. Alfred Kazin must be understood as part of that phenomenon and *A Walker in the City* as one of its key triumphs, being at once one of the works of art defining the movement and an explanation of the movement's existence.

Sources for Further Study

Byam, M. S. Review in *Library Journal*. LXXVI (October 1, 1951), p. 1560.

Edman, Irwin. Review in *The New York Times Book Review*. LVI (October 28, 1951), p. 1.

Gill, Brendan. Review in *The New Yorker*. XXVII (November 17, 1951), p. 180.

Handlin, Oscar. Review in *The Saturday Review of Literature*. XXXIV (November 17, 1951), p. 14.

Rolo, C. J. Review in *Atlantic Monthly*. CLXXXIX (January, 1952), p. 88.

Sugrue, Thomas. Review in *New York Herald-Tribune Book Review*. November 4, 1951, p. 6.

Murray Sachs

THE WAY THE FUTURE WAS
A Memoir

Author: Frederik Pohl (1919-   )
Type of work: Memoir
Time of work: 1919-1977
Locale: Primarily New York City
First published: 1978

Principal personage:
FREDERIK POHL, a writer and editor

Form and Content

Growing up in a poor family in the 1920's and 1930's meant that Frederik Pohl had to find entertainment in his surroundings—most of his youth was spent in Brooklyn—and in vicarious adventure. Pohl learned to read at an early age and soon discovered the pulp magazines of the period. These offered a wide variety of adventure and romance and, despite some atrocious writing, occasionally had good stories by capable writers. Secondhand copies, sold for a nickel or dime in used-book stores, were often within boys' budgets, and a chance encounter with *Science Wonder Stories Quarterly* was the beginning of Pohl's lifelong infatuation.

The catholicity of his interests did not translate into scholarly success, and he left Brooklyn Technical High School without graduating. He had, however, found that there were other science-fiction fans. His best friend, Dirk Wylie, provided more reading material and the idea that there might be others who shared their fascination. Their search for such people led them into the early organizations of science-fiction fans. The Science Fiction League, organized by Hugo Gernsback, editor of such magazines as *Amazing Stories* and *Wonder Stories*, was started to improve circulation; fan organizations grew by the mid-1970's to include tens of thousands of people in a nationwide network.

Pohl was an eager member of the league from its beginning, but along with some other fans—notably Donald A. Wollheim, who was to become a major figure in the genre—he was quick to organize new groups. These clubs published amateur magazines (called "fanzines" by the cognoscenti), which provided Pohl with his first opportunities in publishing and editing. The most famous of the clubs which Pohl helped to organize, the Futurians, was founded in 1937. In addition to Pohl and Wollheim, the original Futurians included Cyril M. Kornbluth and Isaac Asimov. Later, Damon Knight became part of the group. These five were among the shapers of science fiction throughout the mid-twentieth century.

At nineteen Pohl was supporting himself by editing *Astonishing Stories* and *Super Science Stories*. Although these cheaply produced pulps did not last long, a career broken only by service in World War II was begun. After the war Pohl set himself up as a literary agent, and he handled the work of most of the major writers of science fiction. Less exploitative than most agents, he went broke.

Pohl was always a prolific writer; although slowed somewhat by the demands of his career as an agent, during the three decades after World War II he wrote many popular and critically acclaimed novels and stories. The best known, *The Space Merchants* (1953), written with his close friend and frequent collaborator, Cyril M. Kornbluth, is generally regarded as a classic. Pohl was also a very successful editor, both presenting original material and reprinting significant stories that had gone out of print—the latter activity was an important contribution for the growing audience attracted to science fiction. Pohl won four Hugos—the highest award given to science-fiction authors—before the publication of his memoirs: in 1966, 1967, and 1968 as best editor and in 1973 for the best short story for "The Meeting," also written with Kornbluth.

The Way the Future Was is organized chronologically from the author's birth in 1919 to 1977, but, perhaps reflecting his background in fiction, Pohl felt free to digress. The result, combined with the lack of an index, makes the book difficult to use as a reference tool. Personal anecdotes concerning the author's loves and adventures, illustrated with photographs of Pohl and his family and friends, are woven into the biographical frame. The two central themes are Pohl's literary career and the growth of fan organizations from the early clubs in New York and the first formal convention, which drew nine people, to the later meetings, which draw several hundred to several thousand and occur regularly all over the industrialized world.

Analysis

The science-fiction genre was long held in disrepute; indeed, critics seemed to believe that if a work was science fiction it could not be worth much. By the 1970's, however, science fiction was becoming respectable and beginning to influence at least part of the literary establishment. The early work in the field, even the pulps and fantastic tales of writers such as Edgar Rice Burroughs, was reevaluated and found to have valuable speculative and imaginative elements. In addition, readers struggling with the arcane jumble of modern literature began to find that there were some outstanding stories in the genre.

The growth in the genre's popularity led to increasing interest in what drew writers and readers to it. In *The Way the Future Was*, Pohl has attempted to analyze his own attraction to the field and to generalize from his experience. The portrayal of the bright, youthful misfit drawn by a sense of wonder to the fantasies of early science fiction is poignant, though sometimes uneven. Pohl also shows some insight into the teenager's desire to be part of a group. His description of the growth of fan organizations is not only a personal tale of a young man seeking the security of belonging but also a variant of the American dream. Pohl helped create a society into which he fit and turned that effort into a very successful career.

Like films in the 1930's, the pulps were an escape from the unpleasant realities of economic difficulties, and fan organizations were a cheap way to socialize. Pohl's memoir is a useful description of growing up in New York during the Depression. As the Depression ended, Pohl and his genre matured and began to reflect the increasing sophistication of technology. Pohl's book *Man Plus* (1976), a tale of humans being physically prepared to live on Mars told from an unexpected point of view, is an excellent example of this change. *The Way the Future Was* is a chronicle of the maturing of Pohl, science fiction, and modern American society. It will be of value to both literary critics and historians.

Throughout the book, Pohl emphasizes the sense of wonder that sets science fiction writers and fans apart from the rest of society. He seems to regard it as axiomatic that every fan is an aspiring writer, and every working author is a part of "fandom." Certainly in the early days it was true—Pohl was one of nine who attended the first convention held in Philadelphia in 1936—and the cognoscenti encouraged it by developing their own jargon and traditions. Those not involved were called, with a touch of scorn, "mundanes." Although Pohl never yields his sense of being the outsider, by the time *The Way the Future Was* was written, science fiction, if still a genre, was extremely popular and profitable. Pohl, like many of his fellows, cherishes the "us-against-them" sense of his youth and clings to it.

Critical Context

Pohl's career calls to mind Georges Clemenceau's remark, "A man who is not a communist at twenty has no heart; a man who is still a communist at forty has no head." A member of the Young Communist League in his youth, he has remained a champion of social justice, but the German-Soviet nonaggression pact of 1939 finished his infatuation with socialism. In his best work, Pohl is a subtle and effective critic of human foibles and society. Unfortunately, *The Way the Future Was* is far from his best. Ideas are sometimes treated superficially, and the book, which gives the impression of having been written in haste, degenerates into episodic reminiscences of prominent authors whom Pohl knew and the failure of his several marriages. Given Pohl's place in the growth of science fiction, he was in a position to provide a much more valuable account of its development.

Pohl also glosses over his own work. He describes the development of ideas for a satire about the advertising industry which became *The Space Merchants*, but other influential works are ignored. For example, neither *Drunkard's Walk* (1961) nor *A Plague of Pythons* (1965) is mentioned. Certainly a memoir is a personal document, but the more personal information is set into the context of the author's times and the more his accomplishments are explicated the more valuable it becomes. Although Pohl did the former well in the first half of the book, context is lost in the second. He did not handle the latter well at any point.

The book is at its best both in style and in content when the author is describing the 1930's and 1940's. Pohl is able to convey the excitement of the young men— there were few women, at least within the group of fans and authors with whom Pohl was acquainted before World War II—who felt themselves to be part of a new movement. Although the first volume of Asimov's autobiography, *In Memory Yet*

Green (1979), covers some of the same ground, Pohl's work provides different insights, particularly into the commercialization of the genre and into the work of an editor.

Sources for Further Study

Aldiss, Brian W., and Harry Harrison, eds. *Hell's Cartographers: Some Personal Histories of Science Fiction Writers*, 1976.

Aldiss, Brian W., and David Wingrove. *Trillion Year Spree: The History of Science Fiction*, 1986.

Knight, Damon. *In Search of Wonder: Essays on Modern Science Fiction*, 1967.

Platt, Charles. *Dream Makers: The Uncommon People Who Write Science Fiction*, 1980.

Rose, Mark. *Alien Encounters: Anatomy of Science Fiction*, 1982.

Smith, Nicholas D., ed. *Philosophers Look at Science Fiction*, 1982.

Wollheim, Donald A. *The Universe Makers: Science Fiction Today*, 1971.

Fred R. van Hartesveldt

THE WAY TO RAINY MOUNTAIN

Author: N. Scott Momaday (1934-   )
Type of work: History/cultural anthropology
Time of work: The early nineteenth century
Locale: Montana and Oklahoma
First published: 1969

Form and Content

The Kiowa tribe emerged from the mountains of Montana soon after horses became available to the people of the northern plains. Early in the nineteenth century they migrated south to Oklahoma, where they fought their final battles with white civilization and were defeated. This is the story which N. Scott Momaday, whose father was a Kiowa, tells in *The Way to Rainy Mountain.* Yet the book's impressionistic methods make it less a history of the Kiowa than a personal meditation on that history in which Momaday employs myth, legend, ethnographic and historical data, and his own memories.

Momaday has included a prologue and an introduction which relate the history of the Kiowa tribe that follows to his own experience, particularly to his grandmother, Aho, who gave him the first accounts of the Kiowa that he ever heard. The book ends with an epilogue, in which he recounts a story of a Kiowa Sun Dance, which he heard from a hundred-year-old woman who actually witnessed it.

Yet the bulk of the book is made up of three movements: "The Setting Out," which describes the origins of the tribe and their acquisition of a religion and a sense of tribal destiny; "The Going On," which recounts legends of the Kiowa heyday on the southern plains; and "The Closing In," in which the old Kiowa freedom is restricted until they and their destiny, in a sense, fall to earth. These three movements are composed of twenty-four numbered sections, each of which includes three very brief pieces: a legend, recollected by the author from the stories of his grandmother; an ethnographic or historical gloss on this legend; and a personal recollection or observation, which is related to the legend or to the gloss or to both.

In the first of these sections, for example, Momaday gives the legend of the origin of the Kiowa tribe, which tells how they emerged from beneath the earth through a hollow log and how some of them were forced to remain underground when a pregnant woman got stuck in the log—an explanation of why the Kiowa have always been a relatively small tribe. This legend is followed by an explanation of the linguistic origin of the tribal name, which derives from a word which means "coming out." Finally, the author relates this story of origin and self-definition to his own memory of the first time he "came out" onto the plains. The juxtaposition of these three elements, in effect, relates Momaday to his Kiowa ancestors by showing the relationship of the tribe's mythic origins to their actual historical experience of "coming out" onto the plains; this was later repeated by Momaday, who, in effect, saw the plains for the first time as the Kiowa saw them.

As the twenty-four sections which compose the book's three principal movements unfold, significant changes in tone and content become noticeable. In "The Setting Out," the legends have to do with the acquisition of power, often understood in terms of language: The Kiowa name themselves in terms of their miraculous origins; they acquire dogs when the first dog speaks to a hunter and saves him from his enemies; a Kiowa girl ascends into the sky and marries the Sun, who becomes the father of her son; the son becomes, in time, a set of miraculous twins who provide the Kiowa with one of the principal elements of their religion; and the Kiowa discover Tai-me, a strange half-animal, half-bird creature who becomes a primary element of the Sun Dance.

In "The Going On," the stories are all concerned with the Kiowa's great freedom on the southern plains and with the horse, which made that freedom possible. Two stories have to do with escape from enemies, one tells of how the "storm spirit" understands the Kiowa language and always passes over the tribe, another is of a hunter's escape from a magic buffalo when a mysterious voice tells him of the animal's weak spot, and the last is the story of a fantastic journey of Kiowa warriors far south into Mexico, where they see "small men with tails," presumably monkeys.

Finally, in "The Closing In," there is a steady decline from the freedom and power of the middle section to stories of death and deprivation. A Kiowa manages to save his brother from the Ute only by his great bravery, but a great war-horse dies of shame when his rider turns him away during a charge against the enemy. Momaday's grandfather, in a rage, shoots an arrow at a rogue horse and accidentally hits another horse. Most telling of all, for no apparent reason—except that the Kiowa no longer seem to respect their ancient religion—the Tai-me bundle, which contains the effigy which represents the god, falls to earth.

Accompanying this story of the rise, triumph, and decline of the Kiowa is the story of the author's discovery of himself as a Kiowa. The journey of the tribe from their place of origin in the mountains of Montana to the cemetery of the Rainy Mountain church, where Momaday's ancestors lie buried, parallels the author's journey. Each of the legends is understood in relation to a similar, illuminating event in the author's own experience. For example, the legend of the acquisition of the god Tai-me by the Kiowa is glossed with Momaday's story of the time he actually saw the Tai-me bundle, and the story of the hunter who miraculously escapes from a magical buffalo when a mysterious voice speaks to him is paralleled by Momaday's story of how he and his father, walking in a game reserve, are chased by a buffalo.

Analysis

Because the Kiowa always were a small tribe, the stories which Momaday tells about them often emphasize a preoccupation with their numbers, and particularly with the danger of tribal disunion. One of the earliest tribal memories is of a quarrel between two chiefs over a slain antelope, which causes one of the chiefs to lead his people away into the darkness of prehistory, never to be seen again. This story is accompanied by that of an antelope drive which succeeds because all the people unite in a common effort.

Yet balanced against the threat of disunion are the grandmothers who appear again and again in the book. The death of Momaday's grandmother Aho brings him back to Rainy Mountain. Spider Grandmother assures the survival of the twin sons of the Sun. The Talyi-da-i is associated with Spider Grandmother and with Keahdi-nekeah, Momaday's father's grandmother. Momaday's grandfather's grandmother Kau-au-ointy and the ancient Ko-sahn, who describes one of the last Sun Dances, are other examples. The grandmothers maintain tribal traditions, and they stand for harmony and tribal unity in the face of all the forces which threaten it.

At the same time, the element which provides Momaday with the means for uniting his own present with the Kiowa past, once Aho is dead, is language. The stories he tells imply, and his own commentaries say explicitly, that the book's ultimate subject is language, which, in his view, is the one miracle-making power available to humanity. His grandmother's strange word *zei-dl-bei* (meaning "frightful") was her way of confronting evil, "a warding off, an exertion of language upon ignorance and disorder." Again and again in the book language is seen in this way: Kiowa are saved from their enemies by the power of language, the god Tai-me gives himself to the Kiowa with a promise, an arrow maker saves himself and his family by using the Kiowa language, the storm god does not attack the Kiowa because he knows their language.

Eventually, however, language loses this redemptive power for the Kiowa, and, not coincidentally, this is the time when the traditional religion of the tribe also can no longer save them. Momaday's juxtaposition of these two events with the general decline of the Kiowa as an independent tribe is related to his conception of language itself. Just as the Kiowa emerge from myth and legend to enter the historical record, so words lose their original metaphoric power and lapse into mere denotation. From that stage the Kiowa language would fall into cliché and die, were it not for the power of the poet, who saves it by making poetry out of stale language, that is, by breathing new metaphorical life into it. Momaday, therefore, may be said to have taken the fragments of Kiowa experience which he remembered from his grandmother's stories or discovered in his reading of history and ethnography and put them into a new artistic whole. The three movements of the book, therefore, suggest a structure of beginning, middle, and end, the birth, life, and death of the Kiowa tribe, but it is the artist's task to create a fourth stage of their journey, beyond the cemetery at Rainy Mountain, in the work of art that is Momaday's book. Language evolves from metaphor through denotation (history and science) to death (cliché), but just as language is rejuvenated in the new metaphors of the poet, so the three movements in the Kiowa journey ("The Setting Out," "The Going On," and "The Closing In") lead inevitably to a fourth stage, which is the book itself.

Furthermore, to understand Momaday's vision of the Kiowa, one must take account of the Kiowa religion as Momaday defines it. That religion is understood in relation to two objects of veneration: the ten bundles of the Talyi-da-i ("Boy Medicine") and the Tai-me bundle. The Talyi-da-i originates in the myth of the boy who was the result of a Kiowa woman's encounter with the Sun and who was reared by Spider Grandmother and miraculously split in two. When one of the twins disappeared into the waters of a lake—that is, became part of the natural world— the other converted himself into the ten bundles of the Talyi-da-i as a kind of eucharistic gift to the Kiowa.

The other myth that produced the Kiowa's religious vision is of the advent of Tai-me, the strange creature who became the god of the Sun Dance. In a sense, Tai-me remained with the Kiowa in the form of a stone effigy which was kept concealed in a bundle and only exposed to the people once a year, when it was suspended from a pole in the Sun Dance lodge. In this effigy form Tai-me is a spiritual presence of the Sun itself, just as the buffalo bull, which is sacrificed for the occasion, is the embodiment of the Sun's physical presence. In other words, the relation of the Sun to the buffalo and to Tai-me is a kind of trinity which, in a sense, corresponds to the God, Son, and Holy Spirit of the Christian Trinity.

Yet it should be noted that the American Indian religious vision is based upon quaternity rather than trinity. Again and again in American Indian cultures there is, for example, an emphasis on four directions, four reasons, four stages of life, or four symbolic colors, quaternities which are often seen to be images of one another. The Kiowa hunters could not be certain of success in the hunt if they did not prove themselves worthy in the Sun Dance; the Sun Dance is based upon a quaternity composed of the Sun, Tai-me, the sacrificed buffalo, and the buffalo herd itself.

At the same time, the relationship of the Tai-me effigy to the sacrificed buffalo of the Sun Dance resembles that of the ten bundles of the Talyi-da-i to the twin who returned to nature by entering the lake, just as the Sun—the spiritual father of the twins—is related to the maternal Spider Grandmother, who in their lives is associated with the natural world.

Critical Context

The Way to Rainy Mountain is a remarkable example of the way traditional tribal materials can be used to achieve a new combination of the traditional and the personal by a literary artist who is sensitive to those materials and determined not to violate them. The most notable achievements by American Indian writers are works which are simultaneously products of a tribal culture and contributions to it. Momaday succeeds in attaining both these ends. His book is the most important definition of the Kiowa identity by a Kiowa writer and a distinguished contribution to the culture of the tribe. At the same time it is a deeply personal work, a product of its author's effort to achieve a sense of what it meant to him to be a modern Kiowa.

Because *The Way to Rainy Mountain*—in an earlier version titled *The Journey of Tai-me* (1967)—was Momaday's first published work, it must be considered crucial in his development as an artist, a necessary first step in the discovery of his origins and thus of himself. Because his example was such a great inspiration to so many young Indian writers—and many of them have affirmed this—and thus so great an inspiration in producing what might be called a modern American Indian literary renaissance, *The Way to Rainy Mountain* must be considered a seminal work.

Beyond the book's significance as an influence on a whole generation of young writers, it must be considered a remarkable achievement as a testament to the uniquely human power of language to work miracles. As such, it is not only a remarkable personal document and a distinguished work of Kiowa literature but also a work of universal significance.

Sources for Further Study

Berner, Robert L. "N. Scott Momaday: Beyond Rainy Mountain," in *American Indian Culture and Research Journal*. III (1979), pp. 57-67.

Lincoln, Kenneth. "Tai-me to Rainy Mountain: The Makings of American Indian Literature," in *American Indian Quarterly*. X (1986), pp. 101-117.

McAlister, Mick. "The Topology of Remembrance in *The Way to Rainy Mountain*," in *Denver Quarterly*. XII (Winter, 1978), pp. 19-31.

Milton, J. R. Review in *Saturday Review*. LII (June 21, 1969), p. 51.

The New Yorker. Review. XLV (May 17, 1969), p. 150.

Papovich, J. Frank. "Landscape, Tradition and Identity in *The Way to Rainy Mountain*," in *Perspectives on Contemporary Literature*. XII (1986), pp. 13-19.

Schubnell, Matthias. *N. Scott Momaday: The Cultural and Literary Background*, 1985.

Trimble, Martha Scott. *N. Scott Momaday*, 1973.

Velie, Alan. *Four American Indian Literary Masters: N. Scott Momaday, James Welch, Leslie Marmon Silko, and Gerald Vizenor*, 1982.

Robert L. Berner

WAYS OF ESCAPE

Author: Graham Greene (1904-   )
Type of work: Autobiography
Time of work: 1929-1980
Locale: Great Britain, Africa, Vietnam, Mexico, Haiti, Antibes, and Argentina
First published: 1980

Principal personage:
GRAHAM GREENE, a writer and an adventurer

Form and Content

Graham Greene's autobiography consists of two volumes: *A Sort of Life* (1971) and *Ways of Escape*. The first volume covers the period from his birth in 1904 to the publication of the novel *Stamboul Train* (also known as *Orient Express*) in 1932. With some overlapping, the second volume traces his growth as a writer from his first published novel, *The Man Within* (1929), to *Doctor Fischer of Geneva: Or, The Bomb Party* (1980). Greene developed about half of the material for *Ways of Escape* from the introductions he had written for the collected edition of his works and from essays that he had published in several British magazines and newspapers.

The autobiographical form of the book is straightforward. Essentially a chronological record of the circumstances in which Greene conceived and wrote his books, *Ways of Escape* also recounts his travels to various trouble spots throughout the world and his reflections upon the political and literary figures who affected his life and writing. Greene incorporates into his narrative several long passages from his private journals as well as occasional dialogues between himself and other people.

Framed by a brief preface and an epilogue, the book is divided into nine main sections and runs 278 pages. Like the first volume of his autobiography, this book lacks an index.

Analysis

The idea of escape is central to an understanding of Greene's life and writing. He sees writing as a form of therapy: "Sometimes I wonder how all those who do not write, compose or paint can manage to escape the madness, the melancholia, the panic fear which is inherent in the human condition." Both his writing and his compulsive travels to dangerous places around the world are ways of escape. Like his fictional characters, Greene enjoys living on the edge of danger, testing his spiritual, psychological, and physical limits. By living intensely, he can evade the deadly boredom and emptiness that threaten his creative sanity.

Greene has carefully excluded from his autobiography details of his personal life. He explains, for example, how he met his wife, Vivien, in *A Sort of Life*, but nowhere does he mention his separation from her in *Ways of Escape*; she simply ceases to exist. Greene is more concerned here with dramatizing the social and political atmosphere in which he created his novels. "Those parts of a life most beloved of columnists," he explains, "remain outside the scope of this book."

One gets the impression from this book that Greene is always at the top of his form, whether writing a new novel or traveling to some remote part of the world. He explains how he set out to write a book that would both please the popular taste and be made into a film, and *Stamboul Train* succeeded in both aims. He also recounts how he tested his youthful bravado by traveling with his twenty-three-year-old cousin Barbara to Liberia, an adventure that was the basis of his travel book *Journey Without Maps* (1936). A statement from his cousin's diary—when Greene became ill in Zigi's Town—captures the tough-minded image of himself that he seeks to project: "I took Graham's temperature again, and it had gone up. I felt quite calm at the thought of Graham's death. To my own horror I felt unemotional about it."

Greene delights in depicting himself in unorthodox poses, whether exploring Africa or writing film criticism. He gives considerable emphasis to his controversial review of Shirley Temple's film *Wee Willie Winkie* (1937), in which he suggests that Twentieth Century-Fox had procured Temple "for immoral purposes" and that she had "a certain adroit coquetry which appealed to middle-aged men." Temple and the studio brought a libel suit against the magazine in which the review appeared and won their case. Nevertheless, Greene takes an obvious delight in having stung the precocious child star and exposed the hypocrisy of the studio; he records the incident as a moral victory.

Although Greene converted to Catholicism in 1926, he had to contend with the label of Catholic writer only after he published *Brighton Rock* in 1938. Insisting that he is not a Catholic writer but a writer who happens to be Catholic, Greene nevertheless brought Catholic characters and themes into almost all of his later works. Given the fixed rules and regulations of the Catholic church at that time, he could put his characters into dynamic situations in which their faith and humanity could be tested to the breaking point. His Catholicism provided him with an excellent dramatic framework for his future novels, stories, and plays.

In *The Power and the Glory* (1940), Greene shocked the public (and the Catholic church) with his depiction of an alcoholic priest who achieves an ambiguous sainthood in his execution. Later, in *The Heart of the Matter* (1948), Greene again tests the limits of orthodox theology by having his Catholic hero, Scobie, commit suicide. Technically, Scobie has damned himself to Hell, but Greene suggests that God can forgive even the hopeless. In his autobiography, Greene expresses a growing weariness over the arguments in Catholic journals as to whether Scobie is saved or damned. Greene also declares his dismay at the response to his novel *A Burnt-Out Case* (1961) about a man who loses his faith in God: "The book appealed too often to weak elements in its readers. Never have I received so many letters from strangers—perhaps the majority of them from women and priests."

That Greene chooses to record these details in his autobiography, however, suggests that he takes a peculiar satisfaction in his ability to stir orthodox Catholics to reassess their beliefs. For example, Greene cites the case of a French priest who pursued him with troubling questions more properly put to a confessor. Beneath the dismay Greene tacitly acknowledges the power of his fiction to bring about such ironic reversals.

Working as a correspondent for *Life* in the early 1950's, Greene made several trips to Vietnam to cover the French invasion of that country. His experiences there led him to write an anti-American novel, *The Quiet American* (1955). Greene met an American attached to an economic-aid mission in Vietnam who lectured him on the importance of finding a native force willing to fight on behalf of the Western powers. Greene transformed this person into the foolish and dangerously naïve hero of his novel, a man whose bookish idealism blinds him to the brutality and murder fostered by American intervention in this country. Like Twentieth Century-Fox, seeking a profit by using Shirley Temple to manipulate the sexual fantasies of her male audience, the American government—as Greene seems to view it—exploits innocent Asian lives in order to strengthen its economic and political hold on the East.

With the publication of *A Burnt-Out Case*, Greene discovered that many of his readers identified him with his hero, a famous architect named Querry. Having lost his faith in God and his interest in his work, Querry seeks refuge from his European fame by going to live in a remote lepers' settlement in the Belgian Congo. Even Greene's friend and fellow Catholic writer Evelyn Waugh read the novel as a sign of Greene's exasperation with his reputation as a Catholic author. Greene admits that there are similarities between Querry and himself. The great irony of the novel, which Greene fails to note, is that it casts a powerful light upon a man who (presumably like Greene himself) seeks anonymity.

Having been in such places as London during the Blitz, Mexico during the persecution of the Catholics, and Vietnam during the war with France, Greene continued his quest for excitement by visiting Haiti in 1963, during the reign of terror of François "Papa Doc" Duvalier. Based upon his experiences there, Greene wrote the novel *The Comedians* (1966). Greene observes, with some pleasure, that Duvalier himself attacked the book in his newspaper, leaving Greene to wonder if he disturbed Duvalier's dreams even as Duvalier's menacing dictatorship disturbed his. Throughout his autobiography, Greene interprets attacks upon his work, especially if made by conventional Catholics, dictators, or American patriots, as signs of their success. As Greene proudly observes, "A pen, as well as a silver bullet, can draw blood."

Greene states that *A Burnt-Out Case* represents the depressive side of his manic-depressive personality. *Travels with My Aunt* (1969), on the other hand, represents his manic side at its height. His new mood was in part the result of the fact that in 1966 he decided to leave England and settle permanently in Antibes. Although the subjects of this novel are old age and death, Greene claims that it is the only book he wrote merely for the fun of it. The heroine, Aunt Augusta, an old woman who lives life to the fullest, travels to the same countries and in the same order as did

Greene himself. A female fantasy version of himself—crusty, vigorous, witty, unconventional, defiant, and eager to be in the center of action—she can, because of her advanced age and sex, behave as she chooses with impunity.

While in Argentina, Greene conceived the plot of his next novel, *The Honorary Consul* (1973): A band of guerrillas mistakenly kidnap a lowly consul in place of an ambassador. He had read an account in the newspapers of the kidnapping of a Paraguayan consul mistaken for the Paraguayan ambassador. The consul was finally released and the matter forgotten, but Greene developed the story into a powerful novel with a more dynamic conclusion. The relationship between fiction and reality has fascinated Greene. In an earlier novel, *Our Man in Havana* (1958), his hero, James Wormold, makes up stories about agents he is supposed to have hired to help him with his work as a British spy in Cuba. One of the fictional characters he creates for his bogus reports to the home office, an aviator named Raul, turns out to be a real person who dies in a plane crash—just as Wormold says he does. As a result, Wormold wonders if he can write human beings into existence.

Greene always wanted to write an espionage novel that was free from the conventional violence of spy novels. His tribute to the unromantic British secret service is *The Human Factor* (1978), a novel based upon the career of Greene's friend, Kim Philby, a double agent who defected to the Soviet Union. Despite Greene's protest that the novel is not a roman à clef, most critics consider the character of Maurice Castle a loose portrait of Philby.

In all of his novels and travel books and especially in his autobiography, fragments of Graham Greene appear and disappear. One reason he wrote his autobiography was to seek out this elusive self, this other: "This book has not been a self-portrait. I leave such a portrait to my friends and enemies. All the same, I did find myself for many years in search of someone who called himself Graham Greene."

Critical Context

The context in which Greene develops his autobiography involves his creative interaction with orthodox Catholicism and with political and military events in England, Mexico, Africa, Vietnam, Cuba, and South America. Although his writing reveals an intensely personal vision of a frightening, suspenseful, and dark world— a human place peopled with sad and suffering men and women who profoundly long for peace—his vision draws upon the public world of the journalist who seeks out social injustice and oppression around the globe.

Coming toward the end of his career, *Ways of Escape* is Greene's attempt to put his literary career into perspective. His reflections on the specific circumstances and people upon which he based his novels and stories not only provide insights into the creative process but also unfold the growth of a writer's mind and career. Combining a fast-paced narrative with dialogue, the book has some of the qualities of Greene's novels; here, however, he is the unmistakable hero of his adventure. The other characters of this book are not only the actual people who moved in and out of Greene's life, but, more important, the characters he created in his novels, short stories, and plays during a period of more than forty years. It is in these fictional people that one discovers the artistic soul of Graham Greene.

Sources for Further Study
Allain, Marie-Françoise. *The Other Man: Conversations with Graham Greene*, 1983.
Allott, Kenneth, and Miriam Farris. *The Art of Graham Greene*, 1963.
Atkins, John. *Graham Greene*, 1966 (revised edition).
DeVitis, A. A. *Graham Greene*, 1986 (revised edition).
Kelly, Richard. *Graham Greene*, 1984.
Stannard, Martin. "In Search of Himselves: The Autobiographical Writings of Graham Greene," in *Prose Studies*. VIII (September, 1985), pp. 139-155.
Zabel, Morton Dauwen. "Graham Greene: The Best and the Worst," in *Craft and Character in Modern Fiction*, 1957.

Richard Kelly

WAYS OF SEEING

Author: John Berger (1926-   )
Type of work: Art history/cultural criticism
First published: 1972

Form and Content

In 1969, the well-known British art critic and historian Sir Kenneth Clark hosted a television series which became the basis of his book *Civilization*. John Berger's *Ways of Seeing* originated in a four-part television program of the same title which was a direct response to Clark and to the conception of art history embodied in Clark's book and programs. By raising questions about the social and economic functions of art, Berger challenged the idea that Western art history could be presented as the work of a series of towering artistic geniuses. A team of five coworkers put the volume together, although Berger's is the dominant authorial presence and *Ways of Seeing* is identified in the contemporary art milieu as "his" book.

The form of *Ways of Seeing* is integral to its content. It comprises seven numbered essays, four of which consist of written texts interspersed with photographic images, while the other three consist solely of images. The text is printed in a bold typeface with the margins left unjustified, contributing to the book's unorthodox look. The essays themselves can be read in any sequence; those that are purely pictorial are intended to generate as many questions as the verbal ones. Thus, the book's form challenges the reader to question the typical linear fashion in which a book is read and the (usually unstated) notion that an argument must be constructed primarily if not exclusively of words.

Ways of Seeing is an argumentative, polemical book. Its challenge to traditional art history is part of a broader questioning of the relationship between past and present in capitalist society. Berger demonstrates in a variety of ways his thesis that techniques for the reproduction of images in twentieth century capitalist society obscure, often to the point of erasing, any meaningful relationship between what reproduced images depict and their historical and social source. The book's title is both ironic—ways of seeing are ways of forgetting—and hopeful: There could be alternative ways of seeing, ones which would embed human beings in a living past with viable connections to the present. *Ways of Seeing*, although primarily critical in its focus, was clearly intended by Berger to be a first step toward such an alternative.

The written essays are the first, third, fifth, and seventh in the book. Placed between them are the three pictorial essays. In the first essay, Berger argues that the twentieth century proliferation of reproduced images of all kinds generates what he calls cultural mystification. He argues that the uniqueness of artworks is destroyed when they can be photographically reproduced and that such techniques obscure art's social and political sources. This in turns cuts people off from their past, making it difficult if not impossible for them to situate themselves in history. Thus, "the entire art of the past has now become a political issue."

In the third and fifth essays, Berger turns his critical attention to the tradition of oil painting as it developed in European art from the Renaissance until the end of the nineteenth century. He is especially concerned to show that oil painting as an art form peculiarly fitted the needs of an emerging bourgeoisie during these centuries. In the third essay, he focuses on a particular genre within painting, the female nude, and demonstrates the ways in which women are depicted and seen differently from men in Western painting. Women are painted to be seen by a spectator who is assumed to be a man; it is a passive role in comparison to the active one given to the male viewer. The female nude in Western painting is a person depicted naked in order to be seen by someone else. Berger concludes that the tradition of oil painting reduces women to being the passive visual property of men.

Similarly, in the fifth essay Berger argues that oil painting is an art form especially adaptable to a society wholly committed to forms of private property. He focuses on the totality of the oil-painting tradition, not merely on the pictures by acknowledged masters but also on the thousands and thousands of canvases which constitute the corpus of Western oil painting. It is an art form intrinsically bound to private property, not only in terms of what oil paintings depict, and who owns them, but also in the extraordinary capacity of oils to capture the look of things.

In the final essay of the book, Berger turns his attention to advertising and to the ways in which images from the tradition of oil painting are used in the generation of publicity to sell products in capitalist society. Such publicity depends on the visual language of oil painting for much of its repertoire of images, but the viewers of advertising images are now potential spectator-buyers rather than actual spectator-owners of individual paintings. By appropriating images from the tradition of oil painting, Berger suggests, advertising preserves the core values of that tradition but in a moribund form.

Many of the ideas in the last three of the written essays are first broached in the pictorial essays, which are placed second, fourth, and sixth in *Ways of Seeing*, that is, before their written counterparts. This organization reinforces the book's opening invocation: "Seeing comes before words." The book's experimental character and its concern to involve its readers in the ongoing process of analyzing image production and ways of seeing are captured by its final words: "To be continued by the reader."

Analysis

Throughout *Ways of Seeing* Berger challenges received assumptions about the meaning of artworks and such attendant notions as beauty, truth, and genius. He argues that photographic techniques for reproducing images have altered the way in which the art of the past is seen. Images of artworks are caught up in the much larger flow of reproduced images which are basic to the cultural life of fully developed capitalist societies. A young woman wearing a T-shirt with an image of Leonardo da Vinci's *Mona Lisa* is one of a number of examples in *Ways of Seeing*. Berger suggests that such duplication of images severs art from its past, thereby destroying the authority works of art once had.

He provides another example of such cultural mystification in his critique of Seymour Slive's analysis of Frans Hals's last two paintings, of the regents and regentesses of the Alms House in the seventeenth century Dutch city of Haarlem. When the art historian emphasizes Hals's personal vision as one which reveals an unchanging human condition, Berger calls this mystification. In contrast to Slive, he thinks that Hals was the first artist to depict the social relations, expressions, and characters created by capitalism. The art historian's language thus severs the paintings from their historical situation. In Berger's opinion, this is a high-cultural instance of the inability of contemporary people to "see" the art of the past and thus to situate themselves in history. This in turn raises a critical question: "To whom does the meaning of the art of the past properly belong? To those who can apply it to their own lives, or to a cultural hierarchy of relic specialists?"

In answering his questions Berger formulates his view of the class function of oil painting. His argument here has two parts. In chapters 3 and 5, Berger relates the development of oil painting to the rise of the bourgeoisie since the fifteenth century. The ways in which oil-painting techniques could be employed to depict the belongings of bourgeois property owners bear constant witness to oil paint's "original propensity to procure the tangible for the immediate pleasure of the owner." According to art critic Peter Fuller, this argument, that from the Renaissance to the nineteenth century there was a special relationship between art and property, has not been refuted and is "established beyond question."

There is a second part to Berger's argument, however, one which appears most clearly in the first chapter of the book. There he claims that new techniques for reproducing images have reduced painting's dominance of the visual arts in the twentieth century. At the same time that painting is mystified, its impact has narrowed to the areas of high culture overseen by academic specialists or has been trivialized in the realms of advertising. Painting is no longer the art form of the bourgeoisie: Rather, it exists in a kind of cultural limbo, not yet accessible in its historical particularity to other classes, no longer reflective of the interests of bourgeois property owners, constantly trivialized in the banalities of publicity.

According to Berger, then, understanding any cultural development must be based upon an analysis of its social foundations. For art critics and historians committed to other critical traditions, such as formal analysis, such a perspective is at best irrelevant, at worst distorting. Berger clearly wanted no part of such traditions of criticism in *Ways of Seeing*. In elaborating a basis for his own theory of art, he dramatically downplayed the focus upon masterpieces central to the ways of seeing he opposed. As he acknowledged in a 1978 essay, "The *Work* of Art," however, the form of the argument in *Ways of Seeing* left an "immense theoretical weakness" in the book: He had failed to make clear the relationship between a work of genius and the entire tradition of oil painting.

The consequence of this weakness is important. *Ways of Seeing* argues that oil painting is preeminently the art form of the bourgeoisie. It also argues that twentieth century methods of reproducing images have severed these paintings from their original social base as well as rendering understanding of their real meanings virtually impossible. How then can one explain the continued power of the great masterpieces of that tradition? Divorced from their social source and mystified by new techniques of image reproduction, they ought to be well-nigh inaccessible, according to the argument in *Ways of Seeing*. Yet they are not, as the many stimulating essays on great masterpieces by Berger himself testify.

A possible way out of this theoretical impasse would be to assume that since capitalist society still flourishes, masterpieces produced within that society ought to remain accessible. Yet Berger argues that in fully developed capitalist society ways of seeing are so profoundly transformed as to render art of the past, even of an earlier capitalist past, inaccessible. It is important to note that in making this argument Berger uses the evidence of paintings themselves (as in his discussion of Hals) to oppose academic interpretations. In relying on the authority of paintings themselves to refute his opponents, however, he employs reproductions of them— something that he is simultaneously asserting has destroyed their authority. Later, in 1978, he invokes the idea of creativeness as something for which any adequate theory of art must account; such notions as creativity were precisely the ones which he refused in *Ways of Seeing*.

Clearly, there is an unresolved contradiction in Berger's critical practice as a whole and in *Ways of Seeing* in particular. While this weakness makes the argument of *Ways of Seeing* less secure than its straightforward, often-assertive prose might initially seem to be, it by no means negates the book's effectiveness as an important intervention in the cultural criticism of the 1970's. *Ways of Seeing* teaches by example as well as by theoretical arguments. It is a fertile source of ideas toward a materialist theory of art and a radical critique of bourgeois culture. It is as well, in its innovative format, accessible style, and open invitation to engage in critical practice, a suggestive model for an alternative use of a new language of images in the twentieth century.

Critical Context

A powerful influence on the argument of *Ways of Seeing* was the famous essay by the German thinker Walter Benjamin, "Das Kunstwerk im Zeitalter seiner Reproduzierbarkeit" ("The Work of Art in the Age of Mechanical Reproduction"). Peter Fuller has argued that Benjamin's influence was indeed too pervasive on Berger and that the contradiction in *Ways of Seeing* stems from contradictions in Benjamin's own thought. That may well be the case. Nevertheless, Benjamin's work also strengthened Berger's commitment to a radical engagement in the critique of twentieth century bourgeois culture. This task links his work with that of others such as the French critic Roland Barthes, whose provocative early essays on bourgeois culture collected as *Mythologies* (1957) were published in English translation in the same year as *Ways of Seeing*. Berger's work also has deep affinities with that of other British Marxist critics whose work began to appear in the 1950's and 1960's, such as the literary scholar Raymond Williams and the historian E. P. Thompson.

Ways of Seeing marks a crucial point in Berger's own multifaceted career as art critic, screenwriter, novelist, and documentary writer. In a series of books written in collaboration with the photographer Jean Mohr, he continued the experiment with books composed of images and texts begun with *Ways of Seeing*. In 1973, Berger went to live in a French village; since then, his work has increasingly focused on a critique of the modern world mediated through an evocation of the peasant experience from village to metropolis. *A Seventh Man* (1975), *Another Way of Telling* (1982), and his two collections of stories, *Pig Earth* (1979) and *Once in Europa* (1987), are all parts of that project.

If there is one theme which runs throughout all Berger's diverse writings, it is best captured in the 1979 preface to the reissue of his book of art criticism *Permanent Red: Essays in Seeing* (1960). Referring to the title of that collection, he wrote that it was meant "to claim that I would never compromise my opposition to bourgeois culture and society."

Sources for Further Study

Berger, John. *Permanent Red: Essays in Seeing*, 1960.

_____. "The *Work* of Art," in *The Sense of Sight: Writings by John Berger*, 1985. Edited by Lloyd Spencer.

Fuller, Peter. *Seeing Berger: A Revaluation of "Ways of Seeing,"* 1981.

Inglis, Fred. "John Berger: Membership, Mannerism, Exile," in *Radical Earnestness: English Social Theory, 1880-1980*, 1982.

Wolff, Janet. "Art as Ideology," in *The Social Production of Art*, 1981.

Michael Messmer

THE WEIGHT OF THE WORLD

Author: Peter Handke (1942-   )
Type of work: Diary
Time of work: November, 1975, to January, 1977
Locale: Paris
First published: Das Gewicht der Welt, 1977 (abridged in translation as *The Weight of the World*, 1984)

Principal personage:
PETER HANDKE, an Austrian writer

Form and Content

Peter Handke, a native of Austria, is one of the most prominent, and at times controversial, authors writing in the German language. He has produced a prodigious amount of work, including plays, poetry, and a number of novels and essays. *The Weight of the World* is his first published diary journal. It is very much a literary text, written as an experiment in aesthetic form. The English translation represents an abridged version of the original German edition. In collaboration with his translator, Handke excised a number of passages—especially those concerning politics and those too difficult to translate—amounting to about ten pages.

The work consists of short entries which have the quality of random notes. Indeed, Handke composed it by writing in a small book which he carried around with him during the period of November, 1975, to January, 1977. At this time he was living with his young daughter in Paris. Some of the entries are noted by both day and month, others by the month only. They are, for the most part, not organized thematically. Interestingly, very few of the entries—with the exception of those pertaining to his daughter—deal with particular individuals or even public events. This is, above all, a journal of the author's inner world, a kind of phenomenological diary: that is, a record of the phenomena of consciousness.

In the preface to the original German edition—which is not included in the English version—Handke indicates that he initially began the notebook with the thought of jotting down ideas for a novel or play he had in mind. He then realized that many of his notes did not seem to fit the plan or scheme for the particular literary work he planned to write. He decided that he wanted to attempt writing down his experiences with as little mediation as possible, without thoughts of some larger project or systematic organization behind the act of formulation. It would be a kind of experimental stream-of-consciousness note-taking, writing almost as a kind of reflex action. In an interview conducted in 1979, Handke said he considered it a kind of "novel" about everyday life.

With this attempt to transcribe his feelings and impressions in an automatic gesture of note-taking, Handke hopes to narrow the gap between experience and its formulation and to achieve thereby a more authentic level of aesthetic discourse.

The truly creative and imaginative fictions of great literature originate in the immediate experience of the writer—in dreams, striking images, and random thoughts—which are then given a formal structure. These fictions generate, in Handke's view, alternative visions of reality and thereby illustrate other possible modes of existence. Such visions allow the individual to achieve a momentary transcendence with respect to the inevitable estrangement of life, and they introduce the possibility of change.

This attempt to create a poetic discourse that liberates rather than alienates the individual represents the major dimension of the theme of language and fiction in Handke's writings. The problem he seeks to address in *The Weight of the World* is a timeless one: that the attempt to formulate an experience often obscures or distorts the feeling that motivated it. The individual's experience of his feelings then becomes inauthentic by virtue of the act of formulation. Every act of writing, especially personal ones, such as writing in a diary, seeks to overcome the distortions inherent in language.

Analysis

Handke is the type of writer who uses his personal, subjective perceptions as a major source for his fiction, and many of the entries in *The Weight of the World* give indications of the kinds of experiences and themes that structure his other fictional texts. Notes concerning states of anxiety and intense visual images dominate the diary and are central to the majority of his writings. He often notes his dream events and reverie images, such as in one of the early notes for November, 1975 ("Dream sounds . . ."), and the initial entry for March 16, 1976 ("In my half-sleep . . ."). These visions, or images, form the basis of much of Handke's writing. To formulate these often-ineffable experiences in language without distorting their essential meaning is the task of his fiction, as he explains in one of the entries for March 6, 1976, which includes another statement of the goal which informs the writing of *The Weight of the World* itself. His ideal of composition would be one in which these feelings and experiences would be transformed—he uses the image of the caterpillar and butterfly—into new poetic images which would also reflect in some way their origins. They would be aesthetic transformations of the "mythic" images of his own consciousness. This artistic point of view suggests that Handke is very much a post-Romantic writer.

The concept of metaphor is central to Handke's notion of fiction, and many of the entries in *The Weight of the World* suggest its importance. Writing serves as an existential act of orientation because it establishes a sense of connection between consciousness (self) and the world (others) and allows the individual to overcome the extreme states of estrangement that inevitably must plague him. For Handke, metaphor—the comparison of two unlike phenomena—creates a relationship between an inner experience or idea and an external event or object, a momentary unity between self and others. He perceives himself thus to be connected through aesthetic language to the world around him. Metaphor clearly performs for him an important existential function. As Handke suggests in the entry for March 31, 1976 ("Never *look* for metaphors!"), such figurative language must be experienced existentially rather than merely conceived or created intellectually.

The condition of half-sleep or semiconscious reverie (*Halbschlafzustand*) is an important poetic state for Handke; it is a time when the division between consciousness and reality is blurred. This reverie state is a major source of Handke's poetic sensibility, and references to it are frequent in *The Weight of the World*. In this condition he is consumed with images and visions that seem to fill his mind. The fundamental existential fact of the inevitable otherness—the alienation—of the self from the world that is felt so intensely during the fully wakened state is not experienced here because consciousness is enveloped in a totality of dreamlike feeling. The initial entry for March 16, 1976 ("In my half-sleep . . ."), and that for March 18, 1976 ("Images in half-sleep . . ."), are typical. Examples of this particular state of consciousness abound in his fiction, especially in earlier texts such as *Die Angst des Tormanns beim Elfmeter* (1970; *The Goalie's Anxiety at the Penalty Kick*, 1972) and *Der kurze Brief zum langen Abschied* (1972; *Short Letter, Long Farewell*, 1974).

Related to this poetic reverie state of half-sleep are the moments of confusions or misperceptions that characterize Handke's waking process. *The Weight of the World* contains numerous entries noting this occurrence. The one described in the March 19, 1976, entry is a good example. The entry for March 7, 1976, is also representative of this phenomenon. Handke awakens, and in this state of half-sleep he interprets the sound of birds flying past his window as that of falling autumn leaves. This misperception signals the division between, to use the author's terms, the inner world (of consciousness) and the outer world (of reality). This rift is, however, not necessarily one that produces a sense of estrangement, because here the difference is bridged in terms of a metaphor ("like falling autumn leaves"). This poetic image used to interpret an actual event points to a central aspect of Handke's vision of the existential role of aesthetic language and fiction. Poetic language—metaphor in the broadest sense—creates a relationship between consciousness and reality that orients, even if only for a moment, the self in the world.

Throughout his diary, Handke notes many examples of his anxiety and fear of death. These are important because they constitute in many respects the existential motivation for his writing. During March, 1976, Handke became ill and was hospitalized for a period. The entries for March 28 suggest his state of mind as he lay in the hospital bed. ("I shut my eyes, but fear opens them.") Other entries for this day indicate his response to such feelings and again reveal the inner world of imagination and aesthetic form as his mode of transcending the experience of alienation. He notes, for example, his need to read literature ("I need something I can read *word for word* . . ."), in this case one of Johann Wolfgang von Goethe's novels. The imaginative act of reading a literary text (as opposed to reading a newspaper) serves as a means of stabilizing and orienting himself; it transports him to an inner world of images. Reading and writing produce in Handke an almost mystical state of harmony within the self. He is an avid reader, and references to other authors (Goethe, Hermann Hesse, Franz Kafka, for example) abound in *The Weight of the World*.

Another entry for March 28 ("Closing my eyes brings sudden relief . . .") indicates a meditative, mystical state of consciousness that recalls both Handke's moments of poetic reverie and his experiences of art and literature. The Greek root of the word "mystical" means to close the eyes and turn inward. He writes that in closing his eyes he has that feeling that there is a connection between his thoughts and feelings that is not there when his eyes are open. In this meditative state, a dreamlike, visionary unity is achieved within the self. This meditation is again clearly similar to the states of calmness gained through reading and writing and suggests that for Handke the domain of authenticity, of "existential truth," is to be found within the self and the imagination and not in the events of the external world.

Handke makes this notion clear in two of the entries for April 22, 1976. The one note ("Memory and yearning . . .") reiterates the theme of the imaginative experience of art. It produces, he writes, a subjective sense of harmony—a revitalized feeling of connection to life—that is lacking in everyday existence. Thought and feeling, body and soul, self and others are fused in the intensity of imagination and emotion. The other entry ("Split personality as a solution . . .") hints at the states of anxiety and fear he experiences which give rise to the need for art as a healing of the split within the self. The drudgery and tedium of everyday housework, he comments, give rise to a fantasy of being someone else so that some relief might be gained from the boredom of routine. The infinite freedom of the imagination again provides escape from the "weight" of finite existence. This thought again indicates the existential origins of Handke's post-Romantic aesthetic sensibility. It also suggests, as is well-known, that there is often a fine line between the condition of schizophrenia and the creative states of the artist.

Another prominent aspect of the journal is Handke's noting of his own and others' movements and gestures. The entry for June 19, 1976 ("For the last few hours . . ."), illustrates what he seeks to capture. He watches two teenagers hugging and kissing and comments on the "ritual" aspects of their behavior: That is, they are imitating unconsciously what they have seen in films, television, and magazines about love. They are thus alienated to a degree from the authentic experience of their own feelings; their emotions are mediated through the social forms established by their environment. The mediation of experience is a major theme in Handke and is, as discussed, a central aspect of the style of *The Weight of the World* itself.

Critical Context

Handke's intention in *The Weight of the World* is best understood in terms of his overall theories concerning language and the role of fiction. For Handke, language, especially concepts and abstraction of experience, can distort the perception of reality. Conceptual signs or forms as well as language that has become automatized can come to generate their own level of "reality" that is distinct from the world as it really is. It is then easy to confuse these semiological "fictions" with the empirical facts of existence. The individual who takes these signs for truth eventually becomes alienated from his experience and becomes, in existential terms, inauthentic.

Handke gives a good example of this idea in what is perhaps his best-known and most compelling work, *Wunschloses Unglück* (1972; *A Sorrow Beyond Dreams*, 1974), a narrative text he wrote as a tribute to his mother, who committed suicide in late 1971. In it, he examines the forms of language that shaped and circumscribed his mother's life and death. With this intention, he explores the larger theme that concerns much of his early writings, that is, the distortion of experience through language and sign. He looks, for example, at the word "woman," a sign which has the denotative meaning of a human female. The connotations of this word, however, involve many levels of personal and societal meaning, implicit social-psychological roles and behavioral expectations that are often subtly conveyed by friends, family, and society.

Having grown up in rural, conservative, and Catholic Austria, Handke's mother came to know the word "woman" as a repressive and confining sign that unconsciously guided her perceptions of herself and others. Since it is a "woman's destiny" to get married and rear a family, her grandfather forbade her to go on in school even though she was an outstanding student. In her early twenties, she came to define herself in terms of the images of "woman" found in the slick fashion magazines and advertisements of the big city. When she later had an affair with a married German solider and became pregnant, she was told that it was her "woman's duty" to be married so that her child would have a legitimate father. She wed someone whom she did not love, and this man became an abusive alcoholic. Her existence as a "woman" became a tale of misery, and she finally took her own life at the age of fifty-one. This seemingly simple word came to fashion its own system of meanings, a level of linguistic reality that circumscribed the actual reality of her life.

In *The Weight of the World*, Handke attempts to use words in a way that is (relatively) free from such restrictive ideological systems, to generate an existentially authentic use of language. At the time Handke was writing the journal, he also began work on a novel, *Die linkshändige Frau* (1976; *The Left-Handed Woman*, 1978), and this latter text shows the influence of the diary in both its narrative style and the main character's search for an authentic identity outside her roles as wife and mother. The critically acclaimed film *Engel über Berlin* (1987; *Wings of Desire*) is a collaboration between German director Wim Wenders and Handke, and its dialogue is greatly influenced by the fragmentary diary style of *The Weight of the World*. Handke has since published two additional journals—*Die Geschichte des Bleistifts* (1982; the story of the pencil) and *Phantasien der Wiederholung* (1983; fantasies)—which continue the thematic and stylistic intent of this earlier work.

Sources for Further Study

Fothergill, Anthony. Review in *The Times Literary Supplement*. November 15, 1985, p. 1297.

Linville, Susan, and Kent Caspar. "Reclaiming the Self: Handke's *The Left-Handed Woman*," in *Literature/Film Quarterly*. XII (1984), pp. 13-21.

Locke, Richard. Review in *The New York Times Book Review*. LXXXIX (July 12, 1984), p. 10.

Schlueter, June. "The Forthcoming Handke," in *The Plays and Novels of Peter Handke*, 1981.

Sharp, Francis Michael. "Literature as Self-Reflection: Thomas Bernhard and Peter Handke," in *World Literature Today*. LV (Autumn, 1981), pp. 603-607.

_____. "Peter Handke," in *Major Figures of Contemporary Austrian Literature*, 1987. Edited by Donald G. Daviau.

Thomas F. Barry

WEST WITH THE NIGHT

Author: Beryl Markham (1902-1986)
Type of work: Autobiography
Time of work: 1904-1936
Locale: Kenya
First published: 1942

> *Principal personages:*
> BERYL MARKHAM, a horsewoman and an aviator
> TOM CAMPBELL BLACK, the aviator who taught Markham to fly
> BROR VON BLIXEN-FINECKE, an aristocratic Dane, the former
>   husband of author Isak Dinesen, and a well-known hunter
> CHARLES CLUTTERBUCK, Markham's father, who loved racehorses
>   and went bankrupt trying to farm in Africa
> DENYS FINCH-HATTON, an English aristrocrat, the famous game
>   hunter and lover of author Isak Dinesen who died in a plane
>   crash
> KIBII (later ARAB RUTA), Markham's childhood friend from the
>   Murani tribe

Form and Content

   West with the Night is the unconventional autobiography of an unconventional woman. British by birth, Beryl Markham grew up on a remote, colonial farm near Njoro, Kenya. Deserted by her mother and largely ignored by her father, she spent her childhood exploring the primitive African landscape with a dog named Buller and children from the Murani tribe. Markham's formal education was limited, but her knowledge of African animals, customs, languages, and geography was extensive. She tracked game and used a spear like a native, she spoke fluent Swahili, and she possessed an almost uncanny understanding of horses. As a young woman, she opened her own stable, where she trained a number of prizewinning thoroughbreds. She also knew many of the important public figures of the day, including Edward, the Prince of Wales, and his brother Prince Henry, as well as local celebrities such as game hunters Bror von Blixen-Finecke and Denys Finch-Hatton. During the early 1930's, Markham learned to fly and became a bush pilot. She delivered mail, passengers, and supplies to much of East Africa; she also scouted game for hunting safaris. In 1936, she became the first person to fly solo from east to west across the Atlantic. These experiences provided the material for *West with the Night*, an account of her life up to age forty, which aviator and author Antoine de Saint-Exupéry encouraged her to write.

   Despite good reviews, *West with the Night* did not become a popular success until Ernest Hemingway's correspondence was published in 1981. Hemingway, who had known Markham in Africa, praised *West with the Night*:

She has written so well, and marvelously well, that I was completely ashamed of myself as a writer. I felt that I was simply a carpenter with words, picking up whatever was furnished on the job and nailing them together and sometimes making an okay pig pen. But [she] can write rings around all of us who consider ourselves . . . writers.

As a result of Hemingway's praise, *West with the Night* was republished in 1983. Critical acclaim followed and the book became a best-seller, forty-one years after it first appeared.

The book's format and panache explain much of its appeal. It is divided into four books, each focusing on a particular period in Markham's life. Chronology as such is relatively unimportant; Markham describes significant moments or memorable experiences rather than marching through her life year by year. Book 1 recounts some of her experiences as a bush pilot in 1935: the delivery of a bottle of oxygen to a mining-town doctor, the search for a colleague whose plane went down in the wilderness, a deathbed visit with a victim of blackwater fever. Interspersed among these episodes are meditations on the African landscape and animals as seen from the air as well as reflections about the joys and dangers of flying across uncharted territory. Book 2 flashes back to Markham's childhood and adolescence; it includes descriptions of a mauling by a neighbor's pet lion, an exciting boar hunt, a confrontation with an arrogant stallion, and the birth of the colt Pegasus. Book 3 traces Markham's struggle to establish herself as a successful trainer of racehorses after she left her father's farm at the age of seventeen. In book 4, Markham describes her flying lessons with Tom Campbell Black, the death of Finch-Hatton, and her elephant-hunting adventures with Blixen. Only in the last two chapters does she discuss the solo flight over the Atlantic which brought to her fame.

Although Markham's experiences provide the framework for the narrative, *West with the Night* is as much a tribute to Africa as it is an account of a woman's life. In fact, for an autobiography the book is remarkably short of routine biographical details. Markham, for example, never mentions her mother, her husbands, or her son. She has no thesis to advance or position to defend. Her thrust is descriptive; she wishes to re-create the Africa that she understood and loved. Her efforts result in a vivid, first-person account of the African landscape, its animals, and its people as it was experienced by a woman of courage, intelligence, and independence during the early part of the century.

Analysis

Although Markham modestly dismisses *West with the Night* as a "remembrance" or a "revisitation," such an evaluation diminishes her skill as a writer. The book is the product of an accomplished, imaginative writer who was part poet and part storyteller. Much of the power of *West with the Night* derives from Markham's ability to establish a strong sense of place. Whether she is describing a racetrack, the interior of an airplane at five thousand feet, or Lake Nakuru, pink with flamingos, her rich, vivid imagery captures the mood and feel of Africa. She can evoke the dreamy spell of "leopard nights" and "lion nights" on the Kenya farm. She can also repulse her readers with the visceral details of life in a Murani village, where goat urine produces a "pungent stench," where brown-eyed cattle have "friendly nostrils" and "slobbery mouths that covered our legs with sticky fluid," and where the village chief, after drinking a gourd of blood and curdled milk "let his belch roll upward from his belly and resound against the morning silence."

Markham's prose is highly metaphorical. Personification and simile are instrumental in conveying the grandiose beauty of the African landscape. As she looks at the world from the campfire, she writes:

> In a sense it was formless. When the low stars shone over it and the moon clothed it in silver fog, it was the way the firmament must have been when the waters had gone and the night of the Fifth Day had fallen on creatures still bewildered by the wonder of their being.

West with the Night is also distinctive because of Markham's flair for narrative. Many episodes in the book assume the form and impact of short stories. Dialogue is common, especially as a device for revealing character. In addition, when the outcome of an event is in doubt Markham paces the action for optimum suspense. For example, when describing a confrontation with an angry bull elephant, she intensifies the moment of climax by extending it; she describes the elephant's scream, the red and black interior of its mouth, and Bror Blixen's maddening refusal to shoot. The result is a chilling and gripping adventure story, intensified because Markham actually experienced it.

Occasionally, Markham distorts the facts if it serves her literary purposes to do so. In one of the most exciting episodes in the book, Wild Child, an ailing filly, is pitted against Wrack, a stronger horse owned by a rival stable. Tension builds as Markham, shifting into the present tense, describes the preparation, the grandstand crush, and finally the race itself, which she captures in slow motion. It is a very effective passage that builds to an exhilarating finish when Wild Child wins. In reality, however, the race as described by Markham never occurred. Wild Child raced Wrack several times. This particular was merely a composite of many races and thus serves as yet another example of Markham's creative power.

Markham's strong narrative impulse was undoubtedly shaped by the stories she heard during her youth. She was especially impressed by her father's stories of the Masai, Kikuyu, and Nandi wars. She was also exposed to the African oral tradition in which animals are the actors; typically, their foolish or wise behavior provides a lesson or helps explain life. In chapter 8, Kibii, a Murani playmate, explains that death came into the world because the Chameleon was slow in delivering a message from God to man. Markham also alludes to the trickster hare that stole milk from the cow and to the rhinoceros that swallowed a quill borrowed from the porcupine. Some of Markham's own animal characters could have appeared in African folktales, particularly the comic ones. Bombafu, a vain parrot, causes his destruction by tricking the farm dogs with his whistle. Balmy, an eccentric filly, refutes "the principles of justice" by luring a foolish zebra foal away from its mother.

Other of the animal encounters Markham describes are probably the by-product of growing up in a culture that lived intimately with animals and accorded them a respect and dignity lacking in the West. Animals are, in fact, the main characters in *West with the Night*, and Markham grants them an intelligence and a complexity of motives that most authors extend only to humans. She is never patronizing or sentimental. Kimba, a big baboon, escapes his chain and screams his "jealous hatred" at the young Markham while trying to claw her eyes. Rhinoceroses take "sadistic pleasure" in scratching—and destroying—telegraph poles. Warthogs can be lured into the open by rustling a scrap of paper at the entrance of their burrows because they find the sound "clearly insulting." Elephant cows, upon hearing the motor of Markham's plane above them, cleverly group themselves so as to conceal the ivory tusks of the bulls. Buller, Markham's dog, after a lifetime of fights, has become "cynical toward life."

Markham's sensitivity to animals is most poignantly revealed in a chapter of book 2, "Royal Exile." In it, Markham spins the real-life tale of her attempt to subjugate a half-wild stallion. The battle for dominance is an extended, painful one for the adolescent girl. Once when the stallion throws her, she suffers a severe concussion. On another occasion, the stallion snatches her by the back, shakes her, and flings her against the wall of his box. Violent as these events are, they are presented sympathetically, for they are told from the horse's point of view. Markham understands that the stallion's unarticulated anger, pride, and loneliness make him both long for and reject friendship. In the end, the mutual tolerance and respect of horse and girl results in a relationship in which neither dominates the other.

Although Markham's life was full and exciting, it was lonely. She established few close relationships with others, and those friends were almost exclusively male. She idolized her father and she had great respect and affection for Kibii, her childhood friend who later followed her from the wilderness to the racetrack and eventually to the airplane hangar. She also enjoyed the company of her aviator colleagues and the safari organizers. Toward most of the rest of white humankind, however, she showed at best bemusement or grudging tolerance. Having matured in a world where survival was the primary goal, Markham had little use for the ignorant or the weak. She felt an abhorrence of people who were ill. She directed her sometimes-grim humor against those whom she believed had acted "stupidly," most notably a lion hunter who died because he had tried to photograph his not-yet-dead trophy; the hunter's ashes, she suspects, now repose "in an urn of Grecian elegance far from any path a creature more ominous than a mouse might choose to wander."

Life in the wilderness gave Markham an understanding of Africa and its elemental forces and rhythms, an understanding which underscored the puniness of most human enterprises. Many passages in *West with the Night* constitute an informal commentary on the folly of man and his pride. She dismisses whites as an "upstart race" for believing they can conquer the continent and for thinking themselves superior to the natives; they have "overlooked the vital soul of Africa herself, from which emanates the true resistance to conquest." The killing of an elephant, she writes, is an act of "eternal impudence" rather than an act of heroism. She wryly punctures man's inflated notions of his own importance by observing that to birds and animals man is an object of pity because he has only two friends, "the dog and the horse." Man, "with an innocence peculiar to himself," is proud of this situation, believing that he has two dumb, but loyal, friends. The dog and the horse, Markham believes, may not be loyal so much as tolerant. Truly, *West with the Night* provides a humbling perspective on man and his achievements.

Critical Context

West with the Night belongs to a small body of literature produced by writers who knew at first hand the rugged beauty, the solitude, the color, the challenges, and the dangers that East Africa offered to its settlers and visitors during the early part of the twentieth century. The most notable of these writers are Elspeth Huxley, the author of *The Flame Trees of Thika* (1974) and *Out in the Midday Sun: My Kenya* (1985); Isak Dinesen, who reminisced about her experiences on a coffee plantation in *Den afrikanske farm* (1937; *Out of Africa*, 1937) and *Skygger på graesset* (1960; *Shadows on the Grass*, 1960); and Ernest Hemingway, who used East Africa as the setting for *The Snows of Kilimanjaro* (1961) and *Green Hills of Africa* (1935) as well as for several of his short stories.

The Africa of Hemingway, Dinesen, and Markham no longer exists. The wild game that Hemingway's characters hunted is now confined to preserves, white colonial settlers such as Dinesen are no longer welcome, and the magnificent forests that Markham remembers are now largely destroyed. All these writers were aware of the changes that were taking place, even as they were writing. In *West with the Night*, Markham notes, "Africa is never the same to anyone who leaves it and returns again."

Yet if the farmers, hunters, fliers, and opportunists who came to East Africa altered the landscape, the writers who recorded the process permanently fixed the public idea of what life was like in the Kenyan colony. Few of these writers equated life in Africa with a life of ease. They did, however, suggest that it was a life which offered adventure, glamour, and excitement in an exotic setting. The characters and authors who lived those lives, whether fictional or real, have now passed into the realm of myth and legend.

Markham herself wrote little else after the publication of *West with the Night*. Between 1943 and 1946, eight stories were published under her name in magazines such as *Collier's* and *The Saturday Evening Post*. Several of these were ghostwritten by Markham's third husband, Raoul Schumacher; several others were undoubtedly collaborative efforts. Clearly, however, four of the stories were largely Markham's: "The Captain and His Horse," "The Splendid Outcast," "Something I Remember," and "The Quitter." Set in East Africa and obviously autobiographical, these stories, anthologized in *The Splendid Outcast: Beryl Markham's African Stories* (1987), should be read as charming supplements to *West with the Night*.

Sources for Further Study

Cournos, John. Review in *The Atlantic Monthly*. CLXX (September, 1942), p. 138.

Fadiman, Clifton. Review in *The New Yorker*. XVIII (June 20, 1942), p. 66.

Fox, James. "The Beryl Markham Mystery," in *Vanity Fair*. XLVII (October, 1984), pp. 88-91.

Lovell, Mary S. *Straight On Till Morning*, 1987.

Markham, Beryl. *The Splendid Outcast: Beryl Markham's African Stories*, 1987. Edited by Mary S. Lovell.

Wells, Linton. Review in *Saturday Review of Literature*. XXV (June 27, 1942), p. 10.

Deanna Zitterkopf

WHAT'S TO BECOME OF THE BOY?
Or, Something to Do with Books

Author: Heinrich Böll (1917-1985)
Type of work: Memoir
Time of work: January 30, 1933 to February 6, 1937
Locale: Cologne, Germany
First published: Was soll aus dem Jungen bloss werden? Oder, Irgendwas mit Büchern, 1981 (English translation, 1984)

Principal personage:
HEINRICH BÖLL, a noted German novelist

Form and Content

What's to Become of the Boy? appeared in English translation only one year before the 1972 Nobel laureate's death. It was his first and only attempt to write a straight autobiography. Heinrich Böll had previously resisted pressures to write in that genre, believing that autobiographies had a natural inclination to distort the past by interpreting events with the benefit of hindsight.

The book is written in a relaxed, conversational style, much as if the reader were sitting across the table from Böll, listening to him reminisce about his adolescent years. It covers the last four years of Böll's formal education. Those years, from 1933 to 1937, parallel the first four years of Nazi rule in Germany. Böll portrays that time against the gloomy backdrop of the Nazi Party's consolidation of its control over German society.

Böll clearly has not done any research into his past, nor is the narrative based upon any diaries, journals, or other documents. Böll is simply recalling, remembering, or reminiscing. Indeed, at the beginning of the book he warns the reader: "All this happened forty-eight to forty-four years ago, and I have no notes or jottings to resort to. . . . I am no longer sure of how some of my personal experiences synchronize with historical events."

Böll gives several examples of his faulty memory. All of them are meant to impress upon the reader that Böll's purpose is not merely to provide a sort of history of the young Heinrich Böll and his times but rather to re-create the mood of those four years as he felt and experienced it. "The mood and the situation I can vouch for, also the facts bound up with the moods and situations," writes Böll, "but, confronted with verifiable historical facts, I cannot vouch for the synchronization."

The conversational style of the book is evident in its format. It is a brief narrative, really only an extended essay. The paperback edition is only eighty-two pages long, approximately nineteen thousand words. There is no introduction or preface. The book simply begins with the statement, "On January 30, 1933, I was fifteen years and six weeks old." From that inauspicious beginning, Böll's memories flow forth unbroken until a date four years later, when he observes that he celebrated passing his final exams by drinking a glass of beer in a nearby tavern. There are no chapter headings, although the narrative is divided into eighteen numbered sections. There is no obvious reason for the subdivisions, unless it is to provide the reader with convenient points at which to stop reading and take a break.

Because the narrative is not based upon any research or documentation and because it does not attempt to give a history of the times, there are no index, bibliography, or footnotes. Also, there are no appendices or other attempts to place the memoir in its historical perspective. The account simply stops, without any conclusion. It is as if Böll, having finished reminiscing, got up from the table and left, leaving his audience to assign whatever meaning they wish to the memories he has just shared with them.

Analysis

Heinrich Böll of *What's to Become of the Boy?* was a young man in his mid- to late teens living something of a carefree, bohemian life in Cologne. As he watched the Nazis come to power and extend their control over every aspect of society, he, like his family, became preoccupied with surviving the Nazi tenure. At first, they believed that the Nazis would soon pass away like other short-lived governments before them. It soon became apparent, however, that the Nazis would remain in power. Böll found a refuge in school—a Roman Catholic school, for he came from a middle-class Catholic family. Although he believed that he learned more from the "school of the streets," he understood clearly that so long as he remained enrolled in school he could avoid being "organized" (compelled to join some Nazi organization). Catholic schools still enjoyed a measure of independence during the late 1930's, which worked to Böll's advantage. His teachers suffered more from what Böll called the "Hindenburg blindness," the unquestioning patriotism of the interwar era, than from any genuine Nazi sympathies.

Böll developed a love-hate relationship with the Catholic church during those years. Indeed, anticlericalism remained a constant theme in his writings after the war. Nevertheless, he did not formally leave the Catholic church until 1976; even then his action was more a rejection of institutionalized middle-class Catholicism than a rejection of Christianity. Most critics agree that Böll remained a moral Christian throughout his life.

Böll's anticlericalism arose from his belief that the Catholic church's actions during the Nazi era were morally bankrupt and opportunistic. Prior to 1933, the Church in Germany had been a focal point of resistance to Nazism. The Nazi Party made its least electoral gains in areas that were predominantly Catholic. In 1933, after Adolf Hitler came to power, the Church, however, signed a covenant with the Nazi government, making peace with it and according the Nazis their first major international recognition.

The Bölls saw the move as a betrayal by the church establishment. Heinrich Böll recalls that some of his family, himself included, considered leaving the Church in protest; yet they did not. After the March, 1933, elections, it had become fashionable for many Germans to leave the Church and join the Nazi Party. The Bölls chose not to leave the Church for fear that such action "might have been misconstrued as homage to the Nazis" rather than as a protest of the church hierarchy's moral failure.

Throughout the book there is a mood of despair, an apathetic tendency to surrender to forces beyond one's control. Böll writes that he found the Church "insufferable" and "disgusting." Yet he was forced by circumstances not only to remain in the Church but also to identify with it openly. Not only did he remain in his Catholic school, because "*that* school," being Catholic, was an effective "hiding place," but also he continued to wear in his lapel the insignia of the Catholic Youth Movement. He did so, he says, not out of any genuine sentiment for the movement, or what it stood for, but because it was a way of defying the Nazis with a minimum of risk to himself.

Böll did not encounter any real persecution because of his quiet protests. From time to time, he had an argument with a classmate or a teacher, but no one ever tried to convert him. He could make "occasional flippant remarks about Hitler and other Nazi bigwigs," and no one ever reported him. Indeed, the school's authorities made it easy for him to avoid openly supporting the Nazis. For example, he was allowed to clean the school library rather than participate in the weekly "National Day" exercises.

Böll's anticlericalism was linked to his antibourgeois bias, which in turn was linked to his family's inability to determine to which class it belonged. Böll recalls that they "were neither true lower middle class nor conscious proletarians, and we had a strong streak of the Bohemian." Their bohemianism caused them to loathe what they identified as middle-class values. Those values, they believed, characterized the Catholic church. Nevertheless, throughout the book one can see that Böll is troubled by the fact that his values, and those of his family, were also largely bourgeois.

The middle class is portrayed by Böll as apathetic, lacking the will to resist the Nazis. In a cowardly manner, they allowed themselves to be terrorized by Hermann Göring, a buffoonish figure who served as minister-president of Prussia during the years covered by Böll's memoir. Böll and his family limited their resistance to remaining practicing Catholics. They showed their sympathies by displaying only a small Nazi flag on compulsory flag days, but display it they did. And when it became necessary to make a further compromise in order to avoid persecution, Böll recalls that a family council was held, at which it was decided that his brother, Alois, would join the Storm Troopers.

Heinrich Böll and his family, like much of the German middle class, lacked the will to resist the Nazis openly, or for that matter, even to leave Germany. At one point, Böll says that he was too much of a coward to risk passive resistance by becoming a conscientious objector. He was well aware of "the mute, stony-faced men released from concentration camps, the idea of possible torture." As for emigrating, "such an idea was simply beyond the realm of our imagination."

What was the cause of the apathy, the moral paralysis, that dominated the Catholic church, the middle class, and even infected Böll and his family? Böll identifies it as the "Hindenburg blindness," using the term to characterize the outlook of the average, decent German. Like the principal of his school and his teachers, they tended to be World War I veterans, "patriotic, not nationalistic, certainly not Nazist." Like the Bölls, they wanted to survive the Nazi era. Unlike the Bölls, however, they sought refuge in an exaggerated patriotism.

The Hindenburg blindness emphasized service to the Fatherland, not to the Nazis. Böll insists, however, that many a decent, patriotic German schoolteacher helped, unwittingly perhaps, make possible Stalingrad and Auschwitz. In effect, school was preparing German youth for death, not life. Böll refused to learn for the sake of dying; thus, he turned to the school of the streets.

Often, the young Böll left his books home and wandered the streets of Cologne. He says that it was the "overriding bourgeois element," the Hindenburg blindness, of his teachers that drove him to the school of the streets. During the last three of the four years chronicled by the book, Böll actually went to school less than half the time. As he roamed the streets, he saw and heard evidence of the Nazis' new order. "Who," he asks, "was that woman screaming on Achter-Gässchen, who that man screaming on Landesberg-Strasse, who on Rosen-Strasse?" Those sounds, and the sight of bloodied towels, led him to conclude that it is in the streets that one learns the real lessons of life.

In the latter third of the narrative, which covers the last two years, 1936 and 1937, Böll notes that material survival became his family's main preoccupation. They moved to cheaper lodgings, took in a boarder, or "furnished gentleman," and sought whatever means possible to augment the meager family income. Economic problems, added to the ever-present Nazis, increased the feeling of gloom. Böll at one point looks ahead to inform the reader that the war eventually brought an end to the perpetual economic crisis by bringing with it a measure of prosperity. Nevertheless, it also increased the feeling of impending doom.

In the summer of 1936, Böll and his family began to take Pervitim, a stimulant that could be purchased over the counter at any local pharmacy. They used it to escape from the reality of their existence. It was cheaper than alcohol and "more spiritual." Böll admits that his mother, his older sister, and he himself became addicted to the drug. He was able to kick the habit during the war, when he could no longer obtain it.

As his graduation drew near, the family became anxious about his future. "What's to become of the boy?" was increasingly a matter of family concern. Someone, Böll cannot remember who, suggested that his future career should have "something to do with books." Perhaps he would take an interest in theology they hoped. The narrative ends with Böll's becoming an apprentice in a bookstore, one "not too big, and not even remotely Nazi."

Critical Context

Much of the significance of Heinrich Böll's *What's to Become of the Boy?* lies in the fact that it chronicles the author's life during those critical years when he formulated his political and social views—views which would later run through both his fiction and nonfiction. Those four years were also the years during which he decided that his life's career would have something to do with books.

In late 1945, after returning to Cologne from service in the army, Böll began writing novels, essays, and radio and stage plays. Most of his literary works were set in the Rhineland, often in the Cologne-Bonn area. They both chronicled and critiqued the resurrection of West Germany. His biting criticism of middle-class values, which he believed had survived the war and dominated the new Germany, won for him praise from Marxist critics and made his books the best-selling West German fiction in East Germany. In the Soviet Union and throughout the East European Communist bloc, he was the best-selling non-Soviet author.

Some critics questioned Böll's harsh portrayal of politicians, police, and the hierarchy of the Catholic church in postwar West Germany. Nevertheless, Böll remained the foe of every form of institutionalized power. In 1972, he openly campaigned on behalf of the Social Democratic Party, but later he became disillusioned with them.

Critics see much that is autobiographical in Böll's fictional works, but *What's to Become of the Boy?* was his only formal autobiography. Why did he choose to limit it to a four-year period? Perhaps he, too, thought that those were the crucial years for the development of his values. *What's to Become of the Boy?* is a key to the greater understanding and appreciation of the whole of Böll's literary output.

Sources for Further Study

Adams, Phoebe-Lou. Review in *The Atlantic*. CCLIV (November, 1984), p. 148.

Barnet, Andrea. Review in *Saturday Review*. X (November/December, 1984), p. 81.

Craig, Gordon A. "Childhood of a Social Critic," in *The New York Times Book Review*. LXXXIX (October 7, 1984), p. 3.

Lehman, David. "In the Shadow of the Nazis," in *Newsweek*. CIV (October 15, 1984), p. 100.

Paul R. Waibel

THE WHITE GODDESS
A Historical Grammar of Poetic Myth

Author: Robert Graves (1895-1985)
Type of work: Literary criticism
First published: 1948

Form and Content

Robert Graves is best known for his historical novels, but he insists that his real calling is poetry. In *The White Goddess*, Graves has written a dense, original narrative addressing several poetical concerns. First there is an analysis of Celtic poetry that is fairly straightforward literary criticism. In it, he focuses particularly on the Welsh epic *Hanes Taliesm*, which he shows to be a blend of Celtic, Christian, and classical mythology, with even a bit of Scandinavian lore added. He also attempts to uncover the pattern of lines. The poem, he believes, is pied—that is, consecutive lines do not necessarily refer to the same thing. Having established a coherent pattern, he then shows that the poem contains an alphabetic code that existed in several versions in Great Britain and Ireland before the introduction of the Latin alphabet. This system was used by the Druids to maintain their secrets.

Within the larger poem, there are smaller ones. Most famous is the tale of a battle of trees, but when the lines recounting this brawl are put together and the trees are associated with symbols, much more meaning can be ascertained. Further, an analysis of the poetry reveals a number of riddles which Graves attempts to resolve. The answers are references to the various mythologies from which the poet has drawn inspiration.

A second theme in *The White Goddess* is the decline in the quality of poetry since ancient times. The failure of modern poets, Graves argues, is the result of the decline in knowledge of myths. Before the modern era, there was a body of literature, including mythology such as the eighth century B.C. *Iliad* and *Odyssey*, which all educated individuals studied and knew well. The power of a poet's work came from invoking the images and symbols of this common heritage, which Graves personifies as the White Goddess. Thus, when a true poem is heard "the hairs stand on end, the eyes water, the throat is constricted, the skin crawls and a shiver runs down the spine."

Modern education has eliminated the common canon and diluted the myth, and attempts to regain that which has been lost are complicated by the efforts of the early poets to keep secret their lore, much of which was regarded as having magical powers. An Irish student seeking to become a master poet started by spending three years learning 150 cipher alphabets.

The final major theme, more personal, is a consideration of poetic inspiration. Graves uses the metaphor of devotion to the White Goddess to portray the obsession that he considers a necessity to a real poet. In mythology, the White Goddess represents a compendium of the various deities of Bronze Age peoples; these divinities had different names but similar rites, powers, and qualities. Emerging out of matriarchal societies, she represents woman as mother, lover, and destroyer. For the poet, she is the personal muse who inspires and praises yet never is satisfied, like the sexually insatiable woman. The best account of the Goddess in literature is to be found in *Metamorphoses* (c. 180-190) by Apuleius. Of the leading English poets, Graves believes only John Skelton and Ben Jonson had the qualities he thinks are required of a chief poet. The only other writer that comes close to the standard is William Blake.

Modern society, Graves argues, is not conducive to poetry. Its focus on domesticity and the workaday world leads to the submerging of the passion on which poetic inspiration feeds. The White Goddess, he says, "is the perpetual 'other woman,'" and modern women lead their male devotees into marital fidelity and commitment to fatherhood. Within this argument a subtheme emerges: the almost exclusively masculine gender of poets (Sappho is a rare exception). Inspiration, however, is equally exclusively feminine, and his rejection of homosexual love as a source of true poetry borders on the homophobic. In Graves's opinion, at least in this book, the central theme of poetry must be heterosexual love and passion.

The White Goddess was originally published in 1948. It contains twenty-four chapters plus, in later editions, a postscript. An enlarged edition in 1966 was the first to be published in the United States, and by 1987 the book was in its twentieth printing. Although the themes are mixed throughout the text, it starts with a relatively narrow focus on the Celtic poetic tradition and mythology and then broadens into a discussion of poetry and inspiration. The degree of erudition displayed by Graves is truly impressive and at times even intimidating.

Analysis

The questions addressed in *The White Goddess* are difficult indeed, but Graves tackles them with a will. It is ironic that he expresses such devotion to and spends such scholarly energy on poetry and yet is much better known for his prose than verse. His study of Celtic lore is comprehensive; while not all serious students of that tradition agree with his analysis of the poets' messages and techniques, his account is logical and persuasive.

The mix of mythological elements—Celtic, classical, and Christian—in the Welsh and Irish literature on which Graves focuses gives a sense of the transfer of ideas among cultures in the Hellenic and Roman eras. His accounts of the language and importance of poets and poetry in ancient Europe support his contention that the inspiration of the White Goddess has failed in modern times, when poetry is written and read mostly by academics. Despite the lack of formal scholarly apparatus, these sections are clearly the result of serious and in-depth study.

Much more speculative and personal are the sections in which Graves attempts to analyze poetic inspiration. Although his insistence that all serious poetry must be based on an interpretation of myth seems applicable to the Celtic tradition from which he draws most of his examples, it is nevertheless very limiting. There are many poets and critics who would argue that poetry may successfully address other themes and traditions. Indeed, Graves himself seems eventually to agree, for he praises in later writings poetry about nature written out of love for the subject.

The strictly structured sexual stereotypes in *The White Goddess* are his least defensible assertions. Graves is unyielding in his claim that poets are men and that they are inspired by women: "It is the imitation of male poetry that causes the false ring in the work of almost all women poets." He also derides the impact of domesticity and permanence in relationships as being destructive to poetic passion. Poetry, he seems to think, arises from an orgiastic frenzy compounded of sexual and blood lusts and expressed in the sacrificial rites of ancient peoples. Without the capacity to fantasize such ceremonies in all of their bloody horrors, no poet living in the ages since can come to grips with the real power of his craft.

Few other critics would go so far. Graves has rejected all but Romantic poetry, and while the passion of creativity does flare brightly among the Romantics, it is difficult to deny a writer of the stature of Alexander Pope the title of poet. Graves's emphasis on the roles of masculinity and femininity is also not widely accepted. While love is often the subject of the most powerful poetry, there is certainly no consensus that that love must be heterosexual. Nor would many students of poetry agree that women rarely if ever reach the heights of poetic skill. Emily Dickinson, Elizabeth Barrett Browning, Christina Rossetti, Sylvia Plath, and many other women have written poetry that is as respected as most of that produced by men. The sexual theme in *The White Goddess* seems to be mostly a quirk of Graves.

When he is analyzing "The Battle of the Trees," Graves's style is much like that of a very literate academic critic. He clearly loves his subject and enjoys writing about it, but real passion shows only as he begins to discuss the loss of myth in modern culture and the devotion to the White Goddess that he believes must inspire any true poet. When he writes of the power of the poet and of the very real sacrifices he must make to his deity, his prose flowers. Not only is it more expressive but it also begins to take on some of the rhythms of poetry.

Critical Context

The White Goddess is, in part, a work of literary criticism and is focused on a tradition that is not widely studied in the modern era. Graves has done useful scholarly work in his effort to explicate the text of the *Hanes Taliesm* and other Celtic poetry. Much research and thought went into this study. Such work is usually done by academics and rarely is written as well as this effort. He has offered interesting and stimulating interpretations, and his book makes a strong contribution to literary criticism.

The more personal sections of the book, in which Graves discusses the qualities of poetic inspiration, are stimulating and will be of interest to those seeking either an inspiration of their own or an understanding of the motivation of other writers. His interpretations are unorthodox but that makes them the more valuable to those looking for their own muses. These sections are also important for what they reveal about Graves, though his standing as a lesser poet may call into question the validity of his speculations on what makes a great one. Perhaps, however, one does not have to achieve great enlightenment to recognize its qualities.

Sources for Further Study

Enright, D. J. *Robert Graves and the Decline of Modernism*, 1960.

Hoffman, Daniel. *Barbarous Knowledge: Myth in the Poetry of Yeats, Graves, and Muir*, 1967.

Kirkham, Michael. *The Poetry of Robert Graves*, 1969.

Seymour-Smith, Martin. *Robert Graves: His Life and Work*, 1983.

Snipes, Katherine. *Robert Graves*, 1979.

Vickery, John B. *Robert Graves and "The White Goddess,"* 1972.

Fred R. van Hartesveldt

WILL'S BOY, SOLO, and A CLOAK OF LIGHT

Author: Wright Morris (1910-   )
Type of work: Memoir
Time of work: 1910-1960
Locale: Omaha, Chicago, Paris, Austria, and Italy
First published: Will's Boy: A Memoir, 1981; *Solo: An American Dreamer in Europe, 1933-1934*, 1983; *A Cloak of Light: Writing My Life*, 1985

> Principal personages:
> WRIGHT MORRIS, a novelist
> WILL MORRIS, his father
> JO KANTOR, Wright's second wife

Form and Content

The two major studies of Wright Morris' work, David Madden's *Wright Morris* (1964) and G. B. Crump's *The Novels of Wright Morris: A Critical Interpretation* (1978), begin with similar statements of puzzlement over the reading public's neglect of this writer. Morris' more than thirty volumes, of which his novels represent more than half, include phototexts, essays, short stories, and memoirs. Despite having won both the National Book Award and the American Book Award, Morris had not by the beginning of the 1980's attracted a sufficient following to warrant the reprinting by commercial presses of even his most ambitious novels. Nevertheless, the decision by the University of Nebraska Press to reprint his work, plus Morris' continued productivity and the appearance in the 1980's of more than half a dozen stories in *The New Yorker*, has resulted in a modest renaissance of interest.

Morris' minimalist approach and understanding of human emotions raised a number of questions, fair or not, about Morris himself and about his intentions as a writer of fiction. A typical reservation was that of Alfred Kazin: Despite Morris' "many symbols, his showy intentions, his pointed and hinted significances," the novels were "without the breath and extension of life." The seeming detachment of Morris' narrators from their material, and of his characters from their lives and from one another, echoed for many readers the cool geometry of the peopleless photographs of Great Plains settings in *The Inhabitants* (1946) and *The Home Place* (1948). The appearance in his eighth decade of the memoirs *Will's Boy, Solo,* and *A Cloak of Light* answers many questions about Morris as a man and a writer, and reinforces his image as a detached observer of human existence, including his own, as well as an ironic humor which accompanies that detachment.

The three volumes cover the period between Morris' birth in Nebraska in 1910 to the end of the summer of 1960, when he is about to begin a new life in California with his second wife, Jo Kantor. *Will's Boy* emphasizes his youthful years in Nebraska and later in Chicago, concluding during his third year at Pomona College. *Solo,* subtitled *An American Dreamer in Europe, 1933-1934,* recounts a *Wanderjahr* spent mainly in Austria and Italy. *A Cloak of Light* deals with Morris' years of struggle to support himself, develop as a writer, and find himself as a man. Although all three volumes, especially the more expansive first and third, use the vignette as their basic structural unit, each is a unique mixture of thematic emphases.

Will's Boy, a slender two hundred pages long, possesses the most evenly flowing chronology (though it seldom refers to specific dates, being a product of recollection rather than of research), the clearest preoccupation with recounting family history, the most humor, and the warmest tone. It contains many examples of Morris as storyteller: how on a crowded baseball field he failed to get Babe Ruth's autograph but managed to come away with the back pocket of Ruth's Yankee uniform; how as a young adolescent in Chicago he received a ceremonial kiss from a stranger who turned out to be Queen Marie of Romania; how he discovered that his former stepmother was a well-advertised hula dancer at the Gaity Theatre. The book's central irony is that though his mother died a few days after his birth and his father neglected him for various women and failed business ventures, Morris reached age seventeen with "abundant optimism," perhaps the unwitting gift of his father, whose inexhaustible scheming inspired the creation of the title character of *My Uncle Dudley* (1942). Nevertheless, the dominant fact of Morris' childhood was loneliness.

Remembering his early life is a solitary task. His infrequent references to dates reflects Morris' own uncertainty about the chronology: An only child and virtually an orphan, he has no family scrapbooks to consult or other minds with which to compare memories. Because he was shunted to so many different people in so many different places, physical movement was the only constant of his young life; it was not until his high school years in Chicago that he could impose some order and meet people who could guide and inspire him. Not coincidentally, it was here that he discovered his interest in art. To show the proximity of his life and art, Morris develops a striking, self-referential technique: He interrupts the narrative by inserting numerous italicized quotations from his published work (especially his novels) to show how important the dislocations of his youth became as inspirations for his artistic vision of life as journeys, brief relationships, and guarded emotions.

Solo—which might have been subtitled "Europe on a Dollar a Day"—in 196 pages portrays a somewhat more self-aware protagonist, but like *Will's Boy* it emphasizes movement and the picaresque view. The basic structure of the narrative follows the travel of Morris the picaro from the United States to Paris, Austria, Italy, Paris, and back to the United States. Changes in time exceed those of geography: From the self-congratulatory optimism of Chicago's 1933 Century of Progress exposition, Morris traveled to Monsieur Deleglise's castle, Schloss Ranna; there medieval routines were far older than the Hopi hat and cigar-store Indian the proprietor valued as emblems of the primitive. Nearly half the narrative describes Morris' winter at Schloss Ranna, and most of the rest of his tour through Italy with a fellow student from Pomona whom he barely knew. Of the three volumes, this one conveys the clearest sense of time: Seasons determine movement. Its first six chapters show an innocent abroad, an escapee from his own life, a young man who jokes with future victims about the coming war. The seventh ironically portrays a "young panhandler" in Paris who deliberately spends his passage money and begs at the American embassy for a free ticket home, who works in the pornographic book racket, who is told by a Spanish dancer that he is "a person of good character," an idea he has never doubted.

A Cloak of Light is the most ambitious and far-reaching of the three volumes. At 306 pages, it is more than half again as long as either *Will's Boy* or *Solo*. Its foreword, coda, two sections of family photographs, italicized quotations from Morris' fiction as well as from the previous volumes of memoirs, and almost three full decades of adult experiences convey the growth of a callow man into a mature one. The topics emphasized are those which shape an adult life: the finding of a spouse, relationships with in-laws, searching for a vocation, and making a living. There is considerable personal success during these years: several Guggenheim fellowships, a National Book Award, invitations to teach and lecture. These personal subjects, however, do not bring with them a sustained sense of intimacy. Morris notes that Catherine Drinker Bowen took offense at "my reluctance to share what I considered my private life," and he gives his readers no closer look at the private man. The narrative once again is made up of brief vignettes, usually no more than a page or two in length: a host of character sketches ranging from Indian chamber maids and village auto mechanics in Mexico to Saul Bellow, Delmore Schwartz, Robert Frost, and Loren Eiseley. The only systematically portrayed character is Morris' second wife, Jo, who dominates the last fifth of the narrative. The narrator's transformation is striking; the excitement of love and a truly intimate human connection enter the narrative for the first time just as Morris claims they first entered his life.

Analysis

Morris recalls at the beginning of *A Cloak of Light* that when he returned from Europe at the age of twenty-four, determined to be a writer, his intention was to draw upon the expatriate adventures he had sought and enjoyed. He found instead that native material, especially from his childhood in Nebraska, dominated his thoughts. The style in which this material appeared on his manuscript pages emphasized compactness, simplicity of language, and the specific in time and place: "Time had not actually stopped, but the movements were slow enough to be photographed. The scene had the characteristics of a still life." It is not coincidental that his early work emphasized photography and prose, leading to *The Inhabitants* and *The Home Place*. This early preoccupation with visual qualities—texture, surface detail, arrangement—has continued to influence Morris' work throughout his career and characterizes *Will's Boy*, *Solo*, and *A Cloak of Light*. Morris does not seek to demonstrate a grand plan for his life, or a sense of steady progression toward some generalization about the American Self, the American Novelist, and the like. These volumes might best be regarded as a series of vignettes whose course is dictated by accident as often as by design. The Morris who spent so much of his early years without much guidance refuses to write about his life as if plot were its essence. Surprise and puzzlement share equal billing with insight and comprehension.

Readers who look for a tight weave of event and commentary will find in the memoirs as in the fiction a lack of overt editorializing. The surface is the message. Above all, the reader will be struck by the absence of psychoanalytic reflection and speculation: Although there are abundant personal histories that invite such treatment, Morris indulges only once, guessing that his first wife (who is never named in the text) had a need for the companionship of older women because her relationship with her mother had never been satisfactory. Though Morris did not become a Europe-steeped writer in the mode of Ernest Hemingway or F. Scott Fitzgerald, his emphasis upon the exact rendering of names, streets, places, and other concrete particulars results in an impression sometimes similar to Hemingway's: Morris' method discredits the habit of abstraction.

Morris' most general and enduring preoccupation is with epistemology: How does one know and with what confidence? Here the distinction between surface and meaning makes itself felt, for the picture created by memory has an elusive quality:

> If I attempt to distinguish between fiction and memory, and press my nose to memory's glass to see more clearly, the remembered image grows more illusive, like the details in a Pointillist painting. . . . In this defect of memory do we have the emergence of imagination? . . . Precisely where memory is frail and emotion is strong, imagination takes fire.

The role of emotion is key, though authorial emotion is not in most of Morris' narratives a subject for overt discussion and some emotions, such as anger, are not even implied. Nevertheless, to see that for Morris the absence of human beings in a photograph of a human habitation makes the human presence all the more powerfully felt is to understand an important feature of his method and to appreciate the subtlety of his implications. He wrote in *A Cloak of Light* that the ideal reader has the "ability to read the book the author believed he had written," that is, the ability to intuit the emotion within the arrangement of particulars. Even so, Morris himself promises no certainty, for memory, the image-maker at the start of the process, cannot be exact. In *Solo*, Morris punctuates his description of an Austrian acquaintance, Hermann Unger: "If I pause here to consider what I have just written, to what extent is it true to what I remember? To what extent is what I remember true to Hermann? [Hermann himself acted] as if he privately had his doubts that he was the person he appeared to be in public." For the observer, the task is no easier. While Morris was making a tour of the South, he became aware that he was seen as a "Northern snooper out to discredit" the region, and in that troubled state of mind he tried to analyze a possible subject, a house:

> Was it a portrait, or a caricature? Did it reveal a state of soul or a state of abuse? I could see now one, now the other, by merely blinking. What was there to be seen was

in the eye of the beholder. . . . It would be weeks before I saw the negative, and many
months would pass before I made a print of what I had seen on the ground glass.
Would that image restore my original impressions, or would they be replaced by
others?

The connection with writing is direct, for Morris regards writing as the process of
making images the mind only incompletely remembers. All is problematic: The
writer struggles to create an image to slow time and flux to a standstill, to embody
intentions and emotions, and the reader struggles to find those intentions and
emotions.

This situation reflects another of his concerns—human separateness. *Will's Boy*
chronicles well the essence of life as he sees it: real human loss whose only compensation is imaginary gain. Human separateness was first embodied for him by his
father, one of the most isolated of men, who becomes the model for lonely
Will Brady in *The Works of Love* (1952). Morris himself admits to being by temperament an isolated person: "I do not take the trouble, in the interests of fraternity,
to go out of my way." Until Jo arrives for the final fifty pages of *A Cloak of Light*,
there are few vignettes which exemplify real human felicity. The sequence of Will
Morris' marriages and affairs and that of his son's early adult infatuations—a taste
for rich girls echoes his father's third marriage, to the dumpy Mrs. Van Meer—hint
that the young Wright had no image of felicity to pursue. There is much evidence
that Morris still views self-revealing friendship, and the Whitmanesque view of
camaraderie, as deeply suspect. In *Solo*, he likens a preference for "the outward
and open rather than the inward and private" to the German longing for the blond, a
vision of human bliss that must be paid for in blood.

The goal of human connectedness, while illusive and perhaps even dangerous in
the social intercourse of individuals, nevertheless seems for Morris to be the purpose of art; it is best illustrated not by individual relationships, but by what Morris
calls "the vernacular structures of American life," the anima contained in the
objects which are built and inhabited. It is a concept Morris early in his artistic life
borrowed from Henry David Thoreau, whom he discovered while living in a pond-
side cabin one Connecticut winter. In the early phototext volumes, he presents
structures as geometric shapes against empty skies or as objects from interiors
largely cut out by the frame of the photograph. Similarly, the background of the
human relationships portrayed in the memoirs is free of almost all emotional
coloration: contemporary history and politics—national, international, and sexual—and the generalizations that make them consistent and comprehensible in
retrospect. The Wright Morris of these memoirs never gets angry, never raises his
voice in celebration or rage. The same seems true of those among whom he lives.
He follows the example of his friend and defender Granville Hicks, whose autobiography, *Part of the Truth* (1965), deemphasizes emotional life so that other truths
can emerge. In compensation for this vision of separateness, Morris in *Will's Boy*
and *A Cloak of Light* suggests that the structures of power in the United States

expand the distances between individuals and that the vernacular structures are to be found in the byways. The dominant image of authority in these volumes, whether it be the Omaha police arresting his foster father or Charles Scribner refusing to make a cash advance, is one of indifference. The dominant image of the vernacular is some form of family, ironically not his own except for the few meetings with his mother's people in Idaho. At a North Carolina conclave of poor whites, Morris discovers anima where he least expected it, and it is beyond his ability to capture: Intimate sympathy, one of the main structures to which Morris' texts attest, derives its existence from an imaginative response having in Morris' case more to do with rural economics than with region, ancestry, sophistication, education, or other common measures. "Hardship," he wrote in another context, "seemed to me indispensable to what I was feeling. There was something in hardship that I valued." This explains why his fiction, though it portrays so many blighted lives and touches by implication many social themes, does not concern itself with the amelioration of those conditions. The same can be said of these memoirs. He names no presidents, political movements, or personal responses to the problems of his time; political connections are coincidental, as in his comment that he signed the contract for *My Uncle Dudley* on the day Pearl Harbor was attacked.

Because Morris from the beginning of his career chose subjects indicative of his regional roots, questions of landscape and history carry significant weight. Many of his reflexes as an outsider seem traceable to his regional identity, but Morris implies that California more than Nebraska fueled his creative impulses. From Omaha he had looked toward Chicago; later, even before he saw California, it had come to seem a "sanctuary of . . . great expectations," while "the pull of the West, a convenient illusion for any duffer with a yen for flight, had become a magnet for me with the discovery of California." Nebraska seems to represent the hardship Morris found necessary as a catalyst: It made him a dreamer who "lacked a transcendent object." It also habituated him to space and change and helped create a writer whose fiction and memoirs depend for their energy upon a certain kind of open landscape unchanged by what may be called the modern world.

The United States has always favored, Morris asserts, "not a writer in the bookish sense at all, but one of great natural forces." Nevertheless, a distinction must be made between the place of inspiration and the art actually produced: Morris' fiction and his memoirs are not ultimately concerned with that landscape even if they draw inspiration from the illusion of freedom it offers. As he notes, "Let the writer come from the plains, if he must, but be smart enough to leave them behind him."

Of history, Morris is also wary: "The past cast its spell over the present" for major American writers, an affliction for all but William Faulkner. For others—and this has long been a problem for writers of a region as history-poor as the West— the past became "a nostalgic myth . . . that . . . cripple[d] the imagination," a situation perhaps better than what Morris sees as its successor, wherein "the role of nostalgia in our literature has dwindled as our great expectations have diminished." The developing writer Morris portrays in these memoirs had nothing about which to be nostalgic: The mobility and spaciousness of his youth was extended by pluck, luck, and three Guggenheim fellowships well into an adulthood which afforded college teaching positions if not bountiful book sales. The memoirs focus upon a mostly solitary male who keeps moving—to Mexico and California and Venice— who avoids the lethal events of midcentury history, and who in the view of some readers has not sufficiently acknowledged the importance of his never-named first wife.

The final and surely inevitable theme of an autobiographical project of such scope is the loss of innocence. For a writer as private as Morris, this is also the most personally revealing subject. Like all of his other themes, it appears in scattered and brief narrative moments and affords neither definitive statements nor a sense of progression toward enlightenment. There are no epiphanies, but often in the most relevant situations—most often romantic—there is the humor of the books' clearest self-assessments: "It hadn't even crossed my mind, until her mother pointed it out, that Joan [Harwood] already had most of the things I planned to give her." Of the theme of artistic maturity, the reader will find that Morris does not know what constitutes the creative act. He can speak of himself only as "seated with pen and paper, my mind a blank until I [begin] to write."

Critical Context

Readers of the modern phenomenon of autobiography-as-rebuttal who are used to authorial self-inflation and self-justification will find Morris' volumes quite different. Morris has no sense of himself as a figure of great importance. He has always been something of an enigma because of the quiet eccentricity of his fiction; whereas he is willing to answer basic questions about himself, the genesis and place of composition of his various major works, the real-life models for some of his protagonists, and his favorite settings and people, he remains a private individual. He tells no tales on others, either: His vignettes of fellow literary figures such as Robert Frost, Saul Bellow, Delmore Schwartz, Leon Howard, Kitty Bowen, and others are sometimes ironic but never unkind. The dominant presence in the three volumes is a man who feels lucky with his life and his accomplishments, who makes no great claims for himself and has no reason to snipe at anyone. There is a kind of modesty throughout the narratives, as if to assert—as his phototexts do— that a careful look will reveal the depth and signficance of the common man's experience.

To the tradition of contemporary writing from the American West, these volumes—especially *Will's Boy* and *A Cloak of Light*—will be distinguished additions because they work so hard to overcome the merely regional. In addition to giving a skillful picture of growing up on the plains in the early part of this century, Morris also makes it clear that a writer can and must escape the limitations of family, region, and history. He transcends the image of the Western writer tied to geography and hampered by lack of sophistication. He does not strike out against the dominant East and its ignorance of and condescension to the West. Instead, the summary in *A Cloak of Light* of the ideas in his critical study *The Territory Ahead* (1958) attempts to integrate all American writing in a cultural context whose largest forces are felt by writers from all regions. Of all Western writers, only Wallace Stegner and Wright Morris have made such serious use, without apology, of Western experience.

Sources for Further Study

Abbey, Edward. Review of *A Cloak of Light* in *The New York Times Book Review.* XC (February 17, 1985), p. 9.

Allen, Bruce. Review of *A Cloak of Light* in *The Christian Science Monitor.* February 28, 1985, p. 20.

Crump, G. B. *The Novels of Wright Morris: A Critical Interpretation*, 1978.

Knoll, Robert E., ed. *Conversations with Wright Morris: Critical Views and Responses*, 1977.

Madden, David. *Wright Morris*, 1964.

Simon, Linda. Review of *A Cloak of Light* in *Library Journal.* CIX (December, 1984), p. 2272.

Kerry Ahearn

WIT AND ITS RELATION TO THE UNCONSCIOUS

Author: Sigmund Freud (1856-1939)
Type of work: Psychology
First published: Der Witz und seine Beziehung zum Unbewussten, 1905 (English
translation, 1916)

Form and Content

Sigmund Freud's specific plans for a psychoanalytic study of wit and verbal
humor probably began when his friend and confidant Wilhelm Fliess, after reading
the proofs of *Die Traumdeutung* (1900; *The Interpretation of Dreams*, 1913), complained that the dreams in the book were too full of jokes. It is probable, however,
that Freud had considered the importance of jokes even before the publication of the
dream book. In an earlier letter to Fliess, Freud had mentioned that he had been putting together a collection of Jewish anecdotes and humorous stories; it was a form
to which he was naturally drawn because of his father's fascination with such tales.

Like *The Interpretation of Dreams*, Freud's *Wit and Its Relation to the Unconscious* (which has also been translated as *Jokes and Their Relation to the Unconscious*) is a classic example of his ability to perceive the psychological significance
of those aspects of human life which many people ignore as trivial, common, or
obvious. The book combines formal scholarly research with Freud's unrelenting,
although often informal, Socratic technique of analyzing data and formulating hypotheses, which are then either dismissed for lack of clarity or polished until
theoretically and empirically sound. Thus, the book often reads more like a recapitulation of Freud's thought processes than a flat statement of the conclusions
themselves.

The study is divided into three major sections: an analytic part which focuses on
the technique of making jokes and their purposes; a synthetic part which deals with
both the origins of jokes in human pleasure and their social motives; and a theoretical part which considers the relation of jokes to dreams and the unconscious and
shows how jokes are related to the broader area of the comic. As is typical of a
formal academic study, the work also includes a brief review of previous research
on wit and humor as well as a bibliography of works consulted and cited.

Although the book is characterized by Freud's lucid and nontechnical style, it has
created more of a translation problem than any of his other works because he is
more concerned with the form of the phenomenon he is studying than usual.
Because so many jokes depend on the play of language and create their impact as a
result of a self-conscious use of words, it is difficult to translate the jokes Freud
cites as examples without losing the very language play that made them jokes in the
first place. Thus, much of what drew Freud's attention to the examples he uses may
be lost on the English-language reader. As a result, translators and commentators
have frequently resorted to English equivalents of the jokes Freud cites. This problem of translation, which makes many of Freud's examples seem ill-suited to their

purpose, may account for this work's relative lack of impact, in spite of the fact that it is perhaps the most ambitious study Freud ever attempted on issues that involve a psychoanalytic approach to aesthetics.

Analysis

The relationship of the study of jokes to a general study of aesthetics can be seen in Freud's opening review of the previous literature. He particularly calls attention to the philosophers Kuno Fischer and Theodor Lipps, who focused on the "playful" nature of jokes and thus on their relationship to the aesthetic freedom to contemplate things "playfully." He also notes that the novelist Jean Paul suggested that jokes often deal with the similarity between dissimilar things, thus linking jokes to the metaphoric process whereby alien ideas are yoked, sometimes violently, together. Finally, Freud notes that both Paul and Lipps comment on the brevity of jokes and the way they often reveal something previously concealed by not saying the thing outright, thus linking jokes to a process similar to that which underlies lyric poetry. It is clear, therefore, that Freud knew from the beginning of his study that the secret of jokes is related to the means by which artworks are both created and appreciated.

As in his study of dreams, Freud grounds his work in a consideration of technique. He begins by using a joke already cited by Lipps from the German author Heinrich Heine. A lottery agent named Hirsch-Hyacinth boasts to Heine of his relations with the very wealthy Baron Rothschild; the lottery agent is particularly proud that Rothschild treats him as his equal, treats him quite "famillionairely." What makes this remark a joke, Freud says, lies not in the thought but in its form, particularly in its creating a composite word out of the words "familiar" and "millionaire."

The technique, according to Freud, who uses the terms he developed earlier in the study of dreams, is a "condensation" of the two words; a "substitution" of the new condensed word then takes place. He then asks whether this process is in every joke and is thus characteristic of the form. Freud immediately finds other aspects of jokes — double meanings, plays on words, and the confusion of metaphorical and literal meanings of words — which he asserts are either special cases of condensation or cases of condensation without substitute formation. Having determined that the tendency toward condensation and economy is the most general attribute of jokes, he then asks from where this tendency comes, what it signifies, and how the pleasure of a joke derives from it.

Next, he moves to a joke that reflects a different technique. Two Jews meet in a bathhouse. When one asks the other if he has taken a bath, the response is, "Is there one missing?" The technique here, Freud says, again using a term from his study of dreams, is "displacement," for the joke depends on the displacement of the emphasis from the word "bath" to the word "taken." The jokes of displacement use the techniques of faulty reasoning, absurdity, indirect representation, and representation by an opposite.

Freud makes a distinction between jokes that are innocent and have no purpose other than to give pleasure and those that have an ulterior motive. There are only two kinds of these so-called tendentious jokes—hostile jokes and obscene jokes. A person who laughs at obscene jokes, according to Freud, is laughing as if at an act of sexual aggression; thus, the joke makes it possible to tolerate an otherwise intolerable action. Similarly, hostile jokes make it possible to commit an aggressive act under the guise of satire.

In spite of the relevance of this discussion of jokes to the study of artistic structures in general, however, the heart of *Wit and Its Relation to the Unconscious* is Freud's analysis of the origin of jokes in the mechanism of pleasure; Freud theorizes that the amount of pleasure a joke gives is proportional to the amount of psychic energy saved by the condensation. For example, by linking two disparate ideas the joke creates a short circuit and thus creates an economy in one's train of thought, much the way a metaphor does.

According to Freud, jokes evolve in three stages. First, there is the child's pleasure in verbal play, a pleasure the child has when it hears or utters strings of words similar in sound but with no other relationships. Second, there is the movement to jest, when the intellect assumes a meaning for the joke—even though the meaning is of no consequence—in order to justify the pleasure the joke gives. Finally, there is the tendentious joke, which Freud defines as a joke with a definite purpose, either hostile or obscene.

Generally speaking, the tendentious joke requires the presence of three people— the one who makes the joke, the one who is the object of the joke, and the hearer of the joke. The tendentious joke is most clearly represented in the dirty joke, according to Freud, for the kind of hostile assault it makes on women would not be tolerated in any other form. Thus, so-called smutty jokes make possible the satisfaction of an instinct that would be otherwise repressed.

In the final section of the study, Freud shifts from a discussion of technique or motive to one of the relation of jokes to dreams and thus to the unconscious. In order to show this relationship Freud reviews the basic premise of *The Interpretation of Dreams*: The frequently absurd "manifest content" of dreams can be understood once one understands the transforming process by which a repressed "latent content" is converted into the dream. The methods of what Freud calls "dream work" are primarily those of condensation and displacement.

Freud theorizes that jokes are developed play, not the expression of repressed wishes as dreams are. Jokes allow the adult to return to the kind of thinking characteristic of childhood. The basic assumption is that children enjoy the pure nonsense of playing with words, but adults are forced to give up this pleasure and use words in a purely denotative way. The only way to enjoy the forbidden childhood pleasure once again is to take an idea to the point of expression and then give it over to unconscious revision. The outcome is at once foolish and meaningful; this compromise is what is called wit.

Nothing is more characteristic of jokes, according to Freud, than this double-sidedness; thanks to the ambiguity of words, the childish play can be made allowable in jests or considered sensible in jokes. Even as the child in the jokester is pleased by the nonsense, the adult in him is satisfied by the meaning. The laughter experienced at the joke or witticism is a release of the energy that previously was used to inhibit or repress the childish desire for nonsense.

In the final chapter of the book, Freud relates jokes to the broader issue of the comic. Here he develops a notion of what he calls "ideational mimetics," that is, the comic nature of repeating or copying an observed action but with an often-comic difference. Examples range from pantomime, which Freud calls the most primitive form of mimetics, to such forms as caricature, parody, and travesty. Freud suggests that the reason one laughs after recognizing that something has been imitated in an exaggerated way derives from the realization of the discrepancy between the two phenomena. Freud's consideration of the comic, a few critics have suggested, is more relevant to the study of art than to his study of jokes: The comic operates in the realm of the preconscious, as art does, rather than in the realm of the unconscious, as do jokes.

Critical Context

Wit and Its Relation to the Unconscious is not one of Freud's most famous or influential books. It is considered a minor contribution compared to the epoch-making *The Interpretation of Dreams*, although it appeared shortly after the famous dream book and makes use of many of the same discoveries. Ernest Jones, one of Freud's biographers, says that *Wit and Its Relation to the Unconscious* is perhaps the least known of Freud's works. Freud claimed, however, that his study of jokes was the first example of the application of psychoanalytic thinking to the issues of aesthetics, and several critics, including Ernst Kris in *Psychoanalytic Explorations in Art* (1952), have argued that it is the model for anyone who wishes to focus on artistic creation along Freudian lines.

In spite of the scope of this study, it has not carried the impact of such less ambitious but seemingly more suggestive studies as "The Relation of the Poet to Day-Dreaming" and "The 'Uncanny.'" Even the relatively esoteric "The Antithetical Sense of Primal Words" has received more consideration, at least by structuralist critics, than *Wit and Its Relation to the Unconscious*.

Those critics and psychoanalysts who have made the most of Freud's joke theories, although with varying degrees of success, are the famous art critic and historian E. H. Gombrich, the psychoanalyst Silvano Arieti, and the literary critic Norman Holland. Gombrich, in a brief essay in 1966, suggested that the joke book provided the basis of a theory of artistic form applicable to modern art, particularly in its focus on form rather than content. Arieti, in a discussion of creativity in 1976, used Freud's study of jokes as an important element of his theories about art. Norman Holland, the most influential of the new Freudian literary critics, based his theory of literature as transformation on Freud's study of jokes.

These studies, however, are minimal in comparison to the many studies which have derived from Freud's other works. In addition, none of them has been completely successful in adapting Freud's theories of wit to a theory about the nature of the artist's creativity or the nature of the reader's response. Too often, attempted explanations of such basic aesthetic processes have the same effect as the attempt to explain a joke; they never quite seem to match in sophistication the sensed complexity of the experience.

Perhaps the most profitable area in which Freud's theories of jokes may yet make a contribution is in the linguistic study of figurative language. It has been pointed out by more than one theorist that the dual process of condensation and displacement which Freud finds characteristic of the structure of jokes corresponds to the means by which human beings construct meaning or respond to meaning in any area of symbolic language—the principles of substitution and combination, which are equivalent, respectively, to the figurative tropes of metonymy (displacement) and metaphor (condensation). In this area, the underlying assumption of Freud's book—that the study of such obvious matters as jokes may stimulate revelations in other areas of human understanding—may yet bear unsuspected fruit.

Sources for Further Study
Arieti, Silvano. *Creativity: The Magic Synthesis*, 1976.
Brenner, Charles. *Elementary Textbook of Psychoanalysis*, 1955.
Gombrich, E. H. "Freud's Aesthetics," in *Literature and Psychoanalysis*, 1983. Edited by Edith Kurzweil and William Phillips.
Holland, Norman. *The Dynamics of Literary Response*, 1968.
Kris, Ernst. *Psychoanalytic Explorations in Art*, 1952.
Lucas, F. L. *Literature and Psychology*, 1951.
Spector, Jack J. *The Aesthetics of Freud: A Study in Psychoanalysis and Art*, 1972.

Charles E. May

THE WOMAN WARRIOR
Memoirs of a Girlhood Among Ghosts

Author: Maxine Hong Kingston (1940-   )
Type of work: Autobiography
Time of work: From the late nineteenth century to the 1970's
Locale: California and the China of myth and memory
First published: 1976

> *Principal personages:*
> MAXINE HONG KINGSTON, the author and narrator
> NO NAME WOMAN, Kingston's aunt, who commits suicide in
>   China after bearing an illegitimate child
> THE WOMAN WARRIOR, a dream figure representing the author
> BRAVE ORCHID, Kingston's mother
> MOON ORCHID, another of Kingston's aunts

Form and Content

   The Woman Warrior is a blend of autobiographical material about the second-generation Chinese-American author and the myths and dreams that constitute her psychic reality. By fusing fact and imagination, Maxine Hong Kingston works toward answers to the central problem articulated at the beginning of the book. This problem is

> to figure out how the invisible world the emigrants built around our childhoods fit in
> solid America. . . . Chinese-Americans, . . . how do you separate what is peculiar to
> childhood, insanities, one family, your mother who marked your growing with stories,
> from what is Chinese?

   The narrative consists of five interlocking sections, each of which explores the central problem from a different perspective.
   The first section, "No Name Woman," tells the story of an aunt who, after bearing an illegitimate child, was forced by neighbors and family to commit suicide. Kingston explains that when she reached puberty, her mother told her the story of No Name Woman as a warning. The story of this aunt is vague and shrouded in the mystery of the unspeakable.
   The next two sections picture strong women who refuse to be victims. No Name Woman is the victim of a community which devalues and severely restricts women; in contrast, the mythical Woman Warrior of the second section, "White Tigers," actively avenges crimes against her community. A Chinese Joan of Arc, she leads an army in defiance of laws which would put her to death for impersonating a man if she were discovered; she also marries for love, gives birth in the saddle, and returns to her family in honor, evading the fate of the Western woman hero. Kingston

explains that the Woman Warrior, also based on her mother's stories, represents her dreams of power and creativity.

The third section, "Shaman," recounts the life of Kingston's mother, Brave Orchid. While still living in China, Brave Orchid battled stiff odds to be graduated with honors from a women's medical college and then practiced her craft against equally stiff odds. Like the Woman Warrior, the Shaman seems to possess superhuman strengths and takes enormous risks. Unlike most Chinese women whose husbands left them to go to America, Brave Orchid eventually follows her husband to "the Gold Mountain" to work at his side.

The fourth section, "At the Western Palace," recounts the life of Brave Orchid's sister Moon Orchid. Like No Name Woman a generation earlier, Moon Orchid is victimized by a community which devalues women. After thirty years in Hong Kong, Moon Orchid follows her sister's advice, coming to San Francisco to find the husband who left her for the Gold Mountain. Now a successful physician, the husband rejects her, and Moon Orchid retreats so far into madness that she is finally hospitalized. With the other psychiatric patients, Moon Orchid is content once more.

The fifth and last section, "A Song for a Barbarian Reed Pipe," concludes the themes introduced in the first four parts of the work. The first episode in this section concerns the author's childhood reticence, so intense that before allowing her teachers to see her school drawings she covers them with layers of chalk and black paint. This silence parallels the silence surrounding No Name Woman, who never tells the name of the man who raped or seduced her and consequently loses her own name. Kingston's silence, however, eventually turns into self-expression. In the second episode, Kingston recalls her mother's superstitious demand that a white druggist, who has mistakenly delivered medicine, recompense the family with gifts. Kingston learns to lie creatively in order to negotiate between the whites, who do not understand her culture, and her mother, who does not understand the white culture. The third episode builds on the first and second; here, the author acts out her mother's role as a shaman, attempting to "cure" a silent classmate by bullying and torturing her. Instead of curing her classmate, however, Kingston herself succumbs to a mysterious illness which confines her to bed for a year. In the next episode, the author considers female victimization once more, concluding that the silences surrounding women and girls make them crazy: "I thought every house had to have its crazy woman or crazy girl, every village its idiot. Who would it be at our house? Probably me. . . . there were adventurous people inside my head to whom I talked." The last episode of "A Song for a Barbarian Reed Pipe" explores Kingston's dream life and the increasing urgency of her need to communicate. In her childhood, Kingston took this urgency as further evidence of her own craziness, but paradoxically, the dreams and the talk are also the means by which she transcends psychic stress.

The last episode of the last section tells the story of the woman poet Ts'ai Yen. Captured and taken into exile by barbarians, she learns their language and music, transforms barbarian idioms into her language, and eventually brings back to her own people poems of great beauty.

Analysis

Kingston's purpose, presented at the beginning of the book, is to unravel her mother's stories and in the process to understand herself. Her method of unraveling these stories is to retell them, retracing both her actual and her mythic ancestry. Because the author's identity and self-expression are determined by the position of women in traditional Chinese and Chinese-American cultures, the major figures in this autobiographical work are the women who have surrounded Kingston in her everyday life and the women who have dominated in her rich dream life. The style of the work, therefore, is partly direct and factual, partly poetic. The Woman Warrior's endurance in a beautiful, harsh, imaginary landscape attests her superhuman strength. No Name Woman, the facts of whose life are sparse, is described in the romantic clichés that Kingston derived in her childhood from both Eastern and Western culture.

The figures of Kingston's dream life, No Name Woman and the Woman Warrior, are painted in broad strokes and function as symbols of female impotence on the one hand and female empowerment on the other. The style of the sections in which Kingston writes about these characters is poetic.

Unlike the dream figures, the factual figures are drawn in realistic detail. Moon Orchid, for example, is described in a complete and laconic account of her life in Hong Kong as a well-off "widow," her awkward but well-intentioned attempts to fit into her sister's family, her timidity when she faces the husband who abandoned her, and finally her madness, which Kingston presents in almost clinical detail.

The most important figures in the work, Brave Orchid and Kingston herself, are depicted in both mythical terms and realistic detail. The narrative of Brave Orchid's life in China has a tone of mystery and distance. In China, Brave Orchid is the hero of any situation in which she finds herself. Beautiful, intelligent, and brave, she is not only the star of her class at the medical college but also its savior from the "sitting ghost," which she exorcises from the dormitory at great personal risk. When she returns to her village as a physician, Brave Orchid is known for both her sophisticated beauty and her skill. She never loses a patient, because her instincts always tell her which patients are doomed, and she refuses to treat them. In contrast, when she moves to the Gold Mountain, she can no longer practice medicine; she becomes an ordinary woman, a foreigner who never quite learns American ways, a laundress, and a mother who knows both successes and failures with her children. Accordingly, the descriptions of Brave Orchid's life in the United States are more pedestrian than the earlier tales.

In terms of technique, the subject of this autobiography is herself the most complex figure in the work. Kingston traces her everyday life in a Chinese-American family, her frustrating but successful work in school, her labor in the family laundry, and her ties with various family members. Kingston's childhood is a constant battle to feel valued, to overcome confusion about Chinese and American customs, and to transcend her own alienation and hostility. There is nothing romantic about these conflicts. Kingston's aunt, Moon Orchid, however, once remarks that the name Maxine sounds like the Chinese word for ink. The child Maxine works out an identity in writing which includes romance and myth, and in keeping with this alternative identity, she entertains herself with daydreams, which she calls "mind movies." In these dreams, she repeats to herself her mother's fantastic stories, imagining herself as the heroes or victims—No Name Woman, the Shaman, the wife-slave, and finally the poet.

On the one hand, the author feels condemned by language: "There is a Chinese word for the female *I*—which is 'slave.' Break the women with their own tongues!" On the other hand, language gives the author power and identity: "The swordswoman and I are not so dissimilar," she concludes. "May my people understand the resemblance soon so that I can return to them." The warrior's parents cut words into her back so that even if the enemy kills her, the skin will bear witness to the wrongs they have suffered. The reporting of wrongs is in itself vengeance, "not the beheading, not the gutting, but the words."

Kingston is consciously representative of all writers belonging to a minority group within a hostile or indifferent dominant culture. In examining the formation of her own identity as a writer, she explores the cognitive dissonance experienced by the nonwhite writer in a white society, by the writer who belongs to a cultural minority, or by the woman writer in a sexist society.

Kingston and her family are culturally adrift. They no longer belong to the old China, but they also do not belong in American society. Racially, they are a minority, but because they live in a Chinese ghetto and are not black, they experience racism indirectly. The author herself feels invisible, misunderstood, and misunderstanding: She has escaped from a culture which she believes maims, kills, and sells girls, but she is surrounded by a culture which demands that she deny the strengths she needs to survive. Caught in a double jeopardy of racism and sexism, she grows up never knowing exactly what is expected of her, struggling to satisfy society and family while preserving her own integrity. She affirms her cultural, racial, and sexual identities, however, by breaking the rules and evading the stereotypes. For example, she writes in English, when a Chinese woman would be expected to keep silence, or at least to write in Chinese.

Like the poems by Ts'ai Yen, Kingston's work cuts across boundaries. The book concludes with a statement which could refer to its own significance:

> Her words seemed to be Chinese, but the barbarians understood their sadness and anger. . . . She brought her songs back from the savage lands, and one of the three that has been passed down to us is "Eighteen Stanzas for a Barbarian Reed Pipe," a song that Chinese sing to their own instruments. It translated well.

Critical Context

Kingston continues the tradition, begun a generation earlier by Jade Snow Wong, of chronicling the cultural lives of Chinese-American women. The first part of a two-part autobiography, *The Woman Warrior* explores the writer's relationships with the other women in her family. The second part of the autobiography, *China Men* (1980), narrates the lives of the men in Kingston's family and explores her relationships with them. Though published separately, the two books were written almost simultaneously. They are remarkable personal and cultural statements, notable for their brilliant narrative technique, which shows the fluid line between autobiography and imaginative literature. The National Book Critics Circle chose *The Woman Warrior* as the best work of nonfiction published in 1976.

Sources for Further Study

Blinde, Patricia Lin. "The Icicle in the Desert: Perspective and Form in the Works of Two Chinese-American Woman Writers," in *MELUS*. VI (Summer, 1979), pp. 51-71.

Homsher, Deborah. "*The Woman Warrior*, by Maxine Hong Kingston: A Bridging of Autobiography and Fiction," in *The Iowa Review*. X (Fall, 1979), pp. 93-98.

Kramer, Jane. Review in *The New York Times Book Review*. LXXXI (November 7, 1976), p. 1.

Myers, Victoria. "The Significant Fictivity of Maxine Hong Kingston's *The Woman Warrior*," in *Biography*. IX (Spring, 1986), pp. 112-125.

Rainwater, Catherine, and William J. Scheick. *Contemporary American Women Writers: Narrative Strategies*, 1985.

Mary S. Pollock

THE WORDS

Author: Jean-Paul Sartre (1905-1980)
Type of work: Autobiography
Time of work: The early twentieth century
Locale: Meudon, France
First published: Les Mots, 1964 (English translation, 1964)

> *Principal personages:*
> JEAN-PAUL SARTRE, a young writer
> ANNE-MARIE, his mother
> LOUISE SCHWEITZER, his grandmother
> CHARLES SCHWEITZER, his grandfather

Form and Content

Jean-Paul Sartre decided, when he was about twenty years old, that at the age of fifty he would write an autobiography. He began writing "Jean-sans-terre" (one without inheritance or possessions) in 1952 and worked on it for nearly a decade. This unpublished volume was conceived from a political point of view. He later referred to it as an ill-natured work, revealing him to be a person uneasy with others in his milieu, one who at last became the Communist he ought to have been. Realizing that this book would require extensive elaboration, he eventually abandoned it in order to do other things.

He restarted the project in 1961, fashioning the book from a different perspective, one more literary and social than political. He aimed to blend the confessional method of Jean-Jacques Rousseau with something not unlike the reflective meditations of Blaise Pascal, bidding farewell to belles lettres with a very literary book about his childhood. He labored over the style, spending more time and effort than he had ever devoted to any previous work. *The Words* reveals the childhood of a precocious and pampered but lonely boy as he begins to perceive the reality of his existence; the style charms the reader by turns of phrases more felicitous than those found in Sartre's previous writings.

A relatively short book (slightly more than two hundred pages), *The Words* is divided into two parts of nearly equal length, "Reading" and "Writing"; it deals to a large extent with Sartre's immersion in language as a child, the development of his interest in literature, and his longing to become a writer. "Reading" relates how he learned the alphabet from his mother and then virtually taught himself to read; "Writing" describes his first efforts to express himself on paper with stories and novels before he was ten years of age. His reading was first directed by his grandfather toward the French classics (he especially liked the plays of Pierre Corneille), but his taste soon led him to prefer cloak-and-dagger romances and tales of swashbuckling heroes. His early writings reflect similar interests: He rewrote the fables of Jean de La Fontaine in Alexandrines; a story, "For a Butterfly," elaborates upon adventures which had appeared in a popular picture magazine. As a child author Sartre often plagiarized, but he managed to liven things up by blending imagination with memory while including long, didactic passages copied directly from the encyclopedia.

Simple in structure, this autobiography expresses Sartre's reflections on his intellectual and emotional development; it flows smoothly and gracefully from beginning to end. The author's view of himself as a child is expressed from the perspective of a mature thinker unembarrassed by the pranks and disgraces of his past, and he writes with a considerable amount of affection about nearly everyone he remembers.

Sartre's tone is casual and informal—essentially conversational—though the style is highly wrought and polished. He touches on a wide variety of topics which affected him during his childhood: the early loss of his father, his relationships with his mother and grandfather, school friends and experiences, the development of his interest in classical music and silent films, and the first glimmers of philosophical reflections which were later to result in the production of an elaborate system of thought. Philosophy, in fact, binds the whole of Sartre's work together, and *The Words* reveals the childhood sensibility and imagination of a person who was to become one of the great French writers of the century.

Analysis

Sartre was an infant when his father died; his mother, Anne-Marie, took her child to live with her parents in Meudon. In spite of her marriage and motherhood, she was treated like an adolescent in the house where she shared a bedroom with her son. As Sartre grew older, he believed that she was less a parental figure than an older sister with whom he could share secrets. His grandmother, Louise, a semi-invalid and ardent reader of spicy novels, seems to have had little influence on the child's development. His grandfather, Charles Schweitzer, an Alsatian professor of German in France and a pioneer in the development of the direct method of teaching foreign languages, proved an extremely important influence, closely supervising the boy's education and youthful development.

Sartre cultivated his precociousness at an early age; having learned the value and rewards of good behavior, he quickly saw how he could manipulate people and situations to his own advantage. His grandfather encouraged him to enjoy the kindness and generosity of others by behaving always like a model child. Salting the jam was one of his worst offenses. He went to church on Sundays to hear good music played by a well-known organist; moments of high spirituality delighted him as he pretended to pray. He generally amused himself by playing at being good: never crying, laughing, or making noise. Sartre later said that he was fortunate to have lost his father, who would probably have crushed him, instilling a strong Superego. As it was, Sartre claimed that he had none. His grandfather, patient and solicitous, encouraged the boy to explore the world of thought and to develop his individuality. Their relationship was very close: Charles Schweitzer appeared to the child as a patriarch resembling God the Father, and the elderly gentleman worshiped his grandson. If their relationship involved a certain degree of playacting, neither wished to step out of his role.

Through simple observation the child became aware of the relations which prevail between the self and others. He noted how members of his family responded to one another; he felt the pangs of loneliness when he was rejected by other children during games in the Luxembourg gardens. An inscription scrawled on a school wall stupefied and frightened young Sartre, for in it his favorite teacher was called an obscene term. Sartre's awareness of the importance of the judgments of others was to lead, many years later, to the development of his philosophical and psychological views on the self and others in *L'Être et le néant* (1943; *Being and Nothingness*, 1956), views which explored conflicts and frustrations in interpersonal relationships.

A further movement toward the development of Sartre's existential position occurred when he became aware, through the study of literature and the encyclopedia, that a writer's destiny is determined only after his death. The totality of an artist's work is viewed as a whole, and the end modifies the observer's perception of the beginning. From an early age, then, Sartre was aware that man is "becoming" rather than "existing." Sometimes, when young Sartre was frustrated, he would make faces at himself in a mirror as a means of protection against the humiliation of rejection; the mirror metaphor was also later to be developed as an important symbol in Sartre's metaphysical system. Psychological implications of it are explored in *Being and Nothingness*; Estelle, a character in Sartre's play *Huis-clos* (1944; *No Exit*, 1946), feels secure only when she views her own reflection.

As Sartre grew older, his mother began to introduce him to classical music by playing the piano in the evening. He quickly came to love Frédéric-François Chopin's ballades and pieces by Robert Schumann, César Franck, and Hector Berlioz. Music merged with film images in his mind when his mother began taking him to the cinema. He was thrilled at seeing the invisible and liked the muteness of the heroes who communicated by means of music. While watching a film, he thought that he touched the absolute. In spite of his grandfather's disapproval, Sartre continued to go frequently with his mother to films: He later thought of the cinema as the new art of the common man for a century without traditions.

Sartre began writing by composing responses in verse to letters from his grandfather, and the two became united by a new bond through literature. His mother taught him the rules of prosody, and he was given a rhyming dictionary, but he soon tired of poetry (an art form which never later interested him), preferring to realize his imagination in prose. His first stories were inspired by the pulp literature of the time—children's books and cheap magazines. He invented extravagant adventures, joining together bits and pieces of tales he had read and embellishing them with commentaries copied directly from other books. Stories of the supernatural terrified him, yet he imitated them. He won his grandfather's disapproval for these frivolous literary activities, but other members of the family found his writings charming. His mother was pleased because he did not make any noise while writing. Sartre later regretted the loss of these early efforts at composition, for they would have revealed to him his entire childhood.

He thus escaped from playacting and the world of the grown-ups by existing in order to write: He knew joy. Proud of his grandson's ambitions, Schweitzer, with some misgivings, voiced approval of the boy's aspirations. He urged him to follow a double career as writer and teacher, moving back and forth from one priestly function to the other. Still rejected by the "little squirts" in Luxembourg, Sartre decided to depict real objects with real words that were penned with a real pen and so become real himself. He had to learn to see and observe, sweating and laboring to make words express the conflicts he found in the world. As a result of discovering the world through language, he took language for the world. Writing became an end in itself: He wrote in order to write. He held secret meetings with the Holy Ghost whom he believed had elected him, branded but without talent, to set up cathedrals of words and build for the ages. He dreamed of fame and glory but feared that his first book would create a scandal and that he would become a public enemy.

Sartre developed his writing in order to be forgiven for his existence: He could appear to the Holy Ghost as a precipitate of language, could be other than himself, other than everything. In order to write, he needed a brain, bones, eyes, arms; he imagined that one day his being, like a sort of larva, would burst open, sending thousands of pages flying, like so many butterflies, to the shelves of the national library. He would be thoroughly at ease, sitting in state with 130 pounds of paper. A man becomes his books; death is buried in the shroud of glory; immortality is attained through the act of writing. He would one day be changed from an individuality as a subject into an object whose existence has the appearance of an unfolding. The future, he thought, was therefore more real than the present. A light-haired boy of the thirtieth century sitting at a window would observe him through a book, and the main question would be one of sincerity. If his acts of writing were not merely gestures and poses, then he would attain a sort of redemption through his work and his existence would have been justified.

In 1948, a professor showed Sartre a slide illustrating a horse galloping, a man walking, an eagle flying, and a motorboat shooting forward. The motorboat gave him the greatest feeling of speed: He thought that at the age of ten his own prow was cleaving the present and yanking him out of it. He was sure of himself and had only one law: to climb, to flee forward, to make progress. A broken tooth convinced him that his misfortunes would be only tests, means for writing a book. The worst was a guarantee of something better; he would derive himself from himself. Sartre fled forward to fulfill the dreams of his youth.

Critical Context

Sartre's autobiography is essentially a semi-Freudian, semiexistential analysis of himself as a child. The incidents and situations he recalls marked his being, uniting to produce his character and personality. It is what might be called "literary auto-biography": Avoiding any direct presentation of sexual matters, it relates his early exploration of the world of books, both good and bad, and his own first efforts to become a writer. Probably no previous author has penned such a detailed account of his own intellectual development.

The Words is often viewed as a sort of confession, an effort made late in life to seek the sources of what he had become. His efforts to create "committed litera-ture" and excite political action from his readers had often been swallowed up by the purely imaginative expression in novels and plays. By the early 1960's, Sartre had to ask himself why. The answers reposed in the past, in the childhood of a precocious and pampered youth. The tales of heroes and buccaneers and the silent films about exotic adventures had left a permanent mark on his mind; try though he might to be an engaged political activist, Sartre could not quell the energies of imagination and fantasy in his spirit.

A concept of the self as perceived both internally through reflection and exter-nally by responses of others, which was elaborated philosophically in *Being and Nothingness*, permeates this entire volume. Observations and insights into a child's developing self-image, along with perceptions of the adults who surrounded him, are related with charm and innocence, spiced occasionally by a barbed comment. Conflict between the self and others is the *sine qua non* of Sartre's works; in *The Words* one finds its genesis.

In this honest and beautiful self-portrait Sartre is sometimes rather evasive. He sought to justify his existence by writing, by becoming a priest of the word; he ended with the disillusioned feeling of having played at "winner loses." He con-tinued to write out of habit, having nothing else to do, cultivating a literary self-indulgence which expressed his changing flow of thought. Not believing himself particularly talented, Sartre wrote in order to save himself, to become a man as good as others but better than none.

Sources for Further Study

Aronson, Ronald. "Introducing a Crisis: *Les Mots*," in *Jean-Paul Sartre: Philoso-phy in the World*, 1980.

Beauvoir, Simone de. *Adieux: A Farewell to Sartre*, 1984.

Brée, Germaine. *Camus and Sartre: Crisis and Commitment*, 1972.

Champigny, Robert. "Sartre on Sartre," in *The Philosophy of Jean-Paul Sartre*, 1981. Edited by Paul Arthur Schilpp.

_____. *Stages on Sartre's Way, 1938-1952*, 1959.

Davies, Howard. "*Les Mots* as *Essai sur le Don*: Contribution to an Origin Myth," in *Yale French Studies*. LXVIII (1985), pp. 57-72.

McMahon, Joseph H. *Humans Being: The World of Jean-Paul Sartre*, 1971.

Raymond M. Archer

THE WORK OF ART
IN THE AGE OF MECHANICAL REPRODUCTION

Author: Walter Benjamin (1892-1940)
Type of work: Art history
First published: "Das Kunstwerk im Zeitalter seiner technischen
Reproduzierbarkeit," 1936, 1955 (English translation, 1968)

Form and Content

"The Work of Art in the Age of Mechanical Reproduction" is a longish essay, divided—in its 1955 version—into fifteen chapters plus a foreword and an afterword. Walter Benjamin's argument progresses from a general discussion of the changes wrought by technological development on the production of art to a more specific discussion of photography and film as singularly modern genres which alter the viewer's relationship to art in general.

The changes Benjamin made in the second version of the essay do not constitute a major rethinking of his thesis; rather, they help to define the chief elements of his message and to place it within the context of European politics. In this context it is important to remember that Benjamin wrote the essay while in exile. For example, in making what had been the first chapter into a foreword and what had been the last chapter into a postscript, Benjamin placed his statements on art within the larger context of remarks on Fascism and war. The foreword shows Benjamin's "redemptive aesthetics," and in it he claims that the concepts he will develop are "completely useless for the purposes of Fascism. They are, on the other hand, useful for the formulation of revolutionary demands in the politics of art." The afterword returns to this larger political question by contrasting reproducible art with the Fascist art form known as war. Fascism aestheticizes war, while Communism politicizes art. Thus, Benjamin has drawn a closed circle around his essay by twice formulating, with variations, a single contrast between Communism and Fascism.

The first five chapters of "The Work of Art in the Age of Mechanical Reproduction" give an extremely compressed history of art in terms of its ever-increasing reproducibility. This history will lead to the point, made later in the essay, that with the invention of photography and film, artworks have reached a point at which they are inseparable from the concept of their being reproduced. This inseparability can be understood in a practical sense: As opposed to most other art forms, films are so costly that their whole production process is ruled from start to finish by the condition that they be reproducible for mass consumption. Yet, in chapter 9, Benjamin also explores film's reproducibility in a formal sense: The actor's method changes from that of creating a role to that of presenting himself. Characters are composed in films from heterogeneous effects and are a pastiche of performances that may occur at widely spaced moments and in widely varying situations. For the film viewer, the fullness and distance (aura) of a stage appearance are replaced by a flickering thinness and the merciless investigation of reality by the camera. Similarly, Benjamin declares that the public's reception of a film is that of the camera. "The audience takes the position of the camera; its approach is that of testing" (chapter 8). Years of theater and film-going had taught Benjamin the difference between a theater audience, which sits in reverent silence, afraid even to cough during a performance, and a film audience, which feels free to exchange quiet comments and critiques during the showing.

This new critical attitude toward art on the part of the public, which the foreword and afterword show to be the real object of Benjamin's analysis, contrasts sharply with the traditional status of artworks. The "aura" of a work both derived from and was responsible for its religious status. (With the nineteenth century notion of art for art's sake, the work of art retained its traditional authority, although the source of that authority was different.) Aura, which Peter Bürger has defined as the work's unapproachability, depends upon the art object's uniqueness and authenticity, both of which by definition disappear in its reproductions. An example of aura would be a religious icon or, in the secular world, the charisma with which a stage actor holds his audience spellbound. Historically, Benjamin sees the increasing reproducibility of artworks as inversely proportional to the strength of their aura, to their religious content and usage, and to their hiddenness from the general public. Reproducible art is always already exhibited to a public. This historical argument takes up the first third of the essay.

For Benjamin, the invention of photography was the turning point in the history of artistic aura. Chapter 6 thus opens with the provocative generalization that "in photography, exhibition value begins to displace cult value all along the line." The use of early photographs for remembrances of the departed provided the new art form with a kind of compensatory aura. Benjamin emphasizes that photography did not replace painting as the leading art form. Rather, it changed the whole conception of what art is and what it is supposed to do. Moving pictures accomplished the same revolution in a much more profound way. The last third of the essay goes into the details of filmic art.

Analysis

Three problems in translating the title of this essay into English are revealing of its essential thesis. (At least two translations of the essay have appeared. The first, based on the earlier version, uses "reproducibility." The second, more widely available in the collection *Illuminations*, 1968, is based on the second version of the essay and carries the title at the head of this article.) English "reproduction" is used for the German *Reproduzierbarkeit*, which actually means "reproducibility." Benjamin points out in the first chapter that the reproduction of certain works of art had always been possible, but that there has now arrived an epoch (*Zeitalter*) of technical reproducibility, of a process which invests the work of art with a new and different nature. The difference is important and hangs together with the second mistranslation, in which *seiner* ("its," that is, the work of art's) is left out. The use of the possessive personal pronoun emphasizes that it is not reproducibility in general that is Benjamin's concern, but rather the reproducibility of those specific artistic genres—photography and film—which are inconceivable without that reproducibility. Indeed, "mechanical reproduction" in general, as Benjamin points out, had begun to alter European civilization and art more than a century before, during the Industrial Revolution. The point, then, is that at a certain point of history works of art that are always already their own reproductions have come to be created.

The third oddity in the translation, the reduction of *technisch* to "mechanical," leads back to the same point. Mechanical reproduction, such as printing and lithography, had failed to change the nature of art or reduce its aura. There was still an original behind all the reproductions. "Technical" reproduction, on the other hand, with its echoes of "technological," refers to a whole different attitude toward the making of art. Film reproduces events and emotions which have never existed. Montage, slow motion, and other techniques alter one's perception of reality, change a drab world into an exciting one:

> Our taverns and our metropolitan streets, our offices and furnished rooms, our railroad stations and our factories appeared to have us locked up hopelessly. Then came film and burst this prison-world by the dynamite of the tenth of a second.

This is "technical," not "mechanical," reproducibility. "Mechanical" would make it appear that Benjamin is concerned with what happens when art is produced by machines. Though the camera is a machine, this fact is not what interests Benjamin. *Technisch*, with its origins in the Greek word *technē*, meaning "craft" or "skill," shows Benjamin's belief that photography will bring about a rejection of the romantic notion of art as the work of genius, and hence will reduce art's aura.

Benjamin's utopian notion of moving pictures was influenced by his knowledge of the films of experimental socialist filmmakers such as Sergey Eisenstein, Dziga Vertov, and his personal acquaintance Asya Lacis. Benjamin's friend Bertolt Brecht, whose revolutionary playwriting techniques Benjamin had analyzed in another essay, "Was ist das episches Theater?" (1939; "What Is Epic Theater?" 1968), had also shown considerable enthusiasm for filmmaking as a way of influencing the proletariat. In fact, Benjamin's entire essay—with the important exception of the concept of aura, which Brecht detested—seems to be summarized in Brecht's remark that film "can be used better than almost anything else to supersede the old kind of untechnical, anti-technical 'glowing art,' with its religious links. The socialization of these means is vital for art." Brecht's idea of film as a more "thinkable" medium than theater shows up clearly in "The Work of Art in the Age of Mechanical Reproduction."

Brecht's epic theater shared with the Russian filmmakers a fondness for the technique of montage. That is, in both genres the part was privileged above the whole, and there was no attempt at disguising the "madeness" of the work of art.

Brecht's goals of destroying linear plot and thus of breaking the emotional involvement of the spectators and with it the effect of Aristotelian catharsis are paralleled in Benjamin's comments on the relative objectivity of the film viewer. Benjamin argues that film's montage technique, which wrenches the viewer from scene to scene in rapid succession, breaks any hold the image may have over the viewer and allows a more critical attitude. Brecht's goal of having the audience think critically about the work of art was also incorporated into Benjamin's view that the film audience takes the position of the camera. All these points are summarized in Benjamin's long metaphor of the difference between faith healer (traditional art) and surgeon (film art):

> The surgeon represents the polar opposite of the magician. . . . The magician maintains the natural distance between the patient and himself; though he reduces it very slightly by the laying on of hands, he greatly increases it by virtue of his authority. The surgeon does exactly the reverse; he greatly diminishes the distance between himself and the patient by penetrating into the patient's body, and increases it but little by the caution with which his hand moves among the organs.

This distance again represents the concept of aura. Most film theorists would reject Benjamin's rather naïve notion that the camera is somehow less distanced and more objective than the painter's brush. Film, like any other art, is staged; it is mimesis, it brings to mind rather than reproduces reality.

Accordingly, with the hindsight of history one is able to note the extreme discrepancy between Benjamin's hopes for film and what really happened. The year of publication of the essay saw the premiere of Leni Riefenstahl's *Triumph des Willens* (*Triumph of the Will*), a milestone in film history that negates every one of Benjamin's points. Rather than show "taverns and metropolitan streets," Riefenstahl showed the Nazi rallies at Nuremberg, along with one sequence of the medieval, auristic sections of the city. Rather than show men and women in the process of work, Riefenstahl celebrated their passive consumption of the Führer's grand illusion. Rather than diminish the aura of its chief actor, Adolf Hitler, Riefenstahl raised it to unbelievable heights. *Triumph of the Will*, in recording the Nazis' aestheticizing politics, was itself the politicized art which Benjamin had hoped the Communists would provide. Nor has the so-called dominant cinema showed any of the hoped-for tendencies. Emotional involvement, aura, and illusion are the heart and soul of most Hollywood films.

In the light of history, then, one can see what is missing from Benjamin's analysis. He has proved himself to be a materialist, but not a dialectical materialist. He had written in the foreword that he was providing "theses about the developmental tendencies of art under present conditions of production." For Karl Marx, conditions of production included the relationships that men enter into in order to produce material goods, including artworks. Benjamin seems here to believe that technological advancements can change the nature of art, without the ownership of the means of production first changing hands. He writes as though film's ability to change art were inevitable and did not depend upon who was making art products for what purpose. Oddly, then, by theorizing the reduction of art's aura Benjamin has himself endowed it with a power far beyond anything the Romantics could conceive of: the power to change history.

Critical Context

The uniqueness of Walter Benjamin's criticism lies in its combination of religious mysticism, philosophy, and politics. Benjamin came to the last category, in the form of Marxism, relatively late in his short life. His politicization can be seen as a symptomatic reaction to the alienation of intellectuals within the Weimar Republic and to the rabid anti-Semitism of the German Right, which would force him first to leave Germany and eventually to take his own life. Marxism remained a kind of protective shell for the unworldly Benjamin, rather than becoming his bone and muscle. He thus had no problem writing simultaneously in two opposing modes, on Brecht's theater of the concrete and on Franz Kafka's metaphysical world in "Franz Kafka" (1943; "Franz Kafka—On the Tenth Anniversary of His Death," 1968).

Yet precisely this balancing act between Jewishness and Marxism, between mysticism and materialism, defines the achievement of "The Work of Art in the Age of Mechanical Reproduction" as well as of Benjamin's other essays. It allows the essay to turn away from the Marxists' focus on the ideological content of works of art to the more elusive question of the influence of historical conditions on the form of artworks and vice versa. Benjamin's criticism in general has had a profound influence on later Marxist cultural critics such as Fredric Jameson. Benjamin's essay fails when measured against its own attempts to foretell the future. As a history of art it is too sketchy and compressed to be counted a success. Yet Benjamin's failures are always more interesting and important than other people's successes.

Interestingly, the importance of Benjamin's essay lies not in the realm of art history but in the realm of Marxist cultural theory. In spite of its utopianism and mysticism, or rather because of its utopianism and mysticism, "The Work of Art in the Age of Mechanical Reproduction" has the same liberating effect upon Marxist criticism as Benjamin had hoped film art would exercise upon the masses' perception of social reality. Marx, as Maynard Solomon notes, had revealed the "petrifaction of human relations in the 'things' of class society. Benjamin tried to show us how to break the spell."

Sources for Further Study

Allen, Richard W. "The Aesthetic Experience of Modernity: Benjamin, Adorno, and Contemporary Film Theory," in *New German Critique*. XL (Winter, 1987), pp. 225-240.

Caraher, Brian G. "The Work of Discourse in the Age of Mechanical Reproduction," in *Works and Days*. II (Spring, 1984), pp. 7-18.

Hansen, Miriam. "Benjamin, Cinema, and Experience: The Blue Flower in the Land of Technology," in *New German Critique*. XL (Winter, 1987), pp. 179-224.

Jennings, Michael W. *Dialectical Images: Walter Benjamin's Theory of Literary Criticism*, 1987.

Kazis, Richard. "Benjamin's Age of Mechanical Reproduction," in *Jump Cut: A Review of Contemporary Cinema*. XV (July 20, 1978), pp. 23-25.

Ridless, Robin. "Walter Benjamin," in *Ideology and Art: Theories of Mass Culture from Walter Benjamin to Umberto Eco*, 1984.

Roberts, Julian. *Walter Benjamin*, 1983.

Wellek, René. "Walter Benjamin's Literary Criticism in his Marxist Phase," in *The Personality of the Critic*, 1973. Edited by Joseph Strelka.

Wolin, Richard. *Walter Benjamin: An Aesthetic of Redemption*, 1982.

Wright, Kathleen. "The Place of the Work of Art in the Age of Technology," in *Southern Journal of Philosophy*. XXII (Winter, 1984), pp. 565-583.

Thomas O. Beebee

THE WRETCHED OF THE EARTH

Author: Frantz Fanon (1925-1961)
Type of work: Psychology
First published: Les Damnés de la terre, 1961 (*The Damned*, 1963; better known as *The Wretched of the Earth*)

Form and Content

In 1954, within a year after accepting a post as head of psychiatric services at the Blida-Joinville Hospital in Algeria, Frantz Fanon faced the outbreak of the Algerian Revolution. If the Martinique-born, French-educated black psychiatrist had any lingering loyalties to France upon his arrival in Algeria, however, he quickly severed his ties after witnessing the effects of French atrocities and torture on Algeria's Muslim population. In 1956, Fanon made an important decision. Determined to take a meaningful stand against Fascism in North Africa, he resigned his post and officially joined the National Liberation Front (FLN). Moreover, from 1956 until his death in 1961, Fanon devoted himself exclusively to the Algerian struggle for independence.

This struggle, which inspired Fanon's political awakening as well as his increasing understanding of the effects of both colonization and decolonization on individuals and nations, began to alter his vision of the world. Although still Manichaean in outlook, he saw a world divided not into black and white but rather into "colonizer" and "colonized." In addition, although his four books, *Peau noire, masques blancs* (1952; *Black Skin, White Masks*, 1967), *Pour la révolution africaine* (1964; *Toward the African Revolution: Political Essays*, 1967), *L'An cinq de la révolution algérienne* (1959; *Studies in a Dying Colonialism*, 1965), and *The Wretched of the Earth*, are all products of his Algerian experience, the problems he discusses are not unique to Algeria; he defines and describes the distortion of human relations which the phenomenon of colonialism produces.

In 1960, one year before his death, Frantz Fanon was diagnosed as having leukemia. At that time, instead of continuing a study he had begun on the revolution and Africa, Fanon began work on what later became known as *The Wretched of the Earth*. He completed the bulk of the manuscript in three hectic months, from March to May of 1961.

Both the seriousness of his illness and his outrage at the atrocities he had observed from inside the revolution, then, contributed significantly to the mood and form of *The Wretched of the Earth*. Although the work traces the psychological and political destruction of colonialism on both the colonizers and the colonized, it is not an empirical description or a sociological explanation of a political phenomenon but rather a call to action to the exploited masses. The tone is both angry and passionate. Consumed by the desire to excite and activate the people as well as to warn of the dangers of more subtle kinds of exploitation, Fanon resorts to an aphoristic style; in his haste, he often indulges in sweeping generalizations unsupported by concrete evidence. The narrative shifts tenses without warning. Also, critics point out that Socialist revolutions for which there are no precedents are prescribed and that the Algerian Revolution is implicitly treated as a model for all Africa. A set of ideals and categories is imposed on a large and diverse continent. Initially published in Paris, although making no concessions to the "European" point of view, the work was intended for the intellectual elite of the Third World. Yet the work is also considered Fanon's most important and influential; it has even been called "one of the great political documents of our time" in its analysis of political development, the genesis and degeneration of nationalist movements and parties, and, perhaps most important, the question of violence in Third World revolutions.

Turning to the work's format, of the book's 316 pages, the famous preface, written by Jean-Paul Sartre, consists of twenty-five pages. While Fanon's audience was the intellectual elite of the Third World, Sartre addressed Europeans, particularly French intellectuals, exhorting them to heed Fanon's warnings:

> You [Europeans], who are so liberal and so humane, who have such an exaggerated adoration of culture that it verges on affectation, you pretend to forget that you own colonies and that in them men are massacred in your name. Fanon reveals to his comrades . . . the solidarity of the people of the mother country and of their representatives in the colonies. Have the courage to read this book, for . . . it will make you ashamed, and shame, as Marx said, is a revolutionary sentiment.

The body of the work consists of five essays and a six-page conclusion. In the first chapter, "Concerning Violence," Fanon discusses his highly controversial concept of the cathartic effect of violence as well as its purifying and creative power. The next chapter, "Spontaneity: Its Strengths and Weaknesses," explores the positive and negative aspects of peasant participation in the struggle for liberation. "The Pitfalls of National Consciousness," Fanon's third chapter, describes the dangerous rise of national bourgeoisies which threaten the unity of newly independent nations. In chapter 4, "On National Culture," Fanon explains the necessity of maintaining a unique national identity by preserving precolonial history and culture. The final chapter, "Colonial War and Mental Disorders," catalogs case histories which reveal the psychological damage caused by the Algerian Revolution's terrorism and violence. Fanon's brief conclusion urges the intelligentsia of the Third World to turn to itself rather than to Europe for solutions to its problems.

Analysis

In Fanon's vision, the colonized, the proletariat of the world, are the damned or wretched of the earth. As a black psychiatrist who chose to become an Algerian citizen, Fanon invented a collective therapy that he believed would save a race of the damned. That therapy is based on the premise that the black man will remain enslaved until he has successfully struggled for and achieved his political freedom. More permanent in its effects than strikes, boycotts, or demonstrations, the armed insurrection of the Algerian people, according to Fanon, would bring about the total transformation of a colony into a community free of any psychological, emotional, or legal subjection; within that society, the colonized would be fully human. Fanon further argues that the entire structure of the Algerian family would change. Relationships between parents and children or between husbands and wives would lose their restrictive, traditional character; Arabic would lose its religious exclusivism, and French would become domesticated. Violence would create a new spiritual unity which would prepare the country for the enormous task of national postwar reconstruction.

The year 1960 marked independence for Algeria. This, for Fanon and for many Africans, however, was considered a false independence, one granted by France to nationalist leaders who still remained her dependents. The division of the Mali Federation between the French Sudan and Senegal was widely interpreted as an indication of the evils of "neocolonialism." In the midst of the independence celebrations, Fanon saw that independence did not necessarily constitute a new beginning but more often merely replaced one species of man with another. The exploited now became the exploiters.

The reluctance of the new African nations to assume the burdens of their revolutionary duty stemmed, according to Fanon, from a lack of understanding of the fundamental nature of the political world. The African elites had no ideological foundation beyond a simple nationalism. In his final work, Fanon offered them an alternative.

The French title of his book, *Les Damnés de la terre* (the damned of the earth), taken from the first line of the *Internationale*, is more richly connotative than its English translation. The wretched of the earth elicit pity, but the damned are beyond hope. The fate of the wretched can be improved by charity, but the damned must be resurrected. In imagery which critics say links him with Arthur Rimbaud and Jean Genet, the damned are the rat pack, the prostitutes and pimps, the brutal peasants, who invade the city through the sewers. When the city goes up in flames, the damned are purified in its fire.

Fanon's discussion of violence combines a psychoanalytic tradition with a Marxist one, but a Marxism revised to encompass a colonial world where the relations of production are themselves a superstructure rooted in the relations of colonialism. In Fanon's view, in the beginning colonization is imposed through violence. The violent reaction it generates among the members of the colonized, however, is then turned inward, taking the form of muscular tension, heightened criminality within their own community, and tribal wars. Hope lies in the redirection of this internalized aggression onto external objects, utilizing this energy for a destruction which purges and purifies. The most powerful reservoir of violence is to be found not in the cities, themselves artificial constructs of colonialism, but in the country among the peasants, the true revolutionaries. Yet Fanon warns that the violent potential of the people must always be channeled by a vanguard which understands its use.

Nevertheless, Fanon has been charged with surrounding his concept of violence with a considerable amount of ambiguity. Critics state that he dodges any responsibility for possible consequences by putting the blame for its use on the other side: The need for violence in the struggle for national liberation is a function of the size of the resident white minorities; it is used by the colonial power in maintaining its hegemony. The type of political action that would bring about ritual purification, however, is never made explicit.

It seems that for Fanon, violence encompasses almost the entire range of political pressure. He explains that while in some situations there is no alternative to armed struggle, elsewhere the struggle may be symbolic only and decolonization will be rapid. By stressing "commitment" to rather than fulfillment of the act, he appears to be maintaining that violence is both an evil to be feared and a good to be desired.

Much of Fanon's anger in *The Wretched of the Earth* is directed against the new bourgeoisies arising after independence. These groups are made up of city-based individuals, sometimes including urban laborers, who were well treated in the colonial period; more often, they are merchants scavenging on neocolonialist ventures. The bourgoisie that Fanon describes is an underdeveloped class—small businessmen, artisans, administrators, university personnel, army officers—that lacks capital or highly trained technical personnel. Consequently, they readily replace the European settlers who have fled and are hostile to any kind of genuine socialism (which might curb their newly found economic power).

In the new states, as material progress declines, the bourgeoisie is often forced to hide behind a popular, charismatic leader, who urges his subjects on to greater effort for a smaller reward. Moreover, the bourgeoisie allows the national party to disintegrate; useful in organizing mass participation in the struggle for independence, it is no longer needed in peacetime. Thus, the new parties become part of the machinery for controlling the people.

Fanon is at his best when describing middle-class structures within the Third World. Nevertheless, his theories weaken when they approach specific methods for destroying the structure, for destroying the dictatorship of the middle class. Believing that the hope for a better future lies in the country, Fanon describes the possibilities for rebuilding more radical national parties based in rural areas. Decentralization would rejuvenate the countryside and "deconsecrate" the capital, hopelessly corrupted by European rule and thought.

Critical Context

Fanon's concept of violence, especially the association of violence with creativity and regeneration, has often been compared with that of Georges Sorel in his *Réflexions sur la violence* (1908; *Reflections on Violence*, 1912). Fanon's debt to Sorel, however, is rather problematic. In Sorel's theory, the proletariat violently asserts itself in an oppressive society without necessarily overthrowing that society. Yet the foundations of Fanon's views differ from Sorel's; according to Fanon, the peasant revolution is not a myth but a reality, a means of overthrowing a system of exploitation. Thus, Fanon maintains that violence is creative in the context of constructive social action.

Fanon's later writings dealing with the future of the Third World contrast sharply with his first book, *Black Skin, White Masks*, which has been described as the diary of a black intellectual recovering from the trauma of a delayed introduction to the white Western world. His second book, *Studies in a Dying Colonialism*, is an extended commentary on a society undergoing a thorough restructuring, a unique description of a colonial people achieving self-determination. By the time of *The Wretched of the Earth*, Fanon is convinced that the Third World's peasantry has replaced the urban proletariat as the dynamic force in modern history. An elaboration of this theory can be found in *Toward the African Revolution*, a collection of Fanon's articles describing the development of his thought from the time of his departure from French bourgeois society to his death in 1961.

It has been said that Fanon's place in political history will depend less on the intrinsic intellectual merits of his works than on its contributions to the creation of a political mood and its emotional association with particular movements. Although his program is vague and his doctrine incomplete, some of his prophecies concerning Africa have been and continue to be fulfilled.

Sources for Further Study
Caute, David. *Fanon*, 1970.
Geismar, Peter. *Fanon*, 1971.
Gendzier, Irene L. *Frantz Fanon: A Critical Study*, 1973.
McCulloch, Joseph. *Black Soul, White Artifact: Fanon's Clinical Psychology and Social Theory*, 1983.
Onwuanibe, Richard C. *A Critique of Revolutionary Humanism: Frantz Fanon*, 1983.
Woddis, Jack. *New Theories of Revolution*, 1972.

Genevieve Slomski

WRITING AND DIFFERENCE

Author: Jacques Derrida (1930-   )
Type of work: Philosophy/linguistics
First published: L'Écriture et la différence, 1967 (English translation, 1978)

Form and Content

In 1967, the French philosopher Jacques Derrida burst upon the scene of philosophy and literary theory with three major publications: *Writing and Difference, La Voix et le phénomène: Introduction au problème du signe dans la phénoménologie de Husserl* (*Speech and Phenomena,* 1973), and *De la grammatologie* (*Of Grammatology,* 1976). In 1966, Derrida had presented the most influential essay to be published in *Writing and Difference,* "Structure, Sign, and Play in the Discourse of the Human Sciences," at the now-famous structuralism conference at The Johns Hopkins University. Among other offices, Derrida has been Director of Studies at the École des Hautes Études en Sciences Sociales in Paris, as well as a visiting professor at the University of California, Irvine. More than a dozen of his books have been translated into English. Derrida's writings constitute an attack on the tradition of Western metaphysics, or what he calls the "metaphysics of presence." Together with his books of 1967 and a set of three major publications in 1972, including *Positions: Entretiens avec Henri Ronse, Julia Kristeva, Jean-Louis Houdebine, Guy Scarpetta* (*Positions,* 1981), *Writing and Difference* constitutes an explicit, logical statement of Derrida's philosophical position. He later deviated from this earlier, analytical style and adopted the nonlinear, innovative style of *Glas* (1974; English translation, 1986) and *La Carte postale: De Socrate à Freud et au-delà* (1980; *The Post Card: From Socrates to Freud and Beyond,* 1987).

Writing and Difference is a collection of eleven essays written between 1959 and 1967 and translated into English by Alan Bass. As Derrida explains in an interview published in *Positions, Writing and Difference* consists of two parts. Though the essays in each part are arranged in the order of their original publication, the fifth essay, " 'Genesis and Structure' and Phenomenology," which appears almost at the center of the volume, was written in 1959. Moreover, the whole book could be inserted in the middle of *Of Grammatology,* so that the first half of the latter book would constitute a preface to the former. This arrangement is important to bear in mind, because the essays in *Writing and Difference* make numerous references to the history and theory of the sign discussed in the first half of *Of Grammatology.* The second half of the latter text, devoted to Jean-Jacques Rousseau's "Essay on the Origin of Languages," would thus become a twelfth essay in *Writing and Difference.* To complicate matters even more, Derrida says that this arrangement can also be inverted, so that *Of Grammatology* is inserted within *Writing and Difference,* because the first six essays of the latter book were published first. The last five essays of *Writing and Difference* are engaged in what Derrida in *Positions* calls the grammatological opening of the major principles of Western philosophy.

As Alan Bass explains in his introduction, this grammatological opening "can be defined as the 'deconstruction' [the undoing, or de-constructing] of philosophy by examining in the most faithful, rigorous way the 'structured genealogy' of all of philosophy's concepts; and to do so in order to determine what issues the history of philosophy has hidden, forbidden, or repressed." In *Writing and Difference*, Derrida sets out to deconstruct what he calls the "logocentric" tradition of Western metaphysics. The "logos," a Greek term defined as the inward rational principle of consciousness, verbal texts, and the natural universe, is privileged in Western philosophy. The privileging of logos involves the idea of "presence." In *Of Grammatology*, Derrida uses the term "phonocentrism," the privileging of voice, to describe the notion that meaning is primarily present within the speaker rather than within writing. Writing, he points out, has traditionally been considered secondary to speech.

Derrida attacks the notion of presence by subverting the structure of oppositions behind it, such as those between speech and writing, meaning and form, soul and body, intelligible and sensible, nature and culture. In the history of philosophy, these oppositions constitute a hierarchy in which the first term is given priority as belonging to logos and thus being of a higher presence. In *On Deconstruction* (1982), Jonathan Culler lists some concepts that depend on the value of presence: "the immediacy of sensation, the presence of ultimate truths to a divine consciousness, the effective presence of an origin in a historical development, a spontaneous or unmediated intuition . . . [and] truth as what subsists behind appearances." Derrida argues that presence is "always already" divided within itself by the "play" of difference.

Derrida says that one should read *Speech and Phenomena* before his two other books of 1967, for it questions the history of metaphysics at its most decisive point: Edmund Husserl's transcendental philosophy. One of the major objects of Derrida's philosophy is to undermine the reality of the transcendental. In the last essay of this book, "Différance," Derrida coins the term *différance*, which is based on the French verb *différer*, to differ (in space) and to defer (to put off in time, or postpone). He uses this term as a means to show how presence, along with truth, transcendentality, consciousness, and other logocentric notions, is rendered absent through a movement of difference and deferral, or that movement in writing through which all meaning is split within itself both temporally and spatially. Derrida thus gives writing priority over speech. As Alan Bass notes, *Speech and Phenomena* could be attached as a long note either to *Of Grammatology* or to *Writing and Difference*.

Derrida says that his writing is "entirely consumed in the reading of other texts." Reading Derrida himself is made difficult by his dense and punning style and by his challenging of accepted notions of meaning and the process of reading. Since *Writing and Difference* does not form a closely woven whole but rather a loosely strung collection of essays, the reader can begin with any one of the essays and still follow the book's overall design and argument.

Analysis

The first five essays of *Writing and Difference* make constant reference to the notion of presence, especially as developed by the two philosophers Martin Heidegger and Edmund Husserl. Derrida's project is the deconstruction of logocentrism, the critical undoing of oppositions such as that between a word's signifier, or sound image, and signified, or concept. In the first essay, "Force and Signification," Derrida asks the rhetorical question, What if "the meaning of meaning (in the general sense of meaning and not in the sense of signalization) is infinite implication, the indefinite referral of signifier to signifier?" For Derrida, the signified is never present in writing, but always postponed and separated from the signifier through the movement of *différance*. The meaning of a word is so ambiguous that its connotations extend to include all the words in the dictionary. Each word comprises a chain of signifiers in which the "transcendental signified" or ultimate meaning is infinitely deferred.

Derrida does not imply, however, that any interpretation of a text is acceptable. Meaning is always determined by its context, but the context itself is boundless. Each word functions by virtue of its repeatability in the context of different sentences, which may in turn be cited within the texts of different writers, with each citation resulting in a change of meaning. Although the combination of boundless context and contextual meaning has led to the deconstructive theory of the openness or indeterminacy of writing, Derrida does not feel excused from the responsibility to interpret texts or to formulate a coherent theory of language.

Nevertheless, the excess of the signifier results in a residue of meaning that the writer's intended meaning cannot totalize, or fully contain. In "Force and Signification," Derrida calls this lack of totalization the "force" of language—a result of *différance*. Deconstructive theory does not propose, however, that *différance* and indeterminacy make meaning the reader's invention, for even the reader must operate within a greater community. In the second essay, "Cogito and the History of Madness," Derrida writes that "this violent liberation of speech," found "at the greatest possible proximity to the abuse that is the usage of speech," creates a madness, or excess, that is outside the totality of history. According to Derrida, therefore, language constitutes a force in its own right that generates meaning spontaneously and largely independently of the speaker.

In his famous essay "Structure, Sign, and Play in the Discourse of the Human Sciences," Derrida elaborates on the deconstruction of the sign, the referent (or that to which the sign refers), and the speaker, each of which has been defined by logocentrism. The sign was traditionally thought to consist of a natural bond between word and meaning, signifier and signified. The word "horse," for example, was thought to refer naturally to horse as a thing and a concept. In the second decade of the twentieth century, however, the Swiss linguist Ferdinand de Saussure developed a new science called semiology, the study of signs. He argued that the bond between signifier and signified is not natural but arbitrary, since different signifiers are used across languages to refer to the same signified. For example, the words *ashvah*, *cheval*, and *"horse,"* in Sanskrit, French, and English respectively, refer to the same thing or concept. Saussure argued that the sign is not a positive naming of a thing but operates through the difference between words within a language system. The word "cat" thus acquires meaning through its difference from the word "mat," not through its relation to a feline animal. As Saussure says in *Cours de linguistique générale* (1916; *Course in General Linguistics*, 1960), "in a language there are only differences, *and no positive terms*."

Building upon Saussurean semiology, Derrida describes an event in the history of the idea of structure that resulted in a split between structuralism and poststructuralism. Structuralism, which developed from semiology, is a mode of literary interpretation that flourished in the 1950's and 1960's. It holds that the meaning of a text results not from a correspondence between sign and referent but from the relations among the elements of the structure of the text itself. The speaker, traditionally thought to be the source of meaning, is replaced by the structure of binary oppositions, such as those between signifier and signified, nature and culture, transcendental and empirical. Structuralism, then, divides the sign from the thing, or referent.

Poststructuralism, initiated in 1966 with Derrida's presentation of "Structure, Sign, and Play in the Discourse of the Human Sciences," divides the signifier from the signified, a division that results in the dispersion of meaning along a chain of signifiers. In analyzing this play of the signifier in the works of other writers, Derrida undermines the logocentric notion of "center," both as the source of meaning, such as the speaker, and as the goal of meaning, such as the transcendental signified. The problem with structuralism for Derrida was that it retained a center which was paradoxically both inside and outside the structure, organizing the structure while somehow escaping structurality itself. Because it is neither inside nor outside, this center can also be called the origin or the end, and it can always be reawakened as a presence.

Although Derrida deconstructs all these logocentric principles, he grants that they are indispensable for unsettling the heritage of logocentrism, for in order to represent deconstruction as superior, the deconstructionist has to appeal to the logocentric values of argument and persuasion. By undermining the structure of philosophical oppositions, Derrida tries to show that logocentric notions of a central presence must be treated as "under erasure," or as though they had methodological importance but no reality.

In the deconstructive argument of "Structure, Sign, and Play in the Discourse of the Human Sciences," the first opposition to be problematized is that between signifier and signified. As Derrida notes, the sign traditionally has derived its meaning as a sign-of-something, a signifier referring to a signified. In the play of signification, however, the difference between signifier and signified is erased, with the signifier itself substituting for the signified. Without the opposition between the intelligible and the sensible, the sign cannot exist. As Derrida puts it, "Play is the disruption of presence." Yet the deconstructionist cannot dispense with the concept of the sign. The effect of this paradox is that the sign is read as if it were still supported by an opposition between sensible and intelligible, still referring to a signified, when apparently this opposition has collapsed and the sign functions only self-referentially within a system of differences.

Derrida discusses two ways of understanding this limit to the totalization of meaning implied by the deconstruction of logocentric values. In the first way, which is classical and thus irrelevant to deconstruction, the infinity of the field of knowledge precludes unification by the finite intellect. In the second way, it is not the infinity of knowledge but the finite nature of language itself that excludes totalization, or the complete containment of meaning. The linguistic field, therefore, must be understood as a field of play, a field of infinite substitutions resulting not from an infinite source but from the absence or lack of a center. Derrida calls this activity "the play of the world."

This movement of play, Derrida says, can also be called the "movement of supplementarity"; on the one hand, it supplies something lacking—an absent center—and on the other, it supplies something additional. That which is lacking is supplemented by a form of discourse that moves the subject beyond his or her finitude to something greater. This vicarious addition of a supplement results in a "floating" signifier. That is, the signified's lack of material form necessitates the "overabundance of the signifier," or the play of signification, by means of which the reader transcends the boundaries of conventional meaning. That the concept is quantitatively poorer than the signifier is the result of its being qualitatively deficient or, what amounts to the same thing, so divorced from its material form that it cannot effectively unite the referent and the reader.

Critical Context

Writing and Difference, as a part of Derrida's first set of major publications in 1967, set the stage for the second set in 1972, consisting of *Positions*, *La Dissemination* (*Dissemination*, 1981), and *Marges de la philosophie* (*Margins of Philosophy*, 1982). In all these works, Derrida's project is to question the assumptions of traditional thematic criticism, which determines the values of a work according to the value of its theme. In *Dissemination*, Derrida says that he rejects the traditional kind of criticism that "makes the text into a form of expression . . . [and] reduces it to its signified theme."

Derridean deconstruction, as the main philosophical tenet of poststructuralism, has led the way in broadening the scope of literary criticism in the second half of the twentieth century, affecting disciplines as diverse as law, theology, and feminism, each of which has become more open in the reading of texts. In his critique of the metaphysics of presence, Derrida deprives the text of its status as a full object and defines it instead as an effect of *différance*. Because he deconstructs meaning as what the author intends, as what codes and conventions determine, and as what the reader experiences either individually or collectively, Derrida has been criticized as being ahistorical, especially by Marxist critics such as Terry Eagleton. Derrida, however, never separates deconstruction from history; he even helped to found an organization in France to ensure that traditional philosophy will continue to be taught in high schools. Deconstruction has also been criticized for being conservative. In his essay "What Does Deconstruction Contribute to Theory of Criticism?" John Ellis argues that in retaining traditional concepts, deconstruction only subverts the old without providing a new theoretical departure.

Derrida's notion of *différance*, in which presence becomes only a trace, has been called a transcendental signified in its own right. Indeed, deconstruction points to a field of unbounded meaning corresponding to a level of language which in Indian aesthetics is called *pashyantī*. At this level of language, the reader experiences the meaning-whole, or *sphoṭa*, of a word as a unity of sound and meaning which, like Derrida's notion of *différance*, is beyond the intelligible and sensible as ordinarily understood. This experience, however, can occur only on the level of transcendental consciousness. Such a state is perhaps more familiar to the artist than to the literary critic, especially the deconstructive critic, who would undermine consciousness itself.

Sources for Further Study

Culler, Jonathan. *On Deconstruction: Theory and Criticism After Structuralism*, 1982.

Eagleton, Terry. *Literary Theory: An Introduction*, 1983.

Ellis, John M. "What Does Deconstruction Contribute to Theory of Criticism?" in *New Literary History*. Winter, 1988, pp. 259-280.

Gasché, Rodolphe. *The Tain of the Mirror: Derrida and the Philosophy of Reflection*, 1986.

Harland, Richard. *Superstructuralism: The Philosophy of Structuralism and Post-Structuralism*, 1987.

Magliola, Robert. *Derrida on the Mend*, 1984.

Norris, Christopher. *Derrida*, 1987.

Staten, Henry. *Wittgenstein and Derrida*, 1984.

Ulmer, Gregory L. *Applied Grammatology: Post(e)-Pedagogy from Jacques Derrida to Joseph Beuys*, 1985.

William S. Haney II

THE YEARS WITH ROSS

Author: James Thurber (1894-1961)
Type of work: Memoir
Time of work: 1925-1951
Locale: New York and Europe
First published: 1959

> *Principal personages:*
> HAROLD ROSS, the founding editor of *The New Yorker*
> JAMES THURBER, a humorist who wrote for *The New Yorker*

Form and Content

During the decade before Harold Ross's death in 1951, several magazines asked James Thurber to contribute essays about Ross and about Thurber's adventures with him in the weekly production of *The New Yorker*. Thurber declined these requests, but in 1957, Charles Morton, of *The Atlantic Monthly*, queried Thurber repeatedly about the possibility of a series of articles on Ross. One of these queries reached Thurber in the Bahamas just as he was giving up the writing of a play on which he had been working for several months. He said yes to Morton and wrote and published in *The Atlantic Monthly* several articles about Ross in 1957 and 1958. Upon realizing, however, that "the restless force named Harold Wallace Ross could not be so easily confined and contained," he elected to amplify the written record of his memories of Ross considerably. In 1959, he published *The Years with Ross*.

Thurber indicates in his foreword to the book that from the beginning he avoided the writing of a formal biography. Nevertheless, many facts of Ross's life—as well as Thurber's—make their way into the book. Its principal device is the anecdote, and Thurber is himself able to supply many of these in building up a very solid—though never solemn—sense of Ross's character. Citations concerning Ross from the letters and works of other people are copious without ever causing the work to seem crowded or chaotic. There was chaos in the life of Ross, but it all runs very smoothly in the prose of Thurber.

Since the center of Ross's life from 1925 onward was *The New Yorker, The Years with Ross* is, among other things, a self-confessed "short informal history" of Ross's magazine. Thurber does not attempt to move chronologically through either the life of Ross or that of *The New Yorker*. He chooses instead a scheme of what he calls "flashbacks and flashforwards." The resultant rhythm of the book is one that accords handsomely with the very nature of Ross's life, the comings to and goings from the office, the constant looking backward and forward from a worried present, a present always filled with the need to get out the next issue and to plan future issues, and with anguish over the possible recriminations from past issues.

In the Atlantic Monthly Press edition, *The Years with Ross* consists of sixteen chapters and 310 pages. The chapters, ranging in length from ten to twenty-nine pages, are wittily titled, alluding to generally Ross's favorite sayings ("Sex Is an Incident," "A Dime a Dozen") or to some aspect of life and work in the offices of *The New Yorker* ("Every Tuesday Afternoon," "The Talk of the Town"). Thurber also includes some twenty-five drawings of his, a number of which serve as either occasion for or illustrations of stories about Ross.

Analysis

In an article concerning *The Years with Ross*, Gilbert Highet refers to it as "clean, first rate reporting" and also suggests that it can be thought of as another chapter in the free-and-easy autobiographical saga begun by Thurber with the publication of *My Life and Hard Times* (1933). What Thurber is principally reporting are the various conflicts he and others had with Ross during their association of twenty-five years at *The New Yorker*. Working in an office near Ross, Thurber was never very far from even those conflicts that did not directly concern him.

Temperamentally and aesthetically, the two were at odds. Thurber's business as both writer and cartoonist was to make people laugh; Ross often acted as if at least a part of his business in life were to avoid laughing (a word Ross used frequently was "grim"). Thurber was fascinated by—and helped envision in the first half of the twentieth century—the battle of the sexes; Ross wanted as much as possible to pretend the battle did not exist, in the hope that it would consequently go away. Sex, for him, was an "incident." Ross often feared that Thurber—and other cartoonists—were sneaking sexual double entendres into their work and that trouble would result. Thurber once did a drawing which came to be known in the offices of *The New Yorker* as "The Lady on the Bookcase." In it there is indeed a lady on a bookcase; below her, in what appears to be a living room, there are two men and a woman. The man in the middle of the trio is addressing the other man (whose gaze is on the lady on the bookcase), saying to him, "That's my first wife up there, and this is the *present* Mrs. Harris." What worried Ross about this drawing was the condition of the lady on the bookcase. Was she alive or dead? Was she stuffed? Thurber's response to what was for Ross a serious and important question is typical of Thurber's responses to serious and important questions from Ross. He reported that the woman had to be alive because his doctor had informed him that it was anatomically impossible for a dead woman to support herself on all fours and his taxidermist had indicated that it was impossible to stuff a woman. Unperturbed by Thurber's rejoinder, Ross replied, "Then, goddam it, what's she doing naked in the house of her former husband and his second wife?" Thurber said that the woman was simply there and disclaimed responsibility for the behavior of the people in his drawings.

Thurber was an artist; Ross was a man deeply distrustful of artists and fairly certain that all of them were either mad or on the brink of madness. Once, at lunch at the Algonquin with Ross, Thurber looked at his menu, acted as if he had never seen such a thing, got to his feet, trembled, and tried to turn pale. Just before he got the joke, Ross said, "It's the goddam menu." Upon realizing that Thurber was once again having him on, Ross said, "Don't do that to me, Thurber. Too many people I know are *really* ready for the bughouse."

From the outset of Thurber's employment with *The New Yorker*, in 1927, he and Ross disagreed about sundry matters of policy and personnel concerning the magazine. Initially, Ross determined that Thurber was the "miracle man," the managing editor for whom he had been searching and would continue to search, the fellow who would make the magazine run smoothly from a central desk. Two of the book's early chapters ("Miracle Men" and "More Miracle Men") deal with Thurber's attempts to disabuse Ross of this notion and with the comedy inherent in Ross's discoveries of numerous other briefly installed miracle men.

Having determined not to try for unity in the book on the basis of a chronological rendering of Ross's life, Thurber decided to attempt what he called a "unity of effect," to be achieved by treating various aspects of Ross's life and career as entities in themselves and by relegating these entities to chapters. The burden of the book is to make Ross come alive on the pages of these chapters, and Thurber does this by telling tale after tale about Ross concerning his paranoia (life, he seemed to think, was principally out to get him), naïveté, profanity, generosity, and, despite attempts on Ross's part to suggest the contrary, sensitivity. In building up the sense of Ross's character, Thurber quotes Ross frequently and, in fact, feels called upon in his foreword to discuss the problem of incorporating Ross's profanity into his text. Thurber indicates that Ross's "goddam" (which Thurber diplomatically spells without the *n*, just as he spells "Jesus" "Geezus") had nothing to do with God. He argues that the absence of that locution from the text would render Ross unrecognizable by those who knew him and inauthentic for those who did not. Although he opts for orthographic softening of Ross's favorite profanities, he insists on adhering to the strictest accuracy when he quotes Ross's letters, notes, and opinion sheets.

Thurber's approach to his subject is generally candid. In no sense is Ross glorified or, for that matter, simplified. Ross comes across as simultaneously credible and incredible, so fascinatingly mixed and rendered are the elements of his character. In 1931, Thurber introduced Ross to Paul Nash, an English painter. After a couple of hours in the company of the editor of *The New Yorker*, Nash said to Thurber, "He is like your skyscrapers. They are unbelievable, but there they are." The paradox of trying to make credible the incredible was brought home to Thurber by Wolcott Gibbs, who, upon hearing that Thurber was going to attempt to write about Ross, said, "If you get him down on paper, nobody will believe it."

Candid though the portrait of Ross is, it is laced with an affection for Ross. In 1938, Ross and Thurber were together in Paris and found themselves trying to talk to the concierge of a building occupied by Ross when he edited *The Stars and Stripes* in 1918. Thurber had some French, but Ross, despite his sojourn in Paris, appears to have had none. Ross attempted to talk to the concierge, who protested, in French, that he did not understand. Informed by Thurber that the man spoke no English, Ross sputtered, "Goddam it, I'm talking slowly and clearly enough!" To modern readers, this remark smacks of an immense obtuseness, ugly Americanism par excellence, and one can easily imagine feeling a genuine disdain for its author. That one does not do so in the context of the book is a tribute to Thurber's skill in managing to present Ross both honestly and sympathetically.

In the book's fifteenth chapter, "Dishonest Abe and the Grand Marshal," Thurber discusses the strangely hostile friendship of Ross and Alexander Woollcott, and by chapter's end one is very clearly inclined to vote for Ross as the more sympathetic figure in the tableau. Once again, however, one can imagine another perspective from which a different vote might be cast. Indeed, Thurber invites readers to just such an imagining, indicating that Woollcott had his partisans in the battle, and making it clear that he himself never really succumbed to Woollcott's considerable charm.

The differences between Ross and Thurber extended to matters of style, and in revealing Ross's editorial modus operandi, Thurber repeatedly illustrates this tension. The urbanity and sophistication with which one has come to associate *The New Yorker* (and which Thurber's own style, as both writer and cartoonist, did much to define) was oddly missing from Ross's own work. Indeed, in writing about what he takes to have been Ross's unsuccessful contributions to the magazine's "Talk of the Town" column, Thurber makes an interesting pronouncement concerning the editor of the *The New Yorker*: "He simply was not a *New Yorker* writer, never got better at it, and in the thirties gave it up, although he persisted in sticking into my copy now and then such pet expressions of his as 'and such' and 'otherwise.' "

Thurber is a highly allusive writer, and he weaves his allusions subtly into his text. Ross appears to have been suspicious of allusions. For one thing, he often missed them. A scrupulously close reader of copy, he once responded in a query sheet to S. J. Perelman's reference in an article to "the woman taken in adultery" by writing, "What woman? Hasn't been previously mentioned." Just as Thurber's cartoons made Ross nervous, redolent as they were likely to be of unacceptable double meanings, so did Thurber's prose unnerve him: Things were likely to be hidden there also.

Another trademark of Thurber's style is his playful way with figures of speech. He once did a series of drawings based on a child's taking literally the metaphorical daily bread of grown-ups, with consequences comical for the viewer and frightening for the child. His writing is constantly alive with the possibilities of language, and he did not hesitate to play when he wrote. In the opening section of the book's fifth chapter, "The Talk of the Town," Thurber imagines what Ross would say if he were alive and reading the chapter as Thurber was composing it. One hears, loud and clear, the voice of Ross speaking from the editorial office of parentheses, cautioning Thurber primarily against the mixing of metaphors. There results a vivid sense of what Ross was looking for in writing, how he went about trying to get it from his writers, and how he was often thwarted by Thurber—although one finally suspects that he *wanted* to be thwarted by Thurber and secretly applauded the stylistic panache of which he himself was not capable. Thurber cites a sentence that has survived from an early prospectus of the magazine: "The *New Yorker* will be the magazine which is not edited for the old lady in Dubuque." It is almost certain that Ross recognized that the realization of such an aim depended largely upon the very stylistic machinations of Thurber and other writers about which he so often groused.

Critical Context

Thurber is sometimes criticized for depicting characters that are two-dimensional and quite alike, a glittering but small gallery of "Thurber men" and "Thurber women." In *The Thurber Album* (1952) and *The Years with Ross*, however, his characterizations both deepen and broaden. Crediting Thurber with a thorough-going portrait of Ross, Robert Morsberger nevertheless argues that the book consists "mainly of brilliant, fragmentary glimpses of the editor." Richard Tobias maintains, though, that *The Years with Ross* is "an inevitable book, a final statement of all Thurber's themes." He argues that the portrait of Ross was anticipated in earlier pieces (Thurber himself maintained that King Clode in *The White Deer*, 1945, was loosely based on Ross, and he attempted a play about Ross in 1948). According to Tobias, there is nothing fragmentary about the portrait of Ross; it is a carefully constructed tableau, which represents an attempt on Thurber's part to make of Ross a modern hero, "Walter Mitty in triumph." Whether one sees a hero in Ross depends upon one's own concept of heroism; what is probably indisputable about *The Years with Ross*, however, is its place in Thurber's oeuvre as a compendium of things he did well.

Sources for Further Study

Coates, Robert M. "*New Yorker* Days," in *Thurber: A Collection of Critical Essays*, 1974. Edited by Charles S. Holmes.

Ford, Corey. *The Time of Laughter*, 1967.

Kramer, Dale. *Ross and the "New Yorker,"* 1952.

Morsberger, Robert E. *James Thurber*, 1964.

Nugent, Elliott. *Events Leading Up to the Comedy*, 1965.

Plimpton, George, and Max Steele. "James Thurber," in *Writers at Work: The Paris Review Interviews*, 1959. Edited by George Plimpton.

Tobias, Richard C. *The Art of James Thurber*, 1969.

Johnny Wink

ZEN AND THE ART OF MOTORCYCLE MAINTENANCE
An Inquiry into Values

Author: Robert M. Pirsig (1928-   )
Type of work: Autobiography
Time of work: 1950-1970
Locale: The northwestern United States
First published: 1974

> *Principal personages:*
> ROBERT PIRSIG, the author and narrator
> CHRIS, his eleven-year-old son
> JOHN and SYLVIA SUTHERLAND, two friends who accompany the
> Pirsigs on the first leg of their motorcycle journey

Form and Content

Despite its title, *Zen and the Art of Motorcycle Maintenance* offers little information about either Zen Buddhism or the maintenance of motorcycles. The author includes a direct warning to this effect, indicating that the book is instead a narrative based on personal experience. The narrative functions on three levels. At its simplest, it is a travelogue describing a cross-country motorcycle trip taken one summer by the narrator, Robert Pirsig, a middle-aged technical writer, and his eleven-year-old son, Chris; their westward journey begins in Minneapolis, goes through the Dakotas to Montana, then over to Oregon and down the California coast.

On another level, the book describes a psychological journey. Years earlier, Pirsig suffered a serious mental breakdown culminating in electric shock therapy that virtually erased his previous personality; now his son is showing early symptoms of psychotic illness. Each is haunted by the ghost of Pirsig's past incarnation, named Phaedrus by Pirsig, and each in his own way is trying to recover a relationship with that self. Their journey literally covers some of the same ground Phaedrus traversed, including the university in Bozeman, Montana, where Phaedrus was a teacher.

Most important, however, the book retraces the theoretical ground of Phaedrus' thoughts, ideas about the split between classical and romantic thinking and how that dichotomy informs the crisis of modern technological life, thoughts which became so strange and which Phaedrus pursued so intensely that they drove him to madness. These ideas represent the book's third level.

Pirsig is not so much remembering Phaedrus' thoughts as he is trying to pick them up and complete them—only this time, without going mad. His pursuit takes the form of a series of meditative soliloquies appropriate to a motorcycle journey, where conversation is difficult but where long solitary bouts of thinking are possible. These soliloquies, while following a generally consistent theme, dip in and out of diverse philosophical systems, from empiricism to Oriental mysticism to pre-Socratic thinking; they give the book its subtitle, *An Inquiry into Values*. He calls them "Chautauquas," for traveling shows popular in the United States at the turn of the century. These shows consisted of a series of talks meant to enlighten and entertain their listeners and ultimately to raise their level of cultural awareness. Pirsig's inquiry into cultural and personal values is driven by a similar aim.

Assigning the book to a particular genre is problematic. Because the work is based on the author's experiences, "autobiography" may be an accurate descriptor, but the book's focus on philosophical ideas and its relative paucity of biographical details make this label somewhat misleading. Yet Pirsig's ideas—though intricate, complex, and even profound—are not argued with the rigorous, systematic care that would be necessary for the book to be classified as philosophy. The unifying theme of the journey, the presence of characters in conflict, and the often-symbolic interaction of setting and theme make this work more than a mere journal or travelogue and have led many critics to call it a novel. That Pirsig's book straddles so many categories is fitting, because the aim of his intellectual and spiritual journey is to break through such divisions and to unite what have been accepted as opposites, such as reason and emotion, science and art.

An interweaving of place and theme is fundamental to the book's forward movement. At the outset, Pirsig declares that he prefers back roads to freeways, because the aim of this motorcycle journey is to make good time, not in the sense of arriving at a destination quickly but in the sense of spending the time well. Traveling secondary roads allows them to cut more deeply into America, to see things more carefully, even though it may also mean hours spent riding on a road that leads nowhere. Pirsig's Chautauquas are often like these routes: long, circuitous roads of thought dissolving into dead ends, yet along the way providing flashes of beauty and brilliance, recognitions of things forgotten.

In Montana, father and son temporarily leave their motorcycles and hike into the high country; the difficulty and danger of their climb and their isolation from civilization mirrors the path that Phaedrus took into the lonely high country of thought that threatened to cut him off from society. When Pirsig decides not to continue their hike all the way to the summit, it represents a psychological turning point; their turning back toward civilization reflects Pirsig's desire not to follow Phaedrus into madness again. Yet the psychological tension mounts when their trip by motorcycle resumes and Chris becomes increasingly moody and rebellious; the tension culminates off the foggy California cliffs in Chris's desire to throw himself into the sea. The fog surrounding father and son objectifies the confusion of their relationship, the treacherousness of the cliffs, the urgency of their situation. The scene calls for a new recognition from Pirsig, a reconciliation of the father, the son, and the ghost of Phaedrus. That reconciliation, which occurs in the final pages of the book, signals that the journey has reached its destination.

Analysis

Perhaps even more than a peripatetic philosopher, Pirsig is a metaphysical detective. He is on the trail of a crime in modern life, a crisis in living that stems from the alienation of what a person is from what he or she does. He sees evidence of this crime in the faces of those around him: in the funeral procession of commuters, who look saddened and numbed; in the vacant, disinterested expression of the mechanic, who instead of repairing Pirsig's motorcycle further damages it; in the cowed, sleepy eyes of university students, who submit to the rules and sacrifice real learning for regurgitation of their professors' dead facts.

Pirsig first traces this condition to the existence of two distinct approaches to life, exemplified by two different attitudes toward motorcycle maintenance. Pirsig is fascinated by the workings of his machine, whereas his traveling companions, John and Sylvia Sutherland, view the mechanics with bewilderment and hostility. They are romantics, interested in the poetry of the ride and not concerned, as a classicist would be, with their machine's form and the functions of its parts. They are running away from technology, a condition which Pirsig suggests is counterproductive, since "the Buddha, the Godhead, resides quite as comfortably in the circuits of a digital computer or the gears of a cycle transmission as he does at the top of a mountain or in the petals of a flower." The classical and romantic modes, the one proceeding primarily by reason and fact and the other by inspiration and intuition, have been in conflict for centuries; Pirsig believes that a synthesis of these modes is the way out of the modern dilemma.

The dilemma is crystallized for Pirsig in the simple question "What is Quality?" which is a restatement of the question Socrates asks Phaedrus in the Platonic dialogue of the same name, a passage which Pirsig includes as the opening epigraph to this book: "And what is good, Phaedrus,/ And what is not good—/ Need we ask anyone to tell us these things?" It is with this question that Pirsig picks up the train of thought begun by his previous self, the ghost he now calls Phaedrus.

As a teacher of rhetoric at the State University of Montana, Phaedrus pursued the question of Quality with passionate intensity, looking first for its definition by trying to codify its presence or absence in student compositions. A lively and unorthodox teacher whose approach could both inspire and anger his students, he launched an experiment wherein he refused to give his students grades for their papers, probing instead for their ideas on what made a good paper good. He eventually concluded that the notion of Quality could be successfully contained neither by a classical formal definition nor by a romantic subjective assessment; rather, he determined that it was the preexisting and all-encompassing source for both classical and romantic thought, making it very much like the divine underlying unity described by Eastern religions.

Phaedrus enrolled in graduate school at the University of Chicago to explore what he believed was an earthshaking discovery, trying to track down, through close readings of Plato and Aristotle, the false step into dualism of all Western thought. The more consumed he became by his theories, the further into madness he traveled, eventually losing all touch with reality, allowing his cigarettes to burn his fingers and leaving a pool of urine on the floor. Ironically, it was technology that "killed" him; he was taken to a mental hospital where electric shock therapy virtually cleared his fervent investigations from his brain.

The narrator, Pirsig, neither completely dismisses nor fully embraces Phaedrus' ideas. His retracing of Phaedrus' path begins as a simple attempt to put this ghost to rest, yet along the way he recovers his desire to resolve the critical dilemma of modern technological life: the separation of subject and object, of what one is from what one does. He is now a writer of computer manuals and a motorcycle hobbyist, two activities which serve to protect him from the overly abstract flight of Phaedrus the student and teacher.

Appropriately, Pirsig's new solution takes a more practical turn; he now argues for right living. Motorcycle maintenance becomes the metaphor for a new attitude toward living with technology, one which he once found most simply and profoundly expressed in a set of instructions for putting together a Japanese bicycle: "Assembly of Japanese bicycle require great peace of mind." The crisis of technology is actually a crisis of the individual; it occurs when a person angrily separates himself from the objects around him. "The real cycle you're working on is a cycle called yourself," Pirsig declares. "The machine that appears to be 'out there' and the person that appears to be 'in here' are not two separate things." Pirsig argues for the integration of Quality into daily life, for a return to a "craftsmanlike self-involved reality" where the worker cares about the work, is in a sense one with it. Though not strictly adhering to orthodox Buddhist principles, this is Pirsig's brand of Zen.

To follow this path and overcome those feelings of hopelessness and isolation endemic to modern life takes "gumption," an old-fashioned quality of spirit that Pirsig acknowledges is now in short supply. Gumption encompasses such virtues as integrity, self-reliance, and feelings of self-worth. He links it to the word "enthusiasm," whose Greek root *enthousiasmos* means "filled with God," or, in Pirsig's terms, Quality. It is, writes Pirsig, "the psychic gasoline that keeps the whole thing going." He explores the means by which one can refuel one's supply of gumption and highlights those traps which can cause it to leak away. Among these traps is the tendency to think one has all the answers, which Pirsig ironically discovers has trapped him, blinding him to the crisis that has been brewing between him and his son. It is only on the last leg of their journey that Pirsig realizes that while he, as the driver, has enjoyed breathtaking views of the scenery around them, Chris, as the passenger, has had to stare into his back the whole trip.

There are times when the reader may feel somewhat like Chris; the narrator's dogged pursuit of his own ideas can be exasperating. For those who, like the Sutherlands, lean toward romanticism and are disinclined to endure the rigors of classical thinking, long stretches of the book may prove simply boring; these readers will find greater satisfaction in the more novelistic side of the book: its dynamic of psychological tension, its story of a man's spiral into madness, and its more poetic descriptions of steps toward spiritual enlightenment. For those who sit on the other side of the classical-romantic division, Pirsig's sometimes sketchy summaries of various scientific and philosophical systems may appear inadequate, at times even inaccurate. Yet few will walk away from a reading of this work unchanged; in giving a detailed account of one man's passionate pursuit of truth, it encourages others to do the same.

Critical Context

After 121 publishers had rejected the manuscript of *Zen and the Art of Motorcycle Maintenance*, one editor decided to accept it, primarily as an act of conscience; the book had forced him to clarify the reason that he was in the publishing business. He offered Pirsig a standard three-thousand-dollar advance, noting that it was probably the last payment the author would receive, because such books never made money. To the surprise of many, the book soared to the top of the best-seller lists. Pirsig was besieged with requests for interviews and offers for film rights and foreign publication. What made this unusual book so popular?

In an afterword written ten years after the book's initial publication, Pirsig explores the reasons for his book's astonishing popularity. He fits *Zen and the Art of Motorcycle Maintenance* into the category of "culture-bearing books," books which serve to move the culture forward. Such an effect can never be planned; a book will almost accidentally coincide with a culture's restless need to change, to challenge old assumptions, and to find new solutions. At the time of this book's publication, the tumultuous 1960's had just concluded. Those who had participated in radical group protests against war, racism, and corporate profit at the expense of humanist values now found themselves faced with individual choices: Should they simply enter the work force and pursue material success as their fathers did, or was there another path they could take? Pirsig writes:

> This book offers another, more serious alternative to material success. It's not so much an alternative as an expansion of the meaning of "success" to something larger than just getting a good job and staying out of trouble. And also something larger than mere freedom. It gives a positive goal to work toward that does not confine. That is the main reason for the book's success, I think. The whole culture happened to be looking for exactly what this book has to offer.

Sources for Further Study

Abbey, Edward. "Zen and the Art of Motorcycle Maintenance," in *The New York Times Book Review*. LXXX (March 30, 1975), p. 6.

Adams, Robert M. "Good Trip," in *The New York Review of Books*. XXI (June 13, 1974), pp. 22-23.

Basalla, George. "Man and Machine," in *Science*. CLXXXVII (January 24, 1975), pp. 248-250.

Schuldenfrei, Richard. "Zen and the Art of Motorcycle Maintenance," in *Harvard Educational Review*. XLV (February, 1975), pp. 95-103.

Steiner, George. "Uneasy Rider," in *The New Yorker*. L (April 15, 1974), pp. 147-150.

Dana Gerhardt

MASTERPLOTS II

NONFICTION
SERIES

TITLE INDEX

I

TITLE INDEX